Computer Accounting

with

Sage 50 2019

[Formerly Peachtree]

Twenty-First Edition

Carol Yacht, M.A.

COMPUTER ACCOUNTING WITH SAGE 50 2019, TWENTY FIRST EDITION

Published by McGraw-Hill Education, 2 Penn Plaza, New York, NY 10121. Copyright ©2020 by McGraw-Hill Education. All rights reserved. Printed in the United States of America. Previous editions ©2020, 2017, and 2016. No part of this publication may be reproduced or distributed in any form or by any means, or stored in a database or retrieval system, without the prior written consent of McGraw-Hill Education, including, but not limited to, in any network or other electronic storage or transmission, or broadcast for distance learning.

Some ancillaries, including electronic and print components, may not be available to customers outside the United States.

This book is printed on acid-free paper.

1 2 3 4 5 6 QVS 23 22 21 20 19

ISBN 978-1-259-91701-1 (bound edition)
MHID 1-259-91701-0 (bound edition)

Executive Portfolio Manager: *Steve Schuetz*
Product Developer: *Sarah Sacco*
Marketing Manager: *Michelle Williams*
Content Project Managers: *Karen Jozefowicz and Jason Stauter*
Buyer: *Susan K. Culbertson*
Design: *Beth Blech*
Content Licensing Specialist: *Melissa Homer*
Cover Image: *©Shutterstock/nnattalli*
Compositor: *SPi Global*

All credits appearing on page or at the end of the book are considered to be an extension of the copyright page.

The Internet addresses listed in the text were accurate at the time of publication. The inclusion of a website does not indicate an endorsement by the authors or McGraw-Hill Education, and McGraw-Hill Education does not guarantee the accuracy of the information presented at these sites.

Software Installation

Install the software that millions of customers choose every year and accountants recommend. Sage provides small and medium-sized business software to **6 million customers worldwide**. Sage North America, a subsidiary of the Sage Group plc, has offices in the U.S. and Canada, employees more than 13,000 people, and operates in 24 countries. Sage 50 is designed for sole proprietorships, partnerships, and corporations with up to 50 employees, and has more than 40 years of industry experience.

EDUCATIONAL VERSION FOR THE CLASSROOM

To obtain a serial number for classroom installation, email SageEducation@sage.com, *or* go online to www.mhhe.com/yacht2019 > Install Sage 50. Read the "For Educators" section. Refer to the Note to Instructors/Schools on page x. If your school is already an Education Alliance Program member, the 2019 software is sent automatically.

SAGE 50 2019: STUDENT VERSION AND EDUCATIONAL VERSION

Student Version

The Student Version is accessible for 14 months. The serial number for installing the student version is **7Ø2FB-58Ø2-9793-2211**. After installation, product activation is required (pages xiii-xiv). Information about installation is also included on the Online Learning Center at www.mhhe.com/yacht2019 > Install Sage 50.

Educational Version

To install the software in the classroom, go to the Sage Education Alliance Program website at http://www.sage.com/us/about-us/education-instructor to learn more about what is available for Educators and the Instructor software. Once you join the Sage Education Alliance Program, SageEducation@sage.com emails a serial number for the "Educational" version.

The two versions, **Student Version** for individual installation and **Educational Version** for classroom installation, include the same features. The Educational Version does <u>not</u> have a time limit, *and* the serial number differs.

 The serial number distinguishes the Educational Version from the Student Version. Sage 50 2019 can be downloaded at http://www.sage.com/us/about-us/education-instructor.

To restore backup files from lower versions of Sage 50, the "Educational" version must be used.

Sage 50 2019 was used to write the textbook. If you have an earlier version of the software installed, refer to page xxii to delete earlier versions.

SYSTEM REQUIREMENTS: www.mhhe.com/yacht2019 > System Requirements

Recommended system configuration

- 2.4 GHz processor (*Intel Core i3 and higher*) for single user and multiple users
- 2 GB of RAM for single user and 4 GB for multiple users

Minimum system requirements

- 2.0 GHz processor for single user and multiple users
- 2 GB of RAM for single user and multiple users
- *Windows® 7, or Windows 8.1, or Windows 10 (Anniversary Update and higher) with the latest updates from Microsoft installed*
- 1 GB of disk space for installation
- Internet Explorer 10.0 and 11.0 supported (*version 11.0 and higher with Sage Payroll Solutions, Sage Payments Solutions and other Connected Services integration*)
- Microsoft®.NET Framework 4.7.1, including DirectX Dependency for .NET; requires an additional 280 MB to 850 MB
- At least high-color (16-bit) SVGA video; Minimum Resolution: 1280x800, Preferred Resolution: 1440x900 or higher; small fonts/DPI settings required
- *All online features/services require high speed Internet access (For best performance download speeds of at least 25mbps and upload speeds of at least 3mbps)*
- *Maximum of 5GB file size for Sage Drive companies*

Integration/compatibility requirements

- Excel®, Outlook®, and Word integration requires Microsoft Excel, Outlook, and Word 2007, 2010, 2013 or 2016 (32-bit versions).
- Office 365 Integration – *Requires Office 365 Business Premium or Enterprise Editions*
- Printers supported by Windows 7, Windows 8 or Windows 10
- In-product demos require Adobe® Flash® Player 11 or greater (*version 18 or higher strongly recommended*)
- Adobe® Reader® 11.0 and higher

Multiuser

- Multiuser environments are supported in Sage 50 Premium Accounting and higher

---

- Multiuser mode is optimized for Windows Server 2008 R2 SP1, Windows Server 2012 or Windows Server 2016 client-server networks; Windows 7, Windows 8.1 or Windows 10 peer-to-peer networks
- A maximum of five licensed named users is allowed for Sage 50 Premium Accounting and 40 named users for Sage 50 Quantum Accounting; a named user account is granted a license when selected in the user maintenance screen
- 2 GB of disk space for installation of components on server

Terminal Services

- Windows Server 2008, Windows Server 2012 or Windows Server 2016 along with Remote Desktop Connection or Remote Desktop Web Connection client is required to run in a Windows Terminal Services environment; no more than 5 named users for Sage 50 Premium Accounting or 40 named users for Sage 50 Quantum Accounting
- Terminal Server requires additional memory when more than one user is running under Windows Terminal Services

Other

- Customer registration and acceptance of License Agreement for Sage 50 Accounting software products
- USB flash or thumb drive for backups

Read Me: Classroom software: To get the serial number for the full, Educational Version with no time limit for classroom installation, email SageEducation@sage.com. Computer lab installation is on page xix. *Or*, go online to http://www.sage.com/us/about-us/education-instructor > **Educators and instructors click here** .

Sage 50 and Firewalls

Sage 50 and its database, Pervasive, can be mistakenly identified as an intrusion threat by many firewall and anti-virus programs. If not addressed properly, this may cause installation to fail or Sage 50 may not start or run properly.

To read information about firewalls and antivirus software, search the Sage Knowledgebase at https://support.na.sage.com/selfservice/microsites/microsite.do > type Firewall > select Sage 50—U.S. Edition 2019 > link to Files to allow through firewall and anti-virus.

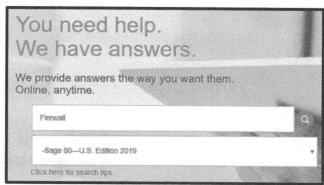

SOFTWARE INSTALLATION

To download Sage 50 2019, refer to the following steps. Depending on the operating system used (Windows 10, 8, 7 or Vista), the installation steps differ slightly. Download steps are also at www.mhhe.com/yacht2019 > Install Sage 50.

Download Sage 50 2019: 472 MB

Sage recommends using Microsoft Edge or Internet Explorer for downloading the software. To download, follow these steps. *Before installing the software, turn off your antivirus program.*

1. Go online to http://www.sage.com/us/about-us/education-instructor. Scroll down the screen to For students > Students click here.

2. In the Sage 50 Accounting—U.S. Edition area, click Register Now. Complete the form > Submit.

3. If necessary, go back to the For students screen. Click Download the software > select **Download 2019 version**. The serial number code is shown on page x, number 9. You can use the Student version for 14 months.

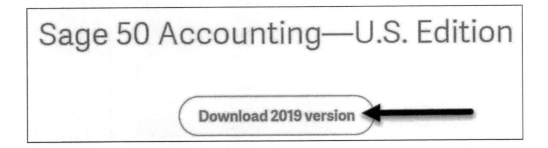

4. Click <Run>. The percentage scale shows how long the download takes.

5. The Sage50 Accounting 2019.0.0 window appears, the Destination folder shows c:\sage\SAGE50_2019_0_0.

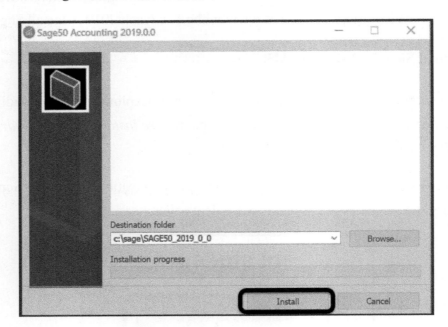

6. After clicking <Install>, the screen prompts "Extracting files." If the User Account Control window appears, click <Yes>. The Welcome to Sage 50 Accounting window appears. Click <Next>.

7. When the License Agreement window appears, click on the box next to I agree to the terms of the license agreement to place a checkmark in it.

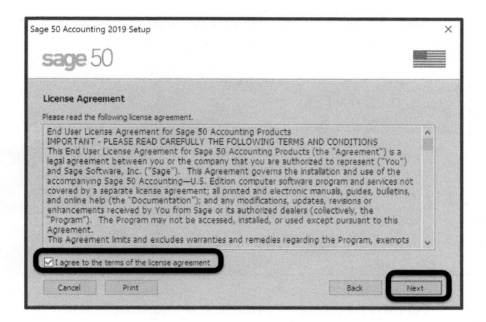

8. After clicking <Next>, the Windows Firewall window appears. Accept the default for Auto configure the Windows Firewall to allow install and run Sage 50 by clicking <Next>.

   NOTE: To read information about firewalls and antivirus software, search the Sage Knowledgebase at https://support.na.sage.com/selfservice/microsites/microsite.do > in the Search the knowledgebase field, type Firewall > in the Products field, select

   Sage 50—U.S. Edition 2019 > click [🔍] > link to Files to allow through firewall and antivirus.

9. The Serial Number window appears. Type **7Ø2FB-58Ø2-9793-2211** in the Serial number field.

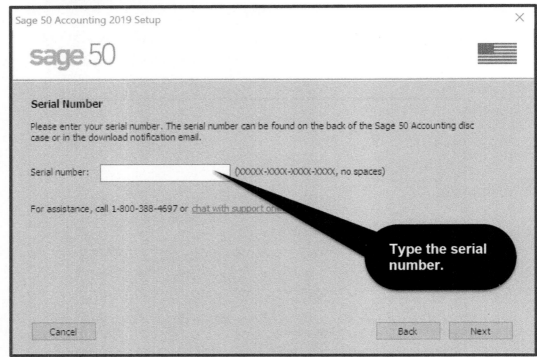

NOTE TO INSTRUCTORS/SCHOOLS: If your school is a member of the Sage Education Alliance Program, Sage 50 2019 is automatically sent to schools. When installing the software, use the serial number emailed by SageEducation@sage.com, 800-256-8807. The website for downloading free classroom software is http://www.sage.com/us/about-us/education-instructor > Educators and instructors click here > Register now> Download the software > Download 2019 version > type Educational version Serial Number provided by Sage Education.

10. After clicking <Next>, the Single computer or Network window appears. Accept the default for Yes by clicking <Next>.
11. The Install Options window appears showing the location for the Sage 50 program and data files.

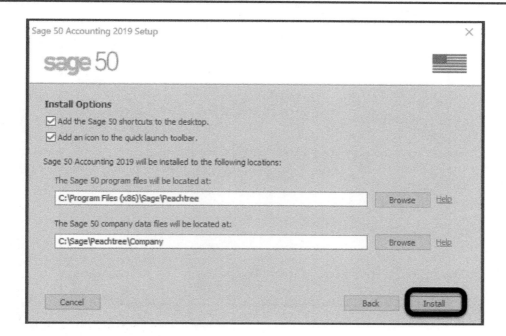

12. After clicking <Install>, the Installing Sage 50 Accounting scale shows the progress of installation. Be patient, installation takes a while.

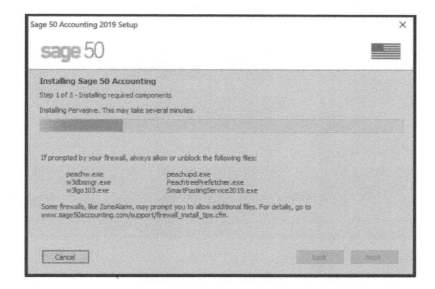

If a Cannot connect to database window appears, click <Cancel>. Install resumes.

13. The Installation Completed window appears.

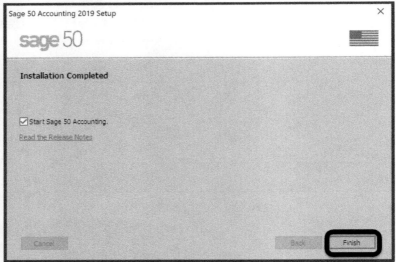

14. After clicking <Finish>, the startup window appears.

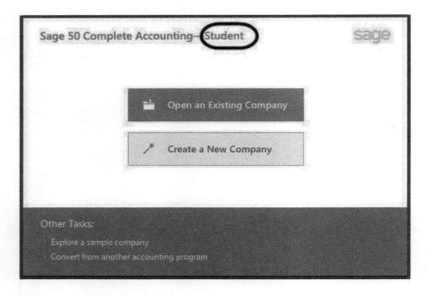

The version students install shows "Student," which can be used for 14 months. The version installed at school may show "Educational" which does not have a time limit. Instructors and schools can email SageEducation@sage.com to receive the serial number for the full

"Educational" version with no time limit. *Except* for the time limit and serial number used during installation, the Student and Educational versions are the same.

15. Complete ***Product Activation***. From the startup window, select Help > Sage 50 Activation, Licensing, and Subscription Options.

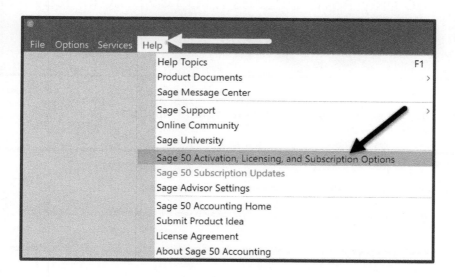

Why do I need to activate?

If you do not complete product activation, Sage 50 will stop working after a few uses. If you start Sage 50 and a screen prompts to activate, follow these steps.

(*Hint:* If you started Sage 50 and a company opened, you can activate from the Help menu.)

Customer ID:

0000000004

a. The Product Activation window appears. Select Activate Online Now. *Or*, if you do not have an Internet connection, select <Activate Manually>.

b. The Activation Complete window appears.

Activation Complete

Your activation is complete. Thank you for choosing Sage 50 Accounting.

Your customer ID is 0000000001. **Important:** Please write this ID down and keep it in a safe place. You will need to have it available whenever you contact Sage.

Sage 50 is ready to give you relevant advice and support when and where you need it. You can get off to a successful start and keep your business running smoothly by accessing these valuable resources:

° The Sage 50 Community - Get answers to questions about using Sage 50 Accounting and participate in discussions about Sage 50 Accounting products in this helpful Community

° Online Training Resources - From our extensive Knowledgebase to custom, onsite training, we offer a variety of ways to learn more about Sage 50. Visit our Education & Training site for details.

° Certified Consultants - Experts in using Sage 50, Certified Consultants can provide guidance on everything from initial setup through year-end processing.

Thank you again for choosing Sage 50 Accounting for your business. If you have questions or need more information, please call 877-495-9904 or visit www.sage50accounting.com.

c. press <Enter>.

16. When Sage 50 starts, the **Student** version startup window shows "Sage 50 Complete Accounting - Student." The Student version is accessible for 14 months.

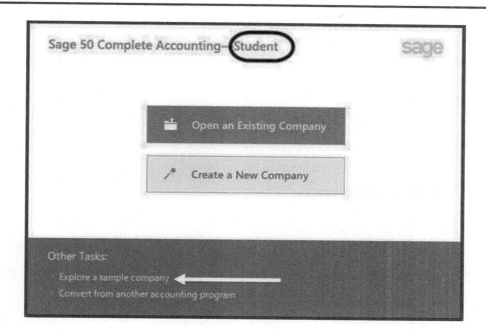

Or, in the classroom, the startup window may show **Educational**. If the school prefers that version, email <u>SageEducation@sage.com</u>. The Educational version is the non-time limited software available for classroom use. Refer to page xix for Computer Lab Installation.

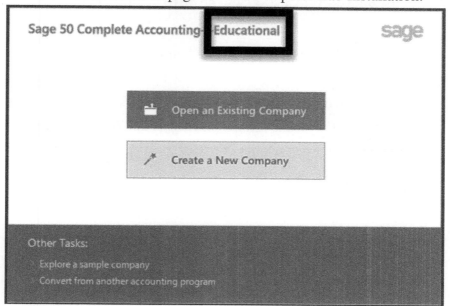

17. Select Explore a sample company. Bellwether Garden Supply is the default.

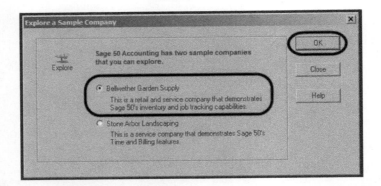

18. Click <OK> *or* press <Enter>. (*Hint:* If a screen prompts You can use this company in the student version of Sage 50 Accounting for the next 14 months and then it will expire, click <OK>. The Student version expiration date is explained below and on the next page.)

Expiration Date, Student Version, Sage 50 2019

To see when the Student Version of Sage 50 2019 expires, do this.

1. From the Menu bar > select Maintain > Company Information.
2. The Maintain Company Information window appears. The expiration date is 14 months after the day you installed the software. For example, the author installed the Sage 50 Student version on August 20, 2018. The expiration date is 14 months later on October 20, 2019.

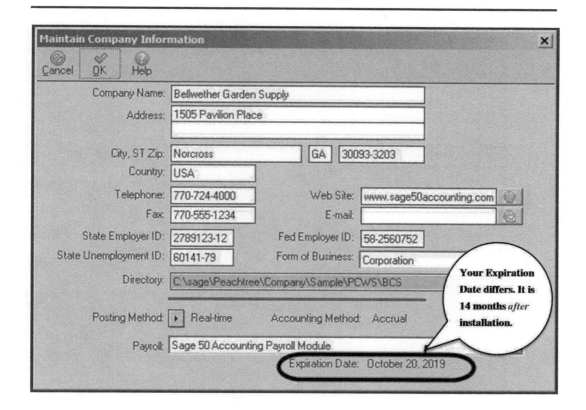

Setting Global Options

Follow these steps to set Sage 50's Global Options. These options will be in effect for all Sage 50 companies.

1. From Sage 50's menu bar, select Options > Global. The <u>A</u>ccounting tab is selected.
   - In the **Decimal Entry** area, Manual and 2 decimal places should be selected in each field.
   - In the **Hide General Ledger Accounts** area, the boxes *must* be unchecked.
   - In the **Other Options** area, Warn if a record was changed but not saved and Recalculate cash balance automatically in Receipts, Payments, and Payroll Entry should be checked.

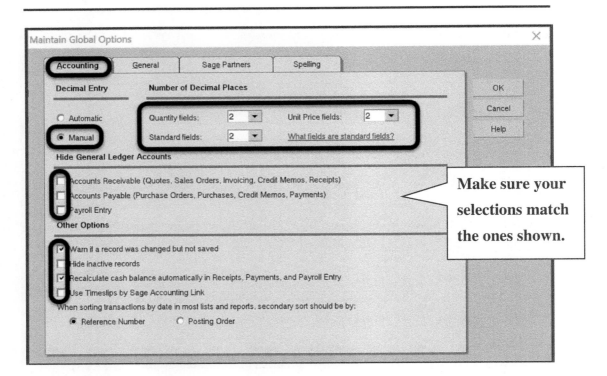

Make sure your selections match the ones shown.

2. Click the <u>G</u>eneral tab. Make sure your screen matches the one shown.

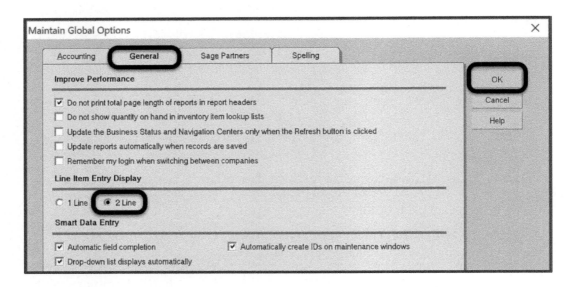

3. Click ⌷OK. The selections made in global options are now set for all companies.

4.   From Sage 50's menu bar, click File > Exit.

Observe that icons have been set up on the desktop for Sage 50: Sage 50 Accounting 2019 and Sage 50 Accounting 2019 Automatic Backup Configuration.

COMPUTER LAB INSTALLATION

Before computer lab installation, make sure all versions of Peachtree or Sage 50 are deleted. Refer to Deleting Sage 50, page xxii.

1.   Sage 50 Accounting 2019 - Educational Version should be installed locally. Do *not* put on server.
2.   Install software on local workstation then ghost (replicate) install. You can put the software on a standard lab image.

If you network Sage 50 2019-Educational Version, you will fall under the 5-seat license rule which will be an issue in a classroom where students may be working on the same data. For classroom installation, it is best to create a lab image.

STUDENT VERSION SOFTWARE

The software included with the textbook is Sage 50 Accounting 2019, Student Version. To see the default location where the currently displayed Sage 50 company resides, follow these steps.

1.   Start Sage 50. Open the sample company, Bellwether Garden Supply.
2.   From the menu bar, select Maintain > Company Information. The Directory field shows where the currently displayed Sage 50 company resides. The Student Version directory is shown below.

Student version Directory:

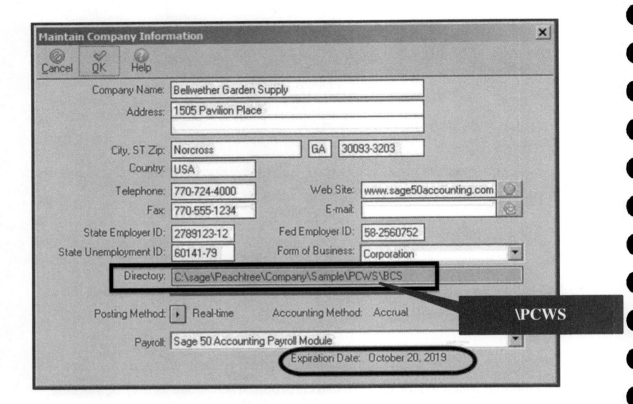

You can use company data in the Student Version for 14 months. After 14 months, the Student Version expires. Your expiration date will differ from the one shown.

> **Read me: Add student name to printouts**
> To add your name to reports, type your name or initials after the Company Name. The Company Name field is shown on Sage 50 printouts.

EDUCATIONAL VERSION SOFTWARE

If you are working in the computer lab, the default directory for Educational Version differs slightly when compared to the Student Version.

The Maintain Company Information window's Directory field differs slightly. Observe that the default folder for the Educational Version is **\PCWE** not **\PCWS**. *Before* adding your name to Bellwether Garden Supply in Chapter 1, the Directory field ends in \BCS. Once your name is added, the Directory field changes to **\belgarsu** (first three letters from the first word (bel), three letters from the second word (gar), two letters from the third word (su). Refer to pages 40-41, Add Your Name to Reports).

Educational version Directory:

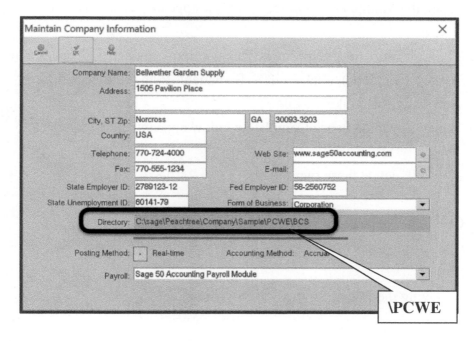

The features of the Student Version and Educational Version are the same, except for the Student Version's 14-month period of use. The serial numbers for installing the Student Version and Education Version also differ.

 On the Educational version, the BCS folder is within the PCW**E** folder. On the Student version, the BCS folder is within the PCW**S** folder. The "E" is for Educational; the "S" for "Student" version.

DELETING SAGE 50

Before uninstalling Sage 50, backup data that you want to keep. Once Sage is uninstalled, all company data files are removed. Follow these steps to delete Sage 50 Accounting 2019. (Use similar steps to delete an earlier version.)

1. Go to Control Panel > Programs and Features > Uninstall Sage 50 Accounting 2019 (*or* other year). The InstallWizard window appears briefly.
2. When the Maintenance Options window appears, select Remove > click <Next>.
3. The Confirm Uninstall prompts This will remove Sage 50 Accounting 2019 (all versions), click <OK>. Be patient. Removing Sage 50 Accounting will take a while.
4. When the Maintenance Complete window appears, click <Finish>.

After uninstall, delete these two folders:

1. C:\Sage
2. C:\Program Files (x86)\Sage

After removing the folders, empty the recycle bin.

Preface

Computer Accounting with Sage 50 2019, 21ˢᵗ Edition, teaches you how to use Sage 50 2019 (formerly Peachtree) software. For more than 40 years[1], Sage has produced award-winning accounting software. The Sage family of software products, which includes Sage 50, is the leading global supplier of business management solutions and services.

Sage operates in 24 countries and serves **6 million small and medium-sized businesses**. Businesses that use Sage 50 include retail stores, healthcare, human resources/payroll, construction/real estate, transportation/distribution, payment processing, nonprofit, manufacturing, public utilities, legal, medical, accounting firms, home office, and personal recordkeeping.

 Read Me: Multi-User Educational Version and Single User Student Version

For the Educational Version serial number, email SageEducation@sage.com. The full **Educational Version** is free to schools, does not have a time limit, and can be installed on multiple computers (http://www.sage.com/us/about-us/education-instructor). Refer to page xix for Computer Lab Installation.

The **Student Version** software can be installed on one computer and is valid for 14 months. The Student Version serial number is **702FB-5802-9793-2211**.

In *Computer Accounting with Sage 50 2019, 21ˢᵗ Edition*, you learn about the relationship between Sage 50 software and fundamental accounting principles, procedures, and business processes.

---

[1]In 1976, Peachtree Accounting Software was available.

The diagram below illustrates the Sage 50 accounting system. Business processes are completed in this order:

- Software is installed.
- Companies are set up.
- Transactions are journalized in the special journals or general journal, then posted to the general ledger and subsidiary ledgers.
- After entering transactions, reports are printed.

Sage 50 is a *double-entry accounting* system. Double-entry accounting means that the equation Assets = Liabilities + Equity is always in balance. Since a debit in one account will be offset by a credit in another account, the sum of all debits is equal to the sum of all credits. To assure double-entry accounting procedures, Sage 50 includes monthly accounting periods, the general journal and special journals, general ledger and subsidiary ledgers, account reconciliation, an audit trail, and numerous financial reports. The Sage 50 accounting system also includes closing the fiscal year.

SAGE 50 2019

The System Requirements for Sage 50 2019 are online at www.mhhe.com/yacht2019 > link to System Requirements. Each textbook includes a copy of the software, Sage 50 2019.

NEW The software, **Sage 50 2019**, is included with every textbook. For software installation instructions, see pages vii-xvi.

NEW Use this serial number **702FB-5802-9793-2211** for installing the Student Version software. The student version is valid for **14 months** and then it expires. The expiration date can be found in the Company Information section of the System Navigation Center and on the Maintain > Company Information window.

NEW After installation, you must activate the software. Refer to Step 15, pages xiii-xiv. The Help menu includes software activation.

Compatible with Windows 10, 8, 7, and Vista. System requirements are on the OLC at www.mhhe.com/yacht2019.

NEW For installation on multiple classroom computers, email SageEducation@sage.com, 800-256-8807; instructor software, www.sage.com/us/about-us/education-instructor. Information for educators is included at www.mhhe.com/yacht2019 > Install Sage 50. Refer to page xix, Computer Lab Installation.

GO GREEN & SAVE is included within the textbook chapters and on the Online Learning Center. There is no need for hard-copy printouts.

NEW   The Online Learning Center at www.mhhe.com/yacht2019 includes the Sage Advisor. The Sage Advisor includes links to Getting started videos, Cheat sheets, Sage University, Show-me-how and New Features.

Online Learning Center at www.mhhe.com/yacht2019 includes three appendixes: Appendix A, Troubleshooting, Appendix C, Review of Accounting Principles; Appendix D, Glossary.

NEW   The Online Learning Center at www.mhhe.com/yacht2019 includes YouTube videos, Narrated PowerPoints, Online quizzes that include Multiple-Choice and True/False questions, QA Templates (end-of-chapter questions and analysis questions), Going to the Net exercises, Assessment Rubrics, Bellwether Garden Supply project, and Practice Set.

How to fix?, **Troubleshooting**, **Comment**, and **Read Me** boxes within chapters identify and help resolve issues. To find How to fix?, Troubleshooting, Comment, and Read Me, use the chapter index.

NEW   Bellwether Garden Supply project includes questions for analyzing the sample company data, identifying software features and functions, and reviewing sample company transactions and reports. The Bellwether Garden Supply project is online at www.mhhe.com/yacht2019.

Sage 50's emphasis on double-entry accounting and business processes is explained throughout the textbook. Accounting skills are applied to all facets of running a business. Students create 12 companies, complete the accounting cycle, and practice computer accounting skills.

Financial Manager Analysis includes the Business Summary of financial ratios and Key Balances from the income statement and balance sheet.

NEW **Source document practice set** online at www.mhhe.com/yacht2019 > Student Edition. Complete the merchandising business practice.

Chapter 8, Stone Arbor Landscaping: Time and Billing. Use Sage 50's time and billing feature to record a time ticket, enter a sales invoice, and record payroll for jobs completed.

Chapters 1-18 include saving Sage 50 reports as Adobe Acrobat PDF files, and exporting reports to Excel.

Payroll tax tables for 50 states. Example payroll withholdings are included in Chapter 4, Employees; Chapter 15, Employees, Payroll, and Account Reconciliation; Exercise 15-1, Student Name Sales and Service; Project 2, Valley Bikes; and Project 4, CL Manufacturing, Inc.

Use Sage 50's import/export feature to copy lists into another company. Sage's modular system design is explained and compared to other accounting information systems. Workflow diagrams illustrate Sage 50's system design.

An accounting software diagram illustrates where Sage 50 fits into the range of accounting software applications.

NEW Sage 50 is compared to QuickBooks Online and Desktop versions.

Computer Accounting with Sage 50 2019, 21st Edition, shows you how to set up service, merchandising, nonprofit, and manufacturing businesses. When the textbook is completed, you have a working familiarity with Sage 50 Complete Accounting 2019 software. You learn how computer accounting and the general ledger accounting cycle work together.

The Part 1, 2, 3, and 4 introductions include a chart showing the chapter number, Sage 50 backups, Excel and Adobe file names, size in kilobytes of each file backed up or saved, and page numbers where each backup, Excel, and Adobe PDF file is completed.

PART 1: EXPLORING SAGE 50 2019

There are two sample companies included with the software: Bellwether Garden Supply and Stone Arbor Landscaping. Bellwether Garden Supply is a retail and service company that demonstrates Sage 50's inventory and job tracking capabilities. Stone Arbor Landscaping is a service company that demonstrates time and billing features.

> **For the Part 1 summary, refer to pages 1-4**. Pages 2-4 include a chart showing chapter numbers, files backed up and saved (.ptb, .pdf, .xlsx), file sizes, and page numbers where work was completed.

Part 1, Chapters 1-8, shows how to backup (save) files, export Sage 50 reports to Excel and save reports as Adobe PDF files. Sage 50's system design is explained. This includes how Sage 50's user interface is organized into general ledger, accounts receivable, accounts payable, inventory, payroll, and job costing modules.

In Part 1 of the textbook, you complete eight chapters that demonstrate how Sage 50 is used. This introduces you to the procedures that will be used with all the chapters of the textbook. Beginning in Part 2, you set up companies from scratch.

Chapter 1, Introduction to Bellwether Garden Supply, includes Sage 50's Navigation Centers and Restore Wizard for opening new or existing companies.

The new Navigation Bar and menu bar selections are explained. Bellwether Garden Supply is updated to March 2019.

Chapter 2, Vendors, shows you how to view accounts payable lists and reports from the Vendors & Purchases Navigation Center as well as custom date filtering and how to add columns to reports. New sections include Receive Inventory from a Purchase Order and Apply to Purchase Order. Sage 50's accounts payable system is explained.

Chapter 3, Customers, shows you how to view customer lists and reports from the Customers & Sales Navigation Center as well as custom date filtering and how to add columns to reports. Chapter 3 includes Sales Orders and Ship Items from a Sales Order. Sage 50's accounts receivable system is explained.

Sage 50's Financial Manager includes financial ratios and key balances.

Chapter 4, Employees, shows you how to navigate Sage 50's Employees & Payroll system.

Chapter 5, General Ledger, Inventory, and Internal Control, shows you Sage 50's budget feature, how selected access for security is used, internal controls, and audit trail. Sage 50's inventory system is also included.

Chapter 6, Job Cost, shows you how to use Sage 50's job cost system.

Chapter 7, Financial Statements, shows the result of work completed in Chapters 1-6.

NEW After Chapter 7, the Bellwether Garden Supply Project can be completed. It is included online at www.mhhe.com/yacht2019.

In Chapter 8, Stone Arbor Landscaping: Time & Billing, you work with a service company that demonstrates Sage 50's time and billing features. In Exercises 8-1 and 8-2, you record time and billing transactions, including a time ticket that is applied to a sales invoice and payroll entry.

PART 2: SAGE 50 2019 FOR SERVICE BUSINESSES

Chapters 9, 10, 11, Project 1, and Project 1A are included in this section of the textbook. The work completed in Chapter 9 is continued in Chapters 10 and 11. The accounting cycle is completed for the fourth quarter of the year and includes adjusting entries and closing the year.

> **For the Part 2 summary, refer to pages 251-256.** Pages 254-256 include a chart showing chapter numbers, files backed up and saved (.ptb, .pdf, .xlsx), file sizes, and page numbers where work was completed.

NEW In Chapter 9, New Company Setup and Beginning Balances, you set up two service companies—James Crosby Designer and Crafts by Student Name with Sage 50's simplified chart of accounts. You use Sage 50's new Company Setup Wizard and enter beginning balances. The companies set up in Chapter 9 continue in Chapters 10 and 11.

In Chapter 10, Maintaining Accounting Records for Service Businesses, you record entries for October in the Write Checks and Receipts windows, use Sage 50's account reconciliation feature and print reports. You also backup, and save reports in Excel and Adobe PDF format.

Chapter 11, Completing Quarterly Activities and Closing the Fiscal Year, you complete transactions for November and December, record adjusting entries, print financial statements, and close the fiscal year.

NEW   Exercises 9-1 through 11-2 include three months of transactions, account reconciliation, adjusting entries, financial statements, Sage 50's closing procedure, and Check Your Figures. Sage 50 reports are backed up, and saved in Adobe PDF format and exported to Excel.

NEW   Project 1, Marcia Westcott, Accounting, is a comprehensive project that reviews what you learned in Chapters 9, 10, and 11.

Project 1A, Student-Designed Service Business, shows you how to design a service business from scratch. You set up the business, choose a chart of accounts, create a balance sheet, write business transactions, complete the computer accounting cycle, and close the fiscal year.

PART 3: SAGE 50 2019 FOR MERCHANDISING BUSINESSES

Chapters 12, 13, 14, 15, Project 2, and Project 2A are included in this section of the textbook. Students set up two merchandising businesses in Chapter 12—Shannon's Service Merchandise *and* Student Name Sales and Service. The work started in Chapter 12 is continued in Chapters 13, 14 and 15.

> **For the Part 3 summary, refer to pages 399-402.** Pages 400-402 include a chart showing chapter numbers, files backed up and saved (.ptb, .pdf, .xlsx), file sizes, and page numbers where work was completed.

In Chapter 12, Vendors & Purchases, use Sage 50's accounts payable system, set up vendor defaults, record inventory purchases and payments from vendors, automatically track vendor discounts, and use vendor credit memos for purchase returns.

In Chapter 13, Customers & Sales, use Sage 50's accounts receivable system, set up customer defaults, record cash and credit sales and receive payments from customers, use credit memos for sales returns.

Chapter 13 includes Financial Manager Analysis. Business summary financial ratios are shown and key balances for income statement and balance sheet accounts.

Chapter 14, Inventory & Services, shows you how to use Sage 50's inventory system.

Chapter 15, Employees, Payroll and Account Reconciliation, shows Sage 50's payroll system using two states, Arizona and Georgia, as an example for payroll withholdings. You set up payroll defaults, add employee information, learn about automatic payroll tax calculations, and complete payroll entry.

Account reconciliation shows you how Sage 50's Accounts Payable, Accounts Receivable, Inventory, and General Ledger systems work together. Chapter 15 includes account reconciliation for both the checking and payroll accounts. Check Your Figure amounts are included for Exercises 12-1 through 15-2.

NEW   Project 2, Valley Bikes, is a comprehensive project that incorporates what you have learned in Chapters 12 through 15. Project 2 includes payroll withholdings for Oregon.

Project 2A, Student-Designed Merchandising Business, asks you to create a merchandising business from scratch.

PART 4: ADVANCED SAGE 50 2019 APPLICATIONS

Chapters 16, 17, 18, Project 3, Project 4, and Project 4A are included in this part of the textbook. Chapter 16, Customizing Forms, shows you how to use Sage 50's design tools. Chapter 17, Import/Export, shows you how to export data from Sage 50 to a word processing program and how to import lists into a company. In Chapter 18, Microsoft Word and Templates, you copy a Sage 50 report to Word and look at vendor, customer, and employee templates included with the software.

> **For the Part 4 summary, refer to pages 617-618**. Page 618 includes a chart showing chapter numbers, files backed up and saved (.ptb, .pdf, .xlsx, .docx, .doc, .txt, .csv), file sizes, and page numbers where work was completed.

Chapter 16, Customizing Forms, includes design tools for report customization.

In Exercises 16-1 and 16-2, forms and financial statements are customized. Chapter 17, Import/Export, includes how to import a chart of accounts into another company and export to a word processing program.

In Exercises 17-1 and 17-2 import lists from Bellwether Garden Supply into the new company set up in Chapter 17.

Chapter 18, Microsoft Word and Templates, includes copying reports to Word, using templates and the write letters feature.

NEW Project 3, Evanston Computer Club, is a nonprofit business.

NEW Project 4, CL Manufacturing, Inc., is the culminating project in your study of Sage 50 2019. Project 4 includes payroll withholdings for Pennsylvania.

Project 4A, Student-Designed Project, instructs you to write another month's transactions for one of the four projects completed.

Each chapter ends with an Index for that chapter. There is also an Index at the end of the book.

CONVENTIONS USED IN TEXTBOOK

As you work through *Computer Accounting with Sage 50 2019, 21e*, you should read and follow the step-by-step instructions. Numerous screen illustrations help you to check your work. The following conventions are used in this textbook:

1. Information that you type appears in boldface; for example, Type **Supplies** in the Account I<u>D</u> field.
2. Keys on the keyboard that should be pressed appear in angle brackets; for example, <Enter>.
3. Sequences of software selections are indicated by a greater than symbol (>).

   Examples:

    > New Bill

   From the menu bar, select File > Close Company.

4. When you see this icon , there is a video, on the textbook website at www.mhhe.com/yacht2019 > Student Edition link > select the appropriate chapter > link to Videos or YouTube > then select the video. The Information Center list includes Sage Advisor videos.

5. This icon— —reminds you to check the Sage 50 work completed.

6. Buttons and picture icons are shown as they appear on the screen. Examples:

About the Author, carol@carolyacht.com and www.mhhe.com/yacht_titles

Carol Yacht is an educator and author of technology-based accounting textbooks. Carol authors Sage Peachtree (21e), Intuit's QuickBooks Online (2/e) and QuickBooks Desktop (9e) textbooks.

Carol taught on the faculties of California State University-Los Angeles, West Los Angeles College, Yavapai College, and Beverly Hills High School. She started using accounting software in her classes in 1980. Carol's teaching career includes first and second year accounting courses, accounting information systems, and computer accounting.

Since 1989, Carol's textbooks have been published by McGraw-Hill. She contributes regularly to professional journals and is the Editor of the American Accounting Association's Teaching, Learning, and Curriculum section's *The Accounting Educator.*

Carol Yacht was an officer of AAA's Two-Year College section and recipient of its Lifetime Achievement Award. She is a board member of the Microsoft Dynamics Academic Alliance; worked for IBM Corporation as an education instruction specialist; serves on AAA's Teaching, Learning, and Curriculum section's research, instructional, and hall of honor award committees; and works for Intuit and Sage as a consultant.

Carol earned her MA degree from California State University-Los Angeles, BS degree from the University of New Mexico, and AS degree from Temple University.

Acknowledgments

I would like to thank the following colleagues for their help in the preparation of this book: Steve Schuetz, Sarah Sacco, and Matt Lowenkron. A special thank you to the following professors.

Nathan Akins, Chattahoochee Technical College

Craig Anderson, Hennepin Technical College

Kathy Anderson, Tidewater Community College

Nat Akins, Chattahoochee Technical College

Kathy Blondell, St. Johns River Comm. College

Ana Boulware, St. Charles Comm. College

Michael Bryan, Tidewater Community College

Jim Burcicki, Penn Foster Career School

Lynda Byrd, Augusta Technical College

Vickie Campbell, Cape Fear CC

Sheree Corkern, Mississippi College

Leonard Cronin, Rochester Comm. College

Emmanuel Danso, Palm Beach State College

Alan Davis, Comm. Coll. of Philadelphia

Dave Davis, Vincennes University

Vaun Day, Central Arizona College

Roger Dimick, Lamar Inst. of Technology

Brenda Douglas, Central Arizona College

Philip Empey, Purdue University-Calumet

Raul Enriquez, Laredo Community College

Bill Gaither, Dawson Community College

Harold Gellis, York College of CUNY

Christopher Gilbert, Glendale College

Marina Grau, Houston Community College

Nancy Greene, University of Cincinnati

Joyce Griffin, Kansas City Kansas CC

Bill Guidera, Texas State Technical College

Jim Hale, Vance-Granville Community Coll.

Pamela Harroff, Georgia Piedmont Tech. Coll.

Mary Hauschen, Moraine Park Tech. Coll.

Paula E. Hegner, Folsom Lake College

Larry Heldreth, Danville Community College

Patricia Henderson, Southside Virginia CC

Betsey Hussey, Helena College

Tynia Kessler, Lake Land College

Jan Ivansek, Lakeland College

Jeff Jackson, San Jacinto College

Robert Jackson, Ivy Tech State College

Stacy Johnson, Iowa Central Comm. Coll.

Dorothy Kennedy, Augusta Technical College

Judy Kidder, Mohave Community College

Mary Kline, Black Hawk College

Vivian Knight, Pima Community College

Linda Kropp, Modesto Junior College

Sara Lagier, American Business College

Jan Lange, MN West Comm. & Tech. Coll.

Bruce Lindsey, Genesee Community Coll.

Susan Looney, Mohave Community Coll.

Susan Lynn, University of Baltimore

Josephine Mathias, Mercer County CC

J. Mike Metzcar, Indiana Wesleyan University

Julie Miller Millmann, Chippewa Valley Tech.

Rania Mousa, University of Evansville

LoAnn Nelson, Lake Region State College

Cory Ng, Comm. College of Philadelphia

Vincent Osaghae, Chicago State University

Susan Pallas, Southeast Community College

Rachel Pernia, Essex County College

Timothy Pearson, West Virginia University

Gerald Peterka, Mt. San Jacinto College

Simon Petravick, Bradley University

Tom Pinckney, Trident Technical College

Susan Pope, University of Akron

Robert Porter, Cape Fear Community College

Shirley Powell, Arkansas State University

Eric Primuth, Cuyahoga Community College

Jeffrey Pullen, Strayer University

Howard Randall, Mission College

Iris Lugo Renta, Interamerican University

Betty J. Reynolds, Arizona Western College

Monique Ring, So. New Hampshire University

Annalee Rothenberg, Tacoma Community Coll.

Helen Roybark, Radford University

Diane Sandefur, Elliott Bookkeeping School

Joann Segovia, Winona State University

Art Shroeder, Louisiana State University

Nancy Shoemake, Rochester Comm. Tech. Coll.

Le Shook, Chipola College

Douglas L. Smith, University of Montevallo

Mona Stephens, University of Phoenix

Charles Strang, Western New Mexico Univ.

Marilyn St. Clair, Weatherford College

Marie Stewart, Newport Business Institute

Maggie Stone, Pima Community College

Mel Sweet, University of Connecticut

Laurie Swinney, University of Nebraska

Eileen Taylor, North Carolina State University

Tom Turner, Des Moines Area Community Coll.

Mazdolyn Winston, Calhoun Community Coll.

W. Brian Voss, Austin Community College

Bruce Whitaker, Diné College

Shandra Ware, Atlanta Technical College

Michele Wiltsie, Hudson Valley Comm. Coll.

Table of Contents

l Table of Contents

The **Timetable for Completion** on the next two pages is a guideline for lecture/discussion/demonstration and hands-on work. Work <u>not</u> completed in class is homework. In most Accounting classes, students can expect to spend approximately two hours outside of class for every hour in class.

Two optional projects are on the textbook's Online Learning Center at www.mhhe.com/yacht2019. Select the Student Edition and then link to Practice Set or Bellwether Garden Supply Project. The Practice Set includes source documents for setting up and completing the accounting cycle for a merchandising business.

Continued

Part 1

Exploring Sage 50 2019

Part 1 introduces the basic features of Sage 50 2019. The purpose of Part 1 is to become familiar with the software rather than test accounting knowledge. Chapters 1 through 8 (Part 1) are an overview of Sage 50's user interface.

Beginning with Chapter 9, computer accounting skills are reviewed in depth. In Chapters 9-18 and Projects 1-4A, 12 businesses are set up from scratch. Part 1, Chapters 1-8, introduces two sample companies that are included with the software: Bellwether Garden Supply and Stone Arbor Landscaping.

Chapter 1: Introduction to Bellwether Garden Supply
Chapter 2: Vendors
Chapter 3: Customers
Chapter 4: Employees
Chapter 5: General Ledger, Inventory, and Internal Control
Chapter 6: Job Cost
Chapter 7: Financial Statements
Chapter 8: Stone Arbor Landscaping: Time & Billing
Bellwether Garden Supply Project, www.mhhe.com/yacht2019 > Student Edition

The work completed with Bellwether Garden Supply is cumulative. That means all work within Chapters 1 through 7, and end-of-chapter exercises, need to be completed. Throughout Part 1, report illustrations and Check Your Figure amounts are shown. To ensure that your work matches the textbook, complete *both* the work within the chapter and the end-of-chapter exercises. The Online Learning Center at www.mhhe.com/yacht2019 > Student Edition includes a Bellwether Garden Supply Project. Complete the project after Chapter 7.

The textbook instructions are written for Sage 50 2019. Sage 50 2019 requires these operating systems – Windows 10, 8.1, or 7. Pages v-vii include system requirements, or go online to www.mhhe.com/yacht2019 > System Requirements. To save reports in PDF format, the latest update of Adobe Acrobat Reader should be used (https://get.adobe.com/reader/).

Windows[1] uses pictures or *icons* to identify tasks. This is known as a *user interface* (*UI*), also known as the *graphical user interface* (*GUI*). For example, Sage uses common icons or symbols to represent tasks: a disk for saving, a question mark for help, a printer for printing, an envelope for email, etc. A *mouse*, *touchpad* or other pointing device is used to perform various tasks. Software design can be described by the acronym *WIMP* -- Windows, Icons, Menus, and Pull-downs.

The chart shows the size of the backup files, Excel files, and PDF files saved in Part 1–Chapters 1 through 8. The textbook shows how to back up to a USB drive. Backups can be made to the desktop, hard drive location, network location or external media.

Chapter	Sage 50 Backup (.ptb) Excel (.xlsx) and Adobe (.pdf)	Kilobytes[2]	Page Nos.
1	bgs.ptb[3]	3,497 KB	23-26
	Chapter 1.ptb	3,498 KB	39-40
	Chapter 1_Employee List.xlsx	15 KB	41-44
	Chapter 1_Employee List.pdf	26 KB	44-45
	Exercise 1-2.ptb	3,473 KB	50
	Exercise 1-2_Employee List.xlsx	13 KB	50
	Exercise 1-2_Employee List.pdf	28 KB	50
	Exercise 1-2_Chart of Accounts.xlsx	17 KB	50
	Exercise 1-2_Chart of Accounts.pdf	31 KB	50

---

[1] Words that are boldfaced and italicized are defined in the Glossary online at www.mhhe.com/yacht2019 > Student Edition > Glossary.

[2] Your backup sizes may differ.

[3] This is the first backup and includes starting data for Bellwether Garden Supply.

Chapter	Sage 50 Backup (.ptb), Excel (.xlsx) and Adobe (.pdf)	Kilobytes	Page Nos.
2	Chapter 2.ptb	3,412 KB	83-84
	Chapter 2_Vendor List and Vendor Ledgers.xlsx	21 KB	84-86
	Chapter 2_Vendor List.pdf	15 KB	86
	Chapter 2_Vendor Ledgers.pdf	27 KB	86
	Exercise 2-2.ptb	3,420 KB	89
	Exercise 2-2_Vendor List_Vendor Ledgers_PO Register.xlsx	25 KB	89
2	Exercise 2-2_Vendor List.pdf	16 KB	89
	Exercise 2-2_Vendor Ledgers.pdf	27 KB	89
	Exercise 2-2_Purchase Order Register.pdf	12 KB	89
3	Chapter 3.ptb	3,471 KB	126
	Exercise 3-2.ptb	3,465 KB	128
	Exercise 3-2_Customer Ledgers.xlsx	19 KB	128
	Exercise 3-2_Customer Ledgers.pdf	34 KB	129
4	Chapter 4.ptb	3,566 KB	149
	Exercise 4-2.ptb	3,560 KB	151
	Exercise 4-2_Payroll Check Register.xlsx	14 KB	151
	Exercise 4-2_Payroll Check Register.pdf	19 KB	151
5	Chapter 5.ptb	3,582 KB	187
	Exercise 5-2.ptb	3,576 KB	188
	Exercise 5-2_General Ledger Trial Balance.xlsx	15 KB	189
	Exercise 5-2_General Ledger Trial Balance.pdf	11 KB	189
6	Chapter 6.ptb	3,620 KB	200
	Exercise 6-2.ptb[4]	3,620 KB	202
	Exercise 6-2_Job Profitability Report.xlsx	17 KB	202
	Exercise 6-2_Job Profitability Report.pdf	26 KB	202
7	No backups in Chapter 7	--	--
	Chapter 7_Financial Statements.xlsx	36 KB	223-226
	Chapter 7_Balance Sheet.pdf	13 KB	226
	Chapter 7_Income Statement.pdf	9 KB	226
	Chapter 7_Gross Profit by Departments.pdf	4 KB	226
	Chapter 7_Statement of Cash Flow.pdf	13 KB	226

[4]The **Exercise 6-2.ptb** backup file is used in Part 4, Chapters 16, 17, and 18. If necessary, backup to external media. Do *not* delete the Exercise 6-2.ptb file.

Chapter	Sage 50 Backup (.ptb), Excel (.xlsx), and Adobe (.pdf)	Kilobytes	Page Nos.
7	Chapter 7_Statement of Retained Earnings.pdf	4 KB	226
	Chapter 7_Statement of Changes in Financial Position.pdf	13 KB	226
OLC	Bellwether Garden Supply Project, www.mhhe.com/yacht2019		
8	Chapter 8.ptb	1,663 KB	243
	Chapter 8_Time Ticket Register.xlsx	14 KB	244-246
	Chapter 8_Time Ticket Register.pdf	20 KB	246
	Exercise 8-1.ptb	1,684 KB	249
	Exercise 8-2_Time and Billing Reports.xlsx	32 KB	249
	Exercise 8-2_Job Ledger.pdf	46 KB	249
	Exercise 8-2_Time Ticket Register.pdf	26 KB	249
	Exercise 8-2_Payroll Time Sheet.pdf	26 KB	249

Chapter 1

Introduction to Bellwether Garden Supply

LEARNING OBJECTIVES

1. Start Sage 50 2019.
2. Explore the sample company, Bellwether Garden Supply.
3. Make sure global options are set ▶.[1]
4. Back up Bellwether Garden Supply data ▶.
5. Restore data with Sage 50's restore Wizard ▶.
6. Operate Sage 50's menus, drop-down lists, toolbar, and navigation bar.
7. Use File Explorer to see file sizes.
8. Export Sage 50 reports to Excel, and save reports as Adobe PDF files.
9. Make three backups, save three Excel files, and three PDF files.[2]

In Chapters 1 through 7 work is cumulative. Complete the work within the chapter and the end-of-chapter exercises. In Parts 2, 3 and 4 (Chapters 9-18, Projects 1-4A), you set up new service, merchandising, nonprofit, and manufacturing companies.

MOUSE AND KEYBOARD BASICS

One of the first decisions is whether to use the mouse or keyboard. The instructions in this book assume that you are using a mouse. When the word click or select is used, it means to use the mouse, but you can also use the

---

[1] ▶ means there is a video at www.mhhe.com/yacht2019 > Student Edition > Chapter 1 > Videos.

[2] Refer to the chart on page 2 for the size of files backed up and saved. Check with your instructor for his or her preference for receiving files—Adobe .pdf, Excel .xlsx, or Sage 50 .ptb backups.

---

keyboard. The instructions that follow explain how to use the mouse or keyboard.

Using the Mouse

- To single click: position the mouse cursor over the selection and click the left mouse button once.
- To double-click: position the mouse cursor over the selection and click the left mouse button twice, quickly.
- Use the right mouse button the same way as the left mouse button.

Using the Keyboard

- If there is an underlined letter on the menu bar, hold down the **<Alt>**[3] key and the underlined letter to make the selection. (*Hint:* Press the **<Alt>** key to underline menu bar letters.)
- If you have already held down the **<Alt>** key and the underlined letter and more selections appear with underlined letters, just type the underlined letter to select the item.

Using Shortcut Keys

Shortcut keys[4] enable you to perform common operations by using two or more keys together. The shortcut keys are shown below and on the next page.

---

[3]The angle brackets are used around words to indicate individual keys on your keyboard; for example, **<Alt>** is for the Alternate key, **<Enter>** for the Enter/Return key, **<Ctrl>** is for the Control key, **<Esc>** is for the Escape key.

[4]Words that are boldface and italics are defined in the Glossary, online at www.mhhe.com/yacht2019 > select Student Edition > Chapter 1 > Appendix D - Glossary.

<Ctrl> + <Letter> Shortcuts	
<Ctrl> + <X>	Cut
<Ctrl> + <C>	Copy
<Ctrl> + <V>	Paste
<Ctrl> + <E>	Delete Record
<Ctrl> + <F>	Find
<Ctrl> + <D>	Find Next
<Ctrl> + <N>	New Company
<Ctrl> + <O>	Open Company
<Ctrl> + <B>	Back Up Company
<Ctrl> + <R>	Restore Company
<Ctrl> + <P>	Print Displayed Report, Invoices, Quotes, etc.
Function Key Shortcuts	
<F1>	Displays the online Help topic for current window
<Shift> + <F1>	Changes mouse pointer to What's This Help selector
<F3>	Find transactions
<F5>	Saves records and posts (or saves) transactions in certain windows
<F7>	Check spelling
<F10>	Toggles between open window and menu bar
<CTRL>+<F4>	Close current document window
<ALT>+<F4>	Closes the application window
<CTRL>+<F6>	Moves to next window
<Shift>+<CTRL>+<F6>	Moves to the previous window

To learn more about Sage 50's shortcuts, use the Help menu. From the menu bar, select Help > Help > Index tab. Type **keyboard shortcuts** in the keyword field, then display the Sage 50 Keyboard Shortcuts. Additional links are listed in the Related topics and What do you want to do next? areas on the Sage 50 Help window.

SAGE 50'S STARTUP WINDOW

Sage 50's startup window displays a number of options.

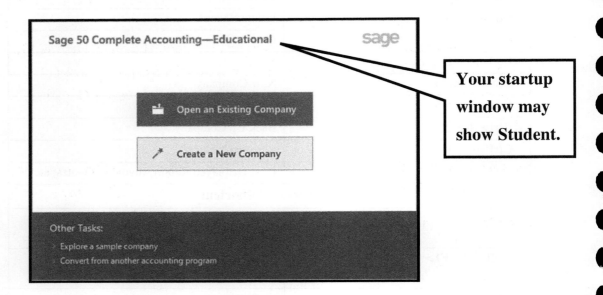

From the startup window, you can Open an existing company, Create a new company, Explore a sample company, and Convert from another accounting program.

Observe that the top-left of the Sage 50 Accounting window has four menu bar

options—

To exit from the startup window select File > Exit; *or*, click on the on the upper right-hand side of the Sage 50 Accounting window.

THE WINDOWS INTERFACE

One of the benefits of Windows is that it standardizes terms and operations used in software programs. Once you learn how to move around Sage, you also know how to use other Windows applications.

To learn more about the Windows user interface, let's look at a Sage window. On the next page, the Sage 50 Accounting window shows the ***Business Status Navigation Center*** (the ***dashboard***) and the menu bar for Bellwether Garden Supply.

For now, let's study the parts of the Business Status Navigation Center. Some features are common to all software programs that are written for Windows. For example, in the upper right corner there is the Minimize ▬ button, Double Window ▣ button, and the Exit or Close ⬛ button. The title bar, window border, and mouse pointer are also common to Windows programs. Other features are specific to Sage: menu bar, toolbar, and the Navigation Bar at the left side of Sage 50's main window which offers access to the Navigation Centers.

Sage 50 includes a Navigation Bar on the left side of the window with nine selections: Business Status, Customers & Sales (the home icon next to it means it is the default page), Vendors & Purchases, Inventory & Services, Employees & Payroll, Banking, Payment Center (fees required), Services (fees required), and System. The Navigation Bar selections open Navigation Centers. For example, the Business Status selection opens the Business Status Navigation Center. The content of the Navigation Centers differ depending on the selection from the Navigation Bar. The Business Status Navigation Center is shown on the next page.

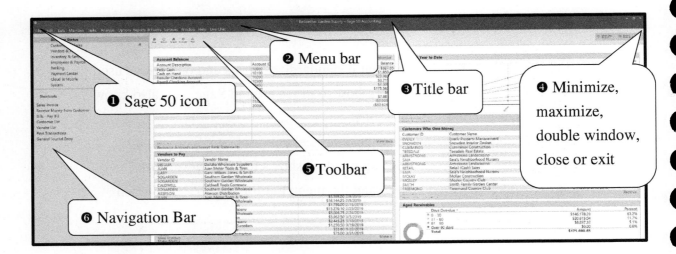

❶ Sage 50 icon: Click on the Sage 50 icon and a menu appears with options such as: Restore, Move, Size, Minimize, Maximize, Close. (Words that are gray are inactive selections.)

❷ Menu Bar: There are 11 active menu bar selections. If your menu bar selections have underlined letters that means you can make a selection by typing **<Alt>** and the underlined letter. For example, if you press the <Alt> key then press the <F> key, the menu bar shows underlined letters as well as the drop-down menu. You can also click with your left-mouse button on the menu bar headings to see a menu of options.

❸ *Title Bar*: The bar is at the top of the window. When a company is open, the name of the company is displayed on the Title Bar. If your window is minimized, you can put your mouse on the Title Bar, click and hold the left mouse button and drag the window around the *desktop*. The title bar shows Bellwether Garden Supply – Sage 50 Accounting.

❹ Minimize ▭, Double Window ▣, or Maximize ▢, and Close or Exit ✕ buttons: Clicking once on Double Window ▣ returns the window to its previous size. This button appears when you maximize the window. After clicking on the Double Window ▣ button, the symbol changes to the Maximize ▢ button. Click once on the Maximize ▢ button to enlarge the window. Click once on the Exit or Close button to close the window, or exit the program.

❺ Toolbar: The gray bar[5] below the Business Status button shows the following selections: Hide, this allows you to hide the Navigation Centers; Refresh, you can update account balances; Customize; Print, you can print the Business Status Navigation Center; System Date is the current date; Period for accounting records. Bellwether defaults to Period 3 – 03/01/19-03/31/19). When Business Status is selected, this toolbar appears.

❻ Navigation Bar: The Navigation Bar includes nine sections: Business Status, Customers & Sales, Vendors & Purchases, Inventory & Services, Employees & Payroll, Banking, Payment Center, Services (Student version; Cloud & Mobile, Educational version), and System.

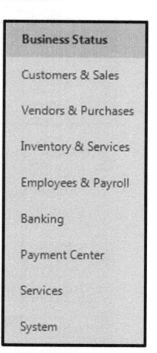

TYPICAL SAGE 50 WINDOWS

When you make a Navigation Bar selection, access is provided to the Navigation Center for each area of the program. For example, when Customers & Sales is selected, a workflow diagram is shown for Customers & Sales tasks, and links to related areas. There is also a tab for Customer Management.

The Maintain Customers/Prospects window shown below is typical of Sage. Information about customers is entered into the Maintain Customers/Prospects

---

[5]Window colors may differ. Check with your instructor if you have a question.

window. There are five sections on this window: ❶ the icon bar, ❷ Previous or next record, ❸ drop-down list (down arrow), ❹ tabs, ❺ information about window.

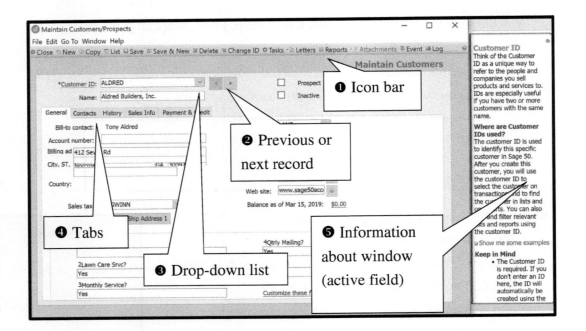

❶ ***Icon bar***[6]: The icon bar shows pictures of commands or additional information that pertains to the window. Some icons are common to all windows while other icons are specific to a particular window.

Close Close: This closes the window without saving any work that has been typed since the last time you saved.

New New: New record or customer.

Copy Copy: Copies customer information.

---

[6]Notice that familiar business items are used for icons: disk for <u>S</u>ave, an X for Delete, a paperclip for Attachments.

List List: List of customers.

Save Save: This saves information you have entered such as addresses, telephone numbers, contacts for vendors, customers, employees, etc.

Save & New Save & New: Save the record and go to a new, blank record.

Delete Delete: If you select this while using a selection from the Maintain menu, the record (customer, vendor, etc.) will be deleted. When you're finished deleting, select Close, in order to delete the records.

Change ID Change ID: When a customer record is displayed on the window, you may change the information for that customer.

Tasks Tasks: Select Tasks to enter a transaction for this customer—Create Quote, Create Sales Order, Create Sales Invoice, Create Receipt.

Letters Letters: Select a form letter or send an e-mail to customer.

Reports Reports: If you click on the down-arrow on the Reports icon, you can select the following customer reports—Aged Receivables, Customer Transaction History, Customer Ledgers, Items Sold to Customers, Job Ledger, Quote Register, Sales Order Register, and Ticket Listing by Customer. (In this example, Maintain > Customers/Prospects > Aldred Builders, Inc. is selected as the customer.)

Attachments Attachments: Use this icon to add attachments for customer record.

Event Event: Select this button in various maintenance windows to create an event. The Create Event window allows you to schedule an event for a customer/prospect, vendor, or employee/sales representative. You can also use the Event log to record notes about telephone calls, meetings, letters, and create a listing of future activity.

Log: Shows you events recorded for an individual over a specified range of time. You can *filter* this list to see only certain types of activities and whether they're completed or not. You can mark activities as completed by placing a mark in the far left column. Double-clicking on any of the *line items* will take you to the Create an Event window. Line items appear on many of Sage 50's windows.

Help: Selecting this icon gives you information specific to the current windows. The window's fields are listed at the bottom of the help message. When you have a question about how to use Sage 50, clicking on the Help icon often answers it.

❷ **Previous or Next Record**: Click on either the left arrow for the previous record; or the right arrow for the next record.

❸ *Drop-Down List*: The down arrow means that this field contains a list of information from which you can make a selection. Many of Sage's windows have drop-down lists that appear when you click on a down arrow next to a field. You can press **<Enter>** or click on an item to select it from the list.

❹ *Tabs*: The tabs that are shown in the Maintain Customers/Prospects window are General, Contacts, History, Sales Info, Payment & Credit. Once a customer is selected, you can select one of these folders to display information about a customer.

THE SAMPLE COMPANY: BELLWETHER GARDEN SUPPLY

Bellwether Garden Supply is one of the sample companies included with Sage 50. To help you become familiar with the software, the sample company is used.

GETTING STARTED

1. To start, click on the desktop icon. If Sage 50 2019 is not installed on your computer, refer to pages vii-xvi for software installation.
2. When Sage 50 was installed, a desktop icon is created. To start, place the mouse pointer on the Sage 50 icon and double-click with the left mouse button. (Or, click Start > go to Apps by name > Sage 50 Accounting 2019.)
3. From the startup window, you can Open an existing company, Create a new company, Explore a sample company, or Convert from another accounting program.

What is the difference between the Educational version and the Student version? The Student version is included with the textbook and can be used for 14 months. The Educational version does <u>not</u> have a time limit, has a *different serial number,* can be installed on multiple computers in the classroom, and is available to instructors and schools. For more information, refer to Student Version and Educational Version, page iv.

4. Select Explore a Sample Company. Sage 2019 has two sample companies: Bellwether Garden Supply and Stone Arbor Landscaping. In Chapters 1–7, you use Bellwether Garden Supply to explore Sage 50. Then, in Chapter 8, you use Stone Arbor Landscaping to see how the time and billing feature works. Make sure that Bellwether Garden Supply is selected.

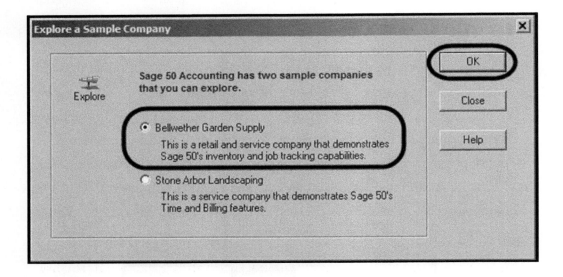

5. Click [OK], *or* press <Enter>. On the Navigation Bar, select

   [**Business Status**]. The Business Status Navigation Center appears. The
   Business Status Navigation Center, also known as the ***Home page*** or
   dashboard, is separated into seven areas. The dashboard lets you see at a
   glance a variety of general business information. Scroll down the window
   to see all of it. Each area has underlined links shown in blue font.

   a. Account Balances – Links include View Account List; Reconcile
      Accounts and Import Bank Statements; View Balance Sheet. You can
      link to reports from the Navigation Centers *or* from the menu bar.

   b. Vendors to Pay – A vendor list is shown with links to View Purchases
      List, Make Multiple Payments, and Make a Payment.

   c. Aged Payables – A graph is shown with links to View Vendor List,
      View Aged Payables Report, Make a Payment, and Make Multiple
      Payments.

   d. Revenue: Year to Date – A graph shows the first quarter of 2019's
      revenue and links to View Income Statement; Edit a Budget; and View
      Account Variance Report.

e. Customers Who Owe Money – A customer list is shown with links to View Sales Invoices List, Write Letters to Customers, Receive Money.

f. Aged Receivables – A graph is shown and links to View Customer List; View Aged Receivables Report; and Receive Payment.

g. Find a Report – Observe that fields are included for Category, Report, and Description. (If necessary, scroll down the Home page.)

DISPLAY PRODUCT INFORMATION

1. From the menu bar, click Help > About Sage 50 Accounting. The About Sage 50 Accounting window shows the copyright information and the Release, Build, Serial Number, Installed Tax Service, and Registered Tax Service. The Release field shows Sage 50 Accounting 2019; the Build No. is 26.0.00.00141S (S for student) *or* Build No. 26.0.00.00141 (E for Educational); Serial Number, Student Version or Educational Version, Customer ID: 000000000X; Installed Tax Service 20180501; Plan Level: None. (The Customer ID shows an X. Substitute the number shown for your Customer ID.)

On the next page, the About Sage 50 Accounting window is shown for the Educational version. Your screen may show Sage 50 Complete Accounting - Student.

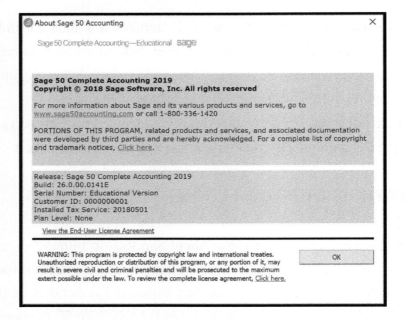

> **Troubleshooting:** If you are using Sage 50 in the classroom or computer lab, the multi-user version may have been installed. When the multi-user version is installed, the Build field ends in E and the Serial Number field shows Educational Version.
> When you install the Student version software included with the textbook on your PC, the Build Number field ends in S and the Serial Number field shows Student Version. The Student Version software is valid for 14 months.

2. Click OK to close.

SETTING GLOBAL OPTIONS ▶[7]

Sage 50's *global options* are in effect for all companies. All companies in Chapters 1-18 and Projects 1-4 require these global options.

---

[7] ▶ means there is a Global Options video. Go online to www.mhhe.com/yacht2019 >Student Edition > Chapter 1 > Videos > Global Options.

1. From the menu bar, select Options > Global. The Maintain Global Options window appears. The <u>A</u>ccounting tab is selected.

    a. In the **Decimal Entry** area, select Manual.
    b. Make sure 2 is shown in the Quantity, Standard and Unit Price fields.
    c. In the **Hide General Ledger Accounts** area, make sure that there are no checkmarks in the boxes. (To uncheck one of the boxes, click on it.)
    d. In the **Other Options** area, a checkmark should be placed next to Warn if a record was changed but not saved; and Recalculate cash balance automatically in Receipts, Payments, and Payroll Entry. Compare your Maintain Global Options > Accounting tab window with the one shown below.

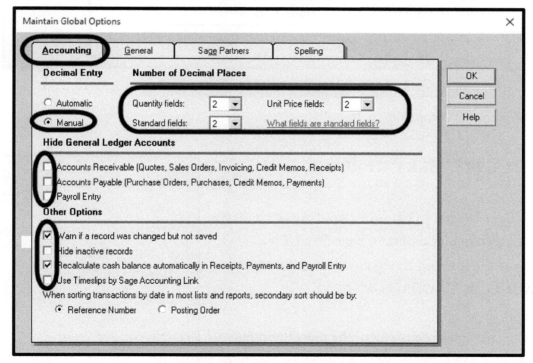

2. Click on the **<u>G</u>eneral** tab. Make sure the Maintain Global Options > <u>G</u>eneral window shows the following selections. The Color Scheme radio buttons are for choosing a different color.

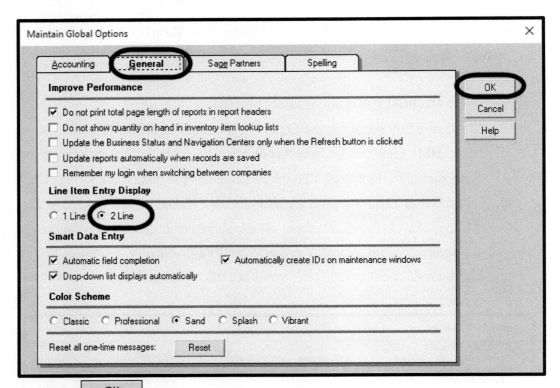

3. Click [OK] to save the global options, which will be in effect for all Sage 50 companies.

SAGE 50'S USER INTERFACE

A User Interface (UI) is the link between a user and a computer program. Sage 50's UI is designed for both Navigation Bar and menu-bar selections.

Business Status

Customers & Sales
Vendors & Purchases
Inventory & Services
Employees & Payroll
Banking
Payment Center
Cloud & Mobile
System

The user interface is one of the most important parts of any software because it determines how easily you can make the program do what you want. Graphical user interfaces (GUIs) that use windows, icons, and pop-up menus are standard on personal computers.

The *Navigation Bar* appears at the left side of the Sage 50 main window and offers access to the *Navigation Centers*. The Navigation Centers provide information about and access to Sage 50. The Navigation Bar includes nine selections: Business Status, Customers & Sales, Vendors & Purchases, Inventory & Services, Employees & Payroll, Banking, Payment Center, Services (Educational version) or Cloud & Mobile (Student version), System. When you click one of the nine selections (for example, Customers & Sales), the panel to the right of the Navigation Bar displays a *workflow diagram* with additional links related to that *module*. Modules organize Sage 50's transaction windows and reports. The menu bar selections – Tasks `Tasks` and Reports & Forms `Reports & Forms` – are also organized by module; for example, the Reports & Forms menu includes Accounts Receivable, Accounts Payable, General Ledger, etc.

Sage 50's modules include Customers & Sales, Vendors & Purchases, Inventory & Services, Employees & Payroll, Banking, and System. The Business Status Navigation Center includes a snapshot of the company. Sage 50's modular design is similar to other accounting software applications. In this textbook, you use the Navigation Bar and menu bar selections to access features of the program. The individual Navigation Bar selections take you to Navigation Centers. For example, if you select Customers & Sales, the tabs for Customers & Sales `Customers & Sales` and Customer Management `Customer Management` appear. The `Customers & Sales` button is the default with the Customer & Sales Tasks Navigation Center shown.

CHART OF ACCOUNTS

A *chart of accounts* is a list of all the account names and account numbers used in the General Ledger. Sage 50's *general ledger module* is the complete collection of accounts (chart of accounts) of a company, transactions associated with these accounts, and account balances for a specified period. In Chapter 5, General Ledger, Inventory, and Internal Control, you will learn more about Sage 50's general ledger module and the chart of accounts. For now, let's view Bellwether's chart of accounts so that you can familiarize yourself with the accounts that will be used in subsequent chapters. Follow these steps to display Bellwether's chart of accounts.

1. From the Navigation Bar, select **Business Status**. In the Account Balances area, link to View Account List. The Account List window appears. The Account List is also called the Chart of Accounts. A partial list is shown.

Account ID	Description	Type	Running Balance
10000	Petty Cash	Cash	$327.55
10100	Cash on Hand	Cash	$1,850.45
10200	Regular Checking Account	Cash	$23,389.83
10300	Payroll Checking Account	Cash	$3,711.09
10400	Savings Account	Cash	$7,500.00
11000	Accounts Receivable	Accounts Receivable	$175,563.10
11100	Contracts Receivable	Accounts Receivable	$0.00
11400	Other Receivables	Accounts Receivable	$7,681.84
11500	Allowance for Doubtful Account	Accounts Receivable	($5,000.00)
12000	Inventory	Inventory	$12,786.56
14000	Prepaid Expenses	Other Current Assets	$14,221.30
14100	Employee Advances	Other Current Assets	$3,000.65
14200	Notes Receivable-Current	Other Current Assets	$11,000.00
14700	Other Current Assets	Other Current Assets	$120.00
15000	Furniture and Fixtures	Fixed Assets	$62,769.25
15100	Equipment	Fixed Assets	$38,738.33
15200	Vehicles	Fixed Assets	$86,273.40
15300	Other Depreciable Property	Fixed Assets	$6,200.96
15400	Leasehold Improvements	Fixed Assets	$0.00
15500	Buildings	Fixed Assets	$185,500.00
15600	Building Improvements	Fixed Assets	$26,500.00
16900	Land	Fixed Assets	$0.00
17000	Accum. Depreciation-Furniture	Accumulated Depreciation	($54,680.57)
17100	Accum. Depreciation-Equipment	Accumulated Depreciation	($33,138.11)
17200	Accum. Depreciation-Vehicles	Accumulated Depreciation	($51,585.26)
17300	Accum. Depreciation-Other	Accumulated Depreciation	($3,788.84)
17400	Accum. Depreciation-Leasehold	Accumulated Depreciation	$0.00
17500	Accum. Depreciation-Buildings	Accumulated Depreciation	($34,483.97)
17600	Accum. Depreciation-Bldg Imp	Accumulated Depreciation	($4,926.28)
19000	Deposits	Other Assets	$15,000.00
19100	Organization Costs	Other Assets	$4,995.10
19150	Accum Amortiz - Organiz Costs	Other Assets	($2,000.00)
19200	Notes Receivable-Noncurrent	Other Assets	$5,004.90
19900	Other Noncurrent Assets	Other Assets	$3,333.00
20000	Accounts Payable	Accounts Payable	($80,626.01)
23000	Accrued Expenses	Other Current Liabilities	($3,022.55)
23100	Sales Tax Payable	Other Current Liabilities	($18,028.06)

The numbers in parentheses are credit balances. The Account List's icon bar includes a Send To selection. When you make that selection, you can send the Account List to Excel, E-mail, or PDF (Adobe Acrobat). Exporting Sage 50 reports to Microsoft Excel is shown on pages 41-44. Saving PDF files is shown on pages 44-45.

2. Close the Account List by clicking ☒ on its title bar.

BACKING UP BELLWETHER GARDEN SUPPLY ▶[8]

Before making changes to Bellwether Garden Supply, you should back up the sample company data. When using Sage 50, information is automatically saved to the hard drive of the computer. In a classroom, a number of students may be using the same computer. This means that when you return to the computer lab or classroom, your data will be gone. ***Backing up*** means saving a copy of the data to a hard drive, network drive, or external media. Backing up ensures that you can start where you left off the last time Sage 50 was used.

When backing up, you have choices—accept the hard-drive default location or back up to a USB flash drive (or other external media). In the steps that follow, backups are made to a USB drive also called flash drives, thumb drives, or pen/stick drives. In this book, the term ***USB drive*** is used to identify USB storage media. USB is an abbreviation of Universal Serial Bus.

Backups should be made each time you complete work. In the textbook, the following backup file names are suggested.
*   For the first backup, *before* any data has been added, the suggested file name is bgs.ptb. [The extension .ptb is added to backups.]
*   Chapter number.ptb for work completed within the chapter.
*   Exercise number.ptb for work completed in the exercises.

When work is completed, back up. This could be before it is shown in the textbook.

---

[8]The arrow indicates there is a video. Go online to www.mhhe.com/yacht2019 > link to Student Edition > select Chapter 1 > Videos > Backup.

> **Comment: Backing up data to the hard-drive default location**
>
> The author suggests backing up the sample company *before* any changes are made. In the textbook, backups are made to *external media* or a USB drive. Backups can also be made to the desktop or other locations.
>
> You may also backup to the default location at C:\Sage\Peachtree\Company\Sample\ PCWS\BCS. (*Hint:* To see the default directory where Bellwether is located, from the menu bar select Maintain > Company Information. The Directory field shows the location of the BCS folder. BCS is the folder where Bellwether Garden Supply data is stored.)
>
> Education Version directory: Directory: C:\Sage\Peachtree\Company\Sample\PCWE\BCS
>
> Student Version directory: C:\Sage\Peachtree\Company\Sample\PCWS\BCS
>
> When you add your name to Bellwether's reports on pages 40-41, the folder where Bellwether data is stored is changed to \belgarsu.
>
> When a backup is made, data is saved to the current point. To distinguish between backups, a different backup name (file name) should be used. Use Sage 50's *restore* feature to retrieve information that was backed up.
>
> In the business world, backups are unique to each business: daily, weekly, monthly. Think of your backups this way and you will see why individual backups at different points in the data are necessary. *You should never leave the computer lab or classroom without backing up your data.*

Follow these steps to back up Bellwether Garden Supply.

The text directions assume that you are backing up to a USB drive. *You can also backup to the desktop, hard drive, or network location. One USB flash, thumb or flash drive, CD-R or DVD-R can be used for all the backups in Chapters 1-18 and the projects.* The chart on pages 2-4 (Part 1 introduction) shows the size of each backup made in Chapters 1-8.

---

1. Insert a USB flash or thumb drive into the USB drive.

2. From the Navigation Bar, click [System]. In the Back Up and Restore Data area, click [Back Up Now]. (*Or,* you can select File > Back Up.) The Back Up Company window appears. If necessary, uncheck the box next to Include company name in the backup file name. Compare your Back Up Company window to the one shown below.

Uncheck Include company name in backup

3. After clicking [Back Up], the Save Backup for Bellwether Garden Supply as window appears.

4. In the Save in field, select your USB drive. The illustration below shows drive F, which is the location of the author's USB drive. Your USB drive

    letter may differ. Type **bgs** in the File name field. Observe that the Save as type field shows that you are making a Sage 50 Backup (*.ptb), which is abbreviated ptb. This is the extension for Sage 50 backups.

Comment

If your Save as type field does *not* show Sage 50 Backup (*.ptb), follow these steps:

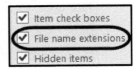

1. Go to File Explorer.
2. From the menu bar, select View. Make sure there is a checkmark next to File name extensions.
3. Close File Explorer.

 Read Me: "Student Version" or "Educational Version"

If you are backing up to the default hard-drive location, the Student Version hard-drive location for backups is C:\Sage\Peachtree\Company\Sample\PCWS\ BCS. If your folder shows ...\Sample\PCWE, you are using the Educational Version's sample company data. Your hard-drive location may differ.

Accept the hard-drive default for backing up. Click , then OK

5. Click Save .

6. A window appears that says This company backup will require approximately 1 diskette. If you are backing up to USB flash drive, this window appears. If backing up to a hard-drive location, a window appears showing the file size.

7. Click OK . When the window prompts Please insert the first disk, click OK . When Back Up Company scale is 100% complete, you have successfully backed up the sample company.

Follow these steps to see the size of the backup file.

1. Go to File Explorer. The folder icon also opens File Explorer.
2. Select your USB drive (or the location where you backed up Bellwether Garden Supply).

   The Name of the file is bgs.ptb; the size of the file is 3,497 KB;[9] and File Type is PTB File. Compare this information to the bcs folder on your hard drive, network drive, USB drive, or DVD. Your backup size may differ.

Name	Type	Size
☐ bgs.ptb	PTB File	3,497 KB

   Refer to the chart on pages 2-4 for estimated back up sizes. Sage 50 backs up to the current point in the data. The author suggests backing up to a USB flash drive or hard drive location.

3. Close File Explorer.

USING SAGE 50'S RESTORE WIZARD ▶[10]

In order to start where you left off the last time you backed up, use the Restore Wizard. Follow these steps to use the Restore Wizard.

1. Start Sage 50. (*Hint:* If another company opens, from the menu bar select File > Close Company to go to the startup window.) Open the sample company, Bellwether Garden Supply.

---

[9]The size of your backup file may differ.

[10]The arrow indicates a video at www.mhhe.com/yacht2019 . Select Student Edition > Chapter 1 > Videos > Restore.

Read Me: What if Bellwether Garden Supply is *not* shown as an existing company *or* when you select Explore a sample company?

Some schools delete company folders from the hard drive. For example, you have a backup file but the company, Bellwether Garden Supply, is *not* listed as a Sage 50 company. Follow these steps to restore *and* create Bellwether from a backup file.

1. If necessary, click File > Close Company to go to the Startup window. To double-check that Bellwether is *not* listed, select Open an existing company. Make sure Bellwether Garden Supply is *not* listed in the Company Name list. Click [Close]. **NOTE:** Complete steps 2, 3, and 4 within this Read Me box if the sample company, Bellwether Garden Supply, *cannot* be opened from the Startup window *or* from the Open an existing company selection.

2. The startup window shows four menu bar options—[File   Options   Services   Help]. Select File > Restore.

3. Browse to the location of your backup file. Click on the backup file to highlight it. Click <Open>, then <Next>.

4. On the Select Company/Choose how to restore your backup window, select Create a new company using the restored data [⦿ Create a new company using the restored data]. The Company Name field shows Bellwether Garden Supply, click <Next>. Continue with step 10, page 30.

2. Insert your USB flash drive. The steps that follow assume you are restoring from a USB drive.

3. From the Navigation Bar > click [System] > [Restore Now]. The Select Backup File window appears > click [Browse]

4. The Open Backup File window appears. In the Look in field, select the location of your USB drive. Select the bgs.ptb file.

5. Click [Open]. The Restore Wizard – Select Backup File window appears showing the location of your backup file, X:\bgs.ptb. (Substitute X for your drive letter.)

6. Click [Next >].

7. The Select Company, Choose how to restore your backup window appears. Observe that Overwrite existing company data is the default. Since Bellwether is open and you are <u>not</u> creating a new company, accept the Overwrite existing company data default. The Company Name field shows Bellwether Garden Supply and the Location shows Bellwether's location. Your Location field may differ.

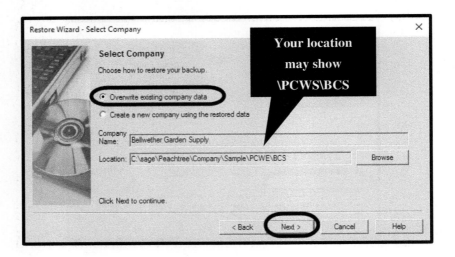

8. Read the information on the Select Company > Choose how to restore your backup window > click ⬚ Next > .

9. The Restore Options window appears. Make sure that the check mark is next to Company Data.

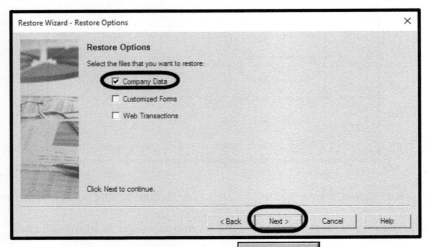

10. On the Restore Options window, click ⬚ Next > .

11. The Confirmation window appears. Read the information. Check the Backup file and Location fields.

12. Click . The window prompts "This process will overwrite and replace existing data permanently. Do you want to continue?"

13. Click **Yes** . When the scale is 100% complete, the Bellwether Garden Supply data is restored. The Bellwether Garden Supply - Sage 50 Accounting window appears. (*Hint:* If a screen prompts that you can use Sage 50 Accounting for 14 months, click <OK>.)

Once Bellwether's files are restored, you are ready to continue using the sample company. *Remember before you exit, make a backup of your work.* The following information demonstrates the horizontal menu bar selections. In this book, you are going to use *both* the menu bar selections and the Navigation Bar.

MENU BAR

The menu bar has 11 active selections: File, Edit, Lists, Maintain, Tasks, Analysis, Options, Reports & Forms, (Services is inactive), Window, Help and Live Chat. (Once a file is restored, the Services menu appears.) Follow these steps to look at each menu bar selection.

1. From the menu bar, click File to see its menu, *or*, press <Alt> + F to display the File menu. If you use <Alt> + F instead of your mouse, notice that the individual letters on the menu bar are underlined. In this example, the mouse is used.

   The File menu allows you to open a company, open previous company, create a new company, close the company, go to the setup guide, print preview, print, create a PDF, go to user login manager (inactive), Back Up, Restore, Automatic Backup, Online Backup/Restore (inactive), select import/export, convert a company, data verification, update encryption, enter payroll formulas, and exit. (The grayed out selections are inactive.)

   Menu choices that are followed by an ***ellipsis*** (…) are associated with ***dialog boxes*** or windows that supply information about a window. An arrow (▶) next to a menu item (Open Previous Company and Payroll Formulas) indicates that there is another menu with additional selections. To cancel the drop-down menu, click File or **<Esc>**.

2. The Edit selection shows Find Transactions.

3. Click Lists to see its menu. The Lists
    selection shows Customers & Sales, Vendors & Purchases, Employees &
    Payroll, Chart of Accounts, General Journal Entries, Inventory & Services,
    Jobs, and Time/Expense. The Lists menu is an alternative to using the
    Navigation Bar.

4. Click Maintain to see its menu.

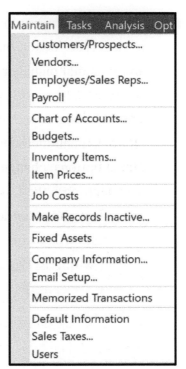

    From the Maintain menu, you can enter, view,
    or edit required information for your company's
    customers or prospects, vendors, employees or
    sales reps, payroll, chart of accounts, budgets,
    inventory items, item prices, job costs, make
    records inactive, fixed assets. (Fixed Assets
    requires that FAS for Sage 50 has been
    purchased). You can edit company information,
    go to email setup, enter memorized
    transactions, go to *default* information, sales
    taxes, and users (passwords and security).
    Defaults are automatically selected. They can
    be changed.

5. Click Tasks to see its menu.

   From the Tasks menu, you can enter quotes and sales orders, sales invoices, invoice time and expenses, receive money, finance charges, select for deposit, issue credit memos, select for purchase orders, purchase orders, purchases/receive inventory, bills, select for payment, payments, write checks, vendor credit memos, account register, record time and expenses, select for payroll entry, payroll entry, make general journal entries, inventory adjustments, assemblies, account reconciliation, void checks, write letters, action items, and system.

6. Click Analysis to see its menu.

   The Analysis menu includes the cash flow manager, collection manager, payment manager, and financial manager.

7. Click Options to see its menu. The Options menu includes setting global options, change the system date, start with the Last Opened Company, and enter default information. The checkmark next to Start with Last Opened Company means that each time you start Sage 50, the last company worked with opens.

8. Click Reports & Forms to see its menu.

    The Reports & Forms menu allows you to *queue* reports for printing or displaying. You can also create and edit the format for forms, reports, and financial statements.

9. Click Window to see its menu. The Window menu allows you to close all windows.

    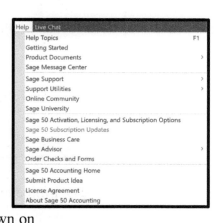

10. Click Help to see its menu.

    The Help menu allows you to open help topics, getting started, product documents, Sage message center, Sage support and utilities, online community, Sage university, Sage activation, Licensing, and subscription options, Sage business care and advisory, order checks and forms, Sage 50 Accounting Home, submit product idea, license agreement, and about Sage 50 accounting. Select About Sage 50 Accounting to display product information. Detailed steps for displaying product information are shown on pages 17-18.

11. Click Live Chat. To get help from Pegg, type a question or message. To close, click <X> on the Pegg tab.

BECOMING AN EMPLOYEE OF BELLWETHER GARDEN SUPPLY

Before adding yourself as an employee of Bellwether Garden Supply, use the Navigation Bar to open the Maintain Employees & Sales Reps window. The Navigation Bar selections include: Business Status, Customers & Sales, Vendors

& Purchases, Inventory & Services, Employees & Payroll, Banking, Payment Center, Services, and System. Follow these steps to add yourself as an employee.

1. On the Navigation Bar, select **Employees & Payroll**. The Employees & Payroll Navigation Center appears.

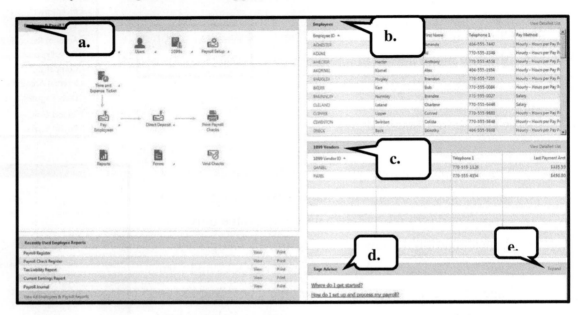

The Employees & Payroll Navigation Center displays information and access points related to the company's employees. It is organized into five sections.

a. Employees & Payroll Tasks: The flowchart shows how Sage 50 processes payroll.

b. Employees: The employee list is shown.

c. 1099 Vendors: Vendors that receive 1099's from Bellwether.

d. Recently Used Employee Reports: Links to payroll reports.

e. Sage Advisor: Link to <u>Expand</u>. The Sage Advisor Getting Started window appears. To watch the videos, go to <u>www.mhhe.com/yacht2019</u> > Sage Advisor Videos.

2. Click 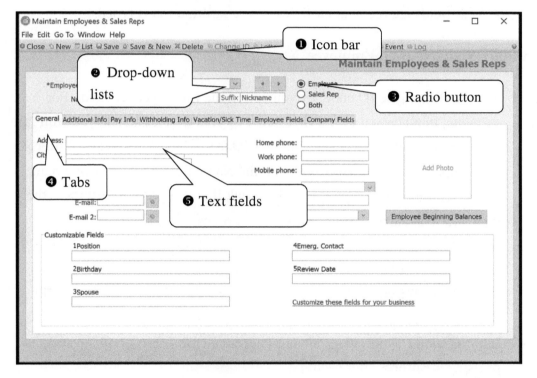 > New Employee. The Maintain Employees & Sales Reps window appears.

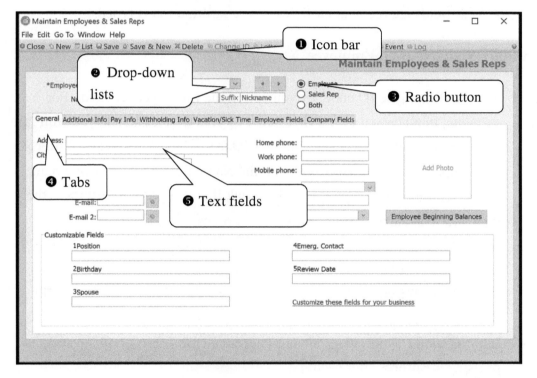

❶ The icon bar at the top of most windows shows graphical representations of commands or functions that are accessible from the window.

❷ Drop-down lists: Click on the down-arrow to see lists. On the Maintain Employees & Sales Reps window, employee IDs are shown. When you are in the text portion of the field, the cursor changes to an I-bar and a question mark <⌶?>. Type a question mark <?> in the field, or click the right mouse button, to display lists.

❸ *Radio Button or Option Button:* These buttons allow you to select one by clicking with the mouse. The default is Employee shown by the radio button next to Employee.

❹ Tabs are common to most windows. They provide a subtitle to the various windows that store and organize information. Here, for example, the information you can choose to track is subdivided into categories: General, Additional Info, Pay Info, Withholding Info, Vacation/Sick Time, Employee Fields, and Company Fields.

❺ Text fields are rectangular fields where information is typed.

Adding Yourself as an Employee

1. Type an Employee ID code for yourself in the Employee ID field. For example, in all caps type the first initial of your first name and your full last name in all capital letters (the author's ID is CYACHT) > press **<Enter>**.[11]

2. Using upper and lowercase letters, in the Name field, type your first name, press **<Enter>** > type your middle initial, if any > press **<Enter>** > then type your last name. Press **<Enter>** five times.[12]

3. In the Address field, type your street address. There are two lines so you can enter an ATTENTION line or PO Box, if necessary. If you are using just one line for your address, press **<Enter>** two times to go to the City, ST, Zip fields.

4. In the City, ST Zip field, type your city, state (two-digits), and zip code, pressing **<Enter>** after each.

5. None of the other information is required. You work with the other fields in Chapter 15, Employees, Payroll, and Account Reconciliation. Click ⌷ Save . To check Employee ID was added, click on the down-arrow.

---

[11]Set up Employee IDs that are consistent with how Bellwether identifies employees. For example, use uppercase for the first initial and last name.

[12]You can use **<Enter>** or **<Tab>** to move between fields. Use **<Shift>+<Enter>** or **<Shift>+<Tab>** to move back a field. You can also hold the **<Alt>** key and press the underlined letter of a text box to move between fields.

6. Click 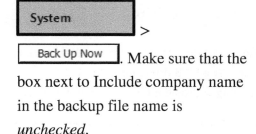 to return to the Employees & Payroll Navigation Center. To

see your name on the Employees list, click Refresh

BACKING UP CHAPTER 1 DATA

Follow these steps to back up Chapter 1 data:

1. Insert your USB flash drive.
2. From the Navigation Bar, click

   System >

   Back Up Now . Make sure that the

   box next to Include company name

   in the backup file name is

   unchecked.

3. Click Back Up .

4. In the Save in field, select the

   appropriate drive letter for your

   USB drive.[13] (*Or,* save to the default

   location or other location.) Type

   Chapter 1 in the File name field.

   Compare your Save Backup for

   Bellwether Garden Supply as

   window with the one shown below.

   (Your Save in field may differ.)

---

[13]If you are having difficulty backing up to USB flash drive, backup to the desktop, then copy
the file to a USB flash drive. Refer to www.mhhe.com/yacht2019 > Troubleshooting Tips >
Problem Backing Up to USB Drive or Other External Media.

5. Click .

6. When the window prompts This company backup will require approximately 1 diskette, click [OK]. When the window prompts Please insert the first disk, click [OK]. When the Back Up Company scale is 100% complete, you have successfully backed up to the current point in Chapter 1. (Step 6 will differ slightly if you are backing up to the default or other hard-drive location.)

 Read Me: Problem Backing Up to USB Drive

If you encounter difficulties backing up to a USB drive, backup to your desktop first. Then copy the backup file from your desktop to a USB drive. Refer to www.mhhe.com/yacht2019 > Troubleshooting > Problem Backing Up to USB Drive or Other External Media.

ADD YOUR NAME TO REPORTS

Your instructor may want to have your name or initials on all report printouts. To do that, follow these steps.

1. From the Navigation Bar > select [System]. If necessary, scroll down the page to Company Maintenance.

2. Click [Edit Company Information Now]. The Maintain Company Information Window appears. In the Company Name field, add your name or initials after Bellwether Garden Supply.

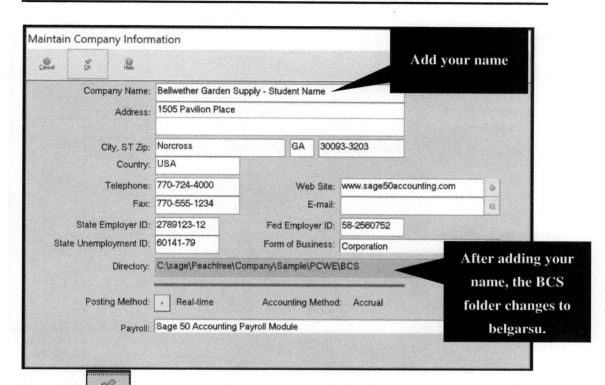

3. Click ![OK]. Your name is added to reports. To see the change from \BCS to \belgarsu, exit Sage 50. Then start Sage and open Bellwether Garden Supply – Your Name. Go to Maintain > Company Information. The Directory field ends in belgarsu.

> Directory: C:\Sage\Peachtree\Company\Sample\PCWE\belgarsu

EXPORTING REPORTS TO EXCEL

On pages 38-39, you added yourself as an employee of Bellwether Garden Supply. To see an Employee List and export the list to Excel, follow these steps. In order to export reports to Excel, you need Excel 2007 or higher.

1. From the Navigation Bar > select Employees & Payroll. In the Recently Used Employee Reports section, link to <u>View All Employees & Payroll Reports</u>. The Select a Report or Form window appears > select Employee List.

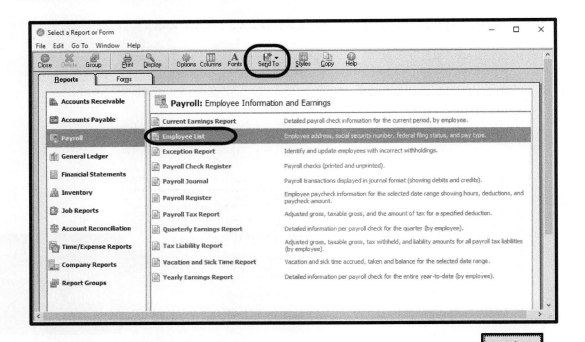

2. On the icon bar, select Send To > then Excel.

   Troubleshooting: If you are using Microsoft Office 365, the Excel icon may be inactive. Display the Sage report > select Edit > Copy > start Excel > open a blank workbook > right click on the sheet > left-click Paste > reformat > save as Chapter 1_Employee List. For more information, go to Appendix A, Troubleshooting, Inactive Excel Icon. On Page v, Integration/compatibility requirements, lists which versions of Microsoft Office work with Sage 50 2019.

3. The Modify Report – Employee List window appears. Accept the defaults by clicking   OK

4. The Copy Report to Excel window appears. Accept the File option, Create a New Microsoft Excel workbook. In the Report header option area, select Show header in Excel worksheet.

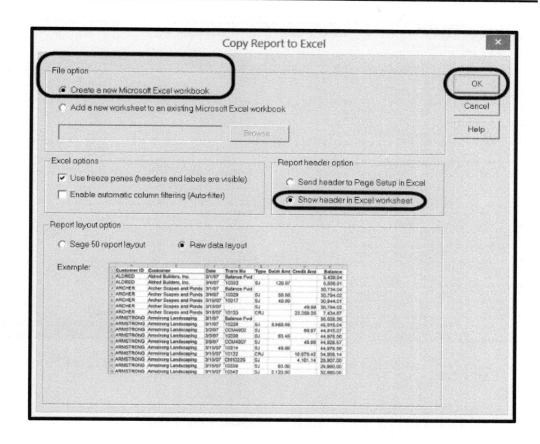

5. Click [OK]. The Copying Employee List to Excel window appears. When the Bellwether Garden Supply Employee List displays, check that your name has been added to the list of employees.

6. Save the Excel worksheet to your USB flash drive. Use **Chapter 1_Employee List.xlsx** as the file name. The Employee List shows Student Name on the title bar. Your name should be shown.

	Employee ID	Employee	Address line 1	Address line 2	City ST ZIP	Masked SS No	Fed Filing Status	Pay Type
					Bellwether Garden Supply - Student Name			
					Employee List			
	Filter Criteria includes: Report order is by ID.							
5	Employee ID	Employee	Address line 1	Address line 2	City ST ZIP	Masked SS No	Fed Filing Status	Pay Type
6	ACHESTER	Amanda W. Chester	4599 West Paces Ferry Road		Atlanta, GA 30328	XXX-XX-1337	Single	Hourly
7	ADUKE	Al L. Duke	3905 Alpharetta Hwy		Alpharetta, GA 30039	XXX-XX-1134	Single	Hourly
8	AHECTER	Anthony H. Hecter	67 Lenox Rd		Atlanta, GA 30319	XXX-XX-5656	Single	Hourly
9	AKORNEL	Alex C. Kornel	847 Clairmont Road		Atlanta, GA 30329	XXX-XX-8778	Married	Hourly
10	BHUGLEY	Brandon A. Hugley	920 Gainesville Hwy		Buford, GA 30518	XXX-XX-8991	Married	Hourly
11	BKERR	Bob G. Kerr	1066 Gwinnett Drive		Lawrenceville, GA 30045	XXX-XX-8992	Single	Hourly
12	BNUNNLEY	Brandee M. Nunnley	2777 Sweetwater Trail		Norcross, GA 30093	XXX-XX-6894	Married	Salaried
13	CLELAND	Charlene M. Leland	834 Chamblee Tucker Rd		Atlanta, GA 30341	XXX-XX-6555	Married	Salaried
14	CLIPPER	Conrad C. Lipper	588 Hammond Dr		Chamblee, GA 30341	XXX-XX-2331	Married	Hourly
15	CSWINTON	Colista A. Swinton	36 Piper Lane		Duluth, GA 30155	XXX-XX-8997	Married	Hourly
16	CYACHT	Carol Yacht					Single	Hourly
17	DBECK	Dorothy L. Beck	3743 North Druid Hills Road		Atlanta, GA 30325	XXX-XX-7745	Married	Hourly
18	DCARTER	Drake V. Carter	1679 Chattahoochee Lane		Flowery Branch, GA 30542	XXX-XX-8990	Single	Hourly
19	DCROCKER	Dennis V. Crocker	3222 Sidney Marcus Blvd		Atlanta, GA 30319	XXX-XX-8526	Single	Hourly
20	DGROSS	Derrick P. Gross	1264 Oak Lane		Lawrenceville, GA 30245-1209	XXX-XX-7746	Married	Salaried
21	DNOVA	Duncan S. Nova	212 Landing Lane		Norcross, GA 30093	XXX-XX-9113	Single	Salaried
22	EADKINS	Elliot U. Adkins	11475 Lakefield Drive		Duluth, GA 30155-1511	XXX-XX-8554	Single	Hourly
23	GCHAPPLE	Griffin E. Chapple	8265 Champlain Ave		Cumming, GA 30028	XXX-XX-5761	Single	Hourly
24	GGARDNER	Giovanni V. Gardner	4328 Old Peachtree Rd		Norcross, GA 30093	XXX-XX-2594	Married	Salaried
25	GKELLOGG	Gary A. Kellogg	522 Neese Road		Woodstock, GA 30188	XXX-XX-8931	Married	Salaried
26	GKEMP	Gordon B. Kemp	634 Winter Chapel Rd		Doraville, GA 30342	XXX-XX-5379	Married	Hourly
27	JBEAMMER	Jasper L. Beammer	21 Pembroke Lane		Hiram, GA 30025	XXX-XX-5162	Single	Hourly
28	JGINN	Joseph W. Ginn	22 Piedmont Rd		Atlanta, GA 30319	XXX-XX-7002	Married	Hourly
29	KALEXANDAR	Kyle B. Alexandar	627 Brookwood Road		Snellville, GA 30039	XXX-XX-8998	Single	Hourly
30	KHARMONY	Kelvin R. Harmony	544 Dunhill Dr		Norcross, GA 30092	XXX-XX-4446	Married	Hourly
31	KIRELAND	Kari M. Ireland	5243 Lupus Lane		Lawrenceville, GA 30044	XXX-XX-3425	Married	Salaried
32	LAKERSON	Lyle E. Akerson	988 Sentinel Lane		Lawrenceville, GA 30365	XXX-XX-8563	Married	Salaried
33	LSWEET	Leonard Sweet	6983 Crabapple Court		Alpharetta, GA 30049	XXX-XX-6399	Married	Hourly
34	MCHAMBERLIN	Mark T. Chamberlin	1015 Velvet Court		Alpharetta, GA 30066-4557	XXX-XX-3325	Single	Salaried
35	MFROST	Melvin H. Frost	275 13th Street	Apt. E-406	Atlanta, GA 30309-0406	XXX-XX-8878	Single	Salaried
36	MMULHERN	Marianna S. Mulhern	256 Mt. Paran Court		Atlanta, GA 30085-1305	XXX-XX-4477	Married	Hourly
37	MRHODES	Matt Q. Rhodes	1220 Neptune Circle		Grayson, GA 30098	XXX-XX-0024	Single	Salaried

(Note, at top left: "Your name is shown." with an arrow pointing to cell A1. A box highlights the CYACHT / Carol Yacht row. Sheet tab: Employee List.)

7.   Exit Excel.

SAVING EMPLOYEE LIST AS AN ADOBE PDF FILE

Check with your instructor to see if he or she would like you to save the
Employee list as a PDF file. If so, follow these steps.

1.   If necessary, go to Reports & Forms > Payroll > Employee
     List > Send To > PDF. To save reports as PDF files, Adobe
     Reader must be installed. If necessary, go online to
     https://get.adobe.com/reader/ and download the free Adobe
     Acrobat Reader. (*Hint:* If you cannot save the Employee List as
     a PDF file, make sure you have the latest Adobe Reader update.)

2.   The Modify Report - Employee List window appears. Click   OK .

3.   The Save As window appears. If necessary, insert your USB drive. Select the USB drive. Type **Chapter 1_Employee List** in the File name field. Observe that the Save as Type field shows Adobe PDF Files (*.pdf).

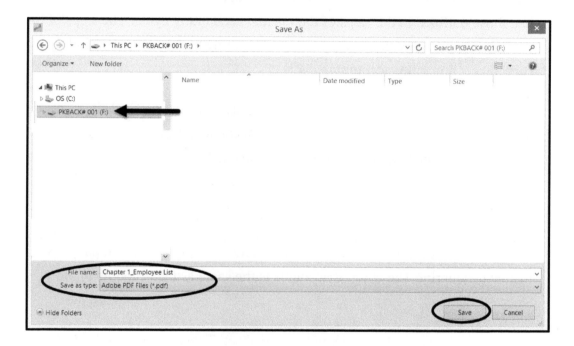

4.   Click [Save]. Close the Select a Report & Form window. Continue or exit Sage 50.

How to Fix? My PDF button is not active. What should I do?

1.   Display the report. Select the Print icon instead of the PDF icon.
2.   The Print window appears. In the Name field, click on the down-arrow.
3.   Select Adobe PDF. Click <OK>. Save the file to your USB drive.

OR, use Excel to save as an Adobe PDF file. The author used Excel 2013.

a.   Open the Excel file, Chapter 1_Employee List.xlsx.
b.   Select File > Save as Adobe PDF > Convert to PDF > type the File name **Chapter 1_Employee List** > Save.

For more information, refer to Appendix A, Troubleshooting, PDF Files and Save Excel as a PDF file.

MANUAL VS. COMPUTERIZED ACCOUNTING

Because there are differences between manual and computerized accounting, notice there are several instances where the procedures used in Sage are different than those outlined in the steps of the manual accounting cycle. The steps of the manual accounting cycle shown in most accounting textbooks differ slightly from Sage's computer accounting cycle.

The differences between the Manual and Computer Accounting Cycle is shown on the next page. The first step of the Computer Accounting Cycle is setting up a new company, which includes the option for selecting a Chart of Accounts. Starting with Chapter 9 you will set up 11 companies from scratch. In Chapters 1-8 you work with the two sample companies that are included with the installation of Sage 50.

The Manual Accounting Cycle does not include creating a new company. In manual accounting, the chart of accounts is the same as the accounts in the general ledger.

Step five of the manual cycle shows a worksheet. There is no worksheet in the computerized cycle. In Sage you can complete account reconciliation. Account reconciliation automates bank reconciliation. Another important difference is that in the Computer Accounting Cycle, the adjusting entries are journalized and posted before printing the financial statements.

In the computerized cycle, Step 10, change accounting periods, is similar to closing the month manually except that the temporary accounts maintain balances so a post-closing trial balance is not available. Sage tracks income and expense data for an entire year. At the end of the year, all revenue and expense accounts are closed to equity. In all Sage 50 companies (including sole proprietorships), a retained earnings account is needed so that posting to the general ledger can be done.

MANUAL ACCOUNTING CYCLE	SAGE'S COMPUTER ACCOUNTING CYCLE
1. Analyze transactions.	1. Create a new company *or* restore A New Company.
2. Journalize entries.	2. Analyze transactions.
3. Post to the ledger.	3. Journalize entries.
4. Prepare unadjusted trial balance.	4. Post to the ledger.
5. Prepare worksheet.	5. Print general ledger trial balance (unadjusted).
6. Prepare financial statements: income statement, statement of changes in owner's equity, and balance sheet.	6. Account reconciliation: reconciling the bank statement.
7. Adjust the ledger accounts: journalize and post adjusting entries.	7. Journalize and post adjusting entries.
8. Close the temporary accounts: journalize and post the closing entries.	8. Print the general ledger trial balance (adjusted).
9. Prepare post-closing trial balance.	9. Print financial statements: balance sheet, income statement, and statement of cash flow.
10. Reverse entries (optional).	10. Change accounting periods.
11. Interpret accounting information	

ONLINE LEARNING CENTER (OLC): www.mhhe.com/yacht2019

Complete end-of-chapter activities at www.mhhe.com/yacht2019 > select Student Edition > then Chapter 1. Link to the appropriate *atom*, for example, Multiple Choice Quiz. Website atoms are underlined. The following chapter resources are available.

1. Quizzes: Multiple Choice Quiz and True or False. Interactive online tests that are graded and can be emailed to your instructor.
2. More Resources:

   a. QA Templates: 10 true/make true questions. Analysis Questions are also included. The Microsoft Word file, with answers, can be emailed to your instructor.
   b. Videos: In Chapter 1, the videos include Global Options, Backup, and Restore. There are also YouTube video links.
   c. Narrated PowerPoints: Listen to narrated PowerPoints.
   d. Going to the Net Exercises: Complete Internet research about accounting careers.
   e. Assessment Rubric: Complete the rubric to review Sage 50's journals, navigation centers, modules, task windows, and reports.

The OLC also includes links to the Appendixes:

- Appendix A: Troubleshooting (Information Center)
- Appendix C: Review of Accounting Principles (Student Edition)
- Appendix D: Glossary (Student Edition). The glossary includes words that are boldfaced and italicized in the chapter.

Exercise 1-1: Follow the instructions below to complete Exercise 1-1:

1. Start Sage. Open the sample company, Bellwether Garden Supply - Student Name.
2. Restore the Chapter 1.ptb file. This backup was made on pages 39-40. For detailed restore steps, refer to pages 27-31. If needed, add your name to Bellwether Garden Supply (refer to pages 40-41, Add Your Name to Reports).

> **Read Me: Do I need to restore?**
>
> If you are working in the computer lab or classroom, open Bellwether Garden Supply - Student Name (your name or another name). Restore the Chapter 1.ptb file from your USB flash drive. Restoring replaces [overwrites] an existing file. If you are working on your own computer or laptop, you can skip restore. On page 38, you added yourself as an employee. Display the employee list. Make sure your name is shown. If *not*, restore.

3. Display Company Information. (*Hint:* Maintain > Company Information; *or* select **System**, Company Maintenance area.) Observe that the Directory field ends in \belgarsu. Why is it different than the Directory field shown on page 41

Directory: `C:\Sage\Peachtree\Company\Sample\PCWE belgarsu`

? (*Hint:* After restarting Bellwether Garden Supply – Student name on page 41, the \belgarsu Directory was shown. Your \Sample folder may show \PCWS; "S" for Student version.)

When you added your name to Bellwether Garden Supply, Sage changed the shortened company name. Shortened company names are comprised of 8 characters: the first three letters from the first and second word (belgar), and two letters from the third word (su). The shortened company name is belgarsu.

4. Continue with Exercise 1-2.

Exercise 1-2: Follow the instructions below to complete Exercise 1-2:

1. Add Sam Conner as a new employee.

Employee ID:	SCONNER [use all capital letters]
Name:	Sam Conner [use upper and lowercase]
Address:	1430 E. Aspen Avenue
City, ST Zip:	Atlanta, GA 30307
Home phone:	770-555-2199

2. Print the Employee List. Select

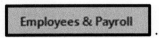

.

Employees				View Detailed List	
Employee ID ⌃	Last Name	First Name	Telephone 1	Pay Method	
ACHESTER	Chester	Amanda	404-555-7447	Hourly - Hours	
ADUKE	Duke	Al	770-555-3349	Hourly - Hours	
AHECTER	Hecter	Anthony	770-555-4558	Hourly - Hours	

In the Employees area, link to <u>View Detailed List</u>. (*Hint:* Click 🔄 Refresh to see Sam Conner.)

3. Click 🖨 Print, then make the selections to print. If necessary, click on Employee ID to display the list in alphabetical order. (*Hint:* The Employee List should also show your name. Adding your name to reports was shown on pages 40-41.) After printing the Employee List, close the Employee List window.

4. Back up. The suggested file name is **Exercise 1-2**. For detailed backing up steps, refer to pages 23-26, steps 1-7.

5. Export the Employee List to Excel. Save. Use **Exercise 1-2_Employee List.xlsx** as the file name. Refer to pages 41-44 for exporting reports to Excel. Click Send To Excel to Create a new Microsoft Excel workbook. If your Excel icon is inactive, refer to Troubleshooting, page 42.

6. Save the Employee List as a PDF file. Use **Exercise 1-2_Employee List.pdf** as the file name. Refer to pages 44-45 for saving files as PDFs.

7. Export the Chart of Accounts to Excel. Use **Exercise 1-2_Chart of Accounts.xlsx** as the file name. (Refer to pages 21-23 for displaying the account list or chart of accounts.)

8. Save the Chart of Accounts as a PDF file. Use **Exercise 1-2_Chart of Accounts.pdf** as the file name.
   Check your figures: Account No. 10200, Regular Checking Account: $23,389.83.

9. Exit.

Comment: Check with your instructor for his or her preference for grading purposes – Excel or PDF reports.

CHAPTER 1 INDEX

Chapter

2 Vendors

LEARNING OBJECTIVES

1. Restore data from Exercise 1-2. This backup was made on page 50. (Refer to the Read me box on page 49, Do I need to restore?)
2. Enter a purchase order.
3. Apply receipt of inventory to existing purchase order.
4. Enter and post a vendor invoice in the Purchases/Receive Inventory window.
5. Go to the Payments window to pay a vendor.
6. Print a check in payment of the vendor invoice.
7. Add a Terms column to the Vendor Ledgers report.
8. Analyze payments and vendor credit memos.
9. Make two backups, save two Excel files, and save five PDF files.[1]

Chapter 2 explains how Sage 50 works with accounts payable transactions and vendors. The first thing you do is select **Vendors & Purchases** to go to the Vendors & Purchases Navigation Center. When Bellwether Garden Supply orders and receives inventory from vendors, Account No. 12000, Inventory, is debited. Accounts Payable and the vendor account are credited.

Vendors offer Bellwether a ***purchase discount*** for purchase invoices paid within a discount period. Purchase discounts are cash discounts from vendors in return for early payment of an invoice. If Bellwether pays an invoice within 10 days,

---

[1]Refer to the chart on page 3 for the size of backups and saved Excel and PDF files.

---

they can deduct two percent from the invoice amount. The purchase discount is
entered when the vendor is paid. If the payment is not made within 10 days, the
full invoice amount is due within 30 days.

GETTING STARTED

Follow these steps to start:

1. Start Sage 50. If an activate window
   appears, follow the screen prompts.
   (For more information, refer to pages
   xiii-xiv.)
2. Since Bellwether Garden Supply -
   Student Name was the last company
   opened, it should start automatically.

(*Hint:* If Bellwether does <u>not</u> open, select File > Close Company to go to
the startup window > Open an Existing Company. Select Bellwether
Garden Supply - Student Name > then <OK>.) On the Options menu,
check that Start with Last Opened Company is checked.

> **Troubleshooting:** Bellwether Garden Supply - Student Name is not listed
on Sage 50's Company Name list.

Refer to the Read Me box on page 28 to review the steps for restoring a
company that is not listed. The steps show how to Create a new company
using restored data.

RESTORING DATA FROM EXERCISE 1-2

On page 50, Exercise 1-2 is backed up. In order to begin where you left off,
restore the Exercise 1-2.ptb file. After completing Exercise 1-2, restore allows
you to start where you left off. For detailed restore steps, refer to pages 27-31.

> **Read Me: Do I need to restore?**
>
> You may be able to skip restore. In Chapter 1 (pages 38-39) and Exercise 1-2 (pages 49-50), you added two employees. Refer to the disk icon 🖫 on the next page to make sure you are starting with the work completed in Chapter 1 and Exercise 1-2. If your employee list and Regular Checking Account's balance agrees with Exercise 1-2, you can skip Restore. Go to the next section, Accounts Payable Tasks. *If you are working in the computer lab or classroom, open Bellwether Garden Supply - Student Name. Restore the Exercise 1-2.ptb file from your USB drive.* Detailed steps are shown on pages 27-31, Using Sage 50's Restore Wizard. Restoring replaces [overwrites] an existing file.

🖫 To make sure you are starting in the appropriate place in the data (Exercise 1-2 backup), display the Employee list. (*Hint:* Navigation Bar >

Employees & Payroll). In the Employees area, link to <u>View Detailed List</u>. Your name and SCONNER should appear. You added yourself as an employee on pages 38-39, and added SCONNER in Exercise 1-2, page 49. Confirm that Account No. 10200, Regular Checking Account, is $23,389.83 (*Hint:* On the Business Status Navigation Center, link to View Account List.)

If you are restoring data from the Student version, you can use Sage 50 2019 for 14 months. From the menu bar, select Maintain > Company Information for the Student version's expiration date.

ACCOUNTS PAYABLE SYSTEM

Sage 50's *Accounts Payable System* provides the summary information needed for the entry that credits Accounts Payable and debits the various asset and expense accounts that the vendor invoices represent. Since Bellwether Garden Supply buys on credit from a number of vendors, the company keeps close track of the amount owed and the due dates of the bills.

Vendor transactions are a five-step process.

1. Maintain Vendors: Set up a new vendor.
2. Purchase Orders: Order items from one of Bellwether's vendors.
3. Purchase Invoices: Receive inventory or services from one of Bellwether's vendors. Apply a purchase order to a purchase invoice.
4. Payments: Pay a vendor or record a cash purchase. (Sage also includes vendor credit memos.)
5. Print Checks: Print a check for payment to a vendor or for expenses.

Before you begin adding accounts payable transactions, examine the Vendors & Purchases Navigation Center. Follow these steps to do that.

1. From the Navigation Bar > select **Vendors & Purchases**. The Vendors & Purchases Navigation Center appears. Vendors & Purchases illustrate Sage 50's **accounts payable module** or accounts payable system. The Vendors & Purchases Navigation Center includes Vendors & Purchases Tasks and its workflow diagram, Vendors, Recently Used Vendor Reports, Aged Payables, and Sage 50 Advisor. (To show the Sage Advisor, click Expand. To watch the videos, go to www.mhhe.com/yacht2019 > Sage Advisor Videos.)

   Modules organize Sage 50's transactions and reports. When the Navigation Bar's Vendors & Purchases selection is made, Sage 50's accounts payable system is shown. The menu bar selections, Tasks and Reports & Forms, are also organized by module; for example, the Reports & Forms menu includes Accounts Receivable, Accounts Payable, General Ledger, etc.

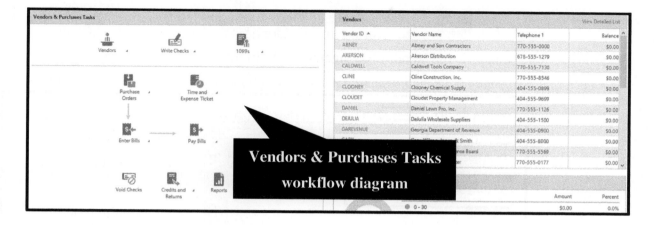

Vendors & Purchases Tasks workflow diagram

The Vendors & Purchases Navigation Center displays information and access points related to the company's vendors. It includes a summary of vendor information, access to recently used vendor reports, and an overview of the company's aged payables. In addition, the Navigation Center shows the flow of vendor-related tasks. You can also link or drill down to various areas. The Vendors & Purchases Navigation Center includes two tabs: Vendors & Purchases and Vendor Management. Vendors & Purchases is the default and shows the workflow diagram for Vendors & Purchases Tasks. The Vendor Management tab lists information regarding transactions and history for an individual vendor, including purchase orders, purchases, and payments.

2. If necessary, click on the Vendors & Purchases tab. In the Vendors area (on the right side of the screen), click ABNEY. The Maintain Vendors window appears with information about Abney and Son Contractors.

3. Click 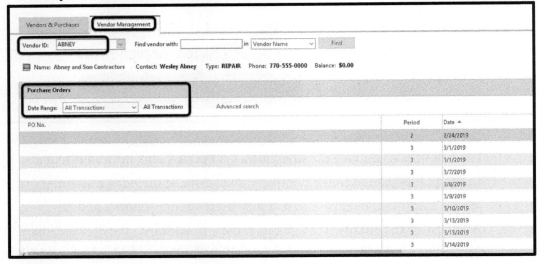[🞩 Close] to return to the Vendors & Purchases Navigation Center.

4. Click on the Vendor Management tab. In the Vendor ID field > select Abney > in the Purchase Order Date Range field > select All Transactions.

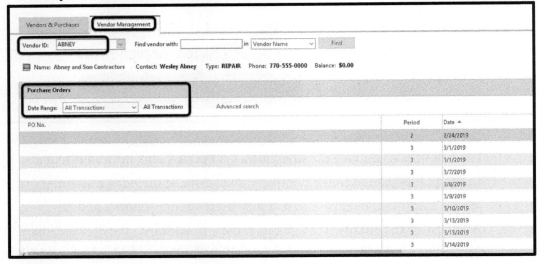

Vendor Management shows historical information about Abney and Son Contractors – Purchase Orders and Payments. If necessary, scroll down.

5. To return to the workflow diagram, select the Vendors & Purchases tab.

The Purchase Order Window

Purchase orders are used to place an order from a vendor. When you post a purchase order, you do not update accounting information. A purchase order is used to request items from a vendor. When the Apply to Purchase Order tab is selected on the Purchases/Receive Inventory window and the transaction is posted, accounting information (inventory, accounts payable subsidiary ledger, general ledger) is updated.

Changing Global Settings for Accounting Behind the Screens

Sage 50 is a double-entry accounting system. There is a selection in Options/Global that allows you to hide general ledger accounts. This is called

Accounting Behind the Screens. The windows in this book show the general ledger accounts. To check the Accounting Behind the Screens settings, follow the steps shown below.

1. From the menu bar > click Options > Global. The <u>A</u>ccounting tab is selected. The boxes in the Hide General Ledger Accounts section *must* be unchecked. (If necessary, click on the boxes to uncheck them.)

Hide General Ledger Accounts

☐ Accounts Receivable (Quotes, Sales Orders, Invoicing, Credit Memos, Receipts)
☐ Accounts Payable (Purchase Orders, Purchases, Credit Memos, Payments)
☐ Payroll Entry

2. Observe that two boxes need to be checked in the Other Options section: Warn if a record was changed but not saved and Recalculate cash balance automatically in Receipts, Payments, and Payroll Entry. Make sure *both* of these Other Options boxes are checked.

Other Options

☑ Warn if a record was changed but not saved
☐ Hide inactive records
☑ Recalculate cash balance automatically in Receipts, Payments, and Payroll Entry
☐ Use Timeslips by Sage Accounting Link

3. Click on the <u>G</u>eneral tab. Make sure your Line Item Entry Display has 2 Line selected; and that the Smart Data Entry area has all three boxes checked.

Line Item Entry Display

○ 1 Line   ⦿ 2 Line

Smart Data Entry

☑ Automatic field completion   ☑ Automatically create IDs on maintenance windows
☑ Drop-down list displays automatically

4. Click [OK]. Once Global Settings are saved by clicking the <OK> button, they are in effect for all companies.

5. From the Vendors & Purchases Navigation Center, select [Purchase Orders] > New Purchase Order. The Purchase Orders window displays.

    If your Purchase Orders window does *not* show an A/P Account lookup

    field [A/P Account 20000] or a GL Account [GL Account] field, the option to hide general ledger accounts is selected. Uncheck the Hide General Ledger

    Accounts boxes in Options > Global. (*Hint: See the instructions on pages 59-60, for changing the global settings.*)

ABNEY		
ABNEY	Abney and Son Contractors	770-555-0000
AKERSON	Akerson Distribution	678-555-1279
CALDWELL	Caldwell Tools Company	770-555-7130
CLINE	Cline Construction, Inc.	770-555-8546
CLOONEY	Clooney Chemical Supply	404-555-0899
CLOUDET	Cloudet Property Management	404-555-9699
DANIEL	Daniel Lawn Pro, Inc.	770-555-1126
DEJULIA	DeJulia Wholesale Suppliers	404-555-1500
GAREVENUE	Georgia Department of Revenue	404-555-0900
GARY	Gary, Wilson, Jones, & Smith	404-555-8000
GWINLICENSE	Gwinnett County License Board	770-555-5569
GWINWATER	Gwinnett County Water	770-555-0177

    OK Cancel Find Next New Sort Help

6. Your cursor is in the Vendor ID lookup field. Type **A** (use capital A). ABNEY displays in the lookup field.

> **Comment:** If the Vendor ID field is not completed, the Automatic Field Completion option is *not* selected. Click Options > Global > General tab. In the Smart Data Entry section, make sure that a check mark is placed next to Automatic field completion. Click [OK] when you are finished.

7. Click on the Date field. Highlight the date, then type **28** press **<Enter>**. Your cursor moves to the Good thru field. Press **<Enter>** to accept the default. Your cursor moves to the PO No. field.

8. Click on the Quantity field. Type **20** as the Quantity.

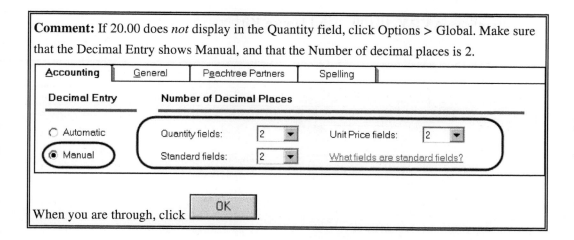

Comment: If 20.00 does *not* display in the Quantity field, click Options > Global. Make sure that the Decimal Entry shows Manual, and that the Number of decimal places is 2.

Accounting	General	Peachtree Partners	Spelling

Decimal Entry   **Number of Decimal Places**

○ Automatic   Quantity fields: 2 ▼   Unit Price fields: 2 ▼

● Manual   Standard fields: 2 ▼   What fields are standard fields?

When you are through, click OK.

9. Press **<Enter>**. Your cursor is in the Item field.
10. Click once on the magnifying-glass icon in the Item field. Click AVRY-10150 Bird Bath - Stone Gothic 2pc. The Description field is automatically completed with detailed information.
11. Press the **<Enter>** key and your cursor moves to the GL Account field. Notice that Account No. 12000 is automatically selected. Account No. 12000 is the Inventory account. The word Inventory is also displayed on the line below the Description. (*Hint:* If Inventory is *not* shown, refer to step 1, page 59.)
12. Press the **<Enter>** key to go to the Unit Price field. The Unit Price of 51.95 automatically displays.
13. Press the **<Enter>** key to go to the Amount field. Sage 50 calculates the quantity times the unit price and enters the result in the Amount field (20 X $51.95 = $1,039.00).
14. Press the **<Enter>** key to go to the Job field. The Job field is also a lookup field. It contains a list of the jobs and their descriptions. Since Bellwether does not apply this purchase to a job, press the **<Enter>** key to skip this field.

Complete the following information:

Quantity: **50**

Item: **AVRY-10100** - Bird House Kit

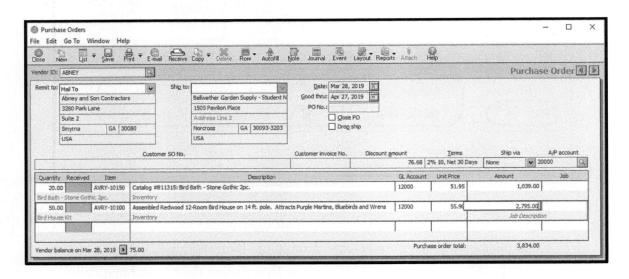

When you selected Abney and Son Contractors, the Vendor Account
Balance as of March 28, 2019 also appears on the lower left side of the
Purchase Orders window. You can drill down
to Abney and Son Contractors vendor ledger
by clicking on the right arrow ( ) in the
Vendor Balance area. Observe that the icon

bar also includes a Reports button.
Click on the down-arrow next to the Reports button.

15. Click . The Accounting Behind the Screens, Purchase Order Journal
     window displays. Compare your Accounting Behind the Screens window to
     the one on the next page. This window shows that Account No. 12000,
     Inventory, was debited for two items and that Accounts Payable was
     credited. (The vendor account, Abney and Sons, is also credited.)

16. Click You are returned to the Purchase Orders window.

Printing Purchase Orders

When you select Print, Sage prints the purchase order and posts it to the

Purchase Order Journal. Save also posts the Purchase Order.

1. Click Print. (*Or,* if you are <u>not</u> going to print, click on the down-arrow next to Print and select Print Preview to display the purchase order.)

2. The Print Forms: Purchase Orders window appears. Accept the default for First PO Number 101 by clicking Print. (If you selected Print Preview, there is a Print Preview button — Print Preview.) Compare your

Purchase Order to the one below. If you are <u>not</u> printing, refer to the How to Fix? on page 65.

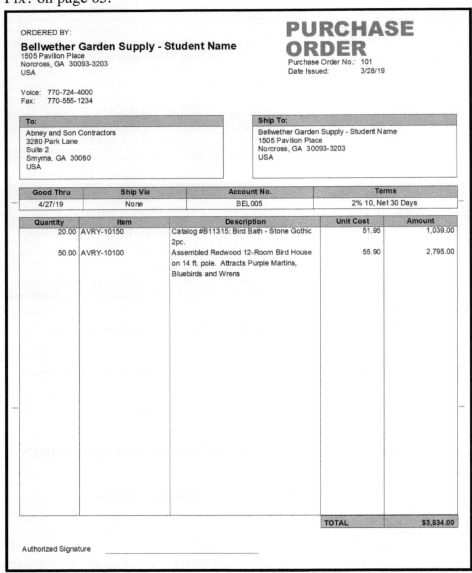

Comment: The purchase order form that printed is called Purchase Order. To print a different form, click [Select Form] Then, select Purchase Order Preprinted as the form to print. When you select a different form, the information is the same but the look of the form changes.

3. If you displayed the report and are printing, click . The Purchase Orders window is ready for the next entry. If you are <u>not</u> printing, refer to the How to fix? Information below.

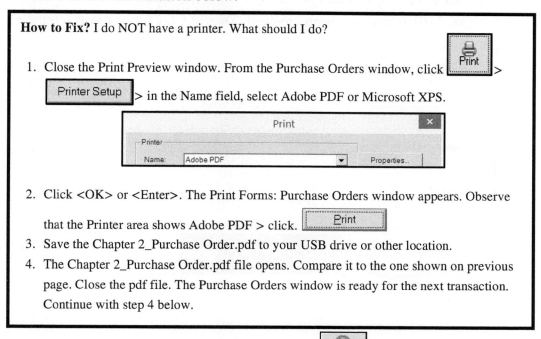

How to Fix? I do NOT have a printer. What should I do?

1. Close the Print Preview window. From the Purchase Orders window, click `Print` > `Printer Setup` > in the Name field, select Adobe PDF or Microsoft XPS.

2. Click <OK> or <Enter>. The Print Forms: Purchase Orders window appears. Observe that the Printer area shows Adobe PDF > click. `Print`

3. Save the Chapter 2_Purchase Order.pdf to your USB drive or other location.

4. The Chapter 2_Purchase Order.pdf file opens. Compare it to the one shown on previous page. Close the pdf file. The Purchase Orders window is ready for the next transaction. Continue with step 4 below.

4. To close the Purchase Orders window, click `Close`.

   ➤ **Troubleshooting:** Selecting `Save` posts and saves Purchase Orders.

   Selecting `Print` also saves and posts Purchase Orders.

Receive Inventory from a Purchase Order

After you have entered a purchase order, the next step is to receive the inventory. Sage 50 allows you to receive a different quantity for an item than you originally ordered. In other words, you can receive less than or more than the originally ordered quantity. Let's see how Bellwether's purchase orders match up to the inventory received.

1. From the Vendors & Purchases Navigation Center > select Purchase Orders > View and Edit Purchase Orders.

2. Double-click DEJULIA, PO No. 10300. Observe that some of the items are received and some are not. For example, six BGS Gardening Handbooks (BOOK-11010) have not been received. Twelve Clay Flower Pots – 6 in. (POTS-30210) were received. The Received field shows items added to inventory.

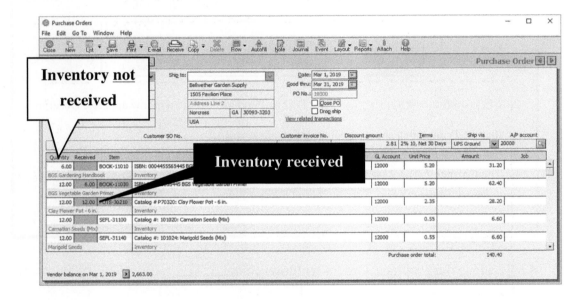

3. Select Reports > Inventory Stock Status Report. The Inventory Stock Status Report shows the Inventory items purchased from DeJulia Wholesale Suppliers, item class, stocking units/measures, quantity on hand, minimum stock order, reorder quantity, and the inventory location.

4. Close the Inventory Stock Status Report.

Apply to Purchase Order

To see if inventory items from PO No. 10300 have been applied, follow these steps.

1. On the Purchase Orders window, click <u>View related transactions</u>.
2. Double-click Purchase 22113. The Purchases/Receive Inventory window appears. (*Hint:* If necessary, enlarge the window.) This is Sage 50's Purchase Journal. Observe that some of the items from PO No. 10300 are shown. (The Apply to Purchase Order No. field shows 10300, the PO number.)

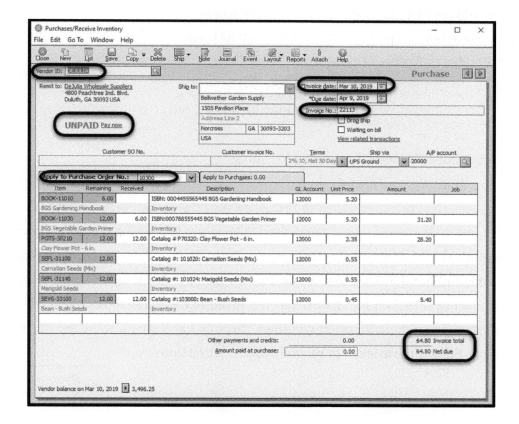

When purchase orders are applied, the transaction appears in Sage 50's Purchase Journal. Click [Journal] to see how the Purchase Journal was

debited and credited. When the Purchases/Receive Inventory window
(Purchase Journal) is posted, the vendor, DeJulia Wholesale Suppliers, is
updated in the vendor ledger, and the controlling account, Accounts
Payable, is updated in the general ledger. Inventory is also updated.
Observe that the Purchases/Receive Inventory window shows Unpaid. Also,
the Invoice total and Net due fields show $64.80 (the items received so far).
The entire purchase order was for $140.40. As of March 10, Bellwether has
not received all the items requested on PO 10300. Payment will be made at
a later date.

From the Purchases/Receive Inventory window, link to <u>View related</u>
<u>transactions</u> to go to Purchase Order 10300. This is the same
Purchases/Receive Inventory window shown on page 67.

3. Close all windows. (*Hint:* From the menu bar, select Window > Close All.)

The Purchases/Receive Inventory Window

In Sage 50, the Purchases/Receive Inventory window is the Purchase Journal.
The Apply to Purchases tab is the default. The lower half of the window shows
fields for Quantity, Item (inventory items), Description, GL Account, Unit Price,
Amount, and Job. Observe that the default for the A/P Account is 20000,
Accounts Payable. The Purchases/Receive Inventory window looks like a
purchase order. Similar to other windows, the icon bar appears at the top of the
window. Follow these steps to record vendor transactions.

1. From the Vendors & Purchases Navigation Center > select >
    New Bill. The Purchases/Receive Inventory window appears. Observe that
    the Apply to Purchases tab is the default. The cursor is in the Vendor ID
    field. To see more lines in the Quantity/Item/Description table, make the

Purchases/Receive Inventory window larger. You can do this by putting your mouse on the bottom border of the window and pulling down. The mouse changes to a double-arrow [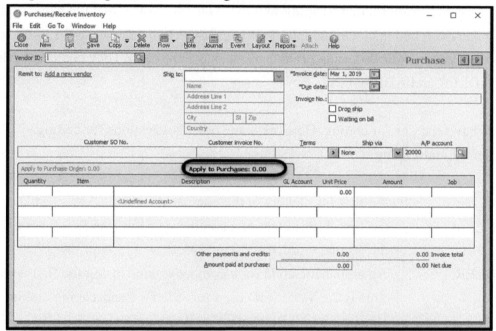]. With the cursor on the bottom border of the window, pull the window down to make it larger. If necessary, repeat this step on the left and right borders.

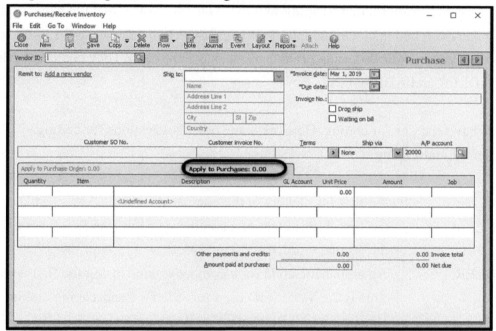

2. With the cursor in the Vendor ID field, press the plus key **<+>** and the Maintain Vendors window appears.

Adding a New Vendor

You are going to enter a new vendor, Adler's Landscaping. Since a ***coding system*** has already been established for Bellwether's vendors, you should continue to use the same one. The coding system used has uppercase letters. To be consistent, Adler's Landscaping will use ADLER. Notice that the name of the company is typed in all capital letters. What if two companies have the same name, such as, Adler's Landscaping and Adler's Suppliers? They could be coded as ADLER and ADLSUPPL.

You have choices for coding. Here are some other suggestions for coding Adler's Landscaping:

ADLE :	the first four letters of the company's name.
ADLL:	the first three letters of a company's name, the first letter of the second word.
ADLER:	An alphabetic code for a company name, using the first word. This is the Vendor ID used for Adler's Landscaping and is consistent with Bellwether's other vendors.

Follow these steps to continue in the Maintain Vendors window:

1. Make sure the Maintain Vendors window is displayed. Type **ADLER** in the Vendor ID field and press **<Enter>**. Your cursor is in the Name field.
2. Type **Adler's Landscaping** in the Name field.

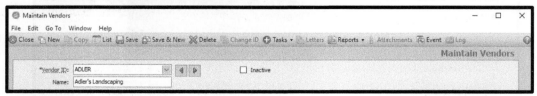

3. Press **<Enter>** two times. Your cursor is in the Contact field. The person who handles sales for Adler's Landscaping is Philip Adler. Type **Philip Adler** and press **<Enter>**.

4. Your cursor is in the Account Number field. Click on the Vendor type field. (Skip the Account Number and Address fields.) The Vendor Type field is used for classifying vendors. In the Vendor Type field, click on the down arrow. Scroll down, then select SUPPLY.

5. Click on the down-arrow in the Expense Account field. Scroll down the list. Select Account No. 57200, Materials Cost. Press **<Enter>**. When Adler's Landscaping is selected as the vendor, Account No. 57200, Materials Cost, will be automatically debited.

   If you need to move between fields to make corrections, use the **<Tab>** key to move forward and the **<Shift> + <Tab>** to move backwards.

6. Click on the Purchase Info tab. Notice that the Vendor ID and Name fields stay the same: ADLER and Adler's Landscaping. Also, observe the

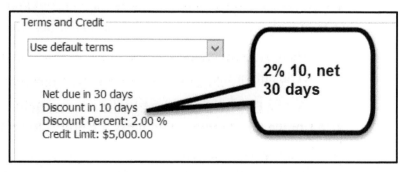

   Terms and Credit are 2% net 10, 30 days. Purchase discounts are described on pages 53-54.

7. Click [Save] > [Close] to return to the Purchases/Receive Inventory window.

Entering a Vendor Invoice

Make sure that the Purchases\Receive Inventory window is displayed and that the cursor is in the Vendor ID field. Follow these steps to enter the transaction.

Date	*Transaction Description*
03/15/2019	Invoice No. AD107 was received from Adler's Landscaping for the purchase of Plant Food, $45. (*Hint:* Debit Account No. 57200, Materials Cost; Credit Account No. 20000, Accounts Payable/Adler's Landscaping.)

1. In the Vendor ID field, click [🔍]. Select ADLER, Adler's Landscaping.
2. Select or type 15 as the date.
3. In the Invoice No. field, type **AD107**.
4. Click on the Quantity field and type **1** and press **<Enter>**.
5. Since you are not purchasing an inventory item, press the **<Enter>** key again.
6. The cursor moves to the Description field. In the Description field, type **Plant Food** and press **<Enter>**.
7. In the GL Account field press **<Enter>** to accept Account No. 57200, the Materials Cost account.
8. In the Unit Price field, type **45** and press **<Enter>**. Compare your Purchases/Receive Inventory window to the one shown on the next page.

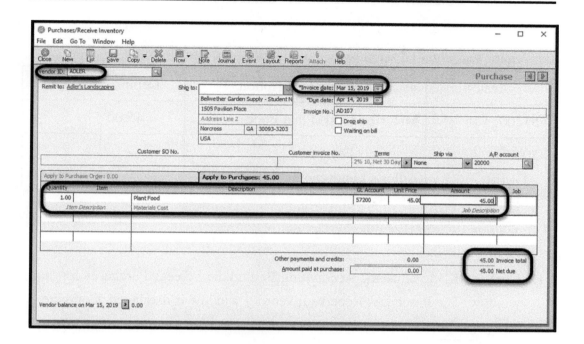

Comment: What if your Purchases/Receive Inventory window does *not* show an A/P Account field or GL Account field?
You should check your Options > Global settings. Make sure that the boxes in the Hide General Ledger Accounts section are unchecked. These steps were shown on page 59, step 1.

Editing a Journal Entry. Observe that the Purchases/Receive Inventory

window includes a [List] icon. Selecting List displays the Purchase List window. From the Purchase List, you can drill down to an entry that you want to edit or change. The Purchases/Receive Inventory window is Sage 50's Purchase Journal. The List icon is included on journal-entry windows.

Posting a Purchase Transaction

When you made this entry in the Purchases/Receive Inventory window, you debited Account No. 57200, Material Cost, which is a General Ledger Cost of Sales account; and credited Accounts Payable/Adler's Landscaping. ADLER is the vendor account. (To see this account distribution, click [Journal].)

Acct. #	Account Description	Debit	Credit
57200	Materials Cost (Plant Food)	45.00	
20000/ ADLER	Accounts Payable/ Adler's Landscaping		45.00

Follow these steps to post this transaction.

1. Click <OK> to close the Accounting Behind the Screens Purchases Journal window. The Purchases/Receive Inventory window is displayed. Compare it to page 73.

2. Click [Save] to post the vendor invoice.

3. Click [Close] to return to the Vendors & Purchases Navigation Center.

> **Read Me:** The Vendors area on the Vendors & Purchases Navigation Center does *not* show the vendor that I added. How do I update the list? The toolbar (above Vendors & Purchases Tasks) includes a button. Click it. Observe that the Vendors list now includes ADLER, Adler's Landscaping.

VENDOR PAYMENTS

When you make a payment to a vendor, use the Payments window. The Payments window is the Cash Disbursements Journal. On pages 70-72, you added a new vendor; then entered and posted an invoice to that vendor on pages 72-74. *Both* the new vendor and invoice *must* be completed *before* a vendor payment can be made.

Date	Transaction Description
03/18/2019	Issued Check No. 10215 to Adler's Landscaping in payment of Invoice No. AD107.

Follow these steps to pay the Adler's Landscaping invoice:

1. From the Vendors & Purchases Navigation Center > Pay Bills > Pay Bill. There are two parts to the Payments window: the check section at the top; and the invoice section at the bottom. In the Vendor ID field, click on the magnifying-glass icon, then select ADLER, Adler's Landscaping. Look at the invoice section. The invoice number AD107 is shown with the amount that Bellwether owes to Adler's Landscaping.

2. Click on the Date field. Type or select **18** > press <Enter>.

3. Click on the Pay box for Invoice AD107. Notice that the check portion of the window is completed. The amount paid is 44.10. This is the amount of the invoice less the 2% discount ($45 -.90 = $44.10).

> ➤ **Troubleshooting:** Observe that the Check/Reference No. field is blank. The check number is assigned when you print. Enter check number 10215 if checks are *not* going to be printed. Checks are printed on pages 77-78

4. To see the Cash Disbursements Journal entry, click [Journal]. Observe the debits and credits. Account distribution is shown below. Click [OK] to close Accounting Behind the Screens.

5. Click [Save] to post the Payments window (Cash Disbursements Journal).

6. Click [Close] to return to the Vendors & Purchases Navigation Center.

When you post this payment, the Accounts Payable account is debited for the full invoice amount ($45), which offsets the credit created when you entered the invoice. The cash account is decreased (credited) by the amount of the check ($44.10) and the Discounts Taken account is increased (credited) for the purchase discount ($.90). Purchase discounts (Account No. 89500 Purchase Disc-Expense Items) was already set up for Bellwether Garden Supply.

Acct. #	Account Description	Debit	Credit
20000/ADLER	Accounts Payable/Adler's Landscaping; Invoice AD107	45.00	
10200	Regular Checking Account (Check Amount)		44.10
89500	Purchase Disc-Expense Items (Discounts Taken)		.90

PRINTING CHECKS

You can print a batch of checks or print one check at a time. Since there is only one check to print, you are going to print an individual check. Sage also includes special check forms to use for printing checks. These may be purchased from Sage. Since you do not have check forms, print the check on a blank piece of paper.

GO GREEN & SAVE: Instead of printing, select Display or Print Preview, and save as an Adobe PDF file or Microsoft XPS file. In other words, you do <u>not</u> need to print hard copy. Check with your instructor for his or her preference. Instead of printing, email PDFs or Microsoft XPS files.

Follow these steps to print a check:

1. From the menu bar, select Reports & Forms > Forms > Checks. The Select a Report or Form window appears.
2. Observe that the For<u>m</u>s tab is selected. If necessary, in the Form Types list, select Checks. In the Forms list, OCR AP Laser Preprinted is automatically selected. (If not, select OCR AP Laser Preprinted.)

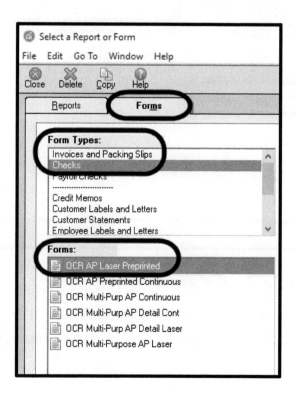

Comment

Step 2 instructs you to select OCR AP Laser Preprinted as the form to print. If this form does *not* print, select another one. The form you select is tied to the kind of printer you are using. Depending on your printer, you may need to make a different selection.

---

3. Double-click OCR AP Laser Preprinted.
4. The Preview and Print Checks window appears. In the Include checks through field, type **3/18/2019**.
5. Type **10215** in the Number the first check field.
6. In the Filter vendors by area, select ADLER to ADLER in the ID fields.
7. Click [**Refresh List**].

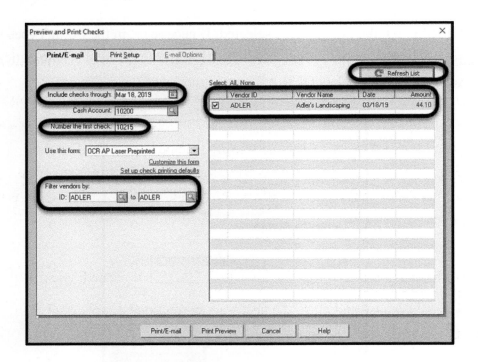

8. Click [Print/E-mail] or [Print Preview]. The check prints or displays. Compare Check No. 10215 to the one shown below. The top half of the check is shown. **If you are NOT connected to a printer, refer to page 65, How to fix.**

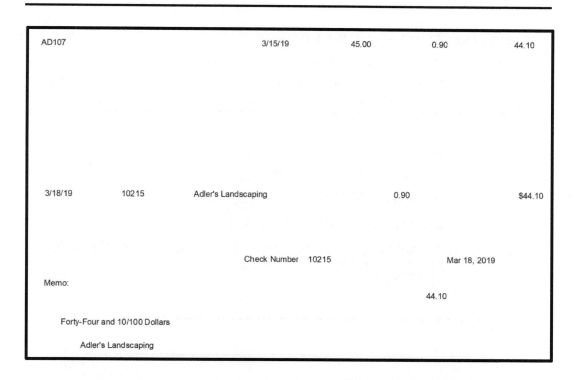

If you print the check, a window displays asking Did the Checks print properly, and is it OK to assign the check numbers to the checks? Make sure the check printed properly and the amount is correct. (See the Payments window on page 75.) The check shows the check stub (top portion) and check portion. When you print Check No. 10215, there is also a bottom portion.

9. If the check printed property, click [Yes]. If needed, click [Cancel] and make the necessary corrections.

10. Close the Select a Report or Form window.

DISPLAYING THE VENDOR LEDGERS

To display the Vendor Ledgers, follow these steps.

1. On the Vendors & Purchases Navigation Center, Recently Used Vendor Reports area > link <u>View All Vendor & Purchases Reports</u> > select Vendor Ledgers > Display (*Or,* in the Recently Used Vendor Reports area, link to View next to Vendor Ledgers.)

2. The Vendor Ledgers displays. To see the terms for the vendor, click Columns. The Vendor Ledgers/Columns window displays. Scroll down the Show list. Select Terms. (Click on the box to place a checkmark.)

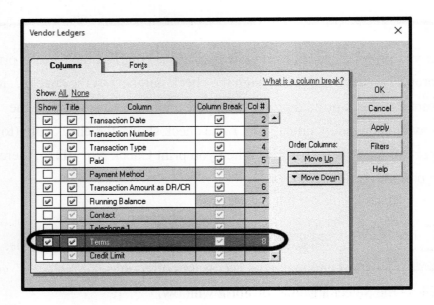

3. After clicking OK, a Terms column is added to the Vendor Ledgers report. A partial Vendor Ledgers report is shown on the next page.

Vendor ID Vendor	Date	Trans No	Type	Paid	Debit Amt	Credit Amt	Balance	Terms
Bellwether Garden Supply - Student Name Vendor Ledgers For the Period From Mar 1, 2019 to Mar 31, 2019								

(Filter Criteria includes: Report order is by ID.)

Vendor ID Vendor	Date	Trans No	Type	Paid	Debit Amt	Credit Amt	Balance	Terms
ABNEY	3/1/19	B1000	PJ			75.00	75.00	2% 10, Net 30
Abney and Son Contractors	3/9/19	B1015	PJ	*		195.65	270.65	
	3/12/19	VCM30001	PJ	*	195.65		75.00	
	3/15/19		CDJ		50.00	50.00	75.00	
ADLER	3/15/19	AD107	PJ	*		45.00	45.00	2% 10, Net 30
Adler's Landscaping	3/18/19	10215	CDJ		0.90	0.90	45.00	
	3/18/19	10215	CDJ		45.00		0.00	
AKERSON	3/1/19	Balance Fw					9,398.75	2% 10, Net 30
Akerson Distribution	3/7/19	VCM30002	PJ	*	27.20		9,371.55	
	3/8/19	4	PJ			5,179.20	14,550.75	
	3/13/19		CDJ		1,000.00	1,000.00	14,550.75	
	3/14/19	B1016	PJ	*		27.20	14,577.95	
CALDWELL	3/1/19	Balance Fw					21,214.10	2% 10, Net 30
Caldwell Tools Company	3/4/19	B1004	PJ			90.00	21,304.10	
	3/6/19	B1017	PJ	*		45.90	21,350.00	
	3/9/19	VCM30003	PJ	*	45.90		21,304.10	

The Vendor Ledger is the Accounts Payable subsidiary ledger. When you entered and posted the vendor invoice (pages 72-74) in the Purchases/Receive Inventory window, the Accounts Payable subsidiary ledger for Adler's Landscaping was credited for $45. Once the invoice was entered, there is a balance of $45. When you posted the payment (step 5, page 76), Sage debited the vendor for the same amount. The balance after posting the payment is zero ($0.00).

VENDOR CREDIT MEMOS

Vendor credit memos are returns to vendors. You can apply vendor credit memos to any existing vendor invoice that has *not* been paid. All entries made on the Vendor Credit Memos window are posted to the general ledger, vendor records, and when applicable, inventory and job records.

Use the ***drill down*** feature to go to the original entry from the vendor ledger. Using the vendor ledger as an example, use drill down to follow the path of an entry to its origin. In Sage 50 reports, you can click transactions to drill down to the window that includes the original transaction information.

1. The vendor ledger should be displayed. Using the vendor, Abney and Son Contractors, put your cursor over the 3/9/19 vendor ledger entry. Your cursor changes to a magnifying-glass with a Z (for zoom) in it.

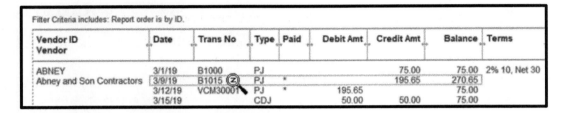

Filter Criteria includes: Report order is by ID.								
Vendor ID **Vendor**	**Date**	**Trans No**	**Type**	**Paid**	**Debit Amt**	**Credit Amt**	**Balance**	**Terms**
ABNEY	3/1/19	B1000	PJ			75.00	75.00	2% 10, Net 30
Abney and Son Contractors	3/9/19	B1015 Ⓩ	PJ	*		195.65	270.65	
	3/12/19	VCM30001	PJ	*	195.65		75.00	
	3/15/19	CDJ			50.00	50.00	75.00	

2. To drill down to the 3/9/19 transaction, double-click on it with your left mouse button. The Purchases/Receive Inventory window appears showing the original purchase of inventory items.

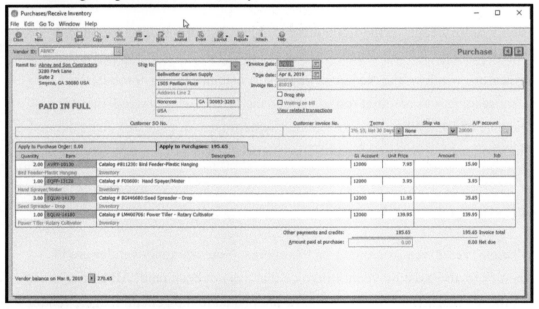

> **Troubleshooting:** On my Purchases/Receive Inventory window, the Quantity, Item, Description, GL Account, Unit Price, and Amount table does *not* show multiple lines. Use the arrows next to the Job field to scroll through the multiple lines. Try enlarging your screen with the cursor. If that doesn't work, read the next paragraph about screen resolution.

3. Click [Close]. You are returned to the Vendor Ledgers. Drill down on the 3/12/19 vendor credit memo (VCM30001). The Vendor Credit Memos window appears. Observe that the Apply to Invoice No. tab shows B1015. This is the same merchandise that was purchased on 3/9/19. (See the Purchases/Receive inventory window.) The returned field shows the items returned.

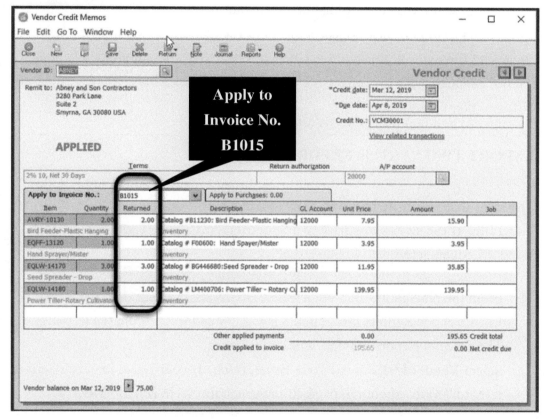

4. Click [Close]. You are returned to the Vendor Ledgers. Click [Close] again to return to the Vendors & Purchases Navigation Center. (*Hint:* You can also select Window > Close All.)

BACKING UP CHAPTER 2 DATA

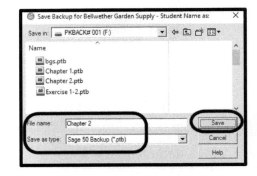

After completing the work within Chapter 2,
back up. The suggested file name is **Chapter
2.ptb**. Detailed steps for backing up data are
shown on pages 23-26.

Backing up saves your data to that point in your
work. Each time you back up, use a different file name; for example, the
suggested file name at this point is Chapter 2.ptb. (Sage 50 automatically adds
the file extension .ptb to backups.) Using a unique name allows you to restore at
different points in the data.

EXPORT TWO SAGE 50 REPORTS TO EXCEL

The steps that follow demonstrate how to add a new worksheet to an existing
Excel file. These steps show how two Sage 50 reports, the Vendor List and the
Vendor Ledgers, are saved to one Excel file.

1. From the Navigation Bar, click **Vendors & Purchases** In the Recently
   Used Vendor Reports area, click <u>View All Vendor & Purchases Reports</u>.
   The Select a Report or Form window appears.
2. Select Vendor List > Se<u>n</u>d To > Excel. (*Hint:* If your Excel icon is inactive,
   refer to Troubleshooting, page 42 *or* Appendix A.) When the Modify
   Report – Vendor List window appears, click **OK**. (*Hint:* You may
   want to display the Vendor list, reformat the columns, then from the
   displayed report click **Excel**)
3. The Copy Report to Excel
   window appears. In the File
   option area make sure Create a

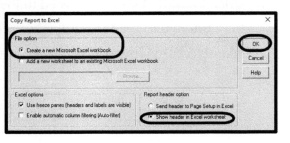

new Microsoft Excel workbook is selected. In the Report header option, Show header in Excel worksheet should also be selected.

4. After clicking [OK], the report is exported to Microsoft Excel. Bellwether Garden Supply's Vendor List is shown.

5. Save the Vendor List. Use **Chapter 2_Vendor List and Vendor Ledgers.xlsx** as the file name. Close the Excel file.

6. Go to Bellwether. (*Hint:* Select a Report or Form.)

7. From the Select a Report or Form window, double-click Vendor Ledgers. The Vendor Ledgers displays. There are two ways to export to Excel.

    a. From the Select a Report or Form window, highlight the report and then select Se<u>n</u>d To Excel.

    b. Display the report and select Excel [Excel]. (This is shown below.)

8. Click [Excel]. On the Copy Report to Excel window, select Add a new worksheet to an existing Microsoft Excel workbook. Select [Browse...] Go to the location of the saved file, Chapter 2_Vendor List and Vendors Ledgers.xlsx. Select [Open]

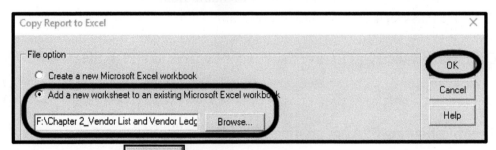

9. After clicking [OK], Bellwether Garden Supply's Vendor Ledgers appear. Observe that the two sheets are shown: Vendor List and Vendor Ledgers (tabs at the bottom of the window.)

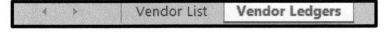

10. Save. The Excel file, Chapter 2_Vendor List and Vendor Ledgers, includes two spreadsheets: the Vendor List and the Vendor Ledgers. Click ⊠ on the title bar to exit Excel and return to Sage 50. Close all windows.

SAVE VENDOR LIST AND VENDOR LEDGERS AS PDF FILES

Follow these steps to save the Vendor List as a PDF file.

1. Go to the Vendor List. From the Reports & Forms menu > Accounts Payable > double-click Vendor List.

2. The Vendor List appears. On the icon bar, click [PDF]. The Save As window appears. Select the location of your USB drive.

➢ **Troubleshooting 1**: If you are having difficulty saving a PDF file, go online to https://get.adobe.com/reader. Update or download the Free Adobe Reader.

➢ **Troubleshooting 2:** Open the Chapter 2_Vendor List and Vendor Ledgers.xlsx file > select the appropriate sheet > select File > Save As an Adobe PDF file.

3. Type **Chapter 2_Vendor List** in the File name field.

4. Click [Save].

5. Complete similar steps to save the Vendor Ledgers as a PDF file. Use the file name **Chapter 2_Vendor Ledgers.pdf**. Close all windows.

➢ **Troubleshooting 3:** After printing PDF files, your printer preferences may change. If necessary, select the appropriate printer. More information is in Appendix A, Troubleshooting, Windows Printer Settings.

ONLINE LEARNING CENTER

Complete the end-of-chapter activities online at www.mhhe.com/yacht2019 > select the Student Edition > Chapter 2.

1. Quizzes: Interactive Multiple-Choice and True/False questions.
2. QA Templates: 10 multiple-choice questions and one analysis question.
3. Listen to narrated PowerPoint slides.
4. Going to the Net exercise: The changing nature of teams in the workplace. An interview with Blake Oliver of FloQast.
5. Assessment Rubric: review journals, navigation centers, modules, and task windows.

The OLC also includes links to the Appendixes:

- Appendix A: Troubleshooting (Information Center)
- Appendix C: Review of Accounting Principles (Student Edition)
- Appendix D: Glossary of Terms (Student Edition)

Exercise 2-1: Follow the instructions below to complete Exercise 2-1.

1. Start Sage 50. Open Bellwether Garden Supply - Student Name [your first and last name].[2]
2. If necessary, restore the Chapter 2.ptb backup file. This file was backed up on page 83.
3. Add the following vendor:

   Vendor ID: OFCSUPPL
   Name: Office Suppliers

---

[2]If Bellwether Garden Supply is *not* shown in the Company Name field, refer to the Read Me box on page 28. If an Activation window appears, follow the screen prompts to activate (pages xiii-xiv).

Contact:	Allen Blair
Vendor Type:	OFFICE
Expense Account:	Account No. 71000, Office Expense

4. Enter the following transaction.

Date	*Transaction Description*
03/15/2019	Invoice No. H788 was received from Office Suppliers for the purchase of five boxes of letter-size file folders, $10.95 each. (*Hint:* Account No. 71000, Office Expense, should be debited.)

5. Post this purchase.
6. Continue with Exercise 2-2.

Exercise 2-2: Follow the instructions below to complete Exercise 2-2.

1. Enter the following transaction.

Date	*Transaction Description*
03/18/19	Pay Office Suppliers for Invoice H788, $53.65. (*Hint:* The payment is less a 2% discount: $54.75 -1.10 = $53.65.)

2. Post the Cash Disbursements Journal. (*Hint:* The Payments window is the Cash Disbursements Journal.)
3. Print Check No. 10216. (*Hint: On the OCR AP Laser Preprinted Filter window, select the payment date and vendor.*)

   If you do NOT have a printer, refer to page 65, How to Fix.

4. Print the Vendor Ledgers. Add a Terms column. Adjust the Vendor Ledgers report so that it prints on one page. (*Hint:* Place the mouse over the column. The cursor changes to a double-arrow. Adjust the column.)

5. Print the March 1, 2019 to March 31, 2019 Purchase Order Register. (*Hint:* The Purchase Order Register is an Accounts Payable report. If necessary, select <Options>, from Mar 1, 2019 to Mar 31, 2019.)

   Check Your Figures: PO No. 10300, $140.40

   PO No. 101, $3,834.00

6. Backup. The suggested file name is **Exercise 2-2.ptb**.

7. Save three Sage 50 reports: Vendor List, Vendors Ledgers, and Purchase Order Register to one Excel file. If your Excel icon is *inactive*, refer to Troubleshooting, page 42. (*Hint:* Refer to pages 84-86, Export Two Sage 50 Reports to One Excel File.) Add the terms column to the Vendor Ledgers. Use **Exercise 2-2_Vendor List_Vendor Ledgers_PO Register.xlsx** as the file name. *(Hint:* You may need to close the Excel file *before* adding the second and third sheets.)

8. Save the Vendor List, Vendor Ledgers, and Purchase Order Register as PDF files. Use **Exercise 2-2_Vendor List**, **Exercise 2-2_Vendor Ledgers.pdf**, **Exercise 2-2_Purchase Order Register.pdf** as the file names.

   Check Your figures: Vendor Ledgers balance: $80,826.01.

9. Close all windows. Exit.

CHAPTER 2 INDEX

Chapter

3   Customers

LEARNING OBJECTIVES

1. Restore data from Exercise 2-2. This backup was made on page 89. (Refer to the Read me box on page 55, Do I need to restore?)
2. Go to the Customers & Sales Navigation Center to enter quotes and sales orders.
3. Enter a sales order and ship items from a sales order.
4. Enter customer terms and record a sales invoice.
5. Print a sales invoice, analyze customer payments and credit memos.
6. Post a customer payment for previously invoiced amounts.
7. Add a Customer Terms column to the Customer Ledgers report.
8. Make two backups, save one Excel file, and one PDF file.[1]

Chapter 3 introduces the basics of how Sage 50 works with customer transactions. First you learn about quotes and ***sales orders***. A sales order is a document containing a list of items or services that a customer wants to buy. When a sales order is posted, no accounting information is updated. Once sales orders are completed, you learn how the information entered in customer maintenance is used when posting entries.

In the Maintain Customers/Prospects window, you set a range of days within which a customer can receive a discount and set the discount percentage. This information will print on the sales invoices you record. The discount is automatically applied when you enter a customer payment within the allotted time. The Collection Manager, included on the Analysis Menu, shows an overview of all outstanding invoices.

---

[1]Refer to page 3 for the size of backups, Excel and PDF files.

GETTING STARTED

1. Start Sage 50. Open Bellwether Garden Supply - Student Name.

   ➢ **Troubleshooting: Bellwether Garden Supply is not listed on Sage 50's Company Name list.**

   Refer to the Read Me box on page 28 to review steps to "Create a new company using the restored data." The steps within the Read Me box show how to restore a backup file and set up a company at the same time.

2. If necessary, restore the Exercise 2-2 file. This file was backed up on page 89.

   To make sure you are starting in the appropriate place in the data (Exercise 2-2 backup) check that these vendors, Adler's Landscaping and Office Suppliers, are shown in the Vendors area of the Vendors & Purchases Navigation

				Paid	Debit Amt	Credit Amt	Balance
ADLER	3/15/19	AD107	PJ	*			45.00	45.00
Adler's Landscaping	3/18/19	10215	CDJ			0.90	0.90	45.00
	3/18/19	10215	CDJ		45.00			0.00
OFCSUPPL	3/15/19	H788	PJ	*			54.75	54.75
Office Suppliers	3/18/19	10216	CDJ			1.10	1.10	54.75
	3/18/19	10216	CDJ		54.75			0.00

   Center. (*Hint:* You may need to click Refresh to update your Vendors list.) The Vendor Ledgers report shows a zero balance for both Adler's Landscaping and Office Suppliers. The Vendor Ledgers Report Total is $80,826.01.

Vendor ID Vendor	Date	Trans No	Type	Paid	Debit Amt	Credit Amt	Balance
SAFESTATE Safe State Insurance Co	3/15/19	10210	CDJ		530.64	530.64	0.00
SOGARDEN Southern Garden Whole	3/1/19	Balance Fwd					31,079.25
	3/4/19	11544	PJ	*		255.65	31,334.90
	3/14/19	SG-11657	PJ			50.90	31,385.80
	3/14/19	SG-11658	PJ			239.85	31,625.65
	3/14/19	10208	CDJ		5.11	5.11	31,625.65
	3/14/19	10208	CDJ		255.65		31,370.00
SOPOWER Southern Power Co.	3/11/19	B1011	PJ			226.88	226.88
STANLEY Stanley Shipping Expres	3/1/19	VCM30009	PJ		103.60		-103.60
	3/12/19	B1012	PJ			19.99	-83.61
SULLEY Sulley Printing	3/5/19	14223	PJ			675.00	675.00
	3/9/19	B1024	PJ			17.10	692.10
WATKINS Watkins Financial Planni	3/2/19	B1013	PJ			60.00	60.00
	3/5/19	VCM30010	PJ		35.35		24.65
Report Total					8,131.74	18,603.12	80,826.01

ACCOUNTS RECEIVABLE SYSTEM

Accounts Receivable represents amounts owed by customers for items or services sold to them when cash is not received at the time of sale. Typically, accounts receivable balances are recorded on sales invoices that include terms of payment. Accounts receivable is used if you are setting up accrued income that customers owe.

The four basic tasks in Accounts Receivable are:

1. Quotes: Allows you to enter a quote for a customer.
2. Sales Orders: Sales orders provide you with a means of tracking backorders for your customers.
3. Sales/Invoicing: When items are ready for shipment, the sales/invoicing window is used.
4. Receive Money from Customers: Used for recording payments from customers. (Sage 50 also includes credits and returns.)

Before adding accounts receivable transactions, examine the Customers & Sales Navigation Center. Follow these steps to do that.

1. From the Navigation Bar > select [Customers & Sales]. The Customers & Sales Navigation Center displays information and access points related to the company's customers. In Sage 50, this represents the *accounts receivable module* or *accounts receivable system*.

    Modules organize Sage 50's transaction windows and reports. When the Navigation Bar's Customers & Sales selection is made, Sage 50's accounts receivable system is shown. The menu bar selections, Tasks and Reports & Forms, are also organized by module; for example, the Reports & Forms menu includes Accounts Receivable, Accounts Payable, General Ledger.

Sage 50's Customers & Sales Navigation Center has two tabs that display information and access points related to Bellwether's customers.

- Customers & Sales The Customers & Sales tab is a summary of customer information, includes access to recently used customer reports and an overview of the company's aged receivables. Scroll down the Customers & Sales window to see the Customers, Recently Used Customer Reports, Aged Receivables, and Sage Advisor.

- Customer Management

  On the Customer Management tab, you can see lists of information regarding transactions and customer history, including invoices, receipts, and finance charges.

  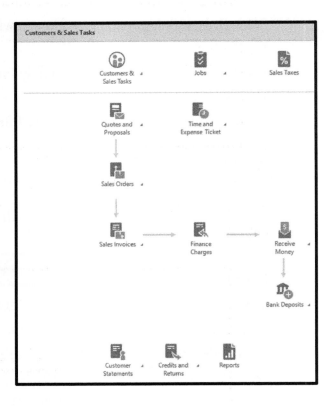

  The Customers & Sales Tasks workflow diagram is shown. If needed, scroll down the window to see all of the Customers & Sales Navigation Center.

Link to a couple of areas to explore the Customers & Sales Navigation Center. Close any open windows, then continue with the next section. (*Hint:* If multiple windows are open, from the menu bar select Window, Close All.)

2. Click on the tab. In the Customer ID field, select ARCHER. On the Customer Management window, there are 3 sections:

- Sales Invoices
- Receipts
- Credit Memos

    In the Receipts > Date Range field > select All Transactions

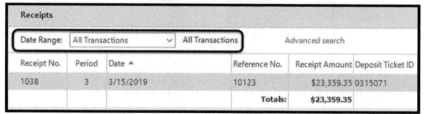

. Archer Scapes and Ponds $23,359.35 receipt amount is shown.

Receipts					
Date Range:	All Transactions	All Transactions		Advanced search	
Receipt No.	Period	Date ▲	Reference No.	Receipt Amount	Deposit Ticket ID
1038	3	3/15/2019	10123	$23,359.35	0315071
			Totals:	$23,359.35	

3. To see detail for Reference No. 10123 > in the Receipts area, drill down on Receipt No. 1038. The Receive Money window appears. The Receive Money window shows a partial payment of $23,359.35. Unpaid amounts are unchecked.

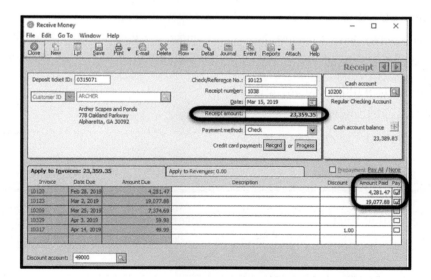

---

4.   After reviewing the Receive Money window, close all windows.

Entering a Quote

When you enter a quote for a customer, you are *not* updating any accounting information or inventory amounts. Sage calculates what the total cost of the sale will be for a customer, including sales tax and freight. You can then print the quote for the customer. Follow these steps to enter a sales quote.

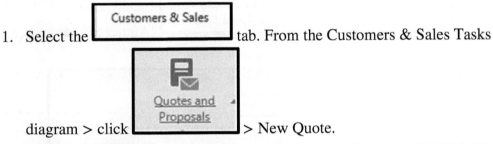

1.   Select the [Customers & Sales] tab. From the Customers & Sales Tasks diagram > click [Quotes and Proposals] > New Quote.

2.   The Quotes window displays. Your cursor is in the Customer ID field. Type **D** (use capital D). Press the **<Enter>** key. Dash Business Systems displays.

3.   Click on the Date field. Type **15** (or select 15). Press the **<Enter>**. The Quote No. field is blank. This is okay. Sage 50 assigns a quote number automatically.

> **Comment:** You can also enter a number that you want to print in the Quote No. field. If you assign your own number, Sage sorts numbers one digit at a time. Therefore, it is a good idea to assign numbers with the same number of digits. For example, Sage sorts numbers in this order:
>
>   1
>   104
>   12
>   2
>   23

4.   Observe that the Customer PO field. Observe that this field is blank. Since this customer does not have a purchase order number, you are going to leave

the field blank. Click on Quantity field. Type **1** and press **<Enter>**. (If the Quantity field shows .01, refer to the steps 1a. and b. on page 19 for setting two decimal places.)

5. In the Item field, select EQFF-13110 Fertilizer Compression Sprayer. (*Hint: Scroll down the Item list to make this selection, or* you can type the item ID.) The Description, GL Account, Unit Price, Tax, and Amount fields are automatically completed.

> **Comment:** If the GL Account field is not displayed on the Quotes window, you need to check your global settings. Refer to step 1c. on page 19 to make sure that the boxes in the Hide General Ledger Accounts section are unchecked (see Options > Global).

6. Click on the Quantity field. Type **4** then select EQWT-15120 Garden Hose - 75 ft. for the item.

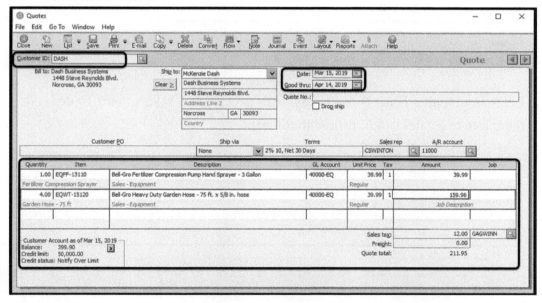

When you selected Dash Business Systems, the Customer Account balance as of March 15, 2019 also appears on the lower left side of the Quotes window, along with the Credit Limit and Credit Status. You can drill down to Dash Business Systems' customer ledger by clicking on the right arrow ( ) in the Customer Account area.

7. To see the journal entry, click 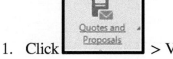. The Quotes Journal lists the sales taxes that are paid for the transaction, the price for each item, and the amount that Bellwether will receive from the customer on this quote. Close the Accounting Behind the Screens window by clicking [OK].

8. Click [Save], then click [Close] to return to the Customers & Sales Navigation Center.

> **Comment:**
>
> When a sales quote is saved, you are *not* posting or updating general ledger accounts. That is handled through the Sales/Invoicing window, which you work with after converting the quote and printing the sales order.

Converting a Quote to a Sales Order

Let's assume that Dash Business Systems accepts this sales quote. To convert the quote to a sales order, follow these steps.

1. Click [Quotes and Proposals] > View and Edit Quotes. The Quote List window appears.

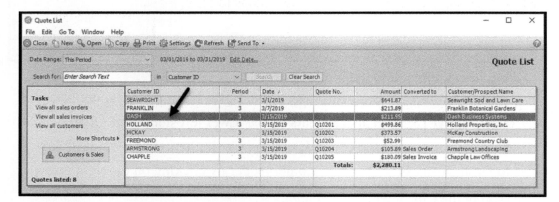

2. Double-click DASH. The Quotes window appears showing the March 15, 2019 quote. Compare this to the Quotes window shown on the previous page.

3. Click [Convert]. There are three options: Sale/Invoice, Sale/Invoice and Print Now, Sales Order. Click on the radio button next to Sales Order. The SO # field is completed automatically.

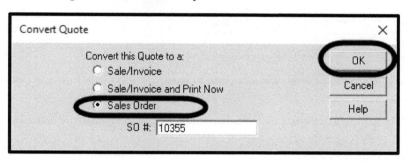

4. Click [OK]. A blank Quotes window appears. Click [Close]. You just converted the sales quote to a sales order. Now you can invoice the customer for shipment.

5. Close all windows. (*Hint:* Select Window > Close All.)

Printing (or Displaying) a Sales Order

Printing a sales order gives you the ability to confirm customer orders and fill these orders more efficiently. Follow these steps to print.

1. From the Customers & Sales Navigation Center > select [Sales Orders] > View and Edit Sales Orders. On the Sales Order List window, double-click DASH, SO 10355. (If needed, scroll down the Sales Order List.) The Quote converted to Sales Order No. 10355 displays.

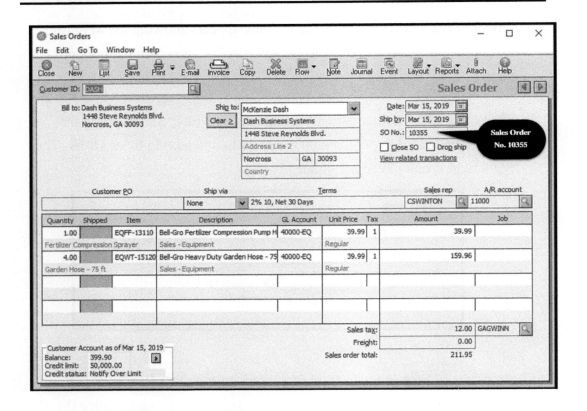

2. Click [Print ▼]. *Or,* click on the down arrow next to Print and select Print Preview. The Print or Preview Forms: Sales Orders window appears. Observe that the Sales Order number is 10355. This agrees with the quote that was converted to a sales order. Sage 50 automatically assigned the sales order number. (*Hint:* If you do <u>not</u> have a printer, see How to Fix on the next page.)

3. Accept the Use this form – Sales Order w/Totals. Click [Print] (*or* [Print Preview]). The sales order starts to print or displays.

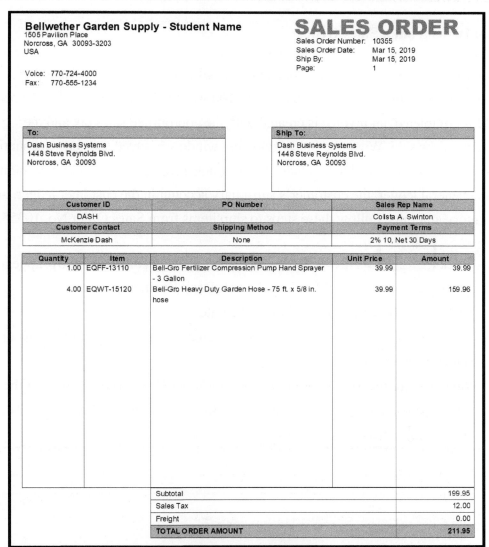

4.   If you previewed the Sales Order, click . (Printing saves and posts.)

How to Fix? I don't have a printer? From the Sales Orders window, select <Print
Preview>. In the Printer area, select <Printer Setup>. Select Adobe PDF or Microsoft XPS
Document Writer. Save to USB drive. For detailed steps, refer to page 65.

---

5.   Close all windows. (*Hint:* From the menu bar, click Window, Close All.)

Ship Items from a Sales Order

To ship items from a sales order, open the Sales/Invoicing window, select the customer, then choose the open sales order you want to invoice. Once the shipped field is completed, an invoice is created with the appropriate sales tax and the amount of the sale. When the Sales/Invoicing window is saved (posted), accounting information is updated. That includes the accounts receivable controlling account in the general ledger, the customer's subsidiary account in the customer ledger, and inventory amounts. Follow these steps to ship items from Sales Order No. 10355.

1. Click ![Sales Invoices] > New Sales Invoice. The Sales/Invoicing window appears.
2. In the Customer ID field, select DASH, Dash Business Systems.
3. In the Date field type **15** (or select the date).
4. The Apply to Sales Order No. tab is selected. Click on the down-arrow and select number 10355.
5. Since we are receiving both items on this Sales Order, type **1** and **4** in the Shipped fields. Once you complete the Shipped fields, the Invoice totals are computed (sales tax and amount paid at sale.)

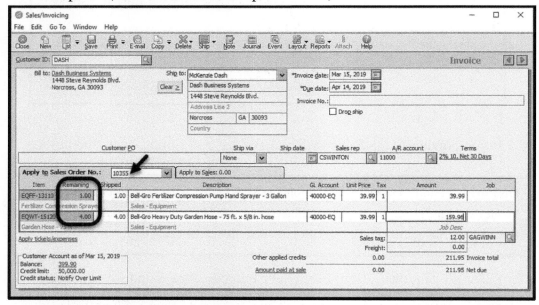

6. To see how this transaction is journalized in the Sales Journal, click .
   After the entry is saved (posted), Cost of Sales is computed. Close the Sales
   Journal window.

7. Click to post. Close the Sales/Invoicing window.

THE MAINTAIN CUSTOMERS/PROSPECTS WINDOW

The first step is to select the customer you are going to invoice and to change
one item of information: the discount percentage offered for timely payment.

1. From the Customers & Sales Navigation Center > > New
   Customer. The Maintain Customers/Prospects window displays. The cursor
   is in the Customer ID field.
2. Click on the down-arrow in the Customer ID field to open the
   customers/prospects list.[2]
3. The customer file you are going to use is Teesdale Real Estate. Click on
   the down-arrow > select **TEESDALE**.

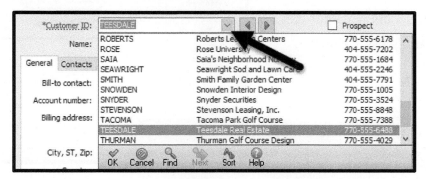

The Maintain Customers/ Prospects window shows a completed record for
Teesdale Real Estate.

---

[2]There are three ways to open the list in a lookup field from the Customer ID field: 1) Press the right mouse
button; 2) type a question mark **<?>**; 3) left-click the down-arrow.

Entering a Discount for a Customer

Because Teesdale Real Estate is such a good customer, Bellwether Garden
Supply is going to increase their discount from 2% to 5%. In accounting, this is
called a *sales discount*. The standard sales discount for Bellwether is 2% if paid
within 10 days. Teesdale's new sales discount is 5% if paid within 15 days. Sales
discounts are applied when payment is received from the customer within the
discount period. In this case, 5% discount if payment is received within 15 days.
Follow these steps to enter a discount for a customer:

1. The Maintain Customers/Prospects window for Teesdale Real Estate should

    be displayed. Click on the Payment & Credit tab 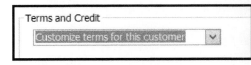.

2. In the Terms and Credit Area (right side of
    window), click on the down-arrow. Select
    Customize terms for this customer.

3. If necessary, click on the radio button next to Due in number of days.

4. Click on the Discount in field.
    Type **15** and press **<Enter>**.
    The cursor moves to the
    Discount percent field.

5. In the Discount percent field,
    type **5** and press **<Enter>**.[3]

---

[3]You should have set two decimal places in Chapter 1 (see page 19, 1 a. and b.).

6. Click [💾 Save]. Close all windows.

Entering a Sale to a Customer

To print or record an invoice, enter a sales invoice for a customer on the Sales/Invoicing window. Similar to a Sales Journal, the Sales/Invoicing window is reserved for sales from credit customers.

Date   *Transaction Description*

03/01/19   Bellwether Garden Supply sold 5 hand sprayer/misters, $49.95, to Teesdale Real Estate, Customer ID, TEESDALE, and cleaned the parking lot, $100, for a total of $149.95 plus $9.00 sales tax; $158.95.

Follow these steps to enter a sales invoice.

1. From the Customers & Sales Navigation Center > [Sales Invoices] > New Sales Invoice. The Sales/Invoicing window appears.

    Use the Sales/Invoicing window for credit sales from customers. The Sales/Invoicing window is for credit customers only. If the transaction involves an accounts receivable credit sale, enter it in the Sales/Invoicing window. The Sales/Invoicing window posts to the Sales Journal.

    The Sales/Invoicing window should be displayed. The cursor is in the Customer ID field. Don't worry if you have forgotten Teesdale's customer ID number because Sage knows it. The Customer ID field has a lookup field.

2. With the cursor in the Customer ID field, click the right mouse button (or type a question mark, **<?>**).

   You may also click 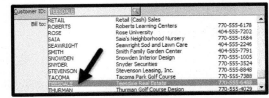.

3. Highlight TEESDALE, Teesdale Real Estate.

4. Click [OK]. The Sales/ Invoicing window appears. Observe that the Bill to and Ship to fields are completed automatically. Sage provides an invoice number when the sales invoice is printed so there is no need to enter an invoice number now.

5. Click on the Invoice date field. If necessary, type **1** for the date.

   Sage offers flexibility when entering dates. For example, you can enter March 1, 2019 as 030119 and the program will format the date correctly. Or, you can enter just the day portion of the date and the date is formatted in the current period. For example, if you're working in March of 2019, you can type 4 in the Invoice date field and the program formats the date as March 4, 2019. You can also use the calendar to select the date.

6. Make sure the Invoice date field shows Mar 1, 2019. Press **<Enter>** two times to go to the Invoice No field. The cursor moves to the Invoice No. field, which you are going to leave blank. Sage 50 will assign an invoice number when you print the sales invoice.

7. Click on the Apply to Sales tab Apply to Sales: 0.00.

8. Click on the Quantity field, type **5** and press **<Enter>**. Your cursor goes to the Item lookup field.

9. Click to open the list of inventory items.

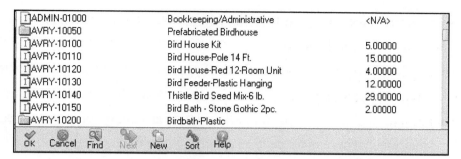

There are two ways to enter transaction lines for an invoice:

- By Inventory Item: Because the price of each inventory item is stored in the Maintain Inventory Items file, you only have to enter the quantity supplied. The program will compute the credit amount.

- By Account Number: If there is no line item set up for a particular commodity you sell, or if you don't use the Inventory module, you can distribute directly against the proper General Ledger account.

10. The Inventory Item list should be open. Let's see what happens if the Sort icon is selected. Click which is located at the bottom of the lookup list on the right side. By selecting Sort, you change the order of the list. The list was sorted by ID number; now the list is sorted alphabetically by name. This feature is available in all lookup lists.

11. Select Hand Sprayer/Mister as the item for this sale. The Item ID, EQFF-13120, displays in the Item field. (*Hint:* You can also type the item ID.)

12. Your cursor should be in the Description field with the following description highlighted: Bell-Gro Plant All-Purpose Plastic Sprayer/Mister. Since you are not going to add a comment or explanation about this inventory item, press **<Enter>** to move to the GL Account field. The default account is Account No. 40000-EQ, Sales – Equipment. The account name, Sales – Equipment, is shown below the transaction line. This account will be credited unless you change the account number in this GL Account field. The debit is automatically made to Accounts Receivable–Teesdale Real Estate.

13. Press **<Enter>** to accept Account No. 40000-EQ. The cursor moves to the Unit Price field and 9.99 is automatically completed. Since the price has

been set up in the Maintain Inventory Items file, the unit price is automatically completed for you.

14. Press **<Enter>** to go to the tax field. Type a **<?>** to display the lookup list. Inventory Item tax types are set up in the Maintain Inventory Item file. This lookup list lets you specify certain items as exempt or having special tax situations. There is no need to specify any special tax situation.

15. Press **<Enter>** to go to the Amount field. Sage calculates the total, $49.95, and enters it in the field.

16. Press **<Enter>** to go to the Job field. The job field also has a lookup list. In Chapter 6, you learn about assigning Jobs.

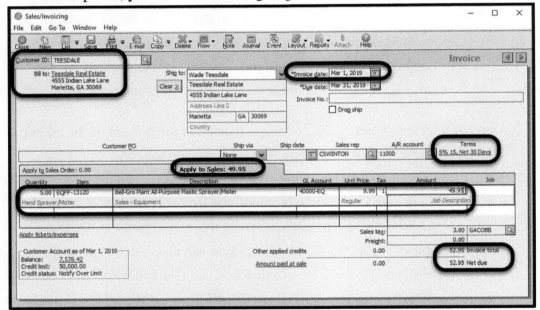

> ➤ **Troubleshooting:** Observe that the Invoice No. field is blank and that the Terms field shows 5% 15, Net 30 Days. The invoice number, similar to the check number, is assigned when you print. If you are <u>not</u> going to print, enter 101 in the Invoice No. field.

Notice that the Invoice Total and Net Due in the lower right of the window shows $52.95. The Invoice Total displays a running total of the customer's account. Accounts Receivable subsidiary ledger is increased (debited).

When you add the next transaction line, this figure will increase. In accounting, two things happen when the Accounts Receivable subsidiary ledger is used.

a. The Accounts Receivable controlling account in the General Ledger is increased by the amount of the credit sale.

b. The credit to the applicable revenue account is offset by a debit to the Customer's account in the Accounts Receivable ledger.

17. To go to a new transaction line, press **<Enter>**.

Distributing Against a Specific Account

In this part of the transaction, Bellwether Garden Supply contracted with Teesdale Real Estate to clean up their parking lot for $100. Because no inventory item is stored in the maintenance records, this transaction is different than the one you just completed (entering a sale to a customer for an inventory item). In this part of the transaction, you need to distribute the amount ($100.00) directly against the Other Income account.

1. Your cursor is in the Quantity field. Since you don't have a quantity number to enter with this transaction, press **<Enter>**. Your cursor should be in the Item field.

2. Press **<Enter>** to leave the Item field blank. Your cursor moves to the Description field.

3. Type **Cleaned parking lot** in the Description field, press **<Enter>**. Your cursor moves to the GL Account field. The default needs to be changed.

4. Type **41000** (for Other Income) and press **<Enter>**. Now the account description below the current transaction line reads Other Income and your cursor moves to the Unit Price field.

The account number that automatically displayed, 40000, Sales, was the default account. Since we want to distribute this revenue to a specific account, 41000, Other Income, you must type this account number (41000); otherwise, the program will accept the default account number.

5. Press **<Enter>** to skip the Unit Price field. Your cursor moves to the Tax field.

6. Press **<Enter>** to accept the default tax code. Your cursor moves to the Amount field.

7. Type **100** and press **<Enter>** two times. Notice the Sales/Invoicing window shows the two amounts entered for this invoice. The Invoice Total, including sales tax, is $158.95.

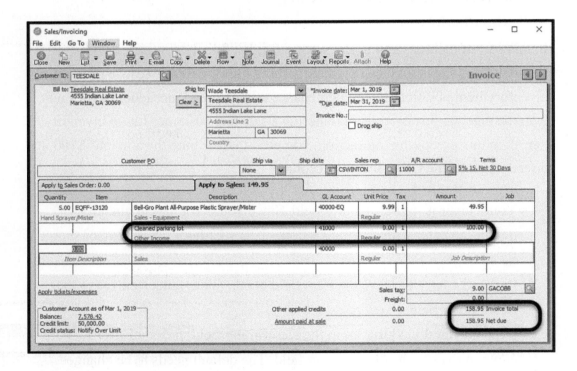

For purposes of this example, the cleaning service is taxed. In some states, services such as cleaning a parking lot would not be subject to sales tax.

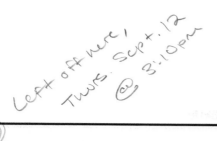
Left off here! Thurs. Sept. 12 @ 3:10pm

Discount Information

In this chapter you changed the sales discount for Teesdale Real Estate. Let's check to make sure that the discount information is current for the invoice you just entered.

1. Link to Terms, <u>5% 15, Net 30 Days</u>. The Terms Information window appears. Since the Discount Amount was computed automatically on the items sold plus sales tax, the Discount

Amount of 7.95 needs to be changed. In Sage 50, you can enter a different sales discount amount.

In this example, the sales discount is calculated on the amount of the items sold which is $149.95. (Refer to the Sales/Invoicing window on page 110.)

Items sold: $49.95 + $100 = $149.95
Times sales discount   .05
Discount Amount   **$7.50**

2. Type **7.50** in the Discount Amount field, then press **<Enter>**.

5% sales discount is $7.50

$149.95 X .05

The Discount Date, March 16, 2019, is the date when the customer must pay to receive the discount. The Displayed Terms are the percentage of discount (5%), the time period in days for receiving the discount (15), and the number of days before the invoice is due (Net 30).

3. Click [OK] to close the Terms Information window.

POSTING THE INVOICE

The sample company, Bellwether Garden Supply, uses *real-time posting*. When real-time posting is used, the transactions that you enter are posted when you select the [Save] icon.

There is another type of posting. It is called *batch posting*. When using batch posting, the transactions you enter are saved to a temporary holding area where you can review them before posting to the general ledger. Follow these steps to save and post the invoice.

1. Click [Save] The Sales/Invoicing window is ready for another transaction.
2. Close all windows.

PRINTING (OR DISPLAYING) INVOICES

Follow these steps to print the invoice for Teesdale Real Estate:

1. From the menu bar, select Reports & Forms > Forms > Invoices and Packing Slips.
2. Observe that the Form Types field shows Invoices and Packing Slips highlighted. In the Forms list, select Invoice.

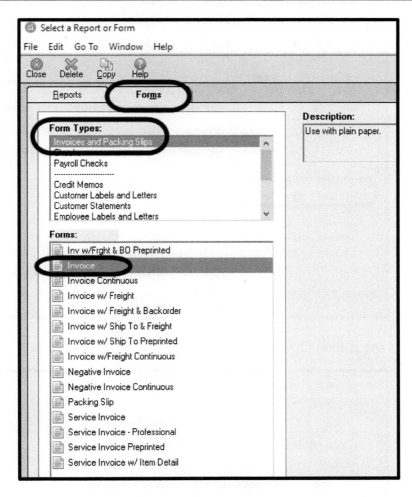

3. Double-click Invoice. The Preview and Print Invoices and Packing Slips window appears.

4. In the through field, type or select 3/1/19.

5. In the Filter customers by field select Teesdale in the ID and to fields.

6. Click ![Refresh List] .

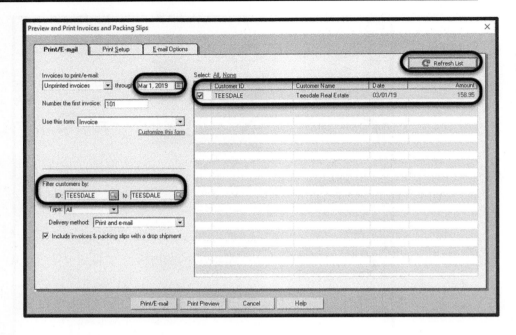

7. Select the <u>E</u>-mail Options tab. Select Print only a paper copy.

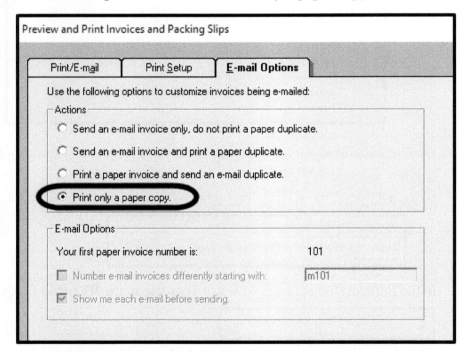

8. Click [Print Preview]. Compare Invoice 101 to the one shown.

Bellwether Garden Supply - Student Name
1505 Pavilion Place
Norcross, GA 30093-3203
USA

Voice: 770-724-4000
Fax: 770-555-1234

INVOICE

Invoice Number: 101
Invoice Date: Mar 1, 2019
Page: 1

Bill To:	Ship to:
Teesdale Real Estate 4555 Indian Lake Lane Marietta, GA 30069	Teesdale Real Estate 4555 Indian Lake Lane Marietta, GA 30069

Customer ID	Customer PO	Payment Terms	
TEESDALE		5% 15, Net 30 Days	
Sales Rep ID	Shipping Method	Ship Date	Due Date
CSWINTON	None		3/31/19

Quantity	Item	Description	Unit Price	Amount
5.00	EQFF-13120	Bell-Gro Plant All-Purpose Plastic Sprayer/Mister	9.99	49.95
		Cleaned parking lot		100.00

Subtotal		149.95
Sales Tax		9.00
Total Invoice Amount		158.95
Payment/Credit Applied		
TOTAL		158.95

Check/Credit Memo No:

9. Click [Print]. If you do <u>not</u> have a printer, go to the Sales/Invoicing

    window – close all windows > [Sales Invoices] > View and Edit Sales Invoices
    > double-click Invoice No. 101 > type **101** in the Invoice No. field > <u>S</u>ave.

Read Me: When I try to print Invoice 101, a Sage 50 Accounting window appears that says There are no forms to preview. What should I do?

1. Click <OK>.
2. Close the Select a Report and Forms window.
3. On the Customers & Sales Navigation Center > select Sales Invoices > View and Edit Sales Invoices.
4. Double-click Teesdale, Invoice 101, to go to the Sales/Invoicing window.
5. Make the selections to Print from the Sales/Invoicing window. Compare Invoice 101 to the one shown above.
6. Close all windows.

Notice the Payment Terms are 5% 15, Net 30 Days. This is the information you entered for Customer Terms on pages 104-105.

10. A message displays asking if the invoice printed and emailed properly. When you answer Yes, Sage updates the invoice number and flags the invoice as printed so that it will not print again. Click **Yes**.

11. Close all windows.

RECEIVE MONEY FROM CUSTOMER

Teesdale Real Estate has sent a check in payment of their invoice. Follow these steps to enter the following transaction.

Date   *Transaction Description*

03/15/19   Received Check No. 8818 from Teesdale Real Estate in payment of Invoice No. 101, $151.45. (*Hint:* The sales discount is applied to the items sold in the amount of $149.95. Refer to Discount Information, step 2, page 111.)

The customer payment is calculated like this:

Items sold:	$149.95
5% sales discount:	(7.50)
Sales tax:	9.00
Customer payment:	$151.45

1. From the Customers & Sales Navigation Center, click >
    Receive Money from Customer. The Receive Money window appears.

    The Receive Money window is also the Cash Receipts Journal. There is a
    table in the lower half of the window that lists distribution lines for the
    current transaction. There is an icon bar at the top of the window. The
    item descriptions and account descriptions appear beneath each
    transaction line. The title bar identifies the window being used. In this
    case, the title bar says, Receive Money.

2. Your cursor is in the Deposit ticket ID field. Type **03/15/19** (the customer
    payment date). This Deposit ticket ID field defaults to the current date
    (today's date) and is used to combine receipts for bank reconciliation. Press
    <Enter>.

3. In the Customer ID field, type the Customer ID for Teesdale: **TEESDALE**
    and press **<Enter>**.

    When you enter a Customer ID, the window shows a list of invoices. When
    the customer is paying for invoiced amounts, you can select an invoice from
    the list. The invoice amounts, including discounts, complete the Apply to
    Invoices table.

4. Click on the Check/Reference No. field. Type **8818** for the customer's
    check number (a Reference number must be entered). Press **<Enter>** key
    two times and the cursor moves to the Date field. Type **15** (or select 15).
    This date is important because it is used to determine if a discount applies.
    For example, if the transaction date for the invoice was March 1, 2019, and
    the discount terms were 5% for 10 days, the customer payment entered for
    March 15, 2019 would miss qualifying for a discount. The discount amount
    is computed automatically and displays the discount when there is one.
5. The terms for Teesdale are 5% 15 days, Net 30. Since March 15, 2019 is
    within the discount period, accept the March 15, 2019 date. Press
    <Enter>. In the Payment method field, select Check. Press **<Enter>**.
6. If the Cash Account field does *not* show Account No. 10200, Regular
    Checking Account, select it. Press **<Enter>**.
7. If necessary, select the Apply to Invoices tab.
8. Click on the Pay box for Invoice 101.

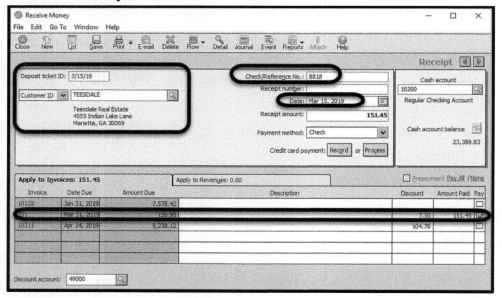

Notice that the Discount field displays the amount of the discount, $7.50.
The discount displays because payment was received within the discount

period (5%, 15 days). Therefore, the customer gets the 5% discount and the amount is automatically entered in the Discount field. Then, the check amount for the invoice is automatically computed: $151.45 (149.95 – 7.50 + 9.00 = $151.45). The Receipt amount in the check portion of the Receive Money window shows 151.45, Teesdale's invoice minus the 5% discount, plus sales tax.

9. Click [Journal] to see the account distribution in the Cash Receipts Journal.

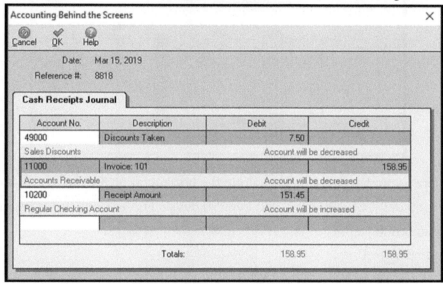

10. Click [OK] to close the Accounting Behind the Screens window.

11. Click [Save] and the customer payment is posted to the Cash Receipts Journal.

12. Close the Receive Money to return to Customers & Sales Navigation Center.

ANALYZING CUSTOMER PAYMENTS

How well does Bellwether Garden Supply manage its collections of payments from customers? To look at customers and aging amounts, use the Collection Manager. Follow these steps to learn how to use the Collection Manager.

1. From the menu bar, click Analysis > Collection Manager. The Collection Aging bar graph appears.

2. In the <u>A</u>s of Date field, type or select 3/15/19.

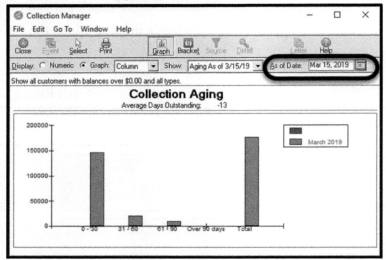

There are four aging brackets along the horizontal or X axis: 0 - 30 days, 31 - 60 days, 61 - 90 days, and over 90 days. The vertical or Y axis shows dollar amounts due.

3. Click Bracket. The Total Bracket table is shown below.

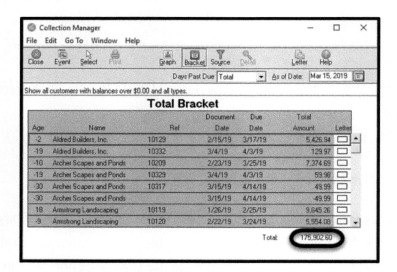

The Total agrees with the Customer Ledgers total on page 124. The Collection Manager's Total Bracket window shows the age of the invoice in days, the customer name, the reference (Ref) number, the document date or transaction date, the due date, the total amount due, and whether a letter was sent.

4. Scroll down the window to highlight the invoice for Teesdale Real Estate

   (Age, -30; Ref, 10311; Amt Due, 5,238.12). Then, click . The Customer Detail window is shown below.

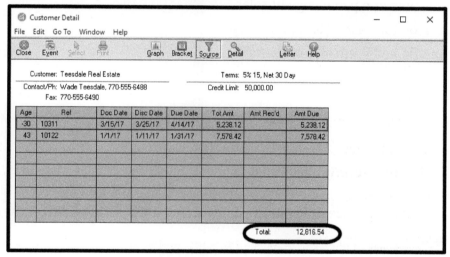

The Total agrees with Teesdale Real Estate's Customer Ledgers balance shown on page 124. At this level you can see all of Teesdale Real Estate's invoices. If you want to send a collection letter you can do that from this

window. By clicking [Letter] on the icon bar you can send a collection letter. (If you print a letter, Sage 50 defaults to a letter addressed to Thurman Golf Course Design.)

5. Click [Close] to exit the Collection Manager.

FINANCIAL MANAGER

The Financial Manager provides a brief, overall financial picture of how the business is performing. The business summary data includes *financial ratios*. These financial ratios are included.

- Cost of sales as a percentage of sales
- Gross profits as a percentage of sales
- Net income as a percentage of sales
- Return on total assets as a percentage
- Return on net worth as a percentage
- Current assets
- Current liabilities
- Current ratio
- Inventory turnover
- Days accounts receivable outstanding

Follow these steps to see the Financial Manager and the ratios that Sage 50 calculates.

1. From the Analysis menu > select Financial Manager. The defaults are March 31, 2019. Business Summary is the default. (If needed, type 033119 as the date.) The Financial Manager includes these sections: Operational Analysis, Resource Management, Profitability, and Working Capital.

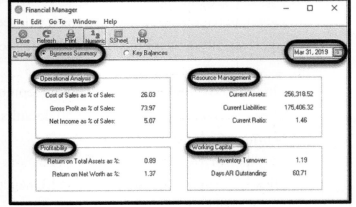

Financial ratios are included within each section.

2.   Review the ratios shown on the Financial Manager, then close all windows.

DISPLAYING THE CUSTOMER LEDGERS

Sage 50's accounts receivable system includes the customer ledgers. ***Customer Ledgers*** lists customers with detail transaction information including outstanding balances for each customer. To display the Customer Ledgers, follow these steps.

1.   From the Customers & Sales Navigation Center, link to <u>View All Customer & Sales Reports</u> in the Recently Used Customer Reports area. The Select a Report or Form window appears.

2.   Double-click Customer Ledgers.

3.   The Customer Ledgers report appears. Click Columns. The Customer Ledgers/Columns window appears. Select Customer Terms.

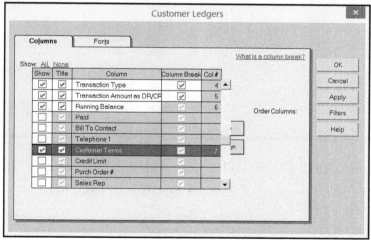

4.   Click OK. A Terms column is added to the Customer Ledgers report. Scroll down the report to TEESDALE. Observe the terms are 5% 15, Net 30 Days and the account balance is $12,816.54. The Customer Detail window on page 121 shows the same balance.

Bellwether Garden Supply - Student Name
Customer Ledgers
For the Period From Mar 1, 2019 to Mar 31, 2019

Filter Criteria includes: Report order is by Name. Report is printed in Detail Format.

Customer ID / Customer	Date	Trans No	Type	Debit Amt	Credit Amt	Balance	Terms
SEAWRIGHT / Seawright Sod and Lawn	3/15/19	10316	SJ	49.99		49.99	2% 10, Net 30 Days
SMITH / Smith Family Garden Ce	3/1/19	Balance Fwd				5,088.49	2% 10, Net 30 Days
	3/10/19	10305	SJ	6,011.64		11,100.13	
	3/15/19	10125, 10305	CRJ	120.23	120.23	11,100.13	
	3/15/19	10125, 10305	CRJ		10,930.16	169.97	
SNOWDEN / Snowden Interior Design	3/1/19	Balance Fwd				7,161.98	2% 10, Net 30 Days
	3/3/19	10303	SJ	387.63		7,549.61	
	3/4/19	31114	CRJ	1.99	1.99	7,549.61	
	3/4/19	31114	CRJ		387.63	7,161.98	
	3/11/19	10306	SJ	184.29		7,346.27	
SNYDER / Snyder Securities	3/1/19	Balance Fwd				2,981.04	2% 10, Net 30 Days
	3/4/19	10334	SJ	59.98		3,041.02	
	3/13/19	CC0006	CRJ	99.98	99.98	3,041.02	
STEVENSON / Stevenson Leasing, Inc.	3/8/19	10318	SJ	49.99		49.99	2% 10, Net 30 Days
	3/12/19	10118	SJ	7,790.42		7,840.41	
TACOMA / Tacoma Park Golf Cours	3/1/19	Balance Fwd				4,675.57	2% 10, Net 30 Days
	3/14/19	10322	SJ	49.99		4,725.56	
	3/15/19	10327	SJ	1,049.01		5,774.57	
TEESDALE / Teesdale Real Estate	3/1/19	Balance Fwd				7,578.42	5% 15, Net 30 Days
	3/1/19	101	SJ	158.95		7,737.37	
	3/15/19	10311	SJ	5,238.12		12,975.49	
	3/15/19	8818	CRJ	7.50	7.50	12,975.49	
	3/15/19	8818	CRJ		158.95	12,816.54	
THURMAN / Thurman Golf Course De	3/1/19	Balance Fwd				3,610.39	2% 10, Net 30 Days
	3/15/19	10343	SJ	9,998.00		13,608.39	
TRENT / Trent Bank and Trust		No Activity				0.00	2% 10, Net 30 Days
WILLIAMS / Williams Industries	3/3/19	4452	CRJ	220.31	220.31	0.00	2% 10, Net 30 Days
	3/5/19	10312V	SJ		939.72	-939.72	
	3/15/19	10312	SJ	939.72		0.00	
Report Total				91,904.25	80,942.32	175,902.60	

The Report Total, 175,902.60, agrees with the Total Bracket table's total on page 120, and Teesdale's Customer Detail total page 121.

CREDIT MEMOS

Credit Memos are issued to customers for returned merchandise or service refunds. Use the Credit Memos window to enter credit memos for customer returns and credits. You can apply credit memos to any existing sales invoice. All entries made on this window are posted to the General Ledger, customer records, if appropriate, and to inventory and job records.

The customer ledgers should be displayed on your screen. Scroll up the customer ledger to Saia's Neighborhood Nursery. Observe that Saia's Neighborhood Nursery has a customer credit memo (CCM4003) on 3/14/19. Follow these steps to see how the credit was applied.

1. The customer ledgers should be displayed. Scroll up the Customer Ledgers window to Saia's Neighborhood Nursery.
2. Double-click on the 3/14/19 CCM4003 transaction to drill down to Credit memos window.

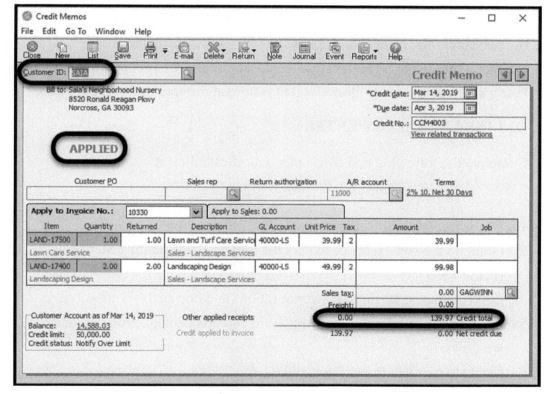

3. Observe that there is a $139.97 Credit total which was applied to Invoice No. 10330. Close the Credit Memos window. You are returned to the Customer Ledgers. The amount of the credit memo is subtracted from the Customer Ledger's balance forward amount: $14,728.00 – 139.97 = $14,588.03.

SAIA	3/1/19	Balance Fwd				14,588.03	2% 10, Net 30 Days
Saia's Neighborhood Nu	3/4/19	10330	SJ	139.97		14,728.00	
	3/14/19	CCM4003	SJ		139.97	14,588.03	←
	3/15/19		SJ		49.99	14,538.04	

4. Close all windows.

BACKING UP CHAPTER 3 DATA

After completing the work within Chapter 3, back up. The suggested file name is **Chapter 3.ptb**. Detailed steps for backing up data are shown on pages 24-26. Backing up saves your data to that point in your work. Each time you back up, use a different file name; for example, the suggested file name at this point is Chapter 3.ptb. (Sage 50 automatically adds the file extension .ptb to backups.) Using a unique file name allows you to restore at different points in the data.

ONLINE LEARNING CENTER

Complete the following end-of-chapter activities online at www.mhhe.com/yacht2019 > Student Edition > Chapter 3.

1. Interactive Multiple-Choice and True/False questions.
2. Going to the Net exercise: Access the Financial Accounting Standards Board (FASB) website.
3. QA Templates: 10 short-answer questions and one analysis question.
5. Assessment Rubric: review journals, navigation centers, modules, and task windows.
6. Listen to narrated PowerPoint slides.

The OLC also includes links to the Appendixes:

* Appendix A: Troubleshooting (Information Center)
* Appendix C: Review of Accounting Principles (Student Edition)
* Appendix D: Glossary of Terms (Student Edition)

Exercise 3-1: Follow the instructions below to complete Exercise 3-1.

1. Start Sage 50. Open Bellwether Garden Supply - Student Name [your first and last name].
2. If necessary, restore data from the end of Chapter 3. This backup was made on page 126.
3. Record the following transaction.

Date	*Transaction Description*
03/03/19	Bellwether Garden Supply sold one Rotary Mower – Riding 4HP to Teesdale Real Estate, Invoice 102, $299.99; plus $18 sales tax; total, $317.99. (*Hint*: If you do <u>not</u> have a printer, type 102 in the Invoice No. field. Select the Apply to Sales tab. Type **1** in the Quantity field > select EQLW-14140 > Bell-Gro Riding Lawn Mower - 4HP as the Item.)

4. Print or post. (*Hint:* When you print from the Sales/Invoicing window, the sales invoice saves and posts. If you do <u>not</u> print, click <Save> to post to the Sales Journal.)
5. Continue with Exercise 3-2.

Exercise 3-2: Follow the instructions below to complete Exercise 3-2.

1. Record the following transaction:

Date	*Transaction Description*
03/15/19	Received Check No. 9915 in the amount of $302.99 from Teesdale Real Estate in payment of Invoice 102. (*Hint: Type **3/15/19** in the Deposit ticket ID field. Remember to use the check number in the Check/Reference field.*

IMPORTANT: Calculate the discount on the item sold. On the Receive Money window, type the appropriate amount in the Discount field. *Do* not *include sales tax in the sales discount calculation.*

2. Post the customer payment.

The 5% discount for Teesdale's 3/15/19 transactions is shown on the Cash Receipts Journal. From

the menu bar, select Reports & Forms > Accounts Receivable > Cash Receipts Journal > Columns > GL Account Description > then <OK>. The Cash Receipts Journal displays with an Account Description column.

3. Print the Customer Ledgers. Add a Customer Terms column to the Customer Ledgers report. Adjust the columns so that the Terms for each customer prints on the same page.

If needed, on the Print window, select Adobe PDF or Microsoft XPS Document Writer as the printer. Refer to page 65, How to Fix. If you save as PDF file, use file name shown in step 6.

4. Back up Exercise 3-2. Use **Exercise 3-2.ptb** as the file name.

5. Export the Customer Ledgers to Excel. Use **Exercise 3-2_Customer Ledgers.xlsx** as the file name. (*Hint:* Refer to pages 41-44, Exporting Reports to Excel. A Terms column should be included on the Customer Ledgers. If your Excel icon is inactive, read Troubleshooting, page 42.)

6. Save the Customer Ledgers as PDF file. Use **Exercise 3-2_Customer Ledgers.pdf** as the file name.

    Check your figures: Customer Ledgers balance, $175,902.60.

7. Exit.

CHAPTER 3 INDEX

Chapter 4 — Employees

LEARNING OBJECTIVES

1. Restore data from Exercise 3-2. (This backup was made on page 128.)
2. Enter and store information using the Maintain Employees/Sales Reps window.
3. Set up default information for payroll.
4. Store information about payroll payment methods.
5. Transfer funds from the regular checking account to the payroll checking account.
6. Enter paychecks in the Payroll Entry window.
7. Print employee paychecks.
8. Make two backups, save one Excel file, and save one PDF file.[1]

In Chapter 4 you learn how Sage 50 processes payroll. Once default and employee maintenance information is set up, payroll is a simple process. The first step in setting up payroll is to go to the **Employees & Payroll** Navigation Center. Sage 50's Employees & Payroll Navigation Center displays information and access points related to the company's employees. It includes a summary of employee information including 1099 vendors and access to recently used employee reports.

---

[1]Refer to the chart on page 3 for the size of backup files and saved Excel and PDF files.

On the left side of the Employees &
Payroll Navigation Center, there is a
workflow diagram showing employee
and payroll tasks, represented by icons.
The Employees & Payroll workflow
diagram is shown on this page.

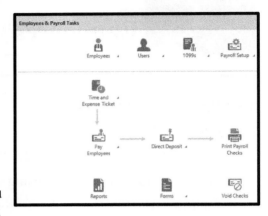

Click the icons to see menus that take you
to various payroll-related tasks. Sage 50's
employees and payroll system is another example of the software's modular
design. Sage 50's modules organize lists, transaction windows, and reports
related to a specific Navigation Bar selection. In Chapter 2, Vendors, you used
Sage 50's accounts payable system. In Chapter 3, Customers, you used Sage
50's accounts receivable system. In this chapter, you see how the payroll system
is organized.

Another way to use Sage 50's modules is to select Tasks or Reports & Forms
from the menu bar. For example, if you select Tasks from the menu bar, observe
that selections for Payroll—Select for Payroll Entry and Payroll Entry—are
listed together. If you select Reports & Forms from the menu bar, there is a
selection for Payroll. Selections from the Tasks and Reports & Forms menus are
also organized by module.

Some of the information that appears in the Employees & Payroll Navigation
Center can be accessed with the drill down feature. Drill down is the act of
following a path to its origin for further analysis. In certain Sage 50 reports, click
on a transaction to drill down to the window that includes the original
transaction information. From financial statements, you can drill down to the
General Ledger report, and then use drill down again to see original transaction

detail. You can also drill down to transaction detail from other Navigation Bar selections.

The diagram below describes the payroll process. These steps show how payroll accounting is set up.

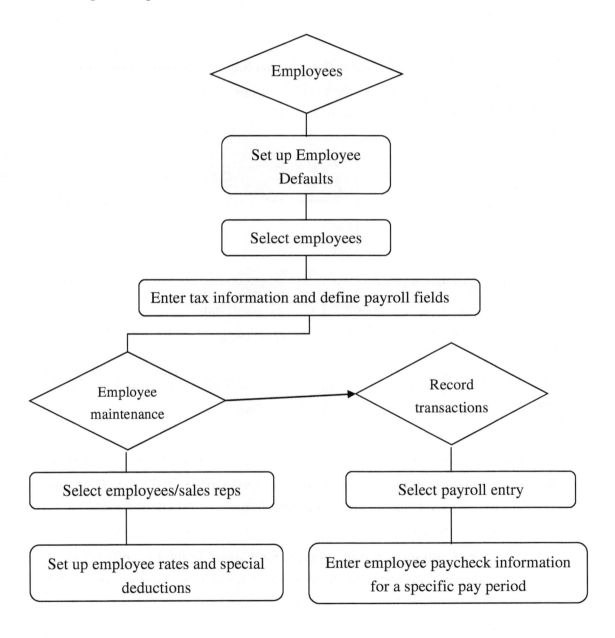

GETTING STARTED

Follow these steps to start:

1. Start Sage 50. Open Bellwether Garden Supply - Student Name [your first and last name].

✓ **Troubleshooting:** If Bellwether Garden Supply - Student Name does not open, or is not shown on the Company Name list, refer to the Read Me box on page 28 to review the steps to "Create a new company using the restored data." To see the Open an Existing Company window, go to the startup window. Select Open an existing company. To make sure Bellwether

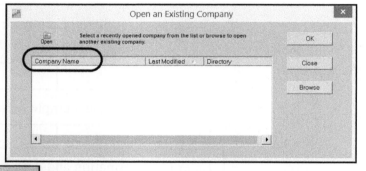

is not listed, click [Browse]. Some schools delete company folders so you may need to restore. Continue with step 2.

2. If necessary, restore data from the Exercise 3-2 back up. The Exercise 3-2.ptb backup was made on page 128. (*Hint:* To verify data, restore data periodically.)

To make sure you are starting in the appropriate place in the data (Exercise 3-2.ptb backup) check the account balance for Teesdale Real Estate.

3. Go to the Customers & Sales Navigation Center. In the Recently Used Customer Reports area, link to <u>View All Customer & Sales Reports</u>. Double-click Customer Ledgers.

4. Scroll down to TEESDALE. The balance for Teesdale Real Estate is $12,816.54.

Bellwether Garden Supply - Student Name
Customer Ledgers
For the Period From Mar 1, 2019 to Mar 31, 2019

Filter Criteria includes: Report order is by ID. Report is printed in Detail Format.

Customer ID Customer	Date	Trans No	Type	Debit Amt	Credit Amt	Balance
TEESDALE	3/1/19	Balance Fwd				7,578.42
Teesdale Real Estate	3/1/19	101	SJ	158.95		7,737.37
	3/3/19	102	SJ	317.99		8,055.36
	3/15/19	10311	SJ	5,238.12		13,293.48
	3/15/19	8818	CRJ	7.50	7.50	13,293.48
	3/15/19	8818	CRJ		158.95	13,134.53
	3/15/19	9915	CRJ	15.00	15.00	13,134.53
	3/15/19	9915	CRJ		317.99	12,816.54

5. Close all windows.

DEFAULT INFORMATION

In Sage, you can set up default information for your business. This information is important for payroll, customer receivables, and vendor payables. Bellwether Garden Supply already has the receivable and payable default information set up. Processing payroll is automatic once defaults are set up.

Follow these steps to set up payroll Default Information:

1. From the Navigation Bar > select **Employees & Payroll** > **Employees** >
    > Set Up Employee Defaults. Compare your Employee Defaults window with the one on the next page.

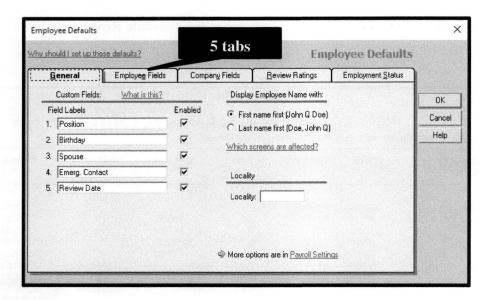

There are five tabs on the Employee Defaults window: General, Employee Fields, Company Fields, Review Ratings, Employment Status. You can set up a lot of information within these tabs. This will make your payroll processing almost automatic.

2. Click on the Employee Fields tab.

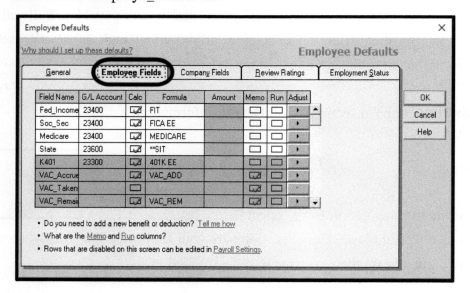

Notice that there are numerous items checked in the Calc column: Fed_Income (FIT), Soc_Sec (FICA EE), Medicare (MEDICARE), State (**SIT), K401 (401K EE), etc. (Scroll down to see the Field Name's complete list.) These fields work together with the payroll tax tables to calculate common employee deductions.

The check marks in the Calc and Memo columns indicate common deductions. Bellwether Garden Supply computes Federal Income Tax, Social Security, Medicare, State Income Taxes, 401K, and vacation deductions. These deductions are calculated according to the appropriate tax tables and formulas entered for payroll deductions, 401K's and vacation calculations.

The accounts affected by paychecks are liability accounts set up specifically to handle these kinds of deductions. Notice that the GL Account field shows the account numbers. All the accounts that are checked off are liability accounts. You can also set up voluntary deductions (called allowances). Voluntary allowances that are individually entered on the employee paycheck could include gas allowances, union dues, and savings bonds.

There is a Memo column with a place to put check marks for amounts that should not be posted to the company's books. The Memo check box is used when you want the employee record to show amounts not on the company's books. An example would be a restaurant business that needed to show employees' tips.

3. Click on the Company Fields tab. The Company Fields tab is for the employer's portion of Soc_Sec_ER (Social Security), Medicare_ER (Medicare), FUTA_ER (Federal Unemployment Tax Act), SUI_ER (State Unemployment Insurance), and K401_ER (401K contribution). The Employee Defaults/Company Fields window is shown on the next page.

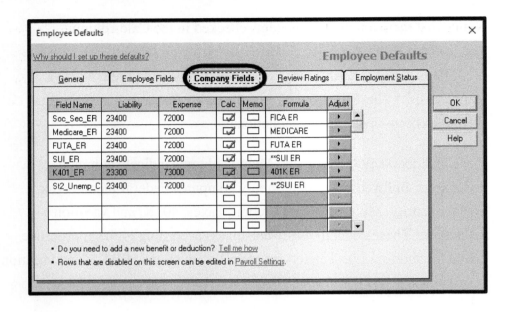

4. Click on the <u>R</u>eview Ratings tab. You can add up to 10 performance ratings.

5. Click on the Employment <u>S</u>tatus tab. This shows different statuses for Bellwether's employees: Current Employee, Terminated, Leave of Absence, etc.

6. Select **OK** to return to the Employees & Payroll Navigation Center.

EMPLOYEE MAINTENANCE

When default information is completed, Sage sets guidelines for processing the company's payroll. On the Maintain Employees/Sales Reps window, information is entered for each employee.

1. From the Employees & Payroll Navigation Center > click > View and Edit Employees. The Employee List appears.

2. Double-click **BNUNNLEY, Nunnley, Brandee.** The Maintain Employees
    & Sales Reps window appears. Read the information in the Employee ID
    box. Let's look at this employee's record. (*Hint:* In Chapter 15, you learn
    about Sage 50's payroll features in more detail.)

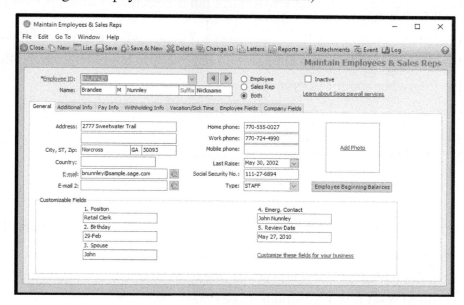

3. Click on the Pay Info tab. Read the information on the Pay Info Tab box.

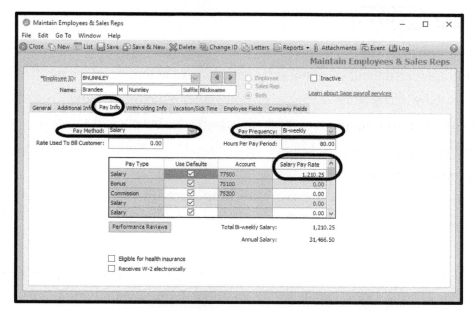

Observe that there is a Performance Reviews button. Select

Performance Reviews to see if any information has been added for this employee. On page 136, the Employee Defaults window included a Review Ratings tab. When the Review Ratings tab is selected up to ten performance ratings can be set up. Click Close . You are returned to the Maintain Employees & Sales Reps window and the Pay Info tab is selected. Notice the following about Ms. Nunnley:

a.   She is paid a salary of $1,210.25.
b.   She is paid bi-weekly (once every two weeks).

4.   Click on the down-arrow in the Employee ID field.
5.   Select employee **DCARTER > Drake V. Carter**. If necessary, select the Pay Info tab. Notice that Mr. Carter is paid an hourly wage of $9.00, overtime pay of $13.50, and special rate of $18.00. Observe that Mr. Carter is paid bi-weekly. Close all windows.

PAYROLL SYSTEM

Once employee default information is set up, Sage automates the payroll process. Now that you have looked at Bellwether's payroll defaults, you can see how easily Sage computes and prints paychecks for hourly and salaried employees.

Transferring Cash to the Payroll Checking Account

Before making a payroll entry, you need to transfer $8,000 from Account No. 10200, Regular Checking Account; to Account No. 10300, the Payroll Checking Account. The following transaction is recorded in the general journal.

Date	Transaction Description
3/29/19	Transfer $8,000 from the regular checking account to the payroll ch10ecking account.

Follow these steps to record this transaction in the general journal.

1. From the Navigation Bar > select **Banking** > General Journal Entry > New General Journal Entry. (*Hint:* You can also link to General Journal Entry in the Shortcuts list.) The General Journal Entry window appears.

2. Select **29** as the date. Click on the Reference field. Type **Transfer** in the Reference field. Press the **<Enter>** key two times.

3. Your cursor is in the GL Account field. Select Account No. 10300, Payroll Checking Account (or you can type **10300**). Press **<Enter>**.

4. Your cursor should be in the Description field. Type **Payroll Checking Account** (or you can type a description) in the Description field. Press **<Enter>**.

5. Type **8000** in the Debit field. Press the **<Enter>** key three times to go to the Account No. field.

6. Your cursor should be in the GL Account field. Select Account No. 10200, Regular Checking Account. Press **<Enter>.**

7. Type **Regular Checking Account** in the Description field. Press the **<Enter>** key two times to go to the Credit field.

8. Your cursor is in the Credit field. Type **8000** in the Credit field. Press **<Enter>**. Observe that at the bottom of the General Journal Entry window, the Out of Balance field shows 0.00. This shows that debits equal credits, therefore, out of balance equals zero.

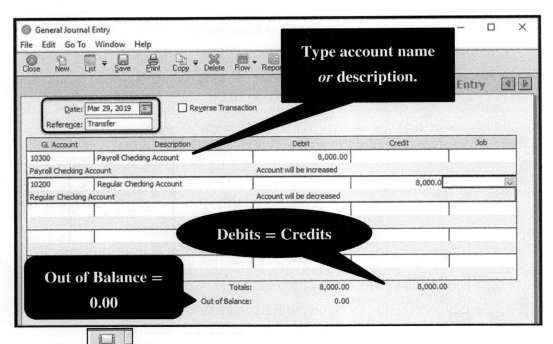

9. Click Save to post the entry to the general ledger.
10. Close the General Journal Entry window.

Payroll Entry for a Salaried Employee

In the next section you enter paychecks for these two employees: Brandee M.
Nunnley and Drake V. Carter. When processing payroll checks, the information
stored in Default Information and in the Maintain Employees file is important.
Processing payroll is simple once you have set the defaults correctly. Follow
these steps to see how a paycheck for a salaried employee is done.

1. From the Navigation Bar > select **Employees & Payroll** > Pay
    Employees >
    Enter Payroll For One Employee. The Payroll Entry window appears.
2. In the Employee ID field, type **BN** for Brandee M. Nunnley and press
    <Enter>.

3. To print a check, leave the Check Number field blank by pressing **<Enter>**. If you type a check number and then print, Duplicate is printed on the check. (*Hint:* If you do <u>not</u> have a printer, type 1294 in the Check Number field.)

4. Type **29** in the <u>D</u>ate field, then press **<Enter>**. (*Remember you can also click on the Calendar icon* 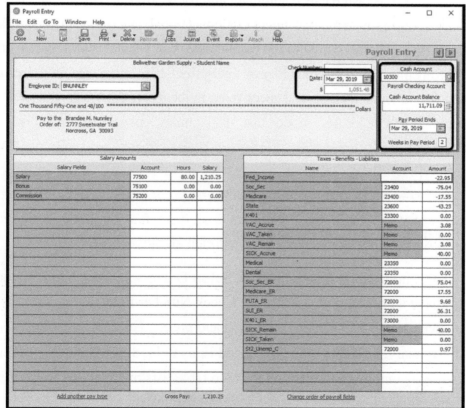 *and select 29. If necessary, enlarge the Payroll Entry window.*) Your cursor goes to the Cash Account field. This check will be charged against the Payroll Checking Account (Account No. 10300) which is displayed in the Cash Account field.

5. Press **<Enter>**. Your cursor is in the P<u>a</u>y Period Ends field. Type **29** then press **<Enter>**. Your cursor goes to the Weeks in Pay Period box. The number 2 is displayed. Ms. Nunnley is on a bi-weekly pay period which means that Ms. Nunnley has two weeks in her pay period.

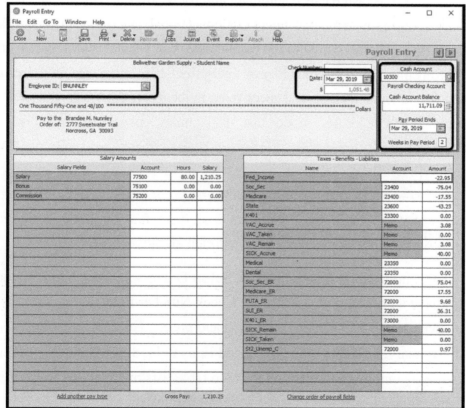

Notice that Brandee M. Nunnley has a Salary Amounts table that includes Salary, Bonus, and Commission. If necessary, these amounts can be adjusted. All of the Taxes - Benefits - Liabilities fields that were completed, which include Fed_ Income, Soc_Sec, Medicare and State tax, etc., have been calculated and display as negative amounts. They display as negative amounts because they decrease the check amount. The amounts shown as positive numbers are *not* deducted from the employee's check. Once payroll defaults and employees are set up, payroll processing is easy. Compare your Payroll Entry window for Brandee M. Nunnley to the one shown on the previous page.

Observe that the Cash Account Balance field on the upper right side of the Payroll Entry window shows 11,711.09. This is because the default is to recalculate the cash balance automatically for receipts, payments, and payroll entries. From the menu bar, select Options, Global, and notice that a check mark <✓> is placed next to the Recalculate cash balance automatically in the Receipts, Payments, and Payroll Entry field. If your balance field does *not* show an amount, then place a check mark in the recalculate cash balance automatically field. Also, notice that Ms. Nunnley's paycheck amount is $1,051.48.

6. Click [Save] to post this payroll entry.

Payroll Entry for an Hourly Employee

1. In the Employee ID field, click 🔍. Select Drake V. Carter. (*Hint:* If you do not have a printer, type 1295 in the Check Number field.)
2. If necessary, type **29** in the Date field and press **<Enter>** two times.
3. If necessary, type **29** in the Pay Period Ends field. Since Drake V. Carter is an hourly employee, the Hours Worked table lists his regular and overtime hours. If necessary, these categories can be adjusted.

4. To see how to adjust the hours that he worked, do the following: in the Hours Worked table, click on Overtime. The Overtime row is highlighted. Make sure your cursor is in the Hours field. Type **3** and press **<Enter>**. Notice that the amounts in the Taxes - Benefits - Liabilities fields are automatically adjusted. The check amount also changed.

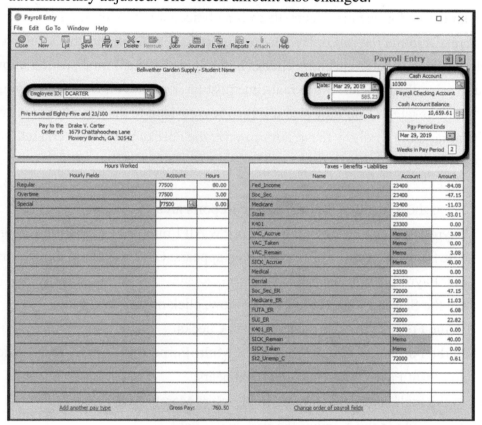

Observe that the Cash Account Balance field on the upper right side of the Payroll Entry window changed to 10,659.61. This is because the default for Sage 50 is to recalculate the cash balance automatically for receipts, payments, and payroll entries. (If your Cash Account Balance did *not* automatically recalculate, refer to Chapter 1, page 19, step 1d; Other Options area, Recalculate cash balance automatically in Receipts, Payments, and Payroll Entry should be *checked*.)

5. Select [Save] to post this paycheck. Close the Payroll Entry window.

Printing Payroll Checks

Similar to vendor disbursements, there is a choice: you may print each check as you enter it in the Payroll Entry window or you can print all the checks at once. Batch posting involves printing checks before posting. Real time posting allows you to print checks later. Since real-time posting is used with Bellwether, you print checks later. (You may also use the Preview icon to display checks instead of printing them.) Follow these steps to print the checks previously entered in the Payroll Entry window.

1. From the Recently Used Employee Reports area of the Employees & Payroll Navigation Center, link to <u>View All Employees & Payroll Reports</u>. The Select a Report or Form window appears. Observe that in the <u>R</u>eports list, Payroll is selected.
2. On the Select a Report or Form window, click on the For<u>m</u>s tab.
3. In the Form Types list, select Payroll Checks.
4. In the Forms list, double-click OCR Multi-Purpose PR Laser. The Preview and Print Payroll Checks window appears.
5. In the Include checks through field, select March 29, 2019.
6. Type **1294** in the Number the first check field.
7. In the Filter employees by field > select ID, Brandee M. Nunnley to Drake V. Carter.
8. Click [Refresh List]. The two employee names, both check marked, appear in the table on the right side of the Preview and Print Payroll Checks window.

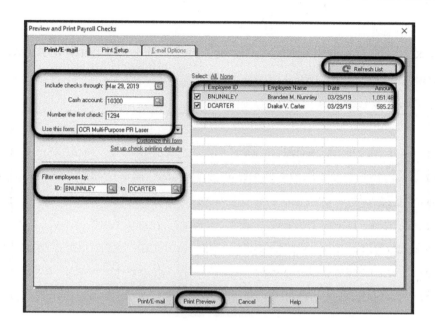

9. After clicking Print Preview, the Print Preview window appears. The top portion of Brandee M. Nunnley's check is shown below.

10. Click 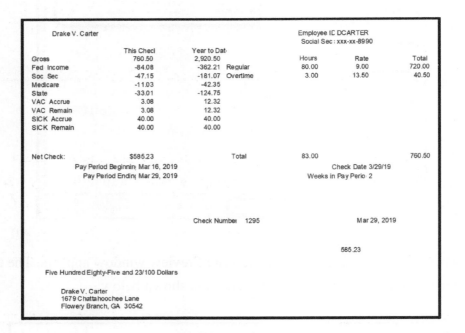 to see Drake V. Carter's check. The top portion of Drake V. Carter's check is shown below.

Drake V. Carter				Employee ID DCARTER		
				Social Sec : xxx-xx-8990		
	This Check	Year to Date		Hours	Rate	Total
Gross	760.50	2,920.50				
Fed Income	-84.08	-362.21	Regular	80.00	9.00	720.00
Soc Sec	-47.15	-181.07	Overtime	3.00	13.50	40.50
Medicare	-11.03	-42.35				
State	-33.01	-124.75				
VAC Accrue	3.08	12.32				
VAC Remain	3.08	12.32				
SICK Accrue	40.00	40.00				
SICK Remain	40.00	40.00				
Net Check:	$585.23		Total	83.00		760.50

Pay Period Beginning Mar 16, 2019 Check Date 3/29/19
Pay Period Ending Mar 29, 2019 Weeks in Pay Period 2

Check Number 1295 Mar 29, 2019

585.23

Five Hundred Eighty-Five and 23/100 Dollars

Drake V. Carter
1679 Chattahoochee Lane
Flowery Branch, GA 30542

11. Click 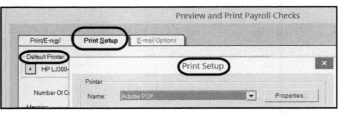 to print Check Nos. 1294 and 1295. Observe that the employee statement information (also known as the pay stub) is printed first, then the check is printed. If needed, on the Preview and Print Payroll Checks window, select the Printer Setup tab. In the Default Printer area, select Adobe PDF or Microsoft XPS Document Writer.

12. A window appears that says Did the Checks print properly and is it is OK to assign the check numbers to the checks? If your checks are correct, click Yes.

13. Close the Select a Report or Form window to return to the Employees & Payroll Navigation Center.

> **Comment:** In Chapter 15, Employees, Payroll, and Account Reconciliation, you learn how to set the defaults for the payroll accounts. Each employee and employer deduction will be set for individual liability accounts and expense accounts. The sample company is used as an example of automatic payroll processing but does *not* reflect correct payroll accounting procedures.

JOURNAL ENTRY FOR PAYROLL

What happens when you post payroll? In the most common case, the Cash Account that you entered in the Payroll Default window is automatically credited for the net paycheck amount when the payroll check is posted. The employee salary expense account is debited for the gross amount of the check and any deductions used are credited. The following table shows the payroll journal entry for the hourly employee, Drake V. Carter.

Account Description	Debit	Credit
Wages Expense (Regular Hours)	720.00	
Wages Expense (Overtime Hours)	40.50	
Federal Payroll Taxes Payable (Fed_Income)		84.08
Social Security (Soc_Sec for the Employee)		47.15
Medicare (Medicare for the Employee)		11.03
State Payroll Taxes Payable		33.01
Payroll Checking Account		585.23

BACKING UP CHAPTER 4 DATA

After completing the work within Chapter 4, back up. The suggested file name is **Chapter 4.ptb**. Detailed steps for backing up data are shown on pages 24-26. Backing up saves data to that point in your work. Each time you back up, use a different file name. The suggested file name at this point is Chapter 4.ptb.

ONLINE LEARNING CENTER

Complete the following end-of-chapter activities online at
www.mhhe.com/yacht2019 > select the Student Edition > Chapter 4.

1. Interactive Multiple-Choice and True/False questions.
2. Going to the Net exercise: Access the All Accounting Careers website.
3. QA Templates: 10 short-answer questions and two analysis questions.
4. Assessment Rubric: Review journals, navigation centers, modules, and task windows.
5. Listen to narrated PowerPoint slides.

The OLC also includes links to the Appendixes:

- Appendix A: Troubleshooting (textbook and OLC)
- Appendix C: Review of Accounting Principles (OLC Student Edition)
- Appendix D: Glossary of Terms (OLC Student Edition)

Exercise 4-1: Follow the instructions below to complete Exercise 4-1:

1. Start Sage 50. Open Bellwether Garden Supply - Student Name [your first and last name].
2. If necessary, restore data from the end of Chapter 4. This back up was made on page 149.
3. Record the following transaction.

Date	Transaction Description
03/29/19	Record paycheck information for Brandon A. Hugley. Mr. Hugley worked 80 regular hours during this pay period. (If you do not have a printer, type 1296 in the Check No. field.)

4. Post the payroll entry.

5. Continue with Exercise 4-2.

Exercise 4-2: Follow the instructions below to complete Exercise 4-2:

1. Record the following transaction:

   Date   *Transaction Description*

   03/29/19   Record paycheck information for Derrick P. Gross. Mr. Gross is a salaried employee. (If you do <u>not</u> have a printer, type 1297 in the Check No. field.)

2. Post the payroll entry.
3. Print Check Nos. 1296 and 1297. (*Hint: Select OCR Multiple-Purpose PR Laser as the form. Type **3/29/19** in the Include checks through field. The Number the first check field should display 1296. If not, type 1296. Filter employees by Brandon A. Hugley to Derrick P. Gross. Click* [Refresh List].) **Not printing? Select Adobe PDF or Microsoft XPS Document Writer as the printer. Refer to page 65, How to Fix.**
4. Print the Payroll Check Register. (*Hint*: In the Recently Used Employee Reports area of the Employees & Payroll Navigation Center, link to <u>Print</u> the Payroll Check Register. Accept the default for This Period.)
5. Close all windows. Back up Exercise 4-2. Use **Exercise 4-2** as the file name.
6. Export the Payroll Check Register to Excel. Use **Exercise 4-2_Payroll Check Register.xlsx** as the file name. If your Excel icon is inactive, read Troubleshooting, page 42.
7. Save the Payroll Check Register as a PDF file. Use **Exercise 4-2_Payroll Check Register.pdf** as the file name.

   Check your figures: Payroll Check Register, 3/1/19 thru 3/31/19, $37,631.02

CHAPTER 4 INDEX

Chapter 5

General Ledger, Inventory, And Internal Control

LEARNING OBJECTIVES

1. Restore data from Exercise 4-2. (This backup was made on page 151.)
2. Use Sage 50's help feature, enter a new account in the Chart of Accounts, and look at Sage 50's budget feature.
3. Record and post a General Journal entry to transfer funds, and display the General Ledger Trial Balance.
4. Set up an Inventory Item and record an inventory adjustment.
5. Look at Sage 50's internal controls, user security and access, and audit trail.
6. Make two backups, save one Excel file, and save one PDF file.

In Chapter 5, Bellwether's general ledger, inventory, and internal control systems are shown. In Parts 2, 3, and 4 (Chapters 9-18 and Projects 1 through 4A), you create 12 new companies, populate the data, and complete the general ledger accounting cycle. The accounting cycle is completed for service, merchandising, nonprofit, and manufacturing businesses. When a new company is set up, the following initial steps are performed: set up a chart of accounts and enter beginning balances or budget amounts. After completing work with the sample companies (Chapters 1-8), you learn how to set up new companies.

Chapter 5 shows how to use the Inventory system. When an inventory item is set up, the General Ledger accounts that are updated by purchases and sales are established. Sage 50's *perpetual inventory* system tracks cost of goods sold, stock levels, sales prices, and vendors. In a perpetual inventory system, an up-to-date record of inventory is maintained, recording each purchase and each sale as they occur. Chapter 5 also shows Sage 50's user security feature. On pages 178-186, Security and Internal Control, you look at how company data is kept secure.

GETTING STARTED

1. Start Sage 50. Open Bellwether Garden Supply - Student Name [your first and last name]. (If Bellwether Garden Supply is not shown, Restore data to Create a new company using the restored data. Refer to the Read Me box on page 28.)

2. Restore data from the Exercise 4-2 backup. This back was completed on page 151, step 5. The steps that follow review the steps for restoring the backup file.

   a. Insert your USB flash drive. From the Navigation Bar > select

   | System | > | Restore Now |.

   b. The Select Backup File window appears. Click | Browse |. Go to the Location of your Exercise 4-2.ptb file and select it. Click

   | Open | > | Next > |

   c. The Select Company window appears. The radio button next to Overwrite an existing company is selected. The Company name field shows Bellwether Garden Supply - Student Name [your first and last name]. The Location field shows the default location on the hard drive for Bellwether Garden Supply. Click | Next > |.

   d. The Restore Options window appears. Make sure that the box next to Company Data is *checked*. Click | Next > |.

   e. The Confirmation window appears. Check the Backup file and Location fields to make sure they are correct. Click | Finish |. When the window prompts "This process will overwrite....", click

   | Yes |. When the Restore Company scale is 100% complete, your data is restored. (*Hint:* If the Student version of Sage 50 prompts that

company data can be used for 14 months, click [OK]. Bellwether
Garden Supply opens.)

💾 To make sure you are starting in the appropriate place in the data
(Exercise 4-2.ptb backup) check the Payroll Check Register. View the
Payroll Check Register from the Employee's & Payroll Navigation
Center. Make sure Check Nos. 1294-1297 are listed.

Bellwether Garden Supply - Student Name
Payroll Check Register
For the Period From Mar 1, 2019 to Mar 31, 2019
Filter Criteria includes: Report order is by Check Date. Report is printed in Detail Format.

Reference	Date	Employee	Amount
1281	3/15/19	Mitchell K. Trotter	681.40
1282	3/15/19	Michelle Y. Wagner	612.75
1283	3/15/19	Nola I. Bigalow	787.54
1284	3/15/19	Ray J. Mosley	740.47
1285	3/15/19	Raffaello M. Saulny	770.44
1286	3/15/19	Steve N. Barkley	694.03
1287	3/15/19	Susan T. Prichard	559.22
1288	3/15/19	Samuel R. Prather	1,148.62
1289	3/15/19	Thatcher G. Leverne	759.00
1290	3/15/19	Tim O. Maske	1,380.01
1291	3/15/19	Tyler F. Riddell	756.11
1292	3/15/19	Virginia L. Ansell	965.72
1293	3/15/19	Vincent O. Kilborune	759.00
1294	3/29/19	Brandee M. Nunnley	1,051.48
1295	3/29/19	Drake V. Carter	585.23
1296	3/29/19	Brandon A. Hugley	650.25
1297	3/29/19	Derrick P. Gross	1,058.87
	3/1/19 thru 3/31/19		37,631.02
	3/1/19 thru 3/31/19		37,631.02

➤ **Troubleshooting:** Payroll Check Register does *not* agree. Make sure you
completed paychecks 1294 through 1297 in Chapter 4, pages 142-151. You
should also check the 3/29/19 transfer, pages 141-142. Select Reports &
Forms > General Ledger > General Journal.

Bellwether Garden Supply - Student Name					
General Journal					
For the Period From Mar 29, 2019 to Mar 29, 2019					
Filter Criteria includes: Report order is by Date. Report is printed with Accounts having Zero Amounts and with shortened descriptions and in Detail Format.					
Date	Account ID	Reference	Trans Description	Debit Amt	Credit Amt
3/29/19	10300	Transfer	Payroll Checking Account	8,000.00	
	10200		Regular Checking Account		8,000.00
		Total		8,000.00	8,000.00

3. Close all windows.

SAGE 50 HELP

Use the Help Topics feature to read about backing up data. The steps below show how to navigate Contents > Getting Started > Other Decisions > Backup strategies. You should also try other selections. Follow these steps to learn more.

1. From the menu bar, select Help > Help Topics. The Sage 50 Help window appears. Sage 50 Help topics are displayed in the *HTML* (Hypertext Markup Language).

2. Click on the Contents tab > then the plus signs (+) next to Getting Started > Other Decisions > Backup Strategies.

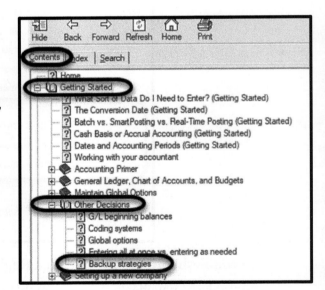

3. The Help window has four panes.

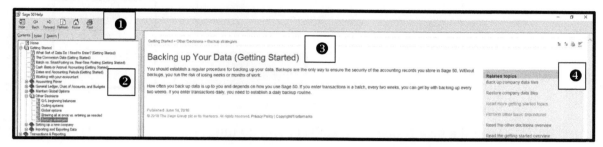

❶ The Toolbar is located below the Sage 50 Help title bar. The toolbar appears on individual windows and contains buttons that include functions: Help, Back, Forward, Home, Print.

❷ The Navigation pane is located on the left side of the Help window. It contains three tabs: Contents, Index, and Search. Use the Navigation pane to browse or search for topics.

❸ In the middle of the Help window is the information about Backing up Your Data (Getting Started). Read the information.

❹ Related Topics includes links for related information.

4. Click [×] on the Sage 50 Help title bar to close the Help window.

Context-sensitive help is also available. For example, select Business Status > View Account List > press the function key F1. The Lists Help window appears. Read the information and explore some of the links: Customize a list, Add a record to a list, Export a list to Microsoft Excel, Convert the list to PDF format, etc. When through, Close All windows.

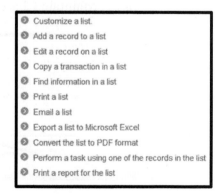

ADD AN ACCOUNT TO THE CHART OF ACCOUNTS

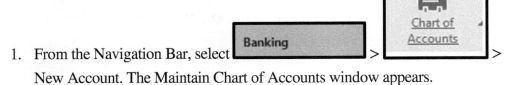

1. From the Navigation Bar, select **Banking** > **Chart of Accounts** > New Account. The Maintain Chart of Accounts window appears.

2. To add a new Money Market account, do this:

   a. In the Account ID field, type **10500** and press **<Enter>**.

   b. Your cursor is in the Description field. Type the name of the account **Money Market Fund**, and press **<Enter>**.

   c. Your cursor is in the Account Type field. There is a drop-down list indicated by a down arrow. The default Account Type is Cash.

In the Account Type field specify the kind of account you are creating; for example, Cash, Cost of Sales, Equity-doesn't close, Equity-gets closed, etc. Select the drop-down list by clicking on the down arrow in the Account Type field to display the list of available account types.

Make sure **Cash** is highlighted and press **<Enter>**. *The Account Type is important; it sorts each account for the financial statements.* Compare your Maintain Chart of Accounts window to the one shown below. (The top portion of the Maintain Chart of Accounts window is shown.)

Account Types categorize accounts on the financial statements. Account 10500 Money Market Fund is a Cash account on the Balance Sheet.

Remember to check the Account Type field. The selection made in the Account Type field classifies accounts on the financial statements.

3. Click |💾 Save| then close the Maintain Chart of Accounts window.

BUDGETS

Bellwether Garden Supply already has a budget set up. To see Bellwether's budget, do the following.

1. From the Navigation Bar, select |Banking| > |Analysis Tools| > View and Edit Budgets.

2. The Maintain Budgets window appears. Observe that the Maintain Budgets window shows an icon bar with an Excel icon— |📊 Excel|. Most Sage 50 reports can be exported to Excel. If your Excel icon is inactive, refer to Troubleshooting, page 42.

The Maintain Budgets window defaults to Income Statement Accounts.

This is shown in the Account Filters/Type field– | Account Filters — Type: Income Statement Accounts ▼ | . The Maintain Budgets window lets you build a forecast of dollar amounts for selected accounts for each fiscal period. You can filter accounts by account type (income statement accounts, expenses, etc.). For example, the amount budgeted to Account No. 40000-AV, Sales - Aviary for 3/31/19 is $7,000.00. Look at the Income Statement to see how close that amount was to the actual sales for Account No. 40000-AV, Sales - Aviary. (*Hint:* The Total column shows the accumulated total for 1/31/19 through 12/31/19.)

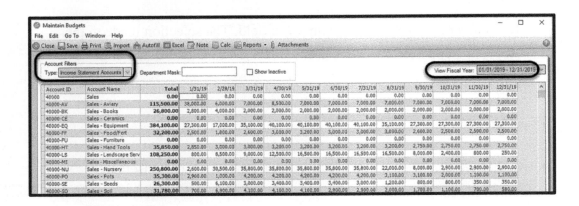

To compare the March 31, 2019 budgeted amount for Account No. 40000, Sales-Aviary to the actual amount, display the <Standard> Income/Budget report.

1. Minimize the Maintain Budgets window.
2. From the menu bar, select Reports & Forms > Financial Statements > then <Standard> Income/Budget.

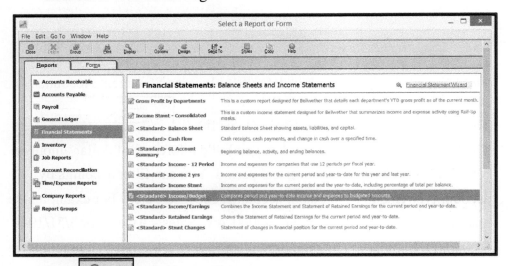

3. Click [Display]. The <Standard> Income/Budget window appears. Observe that the title of the report shows Income Statement, Compared with Budget. Observe that Sales - Aviary for the Current Month Actual is 7,127.71. The

Current Month Budget shows 7,000.00. The Total Revenues section is shown. Current Month Actual, Budget and Variance; and Year to Date Actual, Budget, and Variance are also shown.

	Current Month	Current Month	Current Month	Year to Date	Year to Date	Year to Date
Bellwether Garden Supply - Student Name						
Income Statement						
Compared with Budget						
For the Three Months Ending March 31, 2019						
Revenues						
Sales	$ 295.00	$ 0.00	295.00	$ 295.00	$ 0.00	295.00
Sales - Aviary	7,127.71	7,000.00	127.71	51,652.86	51,000.00	652.86
Sales - Books	149.75	2,000.00	(1,850.25)	7,293.10	8,800.00	(1,506.90)
Sales - Ceramics	0.00	0.00	0.00	0.00	0.00	0.00
Sales - Equipment	17,848.80	35,100.00	(17,251.20)	60,202.29	79,400.00	(19,197.71)
Sales - Food/Fert	1,176.86	2,600.00	(1,423.14)	5,374.05	6,900.00	(1,525.95)
Sales - Furniture	0.00	0.00	0.00	0.00	0.00	0.00
Sales - Hand Tools	729.67	3,000.00	(2,270.33)	7,058.12	8,850.00	(1,791.88)
Sales - Landscape Services	17,467.43	9,000.00	8,467.43	26,975.53	18,300.00	8,675.53
Sales - Miscellaneous	0.00	0.00	0.00	45.00	0.00	45.00
Sales - Nursery	33,795.03	35,800.00	(2,004.97)	67,637.11	68,900.00	(1,262.89)
Sales - Pots	7,919.31	4,200.00	3,719.31	11,483.74	8,100.00	3,383.74
Sales - Seeds	1,457.43	3,000.00	(1,542.57)	8,661.39	9,600.00	(938.61)
Sales - Soil	724.92	4,100.00	(3,375.08)	9,152.45	11,700.00	(2,547.55)
Sales - Statuary	0.00	0.00	0.00	0.00	0.00	0.00
Sales - Topiary	0.00	0.00	0.00	0.00	0.00	0.00
Interest Income	0.00	0.00	0.00	0.00	0.00	0.00
Other Income	100.00	0.00	100.00	25,600.00	25,000.00	600.00
Finance Charge Income	0.00	0.00	0.00	0.00	0.00	0.00
Sales Returns and Allowances	0.00	0.00	0.00	0.00	0.00	0.00
Sales Discounts	(145.72)	0.00	(145.72)	(155.62)	0.00	(155.62)
Total Revenues	88,646.19	105,800.00	(17,153.81)	281,275.02	296,550.00	(15,274.98)

What does the Income/Budget report show? For the Current Month, March 31, 2019, the budgeted amount of $7,000 was exceeded by the actual sales amount of $7,127.71 for Sales-Aviary. The current month variance is 127.71—sales exceeded the budget by that amount. Amounts shown in parentheses indicate that sales were lower than budgeted amounts.

4. Close all windows.

GENERAL JOURNAL

To open the Money Market Fund, transfer $4,500 from Bellwether's regular checking account to Account No. 10500, Money Market Fund. Also, transfer $1,000 from Bellwether's regular checking account to the payroll checking account (10300, Payroll Checking Account). The transfer of funds is recorded in the General Journal, and then posted to the General Ledger.

Date	Transaction Description
03/15/19	Transfer $4,500 to the Money Market Fund and $1,000 to the Payroll Checking Account from the Regular Checking Account.

1. From the Banking Navigation Center, select > New General Journal Entry. (*Or,* from the Navigation Bar, link to General Journal Entry.) The General Journal Entry window appears.

2. In the Date field, type **3/15/19** or select the day. Press **<Enter>**.

3. Your cursor is in the Reference field. Type **Transfer** and press **<Enter>** two times.

4. Your cursor is in the GL Account field. Type the account number for the Money Market Fund account, **10500**, and press the **<Enter>** or **<Tab>**. Observe that Money Market Fund appears below the account number.

5. Type **Money Market Fund** in the Description field. In this textbook, the account name is used as the description. You may prefer to type a description instead; for example, Established money market account. When a description is typed, it will repeat automatically on each Description line. Press **<Enter>** or **<Tab>** to go to the Debit field.

6. You are going to increase this account by $4,500. Type a debit amount of **4500** and press **<Enter>** three times. (It doesn't matter whether you type the debit or credit part of the entry first.) Notice that the Totals field displays 4,500.00 below the Debit column. The Out of Balance amount beneath it totals 4,500.00.

7. Your cursor is in the Account No. field. Type **10300** and press **<Enter>**. Payroll Checking Account displays on the line below the account number. Type **Payroll Checking Account** in the Description field. Press **<Enter>** to go to the Debit field.

8. Type **1000** in the Debit field. Press **<Enter>** three times.

9. Your cursor is in the Account No. field. Type **10200** > press **<Enter>**.
    Type **Regular Checking Account** in the Description field. Press **<Enter>**
    two times to go to the Credit field.

10. Type **5500** in the Credit field > press **<Enter>**. Notice that the Totals
    field beneath the Credit column displays 5,500.00. The Out of Balance
    amount equals zero (0.00). This means that the General Journal is in
    balance and can be posted.

11. Click [Save] to post to the General Ledger. Close the General Journal
    Entry window.

Follow these steps to check that the account transfers have been made.

1. From the menu bar, select Reports & Forms > General Ledger. The Select
    a Report or Form window displays.

2. In the General Ledger: Account Information List > double-click General
    Ledger Trial Balance. The General Ledger Trial Balance is shown on the
    next two pages.

Bellwether Garden Supply - Student Name
General Ledger Trial Balance
As of Mar 31, 2019

Filter Criteria includes: Report order is by ID. Report is printed in Detail Format.

Account ID	Account Description	Debit Amt	Credit Amt
10000	Petty Cash	327.55	
10100	Cash on Hand	1,850.45	
10200	Regular Checking Account	10,246.52	
10300	Payroll Checking Account	9,365.26	
10400	Savings Account	7,500.00	
10500	Money Market Fund	4,500.00	
11000	Accounts Receivable	175,775.05	
11400	Other Receivables	7,681.84	
11500	Allowance for Doubtful Account		5,000.00
12000	Inventory	12,547.11	
14000	Prepaid Expenses	14,221.30	
14100	Employee Advances	3,000.65	
14200	Notes Receivable-Current	11,000.00	
14700	Other Current Assets	120.00	
15000	Furniture and Fixtures	62,769.25	
15100	Equipment	38,738.33	
15200	Vehicles	86,273.40	
15300	Other Depreciable Property	6,200.96	
15500	Buildings	185,500.00	
15600	Building Improvements	26,500.00	
17000	Accum. Depreciation-Furniture		54,680.57
17100	Accum. Depreciation-Equipment		33,138.11
17200	Accum. Depreciation-Vehicles		51,585.26
17300	Accum. Depreciation-Other		3,788.84
17500	Accum. Depreciation-Buildings		34,483.97
17600	Accum. Depreciation-Bldg Imp		4,926.28
19000	Deposits	15,000.00	
19100	Organization Costs	4,995.10	
19150	Accum Amortiz - Organiz Costs		2,000.00
19200	Notes Receivable- Noncurrent	5,004.90	
19900	Other Noncurrent Assets	3,333.00	
20000	Accounts Payable		80,626.01
23000	Accrued Expenses		3,022.55
23100	Sales Tax Payable		18,067.08
23200	Wages Payable		2,320.30
23300	401 K Deductions Payable		2,490.32
23350	Health Insurance Payable	530.64	
23400	Federal Payroll Taxes Payable		41,791.17
23500	FUTA Tax Payable		258.20
23600	State Payroll Taxes Payable		6,857.05
23700	SUTA Tax Payable		658.67
23800	Local Payroll Taxes Payable		113.25
23900	Income Taxes Payable		11,045.75
24000	Other Taxes Payable		2,640.15
24100	Current Portion Long-Term Debt		5,167.00
24300	Contracts Payable- Current		2,000.00
24700	Other Current Liabilities		54.00
27000	Notes Payable-Noncurrent		4,000.00
39003	Common Stock		5,000.00
39004	Paid-in Capital		100,000.00
39005	Retained Earnings		189,037.60
40000	Sales		295.00
40000-AV	Sales - Aviary		51,652.86
40000-BK	Sales - Books		7,293.10
40000-EQ	Sales - Equipment		60,202.29
40000-FF	Sales - Food/Fert		5,374.05
40000-HT	Sales - Hand Tools		7,058.12
40000-LS	Sales - Landscape Services		26,975.53
40000-MI	Sales - Miscellaneous		45.00
40000-NU	Sales - Nursery		67,637.11
40000-PO	Sales - Pots		11,483.74
40000-SE	Sales - Seeds		8,661.39
40000-SO	Sales - Soil		9,152.45
41000	Other Income		25,600.00
49000	Sales Discounts	155.62	

Account ID	Account Description	Debit Amt	Credit Amt
	Bellwether Garden Supply - Student Name		
	General Ledger Trial Balance		
	As of Mar 31, 2019		
	Filter Criteria includes: Report order is by ID. Report is printed in Detail Format.		
50000	Product Cost		68.50
50000-AV	Product Cost - Aviary	20,821.45	
50000-BK	Product Cost - Books	2,361.37	
50000-EQ	Product Cost - Equipment	24,154.95	
50000-FF	Product Cost - Food/Fert	2,127.54	
50000-HT	Product Cost - Hand Tools	2,813.85	
50000-PO	Product Cost - Pots	3,423.60	
50000-SE	Product Cost - Seeds	3,450.65	
50000-SO	Product Cost - Soil	4,075.97	
57000-NU	Direct Labor - Nursery	3,062.50	
57200	Materials Cost	1,397.45	
57200-NU	Materials Cost - Nursery	9,668.50	
57300-LS	Subcontractors - Landscaping	335.50	
57500	Freight	50.00	
60000	Advertising Expense	1,325.00	
61000	Auto Expenses	274.56	
61500	Bad Debt Expense	1,341.09	
62000	Bank Charges	18.00	
64000	Depreciation Expense	8,394.00	
68500	Legal and Professional Expense	510.00	
69000	Licenses Expense	150.00	
70000	Maintenance Expense	75.00	
71000	Office Expense	534.64	
72000	Payroll Tax Exp	15,857.60	
74000	Rent or Lease Expense	1,100.00	
74500	Repairs Expense	3,694.00	
75500	Supplies Expense	2,873.42	
77000	Utilities Expense	303.45	
77500	Wages Expense	138,465.46	
89000	Other Expense	464.90	
89500	Purchase Disc- Expense Items		10.11
	Total:	**946,261.38**	**946,261.38**

On page 164, Account No. 10200, Regular Checking Account, has a debit balance of $10,246.52; Account No. 10300, Payroll Checking Account, has a debit balance of $9,365.26; and Account No. 10500, Money Market Fund, has a debit balance of $4,500.00. This shows that the General Journal entry that you completed is posted correctly. To see the rest of the General Ledger Trial Balance, scroll down the General Ledger Trial Balance window.

3. Close all windows.

How to fix? What if an account balance does <u>not</u> agree with the General Ledger Trial Balance shown on pages 164-165? Suggestions follow.

- Determine the difference in the amounts. Is the difference the amount of an entry? Refer to Audit Trail Report on page 185. For example, display the Audit Trail for the month(s)/year you have been completing work.
- Did you record an entry twice? For example, display the general journal. If you

  recorded an entry twice, drill down to the original entry, then select [Delete] to remove the entry. (*Hint:* To check if you duplicated an entry, you could also display the Customer and Vendor Ledgers.)
- Did you forget to record an entry? Both work within the chapter and the exercises should be completed.
- If needed, restore an earlier backup file and then continue from that point. Refer to the chart on pages 2-3 for the backups made in Chapters 1-5.

SETTING UP AN INVENTORY ITEM

This part of Chapter 5 explains the Inventory system. The sample company, Bellwether Garden Supply, has decided to track cleaning supplies as stock inventory items and to bill clients for supplies used. First, you need to enter the cleaning supplies they stock as Inventory Items.

Sage 50's Inventory & Services Navigation Center shows Sage 50's *Inventory System*, another module within the software. The Navigation Bar's

[Inventory & Services] selection displays information and access points related to the company's inventory items. It includes a summary of item information, access to recently used inventory reports, and a graphic analysis of how the cost of sales is trending. In addition, the Inventory & Services Navigation Center shows the flow of inventory-related tasks and takes you where you need to go to perform those tasks. Observe that drill down links are also available. If necessary, scroll down and across the Inventory & Services Navigation Center window to see all the areas.

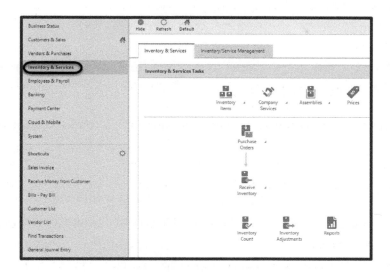

The Inventory & Services Navigation Center also includes an Inventory/Service Management tab. The Inventory and Service Management selection is a dashboard that allows you to quickly find and view information about inventory and service items. This helps you do research, make comparisons, and make decisions regarding the items sold and the services offered by the business.

Follow these steps to set up an Inventory Item:

1. From the Inventory & Services Navigation Center, select > New Inventory Item. The Maintain Inventory Items window displays and information about inventory. Read the Item ID information.
2. In the Item ID field, type **AVRY-10300** — the first four characters should be in uppercase and press **<Enter>**. Read the Description information.
3. In the Description field, type **Oriole Feeder** and press **<Enter>**. As information appears about each field, read it.
4. In the Item Class field, select Stock item.

Inventory Types

If you click on the down-arrow next to the Item field, observe that there are several types of Inventory Items or item classes:

➢ Stock item: For traditional inventory items that are tracked for quantities, average costs, vendors, low stock points, etc. Once an item is assigned to this class, it cannot be changed.

➢ Master Stock Item: Use this item class when you want to set up a group of related stock items that have similar characteristics or attributes. A master stock item is a special item that does not represent inventory you stock but rather contains item attributes shared with a number of substock items.

➢ Non-stock item: For items that you buy or sell but do not put into inventory. Quantities, descriptions, and unit prices are printed on invoices and purchase orders, but quantities on hand are not tracked. You can assign a cost of goods General Ledger account to non-stock items, but it is not affected by a costing method.

➢ Description only: Use this item class when nothing is tracked except the description. For example, "comments" can be added to sales or purchase transactions as description-only items.

➢ Service: For services you perform and sell, such as monthly maintenance work. You can enter a cost for the service used in the course of performing the service.

➢ Labor: For labor that is part of an assembly item or for outside labor that you use for projects; you can enter a cost for the service. In the case of assembly items, this labor will become part of the cost of goods for the assembled item.

➢ Assembly: For items that consist of components that can be built or dismantled. For each assembly item, select the Bill of Materials tab. Define the components of the assembly before clicking Save. Once a transaction uses an assembly, it cannot be changed.

➤ Activity item: For different types of work that are performed for a customer or job. For example, these are useful for law firms that want to track employee time for a customer and job and then bill the customer. Activity items are used in Time & Billing and are recorded on employee or vendor time tickets.

➤ Charge item: Used to identify items that are expenses recorded by an employee or vendor when various services are performed for a customer or job. Charge items are used in Time & Billing and are recorded on employee or vendor expense tickets. Use charge items when you plan on billing customers for reimbursable expenses.

Follow these steps to continue setting up an Inventory Item:

1. If necessary, press the **<Enter>** key to go to the Description field. Type **Oriole Feeder** and press **<Enter>**. Read the information about each field.

2. Go to the Price Level 1 field. Click on the right arrow button in this field. The Multiple Price Levels window appears. In the Price Level 1 row > click on the Price field > type **15** on the Price Level 1 row > press **<Enter>**. You can set up ten different sales prices per item.

3. After clicking ☑ OK , close the Multiple Price Levels window. The Price level 1 field shows 15.00.

4. Click on the Last Unit Cost field. Type **7** and press **<Enter>**. (*Hint:* Delete 0.00 in the Last Unit Cost field, then type 7.)

5. Observe that the Cost Method is FIFO. Sage 50 includes three inventory cost methods: FIFO, LIFO and Average. Press **<Enter>**.

6. Your cursor is in the GL Sales Account field. Click 🔍, then select Account No. 40000-AV, Sales – Aviary, as the sales account. Press **<Enter>**.

7. Accept the default for the GL Inventory Acct, Account No. 12000, Inventory, by pressing **<Enter>**.

8. Your cursor is in the GL Cost of Sales Acct field. Select Account No. 50000-AV, Product Cost – Aviary, as the product cost account. Press **<Enter>**.

9. Click 🔍 in the Item Ta<u>x</u> Type field. Observe that the default, 1, means that this is a regular, taxable item. Press **<Enter>**. UPC/SKU information pops up. Read the information.

10. Click on the Item Type field. The Item Type is a way of classifying similar inventory items for sorting and printing reports. Select SUPPLY. Press **<Enter>**.

11. Your cursor is in the Location field. Select AISLE 1. Press **<Enter>**.

12. Your cursor is in the Stocking U/M field. Select Each and press **<Enter>** two times.

13. Your cursor is in the Minimum Stock field. Type **6** and press **<Enter>**.

14. Your cursor is in the Reorder Quantity field. Type **6** and press **<Enter>**

15. Select DEJULIA, DeJulia Wholesale Suppliers as the Preferred <u>V</u>endor ID. Leave the Buyer ID field blank. Your Maintain Inventory Items window should agree with the one shown on the next page.

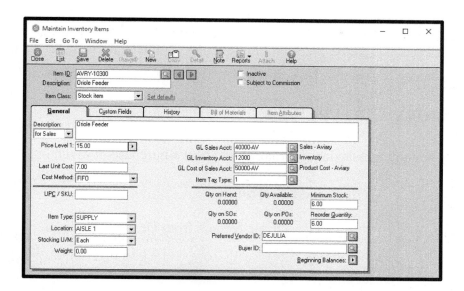

When you purchase inventory stock items from a vendor, this is the Purchase Journal entry: debit the Inventory account and credit Accounts Payable/Vendor account. When you sell Inventory stock items on account, a compound Sales Journal entry is recorded.

➢ Debit Accounts Receivable and Cost of Sales accounts.
➢ Credit Sales, Sales Tax Payable, and Inventory accounts.

The Maintain Inventory Items window should be displayed. Observe that you set the following account defaults for this stock item.

GL Sales Acct	40000-AV	Sales - Aviary
GL Inventory Acct	12000	Inventory
GL Cost of Sales Acct	50000-AV	Product Cost - Aviary

You also selected a preferred vendor. The Preferred Vendor ID field should display DEJULIA, which is the Vendor ID for DeJulia Wholesale Suppliers. Bellwether purchases oriole feeders from this vendor.

16. Click ![Save] Close the Maintian Inventory Items window to return to the Inventory & Services Navigation Center.

INVENTORY AND PURCHASES

In the following transaction, journalize and post a purchase of inventory.

Date   *Transaction Description*

03/17/19   Purchased 6 Oriole feeders from DeJulia Wholesale Suppliers, Invoice No. 55522, at a unit price of $7, for a total of $42.

1. From the Navigation Bar, click **Vendors & Purchases** > **Enter Bills** > New Bill. The Purchases/Receive Inventory window displays. If your GL Account field and A/P Account fields do *not* display on the Purchases/Receive Inventory window, see the instructions on page 19, step 1c, Hide General Ledger Accounts area.
2. In the Vendor ID field, type **DEJULIA** and press **<Enter>** (or use the lookup icon to find DeJulia Wholesale Suppliers).
3. Click on the Invoice date field. Type or select **19** as the date.
4. In the Invoice No. field, type **55522** and press **<Enter>**. This is a required field.
5. Click on the Apply to Purchases tab.
6. Click on the Quantity field. Type **6** and press **<Enter>**.
7. Your cursor is in the Item field. Type or select the code you just created, **AVRY-10300** and press **<Enter>** three times. The description and the GL Account automatically default to the information you assigned in the Maintain Inventory Items window.

8. To see how this inventory purchase is journalized, click 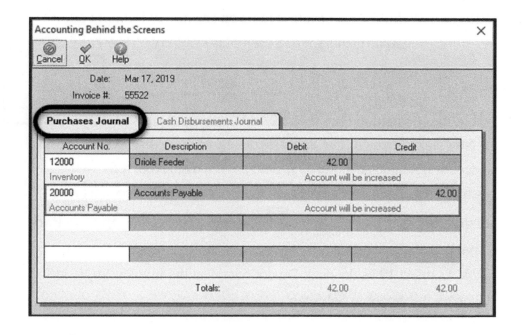 . The Accounting Behind the Screens, Purchases Journal appears: Account No. 12000, Inventory, is debited for 42.00; Account No. 20000, Accounts Payable is credited for 42.00. The vendor, DeJulia Wholesale Suppliers is also credited. The entry to the vendor is shown in the Vendor Ledgers.

9. Click [OK] to return to the Purchases/Receive Inventory window.

10. Click [Save] to post this purchase. Close the Purchases/Receive Inventory window.

INVENTORY AND SALES

When a stock item is sold, Sage updates Accounts Receivable and computes the Cost of Goods Sold (product cost), using one of three costing methods. In the General Ledger, a single entry encompassing all sales in the current period is made to the Product Cost account. This entry is dated the last day of the accounting period. Henton Park Apartments wants three Oriole feeders. The following steps show you how to invoice Henton Park Apartments for three Oriole feeders.

Date   *Transaction Description*

03/17/19   Sold three Oriole feeders on account to Henton Park
                   Apartments for $15 each plus sales tax.

1. From the Navigation Bar, click [Customers & Sales] > [Sales Invoices]
    > New Sales Invoice. The Sales/Invoicing window displays. (If the GL
    Account field and A/R Account field are *not* displayed, refer to the
    instructions on page 19 step 1c, Hide General Ledger Accounts area.)
2. In the Customer ID field, click [🔍] and select **HENTON, Henton Park
    Apartments**.
3. Type or select **19** as the date. Do not complete the Invoice No. field.
4. Click on the Apply to Sales tab.

5. Click on the Quantity field. Type **3** and press **<Enter>**.

6. The cursor is in the Item field. Type **AVRY-10300** and press **<Enter>** five times. (*Hint:* This is the inventory item added on page 167. Observe that the default GL Account is Account No. 40000-AV, Sales - Aviary. If the GL Account is <u>not</u> 40000-AV, you did <u>not</u> complete step 6, page 170. In the GL Account field, select 40000-AV *or* redo step 6, page 170.)

Sage computes the amount based on the quantity times the sales price that was established when setting up the inventory item. All the other lines for this invoice are automatically completed based on the inventory item information.

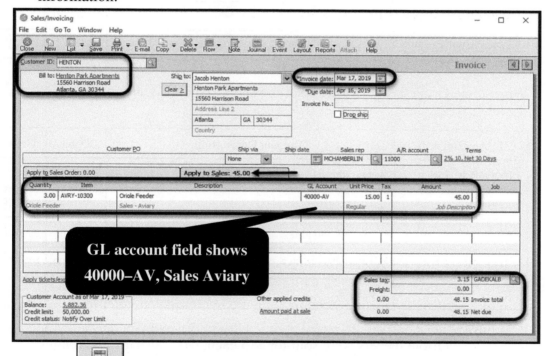

7. Click [Journal] to see how this entry is recorded in the Sales Journal. To see the whole entry, scroll down Accounting Behind the Screens. Observe that in a perpetual inventory system, the cost of sales accounts (50000-AV, Product Cost-Aviary; and 12000, Inventory) are "To be calculated." Once

the sales invoice is posted, the cost of sales amounts will be calculated.

Click [OK] to close the Accounting Behind the Screens window.

8. Click [Save] to post this sales invoice. Close the Sales/Invoicing window to return to the Customers & Sales Navigation Center.

When Bellwether purchased six Oriole Feeders, an inventory stock item, the entry is recorded in the Purchase Journal.

Account #	Account Description	Debit	Credit
12000/AVRY-10300	Inventory	42.00	
20000/DEJULIA	Accounts Payable/DeJulia Wholesale Suppliers		42.00

When three Oriole Feeders were sold, the entry in the Sales Journal is:

Account #	Account Description	Debit	Credit
11000/HENTON	Accts. Rec./Henton Park Apartments	48.15	
40000-AV	Sales-Aviary		45.00
23100	Sales Tax Payable		3.15
50000-AV	Product Cost-Aviary	21.00	
12000	Inventory		21.00

When three Oriole feeders were sold for $15 each, plus sales tax, the total is $48.15 ($45 + $3.15). When Bellwether Garden Supply bought the Oriole Feeders from the vendor (DeJulia Wholesale Suppliers), they paid $7 each. The last two lines of the journal entry (Account nos. 50000-AV and 12000) reflect the product cost of the stock items, $7 X 3 = $21. The journal entries shown above are examples of how purchases and sales are recorded in Sage 50's perpetual inventory system.

INVENTORY ADJUSTMENTS

It may become necessary to adjust the amount of Inventory Items due to faulty records, pilferage, spoilage, or inventory changes. You use the Inventory Adjustment Journal to make inventory adjustment entries. In the example that follows, one of Bellwether's employees dropped two bird house kits which damaged them beyond repair. To adjust inventory for this loss, follow these steps.

1. From the Navigation Bar, click **Inventory & Services** > **Inventory Adjustments**.
    The Inventory Adjustments window appears.
2. Type **AVRY-10100** (for Bird House Kit) in the Item ID field and press **<Enter>**.
3. In the Date field, type **15** or select the day.
4. Type **-2** in the Adjust quantity by field to decrease the current inventory by two. Press the **<Enter>** key. The New Quantity field shows that you have 28.00 bird house kits.
5. Type **Damaged** as the Reason to Adjust.
6. Click **Save** to post this adjustment, then close the Inventory Adjustments window.

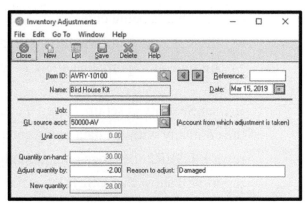

Adjustments to inventory, like the one just made, only affect the average cost of the item. For example, let's say you purchased two bird house kits at $30 each and then damaged one. For accounting purposes you now have one bird house kit that costs $30.

SECURITY AND INTERNAL CONTROL

Internal control is an integrated system of people, processes, and procedures that minimize or eliminate business risks, protect assets, facilitate reliable accounting, and promote efficient operations. If changes are made to company records, Sage 50's *audit trail* provides documentation. An audit trail records all entries and changes related to the company's data, including actions by specific users. Sage 50 has several methods to track information – a combination of the general ledger, journals, reports, and financial statements are used to trace transactions and balances. If you want to track when an action is performed, the audit trail provides that information. The audit trail provides accountability of users, deters users from fraudulent activity or mistakes, and tracks transaction history. Four internal control methods are used:

- Setting up user names, passwords, and access rights.
- The ability to associate the user currently logged into the company with the data that is being entered.
- Limit access to information in Sage 50's Navigation Centers.
- Audit Trail reports that show what each user entered.

If User Security is set up, Sage 50 can associate the user currently logged into the company with the data being entered. For example, USER1 adds a customer record. USER2 then logs on and modifies the customer record. The Audit Trail report will show that USER2 was the last person who worked with the customer record, and it will display what was changed. By limiting access to accounting data, the user security feature addresses an important purpose of internal control. Assigning users to one Navigation Center increases the accuracy of records and reports. Also, since one user assumes responsibility for repetitive tasks, the efficiency of operations increases. User security reduces the business's risk of users changing or deleting data inappropriately. User security allows the company to track who has performed various maintenance and recording tasks.

User Security and Access to the Sage 50 Navigation Centers

If you are an administrator responsible for setting up and maintaining user access, you can choose settings that will limit access to information in Navigation Centers. For example, if you want a user to have limited access to company revenue information, you could make sure the user has no access to the general ledger master list and transaction list reports or financial statements. However, you might want that same user to be able to view company budgets but not change them in any way. You can fine-tune settings to give users exactly the kind of access you want them to have. The Selected AccessRole Setup window has embedded Help for each security setting. Just select a setting to see Help about it. This will aid you in deciding which areas users have access to and which areas are not accessible.

Selected Access

The Selected Access window allows the administrator to grant rights to work in certain areas of the Sage 50 program within the current company. Sage 50 program areas include the following roles:

- Customers & Sales
- Vendors & Purchases
- Inventory & Services
- Employees & Payroll

- Banking & General Ledger
- System

In addition to full or no access, the administrator can set different levels of access within subareas such as maintenance, tasks, and reports. For example, in the Customers & Sales area, the administrator could choose to give a user limited access to Customer Information or Customer Beginning Balances. Drop-down lists let the administrator set different access levels for different subareas of the program; for example, Payments; Write Checks.

User Security

Sage 50 allows custom access for different individuals. If you want to take advantage of this security feature, you set up user rights for each person who will be using Sage 50. When set up, each user is issued a user name and password that will be required before opening and working with company data.

Once user names and passwords are set up, Sage 50 prompts each user for a user name and password whenever he or she opens a company. As long as users properly enter their passwords, they can access the areas of the program to which they have rights.

Setting Up Company Users, Passwords, and Access Rights

In order to have data security and password protection, you need to set up user records. When user names and passwords are set up, Sage 50 prompts you for a user name and password when you open a company. This is a two-step process:

- Set up the company administrator.
- Set up individual users.

The steps below are for example purposes only. *Remember, if you set up a user name and password you have to use it each time you start Sage 50.* To learn about setting up company users, passwords, and access rights, go to the following Help windows.

1. From Sage 50's menu bar select, Help > Help Topics > Index tab.
2. Type **Password** in the Type in the keyword to find field. Select setting up, click [Display].
3. The Set Up Company Users, Passwords, and Access Rights window appears. Enlarge the window. In the right pane, link to Setting up the first user (administrator). Read the information.
4. Link to Setting up additional company users. Read the information.
5. Link to Setting up users with selected access. Read the information. This Help window explains how to set up users, passwords and access rights. Check with your instructor to see if he or she would like you do this.

Note: Passwords must be at least seven characters. They must contain both numbers and letters. An example of a strong password is MLsmith707. Passwords are *case sensitive*. You need to remember if letters are capitalized or not.

6. Click [×] on the Sage 50 Help title bar to close.

Audit Trail Report

The Audit trail is an historical record of financial data that is used to examine the data's correctness. Sage 50's audit trail feature records all entries and changes related to company data, including actions by specific users. The Audit Trail report can trace fraudulent activity and other accounting adjustments you may not know were completed.

The System Navigation Center shows a link to <u>Run Audit Trail report</u>. Once date options are selected, the Audit Trail Report can be viewed from this link, or from the Reports & Forms, Company selection. On page

185, the Audit Trial Report is displayed from the Reports & Forms menu.

The audit trail feature records the following items with each activity performed while operating in the Sage 50 company:

- Date: System (computer) date of action.
- Time: System (computer) time of action.
- User Name: User Name (if available); otherwise, Sage 50 displays "Not Available."
- Action: Add, Change, or Delete.
- Window/Description: Window where action occurred or name of system function implemented (for example, Backup Company Data Files, Maintain Employees & Sales Reps).

- Transaction ID: For maintenance records, the ID associated with the record; for tasks, the ID associated with the transaction after change. (*Hint:* To see entire column, widen it.)
- Transaction Reference: Reference number associated with the transaction after change.
- Amount: Amount of transaction after change.

Sage 50's audit trail tracks the following:

1. Records and Transactions: Records include customers, vendors, employees, inventory items, etc. Transactions include quotes, sales orders, invoices, payments, general journal entries, inventory adjustments, etc. These include:
   - adding records or transactions (when Save is selected).
   - editing records or transactions (when Save is selected).
   - deleting records or transactions (when Delete is selected).
   - entering or maintaining record beginning balances (when OK or Save is selected).
   - voiding checks and paychecks.
   - making payments in Cash Manager and Payment Manager.
2. Miscellaneous Actions
   - reconciling accounts.
   - maintaining company information and options.
   - maintaining and loading user-maintained and Sage 50-maintained payroll tax tables.
   - importing data into the company.
   - adding transactions using Dynamic Data Exchange (DDE).
3. System Functions
   - posting and unposting journals (Batch mode only).
   - closing the fiscal year.

- closing the payroll tax year.
- backing up company data.

Displaying the Audit Trail Report & Find Transactions Report

Follow these steps to print an Audit Trail Report.

1. From the menu bar, select Reports & Forms > Company. The Select a Report or Form window appears. The Audit Trail Report is the default.

2. Click 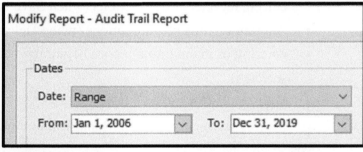.

3. In the Date field, select Range.

4. Type **1/1/2006** in the From field. Press **<Tab>**.

5. Type **12/31/2019** in the To field. Press **<Tab>**.

> **Troubleshooting:** If your current date is *after* 12/31/2019, type today's date in the To field. The Audit Trail Report shows the dates that you recorded entries.

Modify Report - Audit Trail Report

Dates

Date: Range

From: Jan 1, 2006   To: Dec 31, 2019

6. Click **OK**. The Audit Trail Report for the period from Jan 1, 2006 to Dec. 31, 2019 (*or, today's date*) appears. Observe that each transaction shows the Date, Time, User Name, Action, Window/ Description, Transaction ID, Transaction Reference, and Amount. If users had been set up, the User Name column would show that. Observe that the work completed in Chapters 1-5 is shown on the Audit Trail Report; for example, the employees added in Chapter 1 (CYACHT, or your name, and SCONNER) the vendors added (Maintain Vendors), purchases (Purchases/Receive Inventory), and payments to ADLER and OFCSUPPL

in Chapter 2. From Chapter 4, the DASH and TEESDALE transactions are also shown. Scroll down the Audit Trail Report to see your work. (Your date column will differ. It shows the date you recorded the entries.) The Audit Trial Report provides a listing of the changes made to the maintenance items and transactions. Depending on when you made additions and changes, your time and date column will differ. The Audit Trail Report shows when the author made changes. If you are working *after* December 31, 2019, your Audit Trail Report may show a different ending date.

Bellwether Garden Supply - Student Name
Audit Trail Report
For the Period From Jan 1, 2006 to Dec 31, 2019

Filter Criteria includes: 1) All Actions.

Date	Time	User Name	Action	Window/Description	Transaction ID	Transaction Reference	Amount
8/20/18	4:50 PM	Not Available	Add	Maintain Employees & Sales	CYACHT		
8/20/18	4:51 PM	Not Available	Change	Backup Company Data Files			
8/20/18	4:55 PM	Not Available	Change	Maintain Company	BCS	Bellwether Garden Supply - Student	
8/20/18	4:56 PM	Not Available	Change	Sage 50 Accounting	*UNNAMED*	User Logon...	
8/20/18	4:57 PM	Not Available	Change	Maintain Company	BELGARSU	Bellwether Garden Supply - Student	
8/20/18	5:10 PM	Not Available	Change	Maintain Company	BELGARSU	Bellwether Garden Supply - Student	
8/20/18	5:14 PM	Not Available	Add	Maintain Employees & Sales	SCONNOR		
8/20/18	5:18 PM	Not Available	Change	Backup Company Data Files			
8/20/18	5:38 PM	Not Available	Change	Maintain Employees & Sales	SCONNOR		
8/20/18	5:39 PM	Not Available	Change	Backup Company Data Files			
8/21/18	12:51 PM	Not Available	Change	Sage 50 Accounting	*UNNAMED*	User Logon...	
8/21/18	2:01 PM	Not Available	Change	Sage 50 Accounting	*UNNAMED*	User Logon...	
8/21/18	2:37 PM	Not Available	Change	Sage 50 Accounting	*UNNAMED*	User Logon...	
8/21/18	2:40 PM	Not Available	Change	Sage 50 Accounting	*UNNAMED*	User Logon...	
8/21/18	2:46 PM	Not Available	Change	Sage 50 Accounting	*UNNAMED*	User Logon...	
8/21/18	2:48 PM	Not Available	Change	Sage 50 Accounting	*UNNAMED*	User Logon...	
8/21/18	3:26 PM	Not Available	Change	Sage 50 Accounting	*UNNAMED*	User Logon...	
8/21/18	3:30 PM	Not Available	Change	Sage 50 Accounting	*UNNAMED*	User Logon...	
8/21/18	3:32 PM	Not Available	Change	Sage 50 Accounting	*UNNAMED*	User Logon...	
8/21/18	3:34 PM	Not Available	Change	Sage 50 Accounting	*UNNAMED*	User Logon...	
8/21/18	3:45 PM	Not Available	Change	Sage 50 Accounting	*UNNAMED*	User Logon...	
8/22/18	10:17 AM	Not Available	Change	Sage 50 Accounting	*UNNAMED*	User Logon...	
8/22/18	10:46 AM	Not Available	Change	Sage 50 Accounting	*UNNAMED*	User Logon...	
8/22/18	11:03 AM	Not Available	Add	Purchase Orders	ABNEY	101	3,834.00
8/22/18	11:45 AM	Not Available	Change	Sage 50 Accounting	*UNNAMED*	User Logon...	
8/22/18	1:15 PM	Not Available	Change	Sage 50 Accounting	*UNNAMED*	User Logon...	
8/22/18	1:19 PM	Not Available	Change	Sage 50 Accounting	*UNNAMED*	User Logon...	
8/22/18	1:23 PM	Not Available	Change	Sage 50 Accounting	*UNNAMED*	User Logon...	
8/22/18	1:24 PM	Not Available	Change	Maintain Company	BELGARSU	Bellwether Garden Supply - Student	
8/22/18	1:26 PM	Not Available	Change	Sage 50 Accounting	*UNNAMED*	User Logon...	
8/22/18	2:10 PM	Not Available	Add	Maintain Vendors	ADLER		
8/22/18	2:14 PM	Not Available	Add	Purchases/Receive Inventory	ADLER	AD107	45.00
8/23/18	10:11 AM	Not Available	Change	Sage 50 Accounting	*UNNAMED*	User Logon...	
8/23/18	10:17 AM	Not Available	Add	Payments	ADLER		44.10
8/23/18	11:50 AM	Not Available	Change	Backup Company Data Files			
8/23/18	12:44 PM	Not Available	Add	Maintain Vendors	OFCSUPPL		
8/23/18	12:53 PM	Not Available	Add	Purchases/Receive Inventory	OFCSUPPL	H788	54.75
8/23/18	12:55 PM	Not Available	Change	Purchases/Receive Inventory	OFCSUPPL	H788	54.75
8/23/18	1:00 PM	Not Available	Add	Payments	OFCSUPPL	10216	53.65
8/23/18	1:04 PM	Not Available	Change	Backup Company Data Files			
8/23/18	2:15 PM	Not Available	Change	Sage 50 Accounting	*UNNAMED*	User Logon...	
8/25/18	9:43 AM	Not Available	Change	Sage 50 Accounting	*UNNAMED*	User Logon...	
8/27/18	12:36 PM	Not Available	Change	Sage 50 Accounting	*UNNAMED*	User Logon...	
8/28/18	1:34 PM	Not Available	Change	Sage 50 Accounting	*UNNAMED*	User Logon...	
8/30/18	9:10 AM	Not Available	Change	Sage 50 Accounting	*UNNAMED*	User Logon...	
8/30/18	9:31 AM	Not Available	Add	Quotes	DASH		211.95
8/30/18	9:34 AM	Not Available	Add	Quotes	DASH	10355	211.95
8/30/18	9:34 AM	Not Available	Add	Auto Purchase Orders	SOGARDEN		191.40
8/30/18	9:34 AM	Not Available	Change	Quotes	DASH		211.95
8/30/18	9:34 AM	Not Available	Change	Convert to Sales Order	DASH		
8/30/18	9:44 AM	Not Available	Change	Sales Orders	DASH	10355	211.95
8/30/18	9:52 AM	Not Available	Add	Sales/Invoicing	DASH		211.95
8/30/18	9:58 AM	Not Available	Change	Maintain Customers/Prospec	TEESDALE		
8/30/18	10:19 AM	Not Available	Add	Sales/Invoicing	TEESDALE		158.95
8/30/18	11:03 AM	Not Available	Add	Receive Money	TEESDALE	8818	151.45

7. Close the Audit Trail Report.

8. From the Select a Report or Form window, select Find Transactions Report from 3/15/19 to 3/15/19. The Find Transactions Report provides a way to easily search for Sage 50 Transactions. You can drill down to the original entry from each transaction.

Bellwether Garden Supply - Student Name
Find Transactions Report
For the Period From Mar 15, 2019 to Mar 15, 2019
Filter Criteria includes: 1) All Transaction Types. Report order is by Date.

Date	Type	Reference	ID	Name	Amount
3/15/19	Credit Memo		ARCHER	Archer Scapes and Ponds	-49.99
3/15/19	Credit Memo		SAIA	Saia's Neighborhood Nursery	-49.99
3/15/19	General Journal Entry	ADJ0303103			0.11
3/15/19	General Journal Entry	Transfer			5,500.00
3/15/19	Inventory Adjustment		AVRY-10100	Bird House Kit	-2.00
3/15/19	Inventory Adjustment		AVRY-10050-SM-HTL	Prefabricated Birdhouse	8.00
3/15/19	Inventory Adjustment		AVRY-10050-LG-EFL	Prefabricated Birdhouse	4.00
3/15/19	Inventory Adjustment		AVRY-10050-SM-EFL	Prefabricated Birdhouse	8.00
3/15/19	Inventory Adjustment		AVRY-10050-SM-PYR	Prefabricated Birdhouse	4.00
3/15/19	Inventory Adjustment		AVRY-10050-SM-HTL	Prefabricated Birdhouse	6.00
3/15/19	Payment		ABNEY	Abney and Son Contractors	50.00
3/15/19	Payment	10210	SAFESTATE	Safe State Insurance Company	530.64
3/15/19	Payment	10212	PAYNE	Payne Enterprises	50.00
3/15/19	Payment	10213	CLINE	Cline Construction, Inc.	100.00
3/15/19	Payment	10214	HAWKINS	DPH Web Design	100.00
3/15/19	Payroll Entry	1250	ACHESTER	Amanda W. Chester	809.22
3/15/19	Payroll Entry	1251	ADUKE	Al L. Duke	379.50
3/15/19	Payroll Entry	1252	AHECTER	Anthony H. Hecter	787.54
3/15/19	Payroll Entry	1253	AKORNEL	Alex C. Kornel	845.06
3/15/19	Payroll Entry	1254	BHUGLEY	Brandon A. Hugley	612.75

9. Close all windows.

BACKING UP CHAPTER 5 DATA

After completing the work within Chapter 5, back up. The suggested file name is **Chapter 5.ptb**. Detailed steps for backing up data are shown on pages 24-26. Backing up saves data to that point in your work. Each time you back up, use a different file name; for example, the suggested file name at this point is Chapter 5.ptb. (Sage 50 automatically adds the file extension .ptb to backups.) Using a unique file name allows you to restore at different points in the data.

ONLINE LEARNING CENTER

Complete the following end-of-chapter activities online at www.mhhe.com/yacht2019 > Student Edition > Chapter 5.

1. Interactive Multiple-Choice and True/False questions.
2. Going to the Net exercise: Go online to the Bookkeeping and Accounting Basics website.
3. QA Templates: 10 multiple-choice questions and three analysis questions.
4. Assessment Rubric: Review journals, navigation centers, modules, and task windows.
5. Listen to narrated PowerPoint slides.

The OLC also includes links to the Appendixes:

- Appendix A: Troubleshooting (textbook and OLC)
- Appendix C: Review of Accounting Principles (OLC Student Edition)
- Appendix D: Glossary of Terms (OLC Student Edition)

Exercise 5-1: Follow the instructions below to complete Exercise 5-1.

1. Start Sage 50. Open Bellwether Garden Supply - Student Name [your first and last name].
2. Restore data from the end of Chapter 5. This back up was made on page 187.
3. Journalize and post the following transactions:

Date	Transaction Description
03/18/19	Transfer $1,200 from the Regular Checking Account to the Payroll Checking Account.
03/19/19	Purchased two (2) Oriole Feeders from DeJulia Wholesale Suppliers, Invoice No. 94977, $14.

4. Continue with Exercise 5-2.

Exercise 5-2: Follow the instructions below to complete Exercise 5-2.

1. Print the General Ledger Trial Balance.

How to Fix? I am NOT connected to a printer. What should I do?

1. Display the General Ledger Trial Balance. Select . In the Name field, click on the down-arrow. Select Adobe PDF *or* Microsoft XPS Document Writer.

2. Save the file to your USB drive. Use the file name shown in step 4.

---

2. Back up Exercise 5-2. Use **Exercise 5-2** as the file name.

3. Export the General Ledger Trial Balance to Excel. Use **Exercise 5-2_General Ledger Trial Balance.xlsx** as the file name.

4. Save the General Ledger Trial Balance as a PDF file. Use **Exercise 5-2_General Ledger Trial Balance.pdf** as the file name. (*Hint:* You may also be able to save PDF files from Excel. Open the Excel file, select File > Save as Adobe PDF.)

Check your figures:

Account No. 10200, Regular Checking Account	$9,046.52
Account No. 10300, Payroll Checking Account	10,565.26
Account No. 11000, Accounts Receivable	175,823.20
Account No. 20000, Accounts Payable	80,682.01

CHAPTER 5 INDEX

Chapter

6 Job Cost

LEARNING OBJECTIVES

1. Restore data from Exercise 5-2. (This backup was made on page 188.)
2. Learn about Sage 50's Job Cost system.
3. Set up a job.
4. Coordinate job costs with purchases, sales, and payroll.
5. Display the Job Profitability Report.
6. Make two backups, save one Excel file, and save one PDF file.

This chapter shows how to use the Job Cost system. In Sage 50, you can assign Job ID codes to purchases, sales, and employee hours. In this way, Sage 50 tracks how each of these factors impacts job costs. The diagram below illustrates how job costing works with purchases, sales, and payroll.

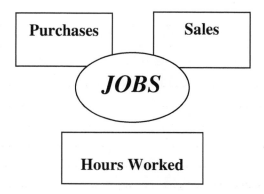

Sage 50's *job costing* feature allows you to track the costs incurred while performing a job. To use job costing, identify the project for which you want to track expenses and income and then determine how much detail is needed.

There are several advantages to using job costing:

- It allows you to track income and expenses for each project the company undertakes. You can create estimates for each job. As you enter invoices for materials or services used in the job through accounts payable, they can be assigned to a job so actual costs can be compared with job estimates.
- You can exercise greater control over costs and revenues by tracking customer invoices and payments received for each job. You can print reports during a job's progress to find out the total amount spent and net revenues due for each job.
- You can also maintain statistics on various jobs including starting date, completion date, and the progress of each job and view these by printing various job-costing reports.
- If phases or cost codes are used, you can generate reports to display this information, showing whether a job is over or under budget for any phase or task involved. This helps control costs by adjusting one phase or task prior to the job's completion.

Job costing gives you greater insight into all the company's jobs or projects so that you know what you are spending, how long it is taking, and how much profit was made on each job. The diagram below shows how Sage 50 organizes job costing.

1) Setup   **2) Tasks**   **3) Reporting**

GETTING STARTED

Bellwether Garden Supply has a customer named Franklin Botanical Gardens. Once a Job ID is set up for Franklin Botanical Gardens, you can track supplies and employee hours charged to this customer.

1. Start Sage 50. Open Bellwether Garden Supply - Student Name. (If Bellwether Garden Supply - Student Name is not shown, Create a new company using the restored data. Refer to the Read me box on page 28.)

2. If necessary, restore data from the Exercise 5-2 backup. (The Exercise 5-2.ptb backup was made on page 188.) Restoring overwrites or replaces an existing file.

💾 To make sure you are starting in the appropriate place in the data (Exercise 5-2.ptb backup) check the General Ledger Trial Balance. A partial trial balance is shown below. The General Ledger Trial Balance was completed in Exercise 5-2, step 1, page 188.

Bellwether Garden Supply - Student Name
General Ledger Trial Balance
As of Mar 31, 2019
Filter Criteria includes: Report order is by ID. Report is printed in Detail Format.

Account ID	Account Description	Debit Amt	Credit Amt
10000	Petty Cash	327.55	
10100	Cash on Hand	1,850.45	
10200	Regular Checking Account	9,046.52	
10300	Payroll Checking Account	10,565.26	
10400	Savings Account	7,500.00	
10500	Money Market Fund	4,500.00	
11000	Accounts Receivable	175,823.20	
11400	Other Receivables	7,681.84	
11500	Allowance for Doubtful Account		5,000.00
12000	Inventory	12,470.31	
14000	Prepaid Expenses	14,221.30	
14100	Employee Advances	3,000.65	
14200	Notes Receivable-Current	11,000.00	

3. From the Navigation Bar, select [Customers & Sales] > [Jobs] > New Job. The Maintain Jobs window appears. Read the Job ID information, and each field explanation as they appear.

4. In the Job ID field > type **FRANKLIN** > press **<Enter>**. *(Use uppercase.)*

5. In the Description field > type **Franklin Botanical Gardens** > press **<Enter>** two times.

6. Type **3/4/19** in the Start Date field > press **<Enter>** to go to the For Customer field. (*Hint:* Or, click on the For Customer field).

7. In the For Customer field, select FRANKLIN.

8. Click on the Job Type field, select LAND. Compare your Maintain Jobs window to the one shown below.

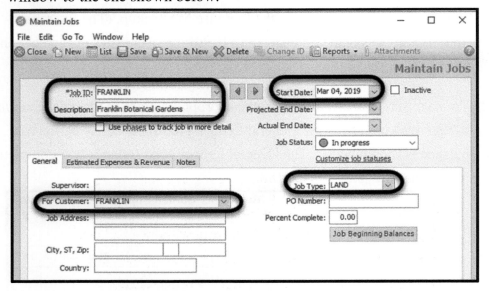

9. Save this job. Close the Maintain Jobs window to return to the Customers & Sales Navigation Center.

JOB COSTING AND PURCHASING: Purchasing Inventory Items for Jobs

This new job has some special circumstances; namely, Franklin Botanical Gardens has a new building overlooking a park. In the park, there are several picnic tables. According to the terms of the contract with Franklin Botanical Gardens, Bellwether Garden Supply purchases and provides a special wood treatment to the picnic benches.

When inventory items are purchased for jobs, you need to do the following:

➢ Record the purchase directly as a job expense. You could indicate a Non-stock or a Description only Inventory Item but not a Stock Item.

➢ Record the purchase into Inventory. When you bill the customer, enter the Item and the Job. The system posts the price as Job revenue and the Cost of Goods Sold as Job Expense.

Date	*Transaction Description*

3/20/19   Invoice No. AD501 was received from Adler's Landscaping for the purchase of special wood treatment, $85; terms 2% 10, Net 30 Days. Apply this purchase to the Franklin Botanical Gardens job.

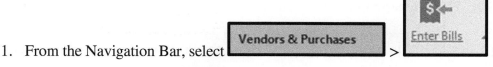

1. From the Navigation Bar, select **Vendors & Purchases** > **Enter Bills** > New Bill. The Purchases/Receive Inventory window displays.

2. Type or select **AD** (Adler's Landscaping) for the Vendor ID.

3. Select or type **20** in the Invoice date field > press **<Enter>**.

4. Type **AD501** for the Invoice No. (This is a *required* field.) Press **<Enter>**.

5. The Apply to Purchases tab is selected. Type **1** in the Quantity field > press **<Enter>** two times.

6. In the Description field, type **Special wood treatment** > press **<Enter>**.

7. Account No. 57200, Materials Cost, is the default account displayed in the GL Account field. In the Unit Price field, type **85** > press **<Enter>** two times.

8. Type or select **FRANKLIN**, the new Job, in the Job field.

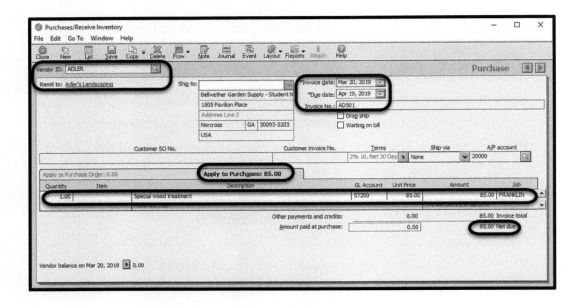

If your GL Account field and A/P Account field are *not* displayed on the Purchases/Receive Inventory window, see the instructions on page 19, step 1c, Hide General Ledger Accounts area.

9. Click [Save] to post this purchase. Close the Purchases/Receive Inventory window to return to the Vendors & Purchases Navigation Center.

JOB COSTING AND SALES

Follow these steps to invoice Franklin Botanical Gardens for a drip irrigation system and apply this sale to Franklin Botanical Gardens, Job ID, FRANKLIN.

Date	*Transaction Description*
3/21/19	Bellwether Garden Supply sold one Bell-Gro Home Irrigation System, Item No. EQWT-15100, to Franklin Botanical Gardens on account, $129.99, plus $9.10 sales tax, total $139.09; terms 2% 10, Net 30 Days.

1. Select > New Sales Invoice. The Sales/Invoicing window displays.

2. In the Customer ID field, click 🔍 > select Franklin Botanical Gardens as the Customer > press **<Enter>**.

3. Select or type **21** in the Invoice date field.

4. If necessary, click on the Apply to Sales tab.

5. Click on the Quantity field, type **1** > press **<Enter>**.

6. In the Item field, type **EQWT-15100** (Drip Irrigation System).

7. Press **<Enter>** until you are in the Job field. (You are accepting all of the displayed information when you do this.)

8. Type or select **FRANKLIN**, the Job ID for Franklin Botanical Gardens.

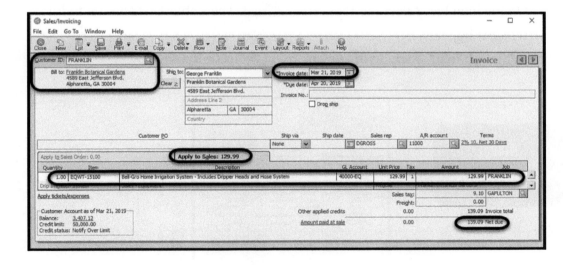

If your GL Account field and A/R Account field are *not* displayed on the Sales/Invoicing window, see the instructions on page 19, 1c, Hide General Ledger Accounts area.

9. Click [Save] to post this invoice. Close the Sales/Invoicing window to return to the Customers & Sales Navigation Center.

JOB COST AND PAYROLL

In the example that follows, one employee applied the special wood treatment to the picnic tables at Franklin Botanical Gardens. The employee spent one hour applying the wood treatment.

1. From the Navigation Bar, select **Employees & Payroll** > **Pay Employees** > Enter Payroll for One Employee. The Payroll Entry window appears.

2. Click 🔍 in the Employee ID field, select Alex C. Kornel > press **\<Enter\>**.

3. Type **29** as the Date > press **\<Enter\>** two times.

4. Type **29** in the Pay Period Ends field.

5. On the icon bar, select the Jobs icon **Jobs**. The Labor Distribution to Jobs window appears.

6. In the Job field, click on the down arrow >select FRANKLIN.

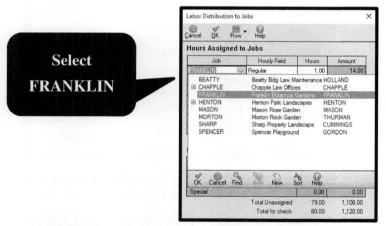

Select **FRANKLIN**

7. Press the **\<Enter\>** key. Type **1** in the Hours field > press **\<Enter\>**. In the Amount field, 14.00 is shown.

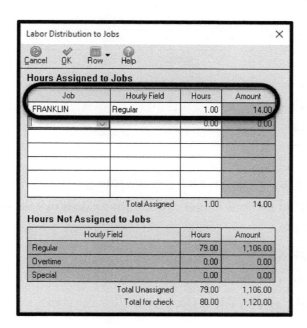

8. Click [✔ OK]. You are returned to the Payroll Entry window.

9. Click [Save] to post the paycheck. Close the Payroll Entry window to return to the Employees & Payroll window.

JOB COST REPORTS

Job cost reports tell you how jobs are progressing. Follow these steps to look at Job Cost Reports.

1. From the menu bar, select Reports & Forms > Jobs. The Select a Report or Form window displays.
2. In the Job Reports: Project Information list, double-click Job Profitability Report. The Job Profitability Report appears.
3. Scroll down to FRANKLIN.

Job ID	Phase ID	Cost Code ID	GL Acct ID	Actual Rev.	Actual Exp.	Profit $	Profit %
FRANKLIN			40000-EQ	129.99			
			50000-EQ		59.95		
			57200		85.00		
			77500		14.00		
				129.99	158.95		
FRANKLIN	Total			129.99	158.95	-28.96	-22.28

The report breaks down each job according to what was spent or earned for each affected general ledger account. It also shows the profit or loss for each job.

4. Close all windows.

BACKING UP CHAPTER 6 DATA

After completing the work within Chapter 6, back up. The suggested file name is **Chapter 6.ptb**. Detailed steps for backing up data are shown on pages 24-26. Backing up saves your data to that point in your work. Each time you back up, use a different file name; for example, the suggested file name at this point is Chapter 6.ptb. (Sage 50 automatically adds the file extension .ptb to backups.) Using a unique file name allows you to restore at different points in the data.

ONLINE LEARNING CENTER

Complete the following end-of-chapter activities online at www.mhhe.com/yacht2019 > Student Edition > Chapter 6.

1. Interactive Multiple-Choice and True/False questions.
2. Going to the Net exercise: Describe Sage 50cloud accounting software.
3. QA Templates: 10 short-answer questions and one analysis question.
4. Assessment Rubric: Review journals, navigation centers, modules, and task windows.

5. Listen to narrated PowerPoint slides.

The OLC also includes links to the Appendixes:

*   Appendix A: Troubleshooting (textbook and OLC)
*   Appendix C: Review of Accounting Principles (OLC Student Edition)
*   Appendix D: Glossary of Terms (OLC Student Edition)

Exercise 6-1: Follow the instructions below to complete Exercise 6-1.

1. Start Sage 50. Open Bellwether Garden Supply - Student Name.
2. If necessary, restore data from the end of Chapter 6. This backup was made on page 200.
3. Journalize and post the following transactions:

Date	Transaction Description
03/26/19	Sold two Bell-Gro Impulse Sprinklers (EQWT-15160) to Franklin Botanical Gardens, $64.18 (includes sales tax); terms 2% 10, Net 30 Days; Job ID Franklin Botanical Gardens.
03/26/19	Invoice No. AD967 was received from Adler's Landscaping for the purchase of one container of special wood treatment for $85; terms 2% 10, Net 30 Days; Job ID Franklin Botanical Gardens. (Debit Materials Cost.)
03/29/19	Amanda W. Chester worked one hour on the Franklin Botanical Gardens job. Apply her paycheck to this job. (*Hint:* Remember to select the appropriate job and hour worked. Refer to pages 198-199, steps 6 and 7. The Job Profitability Report completed in Exercise 6-2 depends on selecting the appropriate job and entering the hour worked.)

4. Continue with Exercise 6-2.

Exercise 6-2: Follow the instructions below to complete Exercise 6-2.

1. Print a Job Profitability Report. (*Hint*: If needed, select Adobe PDF or Microsoft XPS Document Writer as the printer. If you save as a PDF file, use the file name shown in step 4. Refer to page 65, How to Fix - I do not have a printer.)

2. Back up Exercise 6-2. Use **Exercise 6-2** as the file name.

Read Me: This backup is important. If you are using external media; for example, a USB drive, do *not* delete the Exercise 6-2.ptb file. You restore the Exercise 6-2.ptb backup file to complete work in Part 4, Chapters 16, 17, and 18.

3. Export the Job Profitability Report to Excel. Use **Exercise 6-2_Job Profitability Report.xlsx** as the file name.

4. Save the Job Profitability Repot as a PDF file. Use **Exercise 6-2_Job Profitability Report.pdf** as the file name.

Check Your Figures: Job Profitability Report, FRANKLIN

Actual Revenue, $189.97
Actual Expenses, $281.85
Profit dollars, -$91.88
Profit percentage, -48.37

CHAPTER 6 INDEX

Chapter

7

Financial Statements

LEARNING OBJECTIVES

1. Restore data from Exercise 6-2. This backup was made on page 202.
2. Explore Sage 50's Help feature.
3. Print the financial statements.
4. Use drill down to go from the income statement to the general ledger, then to the original entry window.
5. Complete Bellwether Garden Supply project online at www.mhhe.com/yacht2019 > Student Edition link.
6. Make an optional backup of Chapter 7, save one Excel file, and save six PDF files. (The Exercise 6-2.ptb backup includes the data needed for Chapter 7.)

FINANCIAL STATEMENTS

In Chapters 1 through 6, you explored the sample company, Bellwether Garden Supply. You learned how Sage's user interface works and how to navigate the software. In Chapters 1 through 6, you also journalized and posted various types of transactions. Beginning with Chapter 9, you learn how to use these features to set up service businesses from scratch.

In Chapter 7, you look at the financial statements. Once journal entries are recorded and posted, financial statements are calculated. Since business managers and owners have the primary responsibility for the organization, they depend on accounting information in the form of financial statements to understand what is happening. The financial statements reflect the current month and year-to-date amounts.

In this chapter, six financial statements are printed.

1. Balance Sheet.
2. Gross Profit by Departments.
3. Income Statement.
4. Statement of Cash Flow.
5. Statement of Retained Earnings.
6. Statement of Changes in Financial Position. Even though current accounting standards do not require a SCFP, Sage 50 includes it. (Refer to Read Me on page 221.)

Balance Sheet

A balance sheet is a list of assets, liabilities, and capital of a business entity as of a specific date, such as the last day of an accounting period or the last day of the year. Each financial statement may be modified to fit your needs. Sage 50 includes a Design icon for that purpose. Later in this chapter, you learn about how to use the Help feature to design financial statements. In Chapter 16, Customizing Forms, you learn more about modifying Sage 50's standard forms.

Gross Profit by Departments

A departmentalized accounting system provides information that management can use to evaluate the profitability or cost effectiveness of a department's activities. The Gross Profit by Departments financial statement is a custom report designed for Bellwether that details each department's year-to-date gross profit as of the current month.

Some of Bellwether's chart of account numbers have a dash, then an AV or a BK. For example, Account No. 40000-AV, Sales - Aviary; and Account No. 40000-BK, Sales - Books show the departmental designation.

Sage 50 includes a feature called masking which allows departmental organization. Custom forms can be designed to accommodate a departmentalized accounting system. The wrench [] to the left of Bellwether's financial statements indicates custom-designed forms.

Income Statement

The income statement is a summary of the revenues and expenses a company accrues over a period of time, such as an accounting period or a year. Only revenue and expense accounts are displayed on the income statement. *Net income* is computed by subtracting total expenses from total revenues. Net income results when revenues exceed expenses. An excess of expenses over revenues results in a *net loss*. Bellwether's net loss for the current month, March 1 through March 31, 2019, is $2,523.21. A net loss is indicated on the income statement with parenthesis ($2,523.21). Bellwether's year-to-date net income is $25,579.22. On page 218, the Income Statement is shown.

In addition to dollar figures, the income statement also includes percentage-of-revenue columns for the current month and year to date. The percentages shown for each expense, total expenses, and net income (or net loss) indicate the relationship of each item to total revenues.

Statement of Cash Flow

The cash flow from operations is roughly the same as income from operations plus depreciation, depletion, and adjusted for any other operating transactions that had no effect on cash during the period. The statement of cash flow also reports cash transactions associated with the purchase or sale of fixed assets (Investing Activities) and cash paid to or received from creditors and owners (Financing Activities).

The statement of cash flow provides the answers to three questions:

1. Where did cash receipts come from?
2. What were cash payments used for?
3. What was the overall change in cash?

Statement of Retained Earnings

The Statement of Retained Earnings shows beginning and ending retained earnings amounts, adjustments made to retained earnings within the report period, and the detail for all Equity-gets closed accounts. The retained earnings balance is the cumulative, lifetime earnings of the company less its cumulative losses and dividends.

Statement of Changes in Financial Position

The statement of changes in financial position describes changes in a company's financial position that may not be obvious from other financial statements. The statement of changes shows the change in working capital, assets, and liabilities for a given period of time. (Sage 50 includes this report. For more information, refer to Read me, page 221.)

Interrelationship of Financial Statements

The financial statements work together. The net income (or net loss) from the income statement is reported on the balance sheet's capital section. The net income or net loss is used to update the balance sheet's capital amount: Capital Beginning of the Year – Net Loss (or + Net Income) = Total Capital.

On the statement of retained earnings, the Ending Retained Earnings balance is $214,616.82. On the balance sheet, if you add the net income $25,579.22 to the balance sheet's retained earnings amount, $189,037.60, the result is

$214,616.82. This amount, $214,616.82, is the same as the Ending Retained Earnings balance on the Statement of Retained Earnings.

The total of all the cash accounts on the Balance Sheet (Petty Cash, Cash on Hand, Regular Checking Account, Payroll Checking Account, Savings Account, and Money-Market Fund) is shown as the Cash Balance at End of Period on the statement of cash flow, $32,060.92. The statement of cash flow uses information from both the balance sheet and income statement.

The statement of changes in financial position uses information from the income statement and balance sheet. No single financial statement tells the entire story. The income statement indicates how much revenue a business has earned during a specific period of time, but it says nothing about how much of that amount has or has not been received in cash. For information about cash and accounts receivable, look at the balance sheet and statement of cash flow.

GETTING STARTED

1. Start Sage 50. Open the sample company, Bellwether Garden Supply - Student Name.
2. If necessary, restore data from the Exercise 6-2 backup. (This backup was made on page 202.) Restoring overwrites or replaces an existing file.

To make sure you are starting in the appropriate place in the data (Exercise 6-2.ptb backup) check the Job Profitability Report. The results for Franklin Botanical Gardens are shown below.

FRANKLIN		40000-EQ	129.99			
			59.98			
		50000-EQ		59.95		
				23.90		
		57200		85.00		
				85.00		
		77500		14.00		
				14.00		
			189.97	281.85		
FRANKLIN	Total		189.97	281.85	-91.88	-48.37

USING SAGE 50'S HELP FEATURE

In Chapter 5 on pages 156-157 you used the Help feature to access sample charts of accounts. Later in Chapter 5, on pages 181-182, you used Sage 50's Help feature to learn about security and internal controls. In this chapter, you learn how to access Sage 50's Help feature to learn more about financial statements.

1. From the menu bar, click Help > Help Topics. The Sage 50 Help window displays. If necessary, click on the Index tab.

2. Type **balance sheet** in the Type in the keyword to find field. Observe that Balance Sheet is highlighted.

3. Click [Display]. Read the information in the right pane. In the Learn more section, link to additional information.

4. If necessary, on the Sage 50 Help title bar click [□] to enlarge the Sage 50 Help window, *or* scroll down. Link to How Transactions Affect the Balance Sheet. In the Learn more area, link to Balance Sheet Format, Debit and Credit, and Measure Income.

5. Click [×] on the Sage 50 Help title bar to close the window.

DISPLAYING THE FINANCIAL STATEMENTS

You have already used the Reports & Forms menu to print reports. In the steps that follow you use the Business Status Navigation Center to print financial statements.

1. From the Navigation Bar, click [**Business Status**]. In the Find a Report area's Category field > select Financial Statements.
2. In the Report field > select <Standard> Balance Sheet.

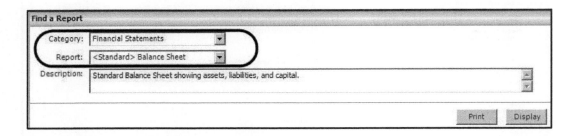

3. Click [Display]. The <Standard> Balance Sheet appears.

   Standard refers to statements that Sage 50 has already set up. As noted in the Help window, Sage 50 has a feature that allows you to design financial statements to fit your company's needs. For example, if you select Financial Statements from the Reports & Forms menu, reports with a wrench [🔧] next to them are customized forms. Compare your balance sheet with the one shown on the next two pages. If you printed the report, observe that a line at the bottom of the reports says "Unaudited – For Management Purposes Only."

Bellwether Garden Supply - Student Name
Balance Sheet
March 31, 2019

ASSETS

Current Assets
Petty Cash	$	327.55
Cash on Hand		1,850.45
Regular Checking Account		9,046.52
Payroll Checking Account		8,836.40
Savings Account		7,500.00
Money Market Fund		4,500.00
Accounts Receivable		176,026.47
Other Receivables		7,681.84
Allowance for Doubtful Account		(5,000.00)
Inventory		12,386.46
Prepaid Expenses		14,221.30
Employee Advances		3,000.65
Notes Receivable-Current		11,000.00
Other Current Assets		120.00

Total Current Assets   251,497.64

Property and Equipment
Furniture and Fixtures	62,769.25
Equipment	38,738.33
Vehicles	86,273.40
Other Depreciable Property	6,200.96
Buildings	185,500.00
Building Improvements	26,500.00
Accum. Depreciation-Furniture	(54,680.57)
Accum. Depreciation-Equipment	(33,138.11)
Accum. Depreciation-Vehicles	(51,585.26)
Accum. Depreciation-Other	(3,788.84)
Accum. Depreciation-Buildings	(34,483.97)
Accum. Depreciation-Bldg Imp	(4,926.28)

Total Property and Equipment   223,378.91

Other Assets
Deposits	15,000.00
Organization Costs	4,995.10
Accum Amortiz - Organiz Costs	(2,000.00)
Notes Receivable- Noncurrent	5,004.90
Other Noncurrent Assets	3,333.00

Total Other Assets   26,333.00

Total Assets $ 501,209.55

LIABILITIES AND CAPITAL

Current Liabilities
Accounts Payable	$	80,852.01
Accrued Expenses		3,022.55
Sales Tax Payable		18,083.53
Wages Payable		2,320.30
401 K Deductions Payable		2,579.92
Health Insurance Payable		(530.64)
Federal Payroll Taxes Payable		42,381.73
FUTA Tax Payable		258.20
State Payroll Taxes Payable		6,946.31
SUTA Tax Payable		658.67
Local Payroll Taxes Payable		113.25

Unaudited - For Management Purposes Only

```
                        Bellwether Garden Supply - Student Name
                                    Balance Sheet
                                   March 31, 2019

Income Taxes Payable                      11,045.75
Other Taxes Payable                        2,640.15
Current Portion Long-Term Debt             5,167.00
Contracts Payable- Current                 2,000.00
Other Current Liabilities                     54.00

Total Current Liabilities                                177,592.73

Long-Term Liabilities
Notes Payable-Noncurrent                   4,000.00

Total Long-Term Liabilities                                4,000.00

Total Liabilities                                        181,592.73

Capital
Common Stock                               5,000.00
Paid-in Capital                          100,000.00
Retained Earnings                        189,037.60
Net Income                                25,579.22

Total Capital                                            319,616.82

Total Liabilities & Capital                        $     501,209.55


                       Unaudited - For Management Purposes Only
```

Follow these steps to display the Gross Profit by Departments financial statement for the current period.

1. Close the Balance Sheet. In the Find a Report area of the Business Status Navigation Center, the Category field shows Financial Statements. In the Report field, select Gross Profit by Departments.

2. Click Display The Departmental Gross Profit Totals report appears. Compare yours with the one shown on the next page.

```
                          Bellwether Garden Supply - Student Name
                               Departmental Gross Profit Totals
                          Year To Date Totals For the Month Ending March 31, 2019

                          Aviary                    Books                  Equipment

Revenues
  Sales                 $   51,697.86  100.00  $   7,293.10  100.00      60,392.26  100.00

  Total Revenues            51,697.86  100.00       7,293.10  100.00      60,392.26  100.00


Cost of Sales
  Product Cost - Aviary     20,954.25   40.53           0.00    0.00          0.00    0.00
  Product Cost - Books           0.00    0.00       2,361.37   32.38          0.00    0.00
  Product Cost - Equipment       0.00    0.00           0.00    0.00     24,238.80   40.14

  Total Cost of Sales       20,954.25   40.53       2,361.37   32.38     24,238.80   40.14

  Gross Profit             30,743.61   59.47       4,931.73   67.62     36,153.46   59.86

                               For Management Purposes Only
```

The Departmental Gross Profit Totals report lists the departmental gross profit totals for the following departments: Aviary, Books, and Equipment.

3. Close the Departmental Gross Profit Totals window.

Departmental Masking

The Departmental Gross Profit report shown above is separated into three departments: Aviary, Books, and Equipment. A feature included in Sage 50 called *masking* allows you to departmentalize financial statements. Masking is the ability to limit information on the report to a single division, department, location, or type code.

1001M01
Account No.
Main Branch
Department

For masking, account numbers could be set up like this.

When you print or display a report, you can filter the report using *wildcard* characters. In this example, you would type *****01 to include all departments ending in 01. You would type ****M** to show only main branch numbers on the report. You could type 10***** to find all asset-type accounts for all branches and departments (assuming your asset accounts all begin with 10).

Wildcards make it easy to select a range of account numbers. In Sage 50, the only valid wildcard character is an asterisk. An asterisk represents any number of characters. You can filter or mask the information that appears on certain general ledger reports. This is done by the use of 15 characters that are allowed in the Account ID field of your general ledger accounts. To see the account masking option, do this.

1. Select Reports & Forms > General Ledger > highlight Chart of Accounts.

2. On the toolbar, click [Options].

3. In the Select a filter area, highlight Department Mask.

4. In the Select an option area, select Use wildcards. Type **10*****.** (*Hint*: After 10, type 5 asterisks.)

5. Click [OK]. The Chart of Accounts appears with account numbers starting with 10.

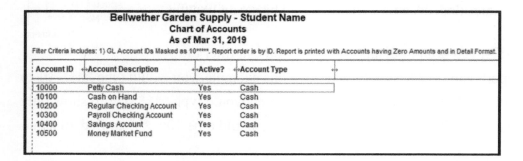

Bellwether Garden Supply - Student Name
Chart of Accounts
As of Mar 31, 2019

Filter Criteria includes: 1) GL Account IDs Masked as 10*****. Report order is by ID. Report is printed with Accounts having Zero Amounts and in Detail Format.

Account ID	Account Description	Active?	Account Type	
10000	Petty Cash	Yes	Cash	
10100	Cash on Hand	Yes	Cash	
10200	Regular Checking Account	Yes	Cash	
10300	Payroll Checking Account	Yes	Cash	
10400	Savings Account	Yes	Cash	
10500	Money Market Fund	Yes	Cash	

6. Close the Chart of Accounts and the Select a Report or Form window.

Bellwether Garden Supply masks departments by adding a suffix for the department name—AV for Aviary, BK for Books, etc.

Follow these steps to display the income statement:

1. In the Find a Report area of the Business Status Navigation Center, the Category field shows Financial Statements. In the Report field > select <Standard> Income Stmnt.

2. Click [Display] When the Income Statement displays > click [Options], then uncheck Show Zero Amounts > [OK].

How to fix? What if your financial statements do <u>not</u> agree? Suggestions follow.

- Determine the difference in the amounts. Is the difference the amount of an entry?
- Display the Audit Trail report for the month(s)/year you have been completing work. A partial Audit Trail Report is shown in Chapter 5, page 185. Verify amounts. Is an entry missing or has an entry been recorded twice? If needed, drill down to the original entry.
- You may also find it useful to display the General Ledger Trial Balance and drill down to specific accounts.
- If needed, restore an earlier backup file and then continue from that point. Refer to the chart on pages 2-4 for the backups made in Chapters 1-7.
- Display the financial statement again and compare to textbook illustration.

The income statement is shown on the next page.

Bellwether Garden Supply - Student Name
Income Statement
For the Three Months Ending March 31, 2019

		Current Month			Year to Date	
Revenues						
Sales	$	295.00	0.33	$	295.00	0.10
Sales - Aviary		7,172.71	8.07		51,697.86	18.36
Sales - Books		149.75	0.17		7,293.10	2.59
Sales - Equipment		18,038.77	20.30		60,392.26	21.45
Sales - Food/Fert		1,176.86	1.32		5,374.05	1.91
Sales - Hand Tools		729.67	0.82		7,058.12	2.51
Sales - Landscape Services		17,467.43	19.65		26,975.53	9.58
Sales - Miscellaneous		0.00	0.00		45.00	0.02
Sales - Nursery		33,795.03	38.02		67,637.11	24.03
Sales - Pots		7,919.31	8.91		11,483.74	4.08
Sales - Seeds		1,457.43	1.64		8,661.39	3.08
Sales - Soil		724.92	0.82		9,152.45	3.25
Other Income		100.00	0.11		25,600.00	9.09
Sales Discounts		(145.72)	(0.16)		(155.62)	(0.06)
Total Revenues		88,881.16	100.00		281,509.99	100.00
Cost of Sales						
Product Cost		(68.50)	(0.08)		(68.50)	(0.02)
Product Cost - Aviary		2,210.60	2.49		20,954.25	7.44
Product Cost - Books		14.27	0.02		2,361.37	0.84
Product Cost - Equipment		7,482.30	8.42		24,238.80	8.61
Product Cost - Food/Fert		466.30	0.52		2,127.54	0.76
Product Cost - Hand Tools		287.15	0.32		2,813.85	1.00
Product Cost - Pots		3,148.60	3.54		3,423.60	1.22
Product Cost - Seeds		584.45	0.66		3,450.65	1.23
Product Cost - Soil		310.72	0.35		4,075.97	1.45
Direct Labor - Nursery		1,750.00	1.97		3,062.50	1.09
Materials Cost		1,567.45	1.76		1,567.45	0.56
Materials Cost - Nursery		5,438.40	6.12		9,668.50	3.43
Subcontractors - Landscaping		335.50	0.38		335.50	0.12
Total Cost of Sales		23,527.24	26.47		78,011.48	27.71
Gross Profit		65,353.92	73.53		203,498.51	72.29
Expenses						
Freight		0.00	0.00		50.00	0.02
Advertising Expense		1,325.00	1.49		1,325.00	0.47
Auto Expenses		274.56	0.31		274.56	0.10
Bad Debt Expense		1,341.09	1.51		1,341.09	0.48
Bank Charges		18.00	0.02		18.00	0.01
Depreciation Expense		2,761.30	3.11		8,394.00	2.98
Legal and Professional Expense		150.00	0.17		510.00	0.18
Licenses Expense		150.00	0.17		150.00	0.05
Maintenance Expense		75.00	0.08		75.00	0.03
Office Expense		534.64	0.60		534.64	0.19
Payroll Tax Exp		5,854.46	6.59		16,115.88	5.72
Rent or Lease Expense		550.00	0.62		1,100.00	0.39
Repairs Expense		125.00	0.14		3,694.00	1.31
Supplies Expense		2,873.42	3.23		2,873.42	1.02
Utilities Expense		303.45	0.34		303.45	0.11
Wages Expense		51,086.42	57.48		140,705.46	49.98
Other Expense		464.90	0.52		464.90	0.17
Purchase Disc- Expense Items		(10.11)	(0.01)		(10.11)	0.00
Total Expenses		67,877.13	76.37		177,919.29	63.20
Net Income	$	(2,523.21)	(2.84)		25,579.22	9.09

For Management Purposes Only

Drill Down from the Income Statement to Original Entry

Follow these steps to follow an account balance from the income statement, to the general ledger, then to the original entry window. This is called drill down.

1. The income statement should be displayed. Place your cursor over 7,172.71, Sales – Aviary

Observe that the cursor becomes a magnifying glass icon with a Z in the middle. (Z is an abbreviation for zoom). Double-click with your left mouse button.

2. The General Ledger Account 40000-AV, Sales - Aviary, appears. From the general ledger you can drill down to the Receive Money window. For example, double click on the 3/5/2019 Cash Receipts Journal (CRJ) entry for $79.96.

| 3/5/19 | CASH0305 | CRJ | Retail (Cash) Sale | 79.96 |

3. This takes you to the Receive Money window. The original entry for 4 Thistle Bird Seed Mix-6 lb. (AVRY-10140) is shown (19.99 x 4 = 79.96). Close the Receive Money window to go back to the General Ledger Account No. 40000-AV.

4. Drill down from one of the Sales Journal (SJ) entries. The Sales/Invoicing window appears.

5. When you are through using drill down, close the Sales/Invoicing window, General Ledger, and Income Statement windows.

Follow these steps to display the Statement of Cash Flow.

1. In the Find a Report area of the Business Status Navigation Center, the Category field shows Financial Statements. In the Report field, select

   <Standard> Cash Flow > Display

2. From the Statement of Cash Flow window, click [Options] > uncheck Show Zero Amounts > [OK]. If printed, observe that the bottom of the report says "Unaudited - For Internal Use Only."

Bellwether Garden Supply - Student Name
Statement of Cash Flow
For the three Months Ended March 31, 2019

	Current Month	Year to Date
Cash Flows from operating activities		
Net Income	$ (2,523.21)	$ 25,579.22
Adjustments to reconcile net income to net cash provided by operating activities		
Accum. Depreciation-Furniture	420.80	1,262.40
Accum. Depreciation-Equipment	385.05	1,265.25
Accum. Depreciation-Vehicles	1,437.89	4,313.67
Accum. Depreciation-Other	64.57	193.71
Accum. Depreciation-Buildings	396.37	1,189.11
Accum. Depreciation-Bldg Imp	56.63	169.87
Accounts Receivable	(11,085.80)	(172,928.03)
Other Receivables	0.00	(3,672.24)
Inventory	13,650.37	6,211.73
Accounts Payable	10,497.38	76,949.26
Sales Tax Payable	4,386.16	15,622.98
401 K Deductions Payable	825.32	2,135.22
Health Insurance Payable	(530.64)	(530.64)
Federal Payroll Taxes Payable	14,617.04	40,794.88
State Payroll Taxes Payable	2,138.64	5,960.98
Other Taxes Payable	50.00	50.00
Other Current Liabilities	150.00	150.00
Total Adjustments	37,459.78	(20,861.85)
Net Cash provided by Operations	34,936.57	4,717.37
Cash Flows from investing activities Used For		
Net cash used in investing	0.00	0.00
Cash Flows from financing activities Proceeds From Used For		
Net cash used in financing	0.00	0.00
Net increase <decrease> in cash	$ 34,936.57	$ 4,717.37
Summary		
Cash Balance at End of Period	$ 32,060.92	$ 32,060.92
Cash Balance at Beg of Period	2,875.54	(27,343.66)
Net Increase <Decrease> in Cash	$ 34,936.46	$ 4,717.26

Unaudited - For Internal Use Only.

3. Close the Statement of Cash Flow.

Follow these steps to display the Statement of Retained Earnings:

1. In the Report field, select <Standard> Retained Earnings.

2. Click [Display]. When the Statement of Retained Earnings displays > click

    [Options] > uncheck Show Zero Amounts > [OK]. The Statement
    of Retained Earnings appears.

	Bellwether Garden Supply - Student Name	
	Statement of Retained Earnings	
	For the Three Months Ending March 31, 2019	
Beginning Retained Earnings	$	189,037.60
Adjustments To Date		0.00
Net Income		25,579.22
Subtotal		214,616.82
Ending Retained Earnings	$	214,616.82

3. Close the Statement of Retained Earnings.

Follow the steps on the next page to print the Statement of Changes in Financial Position.

 Read Me: Statement of Changes in Financial Position

Sage 50 includes the Statement of Changes in Financial Position even though current accounting standards require that a statement of cash flow is needed as part of a full set of financial statements in place of a statement of changes in financial position.

---

1. In the Report field, select \<Standard\> Stmnt Changes > [Display] Select the option to uncheck Show Zero amounts.

Bellwether Garden Supply - Student Name
Statement of Changes in Financial Position
For the three months ended March 31, 2019

	Current Month	Year To Date
Sources of Working Capital		
Net Income	$ (2,523.21)	$ 25,579.22
Add back items not requiring working capital		
Accum. Depreciation-Furniture	420.76	1,262.36
Accum. Depreciation-Equipment	384.99	1,265.19
Accum. Depreciation-Vehicles	1,437.89	4,313.67
Accum. Depreciation-Other	64.57	193.71
Accum. Depreciation-Buildings	396.36	1,189.10
Accum. Depreciation-Bldg Imp	56.63	169.87
Working capital from operations	237.99	33,973.12
Other sources		
Total sources	237.99	33,973.12
Uses of working capital		
Total uses	0.00	0.00
Net change	$ 237.99	$ 33,973.12
Analysis of componants of changes		
Increase \<Decrease\> in Current Assets		
Petty Cash	$ 227.55	$ 227.55
Regular Checking Account	(631.21)	(2,280.03)
Payroll Checking Account	30,840.12	2,269.74
Money Market Fund	4,500.00	4,500.00
Accounts Receivable	11,085.80	172,928.03
Other Receivables	0.00	3,672.24
Inventory	(13,650.37)	(6,211.73)
\<Increase\> Decrease in Current Liabilities		
Accounts Payable	(10,497.38)	(76,949.26)
Sales Tax Payable	(4,386.16)	(15,622.98)
401 K Deductions Payable	(825.32)	(2,135.22)
Health Insurance Payable	530.64	530.64
Federal Payroll Taxes Payable	(14,617.04)	(40,794.88)
State Payroll Taxes Payable	(2,138.64)	(5,960.98)
Other Taxes Payable	(50.00)	(50.00)
Other Current Liabilities	(150.00)	(150.00)
Net change	$ 237.99	$ 33,973.12

For Management Purposes Only

> **How to Fix?** I do NOT have a printer. What should I do?
>
> 1. Display the financial statement > select . In the Name field, click on the down-arrow.
> 2. Select Adobe PDF *or* Microsoft XPS Document Writer.
>
> 3. Save the file to your USB drive.
> 4. Verify your displayed reports with those shown on pages 213-222.
>
> If needed, the PDF or XPS file can be emailed to your instructor. When selecting an Adobe PDF or XPS file, no printer is required.

2. If instructed, print or save. Close all windows.

BACKING UP CHAPTER 7 DATA (Optional Backup)

You have not added any new data in Chapter 7. If you would prefer to make a backup, the suggested file name is **Chapter 7.ptb**. Detailed steps for backing up data are shown on pages 24-26.

Backing up saves your data to that point in your work. Each time you back up, use a different file name; for example, the suggested file name at this point is Chapter 7.ptb. (Sage 50 automatically adds the file extension .ptb to backups.) Using a unique file name allows you to restore at different points in the data.

EXPORT FINANCIAL STATEMENTS TO EXCEL

Follow these steps to have separate sheets for each financial statement on one Excel workbook.

---

1. Display the \<Standard\> Balance Sheet > click Excel.

2. The Copy Report to Excel window appears. The default File Option is Create a new Microsoft Excel workbook. The Default Report header option is Show header in Excel worksheet. If necessary, make these selections.

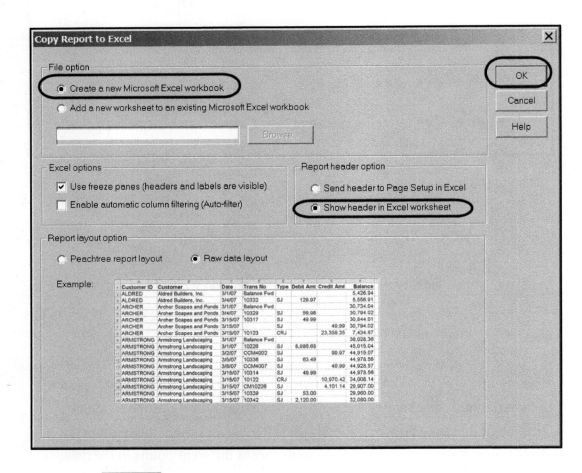

3. Click OK. The Balance Sheet appears as an Excel workbook.

4. Save. Use the file name **Chapter 7_Financial Statements.xlsx**. Minimize Excel.

5. Close Sage 50's Balance Sheet.

6. Display the <Standard> Income Statement. From the displayed Income Statement, click [Excel].

7. On the Copy Report to Excel window, select Add a new worksheet to an Existing Microsoft Excel workbook. Then, Browse to the location of the saved file (Chapter 7_Financial Statements.xlsx). Double-click on the Chapter 7_Financial Statements file (or highlight it and click <Open>).

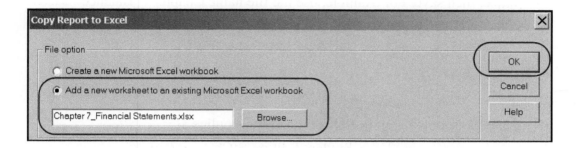

8. Click [OK]. Maximize Excel. (From the taskbar, click on the Microsoft Excel button.) Observe that the Excel file shows two sheets—Balance Sheet and Income Stmnt — [Balance Sheet | Income Stmnt]. (*Hint:* You may need to save each sheet, then exit Excel before exporting the next financial statement.)

9. Save. Add the following financial statements to the Excel file: Gross Profit by Departments, Statement of Cash Flow, Retained Earnings Statement, and Statement of Changes in Financial Position. When you are finished, the Excel file should have 6 sheets: Balance Sheet, Income Stmnt, Gross Profit by Departments, Cash Flow, Retained Earnings, Stmnt Changes.

Check your figures:

Total Liabilities & Capital	$501,209.55
Year to Date Gross Profit	203,498.51

Year-to-date Net Income	$25,579.22
Year-to-date Net Increase in Cash	$4,717.26
Ending Retained Earnings	$214,616.82

10.   Save. Exit Excel.

11.   Save the financial statements as PDF files. Use the financial statement's name, then save. For example, use the file name Chapter 7_Balance Sheet.pdf, Chapter 7_Income Statement, etc.

ONLINE LEARNING CENTER

Complete the following end-of-chapter activities online at www.mhhe.com/yacht2019 > Student Edition > Chapter 7.

1.   Interactive Multiple-Choice and True/False questions.
2.   Going to the Net exercise: Access the article How to Value Stocks: How to Read a Balance Sheet.
3.   QA Templates: 10 true/make true questions and three analysis questions.
4.   Assessment Rubric: Review journals, navigation centers, modules, and task windows.
5.   Listen to narrated PowerPoint slides.
6.   Bellwether Garden Supply Project.

The OLC also includes links to the Appendixes:

- Appendix A: Troubleshooting (textbook and OLC)
- Appendix C: Review of Accounting Principles (OLC Student Edition)
- Appendix D: Glossary of Terms (OLC Student Edition)

Exercise 7-1: Answer the following questions about the balance sheet and income statement:

1. The total assets are: _506,209.55_
2. The total capital is: _319,616.82_
3. Indicate the amount of the net income or
   (net loss) for the month of March: _(2,523.21)_
4. The current month's gross profit is: _65,353.92_
5. The current month's total expenses are: _67,877.13_

Exercise 7-2: Answer the following questions about the statement of cash flow and the statement of retained earnings:

1. The current month's cash balance at the
   beginning of the period is: _2,875,54_
2. The year-to-date's cash balance at the
   beginning of the period is: _27,343,66_
3. The cash balance at end of period for the
   current month is: _32,060,92_
4. The beginning Retained Earnings balance is: _189,037.60_
5. The ending Retained Earnings balance is: _214,616.82_

BELLWETHER GARDEN SUPPLY PROJECT

To answer questions about Bellwether Garden Supply, go online to
www.mhhe.com/yacht2019 > Student Edition > link to Bellwether Garden
Supply Project. In this project, you examine Bellwether's transactions, reports,
and internal controls. The project includes comparing controlling account
balances to the subsidiary ledgers and describing why some balances may differ.

CHAPTER 7 INDEX

Chapter 8

Stone Arbor Landscaping: Time & Billing

LEARNING OBJECTIVES

1. Start the sample company, Stone Arbor Landscaping.
2. Explore Sage 50's time and billing feature.
3. Use the time and billing feature to complete a time ticket, sales invoice, and payroll entry.
4. Make two backups, save two Excel files, and save four PDF files.

STONE ARBOR LANDSCAPING

When you installed Sage 50, two sample companies were included with the software: Bellwether Garden Supply and Stone Arbor Landscaping. In Chapters 1–7 you worked with Bellwether Garden Supply. Chapter 8 focuses on how Stone Arbor Landscaping uses the time and billing feature.

TIME & BILLING

Time & Billing tracks time spent on various tasks, records internal use of company resources associated with customers or jobs, and manages administrative activities and overhead expenses. Recorded time and expenses can be billed later to customers. Timed activities can also be applied to an employee's paycheck. The purpose of Sage 50's time and billing feature is to provide the tools to record customer-related work or expenses.

Customers: Time and expenses can be associated with customers that you intend to bill later in Sales/Invoicing. Record time and expenses for customers only if you are not using job costing.

Jobs: If Job Costs are tracked, you can record time and expenses for jobs, phases, or cost codes. Then, you can apply billable time and expense items to the customer's invoice. The advantage of recording time and expense for jobs is that you can track details related to the completion of the project, including overhead and labor costs, and manage job profitability in reports.

Administrative: You can track internal activities to manage process control and overhead costs. You may want to track the number of hours an employee spends preparing proposals or bookkeeping. Or, you may want to track an employee's mileage or travel expenses.

To track time and expenses, Sage uses two forms or tickets: the time ticket and the expense ticket. Each ticket type can be specific to a customer, job, or non-billable administrative tasks. Each ticket has its own special type of inventory item: the activity item for time tickets and the charge item for expense tickets.

Time Tickets

Time tickets are used to record time-based activities such as research or consultations. They record the activities of either an employee or a vendor. The two methods of entering time ticket information are weekly or daily.

The billing rate used for a recorded activity can be based on the employee who records the ticket or one of the five billing rates assigned to the activity item. Or, you can record the billing at the time you enter the time ticket.

Expense Tickets

Expense tickets are used to track and aid in the recovery of customer-related expenses. These expenses are *not* based on time. Expenses can be based on the various charges related to the service being offered. For example, if you were an accountant, you might charge your client for copying fees or faxing fees.

Both time and expense tickets can be used in the Sales/Invoicing window to bill customers. The Sales/Invoicing window includes a feature called Apply Tickets/Reimbursable Expenses which takes you to the time and billing feature. The rate for expense tickets is determined by the unit price of the charge item multiplied by the quantity. The chart shows how time and billing works.

Time & Billing Ticket Types			
Ticket Type	Inventory Item Class	Examples	Billing Amount Equals
Time Ticket	Activity Item	Research, Consultants, Writing Reports	Billing Rate Times Activity Divisions
Expense Ticket	Charge Item	Copying, Faxing, Court Fees	Unit Price of the Charge Item Times Quantity

GETTING STARTED

1. Start Sage 50. From the startup window, select Explore a sample company. (*Hint:* If another company opens, select File > Close Company. Stone Arbor Landscaping will be listed in the Company Name list after the first time it is opened.)

2. The Explore a Sample Company window appears. Select Stone Arbor Landscaping.

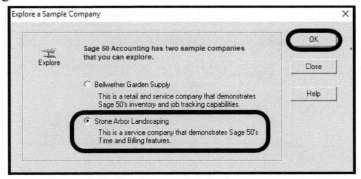

Troubleshooting: When opening Stone Arbor Landscaping, if the screens shown on the next page appear, click <Yes>.

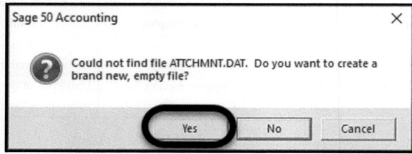

Software Expiration. If you are using the Student Version of Sage 50 2019 included with the textbook, a Sage 50 Accounting window appears that says "You can use this company in the student version of Sage 50 for the next 14 months and then it will expire. The company's expiration date can be found in the Company Information section of the System Navigation Center." For more information about the expiration date, refer to pages xvi-xvii, Expiration Date, Student Version, Sage 50 2019.

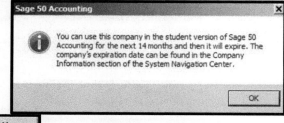

3. Click [OK]. Starting Stone Arbor Landscaping takes a few moments. The title bar shows Stone Arbor Landscaping – Sage 50 Accounting. The Customers & Sales Navigation Center is shown.

ADD YOUR NAME TO REPORTS

To add your name to reports, follow these steps.

1. From the Navigation Bar, select **System**. If necessary, scroll down the page to Company Maintenance.

2. Click **Edit Company Information Now**. The Maintain Company Information Window appears. In the Company Name field, add your name or initials after Stone Arbor Landscaping.

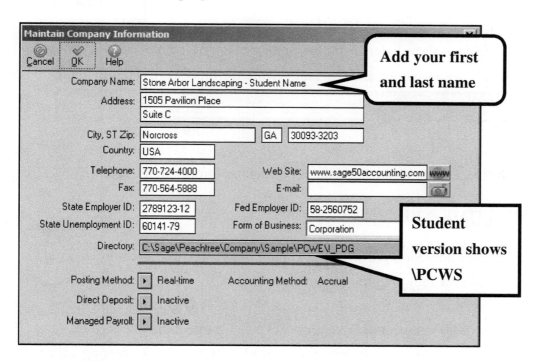

3. Click **OK**. Click File > Exit Sage 50. (Exit so you can see how the Maintain Company Information window changes.)

4. Start Sage 50 > **Open an Existing Company**. Open Stone Arbor Landscaping - Student Name (your first and last name.) In the Last Modified field, the current date is shown. Your date will differ.

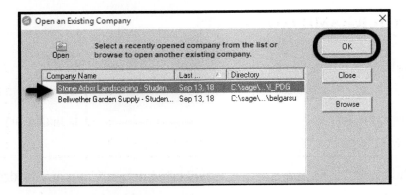

5. Display the Maintain Company Information window (Maintain > Company Information). Observe that the Directory field has changed. After adding your name to the Stone Arbor Landscaping, the Directory field ends in **\stoarbla** – three letters from the first word (**sto**ne), three letters from the second word (**arb**or), and two letters from the third word (**la**ndscaping).

6. Click [OK] to close the Maintain Company Information window.

USING TIME & BILLING

Let's look at how Stone Arbor Landscaping has set up time and billing. First, they set up how they are going to invoice for their services. There are two special inventory item classes for Time & Billing: *activity items* and *charge items*. Activity items are used on time tickets. Charge items are used on expense tickets. These inventory items must be set up prior to entering a time or expense ticket. There are four steps to complete Time & Billing.

Step 1: Set up the inventory item.
Step 2: Enter the time ticket.
Step 3: Record the sales invoice.
Step 4: Payroll.

Inventory Item Maintenance

You use maintenance windows to set up defaults. Follow these steps to look at the inventory maintenance information for Stone Arbor Landscaping.

1. From the Navigation Bar, click 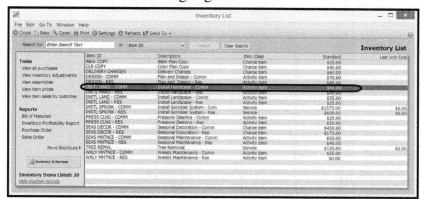 >
   View and Edit Inventory Items. The Inventory List appears. Click once on
   INSTL HARD – COMM to highlight it.

2. Double-click INSTL HARD – COMM. The Maintain Inventory Items
   window appears for INSTL HARD – COMM, Install Hardscape – Comm.
   If the Sage Advisor appears, read it. To close it, click ⊗.

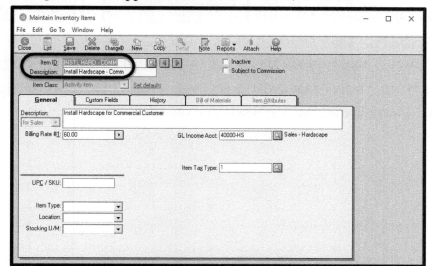

Review the information on the Maintain Inventory Items window. As you move to different fields, read the information that explains each field (Item ID, Description, etc.). Observe that $60.00 is shown in the Billing Rate #1 field. Click on the right-arrow to see other billing rates, then close the Multiple Price Levels window. The GL Income Acct is Account No. 40000-HS, Sales – Hardscape. The Item Tax Type is 1 (for Taxable). This maintenance window is similar to ones that you have set up before.

Remember, defaults are set up in maintenance windows.

3. Close all windows to return to the Inventory & Services Navigation Center.

Time Ticket

The Time Ticket shows how much was billed to the customer. To see how time is billed, look at a job that Alan Hardman has already completed.
Follow these steps to see time tickets.

1. From the Navigation Bar, click [Employees & Payroll] > [Time and Expense Ticket] > View and Edit Time Tickets. The Time Tickets List window appears.
2. Scroll down. Select Ticket No. 282, 3/12/2019, AHARDMAN, INSTL HARD –COMM, OHARA, 03-Installation. A partial Time Tickets List window is shown on the next page.

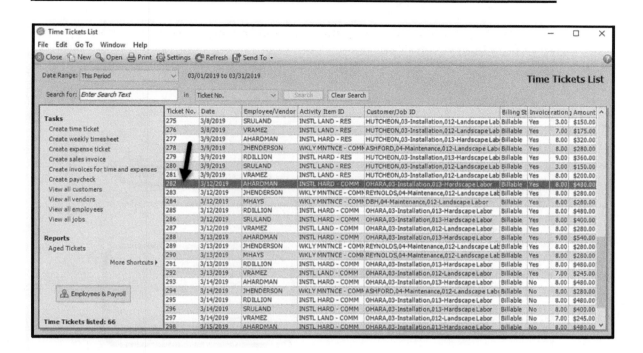

3. Click [🔍 Open]. The Time Tickets window appears. Notice that the Activity
    Item is for **INSTL HARD – COMM**, Activity name is Install Hardscape –
    Comm, and that the Job name is O'Hara Homes Contract. The Invoice
    description is Installation of Decking/Patio. Mr. Hardman worked for eight
    hours on March 12, 2019; and the Billing amount is 480.00. The Time
    Tickets window shows one instance, March 12, 2019 (refer to the Ticket
    date field.)

4. Click 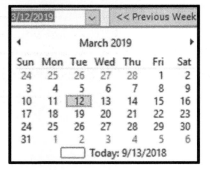 . The Time Ticket Weekly Timesheet Entry window appears. In the Week including field, click on the down arrow. The calendar appears. Select March 12, 2019. (*Hint:* The Week including field may default to the current date. To select the date, use the calendar.)

The Time Ticket Weekly Timesheet Entry window is shown on the next page. The OHara job completed on 3/12 is shown.

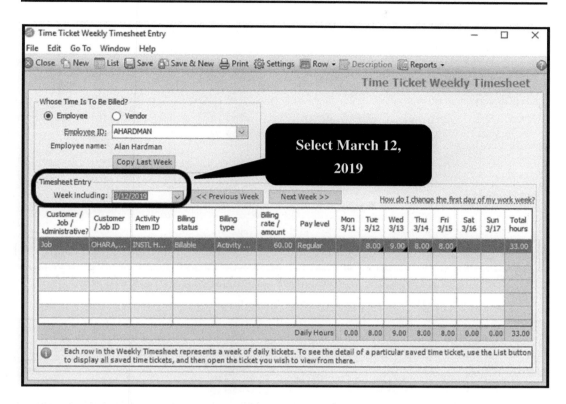

5. Close all windows.

Sales Invoice

In order to see how Mr. Hardman's charges were billed to the customer, O'Hara Homes, follow these steps.

1. From the Navigation Bar, click **Customers & Sales** > Sales Invoice > View and Edit Sales Invoices. The Sales Invoice List appears. Click on OHARA, Invoice No. 1008, 3/13/2019 to highlight it.

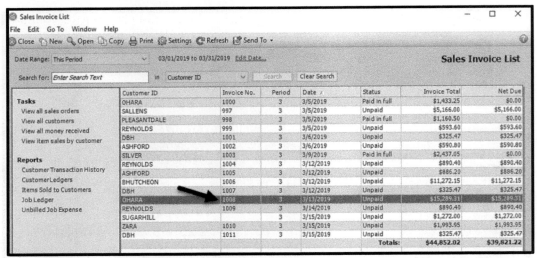

2. Double-click OHARA, Invoice 1008. A partial Sales/Invoicing window appears. Scroll down to see all of it, *or* enlarge the Sales/Invoicing window.

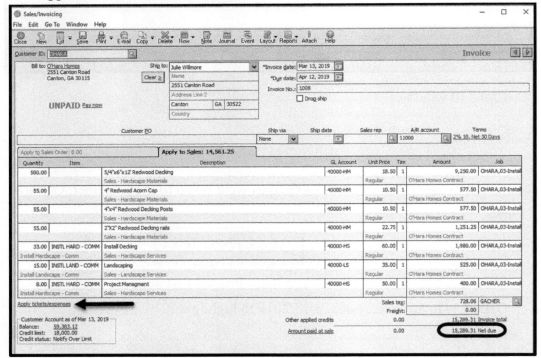

3. Link to <u>Apply tickets/expenses</u>. (*Hint: This is located in the lower left of the window.*)

4. The Apply Tickets/Reimbursable Expenses window appears. Observe that Alan Hardman's work is billed, along with other employees that worked on this customer's job.

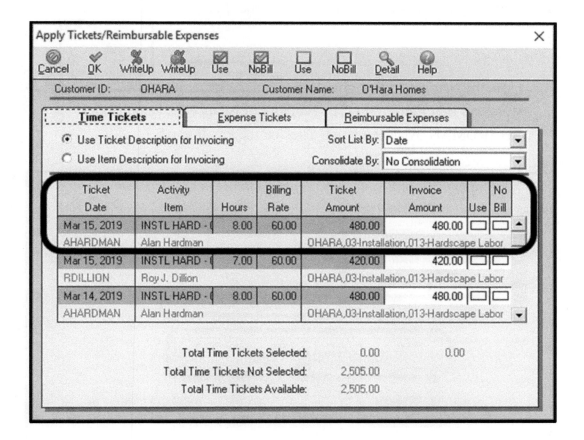

The time ticket shows Alan Hardman's Ticket Amount of 480.00 for 8 hours at a billing rate of $60.00 ($60 x 8 = $480).

5. Click [OK] to close the Apply Tickets/Reimbursable Expenses window. You are returned to the O'Hara Homes Sales/Invoicing window.

6. Close all windows to return to the Customers & Sales Navigation Center.

Payroll

Payroll also needs to be set up. You do this by selecting Hourly-Time Ticket Hours for employees. Let's see how Stone Arbor Landscaping sets this up.

1.   From the Navigation Bar, click **Employees & Payroll** > **Employees** >
     View and Edit Employees. The Employee List appears. Double-click
     AHARDMAN, Alan Hardman. Click on the Pay Info tab.

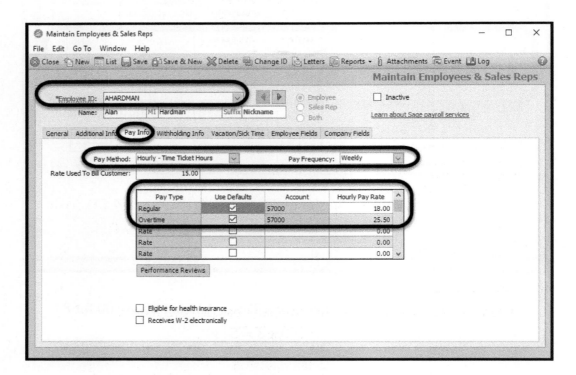

Observe that Mr. Hardman's Pay Method is Hourly – Time Ticket Hours. He is paid weekly. Also notice that Mr. Hardman's regular pay account number is 57000.

2.   Close all windows. If prompted, do not save this record.

BACKING UP CHAPTER 8 DATA

Follow these steps to back up Chapter 8 data:

1. If necessary, insert your USB flash drive. From the System Navigation Center, link to | Back Up Now |. Make sure that the box next to Include company name in the backup file name is *unchecked*.

2. Click | Back Up |.
3. In the Save in field, select the appropriate drive letter for your USB drive. (*Or*, save to the hard-drive default location or other location.) Type **Chapter 8** in the File name field.
4. Click | Save |.
5. When the window prompts This company backup will require approximately 1 diskette, click | OK |. When the window prompts Please insert the first disk, click | OK |. When the Back Up Company scale is 100% complete, you have successfully backed up to the current point in Chapter 8. (Step 5 will differ slightly if you are backing up to the default or other hard-drive location.)

EXPORT TIME TICKET REGISTER TO EXCEL

Follow these steps to export the Time Ticket Register to Excel.

1. From the Reports & Forms menu, select Time/Expense > highlight Time Ticket Register

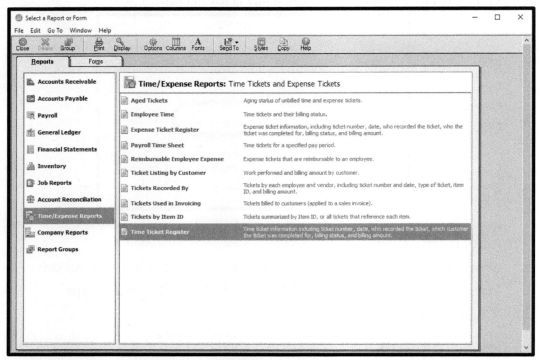

2. Click Send To, Excel.

Troubleshooting: If you are using Microsoft Office 365, the Excel icon may be inactive. Display the Sage report > select Edit > Copy > start Excel > open a blank workbook > right click on the sheet > left-click Paste > reformat > save as Chapter 8_Time Ticket Register. On page v, Integration/compatibility requirements lists which versions of Microsoft Office work with Sage 50 2019.

3.   The Modify Report – Time Ticket Register window appears, click

OK

4.   The Copy Report to Excel window appears. In the File option area, make sure Create a new Microsoft Excel workbook is selected.

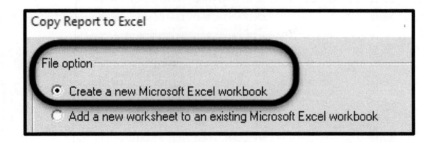

5.   In the Report header option area, Show header in Excel worksheet should be selected.

6.   Click   OK . Stone Arbor Landscaping's Time Ticket Register is exported to Excel. Scroll down the Register. Ticket No. 282 for AHardman is shown. The Time Tickets List window on page 237 also shows this job. A partial Time Ticket Register is shown on the next page.

Stone Arbor Landscaping - Student Name
Time Ticket Register
For the Period From Mar 1, 2019 to Mar 31, 2019
Filter Criteria includes: Report order is by Ticket Number.

Ticket Number	Ticket Date	Recorded by ID	Item ID	Completed for ID	Billing Status	Billing Amount
234	3/1/19	JWHITE	DESIGN - COMM	SILVER	Billable	490.00
235	3/1/19	AHARDMAN	INSTL HARD - CO	SALLENS	Billable	540.00
236	3/1/19	JHENDERSON	WKLY MNTNCE -	ASHFORD,04-Mai	Billable	280.00
237	3/1/19	MHAYS	INSTL LAND - CO	OHARA,03-Installa	Billable	280.00
238	3/1/19	RDILLION	INSTL HARD - CO	SALLENS	Billable	540.00
239	3/1/19	VRAMEZ	PRESS CLNG - CO	PLEASANTDALE	Billable	140.00
240	3/2/19	JWHITE	DESIGN - COMM	SILVER	Billable	490.00
241	3/2/19	AHARDMAN	INSTL HARD - CO	SALLENS	Billable	540.00
242	3/2/19	JHENDERSON	WKLY MNTNCE -	ASHFORD,04-Mai	Billable	280.00
243	3/2/19	MHAYS	INSTL LAND - CO	OHARA,03-Installa	Billable	245.00
244	3/2/19	RDILLION	INSTL HARD - CO	SALLENS	Billable	540.00
245	3/2/19	VRAMEZ	PRESS CLNG - CO	PLEASANTDALE	Billable	120.00
246	3/5/19	KGREENE	DESIGN - COMM	ZARA	Billable	490.00
247	3/5/19	JWHITE	DESIGN - COMM	SILVER	Billable	420.00
248	3/5/19	AHARDMAN	INSTL LAND - RES	HUTCHEON,03-In	Billable	175.00
249	3/5/19	JHENDERSON	WKLY MNTNCE -	REYNOLDS,04-Ma	Billable	280.00
250	3/5/19	MHAYS	WKLY MNTNCE -	DBH,04-Maintenan	Billable	280.00
251	3/5/19	RDILLION	INSTL HARD - RES	HUTCHEON,03-In	Billable	320.00
252	3/5/19	SRULAND	INSTL LAND - RES	HUTCHEON,03-In	Billable	300.00
253	3/5/19	VRAMEZ	INSTL LAND - RES	HUTCHEON,03-In	Billable	200.00
255	3/6/19	KGREENE	DESIGN - COMM	ZARA	Billable	490.00
256	3/6/19	JWHITE	DESIGN - COMM	SILVER	Billable	420.00
257	3/6/19	AHARDMAN	INSTL LAND - RES	HUTCHEON,03-In	Billable	175.00
258	3/6/19	JHENDERSON	WKLY MNTNCE -	REYNOLDS,04-Ma	Billable	280.00
259	3/6/19	MHAYS	WKLY MNTNCE -	REYNOLDS,04-Ma	Billable	280.00
260	3/6/19	RDILLION	INSTL HARD - RES	HUTCHEON,03-In	Billable	320.00
261	3/6/19	SRULAND	INSTL LAND - RES	HUTCHEON,03-In	Billable	150.00
262	3/6/19	VRAMEZ	INSTL LAND - RES	HUTCHEON,03-In	Billable	175.00
263	3/7/19	KGREENE	DESIGN - COMM	ZARA	Billable	420.00
264	3/7/19	AHARDMAN	INSTL LAND - RES	HUTCHEON,03-In	Billable	50.00
265	3/7/19	AHARDMAN	INSTL HARD - RES	HUTCHEON,03-In	Billable	360.00
267	3/7/19	JHENDERSON	WKLY MNTNCE -	ASHFORD,04-Mai	Billable	280.00
268	3/7/19	RDILLION	INSTL HARD - RES	HUTCHEON,03-In	Billable	320.00
269	3/7/19	SRULAND	INSTL LAND - RES	HUTCHEON,03-In	Billable	150.00
270	3/7/19	VRAMEZ	INSTL LAND - RES	HUTCHEON,03-In	Billable	200.00
271	3/8/19	KGREENE	DESIGN - COMM	ZARA	Billable	490.00
272	3/8/19	AHARDMAN	INSTL HARD - RES	HUTCHEON,03-In	Billable	360.00
273	3/8/19	JHENDERSON	WKLY MNTNCE -	ASHFORD,04-Mai	Billable	280.00
274	3/8/19	RDILLION	INSTL HARD - RES	HUTCHEON,03-In	Billable	360.00
275	3/8/19	SRULAND	INSTL LAND - RES	HUTCHEON,03-In	Billable	150.00
276	3/8/19	VRAMEZ	INSTL LAND - RES	HUTCHEON,03-In	Billable	175.00
277	3/9/19	AHARDMAN	INSTL HARD - RES	HUTCHEON,03-In	Billable	320.00
278	3/9/19	JHENDERSON	WKLY MNTNCE -	ASHFORD,04-Mai	Billable	280.00
279	3/9/19	RDILLION	INSTL HARD - RES	HUTCHEON,03-In	Billable	360.00
280	3/9/19	SRULAND	INSTL LAND - RES	HUTCHEON,03-In	Billable	150.00
281	3/9/19	VRAMEZ	INSTL LAND - RES	HUTCHEON,03-In	Billable	200.00
282	3/12/19	AHARDMAN	INSTL HARD - CO	OHARA,03-Installa	Billable	480.00
283	3/12/19	JHENDERSON	WKLY MNTNCE -	REYNOLDS,04-Ma	Billable	280.00
284	3/12/19	MHAYS	WKLY MNTNCE -	DBH,04-Maintenan	Billable	280.00
285	3/12/19	RDILLION	INSTL HARD - CO	OHARA,03-Installa	Billable	480.00
286	3/12/19	SRULAND	INSTL HARD - CO	OHARA,03-Installa	Billable	400.00
287	3/12/19	VRAMEZ	INSTL LAND - CO	OHARA,03-Installa	Billable	280.00
288	3/13/19	AHARDMAN	INSTL HARD - CO	OHARA,03-Installa	Billable	540.00
289	3/13/19	JHENDERSON	WKLY MNTNCE -	REYNOLDS,04-Ma	Billable	280.00
290	3/13/19	MHAYS	WKLY MNTNCE -	REYNOLDS,04-Ma	Billable	280.00

7. Save. Use the file name **Chapter 8_Time Ticket Register.xlsx**. Close all windows.

8. Save the Time Ticket Register as a PDF file. Use **Chapter 8_Time Ticket Register.pdf** as the file name.

ONLINE LEARNING CENTER

Complete the following end-of-chapter activities online at
www.mhhe.com/yacht2019 > Student Edition > Chapter 8.

1. Interactive Multiple-Choice and True/False questions.
2. Going to the Net exercise: Access the Sage Support Resources website and
    watch a video.
3. QA Templates: 10 multiple choice questions and one analysis question.
4. Assessment Rubric: Review journals, navigation centers, modules, and task
    windows.
5. Listen to narrated PowerPoint slides.

The OLC also includes links to the Appendixes:

•   Appendix A: Troubleshooting (textbook and OLC)
•   Appendix C: Review of Accounting Principles (OLC Student Edition)
•   Appendix D: Glossary of Terms (OLC Student Edition)

Exercise 8-1: Complete the following time ticket, sales invoice, and payroll
entry.

1. If necessary, restore the Chapter 8.ptb file (backup on page 243).
2. Enter a new time ticket for the employee, Mike E. Hays. Complete the
    following Time Ticket fields.

    Employee ID: Mike E. Hays
    To be applied: Against a Job
    Job ID: DBH
              04-Maintenance
              012 Landscape Labor

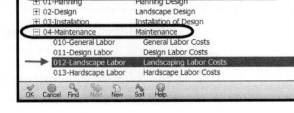

Hint: Click on the plus sign next to DBH to expand the list. Expand 04-

Maintenance, then select 012 Landscape Labor.

Activity item:	Weekly Maintenance - Comm
Invoice description:	Weekly Maintenance
Ticket Date:	Mar 15, 2019
Duration:	8:00
Billing status:	Billable
Billing type:	Activity Rate

3. Save the Time Ticket.
4. Record the following sales invoice.

Date	*Description*
03/22/19	Apply the completed time ticket to Invoice 1019. (*Hint:* Enter a new sales invoice.) On the Sales/Invoicing window, complete these fields:

Customer ID:	DBH Enterprises
Date:	March 22, 2019
Invoice No.:	1019

Link to Apply tickets/expenses. The Apply Tickets/Reimbursable Expenses window appears showing the Time Ticket information. Select the Use box to place a checkmark in it. Click <OK>. The Apply to Sales portion of the Sales/Invoicing window is completed. Observe that the Net due shows $295.40. Post the sales invoice.

5. Display the Time Ticket for Mike E. Hays. Observe that Invoice No. 1019 is applied.
6. Record the following payroll entry.

03/23/19   Pay employee, Mike E. Hays for 24 regular hours. Select the Jobs icon to see the two jobs Mr. Hays completed during this pay period. Post the payroll entry.

7.   Backup. The suggested file name is **Exercise 8-1**.

Exercise 8-2:   To complete Exercise 8-2, do the following.

1.   If necessary, restore the Exercise 8-1.ptb backup file.
2.   Print the Job Ledger Report. (*Hint:* Reports & Forms > Jobs > Job Ledger.

How to Fix? I don't have a printer?

Select <Print>, then in the Name field, Adobe PDF or Microsoft XPS Document Writer. Save to USB drive. For detailed steps, refer to page 65. Use for steps 2 through 4. If you save as PDF files, use the file names shown in step 6.

---

3.   Print the Time Ticket Register. (*Hint:* Reports & Forms > Time/Expense Reports > Time Ticket Register.)

4.   Print the Payroll Time Sheet. (*Hint:* Reports & Forms > Time/Expense Reports > Payroll Time Sheet. Select [Options]. The Pay End Date is 3/15/19.

5.   Save the three Time & Billing Reports as an Excel file: Job Ledger, Time Ticket Register, and Payroll Time Sheet. The suggested file name is **Exercise 8-2_Time and Billing Reports.xlsx**.

6.   Save three PDF files: **Exercise 8-2_Job Ledger.pdf**, **Exercise 8-2_Time Ticket Register.pdf**, and **Exercise 8-2_Payroll Time Sheet.pdf**.

CHAPTER 8 INDEX

Part 2

Sage 50 2019 for Service Businesses

In Part 2 of *Computer Accounting with Sage 50 2019, 21th Edition,* you are the owner of an accounting practice. Your accounting business does monthly record keeping for local service businesses.

In Chapters 9, 10, 11, Projects 1 and 1A (Part 2), you use Sage 50 to set up four service businesses, complete the accounting cycle, and close the fiscal year. In Part 2, entries are recorded in the Receive Money window (Cash Receipts Journal) and the Write Checks window (Cash Disbursements Journal). Also, adjusting entries are recorded in the General Journal. At the end of each month, you reconcile the bank statement and print the general ledger trial balance and financial statements. At the end of the fourth quarter, you use Sage 50 to complete end-of-quarter adjusting entries, print the adjusted trial balance, print financial statements, close the fiscal year, and print a postclosing trial balance.

After entering deposits and payments, the next step is to post them to the general ledger. One of the best features of a computerized accounting system is how quickly *posting* is done. Once entries are recorded and checked for accuracy, posting is a click of the mouse. Then, account balances are calculated and financial statements are completed. The diagram below illustrates this process.

Journalize and Post   **General Ledger**   **Financial Statements**

This illustration shows the *Sage 50 accounting system*.

- Software is installed.
- Companies are set up.
- Transactions are journalized in the general journal or special journals, and then posted to the general ledger and subsidiary ledgers.
- After entering transactions, reports are printed.

Sage 50 is a *double-entry accounting* system which means that the equation Assets = Liabilities + Equity is always in balance. Since a debit in one account will be offset by a credit in another account, the sum of all debits is equal to the sum of all credits.

To assure double-entry accounting procedures, Sage 50 includes accounting periods and the fiscal year, the general journal and special journals, general ledger and subsidiary ledgers, account reconciliation, an audit trail, and financial reports. The Sage 50 accounting system also includes closing the fiscal year.

In Part 2, you set up companies, journalize transactions in the Cash Receipts and Cash Disbursements Journals, post to the General Ledger, complete account reconciliation, print the Financial Statements, and close the fiscal year.

The accounting cycle is completed for the fourth quarter. The accuracy of your general ledger and financial statement reports depends on the accuracy of the entries recorded on the Write Checks (Cash Disbursements Journal) and Receive Money (Cash Receipts Journal) windows. Once entries are posted, account reconciliation is completed.

Chapters 9, 10 and 11 work together. The service businesses set up in Chapter 9 are continued in Chapters 10 and 11. Part 2 ends with two comprehensive projects.

Chapter 9:   New Company Setup and Beginning Balances
Chapter 10:   Maintaining Accounting Records for Service Businesses
Chapter 11:   Completing Quarterly Activities and Closing the Fiscal Year
Project 1:   Marcia Westcott, Accounting
Project 1A: Student-Designed Service Business

Part 2 includes three chapters and two projects: Chapters 9, 10, and 11 and Projects 1 and 1A. In Chapters 9, 10, and 11, you set up two service businesses from scratch—James Crosby Designer and Crafts by Student Name (after Crafts by, students add first and last name).

You complete accounting tasks for the fourth quarter–October, November and December 2019. You also complete end-of-quarter adjusting entries. At the end of Chapter 9, a new service business is set up in Exercise 9-1. The service business set up in Exercise 9-1 is continued in Exercises 9-2, 10-1, 10-2, 11-1 and 11-2.

In Project 1, you complete the accounting cycle for Marcia Westcott, Accounting. This project gives you an opportunity to apply what you have learned in Chapters 9, 10, and 11. At the end of Project 1, there is a Check Your Progress assessment.

Project 1A is an opportunity to design a service business of your own. You select a chart of accounts, write and journalize transactions, reconcile the bank statement, and complete the accounting cycle for the business.

The chart below and on pages 255-256 shows the size of the backups, Excel files, and PDF files saved in Part 2–Chapters 9, 10, 11, and Project 1. The textbook shows how to back up to a USB drive. Backups can be made to the desktop, hard drive location, network location or external media.

Chapter	Sage 50 Backup (.ptb) Excel (.xlsx) and Adobe (.pdf)	Kilobytes	Page Nos.
9	Chapter 9 Chart of Accounts.ptb	918 KB	276-278
	Chapter 9 Beginning Balances.ptb	922 KB	292-293
	Chapter 9_Chart of Accounts and Beginning Balances.xlsx	17 KB	293-295
	Chapter 9_Balance Sheet.pdf	5 KB	296
	Chapter 9_Chart of Accounts.pdf	8 KB	296
	Exercise 9-1.ptb	914 KB	300
	Exercise 9-2.ptb	917 KB	303
	Exercise 9-2_Chart of Accounts and Beginning Balances.xlsx	17 KB	303
	Exercise 9-2_Chart of Accounts.pdf	8 KB	303
	Exercise 9-2_Balance Sheet.pdf	4 KB	303
10	Chapter 10 Transaction Register October.ptb	966 KB	315-316
	Chapter 10 October.ptb	1,010 KB	329
	Chapter 10_October Trial Balance and Financial Statements.xlsx	21 KB	329-331
	Chapter 10_October Trial Balance.pdf	11 KB	331

Chapter	Sage 50 Backup (.ptb), Excel (.xlsx), and Adobe (.pdf)	Kilobytes	Page Nos.
10	Chapter 10_October Income Statement.pdf	11 KB	331
	Chapter 10_October Balance Sheet.pdf	11 KB	331
	Exercise 10-1.ptb	950 KB	333
	Exercise 10-2.ptb	958 KB	335
	Exercise 10-2_October Trial Balance and Financial Statements.xlsx.	20 KB	335
	Exercise 10-2_October Trial Balance.pdf	6 KB	335
	Exercise 10-2_October Balance Sheet.pdf	4 KB	335
	Exercise 10-2_October Income Statement.pdf	5 KB	335
11	Chapter 11 November.ptb	1,013 KB	350
	Chapter 11 December UTB.ptb	1,030 KB	357
	Chapter 11 December.ptb	1,030 KB	367
	Chapter 11_Adjusted Trial Balance and Financial Statements.xlsx	29 KB	368-369
	Chapter 11_Adjusted Trial Balance.pdf	14 KB	369
	Chapter 11_December Balance Sheet.pdf	11 KB	369
	Chapter 11_December Income Statement.pdf	12 KB	369
	Chapter 11_December Statement of Cash Flow.pdf	12 KB	369
	Chapter 11_December Statement of Retained Earnings.pdf	8 KB	369
	Chapter 11 EOY.ptb	1,039 KB	376
	Chapter 11_Postclosing Trial Balance.xlsx	12 KB	376
	Chapter 11_Postclosing Trial Balance.pdf	12 KB	376
	Asset depreciation.xlsx (Going to the Net)	15 KB	OLC
	Exercise 11-1.ptb	976 KB	380
	Exercise 11-2 Unadjusted Trial Balance.ptb	1,012 KB	383
	Exercise 11-2 Financial Statements.ptb	1,104 KB	383

Chapter/ Project	Sage 50 Backup (.ptb), Excel (.xlsx), and Adobe (.pdf)	Kilobytes	Page Nos.
11	Exercise 11-2_Adjusted Trial Balance and Financial Statements.xlsx	28 KB	383
	Exercise 11-2_Adjusted Trial Balance.pdf	13 KB	384
	Exercise 11-2_Balance Sheet.pdf	10 KB	384
	Exercise 11-2_Income Statement.pdf	12 KB	384
	Exercise 11-2_Statement of Cash Flow.pdf	11 KB	384
	Exercise 11-2_Statement of Retained Earnings.pdf	4 KB	384
	Exercise 11-2 End of Year.ptb	1,022 KB	384
	Exercise 11-2_Postclosing Trial Balance.xlsx	12 KB	384
	Exercise 11-2_Postclosing Trial Balance.pdf	11 KB	384
Project 1	Marcia Westcott Chart of Accounts.ptb	915 KB	390
	Marcia Westcott Beginning Balances.ptb	917 KB	392
	Marcia Westcott UTB.ptb	976 KB	394
	Marcia Westcott December.ptb	976 KB	395
	Marcia Westcott_Adjusted Trial Balance and Financial Statements.xlsx	28 KB	395
	Project 1_Adjusted Trial Balance.pdf	13 KB	395
	Project 1_Balance Sheet.pdf	11 KB	395
	Project 1_Income Statement.pdf	11 KB	395
	Project 1_Statement of Cash Flow.pdf	12 KB	395
	Project 1_Statement of Retained Earnings.pdf	8 KB	395
	Marcia Westcott EOY.ptb	984 KB	395
	Marcia Westcott_Postclosing Trial Balance.xlsx	12 KB	395
	Project 1_Postclosing Trial Balance.pdf	12 KB	395

Chapter 9

New Company Setup and Beginning Balances

LEARNING OBJECTIVES

1. Set up company information for James Crosby Designer.
2. Select a Service Company from the simplified chart of accounts list.
3. Edit the chart of accounts and enter beginning balances.
4. Use File Explorer to see the company's file size.
5. Make four backups, save two Excel files, and save four PDF files.[1]

Chapter 9 begins Part 2 of the book–Sage 50 2019 for Service Businesses. The chapters in Part 2 work together. The service businesses set up in Chapter 9 are continued in Chapters 10 and 11. The two businesses set up in Chapter 9 are James Crosby [your first and last name] Designer, and another service business in Exercise 9-1, Crafts by your first and last name. In Chapter 9, you set up a service business using one of Sage 50's sample companies. Then, edit a chart of accounts and enter beginning balances. When setting up companies, use your first and last name; for example, Your Name Designer and Crafts by Your Name.

GETTING STARTED: NEW COMPANY SETUP

James Crosby is a designer and educator. His sources of income are design work, book royalties, and part-time teaching at Milwaukee Community College. He is single and has no dependents.

---

[1]Refer to page 254 for the file names and size of backups, Excel and PDF files.

▶ Follow these steps to set up the company, James Crosby Designer. (*Hint:* The arrow indicates a video at www.mhhe.com/yacht2019. Link to Student Edition > select Chapter 9 > Videos > Set up a new company.)

1. Start Sage 50. (If a company opens, click File > Close Company.)

2. At the startup window, click [🪄 **Create a New Company**]. The Create a New Company window appears. Read the information.

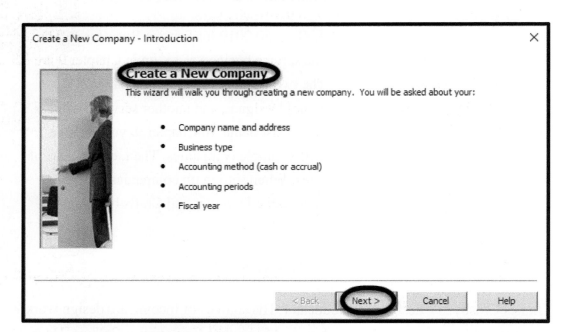

3. After clicking [Next >], type the company information shown on the next page. Press the **\<Tab\>** or **\<Enter\>** key between each field.

Company Information

Company Name:	**James Crosby Designer (use your name)**[2]
Address Line 1:	**788 Lake Drive**
City, State, Zip:	**Milwaukee, WI 53205**
Country:	**USA**
Telephone:	**414-555-8990**
Fax:	**414-555-1900**
Business Type:	Select Sole Proprietorship
Web Site:	**www.jamescrosby.com**
E-Mail:	**info@jamescrosby.com**

Compare your Create a New Company - Company Information window to the one shown. *The company name field should include your first and last name Designer. Do not complete the ID fields. (Hint: Observe that there is a red asterisk next to Company Name. The asterisk indicates a required field.)*

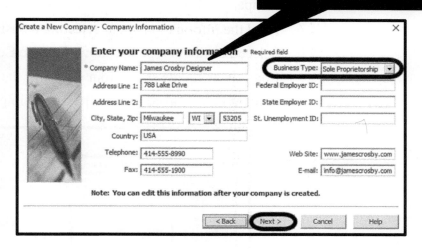

4. Check the company information > click Next > . The Select a method to create your company window appears.

[2]Boldface indicates information that you type. Substitute your name for James Crosby. If you use your first and last name Designer as the company name, Sage 50 printouts show your name.

5. Accept the default to Use a sample business that closely matches your company (**Most companies choose this**). Click Next > .

6. Read the information about selecting a business type. Observe that the Select a business type list shows Service Company selected, and that the Chart of Accounts shows four digits for the account numbers. Four-digit account numbers are used with Sage's simplified chart of accounts.

7. Make sure that Simplified types, Service Company is highlighted, and the Chart of Accounts numbers show 4 digits > click Next > .

8. Accept the default for Accrual, by clicking Next > . The Choose a
    posting method window appears. Real Time posting is the default.

9. Accept the default for Real Time posting, by clicking Next >. The Choose an accounting period structure window appears.

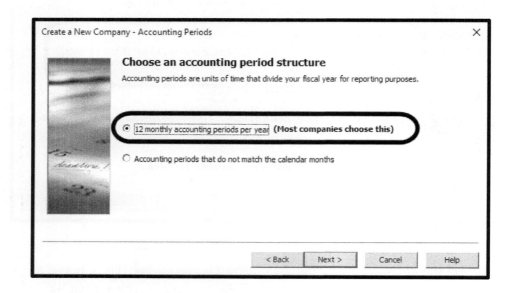

10. Accept the default for 12 monthly accounting periods per year by clicking Next >. The Choose the first period of your fiscal year window appears. **Select 2019** (if necessary).

11. Make sure the Choose the first period of your fiscal year window shows **January 2019**. **This window is important. The year cannot be changed after your company is created**. Click [Next >]. You are ready to create your company window appears.

12. Read the information on the Finish window. Click [Finish]. If the screen prompts You can use this company in the student version of Sage 50 Accounting for the next 14 months and then it will expire, click [OK]. After a few moments (be patient), the James Crosby Designer - Sage 50 Accounting window appears. (Substitute your first and last name for James Crosby.)

13. When the Setup Guide window appears, read the information. Click on the box next to [✓ Don't show this screen at startup.] > click [Close]. When the Sage 50 Setup Guide appears, click on the box next to Do not display this message again [✓ Do not display this message again.], then [OK] to close it. If the Sage Advisor Getting Started window appears in the right pane, click on [⊗] to close it. To watch the videos, go to www.mhhe.com/yacht2019 > Sage Advisor Videos.

14. On the Navigation Bar, click . To set the Business Status Navigation Center as your default page, from the toolbar click

    . When you open James Crosby Designer, the Business Status Navigation Center will appear.

15. On the toolbar (right side of window), click on the Period button

    . The Change Accounting Period window appears. Click 10 – Oct 01, 2019 to Oct 31, 2019 to highlight it.

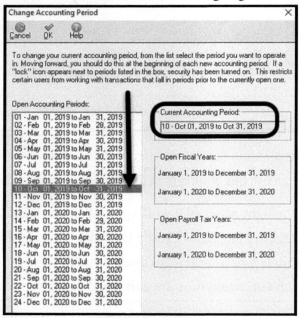

    Selecting the accounting period sets up the month for recording transactions.

16. Make sure Period 10 is selected. October 2019 is the first

    month for recording transactions >click [OK]. If a window prompts that transactions may need to be reviewed, click on the box next to Do not display this message again. Then, click [No].

17. Check that Period 10 – 10/01/19-10/31/19 appears on the toolbar

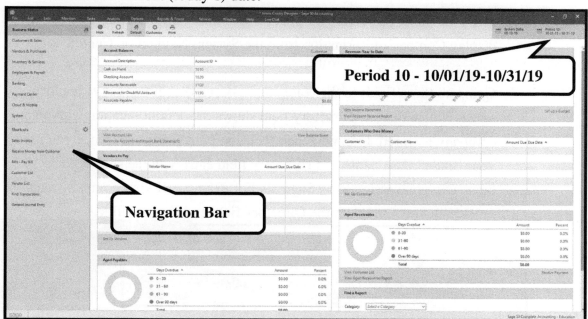

. The Period appears next to the System Date, which is the current (today's) date.

Read Me: *What is Sage 50's shortened name?*

1. From the menu bar, select Help > Support Utilities > File Statistics. The company's shortened name is shown on the title bar. The Data File Statistics for XXXXXXDE window appears. (Substitute the Xs with your shortened name.) This represents the shortened name of the open company. Observe that there is also a Directory field at the bottom of the Data File Statistics window. The directory where James Crosby Designer resides on the computer is C:\sage\Peachtree\Company\jamcrode. (Since you used your first and last name, the first six letters of the shortened name will differ.)

2. Click OK to close the Data File Statistics window.

Company Maintenance Information

Follow these steps to see information.

1. From the menu bar, select Maintain > Company Information. You can also display Company Information from the System Navigation Center.

2. Compare these fields to the company information below. They should agree. Notice that the Directory field shows the default location where your company is stored: C:\sage\Peachtree\ Company\jamcrode. Since you used your first and last name, the Directory field ends with the shortened company name assigned by Sage 50. For example, if your company name is Janet Williams Designer, the Directory field ends in \janwilde.

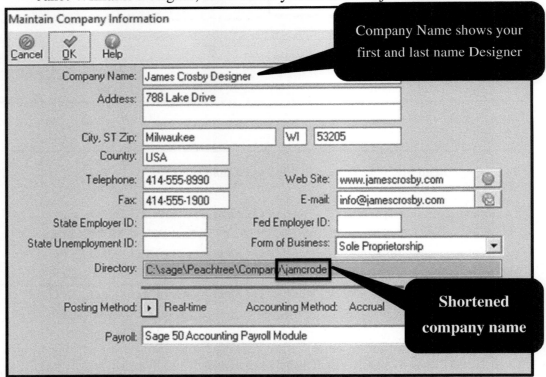

3. Click [OK] to return to the Business Status Navigation Center.

CHART OF ACCOUNTS

The chart of accounts is a list of all the accounts in the general ledger. When you selected Service Company from the list of business types, a chart of accounts was included. Follow these steps to edit the sample chart of accounts.

Delete Accounts

1. From the Business Status Navigation Center, link to <u>View Account List</u>. The Account List appears. (*Or,* you can use the menu bar. Select Maintain > Chart of Accounts > in the Account ID field, click the down-arrow, continue with step 2.)
2. Double click Account ID, 1150, Allowance for Doubtful Account. The Maintain Chart of Accounts window appears.

3. Click Delete .
4. Sage 50 Accounting – Are you sure you want to delete this record? appears.

5. Click Yes .

6. Delete the accounts shown on the chart below. (*Hint:* On the Maintain Chart of Accounts window, type the account number in the Account ID field to expedite editing the chart of accounts.)

Acct. ID	Account Description
2310	Sales Tax Payable
2320	Deductions Payable
2330	Federal Payroll Taxes Payable
2340	FUTA Payable
2350	State Payroll Taxes Payable
2360	SUTA Payable
2370	Local Taxes Payable
2500	Current Portion Long-Term Debt
2700	Long-Term Debt-Noncurrent
4300	Other Income
5900	Inventory Adjustments
6050	Employee Benefit Programs Exp
6250	Other Taxes Expense
6650	Commissions and Fees Expense
7100	Gain/Loss - Sale of Assets Exp

Change Accounts

1. On the Maintain Chart of Accounts window, type **3920** > Press <Tab> or <Enter>. Owner's Contribution appears in the Description field.

2. Type **James Crosby, Capital** (use your first and last name, Capital). Press
   <Tab> or <Enter>.

3. In the Account Type field, click the down arrow. Select Equity-doesn't
   close.

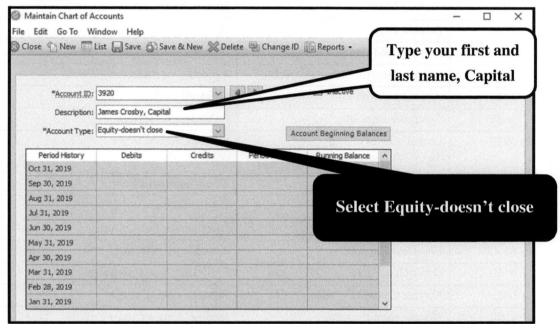

> **Read Me: The Account Type is important**. Make sure the Capital account shows
> **Equity-doesn't close.** The Account Type determines how the account is used and where
> it appears on financial reports. The Account Type classifies the account for financial reports *and* the
> automatic closing process. Once you set up an account and post transactions, you should be very
> careful about changing the account type. Changing the account type could cause your financial
> reporting to be incorrect or inconsistent. If you need to change the account type, you should make the
> account inactive and create a new account with the correct account type.

4. Click 🖫 Save .

5. Change the names of the accounts shown below. (*Hint:* When you change the Account Description, the Account Type does not need to be changed.

Acct. ID	Account Description	New Account Description
1010	Cash on Hand	**Money Market Account**
1400	Prepaid Expenses	**Prepaid Rent**
1500	Property and Equipment	**Computer Equipment**
1900	Accum. Depreciation – Prop&Eqt	**Accum. Depreciation – Comp Eqt**
2000	Accounts Payable	**VISA Payable**
2400	Customer Deposits	**Publisher Advances**
3930	Owner's Draw	**James Crosby, Draw** (your name, Draw)
4000	Professional Fees	**Teaching Income**
4050	Sales of Materials	**Royalty Income**
6100	Payroll Tax Expense	**Dues and Subscriptions**
6150	Bad Debt Expense	**Auto Registration**
6550	Other Office Expense	**Long Distance Company**
6850	Service Charge Expense	**Bank Service Charge**
7050	Depreciation Expense	**Deprec. Exp. - Comp Eqt**

Add Accounts

1. On the Maintain Chart of Accounts window, click [New].
2. In the Account ID field, type **1040** and press **<Enter>**.
3. In the Description field, type **IRA Savings Account** and press **<Enter>**.
4. In the Account Type field, Cash is the default. Click on the down arrow. A list of account types drops down. Make sure that Cash is highlighted. If not, click once on Cash to select it.

On the right side of the Maintain Chart of Accounts window is an explanation of Account Type (if necessary, go to the Account Type field). Read the information. (*Hint*: If necessary, click on Advisor – vertical bar on the right side of Maintain Chart of Accounts.)

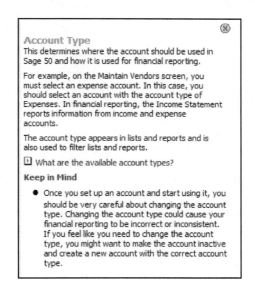

Read Me: *Why is the Account Type field important?*

Observe that the Account Type field shows Cash for the IRA Savings Account. This is an important field – the Account Type field classifies each account for the financial statements. For example, Account No. 1040, IRA Savings Account, is classified as Cash, which means this account will appear on the Balance Sheet and Statement of Cash Flow, but *not* on the Income Statement or Statement of Retained Earnings. The companies you set up in Chapter 9 continue in Chapters 10 and 11. If you select the *wrong* Account Type, transactions will post incorrectly and the financial statements will be inaccurate. The automatic closing process is also affected because Account Type selections affect the postclosing trial balance. *When using accounting software, each process relates to the next step.*

---

5. Click [Save & New] . (*Hint:* What is the difference between Save & New and Save? If you click Save, the Account Type does not change. If you have a couple of accounts with the same Account Type, click Save, then change the Account ID and Description. The Account Type stays the same.)

Important – Account Type field. The Account Type field determines where the accounts appear on financial statements. For example, the Income Statement lists information from the Income and Expense accounts. Make sure you select the account types shown below.

Add the following accounts:

Acct. ID	Account Description	Account Type
1045	WI State Retirement	Cash
1300	Prepaid Insurance	Other Current Assets
1450	Supplies	Other Current Assets
1510	Furniture	Fixed Assets
1520	Automobile	Fixed Assets
1910	Accum. Depreciation – Furnitur	Accumulated Depreciation
1920	Accum. Depreciation – Automobi	Accumulated Depreciation
6560	Internet Service Provider	Expenses
7060	Deprec. Exp. - Furniture	Expenses
7070	Deprec. Exp. - Automobile	Expenses

6. Click [Close] after completing the Chart of Accounts. If necessary, close all windows. You are returned to the Business Status Navigation Center.

Display the Chart of Accounts

1. From the menu bar, click Reports & Forms > General Ledger. Click on the

   Chart of Accounts to highlight it > select .

James Crosby Designer
Chart of Accounts
As of Oct 31, 2019

Filter Criteria includes: Report order is by ID. Report is printed with Accounts having Zero Amounts and in Deta

Account ID	Account Description	Active?	Account Type
1010	Money Market Account	Yes	Cash
1020	Checking Account	Yes	Cash
1040	IRA Savings Account	Yes	Cash
1045	WI State Retirement	Yes	Cash
1100	Accounts Receivable	Yes	Accounts Receivable
1200	Inventory	Yes	Inventory
1300	Prepaid Insurance	Yes	Other Current Assets
1400	Prepaid Rent	Yes	Other Current Assets
1450	Supplies	Yes	Other Current Assets
1500	Computer Equipment	Yes	Fixed Assets
1510	Furniture	Yes	Fixed Assets
1520	Automobile	Yes	Fixed Assets
1900	Accum. Depreciation - Comp Eqt	Yes	Accumulated Depreciation
1910	Accum. Depreciation - Furnitur	Yes	Accumulated Depreciation
1920	Accum. Depreciation - Automobi	Yes	Accumulated Depreciation
2000	VISA Payable	Yes	Accounts Payable
2380	Income Taxes Payable	Yes	Other Current Liabilities
2400	Publisher Advances	Yes	Other Current Liabilities
3910	Retained Earnings	Yes	Equity-Retained Earnings
3920	James Crosby, Capital	Yes	Equity-doesn't close
3930	James Crosby, Draw	Yes	Equity-gets closed
4000	Teaching Income	Yes	Income
4050	Royalty Income	Yes	Income
4100	Interest Income	Yes	Income
4200	Finance Charge Income	Yes	Income
4900	Sales/Fees Discounts	Yes	Income
5000	Cost of Sales	Yes	Cost of Sales
5400	Cost of Sales-Salary & Wage	Yes	Cost of Sales
6000	Wages Expense	Yes	Expenses
6100	Dues and Subscriptions	Yes	Expenses
6150	Auto Registration	Yes	Expenses
6200	Income Tax Expense	Yes	Expenses
6300	Rent or Lease Expense	Yes	Expenses
6350	Maintenance & Repairs Expense	Yes	Expenses
6400	Utilities Expense	Yes	Expenses
6450	Office Supplies Expense	Yes	Expenses
6500	Telephone Expense	Yes	Expenses
6550	Long Distance Company	Yes	Expenses
6560	Internet Service Provider	Yes	Expenses
6600	Advertising Expense	Yes	Expenses
6800	Freight Expense	Yes	Expenses
6850	Bank Service Charge	Yes	Expenses
6900	Purchase Disc-Expense Items	Yes	Expenses
6950	Insurance Expense	Yes	Expenses
7050	Deprec. Exp. - Comp Eqt	Yes	Expenses
7060	Deprec. Exp. - Furniture	Yes	Expenses
7070	Deprec. Exp. - Automobile	Yes	Expenses

> **How to Fix? Width of columns:** Move the mouse to the blue arrows ⊕ between columns. The cursor becomes a crossbar. Left click on the crossbar and drag the mouse to the right. After you have adjusted the Account Description column, click on the Print icon.

Carefully check the Account Type column. Account types classify each account for the financial statements. Observe that the chart of accounts is dated As of Oct 31, 2019. Since Sage 50 posts on the last day of the month, your reports will show October 31, 2019 as the date. James Crosby's chart of accounts includes Account No. 3910, Retained Earnings. At the end of every fiscal year, the temporary owner's equity accounts (revenues, expenses, and drawing) are closed to a permanent owner's equity account. There are two permanent owner's equity accounts: the owner's capital account and the Retained Earnings. Sage 50 closes the temporary accounts to Retained Earnings. This will be discussed in more detail in Chapter 11 when you close the fiscal year. In order to post to the general ledger, a Retained Earnings account is required.

2. To print the Chart of Accounts, click ⎙ Print . When the Print window appears, make the selections to print. (*Hint:* If you do not have a printer, you can save the Chart of Accounts as an Adobe PDF or Microsoft XPS Document Writer file instead of printing.)

   GO GREEN & SAVE: Instead of printing, select Display, and save as an Adobe PDF file or Microsoft XPS file. In other words, you do not need to print hard copy. Check with your instructor for his or her preference. Instead of printing, email PDFs or Microsoft XPS files.

3. Click ⊗ Close two times to return to the Business Status Navigation Center. If you need to edit the Chart of Accounts, select Maintain, then Chart of Accounts, *or* from the Business Status Navigation Center, link to View Account List.

When using accounting software, each step in the process affects the next step – setting up the company affects the chart of accounts, the chart of accounts affects beginning balances, those balances influence transaction processing, and posting affects financial reporting and the closing process. The steps in the computer accounting cycle work together to produce a company's financial records.

The work completed in Chapter 9 continues in Chapters 10 and 11. In this chapter, the Chart of Accounts (page 273) and Beginning Balance Sheet (pages 283-284) are important to accurate processing in the next two chapters.

BACKING UP THE CHART OF ACCOUNTS

Backing up data means saving it to a hard drive location or external media. Saving data (backing up) means that it will be available when you want to work again. In this textbook, detailed steps are shown for backing up to a USB drive. The chart on pages 254-256 shows the size of Part 2 backup files (Chapters 9, 10, 11 and Project 1).

When this backup is done, you are saving the new company set up information (pages 258-265) and the revised chart of accounts (pages 267-274). In the next section, detailed steps are shown for backing up your data to this point.

> **Comment: Backup & Restore**
>
> When a backup is made, you are saving to the current point. Each backup should have a different backup name (file name) to distinguish one backup from another. In this way, if you need to restore to an earlier backup, you have the data for that purpose. Remember, you can Restore if you need to go back to an earlier point in the company's data. Without a backup file, you cannot go back to an earlier point. Since Chapters 9, 10, and 11 work together, your backup files are important. In the business world, backups are unique to each business: daily, weekly, monthly. *Remember, back up before you leave the computer lab!*

Follow these steps to back up James Crosby's company and the chart of accounts.

1. Insert your USB flash drive. From the Navigation Bar, click

    > . Make sure that the box next to Include company name in the backup file name is *unchecked*.

2. Click Back Up .

3. Go to the location of your USB drive. (*Or,* backup to the hard-drive or other location.) Type **Chapter 9 Chart of Accounts** in the File name field.

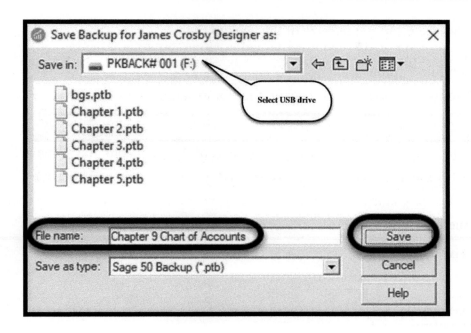

4. Click Save .

5. When the window prompts This company backup will require

   approximately 1 diskette, click OK . When the window prompts

   Please insert the first disk, click OK . When the Back Up Company

   scale is 100% complete, you have successfully backed up to the current

   point in Chapter 9. (This step will differ slightly if you are backing up to the

   default or other hard-drive location.)

    Read Me: Problem Backing Up to USB Drive

If you encounter difficulties backing up to an external USB drive, backup to your desktop first.
Then, copy the backup file from the desktop to the USB drive.

Follow these steps to see the size of the backup file.

1. Open File Explorer.
2. Go to the location of your backup file; for example, the USB drive.

The Name of the file is Chapter 9 Chart of Accounts.ptb, the Type is PTB file, the Size of the file is 918 KB. (Your file size may differ.) Backups can also be made to a hard drive, network location, or external media. Close Explorer.

How to Fix? .PTB extension

If you do *not* have a .PTB extension, follow these steps:

1. Go to File Explorer – . Select View > File name extensions should be checked – ☑ File name extensions

2. Close File Explorer. Your files will now show extensions.

RESTORING COMPANY DATA

After completing new company setup and editing the chart of accounts, you backed up (saved) James Crosby Designer company information. In order to start where you left off the last time you backed up, use the Restore Wizard.

In the steps that follow you are shown how to restore a backup file (.ptb extension). This backup was made on pages 276-277. Sage 50 backups are compressed files which means that the file is made smaller.

1. If necessary, insert your USB flash drive. Start Sage 50.
2. These instructions assume that the James Crosby [your name] Designer - Sage 50 Accounting window appears. If *not*, click File > Close Company.

   If a screen prompts to keep two companies open, select No . Open James Crosby [your name] Designer.

> **Troubleshooting: What if James Crosby Designer (or another name Designer) is not shown on the title bar?**

a. Click File > Close Company.

b. From the startup window, select [⬆ Open an Existing Company].

c. Click [Browse]. The Open Company window appears.

d. If James Crosby Designer (or, other name Designer) is shown select it, and then click [OK]. Go to page 280, step 3, and follow the steps to restore your data.

e. If *no Designer company is shown*, click [Cancel] then [Close].

f. There are four menu bar options--[File   Options   Services   Help]. Select File > Restore.

g. The Select Backup File window appears. Click [Browse]. In the Look in field, select the appropriate location of your backup file; for example, your USB drive.

File Options Services Help	
Open Company...	Ctrl+O
Open Previous Company	▶
New Company...	Ctrl+N
Restore...	Ctrl+R
Online Backup/Restore...	
Convert a Company...	
Exit	

h. Select the Chapter 9 Chart of Accounts.ptb backup file > click [Open].

i. Make sure the Location field shows the Chapter 9 Chart of Accounts.ptb backup file. Click [Next >].

j. The Select Company window appears. Click on the radio button next to Create a new company using the restored data.

Read Me

Observe that there are two options on the Select Company window: Overwrite existing company data *or* Create a new company using restored data. If you select Create a new company using restored data, the company will be named exactly the same as the backup file selected. Let's say you want to restore a backup file for a company that was *not* set up in Sage 50. Some computer labs delete directories from the hard drive. For example, you have a backup file but the company, James Crosby [or your name *or* other student name] Designer, is *not* listed as a Sage 50 company. If you start Sage 50 and you *cannot* select the appropriate company, use the Restore Wizard's Create a new company using the restored data selection to restore and set up the company.

k. The Company Name field shows James Crosby Designer. The Location field shows the location of your backup file. The last two letters of the location field shows "de." Continue with step 7 on page 281.

3. From the Navigation Bar, select **System** > click **Restore Now** The Select Backup File window appears.

4. Click **Browse**. The Open Backup File window appears. Go to the Location of your Chapter 9 Chart of Accounts.ptb file and select it.

5. Click [Open] The Select Backup File window shows the location of your backup file, X:\Chapter 9 Chart of Accounts.ptb. (Substitute X for your drive letter.) Click [Next >].

6. The Select Company window appears. The radio button next to Overwrite existing company data is selected. The Company Name field shows James Crosby Designer (*or,* your first and last name, Designer). The Location field shows the default location on the hard drive for James Crosby Designer – C:\sage\Peachtree\Company\jamcrode.

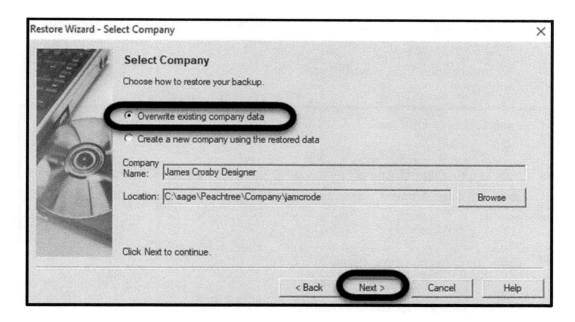

7. Click [Next >]. The Restore Options window appears. Make sure that the box next to Company Data is checked. Click [Next >].

8. The Confirmation window appears. Check the Backup file and Location fields to make sure they are correct. Click [Finish].

9.   A window prompts "This process will overwrite and replace existing data permanently."

10.   Click . When the scale is 100% complete, James Crosby [your name] Designer data is restored. (*Hint:* If a screen prompts that You can use this company in the student version of Sage 50 Accounting for the next 14 months and then it will expire, click <OK>.)

Comment: Global Options

On page xvii (number 1), you are instructed to select manual and 2 decimal places in the Decimal Entry and Number of Decimal Places fields. If you did *not* do this, follow these steps:

1.   From the menu bar, click Options > Global.
2.   In the Decimal Entry field, click Manual. When Manual is selected, a black circle is placed within a circle (radio button).
3.   In the Quantity fields, Standard fields, and Unit Price fields make sure **2** is selected.
4.   The boxes in the Hide General Accounts area should be *unchecked*.
5.   Click OK .

In order for your windows to look like the ones shown in this textbook, you need to have the *same* global settings as the ones shown on pages xvii-xviii, steps 1-3. When global options are selected, this feature is in effect for all companies.

ENTERING CHART OF ACCOUNTS BEGINNING BALANCES

Mr. Crosby hired you to do his monthly record keeping. In order to begin accounting tasks for Mr. Crosby, you asked him for a ***Balance Sheet***. A Balance Sheet lists the types and amounts of assets, liabilities, and equity as of a specific date. A balance sheet is also called a ***statement of financial position***.

James Crosby Designer Balance Sheet, **October 1, 2019**		
ASSETS		
Current Assets		
1010 - Money Market Account	$ 10,700.00	
1020 - Checking Account	13,750.75	
1040 - IRA Savings Account	27,730.35	
1045 - WI State Retirement	35,612.00	
1300 - Prepaid Insurance	2,100.00	
1400 - Prepaid Rent	600.00	
1450 - Supplies	<u>1,771.83</u>	
Total Current Assets		$ 92,264.93
Property and Equipment		
1500 - Computer Equipment	$ 6,800.00	
1510 - Furniture	5,000.00	
1520 - Automobile	<u>19,000.00</u>	
Total Property and Equipment		<u>30,800.00</u>
Total Assets		<u>$ 123,064.93</u>

LIABILITIES AND CAPITAL		
Current Liabilities		
2000 - VISA Payable	$ 5,250.65	
Total Current Liabilities		$ 5,250.65
Capital		
3920 - James Crosby, Capital		117,814.28
Total Liabilities and Capital		$ 123,064.93

The information on this Balance Sheet is the basis for recording Mr. Crosby's beginning balances.

1. From the menu bar, select Maintain > Chart of Accounts >
    Account Beginning Balances.

> Observe that the balance sheet on page 283 is dated October 1, 2019. **Beginning balances must be set for the previous month–September 1 through 30, 2019**. You select 9/1/19 through 9/30/19 because Sage 50 posts on the last day of the month. When 9/1/19 through 9/30/19 is selected as the chart of accounts beginning balance period, transaction windows start on October 1, 2019, and reports are dated October 31, 2019. **The September 30 ending balance is the October 1 beginning balance.**
>
> In Chapter 11, you print end-of-year financial statements. In order for your end-of-year financial statements to show the correct current month and year-to-date amounts, you *must* enter beginning balances for the previous month. **Select From 9/1/19 through 9/30/19 as the period for setting beginning balances**. *The beginning balance period cannot be changed later.*

2. Scroll down the Select Period list. Click From 9/1/19 through 9/30/19 to highlight it.

IMPORTANT: Check the Select Period window. The period you select should be From 9/1/19 through 9/30/19. The period selected affects financial statement current month and year-to-date account balances. Make sure that **From 9/1/19 through 9/30/19** is selected. *The beginning balance period* cannot *be changed later.*

3. On the Select Period window, make sure that you have selected **From 9/1/19 through 9/30/19**. You *cannot* change the period later. Click OK .

4. The Chart of Accounts Beginning Balances window appears. Observe that **Beginning Balances as of September 30, 2019** is shown. For Account ID 1010, Money Market Account, type **10700** in the Assets, Expenses field. Press **<Enter>**.

5. Account No. 1020, Checking Account is selected. Type **13750.75** and press **<Enter>**.

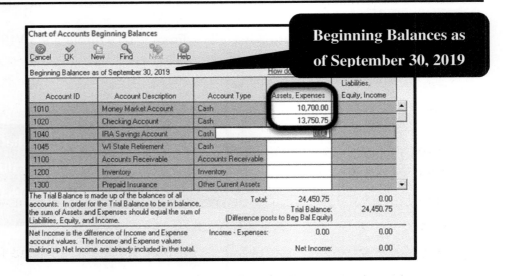

Beginning Balances as of September 30, 2019

Continue entering the beginning balances using the Balance Sheet on pages 283-284. If necessary, for credit balances, click on the Liabilities, Equity, Income field. When you are finished, the Assets, Expenses column equals the Liabilities, Equity, and Income column. This indicates that there are equal debits and credits.

Compare your completed Chart of Accounts Beginning Balances window with the one shown below.

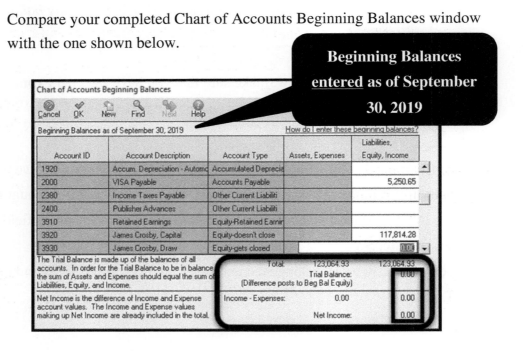

Beginning Balances entered as of September 30, 2019

> **How to Fix?**
> What if your Trial Balance, Income-Expenses, and Net Income does *not* show 0.00? Make sure that debit balances for assets and credit balances for liabilities and capital accounts are entered correctly.

> **Make sure that your beginning balances are as of September 30, 2019. If you enter your balances for the wrong month (period), your financial statements will not show the current month and year-to-date amounts correctly. Remember, Chapters 9, 10 and 11 work together. If beginning balances are incorrect in Chapter 9, Chapters 10 and 11 financial statements will be incorrect.**

6. Click [OK]. A window appears briefly that says Creating Journal Entries.

7. At the Maintain Chart of Accounts window, click [Close] to return to the Business Status Navigation Center.

   To check your chart of accounts beginning balances, select Maintain > Chart of Accounts > [Account Beginning Balances] > then select the From 9/1/19 through 9/30/19 > [OK]. Make any needed corrections. Refer to pages 283-287 for entering the chart of accounts beginning balances. When through, click [OK].

8. Close the Maintain Chart of Accounts window.

Display the September 30, 2019 Balance Sheet

The beginning balances for James Crosby Designer were shown on the October 1, 2019 Balance Sheet. It's important to record account beginning balances for

---

the month *before* the business's start date. That means you should make sure that you entered the appropriate period for beginning balances—From 9/1/19 through 9/30/19 (refer to steps 1 and 2, pages 284-285). To check that you entered account beginning balances as of September 30, 2019, follow these steps. September 30 ending balances are October 1 beginning balances.

1. From the menu bar, select Reports & Forms > Financial Statements > double-click <Standard> Balance Sheet.
2. The Options window appears. In the Time Frame field, select Range.
3. In the From field, select Period 9, (9/1/19). In the To Field, select Period 9, (9/30/19).

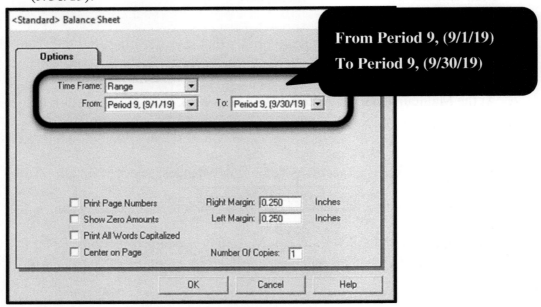

4. Click [OK]. Compare the balance sheet with the one shown on the next page. The September 30, 2019 account balances match the ones shown on the October 1, 2019 balance sheet. If your account balances do not agree, or if they show zeroes, you should redo the account beginning balances. (*Hint:* Restore the Chapter 9 Chart of Accounts.ptb file. Redo steps 1-7, pages 284-287.)

James Crosby Designer
Balance Sheet
September 30, 2019

ASSETS

Current Assets			
Money Market Account	$	10,700.00	
Checking Account		13,750.75	
IRA Savings Account		27,730.35	
WI State Retirement		35,612.00	
Prepaid Insurance		2,100.00	
Prepaid Rent		600.00	
Supplies		1,771.83	
Total Current Assets			92,264.93
Property and Equipment			
Computer Equipment		6,800.00	
Furniture		5,000.00	
Automobile		19,000.00	
Total Property and Equipment			30,800.00
Other Assets			
Total Other Assets			0.00
Total Assets		$	123,064.93

LIABILITIES AND CAPITAL

Current Liabilities			
VISA Payable	$	5,250.65	
Total Current Liabilities			5,250.65
Long-Term Liabilities			
Total Long-Term Liabilities			0.00
Total Liabilities			5,250.65
Capital			
James Crosby, Capital		117,814.28	
Net Income		0.00	
Total Capital			117,814.28
Total Liabilities & Capital		$	123,064.93

Unaudited - For Management Purposes Only

Observe when you print the report, "Unaudited - For Management Purposes Only" is shown at the bottom.

➢ **Troubleshooting: The companies set up in Chapter 9 continue in Chapters 10 and 11. If account beginning balances are <u>not</u> set up for September 30, 2019, your financial statements year-to-date column in Chapter 11 will not show the correct account balances.**

4. Close the Balance Sheet and the Select a Report or Form windows.

5. On the Business Status Navigation Center's toolbar, click 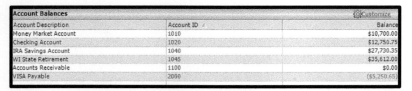. Notice that the account balances are updated. Balances shown in red are credit balances.

Account Balances		{Customize}
Account Description	Account ID	Balance
Money Market Account	1010	$10,700.00
Checking Account	1020	$12,750.75
IRA Savings Account	1040	$27,730.35
WI State Retirement	1045	$35,612.00
Accounts Receivable	1100	$0.00
VISA Payable	2000	($5,250.65)

6. Link to <u>View Account List</u> to see all the accounts and their Running Balance. A partial Account List is shown below. (*Hint:* Accounts shown in red with a parenthesis are credit balances.) These account balances agree with the Balance Sheet shown on page 289.

7. Close the Account List.

USING FILE EXPLORER TO SEE THE FILE SIZE

To see the size of the James Crosby Designer file, following these steps.

1. Open File Explorer – 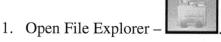.
2. Go to the location of the company data. The default location is C:\sage\Peachtree\Company. Open the Company folder.
3. Right-click on the jamcrode folder, *or* the folder with your shortened name. (*Hint:* Sage 50 shortens the company name using the first three letters of the first word, first three letters from the second word, and two letters from the third word. There are eight characters in the shortened company name.)
4. Left-click Properties. The default location is drive C. The title bar shows the shortened company name.

Observe that the size of the file is 26.2 MB (27,525,660 bytes). To save all the data contained in the James Crosby [or your name] folder, use File Explorer to copy, then paste the jamcrode folder from drive C to a USB drive, CD, or DVD. (Your file size may differ from the jamcrode Properties window. This is okay.)

5. When you are finished comparing your properties window, click OK , then ✕ on the Explorer title bar.

BACKING UP BEGINNING BALANCES

Follow these steps to back up the work completed so far. This backup saves the James Crosby Designer company set up on pages 258-265, the chart of accounts (pages 267-274), and the beginning balances (pages 283-287).

The idea is to make periodic backups so that you can go back to an earlier point in the data. Use a different file name for each backup so that you can distinguish one file from another one.

1. If necessary, close all windows and insert your USB flash drive. From the System Navigation Center, select Back Up Now . (*Or,* from the menu bar, select File > Back Up.)

2. If necessary, uncheck the box next to Include company name in the backup file name. Click Back Up .

3. In the Save in field, go to the location of your USB drive.

4. Type **Chapter 9 Beginning Balances** in the File name field.

File name:	Chapter 9 Beginning Balances		Save
Save as type:	Sage 50 Backup (*.ptb)	⌄	Cancel
			Help

Type the file name.

5. Click [Save] .

6. When the window prompts that This company backup will require approximately 1 diskette, click [OK] . Click [OK] again when the window prompts Please insert the first disk. When the Back Up Company scale is 100% complete, you have successfully backed up to this point in Chapter 9. (This step will differ slightly if you are backing up to the default or other hard drive location.)

In Chapter 9, you learned how to set up a new Sage 50 company, edit the chart of accounts, and how to use information from a balance sheet to enter beginning balances. Because two files were backed up in Chapter 9—the Chapter 9 Chart of Accounts.ptb file and the Chapter 9 Beginning Balances.ptb file—you could restore either file to start at that point in the data. For example, what if you notice a mistake and need to start at an earlier place in the data? By saving two files, you have two different backup files to restore. *Remember, in the business world backups are made frequently.*

EXPORT THE CHART OF ACCOUNTS AND BEGINNING BALANCES TO EXCEL

1. From the menu bar, select Reports & Forms > General Ledger > double-click Chart of Accounts. The Chart of Accounts appears. If needed, expand the Accounts Description and Account Type columns. (Click [↔] to widen the column.)

   Troubleshooting: If you are using Microsoft Office 365, the Excel icon may be inactive. Display the Sage report > select Edit > Copy > start Excel > open a blank workbook > right click on the sheet > left-click Paste >

reformat > save as Chapter 9_Chart of Accounts and Beginning Balances. For more information, go to Appendix A, Troubleshooting, Inactive Excel Icon. On page v, Integration/compatibility requirements lists which versions of Microsoft Office are compatible with Sage 50 2019.

2. Click 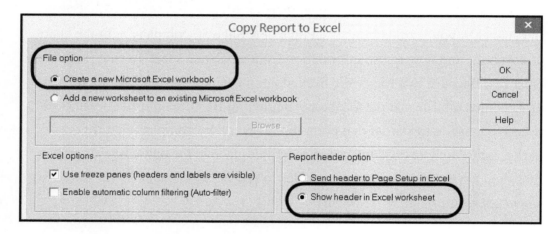 . On the Copy Report to Excel window, in the file option area, Create a new Microsoft Excel workbook is selected. In the Report header option field, Show header in Excel worksheet should be selected.

(If an "unexpected error" appears, do not select Show header.)

3. Click ⬛ OK . The chart of accounts exports to Excel.
4. Save. Use the file name **Chapter 9_Chart of Accounts and Beginning Balances.xlsx**. (*Hint:* If you are using Excel 2003, your file extension is .xls.). If necessary, exit Excel.
5. Go back to the Select a Report or Form window. In the Reports list, select Financial Statements > double-click <Standard> Balance Sheet. Change the date range to Period 9, 9/1/2019 to 9/30/2019. (Refer to page 288, steps 1-3.) Click ⬛ OK .

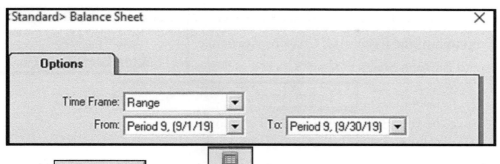

6. Click [OK] > select [Excel]. On the Copy Report to Excel window, select Add a new worksheet to an existing Microsoft Excel workbook.

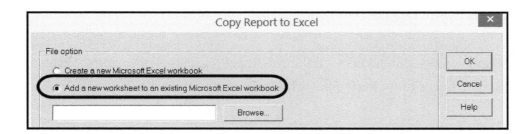

7. Click [Browse...] to go to the location of the Chapter 9_Chart of Accounts and Beginning Balances.xlsx file. Click [Open]. You are returned to the Copy Report to Excel window. Observe that the Browse field shows the location of the Chapter 9_Chart of Accounts and Beginning Balances file.

Go to the location of your Excel file.

8. Click [OK].

9. The September 30, 2019 balance sheet is exported to Excel.

10. Observe that two sheets are shown at the bottom of the Excel file: Chart of Accounts and Balance Sheet.

> James Crosby Designer
> **Balance Sheet**
> September 30, 2019

> **Chart of Accounts**   Balance Sheet

11. Save the file. Exit Excel. Close all windows.

SAVE PDF FILES

Follow these steps to save the September 30, 2019 Balance Sheet and Chart of Accounts as Adobe PDF file.

1. Display the <Standard> Balance Sheet. Change the Time Frame to Range. Select From Period 9, (9/1/19) To Period 9, (9/30/19).

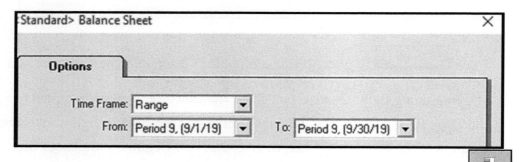

2. Click <OK>. The September 30, 2019 Balance Sheet appears. Click PDF . (*Hint:* If the PDF icon is not active, select Print > in the Name field, select Adobe PDF > click <OK>.) Select your USB drive. Save the file. The suggested file name is **Chapter 9_Balance Sheet.pdf**. (*Hint:* The September 30 ending balances are the October 1, 2019 beginning balances.) Compare the balance sheet to the one shown on page 289.
3. Display the Chart of Accounts. Save as a PDF file. The suggested file name is **Chapter 9_Chart of Accounts.pdf.** (*Hint:* Sage automatically dates

reports the last day of the month. By default, the Chart of Accounts is dated October 31, 2019.)

4. Exit Sage 50.

ONLINE LEARNING CENTER

Complete end-of-chapter activities at www.mhhe.com/yacht2019 > Student Edition > Chapter 9.

1. Quizzes: Multiple Choice Quiz and True or False. Interactive online tests that are graded and can be emailed to your instructor.
2. More Resources:

    a. Going to the Net Exercises: Access Wikipedia's Chart of Accounts website.
    b. QA Templates: 10 multiple-choice questions and two Analysis Questions.
    c. Assessment Rubric: Complete the rubric to review Sage 50's journals, navigation centers, modules, task windows, and reports.
    d. Listen to narrated PowerPoint slides.
    e. Videos: In Chapter 9, the video is New Company Set Up. Watch the videos using an Internet browser.

➢ Information Center > Sage Advisor Videos

The OLC also includes links to the Appendixes:

- Appendix A: Troubleshooting (textbook and OLC)
- Appendix C: Review of Accounting Principles (OLC Student Edition)
- Appendix D: Glossary (OLC Student Edition)

298 Chapter 9

Exercise 9-1: Follow the instructions below to complete Exercise 9-1:

1. Start Sage 50. If James Crosby [your name] Designer or other company opens, select File > New Company. When the window prompts, Do you want to keep James Crosby (your name) Designer open?, click <kbd>No</kbd>. The Create a New Company – Introduction window appears. Click <kbd>Next ></kbd>. (*Or,* from the startup window, select <kbd>✎ Create a New Company</kbd>.)

2. Type the following company information:

Company Name:	Crafts by Your Name (*Use your first and last name*)
Address Line 1:	Your address
City, State, Zip	Your city, Your State, Your Zip code
Country:	USA
Telephone:	Your telephone number
Fax:	Your fax number (if any)
Business Type:	Sole Proprietorship
E-mail:	Type your email address

   Leave the Tax ID Numbers fields blank.

   The Company Name field should show Crafts by *your first and last name.* The Business Type field shows Sole Proprietorship.

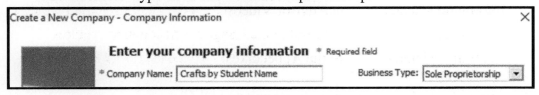

3. Click <kbd>Next ></kbd>. At the Select a method to create your company window, select Copy settings from an existing Sage 50 Accounting company.

---

handwritten: ∂∂ chapter = 9.1 exercises = 9.2

4. Click Next > .

5. Highlight James Crosby [or your name] Designer, then click Next > .

6. At the Copy Company Information window, accept the default selections by clicking Next > .

7. Accept the default for accrual accounting by clicking Next > .

8. Accept the default for Real Time posting by clicking Next > .

9. At the You are ready to create your company window, click Finish . If the screen prompts You can use this company in the student version of Sage 50 Accounting for the next 14 months and then it will expire, click OK .

10. If the Setup Guide window appears, click on the box next to Don't show this screen at startup. Click Close . Close the Getting Started window.

11. The Crafts by your first and last name - Sage 50 Accounting window appears. Make sure the period is Period 10 - 10/01/19-10/31/19 –

    Period 10:
    10-01-19 - 10-31-19

12. Make the following changes to the Chart of Accounts:

a. Change the name of the following accounts:
- Account No. 1020, Checking Account to County Bank
- Account No. 2000, VISA Payable to Accounts Payable
- Account No. 3920, James Crosby, Capital to Your Name, Capital (Make sure the Account Type is Equity-doesn't close)
- Account No. 3930, James Crosby, Draw to Your Name, Draw
- Account No. 4050, Royalty Income to Crafts Income
- Account No. 6800, Freight Expense to Conference Expense

b. Delete the following accounts:
- Account No. 1010, Money Market Account
- Account No. 1040, IRA Savings Account
- Account No. 1045, WI State Retirement
- Account No. 2400, Publisher Advances

c. Add the following accounts:
- Account No. 6180, Automobile Expense
- Account No. 6420, Water and Power Expense
- Account No. 7400, Postage Expense

13. Print the chart of accounts.

How to Fix? I do NOT have a printer.

1. Select > in the Name field > click on the down-arrow.
2. Select Adobe PDF *or* Microsoft XPS Document Writer.

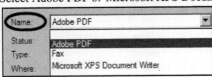

3. Save the file to your USB drive.

If needed, the PDF or XPS file can be emailed to your instructor. When selecting an Adobe PDF or XPS file, no printer is required.

14. Backup. The suggested file name is **Exercise 9-1**.

15. Click File > Exit or continue.

Exercise 9-2: Follow the instructions below to complete Exercise 9-2. Exercise 9-1 *must* be completed before starting Exercise 9-2.

1. Start Sage. If necessary, open the company that you set up in Exercise 9-1, Crafts by Your Name. (*Hint:* If a different company opens, select File > Open Previous Company. When the screen prompts do you want to open two companies, select <No>.)
2. If necessary, restore the Exercise 9-1.ptb file.[3] If you are continuing from Exercise 9-1, you do <u>not</u> need to restore.
3. Use the Balance Sheet on the next page to record chart of accounts beginning balances. (*Hint:* Select **9/1/19 through 9/30/19** as the period for entering chart of accounts beginning balances. Enter beginning balances as of September 30, 2019.)

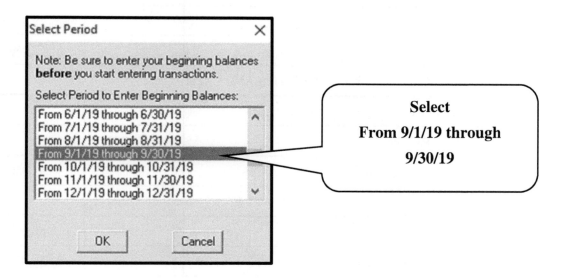

---

[3]You can restore from your back up file even if *no* Sage 50 company exists. Refer to Troubleshooting, pages 279-280.

Crafts by Your Name		
Balance Sheet, October 1, 2019		
ASSETS		
Current Assets		
County Bank	$19,500.00	
Prepaid Insurance	1,000.00	
Prepaid Rent	700.00	
Supplies	850.00	
Total Current Assets		$22,050.00
Property and Equipment		
Computer Equipment	6,500.00	
Furniture	3,500.00	
Automobile	19,000.00	
Total Property and Equipment		29,000.00
Total Assets		$ 51,050.00
LIABILITIES AND CAPITAL		
Current Liabilities		
Accounts Payable	$1,050.00	
Total Current Liabilities		$1,050.00
Capital		
Your Name, Capital		50,000.00
Total Liabilities and Capital		$ 51,050.00

4. Print the September 30, 2019 balance sheet.

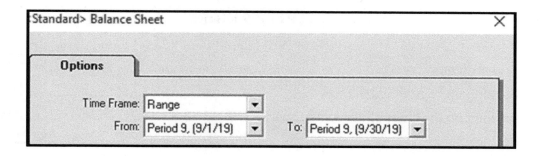

CHECK YOUR FIGURES: Chart of Accounts & Balance Sheet

    Account No. 3930, Student Name, Draw

    Account No. 4050, Crafts Income

    Account No. 7400, Postage Expense

    Account No. 1020, County Bank, $19,500

    Account No. 3920, Student Name, Capital, $50,000

5.   Backup. The suggested filename is **Exercise 9-2**.

6.   Export the chart of accounts and balance sheet to Excel. Use the file name **Exercise 9-2_Chart of Accounts and Beginning Balances.xlsx**. Change the date on the balance sheet to September 30, 2019.

7.   Save the Chart of Accounts and September 30, 2019 Balance Sheet as PDF files. Use the file names **Exercise 9-2_Chart of Accounts.pdf** and **Exercise 9-2_Balance Sheet.pdf** as the file names.

CHAPTER 9 INDEX

Chapter 10

Maintaining Accounting Records For Service Businesses

LEARNING OBJECTIVES

1. Restore data from Chapter 9. (This backup was made on pages 292-293.)[1]
2. Record and post deposits, checks and ATMs.
3. Complete account reconciliation.
4. Display the Account Register.
5. Display the Cash Receipts Journal, Cash Disbursements Journal, and General Journal.
6. Display the general ledger trial balance.
7. Print financial statements.
8. Make four backups, save two Excel files, and save six PDF files.[2]

In Chapter 10, you continue the work started in Chapter 9. You complete the computer accounting cycle for the month of October using your client's transaction register and bank statement as *source documents*. Source documents are used to show written evidence of a business transaction. For James Crosby Designer, the source documents used are his transaction register and bank statement. The *transaction register* shows Mr. Crosby's checking account activity.

Remember, Chapter 9 must be completed before starting Chapter 10.

---

[1] All activities in Chapter 9 must be completed before starting Chapter 10.

[2] Refer to the chart on pages 254-255 for backups, Excel, and PDF files.

GETTING STARTED

Follow the steps on the next page to continue using James Crosby [your first and last name] Designer company data.

1. Start Sage 50. Open James Crosby Designer [or another name Designer]. (*Hint:* If a different company opens, select File > Open a Previous Company > select James Crosby Designer. When the window prompts, Do you want to keep [company name] open?, click No . If you prefer to keep two companies open, click Yes .)

2. If necessary, restore the Chapter 9 Beginning Balances.ptb backup file. This backup was made on pages 292-293.[3]

> **Read Me: Do I need to restore?** If you are working on your own PC or laptop, you may want to skip restore. Refer to the disk icon to make sure you are starting with the work completed in Chapter 9. *If you are working in the computer lab or classroom, start James Crosby Designer [or other name Designer]. Restore the Chapter 9 Beginning Balances.ptb file from your USB drive.*

To make sure you are starting in the appropriate place in the data (Chapter 9 Beginning Balances.ptb backup) check the balance sheet. A partial balance sheet is shown on the next page. The complete balance sheet is shown on page 289.

Unless you change the date range, the balance sheet shows October 31, 2019. Sage 50 dates reports the last day of the period (month). For the balance sheet shown on page 289, you changed the date range to check that you entered beginning balances as of September 30.

---

[3]You can restore from your back up file even if *no* designer company exists. Refer to Troubleshooting, pages 279-280.

```
                                            James Crosby Designer
                                               Balance Sheet
                                             September 30, 2019

                                                  ASSETS

        Current Assets
          Money Market Account          $        10,700.00
          Checking Account                       13,750.75
          IRA Savings Account                     27,730.35
          WI State Retirement                    35,612.00
          Prepaid Insurance                       2,100.00
          Prepaid Rent                              600.00
          Supplies                               1,771.83

          Total Current Assets                                    92,264.93

        Property and Equipment
          Computer Equipment                      6,800.00
          Furniture                               5,000.00
          Automobile                             19,000.00

          Total Property and Equipment                            30,800.00

        Other Assets

          Total Other Assets                                          0.00

          Total Assets                   $                       123,064.93
```

RECORDING DEPOSITS, CHECKS AND ATMs

In Sage, the Receive Money window is used to record deposits. When you save a
receipt, Sage automatically journalizes the entry in the Cash Receipts Journal.
When Mr. Crosby writes a check, the disbursement is recorded in the Write
Checks window. When you save the check or ATM, the entry is automatically
journalized in the Cash Disbursements Journal and posted to the appropriate
general ledger accounts.

Sage 50's Write Checks window is a simplified version of the Payments
window. In this chapter, use the Write Checks window to issue a check for
expenses, assets, owner's draw, or ATM withdrawals.

Mr. Crosby's transaction register has the information necessary to record entries
for the month of October. Since Mr. Crosby is a new client, information from his
Balance Sheet was used for an opening entry. His transaction register lists the
information for the rest of the month.

Follow these steps to show the cash balance on the Receive Money window and Payments window.

1. Click Options > Global. Make sure the box next to Recalculate cash balance automatically in Receipts, Payments, and Payroll is checked.

Other Options

☑ Warn if a record was changed but not saved

☐ Hide inactive records

☑ Recalculate cash balance automatically in Receipts, Payments, and Payroll Entry

☐ Use Timeslips Accounting Link

2. Click [OK]. When you use the Receive Money window or Write Checks window, the transaction register balance agrees with the Cash Account balance shown.

Mr. Crosby's transaction register shows an October 1 deposit of $11,000. A section of Mr. Crosby's transaction register is shown.

Check Number	Date	Description of Transaction	Payment	Deposit	Balance
	9/30				13,750.75
	10/1	Deposit (publisher's advance)		11,000.00	24,750.75

▶ Use these steps to record the October 1 deposit from the transaction register. (The arrow indicates a video at www.mhhe.com/yacht2019 > Student Edition > Chapter 10 > Videos > Deposits.)

1. Select Tasks > Receive Money. The Select a Cash Account window displays. If necessary, click on the down arrow to select Checking Account.

Select a Cash Account ✕

OK

Cancel

Help

Please select a cash account to use for this transaction.

Checking Account ▾

2. Click [OK]. The Receive Money window displays. (*Hint:* If a pop-up message appears, read it. Then close.)

3. Your cursor is in the Deposit ticket ID field. Type **10/1/19**. (*Hint: Use the date of the deposit for the Deposit ticket ID field.*)

4. Click on the Name field. Type **Deposit** in the Name field.

5. Click on the Check/Reference No. field. Type **Advance** in the Check/Reference No. field. Press **<Enter>** two times.

6. Accept the default for Oct 1, 2019 in the Date field by pressing **<Enter>**. Verify that the Payment Method is Check and that Account 1020, Checking Account, is displayed in the Cash account field. The Cash Account Balance field displays 13,750.75. This agrees with the partial transaction register balance shown on page 308 and the Checking Account balance shown on the Balance Sheet, page 307.

7. Make sure that the Apply to Revenues tab is selected. Click once on the Quantity field. Type **1** in the Quantity field. Press the **<Enter>** key two times.

8. Type **Publisher's advance** in the Description field. Press **<Enter>**.

9. Click [ ] in the GL Account field. Select Account No. 2400, Publisher Advances. (*Hint:* In the GL Account field, you can also type 2400.)

10. Type **11000** in the Unit Price field.

How to Fix? 11,000.00 does not appear in the Unit Price field.

1. From the menu bar, click Options > Global.
2. In the Decimal Entry field > click Manual. When Manual is selected, a black circle is placed within a circle (radio button).
3. The Quantity fields, Standard fields, and Unit Price fields, should have **2** selected.
4. Make sure the boxes in the Hide General Ledger Accounts section are *unchecked.*
5. Click [OK].

When global options are selected, this feature is in effect for all companies.

---

11.   Press the **<Enter>** key two times. (*Hint:* If the GL Account field is not shown, refer to the How to Fix box. In order to show account numbers (1020 is debited; 2400 is credited), the boxes in the Hide General Ledger Accounts area must be *unchecked.*)

12.   Click 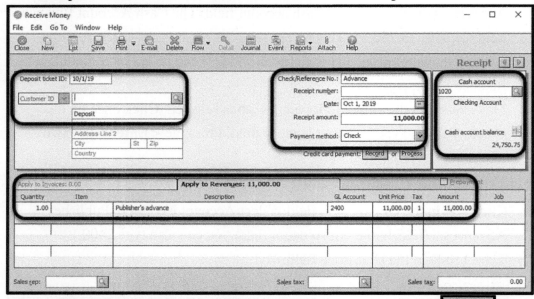 **Save** to post this entry. After you post, the Cash account balance field shows the same balance, $24,750.75, as the partial transaction register shown on the next page. The Receive Money window is ready for another entry. When the entry is saved, it is posted to the general ledger. The Cash Receipts Journal shows the debits and credits for this deposit.

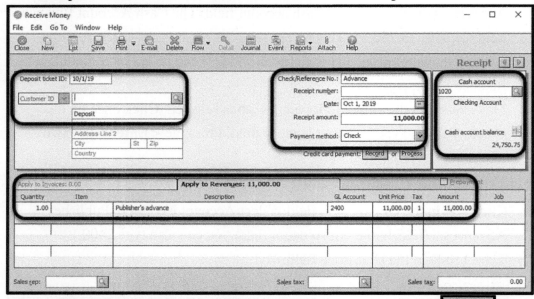

13.   Click **Close**. On the Business Status Navigation Center, click **Refresh**. The Checking account balance shows $24,750.75. The same balance as the Cash account balance on the Receive Money window.

Account Balances		Customize
Account Description	Account ID ▲	Balance
Money Market Account	1010	$10,700.00
Checking Account	1020	$24,750.75
IRA Savings Account	1040	$27,730.35

▶ For Check No. 4001, use Write Checks. (www.mhhe.com/yacht2019 > Student Edition > Chapter 10 > Videos > Checks.) A section of the transaction register is shown below. *Italics, and a broken line, indicate entries that have already been entered and saved.*

Ck. No.	Date	Description of Transaction	Payment	Deposit	Balance
	9/30				*13,750.75*
	10/1			*11,000.00*	*24,750.75*
4001	**10/2**	**Transfer to Money Market Account**	**6,000.00**		**18,750.75**

From the Navigation Bar, click

Banking . Observe that the Banking Tasks diagram appears. In this chapter you focus on banking; in Chapters 12-15, you work with customers and vendors and record customer receipts and vendor payments.

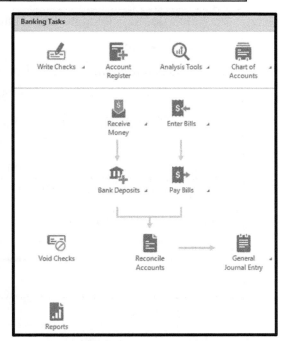

Navigation Bar or Menu Bar? In this textbook, you use *both* menu bar selections and the Navigation Bar. Throughout the textbook, these two methods are shown.

Use these steps to enter Check No. 4001 and post to the Cash Disbursements Journal.

1. From the Banking Navigation Center, click **Write Checks** > New Check. The Select a Cash Account window appears. If necessary, click on the down-arrow to select the Checking Account.

2. Click OK .

3. The Write Checks window displays. Click on the Pay to the order of, Name field. Type **Money Market Account**.

4. Click 🔍 in the Expense account field. The Chart of Accounts list is displayed. Even though you are *not* charging Check No. 4001 against an expense account, you use the Expense Account field to select the appropriate account to debit. Select Account No.1010, Money Market Account. The Description field is automatically completed with Money Market Account.

5. Click on the Check number field. Type **4001** in the Check number field and press **<Enter>**.

6. Type **2** in the Date field and press **<Enter>**. Verify that the Cash Account Balance field shows $24,750.75. This agrees with the partial transaction register on page 311 (beginning balance plus publisher's advance, $13,750.75 + 11,000 = $24,750.75. If the Cash Account Balance field does not agree with your transaction register, see the instructions on page 308, steps 1 and 2, for setting the global options for recalculating the cash balance for receipts, payments, and payroll.

7. Type **6000** in the $ field. Press **<Enter>**. The check is completed.

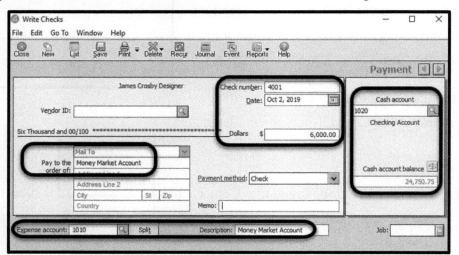

8. Click [Save] to post to the general ledger. The debits and credits for this entry are in the Cash Disbursements Journal. Verify that the Cash Account Balance field displays the October 2 balance. This is the same balance, $18,750.75, as the partial transaction register on page 311. You are ready for the next entry. (*Hint: you may need to change the date to 10/2/19 to see the correct cash balance.*)

9. Click [Close] to return to the Banking Navigation Center.

> **Comment:** Sage automatically completes the Check number field once the first number is typed. After typing another reference in the Check number field (for example, ATM), you need to type the appropriate check number. ATM is an acronym for Automated Teller Machine. When an ATM card is used, cash is withdrawn from the checking account.

Source documents are used to show written evidence of a business transaction. Examples of source documents are sales invoices, purchase invoices, and in this case, Mr. Crosby's transaction registers which show checking account activity. Starting with the ATM withdrawal on October 3 for $200, record the entries shown on the transaction register on pages 314 and 315 in the Write Checks window (Banking Navigation Center) or the Receive Money window (Tasks > Receive Money). Assign each entry on the transaction register an appropriate account number from Mr. Crosby's Chart of Accounts. Record individual entries for each check number, deposit, or ATM transaction.

Each deposit (cash or check received) is a debit to Account No. 1020, Checking Account, and is recorded on the Receive Money window (Cash Receipts Journal). On the Receive Money window, select the appropriate general ledger account for the credit part of the entry. The offsetting debit is automatically entered in Account No. 1020, Checking Account.

Each payment (check issued and ATM withdrawal) listed on the transaction register is a credit to Account No. 1020, Checking Account, and is recorded on the Write Checks window (Cash Disbursements Journal). On the Write Checks window, you select the appropriate general ledger account for the debit part of the entry. The offsetting credit is automatically entered in Account No. 1020, Checking Account.

After recording each check, deposit, or ATM, you should verify that the Balance field on the Write Checks window and Receive Money window agrees with the transaction register balances below and on page 315. You have already recorded the first two entries for October 1 and October 2. Continue recording entries with the October 3 ATM transaction.

Remember, click [Save] *to post each entry (ATMs, Deposits, Checks). The transaction register entries are listed individually on the table below and on page 315.*

> **Read Me:** *Why should I use Write Checks instead of the Payments window?* The Write Checks window is a simplified version of the Payments window. Both Write Checks and Payments post to the Cash Disbursements Journal. In Chapter 10, you use the Write Checks window for checks and ATM withdrawals.

Start with the 10/3 ATM. (Italics indicate entries that are recorded.)

Ck. No.	Date	Description of Transaction	Payment	Deposit	Balance
	9/30				*13,750.75*
	10/1			*11,000.00*	*24,750.75*
	10/2		*6,000.00*		*18,750.75*
	10/3	ATM[4]	200.00		**18,550.75**

[4]For ATMs select Account 3930, Your name, Draw. Type **ATM i**n the Check number and Pay to the order of fields.

	10/4	Deposit (book royalty)		3,965.05	22,515.80
4002	10/4	Office Supplies on Main (computer equipment)	1,105.68		21,410.12
4003	10/9	U.S. Post Office[5]	49.00		21,361.12
4004	10/9	Verde News; debit 6100 Dues and Subscriptions	45.00		21,316.12
4005	10/9	RVP Gas (utilities)	39.64		21,276.48
4006	10/10	Water and Power Company, add 6420 Water and Power Expense	98.59		21,177.89
4007	10/10	Local Telephone (telephone expense)	35.00		21,142.89
4008	10/10	Long Distance Company	46.20		21,096.69
	10/13	Deposit (Milwaukee Community College)		2,716.19	23,812.88
	10/14	ATM (Read warning, click <OK>.	400.00		23,412.88
4009	10/15	Auto Parts - car headlight; add account 6180 Automobile Expense	201.00		23,211.88
4010	10/17	Phil Sanchez (install headlight; automobile expense)	110.00		23,101.88
4011	10/29	Dept. of Transportation (auto registration)	210.00		22,891.88
4012	10/29	Suppliers Plus (letterhead and envelopes); debit 1450, Supplies	215.98		22,675.90
4013	10/30	Internet Service Provider	29.99		22,645.91

BACKING UP THE OCTOBER TRANSACTION REGISTER

1. If necessary, close all windows and insert your USB flash drive. From the System Navigation Center, select [Back Up Now]. (*Or,* from the menu bar, select File > Back Up. If necessary, uncheck the box next to Include company name in the backup file name. Click [Back Up]).

---

[5]Add account 7400, Postage Expense. (*Hint*: In the Expense Account field, click 🔍 > [New] > Account Type > Expenses.)

2. In the Save in field, go to the location of your USB drive or back up to another location. Type **Chapter 10 Transaction Register October** in the File name field.

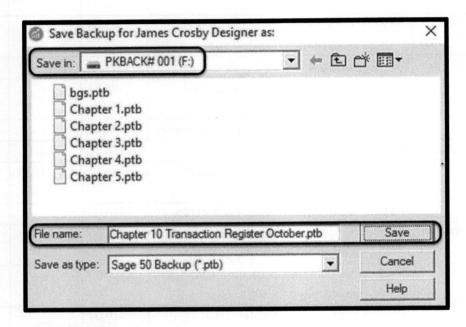

3. Click [Save]. When the window prompts that This company backup will require approximately 1 diskette, click [OK]. When the window prompts please insert the first disk, click [OK]. When the Back Up Company scale is 100% complete, you have backed up to this point in Chapter 10. (This step differs if you are backing up to the default or other hard drive location.)

ACCOUNT RECONCILIATION

James Crosby receives a bank statement every month for his checking account (Account No. 1020). The bank statement shows which checks, ATMs, and deposits cleared the bank. Use Account Reconciliation to reconcile the bank statement.

Statement of Account			James Crosby Designer
Checking Account			788 Lake Drive
October 1 to October 31, 2019	Account No. 348822-33		Milwaukee, WI 53205
REGULAR CHECKING			
Previous Balance		$ 13,750.75	
3 Deposits (+)		17,681.24	
9 checks (-)		7,690.47	
2 Other Deductions (-)		600.00	
Service Charges (-)	10/31/19	10.00	
Ending Balance	10/31/19	**$23,131.52**	
DEPOSITS			
	10/4/19	11,000.00	
	10/7/19	3,965.05	
	10/17/19	2,716.19	
CHECKS (Asterisk * indicates break in check number sequence)			
	10/2/19	4001	6,000.00
	10/6/19	4002	1,105.68
	10/15/19	4003	49.00
	10/16/19	4004	45.00
	10/16/19	4006*	98.59
	10/17/19	4007	35.00
	10/20/19	4008	46.20
	10/23/19	4009	201.00
	10/30/19	4010	110.00
OTHER DEDUCTIONS (ATM's)			
	10/3/19	ATM	200.00
	10/14/19	ATM	400.00

Follow these steps to reconcile Mr. Crosby's bank statement balance to Account No. 1020, Checking Account.

1. From the Navigation Bar, select > . The
    Account Reconciliation window appears.

2. In the Account to Reconcile field, select Account No. 1020, Checking
    Account. If necessary, enlarge the window.

3. On the Account Reconciliation window, click on the up-arrow ⬆ next to
    Statement Ending Balance to expand the area. Type **10** in the Service
    Charges field. The Date defaults to October 31, 2019. In the Account field,
    select Account No. 6850, Bank Service Charge.

4. In the Statement Ending Balance field (at the bottom of the window), type
    23131.52. (This is the ending balance on Mr. Crosby's bank statement.)

5. In the Deposit/Bank Credit; Check/Bank Debit table, place a checkmark
    <✓> in the Status column for each deposit, check, and ATM that is listed
    on the bank statement. For each deposit, check, and ATM cleared, the
    Status column shows a checkmark. Do not check off the outstanding
    checks: 4005, 4011, 4012, 4013.

Comment: Observe that the Unreconciled Difference is zero (0.00). This zero balance is proof
that Account No. 1020, Checking Account, is reconciled. The GL (System) Balance is
$22,635.91. The transaction register on page 315 shows an October 30 balance of $22,645.91.
When you subtract the service charge of $10, the transaction register balance (22,645.91 – 10 =
22,635.91) agrees with the GL (System) Balance shown on the Account Reconciliation
window.

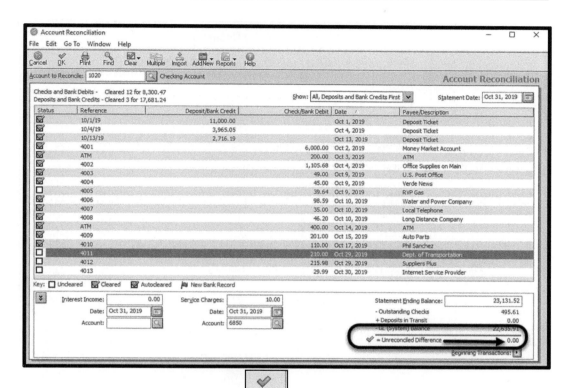

6. When you are finished, click [OK]. The Account Reconciliation feature adjusts Mr. Crosby's bank statement. Another name for this is ***bank reconciliation*** – the process of bringing the balance of the bank statement and the balance of the cash account into agreement. The Account Reconciliation can be used with other accounts, too.

DISPLAYING THE ACCOUNT REGISTER

Entries for deposits and withdrawals are shown on the Account Register.

1. From the Banking Navigation Center's Recently Used Banking Reports area, select View Account Register. Compare your Account Register to the one shown on the next page.

<table>
<tr><td colspan="7" align="center">**James Crosby Designer**
Account Register
For the Period From Oct 1, 2019 to Oct 31, 2019
1020 - Checking Account</td></tr>
</table>

Filter Criteria includes: Report order is by Date.

Date	Trans No	Type	Trans Desc	Deposit Amt	Withdrawal Amt	Balance
			Beginning Balance			13,750.75
10/1/19	10/1/19	Deposit	Deposit	11,000.00		24,750.75
10/2/19	4001	Withdraw	Money Market Account		6,000.00	18,750.75
10/3/19	ATM	Withdraw	ATM		200.00	18,550.75
10/4/19	10/4/19	Deposit	Deposit	3,965.05		22,515.80
10/4/19	4002	Withdraw	Office Supplies on Main		1,105.68	21,410.12
10/9/19	4003	Withdraw	U.S. Post Office		49.00	21,361.12
10/9/19	4004	Withdraw	Verde News		45.00	21,316.12
10/9/19	4005	Withdraw	RVP Gas		39.64	21,276.48
10/10/19	4006	Withdraw	Water and Power Company		98.59	21,177.89
10/10/19	4007	Withdraw	Local Telephone		35.00	21,142.89
10/10/19	4008	Withdraw	Long Distance Company		46.20	21,096.69
10/13/19	10/13/19	Deposit	Deposit	2,716.19		23,812.88
10/14/19	ATM	Withdraw	ATM		400.00	23,412.88
10/15/19	4009	Withdraw	Auto Parts		201.00	23,211.88
10/17/19	4010	Withdraw	Phil Sanchez		110.00	23,101.88
10/29/19	4011	Withdraw	Dept. of Transportation		210.00	22,891.88
10/29/19	4012	Withdraw	Suppliers Plus		215.98	22,675.90
10/30/19	4013	Withdraw	Internet Service Provider		29.99	22,645.91
10/31/19	10/31/19	Other	Service Charge		10.00	22,635.91
			Total	**17,681.24**	**8,796.08**	

2. The Account Register and Mr. Crosby's transaction register on pages 314-315 show the same results, *except* for the 10/31/19 service charge of 10.00. Similar to the transaction register, the Account Register lists deposits (receive money or receipts) and withdrawals (checks and ATMs). If you notice a discrepancy use drill down to follow the path of the entry's origin. Follow these steps to use drill down.

   a. Double-click on the 10/4/19 Deposit of $3,965.05. Notice that your cursor turns into a magnifying glass with a Z in the center.

10/4/19	10/4/19	Deposit	Deposit	3,965.05 ⓩ	22,515.80

   b. The Receive Money window appears with the October 4, 2019 deposit shown.

   c. If there is no need to make a correction, close the Receive Money window. You are returned to the Account Register window. Observe that the Account Register shows the Beginning Balance, Deposits, and

Withdrawals (Checks, ATMs, bank service charge). It is okay if the Trans Desc (transaction descriptions) differs.

You can also drill down from the Account Register to the Write Checks, Receive Money, or General Journal windows. Drill down shows the original entry. For example, if you double-click on the check number, you go to the Write Checks window; if you double-click on the 10/31/19 entry for the service charge (10.00) you go to the General Journal Entry window.

3. Close the Account Register and any other open windows.
4. Follow these steps to display the General Journal.

    a. From the menu bar, click Reports & Forms > General Ledger.

    b. Click General Journal > Display .

James Crosby Designer
General Journal
For the Period From Oct 1, 2019 to Oct 31, 2019
Filter Criteria includes: Report order is by Date. Report is printed with Accounts having Zero Amounts and with shortened descriptions and in Detail Format.

Date	Account ID	Reference	Trans Description	Debit Amt	Credit Amt
10/31/19	1020	10/31/19	Service Charge		10.00
	6850		Service Charge	10.00	
		Total		10.00	10.00

    c. Close the General Journal report.

PRINTING THE CASH RECEIPTS JOURNAL

Follow these steps to print the Cash Receipts Journal.

1. From the Select a Report or Form window, select Accounts Receivable in the Reports area. (*Hint:* From the menu bar, select Reports & Forms > Accounts Receivable.)

2. Double-click Cash Receipts Journal. The Cash Receipts Journal appears.

   ➤ **Troubleshooting: Why does my Cash Receipts Journal show blue lines between columns?** In the textbook, most of the report illustrations are done with the PDF file image.

James Crosby Designer
Cash Receipts Journal
For the Period From Oct 1, 2019 to Oct 31, 2019

Filter Criteria includes: Report order is by Check Date. Report is printed in Detail Format.

Date	Account ID	Transaction Ref	Line Description	Debit Amnt	Credit Amnt
10/1/19	2400	Advance	Publisher's advance		11,000.00
	1020		Deposit	11,000.00	
10/4/19	4050	Book royalty	Book royalty		3,965.05
	1020		Deposit	3,965.05	
10/13/19	4000	Milwaukee CC	Teaching income		2,716.19
	1020		Deposit	2,716.19	
				17,681.24	17,681.24

Comment

The information in the Transaction Ref column may differ. The Transaction Ref column shows the same information as what you typed in the Check/Reference No. field of the Receive Money window.

3. Close the Cash Receipts Journal.

PRINTING THE CASH DISBURSEMENTS JOURNAL

1. The Select a Report or Form window should be displayed. In the Reports area, highlight Accounts Payable.
2. Double-click the Cash Disbursements Journal.

			James Crosby Designer		

James Crosby Designer
Cash Disbursements Journal
For the Period From Oct 1, 2019 to Oct 31, 2019
Filter Criteria includes: Report order is by Date. Report is printed in Detail Format.

Date	Check #	Account ID	Line Description	Debit Amount	Credit Amount
10/2/19	4001	1010	Money Market Account	6,000.00	
		1020	Money Market Account		6,000.00
10/3/19	ATM	3930	James Crosby, Draw	200.00	
		1020	ATM		200.00
10/4/19	4002	1500	Computer Equipment	1,105.68	
		1020	Office Supplies on Main		1,105.68
10/9/19	4003	7400	Postage Expense	49.00	
		1020	U.S. Post Office		49.00
10/9/19	4004	6100	Dues and Subscriptions	45.00	
		1020	Verde News		45.00
10/9/19	4005	6400	Utilities Expense	39.64	
		1020	RVP Gas		39.64
10/10/19	4006	6420	Water and Power Expense	98.59	
		1020	Water and Power Company		98.59
10/10/19	4007	6500	Telephone Expense	35.00	
		1020	Local Telephone		35.00
10/10/19	4008	6550	Long Distance Company	46.20	
		1020	Long Distance Company		46.20
10/14/19	ATM	3930	James Crosby, Draw	400.00	
		1020	ATM		400.00
10/15/19	4009	6180	Automobile Expense	201.00	
		1020	Auto Parts		201.00
10/17/19	4010	6180	Automobile Expense	110.00	
		1020	Phil Sanchez		110.00
10/29/19	4011	6150	Auto Registration	210.00	
		1020	Dept. of Transportation		210.00
10/29/19	4012	1450	Supplies	215.98	
		1020	Suppliers Plus		215.98
10/30/19	4013	6560	Internet Service Provider	29.99	
		1020	Internet Service Provider		29.99
	Total			**8,786.08**	**8,786.08**

3. Close the Cash Disbursements Journal; close the Select a Report or Form window.

EDITING JOURNAL ENTRIES

Compare your journal entries to the ones shown on pages 322–323. Some of the Line Descriptions may differ. This is okay. If your dates, check numbers, or account numbers are different, you should edit the journal entry. Follow these steps to edit the Cash Receipts Journal:

1. From the menu bar, click Tasks > Receive Money. The Receive Money window displays.

2. Click List . The Receipt List window appears showing the three deposits and the total.

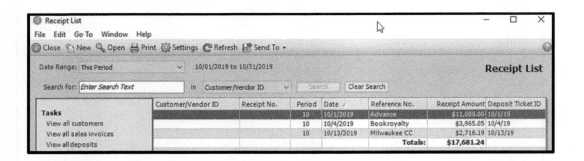

3. If you need to edit a deposit, double-click on it to drill down to the original entry on the Receive Money window.

4. Make any necessary corrections, then click Save to post.

5. Close all windows. (*Hint:* From the menu bar, select Window > Close All.)

6. Editing the Cash Disbursements Journal is similar. Go to Write Checks > View and Edit Checks. The Write Checks List appears. Drill down to the check or ATM that needs to be edited.

7. Close all windows.

DISPLAYING THE GENERAL LEDGER TRIAL BALANCE

Follow these steps to display the General Ledger Trial Balance.

1. From the menu bar, click Reports & Forms > General Ledger > General Ledger Trial Balance.

2. Click [Display]. Compare your General Ledger Trial Balance with the one shown below.

James Crosby Designer
General Ledger Trial Balance
As of Oct 31, 2019

Filter Criteria includes: Report order is by ID. Report is printed in Detail Format.

Account ID	Account Description	Debit Amt	Credit Amt
1010	Money Market Account	16,700.00	
1020	Checking Account	22,635.91	
1040	IRA Savings Account	27,730.35	
1045	WI State Retirement	35,612.00	
1300	Prepaid Insurance	2,100.00	
1400	Prepaid Rent	600.00	
1450	Supplies	1,987.81	
1500	Computer Equipment	7,905.68	
1510	Furniture	5,000.00	
1520	Automobile	19,000.00	
2000	VISA Payable		5,250.65
2400	Publisher Advances		11,000.00
3920	James Crosby, Capital		117,814.28
3930	James Crosby, Draw	600.00	
4000	Teaching Income		2,716.19
4050	Royalty Income		3,965.05
6100	Dues and Subscriptions	45.00	
6150	Auto Registration	210.00	
6180	Automobile Expense	311.00	
6400	Utilities Expense	39.64	
6420	Water and Power Expense	98.59	
6500	Telephone Expense	35.00	
6550	Long Distance Company	46.20	
6560	Internet Service Provider	29.99	
6850	Bank Service Charge	10.00	
7400	Postage Expense	49.00	
	Total:	**140,746.17**	**140,746.17**

3. To print the general ledger trial balance, select [Print], then make the selections to print (or save as a PDF or Microsoft XPS file.)

Observe that the Checking Account (Account No. 1020) balance on the General Ledger Trial Balance and the GL (System) Balance on the Account Reconciliation window on page 319 are the same: 22,635.91.

PRINTING FINANCIAL STATEMENTS

The Computer Accounting Cycle shows that adjusting entries are needed at this point. (See the Computer Accounting Cycle on page 47.) There is no need to complete adjusting entries at the end of October since quarterly adjusting entries are done on December 31, 2019. Instead, print Mr. Crosby's financial statements.

Print the following financial statements:

1. <Standard> Balance Sheet. (*Hint:* Reports & Forms > Financial Statements. *Or,* from the Business Status Navigation Center's Find a Report area, in the *Select a Category* field, select Financial Statements. In the *Select a Report* field, select <Standard> Balance Sheet. Click [Display]. The October 31, 2019 balance sheet is shown on the next page.

	James Crosby Designer	
	Balance Sheet	
	October 31, 2019	

ASSETS

Current Assets		
Money Market Account	$ 16,700.00	
Checking Account	22,635.91	
IRA Savings Account	27,730.35	
WI State Retirement	35,612.00	
Prepaid Insurance	2,100.00	
Prepaid Rent	600.00	
Supplies	1,987.81	
Total Current Assets		107,366.07
Property and Equipment		
Computer Equipment	7,905.68	
Furniture	5,000.00	
Automobile	19,000.00	
Total Property and Equipment		31,905.68
Other Assets		
Total Other Assets		0.00
Total Assets	$	139,271.75

LIABILITIES AND CAPITAL

Current Liabilities		
VISA Payable	$ 5,250.65	
Publisher Advances	11,000.00	
Total Current Liabilities		16,250.65
Long-Term Liabilities		
Total Long-Term Liabilities		0.00
Total Liabilities		16,250.65
Capital		
James Crosby, Capital	117,814.28	
James Crosby, Draw	(600.00)	
Net Income	5,806.82	
Total Capital		123,021.10
Total Liabilities & Capital	$	139,271.75

Unaudited - For Management Purposes Only

2. Display or print the <Standard> Income Stmnt.

> **Comment:** To print an Income Statement without zero balances, select , uncheck Show Zero Amounts.

	James Crosby Designer Income Statement For the Ten Months Ending October 31, 2019				
	Current Month			Year to Date	
Revenues					
Teaching Income	$ 2,716.19	40.65	$	2,716.19	40.65
Royalty Income	3,965.05	59.35		3,965.05	59.35
Total Revenues	6,681.24	100.00		6,681.24	100.00
Cost of Sales					
Total Cost of Sales	0.00	0.00		0.00	0.00
Gross Profit	6,681.24	100.00		6,681.24	100.00
Expenses					
Dues and Subscriptions	45.00	0.67		45.00	0.67
Auto Registration	210.00	3.14		210.00	3.14
Automobile Expense	311.00	4.65		311.00	4.65
Utilities Expense	39.64	0.59		39.64	0.59
Water and Power Expense	98.59	1.48		98.59	1.48
Telephone Expense	35.00	0.52		35.00	0.52
Long Distance Company	46.20	0.69		46.20	0.69
Internet Service Provider	29.99	0.45		29.99	0.45
Bank Service Charge	10.00	0.15		10.00	0.15
Postage Expense	49.00	0.73		49.00	0.73
Total Expenses	874.42	13.09		874.42	13.09
Net Income	$ 5,806.82	86.91	$	5,806.82	86.91

For Management Purposes Only

Observe that both the balance sheet and income statement include a line at the bottom of the report that says "For Management Purposes Only." In addition to dollar amounts, observe that the income statement also includes percentage of revenue columns for both the current month and the year to date. The percentages shown for each expense, total expenses, and net income indicate the percentage of each expense or revenue account divided by total revenues.

For example, here is how 13.09% was calculated for Total Expenses:

$874.42 \div 6,681.24 = 13.09\%$

At the end of the quarter (in Chapter 11), more financial statements are printed.

BACKING UP CHAPTER 10 DATA

Backup your data to this point. The suggested file name is **Chapter 10 October**. This backup saves the following data: new company set up (pages 258-265), chart of accounts (pages 267-274), beginning balances (pages 283-287), the entries recorded in the Receive Money and Write Checks windows (refer to the transaction register, pages 314-315); Account Reconciliation (pages 316-319); the Account Register, General Journal, Cash Receipts Journal, Cash Disbursements Journal, the General Ledger Trial Balance, and Financial Statements (pages 319-329).

Each backup allows you to restore data to different points. Observe that each time you backup, the instructions show a different file name. This allows you to distinguish one backup file from another one.

EXPORT THE GENERAL LEDGER TRIAL BALANCE, INCOME STATEMENT AND BALANCE SHEET TO EXCEL

Follow the steps on the next page to export the October general ledger trial balance and financial statements to Excel.

1. Display the General Ledger Trial Balance.

2. Click **Excel**. On the Copy Report to Excel window, in the file option area, Create a new Microsoft Excel workbook should be selected. In the Report header option field, Show header in Excel worksheet is selected.

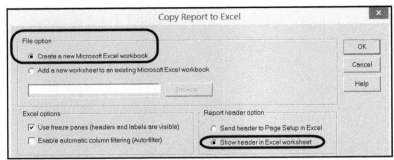

(If an "unexpected error" message appears, do not select Show header.)

3.   Click **OK**. The general ledger trial balance appears in Excel. Save. Use the file name **Chapter 10_October Trial Balance and Financial Statements.xlsx**.

4.   Maximize Sage 50. Go to the Select a Report or Form window. Select Financial Statements. Double-click <Standard> Income Statement. Uncheck Show Zero Amounts. Click **OK**. On the Income Statement window, click **Excel**.

5.   On the Copy Report to Excel window, select Add a new worksheet to an existing Microsoft Excel workbook. Click **Browse...** to go to the location of the saved file. Click **Open**.

6.   Click **OK**. Go to Sage 50 and add the <Standard> Balance Sheet to the Excel file.

7.   Click **OK**. The Excel file opens. Observe that three sheets are shown at the bottom: General Ledger Trial Balance, Income Stmnt, Balance Sheet.

| ◄ ◄ ► ►| | General Ledger Trial Balance | Income Stmnt | **Balance Sheet** |

8.   Save the Excel file. Exit Excel. Close all Sage 50 windows.

SAVE GENERAL LEDGER TRIAL BALANCE AND FINANCIAL STATEMENTS AS PDF FILES

1. Display the General Ledger Trial Balance. Click [PDF]. Save the **Chapter 10_October Trial Balance.pdf**.

2. Display the <Standard> Balance Sheet. Click [PDF]. Save the **Chapter 10_October Balance Sheet.pdf**.

3. Display the <Standard> Income Statement. Click [PDF]. Save the **Chapter 10_October Income Statement.pdf**.

ONLINE LEARNING CENTER

Complete the following end-of-chapter activities online at www.mhhe.com/yacht2019 > Student Edition > Chapter 10.

1. Quizzes: Interactive Multiple-Choice and True/False questions.
2. Going to the Net exercise: Access the Sage Business Cloud website.
3. QA Templates: 10 short-answer questions and one analysis question.
4. Assessment Rubric: review journals, navigation centers, modules, and task windows.
5. Listen to narrated PowerPoint slides.
6. Videos: Recording checks and deposits.

➤ Information Center > Sage Advisor Videos

The OLC also includes links to the Appendixes:

- Appendix A: Troubleshooting (textbook and OLC)
- Appendix C: Review of Accounting Principles (OLC Student Edition)
- Appendix D: Glossary of Terms (OLC Student Edition)

Exercise 10-1: Follow the instructions below to complete Exercise 10-1. Exercises 9-1 and 9-2 *must* be completed before starting Exercise 10-1.

1. Start Sage. Open the company that you set up in Exercise 9-1, Crafts by Your Name. The suggested company name for Exercise 9-1, page 298, is Crafts by your first and last name. (*Hint*: If a different company opens, select File > Open Previous Company. Select No to opening two companies.)

2. If necessary, restore the Exercise 9-2.ptb file.[6] This backup was made on page 303. *Or,* if you are using your own individual PC or laptop, select File, Open Previous Company to resume work with Crafts by Student Name (your first and last name).

3. To make sure you are starting in the correct place, display the Balance Sheet. Compare it to October 1, 2019 balance sheet on page 302.

How to Fix? Check that beginning balances are entered for September 30, 2019

1. To display the September 30, 2019 Balance Sheet, change the Range of dates to From Period 9, (9/1/19) To Period 9, (9/30/19).

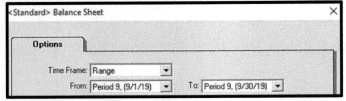

2. The September 30, 2019 balance sheet displays.

In order for the current month and year-to-date balances to post correctly from the general ledger to the financial statements, beginning balances must be entered for September 30, 2019. If you do <u>not</u> have a September 30, 2019 balance sheet, restore the Exercise 9-1.ptb file and redo the chart of accounts beginning balances, pages 301-303, Exercise 9-2.

---

[6]You can restore from your back up file even if *no* Sage 50 company exists. Refer to Troubleshooting, pages 279-280.

4. Use the transaction register below to record and post checks, ATMs, and deposits. (*Hint:* From the Banking Navigation Center, use Write Checks for checks and ATMs. From the menu bar, use Tasks > Receive Money for deposits.) The balance brought forward is Account 1020, County Bank's balance of $19,500.

		Transaction Register			
Ck. No.	Date	Description of Transaction	Payment	Deposit	Balance
	9/30/19	*Balance brought forward*			*19,500.00*
	10/1/19	Deposit (Crafts Income)		2,300.00	21,800.00
	10/2/19	ATM	100.00		21,700.00
1001	10/3/19	Accounts Payable	1,050.00		20,650.00
	10/8/19	Deposit (Teaching Income)		2,105.00	22,755.00
1002	10/9/19	Utilities Company; debit 6400 Utilities Expense	45.80		22,709.20
1003	10/10/19	Lake Advertising	115.00		22,594.20
1004	10/13/19	U.S. Post Office	49.00		22,545.20
1005	10/13/19	Crafts Workshop; debit 6800 Conference Expense	195.00		22,350.20
1006	10/15/19	SIM Telephone	55.15		22,295.05
1007	10/16/19	DSL Service; debit 6560 Internet Service Provider	29.95		22,265.10
	10/20/19	ATM	100.00		22,165.10
1008	10/28/19	Basic Office Supplies; debit 1450 Supplies	137.80		22,027.30
	10/30/19	ATM	200.00		21,827.30

5. Backup. The suggested file name is **Exercise 10-1**.

Exercise 10-2: Follow the instructions below to complete Exercise 10-2. Exercises 9-1, 9-2, and 10-1 must be completed before starting Exercise 10-2.

1. If necessary, start Sage. Open the company that you set up in Exercise 9-1, Crafts by Your Name. (If necessary, restore the Exercise 10-1.ptb backup file.)
2. Use the Bank Statement below to complete Account Reconciliation. *Record the bank service charge on the Account Reconciliation window.* (*Hint:* Click ⬆ to expand the Account Reconciliation window.)

Statement of Account			Crafts by Your Name	
County Bank			Your Address	
October 1 to October 31, 2019		Account No. 04-321822	Your City, State, Zip	
REGULAR CHECKING				
Previous Balance	9/30/19	19,500.00		
2 Deposits(+)		4,405.00		
6 Checks (-)		1,484.75		
3 Other Deductions (-)		400.00		
Service Charges (-)	10/31/19	12.00		
Ending Balance	10/31/19	**22,008.25**		
DEPOSITS				
	10/6/19	2,300.00	10/8/19	2,105.00
CHECKS (Asterisk * indicates break in check number sequence)				
	10/10/19	1001	1,050.00	
	10/10/19	1002	45.80	
	10/24/19	1003	115.00	
	10/24/19	1004	49.00	

	10/27/19	1005	195.00	
	10/30/19	1007*	29.95	
OTHER DEDUCTIONS (ATM's)				
	10/2/19		100.00	
	10/20/19		100.00	
	10/30/19		200.00	

3. Print an Account Reconciliation report. (*Hint:* Reports & Forms > Account Reconciliation.) If you are not connected to a printer, refer to the How to Fix box on page 300.

4. Print the Account Register, General Journal, Cash Receipts Journal, Cash Disbursements Journal, General Ledger Trial Balance, Balance Sheet, and Income Statement.

Check Your Figures:

Account No 1020, County Bank	$21,815.30
Total Liabilities & Capital	$53,503.10
Net Income	$3,903.10

5. Backup. The suggested file name is **Exercise 10-2**.

6. Export the General Ledger Trial Balance, Income Statement and Balance Sheet to Excel. Use the file name **Exercise 10-2_October Trial Balance and Financial Statements.xlsx**.

7. Save the General Ledger Trial Balance, Balance Sheet and Income Statement as PDF files. Use the files names **Exercise 10-2_October Trial Balance.pdf**, **Exercise 10-2_October Balance Sheet.pdf** and **Exercise 10-2_October Income Statement.pdf** as the file names. (Your instructor may also require additional PDFs: Account Reconciliation report, Account Register, General Journal, Cash Disbursements Journal and Cash Receipts Journal). When through, Exit.

CHAPTER 10 INDEX

Chapter 11 | Completing Quarterly Activities and Closing the Fiscal Year

LEARNING OBJECTIVES

1. Restore data from Chapter 10.[1] (This backup was made on page 329.)
2. Define Sage 50's General Ledger System.
3. Change accounting periods; record and post deposits, checks, and ATM transactions for November and December.
4. Complete account reconciliation.
5. Display Sage 50's data file statistics window.
6. Print a General Ledger Trial Balance (unadjusted).
7. Journalize and post end-of-quarter adjusting entries in the General Journal.
8. Print the Adjusted Trial Balance and financial statements.
9. Close the fiscal year, and print a Postclosing Trial Balance.
10. Make eight backups, save four Excel files, and save 12 PDF files.[2]

Chapters 9, 10 and 11 work together. In Chapter 11 you continue recording financial information for James Crosby Designer. You complete the computer accounting cycle for November and December. Mr. Crosby's transaction registers and bank statements are used as source documents. At the end of December, which is also the end of the fourth quarter, you complete adjusting entries, print financial statements, and close the fiscal year.

GENERAL LEDGER SYSTEM (GL)

Sage 50's *General Ledger System* is the complete collection of accounts (chart of accounts) of a company, transactions associated with these accounts, and

---

[1]All activities in Chapters 9 and 10 must be completed before starting Chapter 11.

[2]For the size of backup files, Excel files, and PDFs, refer to the chart on pages 255-256.

account balances for a specified period of time. In Sage 50, the GL is the combination of all journal entries that have been recorded and posted. The account balances are shown on the company's financial statements.

Similar to other modules, the General Ledger System is organized within Sage 50's interface. On the Reports & Forms menu, the General Ledger selection shows the GL system in one place: Chart of Accounts, General Journal, General Ledger, etc. The Navigation Bar's Banking selection shows the Account Register, Chart of Accounts, General Journal Entry (three icons associated with the GL system). The journal associated with the General Ledger System is the general journal. Observe that the Tasks menu includes General Journal Entry in one section-- General Journal Entry... .

The steps of the computer accounting cycle that are completed in Chapter 11 are shown below.

Sage 50's Computer Accounting Cycle
1. Change accounting periods.
2. Journalize entries.
3. Post entries to the General Ledger.
4. Account Reconciliation.
5. Print the General Ledger Trial Balance (unadjusted).
6. Journalize and post adjusting entries.
7. Print the General Ledger Trial Balance (adjusted).
8. Print the financial statements: Balance Sheet, Income Statement, Statement of Cash Flow, and Statement of Retained Earnings.
9. Close the fiscal year.
10. Interpret accounting information.

GETTING STARTED

Follow these steps to continue using James Crosby's company data.

1. Start Sage 50. Open an existing company, James Crosby Designer (or your name Designer).[3] (*Hint:* If a different company opens, select File > Open a Previous Company. Select James Crosby [your name] Designer. If the screen prompts Do you want to keep Crafts by Your Name open?, click [No].)

2. If necessary, restore the Chapter 10 October.ptb backup file. This backup was made on page 329.

To make sure you are starting in the appropriate place in the data (Chapter 10 October.ptb backup), display the General Ledger Trial Balance. This is also shown on page 325.

James Crosby Designer
General Ledger Trial Balance
As of Oct 31, 2019

Filter Criteria includes: Report order is by ID. Report is printed in Detail Format.

Account ID	Account Description	Debit Amt	Credit Amt
1010	Money Market Account	16,700.00	
1020	Checking Account	22,635.91	
1040	IRA Savings Account	27,730.35	
1045	WI State Retirement	35,612.00	
1300	Prepaid Insurance	2,100.00	
1400	Prepaid Rent	600.00	
1450	Supplies	1,987.81	
1500	Computer Equipment	7,905.68	
1510	Furniture	5,000.00	
1520	Automobile	19,000.00	
2000	VISA Payable		5,250.65
2400	Publisher Advances		11,000.00
3920	James Crosby, Capital		117,814.28
3930	James Crosby, Draw	600.00	
4000	Teaching Income		2,716.19
4050	Royalty Income		3,965.05
6100	Dues and Subscriptions	45.00	
6150	Auto Registration	210.00	
6180	Automobile Expense	311.00	
6400	Utilities Expense	39.64	
6420	Water and Power Expense	98.59	
6500	Telephone Expense	35.00	
6550	Long Distance Company	46.20	
6580	Internet Service Provider	29.99	
6850	Bank Service Charge	10.00	
7400	Postage Expense	49.00	
	Total:	**140,746.17**	**140,746.17**

---

[3]You can restore from your back up file even if *no* designer company exists. Refer to Troubleshooting, pages 279-280.

3. Follow these steps to change accounting periods:

a. From the menu bar, select Tasks > System.

b. From the System menu, select Change Accounting Period.

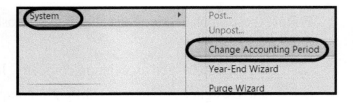

> **Comment: Can I Unpost journal entries?** If your company is operating in the Batch Posting Method, you can Unpost journal entries to edit a batch of transactions. Because you are using Real Time posting, you <u>cannot Unpost</u>.

c. From the Open Accounting Periods list, select 11-Nov 01, 2019 to Nov 30, 2019.

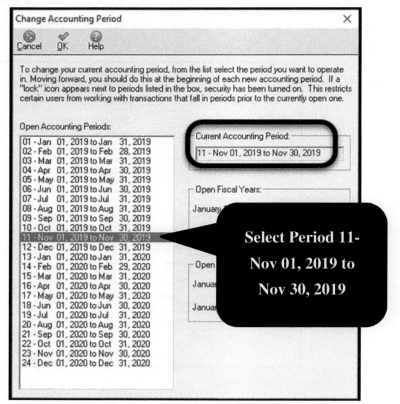

d. Make sure period 11 - Nov 01, 2019 to Nov 30, 2019 is selected. Click [✓ OK]. Click [No] when the Would you like to print your reports before continuing? window appears. If a Sage 50 Accounting prompt appears, read it, then click <No>. You can also select Do not display this message again.

e. Select [Business Status]. The toolbar shows [Period 11: 11-01-19 - 11-30-19].

When accounting periods are changed, windows and reports are updated to November.

TRANSACTION REGISTER AND BANK STATEMENT: NOVEMBER 2019

Use Mr. Crosby's transaction register to journalize and post transactions for the month of November. (*Hint: Use Write Checks* from the Banking Navigation Center *for recording checks and ATMs; use Receive Money from the Tasks menu for recording deposits. Remember to Save after each transaction.* Saving posts the entry to the appropriate journal and the general ledger.) Italics and a broken line, indicate entries that have already been made. Start with the 11/3 Deposit.

Comment: Before journalizing November's entries, make sure that you are starting with correct data. To do that, display the General Ledger Trial Balance and compare it to the one shown on page 325 in Chapter 10. Since you changed accounting periods, your trial balance will be dated November 30. Verify that Account No. 1020, Checking Account, shows a balance of $22,635.91 which is the same as the starting balance on the transaction register below.

		Transaction Register James Crosby Designer			
Check Number	**Date**	**Description of Transaction**	**Payment**	**Deposit**	**Balance**
	10/31	*Starting balance (includes Bank Service Charge)*	*10.00*		*22,635.91*
	11/3	Deposit (book royalty)		2,455.85	25,091.76

	11/5	ATM	200.00		24,891.76
	11/6	Deposit (Milwaukee CC)		2,716.19	27,607.95
4014	11/11	Water and Power Company	90.50		27,517.45
4015	11/11	RVP Gas	53.90		27,463.55
4016	11/12	Local Telephone	45.08		27,418.47
4017	11/14	Long Distance Company	81.50		27,336.97
	11/16	ATM	200.00		27,136.97
4018	11/27	VISA card payment	5,250.65		21,886.32
4019	11/28	Internet Service Provider	29.99		21,856.33
	11/28	ATM	200.00		21,656.33

Follow these steps to complete the computer accounting cycle.

1. Use Mr. Crosby's bank statement to complete the account reconciliation.

Statement of Account			James Crosby Designer		
Checking Account			788 Lake Drive		
November 1 to November 30, 2019		Account No. 344822-33	Milwaukee, WI 53205		
REGULAR CHECKING					
Previous Balance	10/31/19		23,131.52		
2 Deposits(+)			5,172.04		
8 checks (-)			766.59		
3 Other deduction (-)			600.00		
Service Charges (-)	11/30/19		10.00		
Ending Balance	11/30/19		**26,926.97**		
DEPOSITS					
	11/3/19		2,455.85		
	11/8/19		2,716.19		

CHECKS (Asterisk * indicates break in check number sequence)			
	11/3/19	4005*	39.64
	11/3/19	4011	210.00
	11/3/19	4012	215.98
	11/5/19	4013	29.99
	11/17/19	4014	90.50
	11/27/19	4015	53.90
	11/28/19	4016	45.08
	11/28/19	4017	81.50
OTHER DEDUCTIONS (ATM's)			
	11/5/19	200.00	
	11/16/19	200.00	
	11/28/19	200.00	

2. Follow these steps to display the Account Register.

    a. From Banking Navigation Center's Recently Used Banking Reports area, select View Account Register. (*Hint:* You can also go to the menu bar selection Reports & Forms > Account Reconciliation > Account Register.)

James Crosby Designer
Account Register
For the Period From Nov 1, 2019 to Nov 30, 2019
1020 - Checking Account

Filter Criteria includes: Report order is by Date.

Date	Trans No	Type	Trans Desc	Deposit Amt	Withdrawal Amt	Balance
			Beginning Balance			22,635.91
11/3/19	11/3/19	Deposit	Deposit	2,455.85		25,091.76
11/5/19	ATM	Withdrawal	ATM		200.00	24,891.76
11/6/19	11/6/19	Deposit	Deposit	2,716.19		27,607.95
11/11/19	4014	Withdrawal	Water and Power Company		90.50	27,517.45
11/11/19	4015	Withdrawal	RVP Gas		53.90	27,463.55
11/12/19	4016	Withdrawal	Local Telephone		45.08	27,418.47
11/14/19	4017	Withdrawal	Long Distance Company		81.50	27,336.97
11/16/19	ATM	Withdrawal	ATM		200.00	27,136.97
11/27/19	4018	Withdrawal	VISA card payment		5,250.65	21,886.32
11/28/19	4019	Withdrawal	Internet Service Provider		29.99	21,856.33
11/28/19	ATM	Withdrawal	ATM		200.00	21,656.33
11/30/19	11/30/19	Other	Service Charge		10.00	21,646.33
			Total	5,172.04	6,161.62	

    b. Compare the Account Register to the transaction register on pages 341-342. If necessary, drill down to make corrections.

3. Close the Account Register report.

4. Follow these steps to print an Account Reconciliation report:

   a. From the menu bar, click Reports & Forms > Account Reconciliation > highlight Account Reconciliation > [Print] or [Display]. If you are printing, the Modify Report – Account Reconciliation window appears. Observe that the As of field shows Current Period, and the GL Account ID field shows 1020.

   b. At the Print window, click [OK].

James Crosby Designer
Account Reconciliation
As of Nov 30, 2019
1020 - Checking Account
Bank Statement Date: November 30, 2019

Filter Criteria includes: Report is printed in Detail Format.

Beginning GL Balance				22,635.91
Add: Cash Receipts				5,172.04
Less: Cash Disbursements				(6,151.62)
Add (Less) Other				(10.00)
Ending GL Balance				21,646.33
Ending Bank Balance				26,926.97
Add back deposits in transit				
Total deposits in transit				
(Less) outstanding checks	Nov 27, 2019	4018	(5,250.65)	
	Nov 28, 2019	4019	(29.99)	
Total outstanding checks				(5,280.64)
Add (Less) Other				
Total other				
Unreconciled difference				0.00
Ending GL Balance				21,646.33

5. Close the account reconciliation report.

6. Print or display the Cash Receipts Journal.

James Crosby Designer
Cash Receipts Journal
For the Period From Nov 1, 2019 to Nov 30, 2019
Filter Criteria includes: Report order is by Check Date. Report is printed in Detail Format.

Date	Account ID	Transaction Ref	Line Description	Debit Amnt	Credit Amnt
11/3/19	4050	Book royalty	Royalty income		2,455.85
	1020		Deposit	2,455.85	
11/6/19	4000	Milwaukee CC	Teaching income		2,716.19
	1020		Deposit	2,716.19	
				5,172.04	5,172.04

7. Print or display your Cash Disbursements Journal and compare it to the one shown.

James Crosby Designer
Cash Disbursements Journal
For the Period From Nov 1, 2019 to Nov 30, 2019
Filter Criteria includes: Report order is by Date. Report is printed in Detail Format.

Date	Check #	Account ID	Line Description	Debit Amount	Credit Amount
11/5/19	ATM	3930	James Crosby, Draw	200.00	
		1020	ATM		200.00
11/11/19	4014	6420	Water and Power Expense	90.50	
		1020	Water and Power Company		90.50
11/11/19	4015	6400	Utilities Expense	53.90	
		1020	RVP Gas		53.90
11/12/19	4016	6500	Telephone Expense	45.08	
		1020	Local Telephone		45.08
11/14/19	4017	6550	Long Distance Company	81.50	
		1020	Long Distance Company		81.50
11/16/19	ATM	3930	James Crosby, Draw	200.00	
		1020	ATM		200.00
11/27/19	4018	2000	VISA Payable	5,250.65	
		1020	VISA card payment		5,250.65
11/28/19	4019	6560	Internet Service Provider	29.99	
		1020	Internet Service Provider		29.99
11/28/19	ATM	3930	James Crosby, Draw	200.00	
		1020	ATM		200.00
	Total			6,151.62	6,151.62

8. Print or display the general journal to see the bank service charge.

James Crosby Designer
General Journal
For the Period From Nov 1, 2019 to Nov 30, 2019
Filter Criteria includes: Report order is by Date. Report is printed with Accounts having Zero Amounts and with shortened descriptions and in Detail Format.

Date	Account ID	Reference	Trans Description	Debit Amt	Credit Amt
11/30/19	1020	11/30/19	Service Charge		10.00
	6850		Service Charge	10.00	
		Total		10.00	10.00

If your journals do not agree with the ones shown, edit the journals and post again. (Refer to page 324 Editing Journal Entries.)

9. Print or display the General Ledger Trial Balance.

James Crosby Designer
General Ledger Trial Balance
As of Nov 30, 2019
Filter Criteria includes: Report order is by ID. Report is printed in Detail Format.

Account ID	Account Description	Debit Amt	Credit Amt
1010	Money Market Account	16,700.00	
1020	Checking Account	21,646.33	
1040	IRA Savings Account	27,730.35	
1045	WI State Retirement	35,612.00	
1300	Prepaid Insurance	2,100.00	
1400	Prepaid Rent	600.00	
1450	Supplies	1,987.81	
1500	Computer Equipment	7,905.68	
1510	Furniture	5,000.00	
1520	Automobile	19,000.00	
2400	Publisher Advances		11,000.00
3920	James Crosby, Capital		117,814.28
3930	James Crosby, Draw	1,200.00	
4000	Teaching Income		5,432.38
4050	Royalty Income		6,420.90
6100	Dues and Subscriptions	45.00	
6150	Auto Registration	210.00	
6180	Automobile Expense	311.00	
6400	Utilities Expense	93.54	
6420	Water and Power Expense	189.09	
6500	Telephone Expense	80.08	
6550	Long Distance Company	127.70	
6560	Internet Service Provider	59.98	
6850	Bank Service Charge	20.00	
7400	Postage Expense	49.00	
	Total:	140,667.56	140,667.56

10.   Print or display the Balance Sheet.

James Crosby Designer
Balance Sheet
November 30, 2019

ASSETS

Current Assets			
Money Market Account	$	16,700.00	
Checking Account		21,646.33	
IRA Savings Account		27,730.35	
WI State Retirement		35,612.00	
Prepaid Insurance		2,100.00	
Prepaid Rent		600.00	
Supplies		1,987.81	
Total Current Assets			106,376.49
Property and Equipment			
Computer Equipment		7,905.68	
Furniture		5,000.00	
Automobile		19,000.00	
Total Property and Equipment			31,905.68
Other Assets			
Total Other Assets			0.00
Total Assets	$		138,282.17

LIABILITIES AND CAPITAL

Current Liabilities			
Publisher Advances	$	11,000.00	
Total Current Liabilities			11,000.00
Long-Term Liabilities			
Total Long-Term Liabilities			0.00
Total Liabilities			11,000.00
Capital			
James Crosby, Capital		117,814.28	
James Crosby, Draw		(1,200.00)	
Net Income		10,667.89	
Total Capital			127,282.17
Total Liabilities & Capital	$		138,282.17

Unaudited - For Management Purposes Only

11. Print or display the Income Statement.

James Crosby Designer
Income Statement
For the Eleven Months Ending November 30, 2019

		Current Month			Year to Date	
Revenues						
Teaching Income	$	2,716.19	52.52	$	5,432.38	45.83
Royalty Income		2,455.85	47.48		6,420.90	54.17
Total Revenues		5,172.04	100.00		11,853.28	100.00
Cost of Sales						
Total Cost of Sales		0.00	0.00		0.00	0.00
Gross Profit		5,172.04	100.00		11,853.28	100.00
Expenses						
Dues and Subscriptions		0.00	0.00		45.00	0.38
Auto Registration		0.00	0.00		210.00	1.77
Automobile Expense		0.00	0.00		311.00	2.62
Utilities Expense		53.90	1.04		93.54	0.79
Water and Power Expense		90.50	1.75		189.09	1.60
Telephone Expense		45.08	0.87		80.08	0.68
Long Distance Company		81.50	1.58		127.70	1.08
Internet Service Provider		29.99	0.58		59.98	0.51
Bank Service Charge		10.00	0.19		20.00	0.17
Postage Expense		0.00	0.00		49.00	0.41
Total Expenses		310.97	6.01		1,185.39	10.00
Net Income	$	4,861.07	93.99	$	10,667.89	90.00

For Management Purposes Only

➢ **Troubleshooting:** Why are my Current Month and Year to Date balances different than the Income Statement shown?

On the Income Statement, the Year to Date column accumulates balances for October *and* November; the Current Month column reflects November only. In Chapter 9, on page 284, step 1, the instructions said "Beginning balances must be set for the previous month, September 1-30, 2019." If you did <u>not</u> set your chart of accounts beginning balances From 9/1/2019 through 9/30/2019, the Current Month and Year to Date columns will differ from those shown above. To see when your beginning balances were set, display the General Ledger from Period 9 (9/1/2019) to Period 11 (11/30/2019).

To display the General Ledger from Sep 1, 2019 to Nov 30, 2019 do this:

a. From the Reports & Forms menu, select General Ledger > General Ledger > Options . In the From field, select Period 9, (9/1/19). The To field shows Period 11, (11/30/19).

b. Click OK .

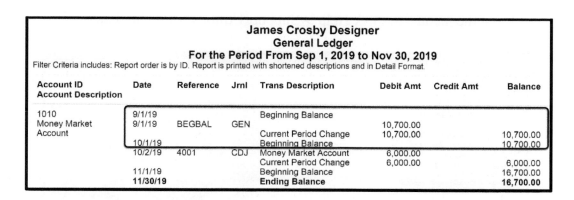

James Crosby Designer
General Ledger
For the Period From Sep 1, 2019 to Nov 30, 2019
Filter Criteria includes: Report order is by ID. Report is printed with shortened descriptions and in Detail Format.

Account ID Account Description	Date	Reference	Jrnl	Trans Description	Debit Amt	Credit Amt	Balance
1010 Money Market Account	9/1/19			Beginning Balance			
	9/1/19	BEGBAL	GEN		10,700.00		
				Current Period Change	10,700.00		10,700.00
	10/1/19			Beginning Balance			10,700.00
	10/2/19	4001	CDJ	Money Market Account	6,000.00		
				Current Period Change	6,000.00		6,000.00
	11/1/19			Beginning Balance			16,700.00
	11/30/19			**Ending Balance**			**16,700.00**

How to Fix? Beginning balances were not set up correctly.

Ask your instructor if points will be deducted if you use one of the backup files available to the instructor. If that is okay, restore the Chapter 10 October.ptb file. Continue on page 339.

OR,

Restore your Chapter 9 Beginning Balances.ptb file. Go to Maintain > Chart of Accounts > Beginning Balances. Delete the beginning balances entered for October [or another incorrect month]. Enter the beginning balances for 9/1/19 through 9/30/19 (refer to page 284). Make sure you have NOT entered the beginning balances twice by displaying the October 31, 2019 balance sheet. (Sage 50 dates reports on the last day of the period or month.) Compare your September 30, 2019 balance sheet to the one shown on page 289. Back up the Chapter 9 Beginning Balances.ptb file. Continue on page 307, Recording Deposits, Checks and ATMs.

BACKING UP NOVEMBER DATA

Back up. The suggested file name is **Chapter 11 November**. This backup saves the work completed for James Crosby [your name] Designer in Chapters 9, 10, and up to this point in Chapter 11.

DATA FILE STATISTICS

To display information about your company data files, follow these steps.

1. From the menu bar, click Help > Support Utilities > File Statistics.

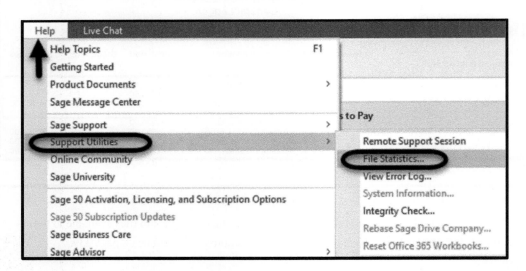

2. The Data File Statistics window lists the number of records and sizes in kilobytes for each data file for the company that is open. It also provides a grand total (scroll down).

   Sage 50 displays the company's shortened name (JAMCRODE) on the title bar.[4] This represents the name of the folder where the opened company resides. Observe that the Directory field shows where the company resides

---

[4]Since you used your first and last name, the company's shortened name will differ.

on your hard drive: C:\Sage\Peachtree\ Company\jamcrode [*or, your shortened name*].

Note: In Chapter 9, pages 291-292, the jamcrode Properties window shows the shortened company name that Sage 50 assigned.

Compare your Data File Statistics window to the one shown below.

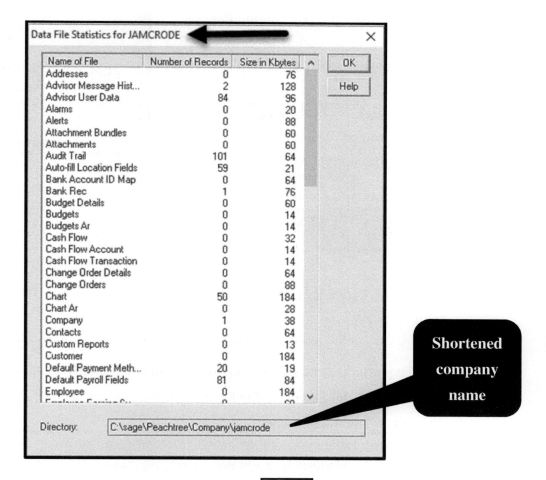

3. To close the Data File Statistics window, click OK .

CHANGING ACCOUNTING PERIODS

Follow these steps to change accounting periods:

1. From the menu bar, select Tasks > System.
2. From the System menu, select Change Accounting Period.

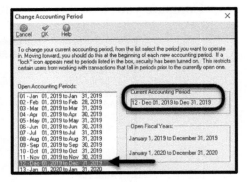

   a. In the Open Accounting Periods list, select period 12 - Dec 01, 2019 to Dec 31, 2019.

   b. Click . When the window prompts Would you like to print your reports before continuing?, click [No]. Observe that the toolbar shows

   Period 12:
   12-01-19 - 12-31-19

TRANSACTION REGISTER AND BANK STATEMENT: DECEMBER 2019

1. To journalize and post transactions for the month of December, use Mr. Crosby's transaction register.

Comment: Before you start journalizing December entries, make sure that you are starting with correct data. To do that, display the General Ledger Trial Balance and compare it to the one shown on page 346. Since you changed accounting periods to December, your General Ledger Trial Balance is dated the last day of the month, December 31, 2019.

Transaction Register James Crosby Designer					
Check Number	Date	Description of Transaction	Payment	Deposit	Balance
	11/30	*Starting balance*			*21,646.33*
	12/3[5]	ATM	400.00		21,246.33
	12/8	Deposit (Milwaukee CC)		2,716.19	23,962.52
4020	12/11	Water and Power Company	75.45		23,887.07
4021	12/11	RVP Gas (utilities)	102.92		23,784.15
4022	12/12	Local Telephone	45.95		23,738.20
4023	12/15	Ur Gallery (business cards; debit 1450 Supplies)	115.25		23,622.95
4024	12/18	Long Distance Company	75.49		23,547.46
4025	12/18	Internet Service Provider	29.99		23,517.47
	12/19	ATM	400.00		23,117.47
	12/29	ATM	400.00		22,717.47

2. Use Mr. Crosby's bank statement to complete account reconciliation.

Statement of Account			James Crosby Designer	
Checking Account			788 Lake Drive	
December 1 to December 31, 2019 Account No. 348822-33			Milwaukee, WI 53205	
REGULAR CHECKING				
Previous Balance	11/30/19	26,926.97		
1 Deposit(+)		2,716.19		
7 Checks (-)		5,695.70		
3 Other Deduction (-)		1,200.00		

[5]Start your journal transactions with the December 3 ATM transaction.

Service Charges (-)	12/31/19	10.00		
Ending Balance	12/31/19	**22,737.46**		
DEPOSITS				
	12/8/19	2,716.19		
CHECKS (Asterisk * indicates break in check number sequence)				
	12/8/19	4018	5,250.65	
	12/8/19	4019	29.99	
	12/22/19	4020	75.45	
	12/29/19	4021	102.92	
	12/29/19	4022	45.95	
	12/31/19	4023	115.25	
	12/31/19	4024	75.49	
OTHER DEDUCTIONS (ATM's)				
	12/3/19	400.00		
	12/19/19	400.00		
	12/29/19	400.00		

2. Display the Account Register.

James Crosby Designer
Account Register
For the Period From Dec 1, 2019 to Dec 31, 2019
1020 - Checking Account

Filter Criteria includes: Report order is by Date.

Date	Trans No	Type	Trans Desc	Deposit Amt	Withdrawal Amt	Balance
			Beginning Balance			21,646.33
12/3/19	ATM	Withdrawal	ATM		400.00	21,246.33
12/8/19	12/8/19	Deposit	Deposit	2,716.19		23,962.52
12/11/19	4020	Withdrawal	Water and Power Company		75.45	23,887.07
12/11/19	4021	Withdrawal	RVP Gas		102.92	23,784.15
12/12/19	4022	Withdrawal	Local Telephone		45.95	23,738.20
12/15/19	4023	Withdrawal	Ur Gallery		115.25	23,622.95
12/18/19	4024	Withdrawal	Long Distance Company		75.49	23,547.46
12/18/19	4025	Withdrawal	Internet Service Provider		29.99	23,517.47
12/19/19	ATM	Withdrawal	ATM		400.00	23,117.47
12/29/19	ATM	Withdrawal	ATM		400.00	22,717.47
12/31/19	12/31/19	Other	Service Charge		10.00	22,707.47
			Total	2,716.19	1,655.05	

3. Print or display the Account Reconciliation report.

James Crosby Designer
Account Reconciliation
As of Dec 31, 2019
1020 - Checking Account
Bank Statement Date: December 31, 2019

Filter Criteria includes: Report is printed in Detail Format.

Beginning GL Balance		21,646.33
Add: Cash Receipts		2,716.19
Less: Cash Disbursements		(1,645.05)
Add (Less) Other		(10.00)
Ending GL Balance		22,707.47
Ending Bank Balance		22,737.46
Add back deposits in transit		
Total deposits in transit		
(Less) outstanding checks		
Dec 18, 2019 4025	(29.99)	
Total outstanding checks		(29.99)
Add (Less) Other		
Total other		
Unreconciled difference		0.00
Ending GL Balance		22,707.47

4. Print or display the General Journal.

James Crosby Designer
General Journal
For the Period From Dec 1, 2019 to Dec 31, 2019

Filter Criteria includes: Report order is by Date. Report is printed with Accounts having Zero Amounts and with shortened descriptions and in Detail Format.

Date	Account ID	Reference	Trans Description	Debit Amt	Credit Amt
12/31/19	1020	12/31/19	Service Charge		10.00
	6850		Service Charge	10.00	
		Total		10.00	10.00

5. Print or display the Cash Receipts Journal.

James Crosby Designer
Cash Receipts Journal
For the Period From Dec 1, 2019 to Dec 31, 2019

Filter Criteria includes: Report order is by Check Date. Report is printed in Detail Format.

Date	Account ID	Transaction Ref	Line Description	Debit Amnt	Credit Amnt
12/8/19	4000	Milwaukee CC	Teaching income		2,716.19
	1020		Deposit	2,716.19	
				2,716.19	**2,716.19**

6. Print or display the Cash Disbursements Journal. Compare your cash disbursements journal to the one shown below.

James Crosby Designer
Cash Disbursements Journal
For the Period From Dec 1, 2019 to Dec 31, 2019

Filter Criteria includes: Report order is by Date. Report is printed in Detail Format.

Date	Check #	Account ID	Line Description	Debit Amount	Credit Amount
12/3/19	ATM	3930	James Crosby, Draw	400.00	
		1020	ATM		400.00
12/11/19	4020	6420	Water and Power Expense	75.45	
		1020	Water and Power Company		75.45
12/11/19	4021	6400	Utilities Expense	102.92	
		1020	RVP Gas		102.92
12/12/19	4022	6500	Telephone Expense	45.95	
		1020	Local Telephone		45.95
12/15/19	4023	1450	Supplies	115.25	
		1020	Ur Gallery		115.25
12/18/19	4024	6550	Long Distance Company	75.49	
		1020	Long Distance Company		75.49
12/18/19	4025	6560	Internet Service Provider	29.99	
		1020	Internet Service Provider		29.99
12/19/19	ATM	3930	James Crosby, Draw	400.00	
		1020	ATM		400.00
12/29/19	ATM	3930	James Crosby, Draw	400.00	
		1020	ATM		400.00
	Total			**1,645.05**	**1,645.05**

If your journals do not agree with the ones shown, edit and post again.

7. Display or print a General Ledger Trial Balance (unadjusted). Compare
   your trial balance to the one shown below.

James Crosby Designer
General Ledger Trial Balance
As of Dec 31, 2019

Filter Criteria includes: Report order is by ID. Report is printed in Detail Format.

Account ID	Account Description	Debit Amt	Credit Amt
1010	Money Market Account	16,700.00	
1020	Checking Account	22,707.47	
1040	IRA Savings Account	27,730.35	
1045	WI State Retirement	35,612.00	
1300	Prepaid Insurance	2,100.00	
1400	Prepaid Rent	600.00	
1450	Supplies	2,103.06	
1500	Computer Equipment	7,905.68	
1510	Furniture	5,000.00	
1520	Automobile	19,000.00	
2400	Publisher Advances		11,000.00
3920	James Crosby, Capital		117,814.28
3930	James Crosby, Draw	2,400.00	
4000	Teaching Income		8,148.57
4050	Royalty Income		6,420.90
6100	Dues and Subscriptions	45.00	
6150	Auto Registration	210.00	
6180	Automobile Expense	311.00	
6400	Utilities Expense	196.46	
6420	Water and Power Expense	264.54	
6500	Telephone Expense	126.03	
6550	Long Distance Company	203.19	
6560	Internet Service Provider	89.97	
6850	Bank Service Charge	30.00	
7400	Postage Expense	49.00	
	Total:	**143,383.75**	**143,383.75**

BACKING UP THE UNADJUSTED TRIAL BALANCE

Back up. The suggested file name is **Chapter 11 December UTB**. (UTB is an
abbreviation for Unadjusted Trial Balance.) This backup saves the work
completed for James Crosby [your name] Designer in Chapters 9, 10, and up to
this point in Chapter 11. After you journalize and post the end-of-quarter
adjusting entries, you print the financial statements.

END-OF-QUARTER ADJUSTING ENTRIES

It is the policy of your accounting firm to record adjusting entries at the end of the quarter. Mr. Crosby's accounting records are complete through December 31, 2019. The adjusting entries are recorded in the General Journal. Use these steps for entering the seven adjusting entries that follow. The first adjusting entries are shown on pages 358-361, steps 1 through 7.

1. From the Banking Navigation Center, select > New General Journal Entry. (*Or,* from the Navigation Bar, link to General Journal Entry. *Or,* from the menu bar, click Tasks > General Journal Entry.)
2. Type **31** in the Date field. Press **<Enter>** three times.
3. In the GL Account field, select the appropriate account to debit. Type the account name in the Description field (or type a description). Press the **<Enter>** key once to go to the Debit field. Type the debit amount, then press the **<Enter>** key three times.
4. In the GL Account field, select the appropriate account to credit. Type the account name in the Description field. (If you typed a description with the debit part of the entry, it appears automatically.) Press the **<Enter>** key two times to go to the Credit field. Type the credit amount. Press the **<Enter>** key.
5. Click [Save] to post each adjusting entry.

Journalize and post the following December 31, 2019 adjusting entries:

1. Office supplies on hand are $1,700.00. (It is the policy of Mr. Crosby's company to do an adjustment for supplies at the end of the quarter.)

Acct. #	Account Name	Debit	Credit
6450	Office Supplies Expense	403.06	
1450	Supplies		403.06

Calculation: Supplies $2,103.06
               Office supplies on hand   - 1,700.00
               Adjustment $ 403.06

2.   Adjust three months of prepaid insurance ($2,100 X 3/12 = $525). Mr.
     Crosby paid a one year insurance premium on 10/1/19.

Acct. #	Account Name	Debit	Credit
6950	Insurance Expense	525.00	
1300	Prepaid Insurance		525.00

3.   Adjust three months of prepaid rent ($200 X 3 = $600.)

Acct. #	Account Name	Debit	Credit
6300	Rent or Lease Expense	600.00	
1400	Prepaid Rent		600.00

4.   Use straight-line depreciation for Mr. Crosby's computer equipment. His
     computer equipment has a three-year service life and a $1,000 salvage
     value. To depreciate computer equipment for the fourth quarter, use this
     calculation: $7,905.68 – $1,000 ÷ 3 years × 3/12 = $575.47

     Computer Equipment, 10/1/19 $6,800.00
     Hardware Upgrade, 10/4/19   1,105.68
     Total computer equipment, 12/31/19 $7,905.68

Acct. #	Account Name	Debit	Credit
7050	Deprec. Exp.- Comp Eqt	575.47	
1900	Accum. Depreciation - Comp Eqt		575.47

5. Use straight-line depreciation to depreciate Mr. Crosby's furniture. His furniture has a 5-year service life and a $500 salvage value. To depreciate furniture for the fourth quarter, use this calculation:

$$\$5,000 - \$500 \div 5 \times 3/12 = \$225.00$$

Acct. #	Account Name	Debit	Credit
7060	Deprec. Exp.- Furniture	225.00	
1910	Accum. Depreciation - Furniture		225.00

6. Mr. Crosby purchased his automobile on October 1, 2019. Use the following adjusting entry. The calculation is: $\$19,000 \times 20\% \times 3/12 = \$950.00$

Acct. #	Account Name	Debit	Credit
7070	Deprec. Exp. - Automobile	950.00	
1920	Accum. Depreciation - Automobile		950.00

7. Mr. Crosby received an $11,000 advance from his publisher. This was recorded as ***unearned revenue***. Unearned revenue is a liability account used to report advance collections from customers or clients. The amount of this adjusting entry is based on Mr. Crosby's royalty statement.

Acct. #	Account Name	Debit	Credit
2400	Publisher Advances	3,500.00	
4050	Royalty Income		3,500.00

8. After journalizing and posting the end-of-quarter adjusting entries, print the General Journal for December 31, 2019. Follow these steps to print your December 31, 2019 General Journal:

   a. From the menu bar, click Reports & Forms > General Ledger. Highlight General Journal.

   b. Click [Display]. The General Journal report appears.

   c. To see the account ID for each account debited and credited, click [Columns]. The General Journal Columns window appears. Select GL Account Description.

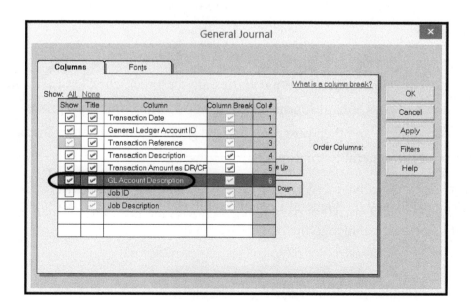

d. Click [OK]. Adjust the report so it appears on one page. Observe that an Account Description column is added. If you used a description on the general journal entry window, you may want to show the account ID on the general journal report. The December 31 adjustments and bank charges, which post on 12/31/19, are shown on the next page.

James Crosby Designer
General Journal
For the Period From Dec 1, 2019 to Dec 31, 2019

Filter Criteria includes: Report order is by Date. Report is printed with Accounts having Zero Amounts and with shortened descriptions and in Detail Format.

Date	Account I	Reference	Trans Description	Debit Amt	Credit A	Account Description
12/31/19	6450		Office Supplies Expense	403.06		Office Supplies Expense
	1450		Supplies		403.06	Supplies
	6950		Insurance Expense	525.00		Insurance Expense
	1300		Prepaid Insurance		525.00	Prepaid Insurance
	6300		Rent or Lease Expense	600.00		Rent or Lease Expense
	1400		Prepaid Rent		600.00	Prepaid Rent
	7050		Deprec. Exp. - Comp Eqt	575.47		Deprec. Exp. - Comp Eqt
	1900		Accum. Depreciation - Co		575.47	Accum. Depreciation - Comp Eqt
	7060		Deprec. Exp. - Furniture	225.00		Deprec. Exp. - Furniture
	1910		Accum. Depreciation - Furn		225.00	Accum. Depreciation - Furnitur
	7070		Deprec. Exp. - Automobile	950.00		Deprec. Exp. - Automobile
	1920		Accum. Depreciation - Auto		950.00	Accum. Depreciation - Automobi
	2400		Publisher Advances	3,500.00		Publisher Advances
	4050		Royalty Income		3,500.00	Royalty Income
12/31/19	1020	12/31/19	Service Charge		10.00	Checking Account
	6850		Service Charge	10.00		Bank Service Charge
		Total		6,788.53	6,788.53	

If any of your general journal entries are incorrect, click [ ] to drill down to the General Journal Entry window. Make the appropriate corrections, and then post your revised general journal entry. Display or print the general journal report.

9. Print or display the General Ledger Trial Balance (adjusted). Compare your adjusted trial balance to the one shown on the next page.

	James Crosby Designer		
	General Ledger Trial Balance		
	As of Dec 31, 2019		

Filter Criteria includes: Report order is by ID. Report is printed in Detail Format.

Account ID	Account Description	Debit Amt	Credit Amt
1010	Money Market Account	16,700.00	
1020	Checking Account	22,707.47	
1040	IRA Savings Account	27,730.35	
1045	WI State Retirement	35,612.00	
1300	Prepaid Insurance	1,575.00	
1450	Supplies	1,700.00	
1500	Computer Equipment	7,905.68	
1510	Furniture	5,000.00	
1520	Automobile	19,000.00	
1900	Accum. Depreciation - Comp Eqt		575.47
1910	Accum. Depreciation - Furnitur		225.00
1920	Accum. Depreciation - Automobi		950.00
2400	Publisher Advances		7,500.00
3920	James Crosby, Capital		117,814.28
3930	James Crosby, Draw	2,400.00	
4000	Teaching Income		8,148.57
4050	Royalty Income		9,920.90
6100	Dues and Subscriptions	45.00	
6150	Auto Registration	210.00	
6180	Automobile Expense	311.00	
6300	Rent or Lease Expense	600.00	
6400	Utilities Expense	196.46	
6420	Water and Power Expense	264.54	
6450	Office Supplies Expense	403.06	
6500	Telephone Expense	126.03	
6550	Long Distance Company	203.19	
6560	Internet Service Provider	89.97	
6850	Bank Service Charge	30.00	
6950	Insurance Expense	525.00	
7050	Deprec. Exp. - Comp Eqt	575.47	
7060	Deprec. Exp. - Furniture	225.00	
7070	Deprec. Exp. - Automobile	950.00	
7400	Postage Expense	49.00	
	Total:	**145,134.22**	**145,134.22**

10. Print or display the Balance Sheet.

James Crosby Designer
Balance Sheet
December 31, 2019

ASSETS

Current Assets		
Money Market Account	$ 16,700.00	
Checking Account	22,707.47	
IRA Savings Account	27,730.35	
WI State Retirement	35,612.00	
Prepaid Insurance	1,575.00	
Supplies	1,700.00	
Total Current Assets		106,024.82
Property and Equipment		
Computer Equipment	7,905.68	
Furniture	5,000.00	
Automobile	19,000.00	
Accum. Depreciation - Comp Eqt	(575.47)	
Accum. Depreciation - Furnitur	(225.00)	
Accum. Depreciation - Automobi	(950.00)	
Total Property and Equipment		30,155.21
Other Assets		
Total Other Assets		0.00
Total Assets	$	136,180.03

LIABILITIES AND CAPITAL

Current Liabilities		
Publisher Advances	$ 7,500.00	
Total Current Liabilities		7,500.00
Long-Term Liabilities		
Total Long-Term Liabilities		0.00
Total Liabilities		7,500.00
Capital		
James Crosby, Capital	117,814.28	
James Crosby, Draw	(2,400.00)	
Net Income	13,265.75	
Total Capital		128,680.03
Total Liabilities & Capital	$	136,180.03

Unaudited - For Management Purposes Only

11. Print or display the Income Statement.

```
                            James Crosby Designer
                             Income Statement
                    For the Twelve Months Ending December 31, 2019
```

	Current Month		Year to Date	
Revenues				
Teaching Income	$ 2,716.19	43.70	$ 8,148.57	45.10
Royalty Income	3,500.00	56.30	9,920.90	54.90
Total Revenues	6,216.19	100.00	18,069.47	100.00
Cost of Sales				
Total Cost of Sales	0.00	0.00	0.00	0.00
Gross Profit	6,216.19	100.00	18,069.47	100.00
Expenses				
Dues and Subscriptions	0.00	0.00	45.00	0.25
Auto Registration	0.00	0.00	210.00	1.16
Automobile Expense	0.00	0.00	311.00	1.72
Rent or Lease Expense	600.00	9.65	600.00	3.32
Utilities Expense	102.92	1.66	196.46	1.09
Water and Power Expense	75.45	1.21	264.54	1.46
Office Supplies Expense	403.06	6.48	403.06	2.23
Telephone Expense	45.95	0.74	126.03	0.70
Long Distance Company	75.49	1.21	203.19	1.12
Internet Service Provider	29.99	0.48	89.97	0.50
Bank Service Charge	10.00	0.16	30.00	0.17
Insurance Expense	525.00	8.45	525.00	2.91
Deprec. Exp. - Comp Eqt	575.47	9.26	575.47	3.18
Deprec. Exp. - Furniture	225.00	3.62	225.00	1.25
Deprec. Exp. - Automobile	950.00	15.28	950.00	5.26
Postage Expense	0.00	0.00	49.00	0.27
Total Expenses	3,618.33	58.21	4,803.72	26.58
Net Income	$ 2,597.86	41.79	$ 13,265.75	73.42

```
                        For Management Purposes Only
```

How to Fix? My Income Statement's Year to Date column does not agree

Check the beginning balances on the general ledger. (Refer to Troubleshooting, pages 348-349.) If you did <u>not</u> enter chart of accounts beginning balances for 9/1/19 through 9/30/19, the Year to Date column does not agree with December's Income Statement or the Statement of Cash Flow on page 367. You can also check your beginning balances by displaying a September 30, 2019 Balance Sheet and comparing it to page 289. After posting transactions for October, November, and December, the chart of accounts beginning balances cannot be changed. What can you do?

Ask your instructor if you can restore the Chapter 11 December.ptb file (or another backup file) that the instructor can provide. Refer to the chart on page 255-256 for the files backed up in Chapter 11. Print or display the financial statements and compare with the textbook.

12. Follow these steps to print or display the Statement of Retained Earnings.

    a. In the Financial Statement list, click <Standard> Retained Earnings to highlight it.

    b. Click [Print] (or to display, click [Options]).

    c. Uncheck Show Zero Amounts. Make the selections to print. Compare your Statement of Retained Earnings to the one shown below.

James Crosby Designer
Statement of Retained Earnings
For the Twelve Months Ending December 31, 2019

Beginning Retained Earnings	$	0.00
Adjustments To Date		0.00
Net Income		13,265.75
Subtotal		13,265.75
James Crosby, Draw		(2,400.00)
Ending Retained Earnings	$	10,865.75

For Management Purposes Only

The Statement of Retained Earnings shows the net income at the end of the quarter, $13,265.75, minus Mr. Crosby's drawing, $2,400. When you close the fiscal year, the Ending Retained Earnings amount, $10,865.75, will be shown on the postclosing trial balance, page 375.

13. Print or display the Statement of Cash Flow. Compare it to the one shown on the next page.

James Crosby Designer
Statement of Cash Flow
For the twelve Months Ended December 31, 2019

	Current Month	Year to Date
Cash Flows from operating activities		
Net Income	$ 2,597.86	$ 13,265.75
Adjustments to reconcile net income to net cash provided by operating activities		
Accum. Depreciation - Comp Eqt	575.47	575.47
Accum. Depreciation - Furnitur	225.00	225.00
Accum. Depreciation - Automobi	950.00	950.00
Prepaid Insurance	525.00	(1,575.00)
Prepaid Rent	600.00	0.00
Supplies	287.81	(1,700.00)
Publisher Advances	(3,500.00)	7,500.00
Total Adjustments	(336.72)	5,975.47
Net Cash provided by Operations	2,261.14	19,241.22
Cash Flows from investing activities		
Used For		
Computer Equipment	0.00	(7,905.68)
Furniture	0.00	(5,000.00)
Automobile	0.00	(19,000.00)
Net cash used in investing	0.00	(31,905.68)
Cash Flows from financing activities		
Proceeds From		
James Crosby, Capital	0.00	117,814.28
Used For		
James Crosby, Draw	(1,200.00)	(2,400.00)
Net cash used in financing	(1,200.00)	115,414.28
Net increase <decrease> in cash	$ 1,061.14	$ 102,749.82
Summary		
Cash Balance at End of Period	$ 102,749.82	$ 102,749.82
Cash Balance at Beg of Period	(101,688.68)	0.00
Net Increase <Decrease> in Cash	$ 1,061.14	$ 102,749.82

Unaudited - For Internal Use Only.

BACKING UP DECEMBER DATA

Backup. The suggested file name is **Chapter 11 December**. (This backup saves the work completed for James Crosby [your name] Designer in Chapters 9, 10, and up to this point in Chapter 11.)

EXPORT FINANCIAL STATEMENTS TO EXCEL AND SAVE PDF FILES

Follow these steps to export the General Ledger Trial Balance (Adjusted), Balance Sheet, Income Statement, Statement of Cash Flow, and Statement of Retained Earnings to Excel and save as Adobe PDF files. For detailed steps exporting multiple reports to Excel, refer to pages 329-331.

1. Display the General Ledger Trial Balance.
2. Export the General Ledger Trial Balance to Excel. Create a new Microsoft Excel workbook.
3. Save. Use **Chapter 11_Adjusted Trial Balance and Financial Statements.xlsx** as the file name.
4. Display the Balance Sheet. Export to Excel. Add a new worksheet to an existing Microsoft Excel workbook. (*Hint:* Add the sheet to the file saved in step 3—Chapter 11_Adjusted Trial Balance and Financial Statements.xlsx.)
5. Display the Income Statement. (*Hint:* Select Options to uncheck Show Zero Amounts.) Export to Excel. Add a new worksheet to an existing Microsoft Excel workbook. *(Hint:* Add the sheet to the file saved in step 3—Chapter 11_Financial Statements.xlsx).
6. Display the Statement of Cash Flow. Export to Excel. Add this sheet to the saved file.
7. Display the Statement of Retained Earnings. Export to Excel. Add this sheet to the saved file.
8. Your Excel file should have five sheets: General Ledger Trial Balance, Balance Sheet, Income Stmnt, Cash Flow, and Retained Earnings.

9. Save the file. Exit Excel.

10. Save the General Ledger Trial Balance, Balance Sheet, Income Statement, Statement of Cash Flow, and Statement of Retained Earnings as PDF files. Use Chapter 11_Adjusted Trial Balance, Chapter 11_December Balance Sheet.pdf, Chapter 11_December Income Statement.pdf, etc. as the file names. (Your instructor may require additional reports saved as PDF files.)

11. Close all Sage 50 windows.

CLOSING THE FISCAL YEAR

The Retained Earnings account is updated at the close of the fiscal year with the ending balance of income and expenses (net income or net loss). The balance in the retained earnings account continues to accrue at the end of each fiscal year. At the end of the year, Sage automatically completes the closing procedure. Follow these steps to close James Crosby's fiscal year:

1. If necessary, start Sage 50, then open James Crosby Designer. (*Hint:* If necessary, restore the Chapter 11 December.ptb file.) From the menu bar, select Tasks > System > Year-End Wizard. (*Hint:* You can also select

)

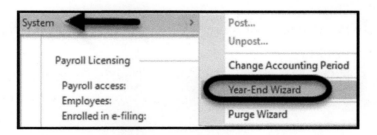

2. The Year-End Wizard - Welcome window appears. Read the information on the Welcome to the Sage 50 Year-End Wizard window.

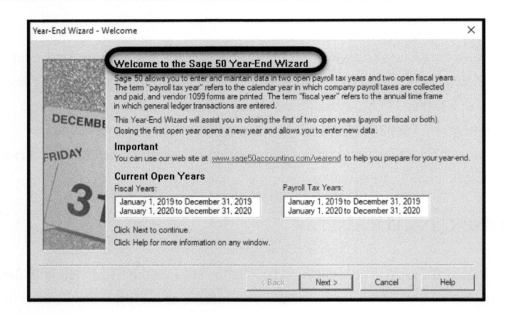

3. Click [Next >]. The Close Options window appears. In the Years to
Close list, Fiscal and Payroll Tax Years is the default. Read the information
on this window.

4.Click .

5. The Print Fiscal Year-End Reports window appears. Read the information on this window. Since you have already printed reports, click Check None to uncheck all.

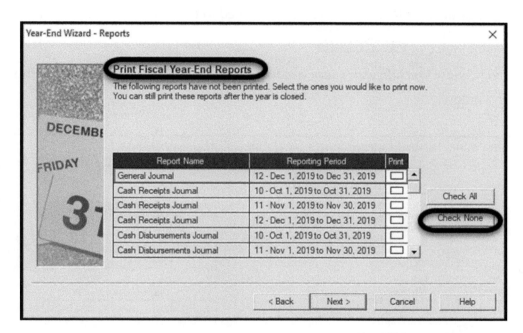

Hint: If you do not *uncheck the boxes, the general ledger prints.*

6. Click Next > .

7. The Internal Accounting Review window appears. Read the information on this window. Click Next > .

8. The Back Up Company Data window appears. You already made a back up on page 367 but you should make another one. Read the information on this window. Click Back Up . The Back Up Company window appears.

9. Observe that the box next to Include company name in the backup file name is checked. Click Back Up .

10. The Save Backup for James Crosby Designer as window appears. Observe that the File name field includes the name of the company and today's date.

11. If necessary, go to the location for backing up. Click [Save]. Click [OK].

12. After the backup is made, you are returned to the Back Up Company Data window. Click [Next >].

13. The New Open Fiscal Years window appears. Read the information on this window.

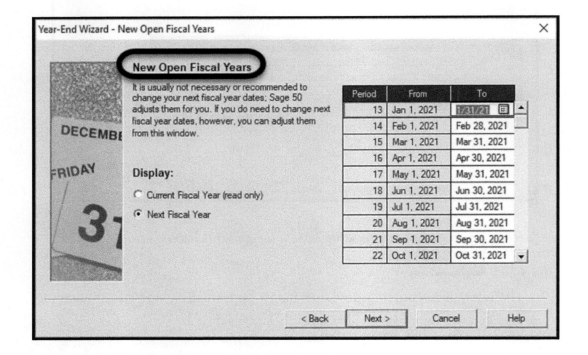

14. Accept the default for Next Fiscal Year by clicking on [Next >].

15. The Important - Confirm Year-End Close window appears. Read the information on this window.

16. Click 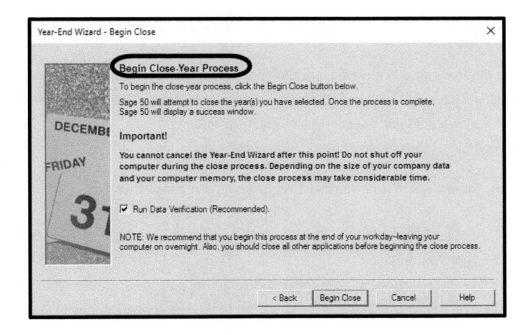 `Next >`.

17. The Begin Close-Year Process window appears. Read the information on this window.

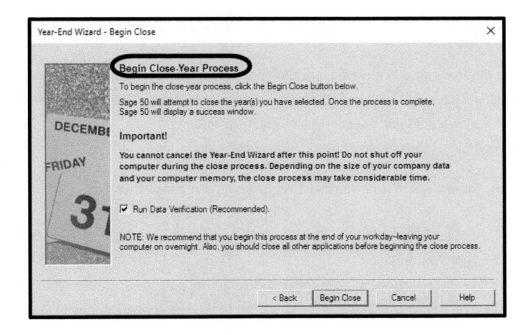

18. Click Begin Close .

19. After a few moments the scale shows 100%. The Congratulations! window appears. Read the information on this window.

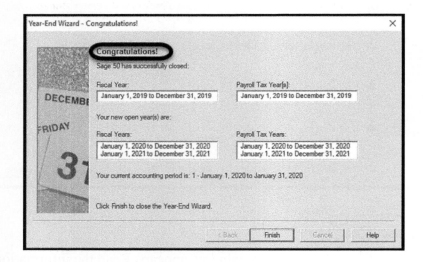

20. Click Finish .

PRINTING THE POSTCLOSING TRIAL BALANCE

After the fiscal year is closed, a postclosing trial balance is printed. Only permanent accounts appear on the postclosing trial balance. All temporary accounts (revenues and expenses) have been closed.

This completes the computer accounting cycle.

Follow these steps to print James Crosby's postclosing trial balance:

1. From the menu bar, select Reports & Forms > General Ledger > General Ledger Trial Balance.
2. Make the selections to print the postclosing trial balance. Compare your general ledger trial balance (postclosing) to the one shown on the next page.

```
                                    James Crosby Designer
                                  General Ledger Trial Balance
                                       As of Jan 31, 2020
Filter Criteria includes: Report order is by ID. Report is printed in Detail Format.

Account ID    Account Description              Debit Amt       Credit Amt

1010          Money Market Account             16,700.00
1020          Checking Account                 22,707.47
1040          IRA Savings Account              27,730.35
1045          WI State Retirement              35,612.00
1300          Prepaid Insurance                 1,575.00
1450          Supplies                          1,700.00
1500          Computer Equipment                7,905.68
1510          Furniture                         5,000.00
1520          Automobile                       19,000.00
1900          Accum. Depreciation - Comp Eqt                      575.47
1910          Accum. Depreciation - Furnitur                      225.00
1920          Accum. Depreciation - Automobi                      950.00
2400          Publisher Advances                                7,500.00
3910          Retained Earnings                                10,865.75
3920          James Crosby, Capital                           117,814.28

              Total:                          137,930.50      137,930.50
```

Observe that the postclosing trial balance is dated January 31, 2019. The balance in Account 3910, Retained Earnings, is Mr. Crosby's year-to-date net income minus the total of his drawing account (13,265.75 – 2,400 = 10,865.75). The Retained Earnings balance was also shown on page 366, Statement of Retained Earnings.

How to Fix? Postclosing trial balance is not the same

On the chart of accounts, the Account Type field is important. Display the chart of accounts and compare your Account Types to the ones shown on page 273. If you need to change the account type, you should make the account inactive and create a new account with the correct Account Type and balance. Then, try to complete the closing process again. If changing the account type does not work, you may need to ask your instructor for an earlier backup. Restore that file and continue work from that point. Refer to the Part 2 introduction, pages 254-256 for the appropriate file to restore. Consult with your instructor about using one of the backup files available to instructors.

BACKING UP YEAR-END DATA

Backup. The suggested file name is **Chapter 11 EOY**. (*Hint:* EOY is an abbreviation of End of Year. If necessary, uncheck Include company name in the backup file name.) When this backup is made, you have saved the work completed for James Crosby [your name] Designer in Chapters 9, 10, and 11.

EXPORT POSTCLOSING TRIAL BALANCE TO EXCEL AND SAVE PDF FILE

Follow these steps to export the postclosing trial balance to Excel.

1. Display the General Ledger Trial Balance.
2. Export to Excel. Create a new Microsoft Excel workbook. Change General Ledger Trial Balance to Postclosing Trial Balance. Change the date to December 31, 2019.
3. Save. Use **Chapter 11_Postclosing Trial Balance.xlsx** as the file name. On the Excel file, change title to Postclosing Trial Balance and date to December 31, 2019.
4. Save the General Ledger Trial Balance (postclosing) as a PDF file. The suggested file name is **Chapter 11_Postclosing Trial Balance.pdf**.
5. Close all windows.

ONLINE LEARNING CENTER

Complete end-of-chapter activities at www.mhhe.com/yacht2019 > Student Edition > Chapter 11.

1. Quizzes: Multiple Choice and True False questions. Interactive online tests that are graded and can be emailed to your instructor.

2. More Resources:

   a. QA Templates: 10 true/make true questions and three Analysis Questions.
   b. Narrated PowerPoints: Listen to narrated PowerPoints.
   c. Going to the Net Exercises: Complete depreciation exercise using the Chapter 11_Asset depreciation schedule1.xlsx file at www.mhhe.com/yacht2019 > Student Edition > Chapter 11 > Going to the Net.
   d. Assessment Rubric: Complete the rubric to review Sage 50's journals, navigation centers, modules, task windows, and reports.

➤ Information Center > Sage Advisor Videos

The OLC also includes links to the Appendixes:
- Appendix A: Troubleshooting (textbook and OLC)
- Appendix C: Review of Accounting Principles (OLC Student Edition)
- Appendix D: Glossary (OLC Student Edition)

Exercise 11-1: Follow the instructions below to complete Exercise 11-1. You must complete Exercises 9-1, 9-2, 10-1, and 10-2 *before* Exercise 11-1.

1. Start Sage 50. Open the company that you started in Exercise 9-1, Crafts by your first and last name. (*Hint:* From the menu bar, select File > Open Previous Company > Crafts by your first and last name. When the screen prompts Do you want to keep James Crosby [or your name] Designer open, click <No>.)

2. If necessary, restore the Exercise 10-2.ptb file.[6] This back up was made on page 335. (*Hint*: To make sure you are starting in the right place, display

---

[6]You can restore from your back up file even if *no* Sage 50 company exists. Refer to Troubleshooting, pages 279-280.

the General Ledger Trial Balance and compare it to Exercise 10-2, step 4, page 335. Compare the County Bank account balance with the 10/31/19 balance on the transaction register below.)

3. Change accounting period to November 1 through November 30, 2019.
4. To record and post checks, ATMs, and deposits, use the transaction register. (*Hint:* Use Write Checks for checks and ATMs; use Receive Money for deposits.)

Transaction Register					
Check Number	**Date**	**Description of Transaction**	**Payment**	**Deposit**	**Balance**
	10/31/19	*Starting balance*			*21,815.30*
	11/2/19	ATM	100.00		21,715.30
	11/3/19	Deposit (Crafts Income)		2,200.00	23,915.30
1009	11/3/19	Albert Maintenance and Repairs	75.00		23,840.30
	11/8/19	Deposit (Teaching income)		2,105.00	25,945.30
1010	11/9/19	Utilities Company	55.75		25,889.55
1011	11/10/19	Lake Advertising	175.00		25,714.55
1012	11/13/19	U.S. Post Office	49.00		25,665.55
1013	11/15/19	SIM Telephone	41.97		25,623.58
1014	11/16/19	DSL Service	29.95		25,593.63
	11/20/19	ATM	100.00		25,493.63
1015	11/28/19	Basic Office Supplies; debit 1450 Supplies	47.80		25,445.83
	11/29/19	ATM	200.00		25,245.83

5. To complete Account Reconciliation, use the Bank Statement on the next page.

Statement of Account County Bank November 1 to November 30, 2019		Account No. 04-321822	Crafts by Your Name Your Address Your city, state, Zip	
REGULAR CHECKING				
Previous Balance	10/31/19	22,008.25		
2 Deposits(+)		4,305.00		
6 Checks (-)		547.70		
3 Other Deductions (-)		400.00		
Service Charges (-)	11/30/19	12.00		
Ending Balance	11/30/19	**25,353.55**		
DEPOSITS				
	11/6/19	2,200.00		
	11/8/19	2,105.00		
CHECKS (Asterisk * indicates break in check number sequence)				
	11/10/19	1006*	55.15	
	11/10/19	1008	137.80	
	11/24/19	1009	75.00	
	11/24/19	1010	55.75	
	11/27/19	1011	175.00	
	11/30/19	1012	49.00	
OTHER DEDUCTIONS (ATM's)				
	11/2/19	100.00		
	11/20/19	100.00		
	11/29/19	200.00		

6. Print an Account Reconciliation report.
7. Print the Account Register.
8. Print the General Journal.
9. Print the Cash Receipts Journal.

10.   Print the Cash Disbursements Journal.

11.   Print the General Ledger Trial Balance.

12.   Print a Balance Sheet and Income Statement.

Check Your Figures:

Account No. 1020, County Bank, $25,233.83

Account No. 3920, Student Name, Capital, $50,000.00

Account No. 3930, Student Name, Draw, $800.00

13.   Backup. The suggested file name is **Exercise 11-1**.

14.   Ask your instructor if you should save these reports as Adobe PDF or Excel files. The suggested file name is Exercise 11-1_November Account Reconcilation.pdf, etc. For the saved Excel files use Exercise 11-1_November Reports.xlsx. Save multiple sheets within one Excel file.

Exercise 11-2: Follow the instructions below to complete Exercise 11-2. Exercises 9-1, 9-2, 10-1, 10-2 and 11-1 *must* be completed before starting Exercise 11-2.

1.   Start Sage. Open the company that you set up in Exercise 9-1 (Crafts by your first and last name).

2.   If necessary, restore Exercise 11-1.[7] To make sure you are starting in the correct place, display the General Ledger Trial Balance (refer to step 11 above).

3.   Change accounting period to December 1 through December 31, 2019.

4.   Use the transaction register to record and post checks, ATMs, and deposits. (*Hint:* On the Business Status Navigation Center, the balance, $25,233.83, should match Account No. 1020 for County Bank. This is the same balance

---

[7]You can restore from your backup file even if *no* Sage 50 company exists. Refer to Troubleshooting, pages 279-280.

as the Transaction Register. You may need to click) Start with the 12/2/19 ATM.

START HERE

Transaction Register					
Check Number	**Date**	**Description of Transaction**	**Payment**	**Deposit**	**Balance**
	11/30/19	*Starting balance*	*12.00*		*25,233,83*
	12/2/19	ATM	100.00		26,133.83
	12/3/19	Deposit (Crafts Income)		2,850.00	27,983.83
1016	12/3/19	Lake Advertising	100.00		27,883.83
	12/7/19	Deposit (Teaching income)		2,105.00	29,988.83
1017	12/8/19	Albert Maintenance and Repairs	75.00		29,913.83
1018	12/9/19	Utilities Company	95.75		29,818.08
1019	12/13/19	U.S. Post Office	49.00		29,769.08
1020	12/15/19	SIM Telephone	45.05		29,724.03
1021	12/16/19	DSL Service	29.95		29,694.08
	12/20/19	ATM	100.00		29,594.08
1022	12/28/19	Basic Office Supplies; debit 1450 Supplies	137.80		29,456,28
	12/30/19	ATM	200.00		29,256.28

typo?

typo?

5. To complete Account Reconciliation, use the Bank Statement on the next page.

Statement of Account			Crafts by Your Name	
County Bank			Your Address	
December 1 to December 31, 2019		Account No. 04-321822	Your City, State, Zip	
REGULAR CHECKING				
Previous Balance	11/30/19	25,353.55		
2 Deposits(+)		4,955.00		
6 Checks (-)		390.47		
3 Other Deductions (-)		400.00		
Service Charges (-)	12/31/19	12.00		
Ending Balance	12/31/19	**29,506.08**		
DEPOSITS				
	12/6/19	2,850.00		
	12/8/19	2,105.00		
CHECKS (Asterisk * indicates break in check number sequence)				
	12/10/19	1013	41.97	
	12/10/19	1014	29.95	
	12/24/19	1015	47.80	
	12/24/19	1016	100.00	
	12/27/19	1017	75.00	
	12/30/19	1018	95.75	
OTHER DEDUCTIONS (ATM's)				
	12/2/19	100.00		
	12/20/19	100.00		
	12/31/19	200.00		

6.   Print an Account Reconciliation report, Account Register, General Journal, Cash Receipts Journal, Cash Disbursements Journal, and General Ledger Trial Balance.

7.   Backup. The suggested file name is **Exercise 11-2 Unadjusted Trial Balance**.

8.   Complete the following end-of-quarter adjusting entries.

   a. Supplies on hand: $850.00.
   b. Depreciation for Computer Equipment: $458.33.
   c. Depreciation for Furniture: $150.00.
   d. Depreciation for the Automobile: $950.00.
   e. Adjust three months prepaid rent: $700.00.
   f. Adjust three months prepaid insurance: $250.00.

9.   Print the December 31, 2019 general journal.

10.   Print the General Ledger Trial Balance (adjusted).

11.   Print the financial statements: Balance Sheet, Income Statement, Statement of Cash Flow, and Statement of Retained Earnings.

   Check Your Figures:
   Account No. 1020, County Bank, $29,244.28
   Account No. 3920, Student Name, Capital, $50,000.00
   Total Liabilities & Capital, $58,285.95
   Net Income, Current Month, $1,716.52; Year to Date, $9,485.95

12.   Backup. The suggested filename is **Exercise 11-2 Financial Statements**.

13.   Export the General Ledger Trial Balance (Adjusted), Balance Sheet, Income Statement, Statement of Cash Flow, and Statement of Retained Earnings to Excel. Use **Exercise 11-2_Adjusted Trial Balance and Financial Statements.xlsx** as the file name.

14. Save the General Ledger Trial Balance (Adjusted), Balance Sheet, Income Statement, Statement of Cash Flow and Statement of Retained Earnings as PDF files. Use Exercise 11-2 and the report's title for each file name.

15. Close the fiscal year.

16. Print the General Ledger Trial Balance (Postclosing).

Check Your Figures:

Account No. 3910, Retained Earnings, $8,285.95

17. Backup. The suggested filename is **Exercise 11-2 End of Year**.

18. Export the Postclosing Trial Balance to Excel. Create a new Microsoft Excel workbook. Change General Ledger Trial Balance to Postclosing Trial Balance. Change the date to December 31, 2019

19. Save. Use **Exercise 11-2_Postclosing Trial Balance.xlsx** as the file name. On the Excel file, change title and date.

20. Save the Postclosing Trial Balance as a PDF file. Use **Exercise 11-2_Postclosing Trial Balance.pdf** as the file name.

CHAPTER 11 INDEX

Project 1

Marcia Westcott, Accounting

In Project 1, you complete the computer accounting cycle for Marcia Westcott, Accounting. Ms. Westcott started her accounting practice on December 1, 2019 in Phoenix, Arizona. Ms. Westcott employs two accounting technicians and one administrative assistant. Ms. Westcott employees are independent contractors. Further study of payroll accounting will be done in Chapter 15.

Marcia Westcott's balance sheet, transaction register, and bank statement are provided as source documents. Remember to make backups at periodic intervals. Project 1 ends with a Check Your Progress assessment.

Step 1: Start Sage 50. If a company opens, select File > New Company. One company should be opened. The Create a New Company – Introduction window appears. Click Next >.

Step 2: Type the following company information:

Company Name:	**Marcia Westcott, Accounting** (substitute your first and last name for Marcia Westcott)
Address Line 1:	**8142 Missouri Avenue**
City, State, Zip	**Phoenix, AZ 85017**
Country:	**USA**
Telephone:	**602-555-6581**
Fax:	**602-555-6583**
Business Type:	Select Sole Proprietorship

Leave the Tax ID Numbers fields blank.

Web Site: www.marciawestcott.com

E-mail: info@marciawestcott.com

- Step 3: Accept the default to Use a sample business type that closely matches your company.

- Step 4: Select Service Company. (*Hint:* Simplified types have four-digit account numbers.)

- Step 5: Accept the default for Accrual accounting.

- Step 6: Accept the default for Real Time posting.

- Step 7: Accept the default for Choose an accounting period structure, 12 monthly accounting periods per year.

- Step 8: The Choose the first period of your fiscal year window appears. Select January 2019.

- Step 9: At the You are ready to create your company window, click
  Finish . If the screen prompts You can use this company in the student version of Sage 50 for the next 14 months and then it will expire, click OK . At the Sage 50 Setup Guide window, click on the box next to Don't show this screen at startup. Click
  Close . Close the Sage Advisor Getting Started window.

- Step 10: Change the accounting period to Period 12 – Dec 01, 2019 to Dec. 31, 2019. (*Hint:* On the toolbar, click > select Period 12.
  The toolbar shows Period 12: 12-01-19 - 12-31-19 . If an Internal Accounting Review screen appears, put a checkmark next to Do not display this message again > click <No>.

- Step 11: Make the following changes to the Chart of Accounts.

Delete these accounts:

- 1010   Cash on Hand
- 1150   Allowance for Doubtful Account
- 2310   Sales Tax Payable
- 2320   Deductions Payable
- 2330   Federal Payroll Taxes Payable
- 2340   FUTA Payable
- 2350   State Payroll Taxes Payable
- 2360   SUTA Payable
- 2370   Local Taxes Payable
- 2400   Customer Deposits
- 2700   Long Term Debt–Noncurrent
- 4300   Other Income
- 5900   Inventory Adjustments
- 6250   Other Taxes Expense
- 6650   Commissions and Fees Expense
- 7100   Gain/Loss – Sale of Assets Exp

Change these accounts:[1]

1020	Checking Account	**Fifth Street Bank**
1400	Prepaid Expenses	**Prepaid Rent**
1500	Property and Equipment	**Computer Equipment**
1900	Accum. Depreciation-Prop&Eqt	**Accum. Depreciation – Comp Eqt**
2500	Current Portion Long-Term Debt	**Notes Payable**
3920	Owner's Contribution	**Marcia Westcott, Capital**

(Use your name; *Account Type: Equity-doesn't close*)

---

[1]New account names are shown in boldface. Click 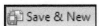 between accounts.

3930	Owner's Draw	**Marcia Westcott, Draw**
		(Use your name)
4000	Professional Fees	**Accounting Fees**
6000	Wages Expense	**Wages Expense – Adm Asst**
6050	Employee Benefit Programs Exp.	**Wages Expense - Acctg Tech**
6150	Bad Debt Expense	**Subscriptions Expense**
6450	Office Supplies Expense	**Supplies Expense**
6550	Other Office Expense	**Internet Service**
7050	Depreciation Expense	**Deprec Exp – Comp Eqt**

Add these accounts:

1450	**Supplies**	Other Current Assets
1510	**Furniture and Fixtures**	Fixed Assets
1520	**Automobile**	Fixed Assets
1910	**Accum. Depreciation – Furn&Fix**	Accum. Depreciation
1920	**Accum. Depreciation – Automobi**	Accum. Depreciation
7060	**Deprec Exp - Furn&Fix**	Expenses
7070	**Deprec Exp - Automobile**	Expenses
7400	**Postage Expense**	Expenses

Step 12: Print or display the Chart of Accounts. Check Account IDs (numbers) and Account Types.

Step 13: Back up the chart of accounts; **Marcia Westcott Chart of Accounts**.

Step 14: Use Marcia Westcott's Balance Sheet to enter the beginning balances.

Important: When selecting the beginning balance period, select From 11/1/19 through 11/30/19—Beginning Balances as of November 30, 2019.

Marcia Westcott, Accounting		
Balance Sheet		
December 1, 2019		
ASSETS		
Current Assets		
Fifth Street Bank	$36,500.00	
Accounts Receivable	17,400.00	
Prepaid Rent	4,000.00	
Supplies	3,300.00	
Total Current Assets		$61,200.00
Property and Equipment		
Computer Equipment	12,600.00	
Furniture and Fixtures	15,000.00	
Automobile	21,500.00	
Total Property and Equipment		49,100.00
Total Assets		$110,300.00
Continued		
LIABILITIES AND CAPITAL		
Current Liabilities		
Accounts Payable	$11,200.00	
Notes Payable	8,400.00	
Total Current Liabilities		19,600.00
Capital		
Marcia Westcott, Capital		90,700.00
Total Liabilities and Capital		$ 110,300.00

Remove check marks I/S & SCF

• Step 15:   To check your beginning balances, display or print the November 30, 2019 balance sheet.

• Step 16:   Back up beginning data; **Marcia Westcott Beginning Balances**.

Step 17:   The transaction register provides the information necessary for December's journal entries.

Stopped here →

$3300.00
105.65
3405.65
3250.00
15565

		Transaction Register			
		Marcia Westcott, Accounting			
Ck. No.	**Date**	**Description of Transaction**	**Payment**	**Deposit**	**Balance**
	11/30	*Starting balance*			*36,500.000*
	12/1	Deposit (accounting fees)		3,500.00	40,000.00
9001	12/1	Fifth Street Bank (Notes Payable)	2,700.00		37,300.00
9002	12/1	AA Office Equipment - laser printer (computer equipment)	625.87		36,674.13
9003	12/9	Administrative Asst.	1,250.00		35,424.13
9004	12/9	Acctg. Technician	690.00		34,734.13
9005	12/12	Penn Office Supplies (letterhead - supplies)	105.65		34,628.48
9006	12/16	Administrative Asst.	1,250.00		33,378.48
9007	12/16	Acctg. Technician	690.00		32,688.48
	12/16	Deposit (accounting fees)		3,500.00	36,188.48
9008	12/17	SW Telephone (telephone bill)	70.47		36,118.01
9009	12/17	U.S. Post Office	49.00		36,069.01
9010	12/17	Journal of Accounting (subscription)	545.00		35,524.01
9011	12/23	Administrative Asst.	1,250.00		34,274.01
9012	12/23	Acctg. Technician	620.00		33,654.01
	12/23	Deposit (accounting fees)		4,000.00	37,654.01
9013	12/24	SPR Electric (utilities bill)	105.20		37,548.81

	12/24	Deposit (accounting fees)		4,000.00	41,548.81
9014	12/30	Administrative Asst.	1,250.00		40,298.81
9015	12/30	Acctg. Technician	750.00		39,548.81
5	12/30	Deposit (payment received from client on account)		1,500.00	41,048.81
9016	12/30	Internet Service	29.99		41,018.82

SAVE!!

Step 18: Marcia Westcott's bank statement is shown below. (*Hint:* Remember to record the bank service charge.)

Statement of Account Fifth Street Bank December 1 to December 31, 2019 Account No. 893-2178		Marcia Westcott, Accounting 8142 Missouri Avenue Phoenix, AZ 85017			
REGULAR CHECKING					
Previous Balance	11/30/19	36,500.000			
4 Deposits(+)		15,000.00			
12 Checks (-)		10,607.19			
Service Charges (-)	12/31/19	25.00			
Ending Balance	12/31/19	**40,867.81**			
DEPOSITS					
12/3/19 $3,500.00	12/17/19 3,500.00	12/27/19 $4,000.00	12/30/19 $4,000.00		
CHECKS (Asterisk * indicates break in check number sequence)					
	12/10/19	9001	2,700.00		
	12/11/19	9002	625.87		
	12/13/19	9003	1,250.00		
	12/13/19	9004	690.00		
	12/17/19	9005	105.65		
	12/17/19	9006	1,250.00		

	12/17/19	9007	690.00	
	12/24/19	9008	70.47	
	12/24/19	9011*	1,250.00	
	12/24/19	9012	620.00	
	12/27/19	9013	105.20	
	12/31/19	9014	1,250.00	

Step 19:   Print an Account Reconciliation report.

Step 20:   Print the Account Register.

Step 21:   Print a General Ledger Trial Balance (unadjusted).

Step 22:   Back up the unadjusted trial balance; **Marcia Westcott UTB**.

Step 23:   Complete these adjusting entries:

    a.   Supplies on hand: $3,250.00.

    b.   Depreciation for Computer Equipment: $353.50.

    c.   Depreciation for Furniture and Fixtures: $166.67.

    d.   Depreciation for the Automobile: $358.33.

    e.   Rent was paid for two months on November 30, 2019. Adjust one month's rent.[2]

SAVE!!

Step 24:   Print the General Journal, Cash Receipts Journal, and Cash Disbursements Journal.

Step 25:   Print the General Ledger Trial Balance (adjusted).

Step 26:   Print the General Ledger. (*Hint: Select Reports & Forms > General Ledger > highlight General Ledger, make the selections to print.*)

---

[2]Refer to the December 1, 2017 Balance Sheet for the account balance in the Prepaid Rent account.

123,478.50

Step 27: Print the financial statements: balance sheet, income statement, statement of retained earnings, and statement of cash flow.

Step 28: Back up December data; **Marcia Westcott December**.

Note: For grading purposes, your instructor may require that you turn in reports. Ask your instructor what type of files they prefer: Adobe (.pdf), Excel (.xlsx), or Sage 50 backup (.ptb).

Step 29: Export the adjusted trial balance, balance sheet, income statement, statement of cash flow, and statement of retained earnings to Excel. Use **Marcia Westcott_Adjusted Trial Balance and Financial Statements.xlsx** as the file name. (Change the name of the General Ledger Trial Balance to Adjusted Trial Balance.)

Step 30: Save the adjusted trial balance and financial statements as PDF files. Use Project 1, then the report's title for the file name; for example, **Project 1_Adjusted Trial Balance**, **Project 1_Balance Sheet.pdf**.

adjusting entries?

Step 31: Close the fiscal year. Continue closing the fiscal year.

Step 32: Print the Postclosing Trial Balance.

Step 33: Back up year-end data; **Marcia Westcott EOY**.

Step 34: Export the postclosing trial balance to Excel. Use **Marcia Westcott_Postclosing Trial Balance.xlsx** as the file name; December 31, 2019 as the data. Change the name of the trial balance.

Step 35: Save the postclosing trial balance as a PDF file. Use **Project 1_Postclosing Trial Balance.pdf** as the file name.

Drop the 2nd file

after adjusting but before closing

Student Name_____ **Date**_____

CHECK YOUR PROGRESS: PROJECT 1, Marcia Westcott, Accounting

1. What are the total debit and credit balances on your unadjusted trial balance?

   122,600.00

2. What are the total debit and credit balances on your adjusted trial balance?

   123,478.50

3. According to your account reconciliation report, what is the Ending GL Balance?

   40,993.82

4. What is the depreciation expense for furniture and fixtures on December 31?

   166.67

5. What is the depreciation expense for computer equipment on December 31?

   353.50

6. What is the amount of total revenues as of December 31?

   15,000.00

7. How much net income (or net loss) is reported on December 31?

   2,765.32

8. What is the account balance in the Supplies account on December 31?

   3,250.00

9. What is the account balance in the Accounts Payable account on December 31?

   1,200.00

10. What is the total liabilities and capital balance on December 31?

    110,365.32

11. Is there an Increase or Decrease in cash for the the month of December?

    Increase

12. Were any Accounts Payable incurred during the month of December? (Circle your answer).

    YES   NO ?

Project

1A   Student-Designed Service Business

In Chapters 9, 10, 11, and Project 1, you learned how to complete the Computer Accounting Cycle for a service business. Project 1A gives you a chance to design a service business of your own.

You create a service business, edit your business's Chart of Accounts, create source documents, and complete the Computer Accounting Cycle. Project 1A also gives you an opportunity to review the software features learned so far.

You should think about the kind of business to create. Since you have been working on sole proprietorship service businesses in Part 2, you may want to design a business similar to these. Service businesses include: accountants, beauty salons, architects, hotels, airlines, cleaning stores, doctors, artists, etc. If you have a checking account and receive a monthly bank statement, you could use your own records for this project.

Before you begin you should design your business. You will need the following:

1. Company information that includes business name, address, and telephone number. (*Hint: Set your company up for Period 12, December 1 - 31, so that you can close the fiscal year.*)
2. One of Sage 50's sample companies.
3. A Chart of Accounts: 25 accounts minimum; 30 maximum.
4. One month's transactions for your business. You will need a Balance Sheet, check register, and bank statement. Your check register should include a minimum of 15 transactions and a maximum of 25. You should have at least four adjusting entries.

McGraw-Hill Education, *Computer Accounting with Sage 50 2019, 21e*

If you don't want to use a check register and bank statement, you could write 15 to 25 narrative transactions.

After you have designed your business, you should follow the steps of Sage 50's Computer Accounting Cycle to complete Project 1A.

For grading purposes, Project 1A should include the following printouts:

Checklist of Printouts
Project 1A
Student-Designed Project
Chart of Accounts
Account Reconciliation
Account Register
General Ledger Trial Balance (unadjusted)
Cash Receipts Journal
Cash Disbursements Journal
December 31, 20XX General Journal
General Ledger Trial Balance (adjusted)
General Ledger
Balance Sheet
Income Statement
Statement of Retained Earnings
Statement of Cash Flow
Postclosing Trial Balance

Part 3

Sage 50 2019 for Merchandising Businesses

In Part 3 of *Computer Accounting with Sage 50 2019*, 21st Edition, your accounting business is hired to do the monthly record keeping for three merchandising businesses: Shannon's Service Merchandise; the end-of-chapter exercise, Your Name Sales and Service; and Valley Bikes. Part 3 includes four chapters and two projects.

Chapter 12: Vendors & Purchases
Chapter 13: Customers & Sales
Chapter 14: Inventory & Services
Chapter 15: Employees, Payroll and Account Reconciliation
Project 2: Valley Bikes
Project 2A: Student-Designed Merchandising Business

Merchandising businesses, also called retail businesses, purchase products ready-made from a vendor and then resell these products to their customers. Items purchased by a retail business for resale are referred to as merchandise. A merchandising business earns revenue from buying and selling goods. Items purchased for use by the business are *not* merchandise; for example, supplies or computer equipment are *not* sold to customers.

In Part 1 you were shown how the sample company, Bellwether Garden Supply, used Sage 50's customer, vendor, payroll, and inventory features. The chapters that follow illustrate these features in detail. Chapters 12 through 15 are cumulative. This means that the businesses you set up in Chapter 12, Shannon's Service Merchandise; and Exercise 12-1, Student Name Sales and Service, are continued in Chapters 13, 14, and 15.

At the end of Part 3, you complete Project 2, Valley Bikes, which reviews Sage 50's merchandising business features. At the end of Project 2, there is a Check Your Progress assessment that your instructor may want you to complete. Project 2A, Student-Designed Merchandising Business, gives you an opportunity to create a merchandising business from scratch.

Chapter	Backup (.ptb extension) and Excel (.xlsx)	Kilobytes	Page Nos.
12	Chapter 12 Chart of Accounts.ptb	927 KB	414-415
	Chapter 12 Starting Balance Sheet.ptb	928 KB	418
	Chapter 12 Begin.ptb	1,007 KB	431
	Chapter 12.ptb	1,051 KB	455
	Chapter 12_CofA_PJ_CDJ_VL_GLTB.xlsx	29 KB	455-457
	Exercise 12-1 Chart of Accounts.ptb	921 KB	460
	Exercise 12-1 Starting Balance Sheet.ptb	922 KB	462
	Exercise 12-1_Chart of Accounts.pdf	32 KB	466
	Exercise 12-1_Dec 31 2018 Balance Sheet.pdf	10 KB	466
	Exercise 12-1.ptb	950 KB	466
	Exercise 12-2.ptb	963 KB	467
	Exercise 12-2_ CofA_PJ_CDJ_VL_GLTB. xlsx	28 KB	467
	Exercise 12-2_Purchase Journal.pdf	11 KB	467
	Exercise 12-2_Cash Disbursements Journal.pdf	12 KB	467
	Exercise 12-2_Vendor Ledgers.pdf	12 KB	467
	Exercise 12-2_General Ledger Trial Balance.pdf	12 KB	467
13	Chapter 13 Begin.ptb	1,047 KB	482
	Chapter 13.ptb	1,066 KB	511
	Chapter 13_SJ_CRJ_CL_GLTB.xlsx	24 KB	511
	Exercise 13-1.ptb	980 KB	514

Chapter	Backup (.ptb extension) and Excel (.xlsx)	Kilobytes	Page Nos.
13	Exercise 13-2.ptb	977 KB	515
	Exercise 13-2_SJ_CRJ_CL_GLTB.xlsx	23 KB	515
	Exercise 13-2_Sales Journal.pdf	45 KB	515
	Exercise 13-2_Cash Receipts Journal.pdf	12 KB	515
	Exercise 13-2_Customer Ledgers.pdf	12 KB	515
	Exercise 13-2_General Ledger Trial Balance.pdf	13 KB	515
14	Chapter 14 Begin.ptb	1,086 KB	526
	Chapter 14.ptb	1,091 KB	539
	Chapter 14_ CL_VL_CGSJ_IAJ_IPR_GLTB.xlsx	30 KB	540
	Exercise 14-1.ptb	1,000 KB	542
	Exercise 14-2_Cash Receipts Journal.pdf	6 KB	542
	Exercise 14-2_Purchase Journal.pdf	6 KB	542
	Exercise 14-2_Cost of Goods Sold Journal.pdf	6 KB	542
	Exercise 14-2_Inventory Adjustment Journal.pdf	6 KB	542
	Exercise 14-2_Inventory Profitability Journal.pdf	6 KB	542
	Exercise 14-2_General Ledger Trial Balance.pdf	6 KB	542
	Exercise 14-2_CRJ_PJ_CGSJ_IAJ_IPR_GLTB.xlsx	29 KB	543
15	Chapter 15 Begin.ptb	1,115 KB	562
	Chapter 15.ptb	1,162 KB	586
	Chapter 15_PayJ_GLTB_BS_IS_SCF.xlsx	33 KB	586
	Exercise 15-1_General Journal.pdf	16 KB	591
	Exercise 15-1.ptb	1,107 KB	591
	Exercise 15-2.ptb	1,047 KB	594
	Exercise 15-2_EL_CL_VL_IVR_PayJ_GLTB_BS_IS_SCF.xlsx	11 KB	594
	Exercise 15-2_Employee List.pdf	11 KB	594

Chapter	Backup (.ptb extension) and Excel (.xlsx)	Kilobytes	Page Nos.
15	Exercise 15-2_Vendor Ledgers.pdf	12 KB	594
	Exercise 15-2_Customer Ledgers.pdf	12 KB	594
	Exercise 15-2_Inventory Valuation Report.pdf	11 KB	594
	Exercise 15-2_Payroll Journal.pdf	21 KB	594
	Exercise 15-2_General Ledger Trial Balance.pdf	14 KB	594
	Exercise 15-2_Balance Sheet.pdf	12 KB	594
	Exercise 15-2_Income Statement.pdf	13 KB	594
	Exercise 15-2_Statement of Cash Flow.pdf	12 KB	594
Project 2	Valley Bikes Chart of Accounts.ptb	926 KB	600
	Valley Bikes_Dec 31 2018 Balance Sheet.pdf	54 KB	601
	Valley Bikes Starting Balance Sheet.ptb	926 KB	601
	Valley Bikes Begin.ptb	973 KB	609
	Valley Bikes January.ptb	1,055 KB	611
	Valley Bikes Financial Statements.ptb	1,054 KB	612
	Valley Bikes_CofA_CL_VL_ GLTB_AcctRec_ BS_ IS_SCF.xlsx	42 KB	612
	Project 2_Chart of Accounts.pdf	23 KB	612
	Project 2_Customer Ledgers.pdf	11 KB	612
	Project 2_Vendor Ledgers.pdf	12 KB	612
	Project 2_General Ledger Trial Balance.pdf	14 KB	612
	Project 2_Account Reconciliation.pdf	11 KB	612
	Project 2_Balance Sheet.pdf	11 KB	612
	Project 2_Income Statement.pdf	12 KB	612
	Project 2_Statement of Cash Flow.pdf	12 KB	612

Chapter 12   Vendors & Purchases

LEARNING OBJECTIVES

1. Set up company information for Shannon's Service Merchandise, a merchandising business.
2. Enter general ledger information–chart of accounts and beginning balances.
3. Enter accounts payable information–vendor defaults and vendor records.
4. Enter inventory information–inventory defaults, inventory items, and inventory beginning balances.
5. Record and post Vendors & Purchases transactions.
6. Make eight backups, save two Excel files, and save five PDF files.[1]

Chapter 12 begins Part 3 of the book, Sage 50 2019 for Merchandising Businesses. Merchandising businesses are retail stores that resell goods and services. In this chapter, you set up a merchandising business called Shannon's Service Merchandise, a partnership owned by Brian Stewart and Shannon Larsen. Mr. Stewart and Ms. Larsen divide their income equally.

Merchandising businesses purchase the merchandise they sell from suppliers known as *vendors*. Vendors are the businesses that offer Shannon's Service Merchandise credit to buy merchandise and/or assets. Purchases made on account from vendors are called *accounts payable transactions*.

Accounts Payable is the amount of money the business owes to suppliers or vendors. When entering a purchase, a vendor code is entered first. The vendor's name and address information, the standard payment terms, and the general

---

[1]Refer to the chart on page 400 for the size of files backed up and saved.

ledger purchase account are automatically entered in the appropriate places. This information can be edited if any changes are needed. This works similarly for accounts receivable.

The diagram below illustrates how vendors are paid.

In Chapter 12, the merchandising businesses that you set up are continued in Chapters 13, 14, and 15.

GETTING STARTED

Shannon's Service Merchandise started operations on January 1, 2019. It is a partnership owned by Brian Stewart and Shannon Larsen and is located in Yuma, AZ. Follow these steps to set up the company.

1. Start Sage 50. If a company opens, select File > New Company. If a screen prompts do you want to keep another company open, click No. (*Hint:* If the startup window appears, select Create a new company.)

2. The Create a New Company – Introduction window appears. Click

    Next > . The Enter your company information window appears.
    (Observe that a red asterisk (*) indicates a required field.) Complete the
    following fields. Press the **<Tab>** key between each field.

Company Name:	**Shannon's Service Merchandise** *(use your first name then Service Merchandise)*
Address Line 1:	**3344 Milton Avenue**
City, State, Zip:	**Yuma, AZ 85366**
Country:	**USA**
Telephone:	**928-555-7744**
Fax:	**928-555-7746**
Business Type:	Select Partnership
Federal Employer ID:	**73-2338811**
State Employer ID:	**14-3997904**
State Unemployment ID:	**1452133-4**
Web Site:	**www.shannonservmdse.biz**
E-mail:	**info@shannonservmdse.biz**

> **Comment:** Use your first name in the Company Name field so that your first name will appear on all printouts.

3. Check the company information, then click . The Select a method to create your Company window appears. Accept the default for Use a sample business type that closely matches your company.

Create a New Company - Setup   ✕

Select a method to create your company

⦿ Use a sample business type that closely matches your company (**Most companies choose this**)

○ Copy settings from an existing Sage 50 Accounting company

○ Convert a company from another accounting program

○ Build your own chart of accounts (**Designed for accountants and advanced users only**)

< Back   Next >   Cancel   Help

4. Click   Next > .

5. Read the information about selecting a business type. Numerous business types are available. Scroll down. In the Detailed types list, select Retail Company. Compare your selection to the one shown on the next page. The detailed types list includes five-digit chart of accounts numbers.

IMPORTANT: Make sure that Retail Company is selected from the **Detailed types** list not the Simplified types list. Check the Chart of Accounts on the right pane. The Detailed types list has a more extensive chart of accounts than the Simplified types list. Observe that the chart of accounts has account numbers with five digits; for example, 10000 – Petty Cash. (The Simplified types list has four-digit account numbers.)

6. Make sure that Retail Company is selected from the Detailed types list. Click [Next >].

7. Read the information about the Accounting Method. Accept the default for Accrual by clicking [Next >].

8. Read the information about Posting Method. Sage 50 Software recommends real-time posting for networked computers. Accept the default for real-time posting by clicking [Next >].

9. At the Choose an accounting period structure window, accept the default for 12 monthly accounting periods per year by clicking [Next >].

10. The Choose the first period of your fiscal year window appears. Select **2019** as the year. **Check this window carefully. You cannot change it later.**

11. Click Next >.

12. The You are ready to create your company window appears. Click Finish. If the screen prompts You can use this company in the student version of Sage 50 for the next 14 months and then it will expire, click OK.

13. The Sage 50 Setup Guide window appears. Click on the box next to Don't show this screen at startup to place a checkmark in it--☑ Don't show this screen at startup. Click Close. Close the Sage Advisor Getting Started window. Shannon's (your first name) Service Merchandise - Sage 50 Accounting appears on the title bar (above the menu bar).

14. The Period shown on the toolbar defaults to the current period (month). (*Hint:* Click on the Period shown on the toolbar to change accounting periods.) Select Period 01-Jan 01,2019 to Jan 31,2019.

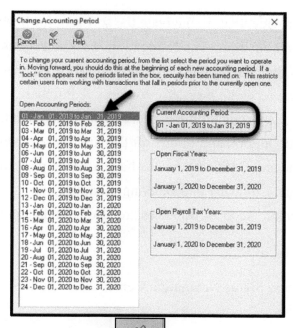

15. After selecting Period 1, click [OK]. The Period shows

 (next to the System Date or current date).

16. Click **Business Status**. The Business Status Navigation Center shows the following sections.

- Account Balances
- Vendors to Pay
- Aged Payables
- Revenue: Year to Date
- Customers Who Owe Money
- Aged Receivables
- Find a Report

In Chapters 12 through 15, you use selections from the Navigation Bar to record transactions.

These selections provide ways to navigate the software for Shannon's Service Merchandise, a retail business. The Navigation Bar's selections show Sage 50's modules: Business Status represents an overview of the company; Customers & Sales is the accounts receivable system; Vendors & Purchases is the accounts payable system, etc. A Navigation Bar is used with other Windows software, for example, Microsoft Outlook and Microsoft Dynamics use a Navigation Bar. QuickBooks Online and Desktop versions have a Home page that includes Vendors, Customers, Company and Banking modules. Similar to Sage 50's Business Status center, Account Balances are also included on QuickBooks' home page.

To make the Business Status Navigation Center the default, on the toolbar, click

 . Business Status shows a home icon

GENERAL LEDGER

Sage 50's general ledger system includes the collection of accounts of a company (chart of accounts), then summarizes the transactions associated with these accounts and their related account balances for a specified period of time. After setting up a new company, the next step is editing the chart of accounts, and then entering the beginning balances. Sage 50's general ledger system is used for that purpose. Think of the general ledger as the core of an accounting system.

The general ledger system is organized within Sage 50's user interface. For example, the Navigation Bar's Banking selection shows general ledger system choices such as the chart of accounts general journal entries, and banking reports. Also, the Reports & Forms menu shows the general ledger system's contents. Most accounting software organizes the user interface into system modules: Accounts Payable (Vendors & Purchases); Accounts Receivable (Customers & Sales), Banking, etc.

The major differences between accounting software applications include the depth of processing, enhanced features and functions, and the size of the *database* (an organized body of related information). As the database gets larger, the depth of processing increases and more features and functions are available. As companies grow in size, their accounting software needs change.

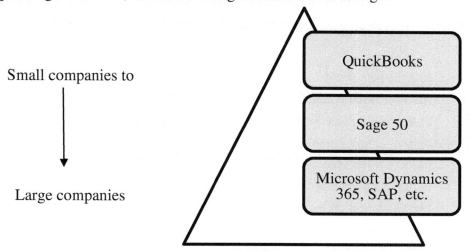

Sage 50 and QuickBooks Online and Desktop are used by small companies. As the company grows, Sage 50, Microsoft Dynamics 365 and NetSuite can be used. Large companies use Microsoft Dynamics 365, SAP and Oracle.

Company size	No. of Employees
Small business	1-50 employees
Mid-sized business	50-500 employees
Large business	500+ employees

Chart of Accounts

From the Navigation Bar, click [**Banking**] > [Chart of Accounts] > View and Edit Accounts.

1. Delete the following accounts. (*Hint:* Double-click on the account, or type the account number, then select [Delete].)

   10000   Petty Cash
   10100   Cash on Hand
   11400   Other Receivables
   14100   Employee Advances
   14200   Notes Receivable-Current
   14700   Other Current Assets
   15200   Automobiles
   15300   Other Depreciable Property
   15400   Leasehold Improvements
   15600   Building Improvements
   16900   Land
   17200   Accum. Depreciation-Automobi
   17300   Accum. Depreciation-Other
   17400   Accum. Depreciation-Leasehol
   17600   Accum. Depreciation-Bldg Imp
   19000   Deposits
   19100   Organization Costs
   19150   Accum. Amortiz -Org. Costs
   19200   Notes Receivable-Noncurrent
   19900   Other Noncurrent Assets
   23300   Deductions Payable
   23800   Local Payroll Taxes Payable

24800 Other Current Liabilities

24900 Suspense-Clearing Account

58000 Cost of Sales-Other

60500 Amortization Expense

61000 Auto Expenses

62500 Cash Over and Short

63000 Charitable Contributions Exp

63500 Commissions and Fees Exp

65000 Employee Benefit Programs Exp

68000 Laundry and Cleaning Exp

73000 Other Taxes

74000 Rent or Lease Expense

76500 Travel Expense

77000 Salaries Expense

2. Change the following accounts.

10200	Regular Checking Account	**Interstate Bank**
10400	Savings Account	**Yuma Savings & Loan**
12000	Product Inventory	**Merchandise Inventory**
14000	Prepaid Expenses	**Prepaid Insurance**
15100	Equipment	**Computers & Equipment**
17000	Accum. Depreciation-Furnitur	**Accum. Depreciation – Furn&Fix**
17100	Accum. Depreciation-Equipmen	**Accum. Depreciation – Comp&Eqt**
24000	Other Taxes Payable	**Soc. Sec. Employee Taxes Payab**
24100	Employee Benefits Payable	**Soc. Sec. Employer Taxes Payab**
24200	Current Portion Long-Term Debt	**Medicare Employee Taxes Payabl**
24400	Customer Deposits	**Medicare Employer Taxes Payabl**
27000	Notes Payable-Noncurrent	**Long-Term Notes Payable**
27400	Other Long Term-Liabilities	**Mortgage Payable**
39006	Partner's Contribution	**Brian Stewart, Capital**
		(Note: Account Type, Equity-doesn't close)

39007	Partner's Draw	**Brian Stewart, Drawing**
40000	Sales-Merchandise	**Sales-Hardware**
40200	Sales-Services	**Sales-Wall**
40400	Sales-Clearance	**Sales-Floor**
40600	Interest Income	**Service Fees**
50000	Cost of Goods Sold	**Cost of Sales-Hardware**
50500	Cost of Sales-Service	**Cost of Sales-Wall**
57000	Cost of Sales-Salaries and Wag	**Cost of Sales-Floor**
64000	Depreciation Expense	**Deprec Exp-Furn & Fixtures**
64500	Dues and Subscription Exp	**Deprec Exp-Computers & Equip**

3. Add the following accounts.   *Account Type*

13000	**Supplies**	Other Current Assets
39008	**Shannon Larsen, Capital**	Equity-doesn't close
39009	**Shannon Larsen, Drawing**	Equity- gets closed
64600	**Deprec Exp-Building**	Expenses
72510	**Soc. Sec. Expense**	Expenses
72520	**Medicare Expense**	Expenses
72530	**FUTA Expense**	Expenses
72540	**SUTA Expense**	Expenses
77600	**Overtime Expense**	Expenses

Backing up the Chart of Accounts

Follow these steps to back up the work completed so far. This backup saves the
new company set up on pages 404-409 and the general ledger chart of accounts,
pages 412-414.

1. Insert your USB flash drive. From the Navigation Bar, select

   System > click Back Up Now . Make sure the box next to Include
   company name in the backup file name is *unchecked.*

2. Click [Back Up].

3. Go to the location of your USB drive. (Or, backup to another location.) Type **Chapter 12 Chart of Accounts** in the File name field.

4. Click [Save]. When the window prompts This company backup will require approximately 1 diskette, click [OK]. When the window prompts Please insert the first disk, click [OK]. When the Back Up Company scale is 100% complete, you have successfully backed up to the current point in Chapter 12. (If you are backing up to the default or another location, this step will differ slightly.)

Beginning Balances

1. From the Maintain Chart of Accounts window, click [Account Beginning Balances]

2. The Select Period window appears. Highlight From 12/1/18 through 12/31/18. Beginning balances *must* be set for the previous month. The starting balance sheet on page 417 is dated January 1, 2019. This means that the period for entering beginning balances must be the *previous month* From 12/1/18 through 12/31/18.

> **Comment:** Select December 1-31, 2018 as your Chart of Accounts Beginning Balance period so that your journals will start on January 1, 2019. Your reports will be dated January 31, 2019. Remember, Sage 50 posts on the last day of the month. The December 31, 2018 account balances are the January 1, 2019 starting balances.

3. Compare your Select Period window to the one shown. Make sure From 12/1/18 through 12/31/18 is selected.

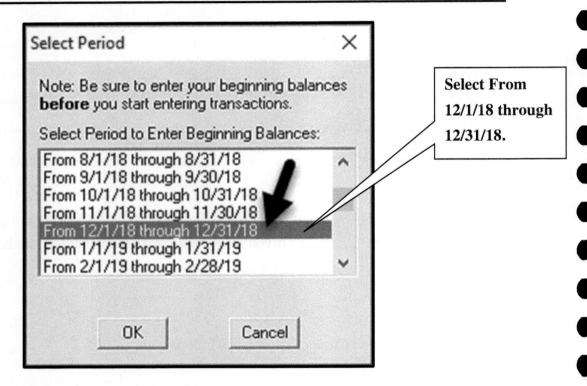

Select From 12/1/18 through 12/31/18.

Check the Select Period window carefully. Once the beginning balance period is selected, you cannot change it later.

4. Click [OK]. The Chart of Accounts Beginning Balances window appears. Observe that this window shows that you are going to enter Beginning Balances as of December 31, 2018.

Beginning Balances as of December 31, 2018.

5. Brian Stewart and Shannon Larsen purchased Shannon's Service Merchandise in December 2018. Use the Balance Sheet on the next page to record the Chart of Accounts Beginning Balances.

Shannon's Service Merchandise		
Balance Sheet, January 1, 2019		
ASSETS		
Current Assets:		
10200 - Interstate Bank	$78,500.00	
10400 - Yuma Savings & Loan	22,000.00	
12000 - Merchandise Inventory	27,740.00	
13000 - Supplies	1,750.00	
14000 - Prepaid Insurance	2,400.00	
Total Current Assets		$132,390.00
Property and Equipment:		
15000 - Furniture and Fixtures	5,000.00	
15100 - Computers & Equipment	7,500.00	
15500 - Building	100,000.00	
Total Property and Equipment		112,500.00
Total Assets		$244,890.00
LIABILITIES AND CAPITAL		
Long-Term Liabilities:		
27000 - Long-Term Notes Payable	20,500.00	
27400 - Mortgage Payable	75,000.00	
Total Long-Term Liabilities		$95,500.00
Capital:		
39006 - Brian Stewart, Capital	74,695.00	
39008 - Shannon Larsen, Capital	74,695.00	
Total Capital		149,390.00
Total Liabilities and Capital		$244,890.00

6. When you are finished entering the beginning balances, click

.

> **Troubleshooting:** To make sure your beginning balances were entered correctly, display the December 31, 2018 balance sheet. (*Hint:* Reports & Forms > Financial Statements > <Standard> Balance Sheet > Options > Time Frame > Range, From Per start (12/1/18) To Per end (12/31/18).

7. Close all windows.

BACKING UP BEGINNING BALANCES

Back up. This backup saves the new company set on pages 404-409; the general ledger chart of accounts, pages 412-414; and the beginning balances, pages 415-418. The suggested file name is **Chapter 12 Starting Balance Sheet**.

ACCOUNTS PAYABLE: VENDORS

The next section shows how to set up Accounts Payable defaults. This is where you set up information about the vendors who offer credit to Shannon's Service Merchandise. Vendors offer Shannon's Service Merchandise a 2 percent discount for invoices paid within 10 days (2% 10, Net 30 Days).

In Chapter 2, Vendors, you used Bellwether Garden Supply to explore Sage 50's accounts payable system. The accounts payable system provides the information needed for the entry that credits the Accounts Payable account and debits asset or expense accounts that vendor invoices represent. Since Shannon's Service

Merchandise buys on credit from various vendors, the business wants to keep track of the amount owed and the due dates of bills. The accounts payable system does that.

1. From the Navigation Bar, select **Vendors & Purchases** > 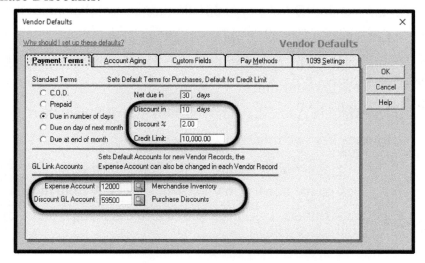 The Sage Advisor Getting Started window appears. If necessary, close the Sage Advisor Getting Started window.

2. Select **Vendors** > Set Up Vendor Defaults. Read, then close pop-up windows.

3. Due in number of days is selected in the Standard Terms list. In the Discount in field, type **10** for the number of days. Press **<Tab>**.

4. In the Discount % field, type **2** then press **<Tab>**.

5. In the Credit Limit field, type **10000** then press **<Tab>**.

6. In the Expense Account field, click 🔍. Select Account No. 12000, Merchandise Inventory.

7. In the Discount GL Account field, click 🔍. Select Account No. 59500, Purchase Discounts.

Make sure that the Expense Account field shows Account No. 12000, Merchandise Inventory; and that the Discount GL Account field shows Account No. 59500, Purchase Discounts. This sets up the default accounts for merchandise purchases and vendor discounts.

In Sage 50, the Merchandise Inventory account contains summary information about the total cost of the merchandise on hand and available for sale. In addition, Sage tracks vendor discounts in Account No. 59500, Purchase Discounts. Sage also keeps a detailed inventory record for each item of merchandise in stock. Sage automatically updates subsidiary records every time there is a change in the Merchandise Inventory account caused by a purchase, sale, or return of merchandise.

8. Click **OK**. You are returned to the Vendors & Payables Navigation Center.

9. Click **Vendors** > New Vendor. The Maintain Vendors window displays. To enter vendor information, follow these steps.

   a. In the Vendor ID field, type **JJH06** (use a zero) then press the **<Enter>** key.
   b. In the Name field, type **James Jarvis Hardware** then press the **<Enter>** key four times.
   c. In the Mailing Address field, type **3001 Clark Street** then press the **<Enter>** key two times.
   d. In the City, ST, Zip field, type **Los Angeles** then press the **<Enter>** key. Click on the down arrow ▼ then select CA from the list of states. Press the **<Enter>** key. Type **90010** as the Zip code, press **<Enter>**.

e. In the Country field, type **USA** then press **\<Enter\>**.

f. In the Vendor Type field, type **hardware** then press **\<Enter\>**.

g. In the 1099 Type field, click on the down arrow 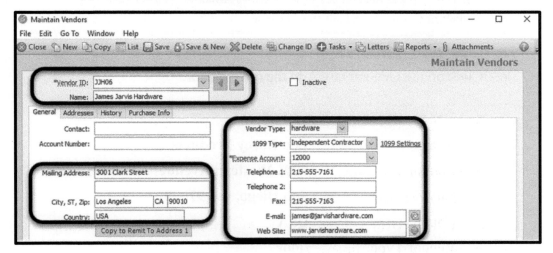 and select Independent Contractor. Press the **\<Enter\>** key. Observe that the Expense Account automatically displays 12000. This is the default Expense Account entered on page 419, step 6.

h. In the Telephone 1 field, type **213-555-7161** then press **\<Enter\>** two times.

i. In the Fax field, type **213-555-7163** then press **\<Enter\>**.

j. In the E-mail field, type **james@jarvishardware.com** and then press **\<Enter\>**.

k. Type **www.jarvishardware.com** in the Web Site field.

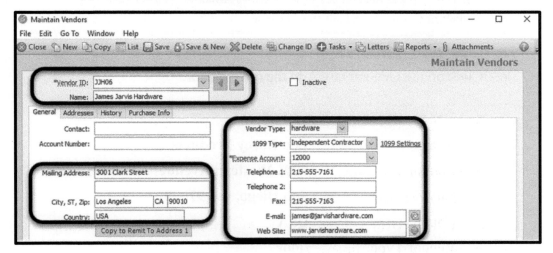

10. Click on the Purchase Info tab. Follow these steps to complete the fields:

a. Type **19-3124884** in the Tax ID Number field. Observe that the credit terms entered on page 419 are shown. Compare your Maintain Vendors/Purchase Info window to the one shown on the next page.

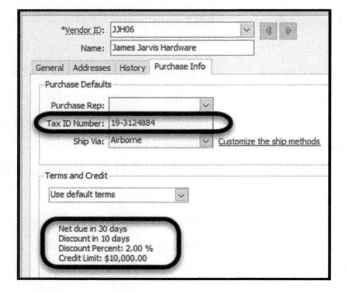

Comment: The Ship Via field on this window shows Airborne. You complete shipping information when you set the defaults for inventory.

b. Click ⬚ Save & New .

c. Click on the General tab. Add the next vendor.

1) Vendor ID: **LLP07**

   Name: **Len Lacey Products**

   Mailing Address: **8201 Western Avenue**

   City, ST, Zip   **San Diego, CA 97022**

   Country: **USA**

   Vendor Type: **floor**

   1099 Type: **Independent Contractor**

   Expense Account: Defaults to 12000

   Telephone 1:   **619-555-1239**

   Fax: **619-555-9317**

   E-mail: **len@laceyproducts.com**

   Web Site: **www.laceyproducts.com**

Purchase Info:

Material mis-statement (handwritten)

Tax ID Number:	**12-8899123**
Terms and Credit:	Defaults to 2% 10 Net 30

2) Vendor ID: **RBF08**

Name:	**Ronny Becker Fabrics**
Mailing Address:	**404 Lauderdale Street**
City, ST, Zip	**Flagstaff, AZ 86001**
Country:	**USA**
Vendor Type:	**wall**
1099 Type:	**Independent Contractor**
Expense Account:	Defaults to 12000
Telephone 1:	**928-555-3518**
Fax:	**928-555-3520**
E-mail:	**ronny@beckerfabrics.net**
Web Site:	**www.beckerfabrics.net**

Purchase Info:

Tax ID Number:	**28-9988377**
Terms and Credit:	Defaults to 2% 10 Net 30

11. Check your vendor information carefully. When you are finished entering vendor information, close the Maintain Vendors window.

How does vendor information work? The diagram on the next page shows how vendor maintenance information, vendor default information and purchases and payments work together.

Vendor Maintenance Information	*Vendor Default Information*
Terms: 2% 10, Net 30 Days	*Accounts*: Accounts Payable; Merchandise Inventory (purchase account); Purchase Discounts (discount GL account); Interstate Bank (cash disbursed).
Purchase Account: Merchandise Inventory	

↓

Purchases/Receive Inventory and Payments

Purchase Order

↓

Check to Vendor

On the Vendors & Purchases Navigation Center, Sage 50 illustrates its accounts payable system. (If necessary, close Sage Advisor.) In Chapter 12, you work with vendors, entering bills, credits and returns, paying vendor bill, and issuing checks for expenses and owners' withdrawals. (*Hint:* To see Vendors, click Refresh .)

Vendors			View Detailed List
Vendor ID ▲	Vendor Name	Telephone 1	Balance
JJH06	James Jarvis Hardware	215-555-7161	$0.00
LLP07	Len Lacey Products	619-555-1239	$0.00
RBF08	Ronny Becker Fabrics	928-555-3518	$0.00

INVENTORY & SERVICES

The Inventory & Services Navigation Center displays information and access points related to the company's inventory items. It includes a summary of item information, access to recently used inventory reports, a graphic analysis of how the cost of sales is trending, the flow of inventory-related tasks and takes you where you need to go to perform those tasks. Sage 50's inventory system is an example of another module within its user interface.

In the next section, default information for inventory items is completed. Because the Merchandise Inventory account is increased or decreased for every purchase, sale or return, its balance in the general ledger is current.

Inventory Defaults

1. From the Navigation Bar, select **Inventory & Services**. Observe how the Inventory & Services Tasks are organized. The workflow diagram illustrates a sequence of connected steps within Sage 50's inventory system.

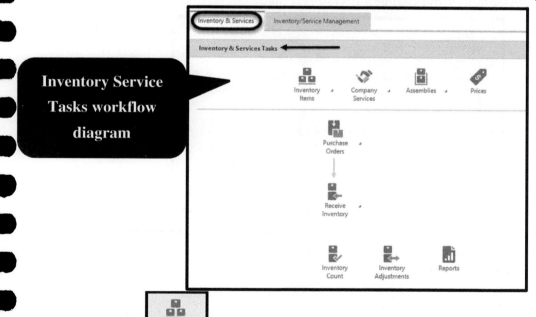

Inventory Service Tasks workflow diagram

2. Click **Inventory Items** > Set Up Inventory Defaults. The Inventory Item Defaults window appears. (If necessary, close the Sage Advisor window.)

3. Click on the General tab. In the Default Item Class field, select Stock item.

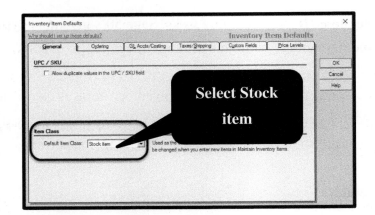

4. Click on the GL Accts/Costing tab. In the Stock item row, click on the down arrow ▼ next to FIFO in the Costing column. Select Average.
5. On the Master Stock item row, change FIFO to Average.
6. On the Assembly row, change FIFO to Average.

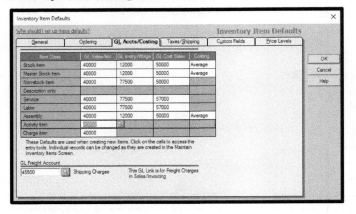

7. Make sure Average is selected in the Costing column. Click | OK |.

Inventory Items

1. Click | Inventory Items | > New Inventory item. Follow these steps to add inventory items.

a. In the Item ID field, type **001hardware**, then press the **<Enter>** key.

b. In the Description field, type **hardware** then press **<Enter>**. In the Item field, Stock item appears automatically. (Refer to step 3, pages 425-426.) Press **<Enter>** two times.

c. In the Description: for Sales field, type **restoration hardware** then press **<Enter>**.

d. Click on the right arrow ▶ in the Price Level 1 field. The Multiple Price Levels window appears. Type **150** in the Price field of Price Level 1, then press **<Enter>**.

e. Click [OK] .

How to Fix?: What if your Price Level 1 field does not display 150.00 but 1.50? Follow these steps to set the decimal point:

1. From the menu bar, click Options > Global. If necessary, select the Accounting tab.

2. In the Decimal Entry field, click Manual. Make sure that the number 2 is shown in the Number of decimal places field. Click [OK] . This sets your decimal place globally. That means from now on all numbers with decimal places will be set automatically; for example, 150 will display as 150.00.

---

f. Type **50** in the Last Unit Cost field. Press **<Enter>**.

g. Accept the default for Account No. 40000, Sales-Hardware as the GL Sales Acct.

h. Accept the default for Account No. 12000, Merchandise Inventory, as the GL Inventory Acct by pressing **<Enter>**

i.   Accept the default for Account No. 50000, Cost of Sales-Hardware as the GL Cost of Sales Acct by pressing **<Enter>** three times.

j.   In the Item Type field, type **hardware** then press **<Enter>** two times.

k.   In the Stocking U/M field (U/M is an abbreviation for Unit of Measure), type **each** then press **<Enter>** two times.

l.   In the Minimum Stock field, type **10** then press **<Enter>**.

m.   In the Reorder Quantity field, type **4** then press **<Enter>**.

n.   In the Preferred Vendor ID field, click . Select James Jarvis Hardware, JJH06, as the vendor. Compare your Maintain Inventory Items window with the one below.

o.   Click .

p.   Click .

Enter the following stock items:

1) Item ID: **002wall**

   Description: **wall**

   Item Class: Stock item

   Description for Sales: **wall coverings**

   Price Level 1:   **100**

   Last Unit Cost: **30**

   Cost Method: Average

   GL Sales Acct: **40200 Sales-Wall**

   GL Inventory Acct: **12000 Merchandise Inventory**

   GL Cost of Sales Acct: **50500 Cost of Sales-Wall**

   Item Type: **wall**

   Stocking U/M: **each**

   Minimum Stock: **10**

   Reorder Quantity: **4**

   Preferred Vendor ID: **RBF08**, Ronny Becker Fabrics

2) Item ID: **003floor**

   Description: **floor**

   Item Class: Stock item

   Description for Sales: **flooring**

   Price Level 1:   **160**

   Last Unit Cost: **54**

   Cost Method: Average

   GL Sales Acct: **40400 Sales-Floor**

   GL Inventory Acct: **12000 Merchandise Inventory**

   GL Cost of Sales Acct: **57000 Cost of Sales-Floor**

   Item Type: **floor**

Stocking U/M:	**each**
Minimum Stock:	**25**
Reorder Quantity:	**10**
Preferred <u>V</u>endor ID:	**LLP07**, Len Lacey Products

2. Save. Then, click on the arrow next to <u>B</u>eginning Balances. The Inventory Beginning Balances window displays. Follow these steps to record beginning balances.

    a. In the Item ID table, click on 001hardware. Press the **<Tab>** key.

    b. In the Quantity field, type **90** then press **<Enter>**.

    c. In the Unit Cost field, type **50** then press **<Enter>**.

    d. The Total Cost field displays 4,500.00. Press the **<Enter>** key.

    e. Enter the beginning balances for walls and floors:

Item ID	*Description*	*Quantity*	*Unit Cost*	*Total Cost*
002wall	wall	148	30	4,440.00
003floor	floor	200	54	10,800.00

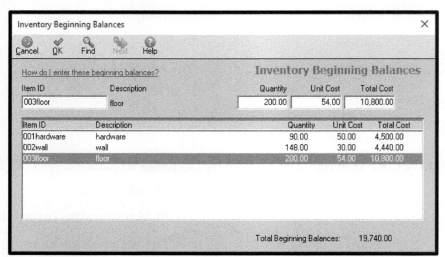

f. Observe that the Total Beginning Balance is 19,740. You add additional inventory in Chapter 14, Inventory & Services.[2] Click .

g. Close the Maintain Inventory Items window.

When you have completed entering Inventory items, the Inventory & Services Navigation Center shows these Inventory items. Click ⟳ Refresh , and if needed close the Sage Advisor.)

Inventory			View Detailed List
Item ID ▲	Description	No. Units Sold	Qty on Hand
001hardware	hardware	0.00	90.00
002wall	wall	0.00	148.00
003floor	floor	0.00	200.00

Inventory/Service Management

On the Inventory & Services Navigation Center, there is a tab for Inventory/Service Management. This page shows Item/Service Information, Purchase Orders, Sales Orders, and Sales Backorders.

BACKING UP YOUR DATA

Back up. This backup saves the new company set on pages 404-409; the general ledger chart of accounts, pages 412-414; the beginning balances, pages 415-418, and accounts payable defaults, vendors, inventory defaults, and inventory items, pages 418-431 The suggested file name is **Chapter 12 Begin**.

VENDORS & PURCHASES: PURCHASES/RECEIVE INVENTORY

The Vendors & Purchases Tasks workflow diagram includes a selection for Enter Bills; New Bill. This selection takes you to the Purchases/Receive

---

[2]If you compare the total beginning balance in inventory, $19,740, to the balance sheet on page 417, observe that the Merchandise Inventory account has a $27,740 balance. Additional inventory valued at $8,000 is added in Chapter 14.

Inventory window. In Sage, all information about a purchase is recorded in the Purchases/Receive Inventory window. Then, Sage takes the necessary information from the window and journalizes the transaction in the Purchase Journal.

In Sage 50, the Purchases/Receive Inventory window is the ***Purchase Journal***. On the Purchases/Receive Inventory window, you can enter vendor purchase invoices or receive inventory for purchase orders. The Purchases/Receive Inventory window includes two tabs.

- **Apply to Purchase Order**: When you select a vendor who has open purchase orders, Sage 50 displays this tab, allowing you to select which purchase order to receive items against.
- **Apply to Purchases**: If you select a vendor with no open purchase orders, by default Sage 50 displays this tab, where you can enter a purchase that did not originate on a purchase order. In addition, if items were included on the purchase invoice that are not included on the purchase order, you can add them here.

After recording vendor purchases in the Purchases/Receive Inventory window, you can display or print the Purchase Journal by selecting Reports, then Accounts Payable and highlighting the Purchase Journal. These steps are included in this chapter. Remember, each time you use the Purchases/Receive Inventory window you are also journalizing in the Purchase Journal.

Purchases are posted both to the General Ledger and to the ***Vendor Ledger*** or ***Accounts Payable Ledger***. You can also apply purchases to Inventory Items or Jobs. Purchases work hand in hand with paying bills. On the Vendors & Purchases Tasks flowchart, Pay Bills is one of the selections. Once you have entered and posted a purchase (vendor invoice), that invoice is available when you enter the Vendor's ID code in Payments. You can select the invoice, then save (post) the payment; Sage distributes the appropriate amounts.

▶ **Recording Purchases: Purchases/Receive Inventory Window**

(*Hint:* This icon, ▶ , means there is a video at www.mhhe.com/yacht2019.)

1. If you exited, start Sage 50. Open Shannon's Service Merchandise and, if necessary, restore the Chapter 12 Begin.ptb backup file.

2. From the Navigation Bar, select **Vendors & Purchases** > **Enter Bills** > New Bill. The Purchases/Receive Inventory window displays. Observe that the window looks like a typical purchase order or invoice form. Check that *both* the A/P Account lookup field and GL Account field are shown on your Purchases/Receive Inventory window. If *not*, read the paragraph below the Purchases/Receive Inventory window.

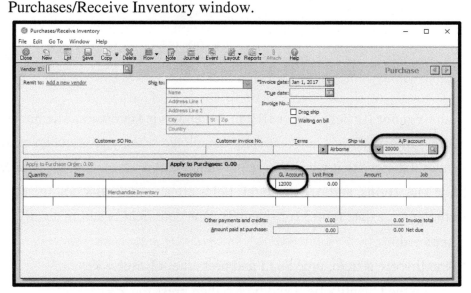

If the A/P Account lookup field and GL Account field are *not* shown, check your global settings. To do that, click Options, Global. If necessary, select the A̲ccounting tab. The boxes in the Hide General Ledger Accounts section *must* be unchecked. (See steps 1-3 pages xvii-xviii, Setting Global Options.)

On the Purchases/Receive Inventory window, your cursor is in the Vendor ID field. There are three ways to select a vendor or add a new vendor.

➢ In the Vendor ID field, type a question mark **<?>**. Vendor list displays.

➢ With the mouse pointer in the Vendor ID field, click on the right mouse button. The vendor list displays.

➢ In the Vendor ID field, click [🔍] and the vendor list displays. The transaction is shown below.

Date	*Transaction Description*
1/3/19	Invoice No. 56JJ was received from James Jarvis Hardware for the purchase of six curtain rods for a unit cost of $50.00 each, and a total of $300.00. (Shannon's Service Merchandise classifies curtain rods as hardware.)

3. In the Vendor ID field, select JJH06, James Jarvis Hardware. The name and address information is automatically completed when you select an existing vendor. Observe that when you select James Jarvis Hardware, the Ship To, Ship Via, Terms, and A/P Account[3] fields are automatically completed.

4. In the Invoice date type **3** (or select 3). Due date field is automatically completed.

5. In the Invoice # field, type **56JJ** and press the **<Enter>** key.

6. Click on the Quantity field and type **6** then press the **<Enter>** key.

7. In the Item field, click [🔍] and select 001hardware. Accept the description. Press the **<Tab>** key. The following purchase information is completed.

---

[3]If the A/P Account lookup field does not display, click Options > Global. The boxes in the Hide General Ledger Accounts section *must* be unchecked.

a. Description field, restoration hardware.

b. GL Account 12000, Merchandise Inventory. (If the account name, Merchandise Inventory does *not* show, go to Options > Global > General tab. In the Line Item Entry Display area, make sure 2 Line is selected > click <OK>. Click on the Purchases/Receive Inventory button on the taskbar to enlarge the window.)

c. Unit Price 50.00.

d. Amount 300.00.

e. Invoice Total and Net Due, 300.00

f. Vendor Balance on Jan 3, 2019 is 0.00.

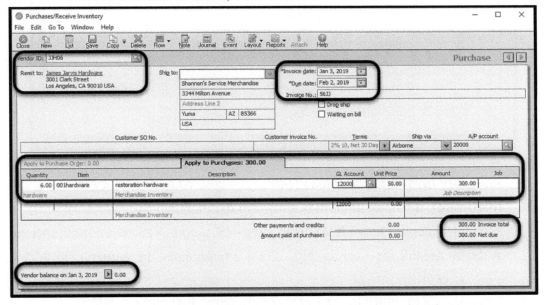

Invoice Total: The Invoice Total keeps a running total of the entry lines you added to the Purchase Journal. Before you post the Purchase Journal, check to see that the amount field is the same as the total invoice amount (Net Due) on the vendor invoice. The total that shows in the Amount field is automatically credited to Account No. 20000, Accounts Payable and the vendor account, James Jarvis Hardware. The information entered on the Purchases/Receive Inventory window is recorded in the Purchase Journal.

8. Click 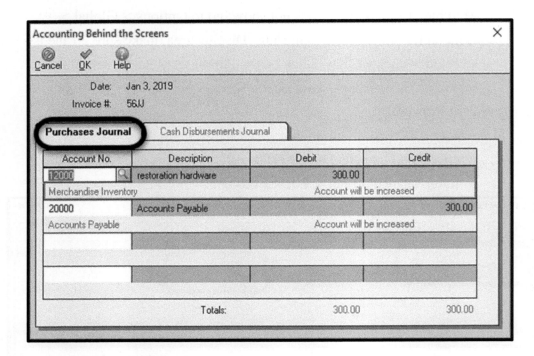 Journal to see this entry in the Purchases Journal.

Inventory Items and Purchases: Since you entered an Inventory Item (hardware), the debit amount is shown in the merchandise inventory account (Account No. 12000). (On page 419, step 6, you set up the Expense Account default for Account No. 12000, Merchandise Inventory.)

9. Click OK to return to the Purchases/Receive Inventory window.

10. Click Save to post this entry. The Purchases/Receive Inventory window is ready for the next transaction. When you enter and post purchases of inventory items, three things happen:

a. The amount or stock level of the item is updated.

b. The *Average Cost* is updated based on the Unit Price entered. Average cost is computed using the *weighted-average method* for inventory. The

Average Cost is used by Sage to compute Cost of Goods Sold when these Inventory Items are entered as Sales.

c. For Stock Type items, the Inventory account is debited and Accounts Payable is credited (debit, Account No. 12000, Merchandise Inventory; credit, Account No. 20000, Accounts Payable/Vendor.)

Additional Purchases

The following transactions need to be entered in the Purchases Journal.

Remember to click [Save] after each transaction to post.

Date	Transaction Description
1/21/19	Invoice 90 was received from Len Lacey Products for the purchase of eight rolls of vinyl flooring at $54 each, for a total of $432. (*Hint: Select 003floor as the inventory item.*)
1/21/19	Invoice 210 was received from Ronny Becker Fabrics for four pairs of curtains at $30 each, for a total vendor invoice of $120. (*Hint: Select 002wall as the inventory item.*)
1/21/19	Invoice 78JJ was received from James Jarvis Hardware for the purchase of 10 curtain rods at $50 each, for a total of $500. (*Hint: Select 001hardware as the inventory item.*)

CASH PURCHASES: Write Checks

Shannon's Service Merchandise pays cash for some purchases. All payments of cash are recorded in the *cash disbursements journal*. Follow these steps to see how cash purchases are entered.

> **Read Me:** The Write Checks window is a simplified version of the Payments
> window. Both the Write Checks window and the Payments window post to the
> Cash Disbursements Journal.

1. From the Vendors & Purchases Navigation Center, click
    \> New Check. When the Select a Cash Account window appears, make
    sure Interstate Bank is selected. Then, click OK . The Write Checks
    window displays.

    Date   *Transaction Description*

    1/24/19   Shannon's Service Merchandise issued check 3030 in the
                 amount of $160 to Lou Klein for cleaning (debit Account No.
                 70000, Maintenance Expense). Print Check No. 3030.

Comment: Your Write Checks window will show a cash account balance in the
Balance field. Your Cash Account Balance field shows the same amount as the January
1, 2019 balance sheet, page 417, Interstate Bank, $87,500.00.

---

2. Click on the Pay to the order of Name field and type **Lou Klein.** On the
    next page, there are steps for printing this check. If you do <u>not</u> have a
    printer, type 3030 in the Check num<u>b</u>er field.
3. Type **24** in the <u>D</u>ate field and press **<Enter>**.
4. Type **160** in the $ field.
5. In the E<u>x</u>pense Account field, select Account No. 70000, Maintenance
    Expense.

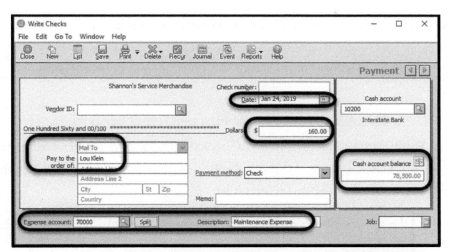

The next section shows you how to print or display Check 3030. If you are <u>not</u> connected to a printer, refer to the How to Fix, page 441; *or type 3030* in the Check num<u>b</u>er field, then click <Save> to post.

Printing (or Displaying) the Check

1. The Write Checks window with Lou Klein's check should be displayed.

2. Click [Print] . (If you are not connected to a printer, click on the down-arrow next to Print and select Print Preview.)

3. The Print Forms: Disbursement Checks window appears. Click [Select Form]. Then select OCR AP Laser Preprinted to highlight it.

> **Comment:** Step 3 instructs you to select OCR AP Laser Preprinted as the form to print. If this form does *not* print, select another one. The form you select is tied to the kind of printer you are using. Depending on your printer, you may need to make a different selection.

4. Click [OK]. Type **3030** in the First check number field.

5. The Print Forms: Disbursements Checks window appears. The Use this form field shows OCR AP Laser Preprinted; the First check number shows 3030.

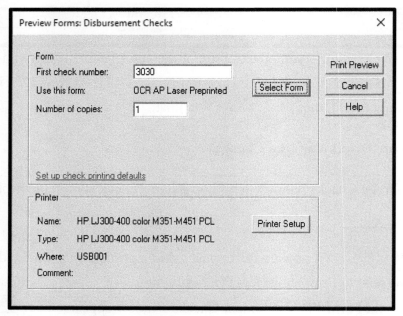

6. Sage 50 automatically sequences check numbers after the first one is entered. Click [Print] (or [Print Preview]). The check starts to print. Printing also posts the check to the Cash Disbursements Journal. If you are <u>not</u> printing, read the How to Fix box on the next page. (*Hint:* You can make sure the check posted by going to the Cash Disbursements Journal – Reports & Forms > Accounts Payable > double-click Cash Disbursements Journal. Check # 3030, Maintenance Expense, is shown for the $160 payment to Lou Klein.)

```
        Maintenance Expense                                                           160.00




1/24/19              3030              Lou Klein                                      $160.00



                                       Check Number   3030                    Jan 24, 2019

Memo:                                                                    160.00


        One Hundred Sixty and 00/100 Dollars

              Lou Klein
```

Comment: If your check does not show the same amount, go back to the Write Checks window and click [List]. Double-click Check No. 3030, 1/24/2019; the Write Checks window appears. Make the necessary corrections. When you reprint Check No. 3030, Duplicate will be shown on the printout.

After you print a check, the Write Checks window is ready for another payment. Remember, the check form that you select is tied to the kind of printer you are using. If necessary, select a different form to print.

How to fix? If you are <u>not</u> connected to a printer, close the print preview window. Type **3030** in the Check number field. Then, click <<u>S</u>ave> on the Write Checks window. The Write Checks window is ready for the next check.

Record the additional payments shown below. Since you are *not* going to print Check Nos. 3031-3035, type the appropriate check number in the Check num<u>b</u>er field on the Write Checks window.

Date	*Transaction Description*
1/24/19	Shannon's Service Merchandise issued Check No. 3031 in the amount of $45.00 to the U.S. Post Office (*Hint: Since you are not going to print checks, type* **3031** *in the Check num<u>b</u>er field. Click* 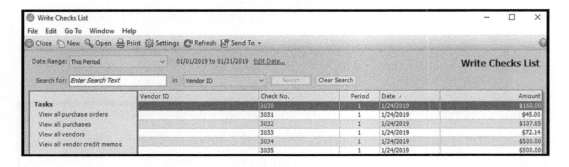 *after each entry.*)
1/24/19	Issued Check No. 3032 in the amount of $107.65 to Green's Office Supplies for letterhead paper, envelopes, and note pads. (Debit Account No. 75500, Supplies Expense.)
1/24/19	Issued Check No. 3033 in the amount of $72.14 to ILM Phone Co.
1/24/19	Issued Check No. 3034 to Brian Stewart for $500.
1/24/19	Issued Check No. 3035 to Shannon Larsen for $500.

8. Click [List] to see if you have issued Check Nos. 3030 through 3035.

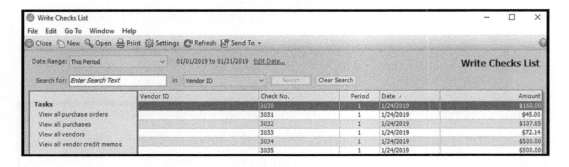

9. If you have any transactions to edit, highlight the line. Double-click. When the Write Checks window appears, make the necessary corrections.

Remember to click for any revised transactions. If no corrections are needed, close the Write Checks List window.

10. Close the Write Checks window and the Write Checks List window.

PURCHASE RETURNS: CREDITS & RETURNS

Sometimes it is necessary to return merchandise that has been purchased from a vendor. A purchase return is entered as a vendor credit memo. The following transaction is for merchandise returned to a vendor:

Date	*Transaction Description*
1/25/19	Returned one roll of vinyl flooring to Len Lacey Products, Invoice 90 and paid the invoice on the same day.

Follow these steps to enter a purchase return:

1. From the Vendors & Purchases Navigation Center, click [Credits and Returns] > New Vendor Credit Memo. The Vendor Credit Memos window appears.
2. In the Vendor ID field, select Len Lacey Products.
3. Type **25** in the Credit date field.
4. Type **VCM90** in the Credit No field. For the credit number you are using the abbreviation VCM for Vendor Credit Memo, then the invoice number.
5. The Apply to Invoice No. tab is selected. Click on the down-arrow to select 90.

Apply to Invoice No.: 90 ▾

The Item, Quantity, Description, GL Account, and Unit Price fields are completed.

6. Type **1** in the Returned field > Press <Enter>. After you type 1 in the Returned field, the Amount field shows 54.00. Also, notice that the Credit Applied to Invoice shows 54.00. This agrees with the Credit Total.

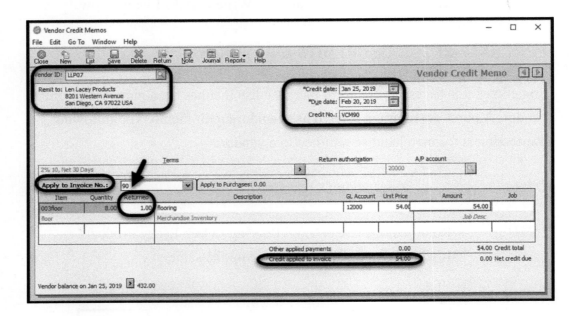

7. To see how the vendor credit memo is journalized, click ⬛ Journal. Notice that Account No. 12000, Merchandise Inventory, is credited for $54.00 and Account No. 20000, Accounts Payable, is debited for $54.00. The Purchases Journal is shown on the next page.

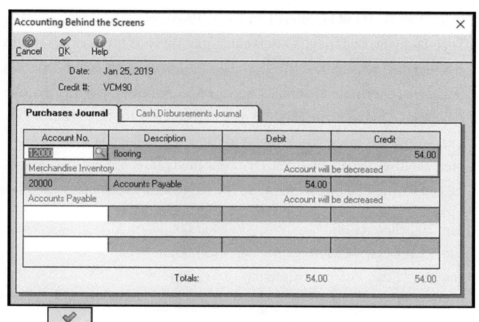

8. Click [OK] to close the Accounting Behind the Screens window.

9. Click [Save] to post, then [Close] the Vendor Credit Memos window.

Paying a Vendor, Minus a Return of Merchandise

How does the return of merchandise affect the payment to the vendor? Follow these steps to pay Invoice No. 90 less the return.

1. From the Vendors & Purchases Navigation Center, select [Pay Bills] > Pay Bill. The Payments window appears.

Date	*Transaction Description*
1/25/19	Shannon's Service Merchandise issued Check No. 3036 to Len Lacey Products in payment of Invoice No. 90 (less the return of merchandise). Print Check No. 3036.

2. In the Vendor ID field, select Len Lacey Products.

3. Type **25** in the Date field. Observe that the Apply to Invoices tab is selected and that the Invoice, 90; Date Due (Feb 20, 2019) and Amount Due 378.00 fields are completed. Shannon's Service Merchandise owes Len Lacey Products $378 ($432, original invoice amount, less the $54 return). Len Lacey Products extends a 2% vendor discount to Shannon's Service Merchandise. Type **7.56** in the Discount field (.02 x 378 = 7.56). Press <Enter>. The Pay box is checked. The payment was calculated as follows:

Jan. 20	Invoice 90	$432.00
Jan. 25	Less, VCM90	(54.00)
Jan. 25	Less, Purchase discount	(7.56)
Total Paid		$370.44

Make sure that Discount field is shows 7.56 and that the Discount Account field shows Account No. 59500, Purchase Discounts. The $ field shows 370.44.

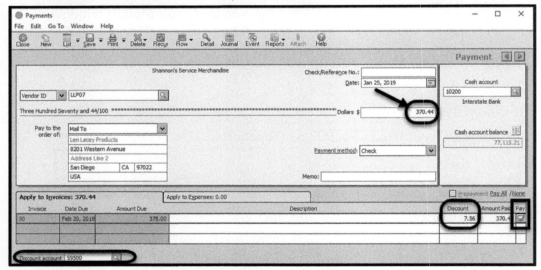

> **Troubleshooting:** What if your Cash Account Balance field does not show an amount? Close the Payments window without saving. Go to Options > Global. A checkmark should be placed next to Recalculate cash

balance automatically in Receipts, Payments, and Payroll Entry. If necessary, click on the appropriate field, then $\boxed{\text{OK}}$. Go back to step 1, on page 445.

4. Click $\boxed{\text{Print}}$ (or select Print Preview).

5. The Print Forms: Disbursement Checks window displays. Type **3036** in the First check number field.

6. The Use this form field shows OCR AP Laser Preprinted. If this selection is *not* made, click $\boxed{\text{Select Form}}$, then select OCR AP Laser Preprinted.

7. Click $\boxed{\text{Print}}$. Check No. 3036 starts to print. Make sure the check amount is $370.44. (*Hint:* If you do <u>not</u> have a printer, click <Cancel> on the Print Forms: Disbursements Checks window. On the Payments window, type **3036** in the Check/Reference No. field > click <Save> to post.)

90			1/21/19	432.00	7.56	370.44

1/25/19	3036	Len Lacey Products		7.56		$370.44

Check Number   3036   Jan 25, 2019

Memo:
                                                          370.44

Three Hundred Seventy and 44/100 Dollars

Len Lacey Products
8201 Western Avenue
San Diego, CA 97022
USA

8. Close the Payments window.

9. Record the following purchase return and payment:

Date	Transaction Description

1/28/19   Returned two curtain rods (001hardware) to James Jarvis Hardware, Invoice No. 78JJ; VCM78JJ. Shannon's Service Merchandise paid $50 each for the two curtain rods; credit total, $100.00.

1/28/19   Issued Check No. 3037 to pay James Jarvis Hardware for Invoice No. 78JJ (minus returned merchandise). (*Hint: Type the check number in the Check/Reference No. field instead of printing it. The discount is 8.00*)

▶ PAYING SPECIFIC VENDOR INVOICES

Once you have entered a vendor invoice in the Purchases/Receive Inventory window, you can apply payments to specific invoices. You enter the vendor invoice using Purchases/Receive Inventory; then when you post, the purchase journal is updated. To pay for the merchandise purchased, you select the specific invoice from the vendor's transaction list. When you print a check, you are also posting to the cash disbursements journal. The journal entry below shows a specific vendor payment.

Account Name	Debit	Credit
Accounts Payable/Ronny Becker Fabrics	$120.00	
Purchase Discounts		$2.40
Interstate Bank		$117.60

You should take advantage of both the Purchases/Receive Inventory and Payments features. Because amounts are disbursed and discounts are tracked automatically, your job is made easier. This also provides a detailed and complete audit trail. An audit trail is the path from the source document to the accounts. The diagram below shows how Purchases/Receive Inventory works together with Payments.

Date   *Transaction Description*

1/28/19   Issued Check No. 3038 to Ronny Becker Fabrics in payment of Invoice No. 210.

Follow these steps to pay vendor invoice 210:

1. From the Payments window, select Ronny Becker Fabrics as the vendor.
2. If necessary, type **3038** in the Check Number field.
3. Type **28** in the Date field.
4. The Apply to Invoices tab should already be selected. For Invoice No. 210, click on the Pay box.
5. Click [Save] to post.

Editing Payments

If you have already paid a vendor, you can edit payments. Follow these steps to see what vendors have been paid.

1. Display the Payments window.

2. Click **List**. The Payment List window appears. Compare your Payment List window to the one shown below.

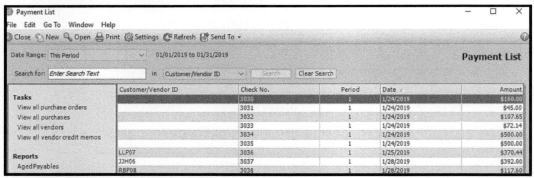

3. If you need to edit a payment, double-click on the appropriate one. Or, if no corrections are needed, close the Payment List window.

4. Make any necessary changes, then post. When you are finished close all windows.

PRINTING THE PURCHASE JOURNAL AND CASH DISBURSEMENTS JOURNAL

Observe that the Vendors & Purchases Navigation Center shows the following sections.

- Vendors & Purchases Tasks: The flowchart that shows the Sage 50's accounts payable system.
- Vendors: Each vendor is shown. You can link to individual vendors or View Detailed List.
- Recently Used Vendor Reports: You can link to view or print vendor reports from this section or View All Vendor & Purchases Reports.

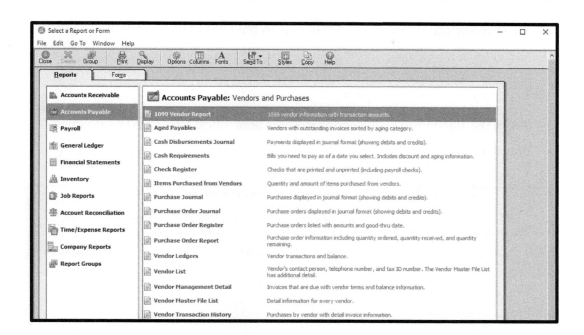

- Aged Payables: From this section, graphs or tables can be viewed.

- Sage Advisor: When you link to <u>Where do I get started?</u> or <u>What type of purchase information can I enter?</u>, the Sage Advisor appears.

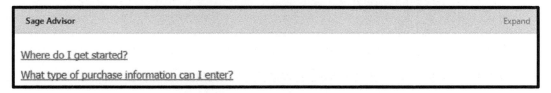

Read the information. Link to <u>Use lists</u> to read the PDF document. To watch the videos, go to www.mhhe.com/yacht2019 > Sage Advisor Videos. Close the Sage Advisor Getting Started window.

1. From the Recently Used Vendor Reports area, click <u>View</u> next to Purchase Journal.

Shannon's Service Merchandise
Purchase Journal
For the Period From Jan 1, 2019 to Jan 31, 2019
Filter Criteria includes: 1) Includes Drop Shipments. Report order is by Date. Report is printed in Detail Format.

Date	Account ID Account Description	Invoice/CM #	Line Description	Debit Amount	Credit Amount
1/3/19	12000 Merchandise Inventory 20000 Accounts Payable	56JJ	restoration hardware James Jarvis Hardware	300.00	300.00
1/21/19	12000 Merchandise Inventory 20000 Accounts Payable	210	wall coverings Ronny Becker Fabrics	120.00	120.00
1/21/19	12000 Merchandise Inventory 20000 Accounts Payable	78JJ	restoration hardware James Jarvis Hardware	500.00	500.00
1/21/19	12000 Merchandise Inventory 20000 Accounts Payable	90	flooring Len Lacey Products	432.00	432.00
1/25/19	12000 Merchandise Inventory 20000 Accounts Payable	VCM90	flooring Len Lacey Products	54.00	54.00
1/28/19	12000 Merchandise Inventory 20000 Accounts Payable	VCM78JJ	restoration hardware James Jarvis Hardware	100.00	100.00
				1,506.00	1,506.00

2. Click <u>View</u> next to the Cash Disbursements Journal.

Shannon's Service Merchandise
Cash Disbursements Journal
For the Period From Jan 1, 2019 to Jan 31, 2019
Filter Criteria includes: Report order is by Date. Report is printed in Detail Format.

Date	Check #	Account ID	Line Description	Debit Amount	Credit Amount
1/24/19	3030	70000	Maintenance Expense	160.00	
		10200	Lou Klein		160.00
1/24/19	3031	73500	Postage Expense	45.00	
		10200	U.S. Post Office		45.00
1/24/19	3032	75500	Supplies Expense	107.65	
		10200	Green's Office Supplies		107.65
1/24/19	3033	76000	Telephone Expense	72.14	
		10200	ILM Phone Co.		72.14
1/24/19	3034	39007	Brian Stewart, Drawing	500.00	
		10200	Brian Stewart		500.00
1/24/19	3035	39009	Shannon Larsen, Drawing	500.00	
		10200	Shannon Larsen		500.00
1/25/19	3036	59500	Discounts Taken		7.56
		20000	Invoice: 90	378.00	
		10200	Len Lacey Products		370.44
1/28/19	3037	59500	Discounts Taken		8.00
		20000	Invoice: 78JJ	400.00	
		10200	James Jarvis Hardware		392.00
1/28/19	3038	59500	Discounts Taken		2.40
		20000	Invoice: 210	120.00	
		10200	Ronny Becker Fabrics		117.60
	Total			2,282.79	2,282.79

Comment: Observe that the Line Description on the Cash Disbursements Journal shows the account name (for example, Account No. 70000, Maintenance Expense) for the debit amount. The person to whom the check was written (Lou Klein) is shown for the amount credited. Your Line Descriptions may differ.

VENDOR LEDGERS

Follow these steps to print a Vendor Ledger for Shannon's Service Merchandise.

1. From the Recently Used Vendor Reports area, link to <u>View All Vendor & Purchases Reports</u>. The Select a Report or Form window appears.

2. Double-click Vendor Ledgers then make the selections to print.

```
                            Shannon's Service Merchandise
                                    Vendor Ledgers
                          For the Period From Jan 1, 2019 to Jan 31, 2019
Filter Criteria includes: Report order is by ID.
```

Vendor ID Vendor	Date	Trans No	Type	Paid	Debit Amt	Credit Amt	Balance
JJH06	1/3/19	56JJ	PJ			300.00	300.00
James Jarvis Hardware	1/21/19	78JJ	PJ	*		500.00	800.00
	1/28/19	VCM78JJ	PJ	*	100.00		700.00
	1/28/19	3037	CDJ		8.00	8.00	700.00
	1/28/19	3037	CDJ		400.00		300.00
LLP07	1/21/19	90	PJ	*		432.00	432.00
Len Lacey Products	1/25/19	VCM90	PJ	*	54.00		378.00
	1/25/19	3036	CDJ		7.56	7.56	378.00
	1/25/19	3036	CDJ		378.00		0.00
RBF08	1/21/19	210	PJ	*		120.00	120.00
Ronny Becker Fabrics	1/28/19	3038	CDJ		2.40	2.40	120.00
	1/28/19	3038	CDJ		120.00		0.00
Report Total					1,069.96	1,369.96	300.00

3. Close the Vendor Ledgers.

PRINTING THE GENERAL LEDGER TRIAL BALANCE

1. In the Reports list, highlight General Ledger > double-click General Ledger Trial Balance.
2. Make the selections to print. Compare your printout with the one shown on the next page.

Troubleshooting Excel: If you are using Microsoft Office 365, the Excel icon may be inactive. Display the Sage report > select Edit > Copy > start Excel > open a blank workbook > right click on the sheet > left-click Paste > reformat > Save. Appendix A, Inactive Excel Icon, includes information.

	Shannon's Service Merchandise		
	General Ledger Trial Balance		
	As of Jan 31, 2019		

Filter Criteria includes: Report order is by ID. Report is printed in Detail Format.

Account ID	Account Description	Debit Amt	Credit Amt
10200	Interstate Bank	76,235.17	
10400	Yuma Savings & Loan	22,000.00	
12000	Merchandise Inventory	28,938.00	
13000	Supplies	1,750.00	
14000	Prepaid Insurance	2,400.00	
15000	Furniture and Fixtures	5,000.00	
15100	Computers & Equipment	7,500.00	
15500	Building	100,000.00	
20000	Accounts Payable		300.00
27000	Long-Term Notes Payable		20,500.00
27400	Mortgage Payable		75,000.00
39006	Brian Stewart, Capital		74,695.00
39007	Brian Stewart, Drawing	500.00	
39008	Shannon Larsen, Capital		74,695.00
39009	Shannon Larsen, Drawing	500.00	
59500	Purchase Discounts		17.96
70000	Maintenance Expense	160.00	
73500	Postage Expense	45.00	
75500	Supplies Expense	107.65	
76000	Telephone Expense	72.14	
	Total:	**245,207.96**	**245,207.96**

3. Close all windows.

BACKING UP CHAPTER 12 DATA

Back up to this point in your data. The suggested file name is **Chapter 12**.

EXPORT REPORTS TO EXCEL

Follow these steps to export the following Sage 50 reports to Excel: Chart of Accounts, Purchase Journal, Cash Disbursements Journal, Vendors Ledgers, General Ledger Trial Balance.

Troubleshooting: If you are using Microsoft Office 365, the Excel icon may be inactive. Display the Sage report > select Edit > Copy > start Excel > open a blank workbook > right click on the sheet > left-click Paste > reformat > Save.

1. From the menu bar, select Reports & Forms > General Ledger > double-click Chart of Accounts. The Chart of Accounts appears. Expand the Account Description column. (Click [⟷] to widen the column.)

2. Click [Excel]. On the Copy Report to Excel window, accept the default for Create a new Microsoft Excel workbook. In the Report header option field, Show header in Excel worksheet is selected.

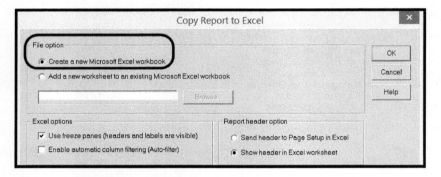

3. Click [OK]. The chart of accounts exports to Excel.

4. Save. Use the file name **Chapter 12_CofA_PJ_CDJ_VL_GLTB. xlsx**. (Abbreviations are Chart of Accounts, Purchase Journal, Cash Disbursements Journal, Vendor Ledgers, and General Ledger Trial Balance.)

5. Go back to Sage 50's Select a Report or Form window. In the Reports list, select Accounts Payable. Double-click Purchase Journal.

6. Click [Excel]. On the Copy Report to Excel window, select Add a new worksheet to an existing Microsoft Excel workbook.

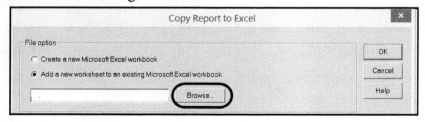

7. Click [Browse...] to go to the appropriate file. (*Hint:* File name is Chapter 12_CofA_PJ_CDJ_VL_GLTB.xlsx.) Click [Open]. You are returned to the Copy Report to Excel window. Observe that the Browse field shows the location of the file selected. Click [OK].

8. Observe that two sheets are shown at the bottom of the Excel file: Chart of Accounts and Purchase Journal. Save the file.

9. Repeat steps 5, 6, 7, and 8 to export the Cash Disbursements Journal, Vendor Ledgers, and General Ledger Trial Balance to the Excel File. There should be five sheets: Chart of Accounts, Purchase Journal, Cash Disbursements Journal, Vendor Ledgers, and General Ledger Trial Balance. When you are through, the Excel file has five sheets.

10. Save. Exit Excel.

    NOTE: If your instructor would like you to save the Chart of Accounts, Purchase Journal, Cash Disbursements Journal, Vendor Ledgers, and General Ledger Trial Balance as PDF files, do that. Depending on your instructor's preference, additional reports could be turned in. The suggested file name is **Chapter 12_Chart of Accounts.pdf**, etc.

ONLINE LEARNING CENTER

Complete end-of-chapter activities at www.mhhe.com/yacht2019 > Student Edition > Chapter 12.

1. Quizzes: Multiple Choice and True False questions. Interactive online tests that are graded and can be emailed to your instructor.

2. More Resources:

   a. QA Templates: Answer 10 true/make true questions and three Analysis Questions.

   b. Videos: Watch the Purchases and Payments video.

    c. Narrated PowerPoints: Listen to the narrated PowerPoints.

    d. Going to the Net Exercises: Watch the YouTube video, Managing Inventory.

    e. Assessment Rubric: Complete the rubric to review Sage 50's journals, navigation centers, modules, task windows, and reports.

➢ Information Center > Sage Advisor Videos.

The OLC also includes links to these Appendixes:

- Appendix A: Troubleshooting (textbook and OLC)
- Appendix C: Review of Accounting Principles (OLC Student Edition)
- Appendix D: Glossary (OLC Student Edition)

Exercise 12-1: Follow the instructions below to complete Exercise 12-1.

1. Start Sage 50. From the menu bar, select File > New Company. (One company should be open.) Set up a retail business using *your last name*; for example, *Your Last Name Sales and Service.* For the address, use 413 Sycamore Lane, Norcross, GA 30092; Telephone, 404-555-3213; Fax, 404-555-3133; Business Type, Sole Proprietorship. For the Tax ID information, use the information below.

Federal Employer ID:	77-4422551
State Employer ID:	23-1488657
State Unemployment ID:	231233-5

Leave the Web Site and E-mail address fields blank.

2. At the New Company – Setup; Chart of Accounts window > select Copy settings from an existing Sage 50 Accounting company.

3. Highlight Shannon's Service Merchandise (*or,* your name Service Merchandise), then click Next > .

4. Observe that the information on the Copy Company Information window includes a selection for Accounting Periods. Since this company is using the same accounting period (January 1 - 31, 2019) as Shannon's Service Merchandise, leave that box checked. For purposes of Exercise 12-1 accept all the defaults on the Copy Company Information window by clicking on Next >.

5. Read the information about the Accounting Method. Accept the default for accrual accounting by clicking on Next >.

6. Accept the default for Real Time posting by clicking on Next >.

7. At the Create a New Company – Finish window, click Finish. If the screen prompts You can use this company in the student version of Sage 50 for the next 14 months and then it will expire, click OK.

8. Close the Setup Guide. (*Hint:* Click on the box next to Don't show this screen at startup to place a checkmark in it.) The Sage Advisor Getting Started window includes PDF documents. You may want to read them. The Online Learning Center's Information Center list includes a link to Sage Advisor Videos. Make sure the Period shows Period 1 - 01/01/19-01/31/19

General Ledger

1. Delete the following accounts:

    3900A   Owner's Draw
    40400   Sales-Floor

Change the following accounts:

10200	Interstate Bank	**Boulevard Bank**
10400	Yuma Savings & Loan	**Enterprise Savings & Loan**
39009	Owner's Contribution	**Student Name, Capital**
		(Equity, doesn't close)
40200	Sales-Wall	**Sales-Tools**
50500	Cost of Sales-Wall	**Cost of Sales-Tools**
57000	Cost of Sales-Floor	**Cost of Sales**

Add the following account:

23755	**SUTA2 Payable**	Other Current Liabilities
39010	**Student Name, Drawing**	Equity-gets closed
72545	**SUTA2 Expense**	Expenses

2. Back up. The suggested file name is **Exercise 12-1 Chart of Accounts**.

3. To record chart of accounts beginning balances, use the Balance Sheet on the next page. You purchased the retail business in December 2018. Select the period From 12/1/18 through 12/31/18. Record beginning balances as of December 31, 2018.

Student Name Sales and Service Balance Sheet. January 1, 2019		
ASSETS		
Current Assets		
10200 – Boulevard Bank	$67,500.00	
10400 - Enterprise Savings & Loan	13,300.00	
12000 - Merchandise Inventory	14,750.00	
13000 - Supplies	1,000.00	
14000 - Prepaid Insurance	2,400.00	
Total Current Assets		$98,950.00
Property and Equipment		
15000 - Furniture and Fixtures	$3,500.00	
15100 - Computers & Equipment	5,500.00	
15500 - Building	85,000.00	
Total Property and Equipment		$94,000.00
Total Assets		$192,950.00
LIABILITIES AND CAPITAL		
Long Term Liabilities		
27000 - Long-Term Notes Payable	10,000.00	
27400 - Mortgage Payable	60,000.00	
Total Long-Term Liabilities		$70,000.00
Capital		
39009 - Student Name, Capital		122,950.00
Total Liabilities and Capital		$192,950.00

4. Print the chart of accounts.

5. Print the December 31, 2018 balance sheet.

6. Back up. The suggested file name is **Exercise 12-1 Starting Balance Sheet**.

Accounts Payable

1. From the Vendors & Purchases Navigation Center, click [Vendors] > Set up Vendor Defaults. Make sure the following defaults are set. If not, set them up.

Standard Terms:	Due in number of days
Net due in:	30 days
Discount in:	10 days
Discount %:	2.00
Credit Limit:	10,000.00
GL Link Accounts:	
Expense Account:	12000 Merchandise Inventory
Discount GL Account:	59500 Purchase Discounts

2. Click [Vendors] > New Vendor. Set up the following vendors:

a.	Vendor ID:	**CPT12**
	Name:	**Charles Peterson Tools**
	Contact:	**Charles Peterson**
	Mailing Address:	**2340 University Avenue**
	City, ST, Zip	**Phoenix, AZ 85120**

Country:	**USA**	
Vendor Type:	**tools**	
1099 Type:	select Independent Contractor	
Expense Account:	12000 Merchandise Inventory	
Telephone 1:	**602-555-3940**	
Fax:	**602-555-3942**	
E-mail:	**info@charlespeterson.com**	
Web Site:	**www.charlespeterson.com**	
Purchase Info:		
Tax ID Number:	**11-3322778**	

b. Vendor ID: **SJH14**

Name:	**Sheila Johnson Hardware**
Contact:	**Sheila Johnson**
Mailing Address:	**8990 Laurel Avenue**
City, ST, Zip	**Los Angeles, CA 90036**
Country:	**USA**
Vendor Type:	**hardware**
1099 Type:	select Independent Contractor
Expense Account:	12000 Merchandise Inventory
Telephone 1:	**310-555-2233**
Fax:	**310-555-5412**
E-mail:	**info@johnsonhardware.net**
Web Site:	**www.johnsonhardware.net**
Purchase Info:	
Tax ID Number:	**66-3144216**

Inventory

1. From the Inventory & Services Navigation Center, click , Set Up Inventory Defaults.
2. On the General tab, the Default Item Class field shows Stock item. If not, select Stock item.
3. Select the GL Accts/Costing tab. If necessary, set up Average as the inventory costing method (Stock item, Master Stock item, Assembly).
4. If necessary, select Account No. 45500, Shipping Charges. This GL Link is for Freight Charges in Sales/Invoicing.

5. Click [Inventory Items] > New Inventory Item. Set up the following inventory stock items:

    a.   Item ID: **002tools**

Description:	**tools**
Item Class:	Stock item
Description for Sales:	**tools**
Price Level 1:	**85**
Last Unit Cost:	**30**
Cost Method:	Average
GL Sales Acct:	**40200 Sales-Tools**
GL Inventory Acct:	**12000 Merchandise Inventory**
GL Cost of Sales Acct:	**50500 Cost of Sales-Tools**
Item Tax Type:	1 Regular Taxable
Item Type:	**tools**
Stocking U/M:	**each**

Minimum Stock: **10**

Reorder Quantity: **4**

Preferred Vendor ID: **CPT12, Charles Peterson Tools**

b. Item ID: **003hardware**

Description: **hardware**

Item Class: Stock item

Description for Sales: **copper hardware**

Price Level 1:   **150**

Last Unit Cost: **50**

Cost Method: Average

GL Sales Acct: **40000 Sales-Hardware**

GL Inventory Acct: **12000 Merchandise Inventory**

Cost of Sales Acct: **50000 Cost of Sales-Hardware**

Item Tax Type: 1 Regular Taxable

Item Type: **hardware**

Stocking U/M: **each**

Minimum Stock: **10**

Reorder Quantity: **4**

Preferred Vendor ID: **SJH14, Sheila Johnson Hardware**

Click on **B**eginning Balances. Record the beginning balances shown below.

Item ID	Description	Quantity	Unit Cost	Total Cost
002tools	tools	175	30	5,250.00
003hardware	hardware	190	50	9,500.00

6. Click [OK] .

7. Save the Chart of Accounts and December 31 2018 Balance Sheet as PDF files. The file names are **Exercise 12-1_Chart of Accounts**, **Exercise 12-1_Dec 31 2018 Balance Sheet**.

8. Back up; **Exercise 12-1**.

Exercise 12-2: Follow the instructions below to complete Exercise 12-2. Exercise 12-1 *must* be completed before starting Exercise 12-2.

1. If necessary, restore the Exercise 12-1.ptb file. (*Hint:* You can restore from your back up file even if <u>no</u> company exists. From the startup window, select File > Restore > location of your backup file. On the Restore Wizard's Select Company window, select *Create a new company using the restored data*. For more information, refer to pages 279-280.)

2. Record the following transactions and print each check.

1/4/19	Invoice No. 480CP was received from Charles Peterson Tools for the purchase of 10 tool kits for a unit cost of $30.
1/4/19	Invoice No. SJH52 was received from Sheila Johnson Hardware for the purchase of 8 hardware sets at a unit cost of $50.
1/6/19	Returned two tool kits to Charles Peterson Tools, Invoice No. 480CP. Paid $30 for each tool kit; VCM480CP.
1/11/19	Issued Boulevard Bank Check No. 2020 to pay Sheila Johnson Hardware for Invoice No. SJH52. (*Hint:* Type the check number, 2020, in the Check/Reference No. field.)
1/11/19	Issued Check No. 2021 to pay Charles Peterson Tools for merchandise purchased on January 3, less the January 6 return, Invoice No. 480CP. (*Hint: Remember to calculate, then type the correct discount amount in the Discount field.*)
1/14/19	Issued Check No. 2022 to Niki Vincent for $125 for cleaning and maintenance.

1/15/19	Issued Check No. 2023 to the U.S. Post Office for $45.
1/15/19	Issued Check No. 2024 to Office Time for $145.72 for cell phone. (Debit Account No. 71000, Office Expense.)
1/15/19	Issued Check No. 2025 to Qwest Telephone for $46.65 to pay the telephone bill.
1/25/19	Issued Check No. 2026 to the owner of the business for $400.

3. Print the Purchase Journal. (*Hint:* If you are not connected to a printer, you can select Adobe PDF or a Microsoft XPS Document Writer in the Print Properties field.)

   GO GREEN & SAVE: Instead of printing, select Display or Print Preview, and save as an Adobe PDF file or Microsoft XPS file. In other words, you do not need to print hard copy. Check with your instructor for his or her preference. Instead of printing, email PDFs or Microsoft XPS files.

4. Print the Cash Disbursements Journal.

5. Print the Vendor Ledgers.

6. Print the General Ledger Trial Balance.

   Check Your Figures:

10200, Boulevard Bank	$66,110.43
12000, Merchandise Inventory	15,390.00
20000, Accounts Payable	0.00
59500, Purchase Discounts	12.80

7. Back up; **Exercise 12-2**.

8. Export the following reports to Excel – Chart of Accounts, Purchase Journal, Cash Disbursements Journal, Vendor Ledgers, and General Ledger Trial balance. File name is **Exercise 12-2_ CofA_PJ_CDJ_VL_ GLTB**.

9. Save these files as PDFs: Purchase Journal, Cash Disbursements Journal, Vendor Ledgers, and General Ledger Trial Balance. The suggested file name is **Exercise 12-2_Purchase Journal.pdf**, etc.

CHAPTER 12 INDEX

Chapter

13 Customers & Sales

LEARNING OBJECTIVES

1. Restore data from Chapter 12. (This backup was made on page 455.)
2. Set up customer default information.
3. Set up sales tax and customer maintenance information.
4. Record credit sales, cash sales, and sales returns.
5. Record customer receipts, partial payments, and edit invoices.
6. Use the Financial Manager to view financial ratios and key Income Statement and Balance Sheet account balances.
7. Make four backups, save two Excel files, and save three PDF files.[1]

In Chapter 12, you learned how to use Sage 50's Purchases/Receive Inventory and Payments features. Now that you have purchased merchandise from vendors, you are ready to sell that merchandise. To do that, you use Sage 50's Customers & Sales Navigation Center.

In Chapter 3, Customers, when you entered a sales invoice for Bellwether Garden Supply, the unit price, description, account number, and sales taxes were automatically calculated for you. (See pages 105-116.)

Before using the Sales/Invoicing window, you need to set up customer defaults, sales tax information, and customer maintenance information. After you set up these defaults, Sage will use this information when you record a sale. Chapter 13 explains how Sage's accounts receivable system works.

---

[1]For the size of files backed up and saved, refer to the chart on pages 400-401.

McGraw-Hill Education, *Computer Accounting with Sage 50 2019, 21e*

Accounts receivable are what customers owe your business. Credit transactions from customers are called *accounts receivable transactions*. Customer receipts work similarly to paying vendor invoices. When a customer pays an existing *invoice* there are two steps:

1. Enter the customer's ID code so that a list of existing invoices for the customer displays.
2. Select the invoice that applies to the customer's check, then select the Pay box.

This diagram illustrates Sage 50's accounts receivable system.

Record, then print a sales invoice.

↓

The customer sends a check to pay for the credit sale.

↓

Select the invoice that applies to the customer's check, then select the pay box.

On the Customers & Sales Navigation Center, Sage 50 illustrates the accounts receivable system. In Chapter 13, you work with customers, sales invoices, credits and returns, and receipts from customers. The Customers & Sales Navigation Center shows the flow of customer-related tasks and takes you where you need to go to perform those tasks. In Sage 50, this represents the accounts receivable module or accounts receivable system. The Customers & Sales workflow diagram is shown below.

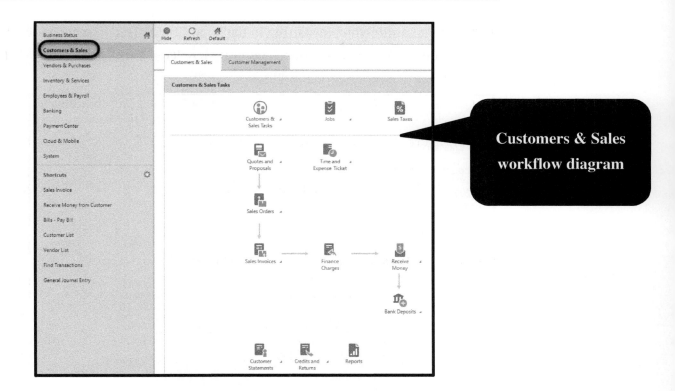

Customers & Sales workflow diagram

GETTING STARTED

1. Start Sage 50. Open Shannon's Service Merchandise, or if you used a unique name, select it. This company was set up in Chapter 12 on pages 404-409. (*Hint:* If another company opens, click File > Open Previous Company > select Shannon's [your name] Service Merchandise. Open one company.)

2. If necessary, restore data from the Chapter 12.ptb file. This file was backed up on page 455.

> **Read Me: Do I need to restore?** If you are working on your own PC or laptop, you may be able to skip restore. Refer to the disk icon 💾 to make sure you are starting with the work completed in Chapter 12. *If you are working in the computer lab, restore the Chapter 12.ptb file from your USB drive.*

To make sure you are starting in the appropriate place in the data (Chapter 12.ptb backup) display the General Ledger Trial Balance.

Shannon's Service Merchandise
General Ledger Trial Balance
As of Jan 31, 2019

Filter Criteria includes: Report order is by ID. Report is printed in Detail Format.

Account ID	Account Description	Debit Amt	Credit Amt
10200	Interstate Bank	76,235.17	
10400	Yuma Savings & Loan	22,000.00	
12000	Merchandise Inventory	28,938.00	
13000	Supplies	1,750.00	
14000	Prepaid Insurance	2,400.00	
15000	Furniture and Fixtures	5,000.00	
15100	Computers & Equipment	7,500.00	
15500	Building	100,000.00	
20000	Accounts Payable		300.00
27000	Long-Term Notes Payable		20,500.00
27400	Mortgage Payable		75,000.00
39006	Brian Stewart, Capital		74,695.00
39007	Brian Stewart, Drawing	500.00	
39008	Shannon Larsen, Capital		74,695.00
39009	Shannon Larsen, Drawing	500.00	
59500	Purchase Discounts		17.96
70000	Maintenance Expense	160.00	
73500	Postage Expense	45.00	
75500	Supplies Expense	107.65	
76000	Telephone Expense	72.14	
	Total:	**245,207.96**	**245,207.96**

This is the same trial balance shown in Chapter 12 on page 455.

Setting Up Customer Defaults

In Chapter 12, you entered General Ledger, Accounts Payable, and Inventory Item defaults. The directions that follow show how to enter customer defaults.

1. From the Navigation Bar, select > **Customers & Sales** >

> Set Up Customer Defaults.

2. If necessary, click on the Discount Percent field. Type **0** (zero) in the Discount Percent field, then press **<Enter>**. Shannon's Service Merchandise does *not* offer a discount to its credit customers.

3. If necessary, type **2500** in the Credit Limit field, press **<Enter>**.

4. Accept the default for GL Sales Account 40000, Sales-Hardware by pressing **<Enter>**. (When you set up individual customers, you will select a GL Sales Account for that customer.)

5. Accept the default for Discount GL Account 49000, Sales Discounts by pressing **<Enter>**.

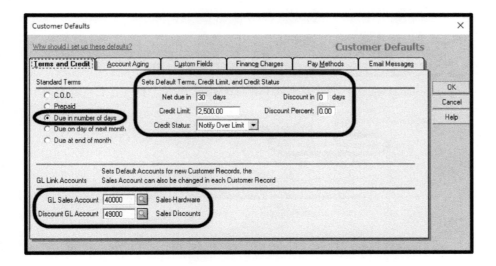

6. Click [OK].

Setting Up Sales Tax Defaults

You can enter sales tax default information for these areas:

➢ Sales Tax Authorities: codes for governments or other tax authorities and their tax rates. These are used to assemble the sales tax codes.

> ➢ Sales Tax Codes: the overall rate applied to taxable items on invoices to customers. This is composed of rates entered as Sales Tax Authorities.

Follow these steps to set up sales tax defaults.

1. From the Customers & Sales Navigation Center, click 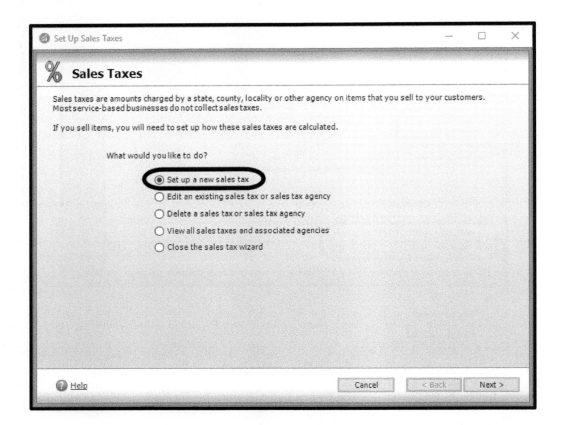 The Sales Taxes window appears. Set up a new sales tax is the default.

2. Click ___Next >___ The Set Up New Sales Tax window appears.
3. Type **8.00**% in the What is the total rate that you will charge? Press **<Enter>.** Accept the default for 1 in the How many individual rates make up this total rate? field.

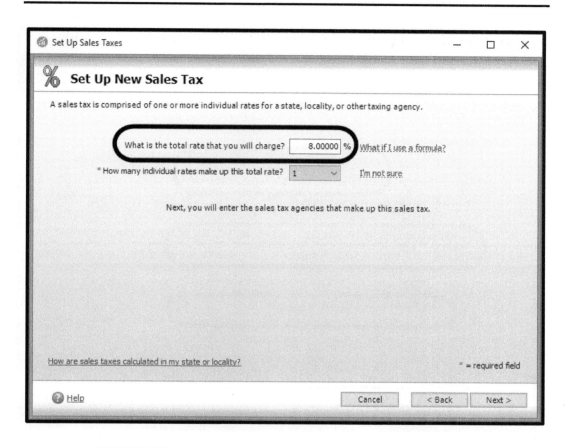

4. Click ⟨Next >⟩. The Add Sales Tax Agency window appears.
5. Type **AZ** in the Sales tax agency ID field. Press **<Enter>**.
6. Type **Arizona Dept. of Revenue** in the Sales tax agency name field.
7. Accept the default by single rate in the How are sales taxes calculated for this agency? field.
8. Type **8.00**% in the Rate field. Press **<Enter>**.
9. Select Account No. 23100, Sales Tax Payable in the Select an account to track sales taxes field. Press **<Enter>**.

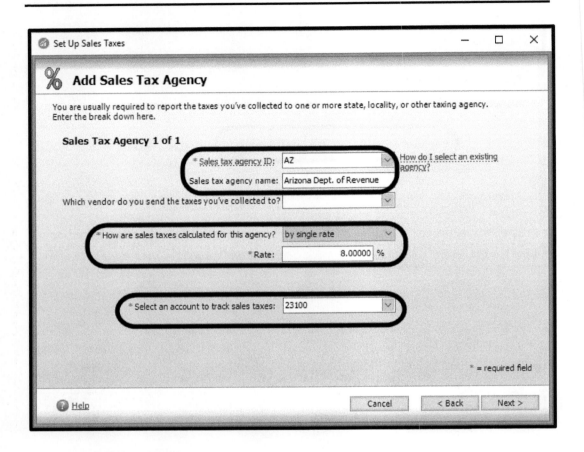

10. Click [Next >] The Sales Tax Entered window appears.

11. Type **AZ** in the Sales tax ID field. Press **<Enter>**.

12. Type **Arizona sales tax** in the Sales tax name field. Compare your Sales Tax Entered window to the one shown on the next page.

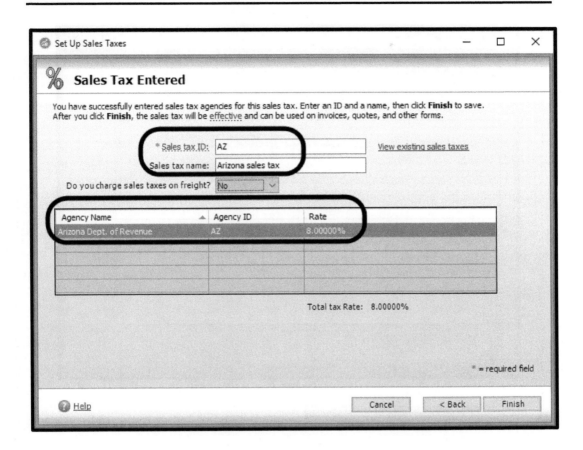

13. Click [Finish]. The Sales Taxes window appears. To make sure you have set up sales taxes for Shannon's Service Merchandise select View all sales taxes and associated agencies

    . Click [Next >]

14. The View All Sales Taxes window appears and shows the sales tax that was set up on pages 474-477. The 8.00% sales tax rate for Arizona is shown. Compare your View All Sales Taxes window with the one shown on the next page.

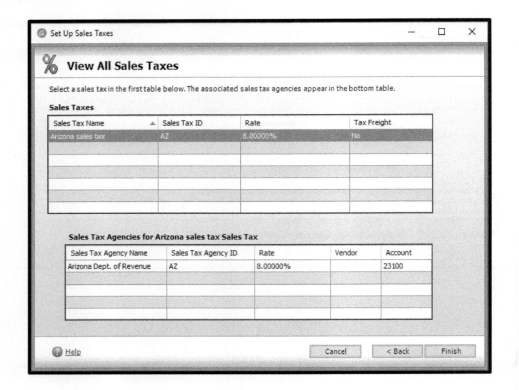

15. Click [Finish]. Click [×] on the title bar to close the Set Up Sales Taxes window.

Setting Up Customer Maintenance Information

To enter default information about your customers, follow these steps:

1. Select [Customers & Sales Tasks] > New Customer. The Maintain Customers/Prospects window appears.
2. Complete the following fields.

> **Customer ID:**   **ap001** (Use lowercase letters and zeroes)
> Name: **Aileen Phinney**

Billing address: **3001 Thomas Avenue**

City, ST, Zip: **Yuma, AZ 85367**

Country: **USA**

Sales tax: Select AZ (for Arizona sales tax)

Customer type: **YUM**[2]

Telephone 1:   **928-555-8822**

Fax: **928-555-2145**

E-mail: **ap@yuma.com**

Web site: **www.yuma.com/aileen**

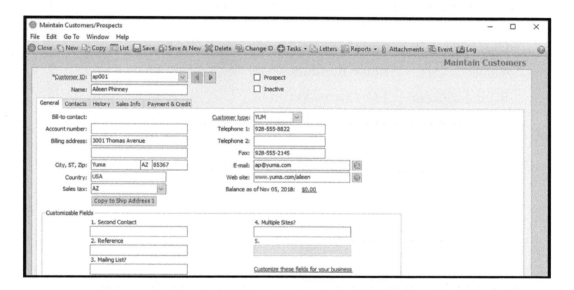

3. Click on the Sales Info tab.

4. In the GL Sales Acct field, if necessary, select Account No. 40000, Sales-
    Hardware.

---

[2]YUM is an abbreviation of Yuma County. Customer Type groups similar customers together.
In this case, customers in Yuma (YUM) are grouped together.

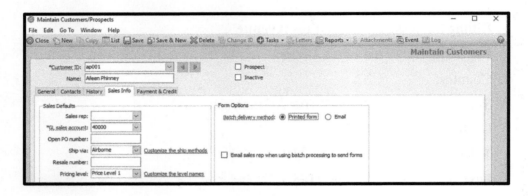

5. Click ☐ Save & New.

6. Click on the General tab. Add in the following customers.

Customer ID:	**bb002**
Name:	**Betsy Bauman**
Billing address:	**134 Citrus Avenue**
City, ST, Zip:	**Yuma, AZ 85366**
Country:	**USA**
Sales tax:	**AZ**
Customer type:	**YUM**
Telephone 1:	**928-555-5422**
Fax:	**928-555-4733**
E-mail:	**betsy@mail.com**
Web site:	**www.mail.com/bauman**

Sales Info: GL Sales Acct 40200, Sales-Wall for Betsy Bauman.

Customer ID:	**dc003**
Name:	**Denise Cobb**
Billing address:	**3354 Meadow Road**
City, ST, Zip:	**Ft. Lauderdale, FL 33310**
Country:	**USA**

Sales tax:	Skip this field--see footnote.[3]
Customer type:	**FL**
Telephone 1:	**954-555-3115**
Fax:	**954-555-5223**
E-mail:	**denise@mail.net**
Web site:	**www.mail.net/deniseC**

Sales Info: GL Sales Acct 40400, Sales-Floor for Denise Cobb

Customer ID:	**jp004**
Name:	**Judi Perin**
Billing address:	**2881 Brockton Road**
City, ST, Zip:	**Yuma, AZ 85365**
Country:	**USA**
Sales tax:	**AZ**
Customer type:	**YUM**
Telephone 1:	**928-555-1133**
Fax:	**928-555-6223**
E-mail:	**perin@yumamail.com**
Web site:	**www.yumamail.com/judi**

Sales Info: GL Sales Acct 40000, Sales-Hardware for Judi Perin.

Customer ID:	**pm005**
Name:	**Peter Martin**
Billing address:	**7133 West Palm Blvd.**
City, ST, Zip:	**Yuma, AZ 85367**
Country:	**USA**
Sales tax:	**AZ**

---

[3]Since this customer is out of state, there is no Sales Tax.

Customer type: **YUM**

Telephone 1:   **928-555-3341**

Fax: **928-555-4115**

E-mail: **peter@mymail.com**

Web site: **www.mymail.com/peter**

Sales Info: GL Sales Acct 40200, Sales-Wall for Peter Martin. Close the Maintain Customers/Prospects window.

BACKING UP YOUR DATA

Back up. This backup saves your data to this point, including Chapter 12 and Chapter 13's work with Shannon's [your first name] Service Merchandise. The suggested file name is **Chapter 13 Begin**.

RECORDING SALES

Two types of sales are entered in Sage 50:

> ➤ Credit sales or invoiced sales—sales where you enter an invoice.
> ➤ Cash sales—sales where you do not enter an invoice.

All the information about a sale is recorded on the Sales/Invoicing window. Then, Sage takes the necessary information from the window and automatically journalizes the transaction in the *sales journal*. Only sales on account are recorded in the sales journal. You can also print sales invoices.

Cash sales are entered on the Receive Money window. Then, Sage takes that information and journalizes the transaction in the *cash receipts journal*.

On the Sales/Invoicing window, enter invoices for the customers stored in Sage's customer file. You entered five credit customers for Shannon's Service

Merchandise. (Click ⟲ Refresh on the Customers & Sales Navigation Center to see the customer list.)

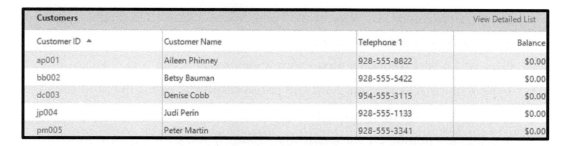

Customers			View Detailed List
Customer ID ▲	Customer Name	Telephone 1	Balance
ap001	Aileen Phinney	928-555-8822	$0.00
bb002	Betsy Bauman	928-555-5422	$0.00
dc003	Denise Cobb	954-555-3115	$0.00
jp004	Judi Perin	928-555-1133	$0.00
pm005	Peter Martin	928-555-3341	$0.00

All journal entries made to the Sales Journal (Sales/Invoicing window) are posted both to the General Ledger and to the Customer Ledger or *Accounts Receivable Ledger*. You can apply transactions to inventory items and jobs. Entering sales works hand in hand with entering receipts. Once an invoice is posted it is simple to show that a customer has paid. Just display the appropriate invoice and click on the Pay box. Sage takes care of all the correct account distributions for you.

▶ Entering Invoices for Credit Sales (Remember, the icon means there is a video at www.mhhe.com/yacht2019.

In the steps that follow, you record the following transaction:

Date   *Transaction Description*

1/7/19   Sold two doorknobs on account to Aileen Phinney; $324 ($300 plus $24, sales tax). (*Hint: Doorknobs are classified as hardware.*)

1. From the Customers & Sales Navigation Center, select [Sales Invoices] > New Sales Invoice. The Sales/Invoicing window appears.

2. Your cursor is in the Customer ID field. Click 🔍 and select **Aileen Phinney**. Sage supplies the customer default information: billing address, payment terms, GL account default, A/R Account default, and the sales tax

code. (*Hint:* If the GL Account field and A/R Account field do not display Account Nos. 40000 and 11000, refer step 1, pages xvii-xviii. The Hide General Ledger Accounts boxes should be unchecked.)

3. Type **7** in the Invoice date field and press **<Enter>**. Since the invoice is printed later, skip the Invoice # field. When the invoice is printed, the invoices are numbered automatically. (**Hint**: *If you do not have a printer, type 101 in the Invoice # field.*)

4. Click on the Quantity field, type **2** and press **<Enter>**.

5. In the Item field, click [icon]. Select **001hardware** for hardware.

6. In the Description field, type **Two doorknobs** and press **<Enter>**. Notice that the GL Account,[4] Unit Price, Amount field, A/R Account, and Sales Tax Code are automatically completed.

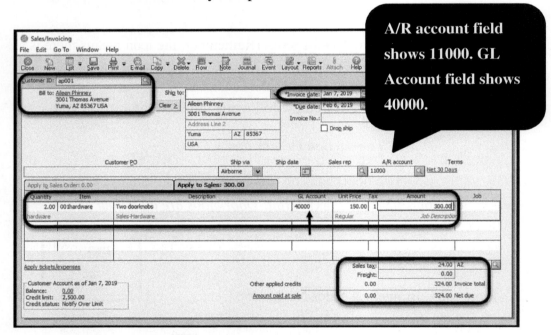

> **A/R account field shows 11000. GL Account field shows 40000.**

---

[4]If the G/L Account field and A/R Account fields are *not* displayed on your Sales/Invoicing window, click Options > Global. Make sure the boxes in the Hide General Ledger Accounts section are unchecked.

Printing Sales Invoices

When sales invoices are printed, you also post the transaction to the Sales Journal. If you do <u>not</u> have a printer, type 101 in the Invoice No. field.

To print or display this sales invoice, follow these steps:

1. Click [Print]. (If you do not have a printer, click on the down-arrow next to Print > select Print Preview.)
2. The Print Forms: Invoices window appears. Click [Select Form].
3. The Print Forms: Invoices/Pkg. Slips window appears. If necessary, select Invoice.
4. Click [OK].
5. The Print Forms [or Preview Forms]: Invoices window appears. The First invoice number field shows 101.

Subsequent invoices are numbered consecutively. The Use this form field shows Invoice.

6. Click [Print] [or [Print Preview]]. The invoice starts to print. (*Hint:* When you print the invoice, it also posts to the sales journal.) If you are not connected to a printer, you post (save) the invoice *after* displaying it. Since you are not printing, an invoice number is not automatically generated. If needed, type the invoice number in the Invoice # field.

Shannon's Service Merchandise
3344 Milton Avenue
Yuma, AZ 85366
USA

INVOICE

Invoice Number:	101
Invoice Date:	Jan 7, 2019
Page:	1

Voice: 928-555-7744
Fax: 928-555-7746

Bill To:	Ship to:
Aileen Phinney 3001 Thomas Avenue Yuma, AZ 85367 USA	Aileen Phinney 3001 Thomas Avenue Yuma, AZ 85367 USA

Customer ID	Customer PO	Payment Terms	
ap001		Net 30 Days	
Sales Rep ID	**Shipping Method**	**Ship Date**	**Due Date**
	Airborne		2/6/19

Quantity	Item	Description	Unit Price	Amount
2.00	001 hardware	Two doorknobs	150.00	300.00

	Subtotal	300.00
	Sales Tax	24.00
	Total Invoice Amount	324.00
Check/Credit Memo No:	Payment/Credit Applied	
	TOTAL	**324.00**

If you are not connected to a printer, close the Print Preview window. On the Sales/Invoicing window, type **101** in the Invoice No. field, select <u>S</u>ave to post.

How to fix?

The form you select is tied to the kind of printer you are using. If your invoice does not print, you should select a different form to print. Refer to step 2 on page 485 to change the form for printing invoices.

---

7. The Sales/Invoicing window is ready for the next sales invoice. (*Hint:* When you printed the invoice, the transaction was posted to the sales journal, accounts receivable account in the general ledger, and customer account in the customer ledger. Once the transaction is posted, cost of sales is also calculated. If you selected <Print Preview> to display the invoice, click <Print> to post.)

8. Record the following credit sales in the Sales/Invoicing window:

Date   *Transaction Description*

1/7/19   Sold four rolls of vinyl flooring on account to Denise Cobb. Print Invoice No. 102. (*Hint: Vinyl flooring is classified as floor. Ms. Cobb's sales invoice shows no tax because this sale is made to an out-of-state customer.*)

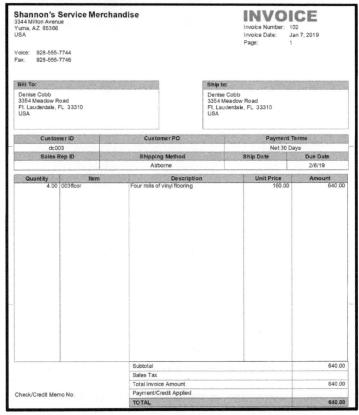

Date	*Transaction Description*

1/7/19   Sold four pairs of curtains on account to Peter Martin. Print Invoice No.103. (*Hint: Curtains are classified as wall.*)

Shannon's Service Merchandise
3344 Milton Avenue
Yuma, AZ 85366
USA

INVOICE

Invoice Number: 103
Invoice Date: Jan 7, 2019
Page: 1

Voice: 928-555-7744
Fax: 928-555-7746

Bill To:	Ship to:
Peter Martin 7133 West Palm Blvd. Yuma, AZ 85367 USA	Peter Martin 7133 West Palm Blvd. Yuma, AZ 85367 USA

Customer ID	Customer PO	Payment Terms	
pm005		Net 30 Days	
Sales Rep ID	**Shipping Method**	**Ship Date**	**Due Date**
	Airborne		2/6/19

Quantity	Item	Description	Unit Price	Amount
4.00	002wall	Four pairs of curtains	100.00	400.00

	Subtotal	400.00
	Sales Tax	32.00
	Total Invoice Amount	432.00
Check/Credit Memo No:	Payment/Credit Applied	
	TOTAL	432.00

Date	Transaction Description

1/7/19   Sold three curtain rods on account to Judi Perin. Print Invoice
            No. 104. (*Hint: Curtain rods are classified as hardware.*)

Shannon's Service Merchandise
3344 Milton Avenue
Yuma, AZ 85366
USA

INVOICE

Invoice Number: 104
Invoice Date: Jan 7, 2019
Page: 1

Voice: 928-555-7744
Fax: 928-555-7746

Bill To:	Ship to:
Judi Perin 2881 Brockton Road Yuma, AZ 85365 USA	Judi Perin 2881 Brockton Road Yuma, AZ 85365 USA

Customer ID	Customer PO	Payment Terms	
jp004		Net 30 Days	
Sales Rep ID	**Shipping Method**	**Ship Date**	**Due Date**
	Airborne		2/6/19

Quantity	Item	Description	Unit Price	Amount
3.00	001 hardware	Three curain rods	150.00	450.00

Subtotal		450.00
Sales Tax		36.00
Total Invoice Amount		486.00
Payment/Credit Applied		
TOTAL		**486.00**

Check/Credit Memo No:

Entering a Service Invoice

Shannon's Service Merchandise sells and repairs household items. When repairs are done, a *service invoice* is used. A service invoice is an alternative to the standard invoice. It is used when you want to create an invoice without inventory items.

Follow these steps to enter a service invoice:

Date	Transaction Description
1/10/19	Repaired curtains for Betsy Bauman, $49.89, plus sales tax of $3.99, for a total of $53.88.

1. From the Sales/Invoicing window, click [Layout]. Then select <Predefined> Service. The Sales/Invoicing window changes to include only the information necessary for a service invoice. This means that you no longer can select inventory items. When you complete the service transaction, click [Layout] again. Then, you are ready to enter an inventory sale on the Sales/Invoicing window.

2. In the Customer ID field, select Betsy Bauman.

3. Type **10** in the Invoice date field, then press **<Enter>**.

4. Click on the Description field. Type **Repair** and press **<Enter>**.

5. In the GL Account field, select Account No. 40600, Service Fees.

6. Type **49.89** in the Amount field. Compare your Sales/Invoicing window to the one shown on the next page.

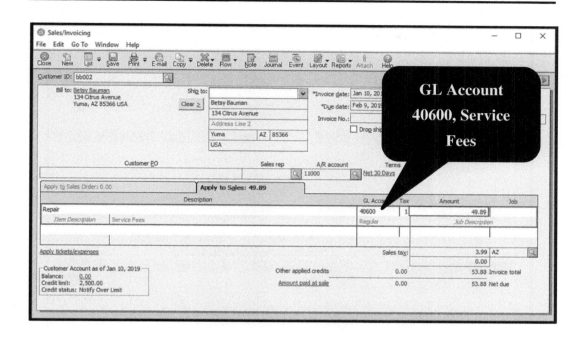

7. Print Invoice No. 105 and compare it to the one shown on the next page.

Shannon's Service Merchandise
3344 Milton Avenue
Yuma, AZ 85366
USA

INVOICE

Invoice Number: 105
Invoice Date: Jan 10, 2019
Page: 1

Voice: 928-555-7744
Fax: 928-555-7746

Bill To:	Ship to:
Betsy Bauman 134 Citrus Avenue Yuma, AZ 85366 USA	Betsy Bauman 134 Citrus Avenue Yuma, AZ 85366 USA

Customer ID	Customer PO	Payment Terms	
bb002		Net 30 Days	
Sales Rep ID	**Shipping Method**	**Ship Date**	**Due Date**
	Airborne		2/9/19

Quantity	Item	Description	Unit Price	Amount
		Repair		49.89
		Subtotal		49.89
		Sales Tax		3.99
		Total Invoice Amount		53.88
		Payment/Credit Applied		
		TOTAL		**53.88**

Check/Credit Memo No:

If you are not connected to a printer, close the Print Preview window. On the Sales/Invoicing window, type **105** in the Invoice No. field, then click <<u>S</u>ave> to post.

8. Click > then <Predefined> Product. Click .

Sales Returns: Credits & Returns

A sales return, or credit memo, is used when merchandise is returned by a customer. Credit memos for sales returns are entered similarly to vendor credit memos.

Before you can apply a credit, you must post the invoice. Invoice Nos. 101–105 were posted to the sales journal when you printed (or saved) the sales invoices (see pages 486-492). This work must be completed *before* you can apply a sales return. When a credit memo is entered, select the customer's ID code and the appropriate invoice number. Then, the return will be applied to that invoice and the customer's account balance will be adjusted.

In the steps that follow, you record the following transaction:

Date	Transaction Description
1/14/19	Peter Martin returned one pair of curtains that he purchased on January 6, Invoice No. 103. He also paid the balance of that invoice.

1. From the Customers & Sales Navigation Center, select > New Credit Memo.
2. In the Customer ID field, select Peter Martin.
3. In the Credit date field, type **14** and press **<Enter>**.
4. Type **CM103** in the Credit No. field. (CM is an abbreviation for Credit Memo. Use the sales invoice number to identify the credit memo.) Press **<Enter>**.
5. The Apply to Invoice No. tab is selected. Click on the down-arrow and select 103.
6. Type **1** in the Returned field. Press **<Enter>**

7. Type **Returned one pair of curtains** in the Description field.

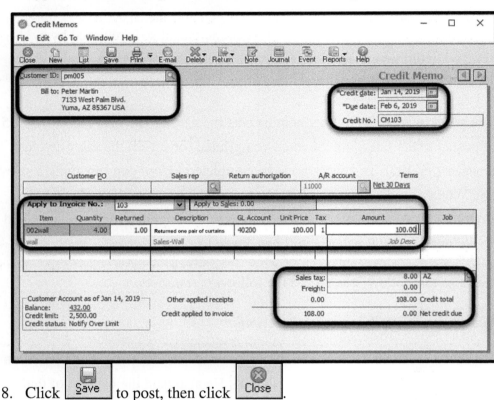

8. Click ![Save] to post, then click ![Close].

Apply a sales return: Follow these steps.

1. From the Customers & Sales Navigation Center, select ![Receive Money] > Receive Money from Customer. At the Select a Cash Account window, accept the default for Interstate Bank by clicking ![OK].

2. On the Receive Money window, type **1/14/19** in the Deposit ticket ID field. Press **<Enter>** two times.

3. In the Customer ID field, select Peter Martin.

4. In the Check/Reference No. field, type **Invoice 103** then press **<Enter>** key two times.

5. In the Date field, type **14**, then press the **<Enter>** key two times.

6. Observe that the Payment method field displays Check, and that the Cash Account field displays Account No. 10200, Interstate Bank. In the Apply to Invoices list, click on the Pay box. The Receipt amount shown is 324.00 ($432 original invoice - $108, return).

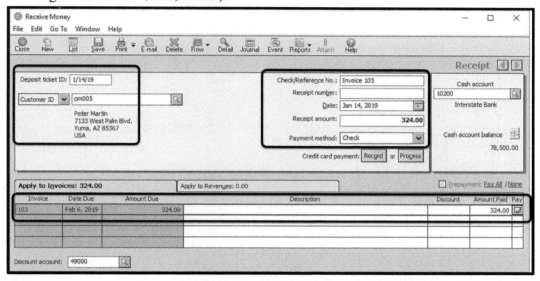

7. Click [Save] to post, then click [Close].

RECORDING RECEIPTS AND CASH SALES

The Receive Money window is used for recording checks, cash, and credit card sales that are received and deposited in the checking account. The information from the Receive Money window is automatically journalized in the Cash Receipts Journal. If the receipt is from a credit customer, then the receipt is posted to the customer's subsidiary ledger as well. There are two categories for receipts that result from sales:

➢ Receipts for which an invoice was entered in the Sales/Invoicing window.
➢ Direct sales receipts for which no invoice was entered in the Sales/Invoicing window.

Entering a Receipt

Date   *Transaction Description*

1/21/19   Shannon's Service Merchandise received a check in the amount of
            $324 from Aileen Phinney in payment of Invoice 101.

Follow these steps to enter this receipt:

1. Select [ ] > Receive Money from Customer. The Receive
    Money window appears.
2. Type **1/21/19** in the Deposit ticket ID field.
3. In the Customer ID field, select Aileen Phinney.
4. In the Check/Reference No. field, type **Invoice 101**. (This is the Invoice
    that is being paid.) Press the **<Enter>** key two times.
5. Type **21** in the Date field.
6. Verify that Account No. 10200, Interstate Bank, is displayed in the Cash
    Account field. The Apply to Invoices tab is selected. Click on the Pay box
    for Invoice 101.

7. Click ⟦Save⟧ to post this receipt. The Receive Money window is ready for another transaction.

In the preceding steps, each customer paid the invoice in full. What if a customer made a partial payment on an invoice?

Date   *Transaction Description*

1/23/19   Judi Perin paid $105 on account, Invoice No. 104.

Follow these steps for partial payment:

1. The Receive Money window should be displayed. Type **1/23/19** in the Deposit ticket ID field.
2. Select Judi Perin as the customer.
3. Type **Invoice 104** in the Check/Reference No. field. Press the **<Enter>** key two times.
4. Type **23** in the Date field. If necessary, in the Payment method field, select Check.

5. Judi Perin's Invoice number, Date Due, and Amount Due display in the Apply to Invoices table. Click on the Amount Paid field. Type **105** in the Amount Paid field and press **<Enter>**. A check mark is automatically placed in the Pay box.

6. Click [Save] to post.

Enter the following receipts:

Date	Transaction Description
1/28/19	Received a check in the amount of $53.88 from Betsy Bauman in full payment of Invoice No. 105.
1/28/19	Received a check in the amount of $640 from Denise Cobb in full payment of Invoice No. 102.

Cash Sales

Follow these steps to record a cash sale.

Date   *Transaction Description*

1/30/19   Sold two pairs of curtains for cash to Bertha Perkins, $200.

1. On the Receive Money window, type **1/30/19** in the Deposit ticket ID field.
2. Click on the Name field, then type **Bertha Perkins**. You do not enter address information for a cash sale.
3. Since this is a cash sale, type **Cash** in the Check/Reference No. field. Press **<Enter>** two times.
4. Type **30** as the date.
5. If necessary, in the Payment method field, select Check.
6. Verify that account 10200, Interstate Bank, is displayed in the Cash Account field.
7. Make sure that the Apply to Revenues tab is selected. (Sage assumes you are going to apply the receipt to revenue unless you select a customer with open invoices. You can also apply a portion of the receipt to both invoices and revenue. You do this by selecting each heading, then entering the distribution information for that portion of the receipt. A running subtotal is kept to show how much of the receipt has been applied.)
8. Type **2** in the Quantity field.
9. Select 002wall as the inventory item.
10. Type **Two pairs of curtains** as the Description and press the **<Enter>** key.
11. Observe that the GL Account field, shows Account No. 40200, Sales-Wall (this is the default account). (*Hint:* Make sure the correct sales account is selected.)
12. In the Sales tax field, select AZ. Observe that 16.00 is automatically calculated in the Sales tax field.

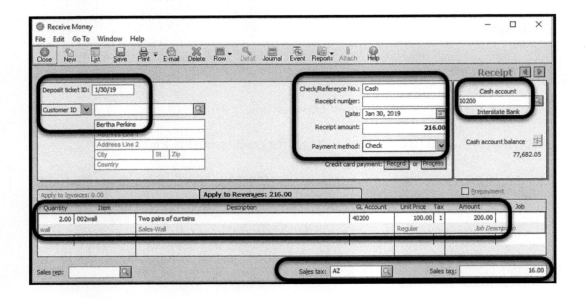

13. Click [Save], then close the Receive Money window.

Finance Charges

Sage 50 includes a feature in the Tasks menu for computing finance or interest charges. This option computes and applies finance charges for customers and/or prints a report listing all finance charges. You use this feature by selecting the Finance Charge option. You may want to try this out on your own. Use the Tasks menu and select Finance Charge to see how this feature works.

PRINTING CUSTOMER FORMS

Sage 50 provides forms for the following types of customer correspondence:

➢ Invoices.
➢ Statements.
➢ Mailing labels.
➢ Collection letters.

These reports can be accessed by selecting Reports & Forms from the menu bar, then Forms. Select a predefined form to print customer information or design your own form. In Part 4 of this book you will learn more about Custom Forms.

Printing Invoices

You can print a single invoice from the Sales/Invoicing window by selecting . This saves and prints the invoice. A batch of invoices can be printed from the Reports & Forms menu by selecting Forms, then Invoices and Packing Slips. There are several types of predefined invoices available for printing customer information or you can design your own form.

Printing Statements

The information that is printed on customer statements is defined in the Statement/Invoices Defaults which are set up from the Maintain menu. You can set up collection letters and also select from these print options.

➢ Whether to print your company name, address, phone, and fax on the statement.
➢ Whether to print zero and credit balance statements.
➢ The minimum balance necessary to print a statement.
➢ The number of grace days before printing a statement.
➢ Whether to print statements for accounts with no activity.

If you want to display customer information before printing, display or print the customer ledger. Statements can be printed from the Reports & Forms menu by selecting Forms, then Invoices and Packing Slips. There are several types of predefined statements available for printing customer account balances. Select the form that best suits your needs. As mentioned before, you can also design your own statement. When the statements stop printing, a message box displays, asking if the statements printed okay and if you want to update the customer file.

Look at your printed statements carefully before you answer Yes to this question. When you answer Yes, Sage records the statement date in the customer record. This is used as the balance brought forward date the next time you print a statement. This way the ending balance on one statement is the same as the beginning balance on the next statement.

You should enter, print, and post all invoices prior to printing statements. In this way the Balance Forward amounts are correct from month to month.

Printing Mailing Labels

Labels can be printed by selecting the Reports & Forms menu, Accounts Receivable, Forms, then Customer Labels and Letters. Select one of the Customer Labels, then print. There are several predefined labels available for printing. You can elect to use these forms or design your own.

➢ Select a range of customers.
➢ Enter all or part of a zip code to limit the mailing labels to customers in a certain area.
➢ Print labels for customers, prospects, or both.
➢ Enter a Status for customers so that you print labels for all, active, or inactive customers.
➢ Enter a Type Code for customers so that only customers of a specific Type Code will print.

Preparing Collection Letters

What if credit customers are slow to pay their bills? Collection letters can play an important role in generating revenue from customers who are slow to pay off their balances. Sometimes just a friendly reminder is all that is needed. The table below shows how important it is to get paid on time because the longer a bill remains unpaid, the less chance there is of collecting.

Number of Days Overdue	Percent Uncollectible
1 to 30 days	2%
31 to 60 days	10%
61 to 90 days	20%
91 to 180 days	30%
181 to 365 days	50%
over 365 days	90%

Collection letters are an effective way to remind customers to pay their unpaid balances. Most customers will pay after they receive a friendly reminder of a past-due account. It is worthwhile to send these letters because past-due amounts can be a burden on a company's cash flow.

Depending on how late the payment is, collection letters vary in tone and urgency. For example, a friendly reminder may be all that's needed for someone who is 30 days past due, but a different letter may be needed for someone who is more than 90 days past due. Remember that while it is important to collect past-due amounts, you would also like to keep the customer.

Sage 50's letters are grouped by lateness of payment and severity of tone. The less than 30 days overdue letter is soft while the 61-90 days overdue letter is much firmer. You may edit all of these letters to suit your needs.

To print a collection letter you use the analysis menu. Follow these steps to do that:

1. From the menu bar, select Analysis > Collection Manager.
2. Type **1/31/19** in the As of Date field. Press **<Enter>**. The Collection Aging bar graph appears.

3. Click . The Total Bracket table lists an invoice for Judi Perin.

4. Click on the Letter box on the Total Bracket table to place a check mark in

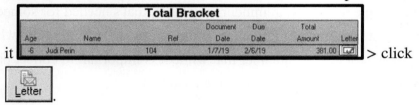

it > click

.

5. The Print Forms: Collection Letters window appears. Click Select Form .

You may want to try one of these selections and see what Sage 50's collection letters look like. The sample letters are sorted as follows.

➢ Overdue < 30 Days - Soft
➢ Overdue >90 Days
➢ Overdue >90 Days – Coll Agency
➢ Overdue 31-60 Days - Medium
➢ Overdue 61-90 Days - Firm

6. Select a form to print, then click ⬚ OK ⬚.

7. Click ⬚ Print ⬚. A collection letter prints. Read the letter that you printed. The collection letter that prints is an example. When the window prompts, Did the collection letters print properly?, click ⬚ Yes ⬚. Since Ms. Perin does *not* have an overdue bill, no amount shows in the letter's Amount Overdue field.

8. Close the Collection Manager.

FINANCIAL MANAGER

The *Financial Manager* provides a brief, overall financial picture of how your business is performing. By default, the first window you see is a numeric table of summary data consisting of various business ratios. Both the Business Summary and Key Balances can be displayed.

1. From the menu bar, select Analysis > Financial Manager.

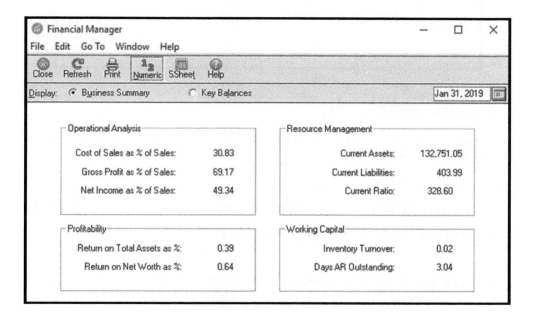

The radio button next to Business Summary is the default. The information is separated into four areas: Operational Analysis, Resource Management, Profitability, and Working Capital. Ratios are shown within each area.

2. Select the Key Balances radio button. Within Key Balances, Specific asset and liability balances are shown. The Operations column shows key balances from the income statement. Current and Year to Date amounts are shown but since Shannon's Service Merchandise data is only for one year, those columns are the same. The cash balance is the total of Interstate Bank and Yuma Savings and Loan: 77,898.05 + 22,000.00 = 99,898.05.

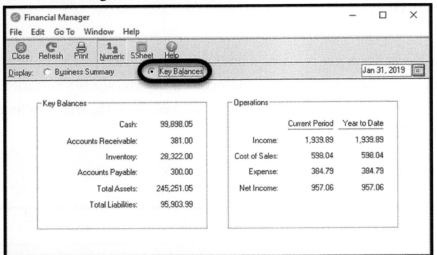

3. Close the Financial Manager.

PRINTING THE SALES JOURNAL

The Sales/Invoicing window is the Sales Journal. Credit sales are recorded in the Sales/Invoicing window. Follow these steps to print the Sales Journal:

1. From the Recently Used Customer Reports area on the Customers & Sales Navigation Center, link to <u>Print</u> or <u>View</u> the Sales Journal.

2. If you linked to <u>Print</u>, If the Modify Report – Sales Journal window appears. Click [OK]. Make the selections to print.

			Shannon's Service Merchandise		
			Sales Journal		
			For the Period From Jan 1, 2019 to Jan 31, 2019		
			Filter Criteria includes: Report order is by Invoice/CM Date. Report is printed in Detail Format.		
Date	**Account ID**	**Invoice/CM #**	**Line Description**	**Debit Amnt**	**Credit Amnt**
1/7/19	23100	101	AZ: Arizona Dept. of Revenue		24.00
	40000		Two doorknobs		300.00
	50000		Cost of sales	100.00	
	12000		Cost of sales		100.00
	11000		Aileen Phinney	324.00	
1/7/19	40400	102	Four rolls of vinyl flooring		640.00
	57000		Cost of sales	216.00	
	12000		Cost of sales		216.00
	11000		Denise Cobb	640.00	
1/7/19	23100	103	AZ: Arizona Dept. of Revenue		32.00
	40200		Four pairs of curtains		400.00
	50500		Cost of sales	120.00	
	12000		Cost of sales		120.00
	11000		Peter Martin	432.00	
1/7/19	23100	104	AZ: Arizona Dept. of Revenue		36.00
	40000		Three curain rods		450.00
	50000		Cost of sales	150.00	
	12000		Cost of sales		150.00
	11000		Judi Perin	486.00	
1/10/19	23100	105	AZ: Arizona Dept. of Revenue		3.99
	40600		Repair		49.89
	11000		Betsy Bauman	53.88	
1/14/19	23100	CM103	AZ: Arizona Dept. of Revenue	8.00	
	40200		Returned one pair of curtains	100.00	
	50500		Cost of sales		30.00
	12000		Cost of sales	30.00	
	11000		Peter Martin		108.00
		Total		**2,659.88**	**2,659.88**

PRINTING THE CASH RECEIPTS JOURNAL

The Receive Money window is the Cash Receipts Journal. Payments from customers and cash sales are recorded in the Receive Money window. Follow these steps to print the Cash Receipts Journal.

1. From the Recently Used Customer Reports area on the Customers & Sales Navigation Center, link to <u>Print</u> or <u>View</u> the Cash Receipts Journal. If the Cash Receipts Journal is not listed, link to <u>View All Customer & Sales</u>

Reports. (Or, from the menu bar select Reports, then Accounts Receivable, then highlight Cash Receipts Journal.)

*****EDUCATIONAL VERSION ONLY*****

Shannon's Service Merchandise
Cash Receipts Journal
For the Period From Jan 1, 2019 to Jan 31, 2019

Filter Criteria includes: Report order is by Check Date. Report is printed in Detail Format.

Date	Account ID	Transaction Ref	Line Description	Debit Amnt	Credit Amnt
1/14/19	11000	Invoice 103	Invoice: 103		324.00
	10200		Peter Martin	324.00	
1/21/19	11000	Invoice 101	Invoice: 101		324.00
	10200		Aileen Phinney	324.00	
1/23/19	11000	Invoice 104	Invoice: 104		105.00
	10200		Judi Perin	105.00	
1/28/19	11000	Invoice 105	Invoice: 105		53.88
	10200		Betsy Bauman	53.88	
1/28/19	11000	Invoice 102	Invoice: 102		640.00
	10200		Denise Cobb	640.00	
1/30/19	23100	Cash	AZ: Arizona Dept. of Revenue		16.00
	40200		Two pairs of curtains		200.00
	50500		Cost of sales	60.00	
	12000		Cost of sales		60.00
	10200		Bertha Perkins	216.00	
				1,722.88	1,722.88

2. If you linked to <u>Print</u>, The Modify Report - Cash Receipts Journal window displays. Click OK . Make the selections to print.

PRINTING THE CUSTOMER LEDGERS

Follow these steps to print the Customer Ledgers for Shannon's Service Merchandise:

1. From the Recently Used Customer Reports area on the Customers & Sales Navigation Center, link to <u>View All Customer & Sales Reports</u>. The Select a Report or Form window appears.

2. In the Accounts Receivable: Customers and Sales list, select Customer Ledgers. Then, make the selections to display or print.

Shannon's Service Merchandise
Customer Ledgers
For the Period From Jan 1, 2019 to Jan 31, 2019

Filter Criteria includes: Report order is by ID. Report is printed in Detail Format.

Customer ID Customer	Date	Trans No	Type	Debit Amt	Credit Amt	Balance
ap001	1/7/19	101	SJ	324.00		324.00
Aileen Phinney	1/21/19	Invoice 101	CRJ		324.00	0.00
bb002	1/10/19	105	SJ	53.88		53.88
Betsy Bauman	1/28/19	Invoice 105	CRJ		53.88	0.00
dc003	1/7/19	102	SJ	640.00		640.00
Denise Cobb	1/28/19	Invoice 102	CRJ		640.00	0.00
jp004	1/7/19	104	SJ	486.00		486.00
Judi Perin	1/23/19	Invoice 104	CRJ		105.00	381.00
pm005	1/7/19	103	SJ	432.00		432.00
Peter Martin	1/14/19	CM103	SJ		108.00	324.00
	1/14/19	Invoice 103	CRJ		324.00	0.00
Report Total				**1,935.88**	**1,554.88**	**381.00**

PRINTING THE GENERAL LEDGER TRIAL BALANCE

1. In the Reports list, highlight General Ledger. Then, in the General Ledger: Account Information list highlight General Ledger Trial Balance.
2. Make the selections to display or print. Compare your general ledger trial balance to the one shown on the next page.

Shannon's Service Merchandise			
General Ledger Trial Balance			
As of Jan 31, 2019			
Filter Criteria includes: Report order is by ID. Report is printed in Detail Format.			
Account ID	**Account Description**	**Debit Amt**	**Credit Amt**
10200	Interstate Bank	77,898.05	
10400	Yuma Savings & Loan	22,000.00	
11000	Accounts Receivable	381.00	
12000	Merchandise Inventory	28,322.00	
13000	Supplies	1,750.00	
14000	Prepaid Insurance	2,400.00	
15000	Furniture and Fixtures	5,000.00	
15100	Computers & Equipment	7,500.00	
15500	Building	100,000.00	
20000	Accounts Payable		300.00
23100	Sales Tax Payable		103.99
27000	Long-Term Notes Payable		20,500.00
27400	Mortgage Payable		75,000.00
39006	Brian Stewart, Capital		74,695.00
39007	Brian Stewart, Drawing	500.00	
39008	Shannon Larsen, Capital		74,695.00
39009	Shannon Larsen, Drawing	500.00	
40000	Sales-Hardware		750.00
40200	Sales-Wall		500.00
40400	Sales-Floor		640.00
40600	Service Fees		49.89
50000	Cost of Sales-Hardware	250.00	
50500	Cost of Sales-Wall	150.00	
57000	Cost of Sales-Floor	216.00	
59500	Purchase Discounts		17.96
70000	Maintenance Expense	160.00	
73500	Postage Expense	45.00	
75500	Supplies Expense	107.65	
76000	Telephone Expense	72.14	
	Total:	**247,251.84**	**247,251.84**

EDITING RECEIPTS

Is your Customer Ledger correct? Judi Perin's account is used to show how to edit the Customer Ledger. Follow these steps to see how the editing feature works:

1. From the Customers & Sales Navigation Center, select > View and Edit Money Received.

2. The Receipt List appears. Click on Invoice 104, $105.00 to highlight it.

3. Click ![Open]. The original Receive Money window with Judi Perin's partial payment appears. Make any necessary corrections, then <Save>.
4. Close the Receive Money window and Receipt List window.

BACKING UP CHAPTER 13 DATA

Back up. (*Hint:* Close all windows before backing up.) This backup saves your data to this point, including Chapter 12 and Chapter 13's work with Shannon's [your first name] Service Merchandise. The suggested file name is **Chapter 13**.

EXPORT REPORTS TO EXCEL

1. Export the following Sage 50 reports to Excel:
    *   Sales Journal
    *   Cash Receipts Journal
    *   Customer Ledgers
    *   General Ledger Trial Balance.
2. Use the file name **Chapter 13_ SJ_ CRJ_ CL_GLTB.xlsx.**

    NOTE: If your instructor would like you to save the Sales Journal, Cash Receipts Journal, Customer Ledgers, and General Ledger Trial Balance as PDF files, do that. The file name is **Chapter 13_Sales Journal.pdf**, etc.

ONLINE LEARNING CENTER

Complete end-of-chapter activities at www.mhhe.com/yacht2019 > Student Edition, then Chapter 13.

1. Quizzes: Multiple Choice and True False questions. Interactive online tests that are graded and can be emailed to your instructor.
2. More Resources:
   a. QA Templates: Answer 10 multiple-choice questions and one Analysis Question.
   b. Videos: Watch the Sales Invoice and Customer Payments videos.
   c. Narrated PowerPoints: Listen to the narrated PowerPoints.
   d. Going to the Net Exercises: Read information about accounts receivable on the Business Owner's Toolkit website.
   e. Assessment Rubric: Complete the rubric to review Sage 50's journals, navigation centers, modules, task windows, and reports.

➢ Information Center > Sage Advisor Videos. The OLC also includes links to the Appendixes:

- Appendix A: Troubleshooting (textbook and OLC)
- Appendix C: Review of Accounting Principles (OLC Student Edition)
- Appendix D: Glossary (OLC Student Edition)

Exercise 13-1: You must complete Exercises 12-1 and 12-2 before starting Exercise 13-1.

1. Start Sage 50. Open the company that you set up in Exercise 12-1 on pages 458-459, Your last name Sales and Service.
2. If necessary, restore your data from Exercise 12-2. (*Hint:* This backup was made on page 467.) To make sure you are starting in the right place, display Exercise 12-2's general ledger trial balance (step 6, page 467).

3. If necessary, enter the following customer defaults.

    a. Standard Terms: Due in number of days

    b. Net due in: 30 days

        Discount in: 0 days

        Discount %:   0.00

        Credit Limit: 2,500.00

        GL Sales Account: 40000 Sales Hardware

        Discount GL Account: 49000 Sales Discounts

4. Set up GA sales taxes. The sales tax rate is 8.00%. (*Hint:* Refer to pages 473-478. Use Georgia Dept. of Revenue and Georgia sales tax.)

5. Enter the following customers:

    a. Customer ID: **ac001**

        Name: **Abby Caron**

        Billing address: **8291 Orange Avenue**

        City, ST, Zip: **Norcross, GA 30092**

        Country: **USA**

        Sales Tax: **GA**

        Customer type: **GWI** (for Gwinnett County)

        Telephone 1:   **770-555-1162**

        Fax: **770-555-3822**

        E-mail: **info@abbycaron.com**

        Web site: **www.abbycaron.com**

        Sales Info: GL Sales Acct 40200, Sales-Tools for Abby Caron.

    b. Customer ID: **bb002**

        Name: **Bobby Berman**

        Billing address: **101 North Fifth Street**

        City, ST, Zip: **Atlanta, GA 30343**

        Country: **USA**

Sales tax:	**GA**
Customer type:	**FUL** (for Fulton County)
Telephone 1:	**404-555-1329**
Fax:	**404-555-5188**
E-mail:	**info@bobbyberman.net**
Web site:	**www.bobbyberman.net**

Sales Info: GL Sales Acct 40000, Sales-Hardware for Bobby Berman.

c.
Customer ID:	**rn003**
Name:	**Roberta Norton**
Billing address:	**2233 Darby Road**
City, ST, Zip:	**Atlanta, GA 30303**
Country:	**USA**
Sales tax:	**GA**
Customer type:	**FUL**
Telephone 1:	**404-555-4144**
Fax:	**404-555-6212**
E-mail:	**info@robertanorton.com**
Web site:	**www.robertanorton.com**

Sales Info: GL Sales Acct 40000, Sales-Hardware for Roberta Norton.

6. Make a backup of your work. Use **Exercise 13-1** as the file name.

Exercise 13-2: Exercise 13-1 must be completed before Exercise 13-2.

1. Start Sage 50. Open your last name Sales and Service company. If necessary, restore the Exercise 13-1.ptb file. Then, record the following transactions.

1/7/19 Sold five tool kits on account to Abby Caron, Customer ac001. Type **101** in the Invoice No. field.

1/7/19   Sold three hardware sets on account to Bobby Berman, Customer bb002.   102

1/7/19   Sold six hardware sets on account to Roberta Norton, Customer rn003.   103

1/10/19   Abby Caron returned one of the tool kits that he purchased on January 7, Invoice No. 101, CM101. Mr. Caron also paid the balance of Invoice 101. (*Hint: This transaction requires two entries*. If necessary, select Account No. 10200, Boulevard Bank as the cash account.)

1/14/19   Received a check in full payment of Invoice No. 102 from Bobby Berman.

1/17/19   Sold two hardware sets *and* two tool kits for cash to Sally Murphy. (*Hint:* Remember to enter two quantities and two items. Make sure GA sales tax is being charged.)

1/18/19   Sold three tool kits for cash to John Martinez.

2.   Print the Sales Journal, Cash Receipts Journal, Customer Ledgers, and General Ledger Trial Balance.

Check Your Figures:

10200, Boulevard Bank:	$67,746.63
11000, Accounts Receivable	972.00
12000, Merchandise Inventory	14,570.00
23100, Sales Tax Payable	193.20
40000, Sales-Hardware	1,650.00
40200, Sales-Tools	765.00

3.   Print the Financial Manager's Business Summary and Key Balances.

4.   Backup. Use **Exercise 13-2** as the file name.

5.   Export the following reports to Excel and save as PDFs: Sales Journal, Cash Receipts Journal, Customer Ledgers, General Ledger Trial Balance. Use **Exercise 13-2_SJ_CRJ_CL_GLTB** (Excel) and Exercise 13-2_Sales Journal, etc. (PDFs).

CHAPTER 13 INDEX

Chapter

14   Inventory & Services

LEARNING OBJECTIVES

1. Restore data from Chapter 13. (This backup was made on page 511.)
2. Enter inventory maintenance and default information.
3. Enter inventory item information, including Sales account, Merchandise Inventory account, and Cost of Sales account.
4. Enter inventory adjustments.
5. Compare Chapter 14's Financial Manager's Business Summary and Key Balances to Chapter 13's Financial Manager.
6. Make three backups, save two Excel files, and save five PDF files.

Merchandise inventory includes all goods owned by the business and held for sale. The account used for merchandise inventory is Account No. 12000, Merchandise Inventory. Sage 50's inventory system tracks inventory items at both the purchasing and sales level. When you set up an inventory item, you establish the General Ledger accounts that are updated by purchases and sales. Sage 50 keeps track of cost of goods sold, stock levels, sales prices, and vendors.

Sage uses a perpetual inventory system. In a perpetual inventory system a *merchandising business* continuously updates inventory each time an item is purchased or sold. Inventory calculations include FIFO, LIFO, and average cost methods. The *FIFO* (first in, first out) method assumes that the items in the beginning inventory are sold first. The *LIFO* (last in, first out) method assumes that the goods received last are sold first. The average cost method (also known as weighted average method) is the default for inventory items sold. The formula used is: Average Cost x Quantity Sold = Cost of Sales.

Sage tracks the inventory items that you buy and sell. After you post, the cost and quantity of each inventory item is updated automatically. Generally, all of your inventory should use the same costing method. Tracking inventory is a three-step process:

➢ Enter item information, including Sales account, Merchandise Inventory account, and Cost of Sales account.
➢ Use item codes when entering purchases and sales. Sage defaults to average cost. You can change the cost method to LIFO (last in, first out) or FIFO (first in, first out).
➢ If necessary, enter inventory adjustments.

Sage does the rest automatically: adjusts inventory levels each time you post a purchase or sale of an inventory item, tracks the cost of each item, and makes a Cost of Goods Sold journal entry at the end of the accounting period.

COST METHODS

There are three types of inventory cost methods: average cost, LIFO, and FIFO. Once you select the costing method for an inventory item, you cannot change it if transactions have been posted. Therefore, if you want to change the cost method for an item with posted transactions, you must enter the item again.

Average Cost

When you set up inventory items for Shannon's Service Merchandise, you selected the Average cost method. In Chapter 12, Shannon's Service Merchandise purchased four pairs of curtains from Ronny Becker Fabrics for $30 each (Invoice 210, page 437). What happens when these curtains are sold?

Purchased four pairs of curtains from Ronny Becker Fabrics at $30 each (Invoice 210, page 437).

Account ID	Account Description, Purchase Invoice 210	Debit	Credit
12000	Merchandise Inventory	120.00	
20000/RBF08	Accounts Payable/Ronny Becker Fabrics		120.00

Sold four pairs of curtains to Peter Martin for $100 each (Invoice 103, page 488).

Account ID	Account Description, Sales Invoice 103	Debit	Credit
50500	Cost of Sales-Wall	120.00	
11000/pm005	Accounts Receivable/Peter Martin	432.00	
12000	Merchandise Inventory		120.00
40200	Sales-Wall		400.00
23100	Sales Tax Payable		32.00

You can see from these journal entries that the Merchandise Inventory account is updated with each purchase and sale. After these transactions, the balance in Merchandise Inventory looks like this:

Merchandise Inventory, Account No. 12000

Purchased inventory	120.00	Sold Inventory	120.00	
Balance	0.00			

LIFO (Last In, First Out)

The LIFO (last in, first out) method of inventory pricing assumes that the last goods received are sold first. LIFO assumes that cost is based on replacement and that the last price paid for merchandise is more accurate. Accountants recommend that you select LIFO when you desire to charge the most recent inventory costs against revenue. LIFO yields the lowest amount of net income in periods of rising costs because the cost of the most recently acquired inventory more closely approximates the replacement cost.

FIFO (First In, First Out)

The FIFO (first in, first out) method of inventory pricing assumes that the items in the beginning inventory are sold first. FIFO costs your sales and values your inventory as if the items you sell are the ones that you have had in stock for the longest time. Accountants recommend that you select FIFO when you desire to charge costs against revenue in the order in which costs occur. FIFO yields a higher amount of profit during periods of rising costs. This happens because merchandise was acquired prior to the increase in cost.

TYPES OF INVENTORY ITEMS

There are nine types of inventory items:

➢ Stock item: This is the default in the Item Class list. It is the traditional inventory item where the program tracks descriptions, unit prices, stock quantities, and cost of sales. Once an item has been designated as a stock item, the type cannot be changed.

➢ Master Stock Item: Sage uses this item class as a special item that does not represent inventory stocked but contains item attributes shared with a number of substock items.

➢ Non-stock item: Sage tracks the description and a unit price for sales. You might use this type for service items such as hours where the unit price is set.

➢ Description only: Sage keeps track of the description of an Inventory Item. This saves time when entering purchases and sales because you don't have to retype the description. You might use this type for service items.

➢ Service: This is for services you can apply to your salary and wages account.

➤ Labor: For labor you can apply to your salary and wages account. You cannot purchase labor items but you can sell them.

➤ Assembly: You can specify items as assembly items and create a bill of materials for a unit made up of component stock or subassembly items.

➤ Activity item: To indicate how time is spent when performing services for a customer, for a job, or for internal administrative work. Activity items are used with the Time & Billing feature.

➤ Charge item: Expenses recorded by an employee or vendor when company resources are used for a customer or job.

GETTING STARTED

In the preceding chapters, you set up inventory items. The instructions that follow show how to add inventory items to Shannon's Service Merchandise.

1. Start Sage 50. Open Shannon's [your first name] Service Merchandise.
2. If necessary, restore data from the Chapter 13.ptb file. (Backup was made on page 511.)

💾 To make sure you are starting in the appropriate place in the data (Chapter 13.ptb backup) display the General Ledger Trial Balance (refer to page 510).

Shannon's Service Merchandise
General Ledger Trial Balance
As of Jan 31, 2019

Filter Criteria includes: Report order is by ID. Report is printed in Detail Format.

Account ID	Account Description	Debit Amt	Credit Amt
10200	Interstate Bank	77,898.05	
10400	Yuma Savings & Loan	22,000.00	
11000	Accounts Receivable	381.00	
12000	Merchandise Inventory	28,322.00	
13000	Supplies	1,750.00	
14000	Prepaid Insurance	2,400.00	
15000	Furniture and Fixtures	5,000.00	
15100	Computers & Equipment	7,500.00	
15500	Building	100,000.00	
20000	Accounts Payable		300.00
23100	Sales Tax Payable		103.99
27000	Long-Term Notes Payable		20,500.00
27400	Mortgage Payable		75,000.00
39006	Brian Stewart, Capital		74,695.00
39007	Brian Stewart, Drawing	500.00	
39008	Shannon Larsen, Capital		74,695.00
39009	Shannon Larsen, Drawing	500.00	
40000	Sales-Hardware		750.00
40200	Sales-Wall		500.00
40400	Sales-Floor		640.00
40600	Service Fees		49.89
50000	Cost of Sales-Hardware	250.00	
50500	Cost of Sales-Wall	150.00	
57000	Cost of Sales-Floor	216.00	
59500	Purchase Discounts		17.96
70000	Maintenance Expense	160.00	
73500	Postage Expense	45.00	
75500	Supplies Expense	107.65	
76000	Telephone Expense	72.14	
	Total:	**247,251.84**	**247,251.84**

INVENTORY DEFAULTS

1. From the Navigation Bar, select >
Set Up Inventory Defaults. The Inventory Item Defaults window displays.
Observe that the General tab shows the Default Item Class as Stock item

Item Class	
Default Item Class:	Stock item

. If Stock item is not selected, select it.

2. Click on the GL Accts/Costing tab. The default for inventory costing is the
Average method. Since this is what Shannon's Service Merchandise uses,
there is no need to make any changes to this window. These inventory
defaults were set up in Chapter 12, pages 425-426.

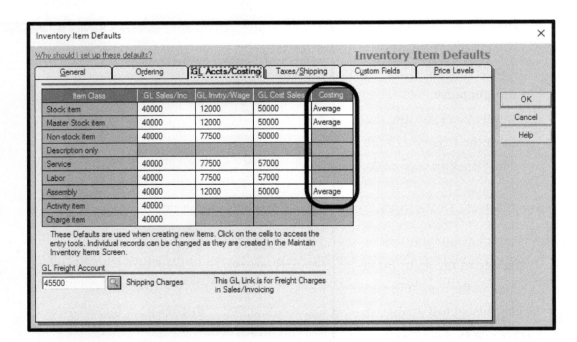

3. Click on the Taxes/Shipping tab.

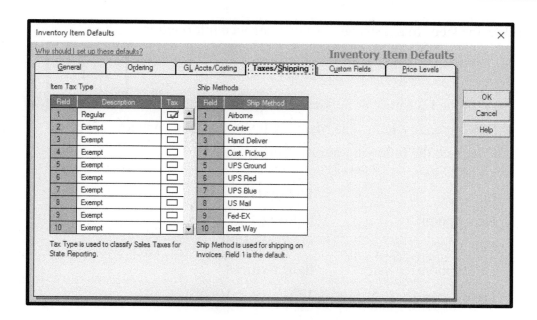

The Regular tax type is selected with a check mark. This is correct because there is an 8% sales tax in Arizona. The Ship Methods that appear on this tab are also shown on the Sales/Invoicing and Purchases/Receive Inventory windows. You can also use these ship methods to set up defaults for customers and vendors.

3. Click [OK] to close this window. (Remember: If you click [Cancel], you close the window without saving any changes.)

ENTERING INVENTORY ITEM MAINTENANCE INFORMATION

Inventory items are set up on the Maintain Inventory Items window. You can establish general ledger accounts, vendors, tax exemptions, sales prices and reorder quantities. The information on the Maintain Inventory Items window displays three active tabs: General, Custom Fields, and History; two tabs are inactive—Bill of Materials, and Item Attributes. Select an active tab to view its fields.

Follow the steps to enter inventory maintenance information.

1. From the Inventory & Services Navigation Center, select [Inventory Items] >
New Inventory Item. The Maintain Inventory Items window appears.
2. Complete the following information:

Item ID:	**004lights**
Description:	**lighting**
Item Class:	Stock Item
Description(for Sales):	**light fixtures**
Price Level 1:	**175**
Last Unit Cost:	**64**
Cost Method:	Average
GL Sales Acct:	Add Account No. **40500 Sales-Lights** (Account Type, Income)
GL Inventory Acct:	12000 Merchandise Inventory
GL Cost of Sales Acct:	Add Account No. **57050 Cost of Sales-Lights** (Account Type, Cost of Sales)
Item Tax Type:	1
Item Type:	**lights**
Stocking U/M:	**each**
Minimum Stock:	**8**
Reorder Quantity:	**4**
Preferred Vendor ID:	

• You need to add a new vendor. Click 🔍 in the Preferred Vendor ID
field > [New]. The Maintain Vendors window displays.

Vendor ID:	**TSS09**

Name:	**Tom's Sales and Service**
Mailing Address:	**3842 Redondo Drive**
City, ST, Zip:	**Yuma, AZ 85368**
Country:	**USA**
Vendor Type:	**lights**
1099 Type:	**Independent Contractor**
Expense Account:	12000 Merchandise Inventory
Telephone 1:	**928-555-4422**
Fax:	**928-555-4438**
E-Mail:	**info@tomsaleserv.com**
Web Address:	**www.tomsaleserv.com**

Purchase Info:

Tax ID Number:	**23-4312138**

a. Click [Save] > Close. You are returned to the Maintain Inventory Items window. In the Preferred Vendor ID field, select Tom's Sales and Service as the vendor. Click

b. Click on the Beginning Balances arrow (lower right corner of the Maintain Inventory Items window.) The Inventory Beginning Balances window displays. Select lighting. Complete the following:

Quantity:	125
Unit Cost:	64.00
Total Cost:	8,000.00 (completed automatically)

3. Observe that the Total Beginning Balances field shows 27,740.00. This amount agrees with the Merchandise Inventory balance on page 417 (Chapter 12's January 1, 2019 balance sheet).

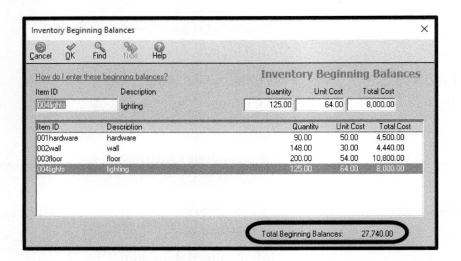

4. Click [OK] to close the Inventory Beginning Balances window.

5. Make sure, TSS09, Tom's Sales and Service, is shown in the Preferred Vendor ID field.

6. Save, then close the Maintain Inventory Items window.

BACKING UP YOUR DATA

Back up. This backup saves your data to this point, including work completed in Chapters 12, 13, and up to this point in Chapter 14 with Shannon's [your first name] Service Merchandise. The suggested file name is **Chapter 14 Begin**.

INVENTORY ADJUSTMENTS

Date	Transaction Description
1/14/19	Tom's Sales and Service sent Invoice No. 112 for the purchase of eight light fixtures for a unit cost of $64 each, and a total of $512.

1. From the Vendors & Purchases Navigation Center, select 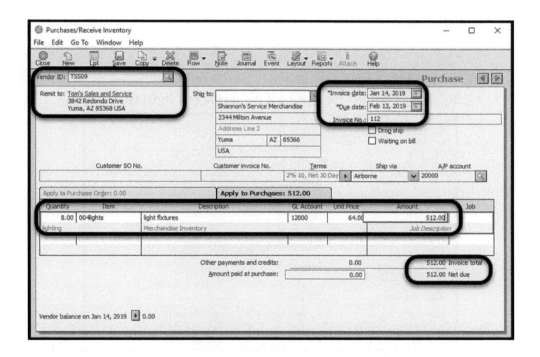 >
    New Bill. The Purchases/Receive Inventory window appears. Record the
    January 14, 2019 transaction.

2. Save to post, then close.

Record the following transaction.

Date	*Transaction Description*
1/16/19	Two light fixtures were damaged when they were dropped on the floor by the owner, Shannon Larsen.

To make an inventory adjustment, follow the steps on the next page.

1. From the Inventory & Services Navigation Center, select . The Inventory Adjustments window appears.

2. In the Item ID field, select lighting.

3. In the Reference field, type **SL** (Shannon Larsen's initials).

4. Type **16** in the Date field.

5. Type **-2** in the Adjust Quantity By field. (After you enter the adjustment, the New quantity is calculated.)

6. In the Reason to Adjust field, type **Two damaged light fixtures**.

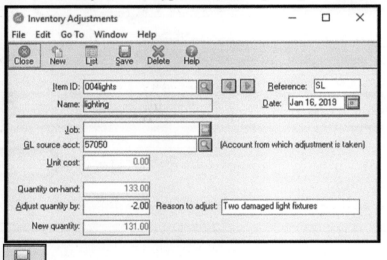

7. Click <img> Save to post, then close the Inventory Adjustments window.

ADDITIONAL TRANSACTIONS

Record the following transactions for Shannon's Service Merchandise.

Date   *Transaction Description*

1/18/19   Sold two doorknobs on account to Aileen Phinney. Type **106** in the Invoice No. field. Subsequent invoices will be numbered automatically. (*Hint: Select hardware as the inventory item for doorknobs. Make sure the Sales Tax field shows 24.00, or 8% of the sales amount for AZ sales taxes.*)

| 1/18/19 | Sold two rolls of vinyl flooring on account to Denise Cobb, Invoice No. 107. There is no sales tax because merchandise is being shipped out of state. |

1/18/19   Sold two pairs of curtains on account to Peter Martin, Invoice No. 108. (*Hint: Select wall as the inventory item for curtains. Remember to check Sales Tax field for 16.00 AZ sales taxes.*)

1/21/19   Shannon's Service Merchandise completed repair work for Betsy Bauman at a cost of $75, plus 6.00 sales taxes, Invoice No. 109. (*Hint: Remember to credit Account No. 40600, Service Fees.*)

1/23/19   Cash sales in the amount of $1,404 ($1,300 plus $104, AZ sales taxes) were deposited at Interstate Bank: 10 pairs of curtains, $1,000; 2 doorknobs, $300. (*Hint: Remember to select AZ in the Sales Tax field.*)

1/25/19   Received a check in the amount of $324 from Aileen Phinney in full payment of Invoice 106.

1/25/19   Received a check in the amount of $216 from Peter Martin in full payment of Invoice No. 108.

1/29/19   Issued Check No. 3039 to CRW Mortgage Co. in the amount of $685.80. Type **685.80** in the Dollars field. To distribute this amount between the principal amount of $587.95 and Interest Expense of $97.85, click [Split].

Split Transaction ×

Cancel OK Add Remove Help

Account No.	Description	Amount	Job
27400	Mortgage Payable	587.95	
67500	Interest Expense	97.85	

Amount Distributed: 685.80
Amount Remaining: 0.00

Transaction Total: 685.80

Click **OK** to accept the split transaction. These steps assume you are using the Write Checks window. (*Hint: On the Write Checks window, type* **3039** *in the Check number field.*)

1/29/19	Issued Check No. 3040 in the amount of $500 to Brian Stewart.
1/29/19	Issued Check No. 3041 in the amount of $500 to Shannon Larsen.
1/30/19	Cash sales in the amount of $2,376 ($2,200 plus $176, AZ sales taxes) were deposited at Interstate Bank: 8 doorknobs, $1,200; 10 pairs of curtains, $1,000. (*Remember to select AZ sales taxes.*)

PRINTING REPORTS

1. Print the Sales Journal. Compare your Sales Journal with the one shown on the next page.

Shannon's Service Merchandise
Sales Journal
For the Period From Jan 1, 2019 to Jan 31, 2019
Filter Criteria includes: Report order is by Invoice/CM Date. Report is printed in Detail Format.

Date	Account ID	Invoice/CM #	Line Description	Debit Amnt	Credit Amnt
1/7/19	23100	101	AZ: Arizona Dept. of Revenue		24.00
	40000		Two doorknobs		300.00
	50000		Cost of sales	100.00	
	12000		Cost of sales		100.00
	11000		Aileen Phinney	324.00	
1/7/19	40400	102	Four rolls of vinyl flooring		640.00
	57000		Cost of sales	216.00	
	12000		Cost of sales		216.00
	11000		Denise Cobb	640.00	
1/7/19	23100	103	AZ: Arizona Dept. of Revenue		32.00
	40200		Four pairs of curtains		400.00
	50500		Cost of sales	120.00	
	12000		Cost of sales		120.00
	11000		Peter Martin	432.00	
1/7/19	23100	104	AZ: Arizona Dept. of Revenue		36.00
	40000		Three curain rods		450.00
	50000		Cost of sales	150.00	
	12000		Cost of sales		150.00
	11000		Judi Perin	486.00	
1/10/19	23100	105	AZ: Arizona Dept. of Revenue		3.99
	40600		Repair		49.89
	11000		Betsy Bauman	53.88	
1/14/19	23100	CM103	AZ: Arizona Dept. of Revenue	8.00	
	40200		Returned one pair of curtains	100.00	
	50500		Cost of sales		30.00
	12000		Cost of sales	30.00	
	11000		Peter Martin		108.00
1/18/19	23100	106	AZ: Arizona Dept. of Revenue		24.00
	40000		Two doorknobs		300.00
	50000		Cost of sales	100.00	
	12000		Cost of sales		100.00
	11000		Aileen Phinney	324.00	
1/18/19	40400	107	Two rolls of vinyl flooring		320.00
	57000		Cost of sales	108.00	
	12000		Cost of sales		108.00
	11000		Denise Cobb	320.00	
1/18/19	23100	108	AZ: Arizona Dept. of Revenue		16.00
	40200		Two pairs of curtains		200.00
	50500		Cost of sales	60.00	
	12000		Cost of sales		60.00
	11000		Peter Martin	216.00	
1/21/19	23100	109	AZ: Arizona Dept. of Revenue		6.00
	40600		Repair		75.00
	11000		Betsy Bauman	81.00	
		Total		3,868.88	3,868.88

If any of your transactions do *not* agree with the Sales Journal, you can
drill-down (🔍) to the original entry, make any needed corrections,
then save and reprint.

2. Print the Cash Receipts Journal.

Shannon's Service Merchandise
Cash Receipts Journal
For the Period From Jan 1, 2019 to Jan 31, 2019

Filter Criteria includes: Report order is by Check Date. Report is printed in Detail Format.

Date	Account ID	Transaction Ref	Line Description	Debit Amnt	Credit Amnt
1/14/19	11000	Invoice 103	Invoice: 103		324.00
	10200		Peter Martin	324.00	
1/21/19	11000	Invoice 101	Invoice: 101		324.00
	10200		Aileen Phinney	324.00	
1/23/19	11000	Invoice 104	Invoice: 104		105.00
	10200		Judi Perin	105.00	
1/23/19	23100	Cash	AZ: Arizona Dept. of Revenue		104.00
	40200		Ten pairs of curtains		1,000.00
	50500		Cost of sales	300.00	
	12000		Cost of sales		300.00
	40000		Two doorknobs		300.00
	50000		Cost of sales	100.00	
	12000		Cost of sales		100.00
	10200		Cash sales	1,404.00	
1/25/19	11000	Invoice 106	Invoice: 106		324.00
	10200		Aileen Phinney	324.00	
1/25/19	11000	Invoice 108	Invoice: 108		216.00
	10200		Peter Martin	216.00	
1/28/19	11000	Invoice 105	Invoice: 105		53.88
	10200		Betsy Bauman	53.88	
1/28/19	11000	Invoice 102	Invoice: 102		640.00
	10200		Denise Cobb	640.00	
1/30/19	23100	Cash	AZ: Arizona Dept. of Revenue		16.00
	40200		Two pairs of curtains		200.00
	50500		Cost of sales	60.00	
	12000		Cost of sales		60.00
	10200		Bertha Perkins	216.00	
1/30/19	23100	Cash	AZ: Arizona Dept. of Revenue		176.00
	40000		Eight doorknobs		1,200.00
	50000		Cost of sales	400.00	
	12000		Cost of sales		400.00
	40200		Ten pairs of curtains		1,000.00
	50500		Cost of sales	300.00	
	12000		Cost of sales		300.00
	10200		Cash sales	2,376.00	
				7,142.88	7,142.88

3. Print the Customer Ledgers.

```
*****EDUCATIONAL VERSION ONLY*****
```

Shannon's Service Merchandise
Customer Ledgers
For the Period From Jan 1, 2019 to Jan 31, 2019

Filter Criteria includes: Report order is by ID. Report is printed in Detail Format.

Customer ID Customer	Date	Trans No	Type	Debit Amt	Credit Amt	Balance
ap001	1/7/19	101	SJ	324.00		324.00
Aileen Phinney	1/18/19	106	SJ	324.00		648.00
	1/21/19	Invoice 101	CRJ		324.00	324.00
	1/25/19	Invoice 106	CRJ		324.00	0.00
bb002	1/10/19	105	SJ	53.88		53.88
Betsy Bauman	1/21/19	109	SJ	81.00		134.88
	1/28/19	Invoice 105	CRJ		53.88	81.00
dc003	1/7/19	102	SJ	640.00		640.00
Denise Cobb	1/18/19	107	SJ	320.00		960.00
	1/28/19	Invoice 102	CRJ		640.00	320.00
jp004	1/7/19	104	SJ	486.00		486.00
Judi Perin	1/23/19	Invoice 104	CRJ		105.00	381.00
pm005	1/7/19	103	SJ	432.00		432.00
Peter Martin	1/14/19	CM103	SJ		108.00	324.00
	1/14/19	Invoice 103	CRJ		324.00	0.00
	1/18/19	108	SJ	216.00		216.00
	1/25/19	Invoice 108	CRJ		216.00	0.00
Report Total				**2,876.88**	**2,094.88**	**782.00**

4. Print the Purchase Journal and compare it to the one shown on the next page.

Shannon's Service Merchandise
Purchase Journal
For the Period From Jan 1, 2019 to Jan 31, 2019
Filter Criteria includes: 1) Includes Drop Shipments. Report order is by Date. Report is printed in Detail Format.

Date	Account ID Account Description	Invoice/CM #	Line Description	Debit Amount	Credit Amount
1/3/19	12000 Merchandise Inventory 20000 Accounts Payable	56JJ	restoration hardware James Jarvis Hardware	300.00	300.00
1/14/19	12000 Merchandise Inventory 20000 Accounts Payable	112	light fixtures Tom's Sales and Service	512.00	512.00
1/21/19	12000 Merchandise Inventory 20000 Accounts Payable	210	wall coverings Ronny Becker Fabrics	120.00	120.00
1/21/19	12000 Merchandise Inventory 20000 Accounts Payable	78JJ	restoration hardware James Jarvis Hardware	500.00	500.00
1/21/19	12000 Merchandise Inventory 20000 Accounts Payable	90	flooring Len Lacey Products	432.00	432.00
1/25/19	12000 Merchandise Inventory 20000 Accounts Payable	VCM90	flooring Len Lacey Products	54.00	54.00
1/28/19	12000 Merchandise Inventory 20000 Accounts Payable	VCM78JJ	restoration hardware James Jarvis Hardware	100.00	100.00
				2,018.00	2,018.00

5. Print the Cash Disbursements Journal and compare it to the one shown on the next page.

			Shannon's Service Merchandise		
			Cash Disbursements Journal		
			For the Period From Jan 1, 2019 to Jan 31, 2019		
Filter Criteria includes: Report order is by Date. Report is printed in Detail Format.					
Date	**Check #**	**Account ID**	**Line Description**	**Debit Amount**	**Credit Amount**
1/24/19	3030	70000	Maintenance Expense	160.00	
		10200	Lou Klein		160.00
1/24/19	3031	73500	Postage Expense	45.00	
		10200	U.S. Post Office		45.00
1/24/19	3032	75500	Supplies Expense	107.65	
		10200	Green's Office Supplies		107.65
1/24/19	3033	76000	Telephone Expense	72.14	
		10200	ILM Phone Co.		72.14
1/24/19	3034	39007	Brian Stewart, Drawing	500.00	
		10200	Brian Stewart		500.00
1/24/19	3035	39009	Shannon Larsen, Drawing	500.00	
		10200	Shannon Larsen		500.00
1/25/19	3036	59500	Discounts Taken		7.56
		20000	Invoice: 90	378.00	
		10200	Len Lacey Products		370.44
1/28/19	3037	59500	Discounts Taken		8.00
		20000	Invoice: 78JJ	400.00	
		10200	James Jarvis Hardware		392.00
1/28/19	3038	59500	Discounts Taken		2.40
		20000	Invoice: 210	120.00	
		10200	Ronny Becker Fabrics		117.60
1/29/19	3039	27400	Mortgage Payable	587.95	
		67500	Interest Expense	97.85	
		10200	CRW Mortgage Co.		685.80
1/29/19	3040	39007	Brian Stewart, Drawing	500.00	
		10200	Brian Stewart		500.00
1/29/19	3041	39009	Shannon Larsen, Drawing	500.00	
		10200	Shannon Larsen		500.00
	Total			**3,968.59**	**3,968.59**

6. Print the Vendor Ledgers.

Shannon's Service Merchandise
Vendor Ledgers
For the Period From Jan 1, 2019 to Jan 31, 2019

Filter Criteria includes: Report order is by ID.

Vendor ID Vendor	Date	Trans No	Type	Paid	Debit Amt	Credit Amt	Balance
JJH06	1/3/19	56JJ	PJ			300.00	300.00
James Jarvis Hardware	1/21/19	78JJ	PJ	*		500.00	800.00
	1/28/19	VCM78JJ	PJ	*	100.00		700.00
	1/28/19	3037	CDJ		8.00	8.00	700.00
	1/28/19	3037	CDJ		400.00		300.00
LLP07	1/21/19	90	PJ	*		432.00	432.00
Len Lacey Products	1/25/19	VCM90	PJ	*	54.00		378.00
	1/25/19	3036	CDJ		7.56	7.56	378.00
	1/25/19	3036	CDJ		378.00		0.00
RBF08	1/21/19	210	PJ	*		120.00	120.00
Ronny Becker Fabrics	1/28/19	3038	CDJ		2.40	2.40	120.00
	1/28/19	3038	CDJ		120.00		0.00
TSS09	1/14/19	112	PJ			512.00	512.00
Tom's Sales and Service							
Report Total					**1,069.96**	**1,881.96**	**812.00**

7. Follow these steps to print the Cost of Goods Sold Journal and the Inventory Adjustment Journal:

   a. From the Reports area of the Select a Report or Form window, select Inventory.

   b. Highlight Cost of Goods Sold Journal, then make the selections to print. Compare your printout to the one shown on the next page.

Shannon's Service Merchandise
Cost of Goods Sold Journal
For the Period From Jan 1, 2019 to Jan 31, 2019
Filter Criteria includes: Report order is by Date. Report is printed in Detail Format and with shortened descriptions.

Date	GL Acct ID	Reference	Qty	Line Description	Debit Amount	Credit Amount
1/7/19	12000	101	2.00	Two doorknobs		100.00
	50000		2.00	Two doorknobs	100.00	
1/7/19	12000	102	4.00	Four rolls of vinyl flooring		216.00
	57000		4.00	Four rolls of vinyl flooring	216.00	
1/7/19	12000	103	4.00	Four pairs of curtains		120.00
	50500		4.00	Four pairs of curtains	120.00	
1/7/19	12000	104	3.00	Three curain rods		150.00
	50000		3.00	Three curain rods	150.00	
1/14/19	12000	CM103	-1.00	Returned one pair of curtains	30.00	
	50500		-1.00	Returned one pair of curtains		30.00
1/18/19	12000	106	2.00	Two doorknobs		100.00
	50000		2.00	Two doorknobs	100.00	
1/18/19	12000	107	2.00	Two rolls of vinyl flooring		108.00
	57000		2.00	Two rolls of vinyl flooring	108.00	
1/18/19	12000	108	2.00	Two pairs of curtains		60.00
	50500		2.00	Two pairs of curtains	60.00	
1/23/19	12000	Cash	10.00	Ten pairs of curtains		300.00
	50500		10.00	Ten pairs of curtains	300.00	
	12000		2.00	Two doorknobs		100.00
	50000		2.00	Two doorknobs	100.00	
1/30/19	12000	Cash	2.00	Two pairs of curtains		60.00
	50500		2.00	Two pairs of curtains	60.00	
	12000		8.00	Eight doorknobs		400.00
	50000		8.00	Eight doorknobs	400.00	
	12000		10.00	Ten pairs of curtains		300.00
	50500		10.00	Ten pairs of curtains	300.00	
		Total			**2,044.00**	**2,044.00**

c. Highlight the Inventory Adjustment Journal, then make the selections to print.

*****EDUCATIONAL VERSION ONLY*****

Shannon's Service Merchandise
Inventory Adjustment Journal
For the Period From Jan 1, 2019 to Jan 31, 2019
Filter Criteria includes: Report order is by Date. Report is printed in Detail Format and with shortened descriptions.

Date	GL Acct ID	Reference	Qty	Line Description	Debit Amount	Credit Amount
1/16/19	12000	SL	-2.00	lighting		128.00
	57050		-2.00	Two damaged light fixtures	128.00	
		Total			**128.00**	**128.00**

8. Print the Inventory Profitability Report.

Shannon's Service Merchandise
Inventory Profitability Report
For the Period From Jan 1, 2019 to Jan 31, 2019
Filter Criteria includes: 1) Stock/Assembly. Report order is by ID. Report is printed with shortened descriptions.

Item ID Item Description	Units Sold	Sales($)	Cost($)	Gross Profit($)	Gross Profit(%)	% of Total
001hardware hardware	17.00	2,550.00	850.00	1,700.00	66.67	40.23
002wall wall	27.00	2,700.00	810.00	1,890.00	70.00	44.72
003floor floor	6.00	960.00	324.00	636.00	66.25	15.05
004lights lighting						
	50.00	6,210.00	1,984.00	4,226.00		100.00

9. Print the General Ledger Trial Balance.

Shannon's Service Merchandise
General Ledger Trial Balance
As of Jan 31, 2019
Filter Criteria includes: Report order is by ID. Report is printed in Detail Format.

Account ID	Account Description	Debit Amt	Credit Amt
10200	Interstate Bank	80,532.25	
10400	Yuma Savings & Loan	22,000.00	
11000	Accounts Receivable	782.00	
12000	Merchandise Inventory	27,338.00	
13000	Supplies	1,750.00	
14000	Prepaid Insurance	2,400.00	
15000	Furniture and Fixtures	5,000.00	
15100	Computers & Equipment	7,500.00	
15500	Building	100,000.00	
20000	Accounts Payable		812.00
23100	Sales Tax Payable		429.99
27000	Long-Term Notes Payable		20,500.00
27400	Mortgage Payable		74,412.05
39006	Brian Stewart, Capital		74,695.00
39007	Brian Stewart, Drawing	1,000.00	
39008	Shannon Larsen, Capital		74,695.00
39009	Shannon Larsen, Drawing	1,000.00	
40000	Sales-Hardware		2,550.00
40200	Sales-Wall		2,700.00
40400	Sales-Floor		960.00
40600	Service Fees		124.89
50000	Cost of Sales-Hardware	850.00	
50500	Cost of Sales-Wall	810.00	
57000	Cost of Sales-Floor	324.00	
57050	Cost of Sales-Lights	128.00	
59500	Purchase Discounts		17.96
67500	Interest Expense	97.85	
70000	Maintenance Expense	160.00	
73500	Postage Expense	45.00	
75500	Supplies Expense	107.65	
76000	Telephone Expense	72.14	
	Total:	**251,896.89**	**251,896.89**

FINANCIAL MANAGER

1. Display the Financial Manager's Business Summary. Compare it to the one shown on page 505 in Chapter 13.

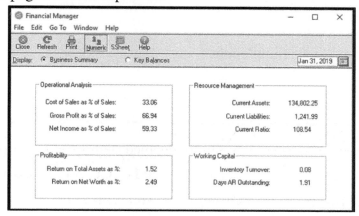

2. Display the Key Balances. Compare it to the one shown on page 506 in Chapter 13.

BACKING UP CHAPTER 14 DATA

If your reports agree with the ones shown, make a backup of Chapter 14 data. If your printouts do not agree with the ones shown, make the necessary corrections. Back up. The suggested file name **Chapter 14**.

EXPORT REPORTS TO EXCEL

1. Export the following Sage 50 reports to Excel.

   - Customer Ledgers
   - Vendor Ledgers
   - Cost of Goods Sold Journal
   - Inventory Adjustment Journal
   - Inventory Profitability Report
   - General Ledger Trial Balance

2. If needed, refer to pages 329-330 for detailed steps to add multiple sheets to one Excel file. Use the file name **Chapter 14_ CL_VL_CGSJ_ IAJ_ IPR_GLTB.xlsx**. If you are using Microsoft Office 365, refer to Appendix A, Inactive Excel Icon.

   NOTE: If your instructor would like you to save reports as PDF files, refer to page 331. The suggested file name is **Chapter 14_Customer Ledgers.pdf**, etc.

ONLINE LEARNING CENTER

Complete end-of-chapter activities at www.mhhe.com/yacht2019 > Student Edition > Chapter 14.

1. Quizzes: Multiple Choice and True False questions. Interactive online tests that are graded and can be emailed to your instructor.
2. More Resources:

   a. QA Templates: Answer 10 short-answer questions and one Analysis Question.
   b. Narrated PowerPoints: Listen to the narrated PowerPoints.
   c. Going to the Net Exercises: Access the BizMov Small Business Guides.

d. Assessment Rubric: Complete the rubric to review Sage 50's journals, navigation centers, modules, task windows, and reports.

➢ Information Center > Sage Advisor Videos.

The OLC also includes links to the Appendixes:

- Appendix A: Troubleshooting (textbook and OLC)
- Appendix C: Review of Accounting Principles (OLC Student Edition)
- Appendix D: Glossary (OLC Student Edition)

Exercise 14-1: You must complete Exercises 12-1, 12-2, 13-1, and 13-2 before starting Exercise 14-1.

1. Start Sage. Open the company that you set up in Exercise 12-1, Your last name Sales and Service.
2. If necessary, restore the data that you backed up in Exercise 13-2. To make sure you are starting in the right place, display Exercise 13-2's general ledger trial balance (step 2, page 515).
3. Complete the following transactions.

1/28/19   Charles Peterson Tools sent Invoice No. 732CP for the purchase of 8 tool kits for a unit cost of $30.

1/30/19   Two tool kits purchased from Charles Peterson Tools on 1/28/19 were accidentally damaged by the owner. (*Hint:* Use your initials.)

1/30/19   Received check in the amount of $972 from Roberta Norton in payment of Invoice No. 103.

1/31/19   Cash Sales in the amount of $4,752, ($4,400 plus $352, GA sales taxes) were deposited at Boulevard Bank: 20 tool kits, $1,700; 18 hardware sets, $2,700.

4. Make a backup of Exercise 14-1. (Use **Exercise 14-1** as the file name.)

Exercise 14-2: Complete Exercise 14-2.

1. Print the Cash Receipts Journal.
2. Print the Purchase Journal.
3. Print the Cost of Goods Sold Journal.
4. Print the Inventory Adjustment Journal.
5. Print the Inventory Profitability Report.
6. Print the General Ledger Trial Balance.

Check Your Figures:

10200, Boulevard Bank	$73,470.63
11000, Accounts Receivable	0.00
12000, Merchandise Inventory	13,250.00
23100, Sales Tax Payable	545.20
50000, Cost of Sales-Hardware	1,450.00
50500, Cost of Sales-Tools	930.00
59500, Purchase Discounts	12.80

7. Export the following reports to Excel and save as PDF files

   a. Cash Receipts Journal
   b. Purchase Journal
   c. Cost of Goods Sold Journal
   d. Inventory Adjustment Journal
   e. Inventory Profitability Report
   f. General Ledger Trial Balance

8. Use the file name **Exercise 14-2_CRJ_PJ_ CGSJ_ IAJ_ IPR_ GLTB**.

9. There is no need to backup Exercise 14-2. The Exercise 14-1.ptb file has the data needed to print Exercise 14-2's reports.

CHAPTER 14 INDEX

Chapter 15

Employees, Payroll, and Account Reconciliation

LEARNING OBJECTIVES

1. Restore data from Chapter 14. (This backup was made on page 539.)
2. Complete the Payroll Setup Wizard, and enter employee and employer default information.
3. Journalize and post Payroll Journal entries, and print paychecks.
4. Reconcile the Interstate Bank account and the Payroll Checking account.
5. Compare the vendor ledgers, customer ledgers, and inventory valuation report to the general ledger's controlling accounts.
6. Print the financial statements.
7. Make four backups, save two Excel files, and save nine PDF files.

Employers withhold local, state, and federal taxes from their employees' paychecks. The amount withheld for federal taxes is determined from tax tables published by the Internal Revenue Service (IRS). Circular E, Employer's Tax Guide, is available from the IRS. It shows the applicable tax tables and forms that are necessary for filing employee payroll information. Sage includes payroll tax tables built into the software. In this chapter you learn how to access and use the payroll tax tables. The amount withheld depends on the employee's earnings and the number of *exemptions or withholding allowances*.

FICA taxes or social security taxes are also deducted. This deduction from wages provides qualified workers who retire at age 62 or older with monthly payments from the federal government. Retirees receive *Medicare* after reaching age 65. In addition to retirement benefits, social security provides payments to the surviving family of a qualified deceased worker.

By January 31 of each year employers are required to issue ***W-2 Forms*** to
employees and to the Internal Revenue Service. The W-2 Form is an annual
report of the employee's wages subject to FICA and federal income tax and
shows the amounts that were withheld.

Using the year 2019 as an example, Social Security is funded by a 12.4% tax on
wages up to $132,900. Half is paid by employers and half is paid by employees.
The employee's W-2 Form shows the Federal Income Tax, State Income Tax,
Social Security, and Medicare withheld. In 2019, yearly income up to $132,900
is subject to the social security portion of the FICA tax. FICA is two taxes — the
Social Security portion and the Medicare portion. Refer to this website
https://www.imercer.com/content/social_security_figures.aspx.

This table compares 2018 and 2019 FICA tax rates and maximum social security
earnings for tax contributions. For purposes of comparison, in 2018 the social
security portion of the FICA tax was based on income up to $128,400; in 2019
that amount is $132,900.

Social Security	2018	2019
FICA tax rate:		
• Social Security for employees	6.2%	6.2%
• Social Security for employers	6.2%	6.2%
• Medicare for employees	1.45%	1.45%
• Medicare for employers	1.45%	1.45%
Maximum Social Security earnings for tax contributions	$128,400	$132,900
Medicare taxable earnings	No limit	No limit

Sage 50's payroll tax calculations are for example purposes only. Payroll
services can be purchased from Sage at https://www.sage.com/en-
us/products/sage-payroll-services/. Employees may also voluntarily deduct other
amounts from wages; for example, U.S. savings bonds, union dues, etc.

It is the purpose of this chapter to show you how to enter payroll default information, add employees, make journal entries for payroll, and print various payroll reports. Once you set up the default information and employee information, Sage automates the payroll process. *The automatic withholding calculations are for example purposes only. They do <u>not</u> reflect accurate amounts.* You establish the following default information for processing payroll:

1. The cash account that is credited when disbursing paychecks. Shannon's Service Merchandise credits Account No. 10300, Payroll Checking Account.
2. The accounts that comprise the employee's fields.
3. The accounts that comprise the employer's fields.
4. The payroll fields that go on the W-2 form.
5. The employee-paid taxes.
6. The employer-paid taxes.

At the Maintain Employees level, you enter the following types of information:

1. The employee name, address, telephone number, and information from the Employee's Withholding Allowance Certificate, Form W-4.
2. Information about employee pay: hourly, salaried, and amount.
3. The tax filing status of the employee for federal, state, and local purposes, including withholding allowances.

When the payroll tables included with Sage 50, Student or Educational versions are used, the payroll tax withholdings are calculated automatically. Once payroll defaults are set up, all you need to do is select the employee you want to pay, date the paycheck and pay period, and post the paycheck. For a yearly fee, Sage 50's payroll tax service offers the appropriate payroll tax withholdings.

The diagram shows the steps for setting up and using Sage's payroll system.

Default and Setup Information

Deductions:	*Cash Account:*
FICA, Federal Payroll Tax,	10300, Payroll Checking
State Payroll Tax	Account

↓

Maintain Employees

Rate of Pay:	*Frequency:*
$12.50 per hour, regular rate	Weekly
$18.75 per hour, overtime rate	

↓

Payroll Journal

Paycheck, net pay: $438.15

Wages Expense	500.00	
FICA: Soc. Sec.		31.00
FICA: Medicare		7.25
Federal Payroll Tax		18.56
State Payroll Tax		5.04
Payroll Checking Account		438.15

Sage 50's payroll tax calculations are for example purposes only. The automatic Social Security tax is calculated as $500.00 X .062 = $31.00. Medicare is calculated as $500 X .0145 = $7.25. The State and Federal Payroll taxes are calculated by Sage 50 and are examples of that employee's withholding tax. The net pay amount, $438.15, is that same as Lynn Gale's paycheck, pages 568-569.

GETTING STARTED

1. Start Sage 50. Open Shannon's [your first name] Service Merchandise. (*Hint:* If a different company opens, select File > Open Previous Company. Open one company.)

2. If necessary, restore the Chapter 14.ptb file. This backup was made on page 539.

To make sure you are starting in the appropriate place in the data (Chapter 14.ptb backup) display the General Ledger Trial Balance. The trial balance is also shown in Chapter 14 on page 538.

Shannon's Service Merchandise
General Ledger Trial Balance
As of Jan 31, 2019

Filter Criteria includes: Report order is by ID. Report is printed in Detail Format.

Account ID	Account Description	Debit Amt	Credit Amt
10200	Interstate Bank	80,532.25	
10400	Yuma Savings & Loan	22,000.00	
11000	Accounts Receivable	782.00	
12000	Merchandise Inventory	27,338.00	
13000	Supplies	1,750.00	
14000	Prepaid Insurance	2,400.00	
15000	Furniture and Fixtures	5,000.00	
15100	Computers & Equipment	7,500.00	
15500	Building	100,000.00	
20000	Accounts Payable		812.00
23100	Sales Tax Payable		429.99
27000	Long-Term Notes Payable		20,500.00
27400	Mortgage Payable		74,412.05
39006	Brian Stewart, Capital		74,695.00
39007	Brian Stewart, Drawing	1,000.00	
39008	Shannon Larsen, Capital		74,695.00
39009	Shannon Larsen, Drawing	1,000.00	
40000	Sales-Hardware		2,550.00
40200	Sales-Wall		2,700.00
40400	Sales-Floor		960.00
40600	Service Fees		124.89
50000	Cost of Sales-Hardware	850.00	
50500	Cost of Sales-Wall	810.00	
57000	Cost of Sales-Floor	324.00	
57050	Cost of Sales-Lights	128.00	
59500	Purchase Discounts		17.96
67500	Interest Expense	97.85	
70000	Maintenance Expense	160.00	
73500	Postage Expense	45.00	
75500	Supplies Expense	107.65	
76000	Telephone Expense	72.14	
	Total:	**251,896.89**	**251,896.89**

Establishing the Payroll Account

In order to establish the payroll checking account, transfer funds from Interstate Bank (Account No. 10200) to the Payroll Checking Account (Account No. 10300). Journalize and post the following General Journal transaction:

Date   *Transaction Description*

01/3/19   Shannon's Service Merchandise transferred $6,500 from Account No. 10200, Interstate Bank, to Account No. 10300, Payroll Checking Account.

After posting this general journal entry, display the general journal. (*Hint: Reports & Forms > General Ledger > General Journal > Display*.) Close all windows.

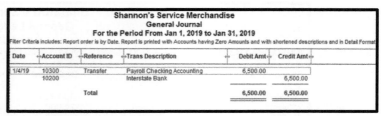

PAYROLL SETUP WIZARD

The Payroll Setup Wizard walks you through setting up most payroll defaults and standard payroll fields. As you answer the prompts, Sage 50 creates most of the common payroll fields used in calculating deductions and taxes.

The Sage 50 Payroll Setup Wizard establishes the following:

- State and locality defaults.
- State unemployment percentage.
- Common federal and state payroll fields for employee-paid and company-paid taxes.
- General ledger account defaults for payroll fields.

- Optional payroll fields for tips, meals, 401K contributions, etc.

1. From the Navigation Bar, select **Employees & Payroll** > **Payroll Setup** > Payroll Setup Wizard. Read the information on the Payroll Setup Wizard window. Observe that the left pane shows Home, Payroll Options, Company Information, Benefits, Taxes, Setup Complete. (Close the sageAdvisor.)

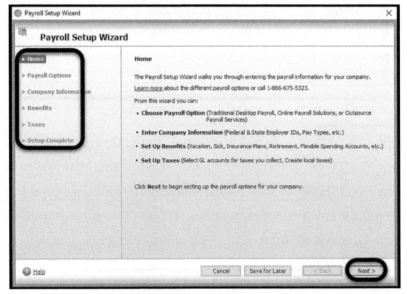

2. Click **Next >**. Payroll Options is selected. Read the information in the Other Payroll Options, Direct Deposit, E-filing, and Full Service Payroll areas.

3. Click **Next >**. Company Information is selected. The Federal Employer ID, State Employer ID, State (AZ), and State Unemployment ID are automatically completed. These fields agree with the company information entered on page 405 in Chapter 12.

4. Type **3.4** in the State Unemployment Rate field. No is the default for Do you want to record employee meals and tips.

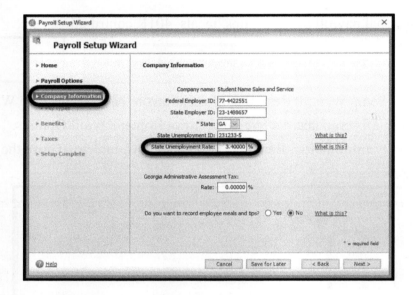

5. Click [Next >]. Pay Types is selected. In the Overtime field, select Account No. 77600 - Overtime Expense. **Check this window carefully**. Account No. 77500 - Wages Expense is shown for the Regular Pay Type, and the Salary Pay Type. Account No. 77600 - Overtime Expense for the Overtime Hourly Pay Type.

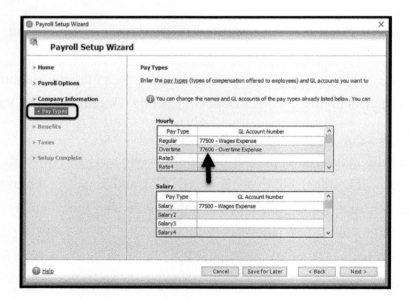

6. Click [Next >]. The Benefits window appears. Do not make any
   selections. Click [Next >] to continue.

7. The Payroll Taxes window appears. Observe that the Tax liability acct no.
   (23400) and Tax Expense acct no. (72000) is selected. To accept these
   defaults, click [Next >].

8. The Setup Complete window appears, click [Finish]. After completing
   employee defaults in the next section, you return to the Payroll Setup
   Wizard to assign employee and company-paid tax fields.

ENTERING EMPLOYEE AND EMPLOYER DEFAULT INFORMATION

1. From the Employees & Payroll Navigation Center, click [Employees] > Set
   Up Employee Defaults. The Employee Defaults window displays. In the
   Employee Defaults window, you enter account numbers that serve as the
   basis for payroll withholdings. There are five tabs:

   ➢ General
   ➢ Employee Fields
   ➢ Company Fields
   ➢ Review Ratings
   ➢ Employment Status

2. Select the Employee Fields tab.

3. The Fed_Income line shows the default G/L Account as 23400 (Federal
   Payroll Taxes Payable) for FIT. Account No. 23400, Federal Payroll Taxes
   Payable, is the correct account for the Fed Income line.

4. Click on the G/L Account field for Soc_Sec and select Account No. 24000,
   Soc. Sec. Employee Taxes Payable.

5. Click on the G/L Account field for MEDICARE and select Account No. 24200, Medicare Employee Taxes Payable.

6. Click on the G/L Account field for St_Income and select Account No. 23600, State Payroll Taxes Payable.

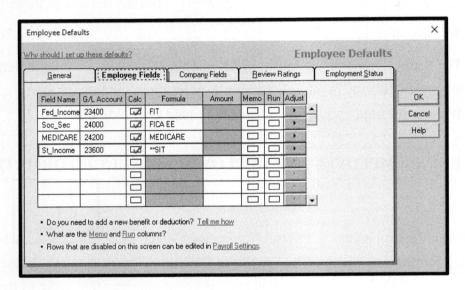

7. Click on the Company Fields tab. Change the following account numbers:

	Liability Column	*Expense Column*
Soc_Sec_C	24100, Soc. Sec. Employer Taxes Payable	72510, Soc. Sec. Expense
Medicare_C	24400, Medicare Employer Taxes Payable	72520, Medicare Expense
Fed_Unemp_C	23500, FUTA Tax Payable	72530, FUTA Expense
State_Unemp_C	23700, SUTA Payable	72540, SUTA Expense

Compare your Employee Defaults/Company Fields window, to the one shown on the next page. Make sure the Liability and Expense accounts are correctly selected.

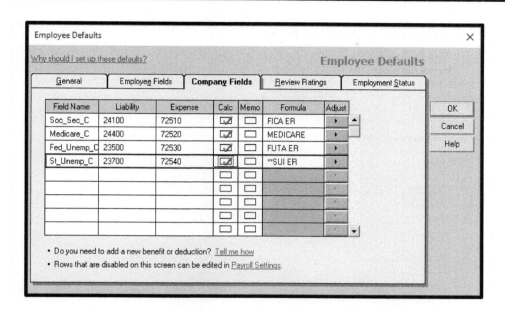

8. Click OK to save your changes and return to the menu bar.

COMPLETING PAYROLL SETUP

After completing the initial payroll setup and entering employee defaults, the next step is to use the Payroll Setup Wizard to assign tax fields. Follow these steps to do that.

1. From the Employees & Payroll Navigation Center, click **Payroll Setup** > Payroll Setup Wizard. On the left pane select Taxes > Assign Tax Fields.

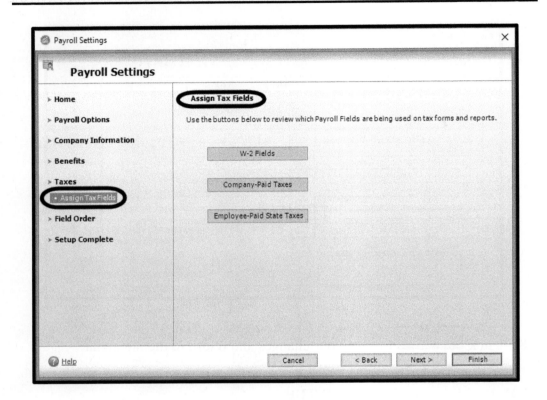

2. The Assign Tax Fields Taxes window appears. There are three buttons: W-2 Fields, Company-Paid Taxes, and Employee-Paid State Taxes. Click

    [W-2 Fields] The Assign Tax Fields for W-2s window appears. These selections appear. (If not, select them.)

Federal income tax withheld:	Fed_Income
Social Security tax withheld:	Soc_Sec
Medicare tax withheld:	MEDICARE
State income tax:	St_Income

    Compare your Assign Tax Fields for W-2s window to the one shown on the next page.

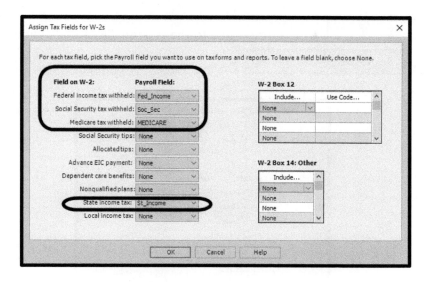

3. Click [OK]. You are returned to the Assign Tax Fields window.

4. Click [Company-Paid Taxes]. The Assign Company-Paid Tax Fields window appears. These selections appear. (If not, select them.)

Federal Unemployment (FUTA): Fed_Unemp_C
State Unemployment (SUTA):   St_Unemp_C

5. Click [OK]. You are returned to the Assign Tax Fields window.

6. Click [Employee-Paid State Taxes]. Do not make any changes.

7. Click [OK]. You are returned to the Assign Tax Fields window. Click [Next >].

8. The Field Order window appears. Do not make any changes. Click [Next >].

9. The Setup Complete window appears. Read the information.

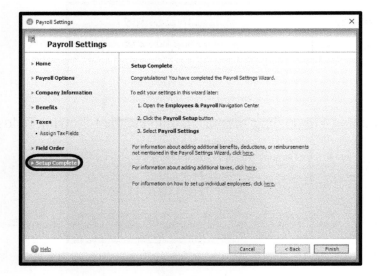

10. Click [Finish].

ENTERING EMPLOYEE MAINTENANCE INFORMATION

The Maintain Employees/Sales Reps window includes information about your employees or sales representatives. The information is displayed as seven tabs: General, Additional Info, Pay Info, Withholding Info, Vacation/Sick Time, Employee Fields, and Company Fields.

1. Select [Employees] > New Employee. The Maintain Employees & Sales Reps window appears. Complete the following fields.

Employee ID:	**A001** (use zeroes)
Name:	**Taryn Anders**
Accept the default for Employee	
Address:	**4600 Miller Valley Road**
City, ST, Zip:	**Yuma, AZ 85365**
E-mail	**taryn@mail.com**
Home phone:	**928-555-2881**
Social Security No	**001-00-2325**
Type:	**FULL**

2. Click on the Withholding Info tab. Complete the following fields.

Filing Status:	Single for Federal, State, and Local
Allowances:	**1** for Federal, State, and Local
State Addl Withholding:	**11.68** (Type **11.68** in the State, Additional Withholding field.)

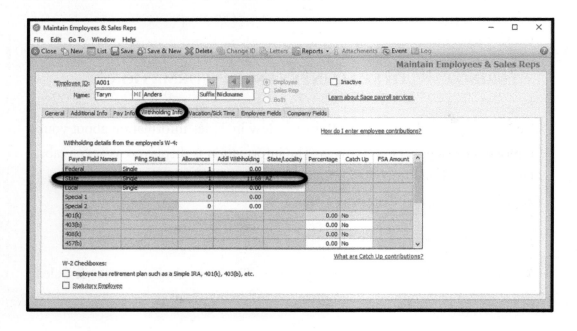

3. Click on the Pay Info tab. Type **12.50** in the Hourly Pay Rate column. Press the **<Enter>** key two times.

4. Type **18.75** in the Hourly Pay Rate column for Overtime. Press the **<Enter>** key. Make sure that the Pay Method field displays Hourly - Hours per Pay Period, the Pay Frequency field displays Weekly, and the Hours Per Pay Period field shows 40.00. Compare your Maintain Employees & Sales Reps/Pay Info window to the one shown on the next page.

5. Select the Employee Fields tab. Notice that the accounts selected for Fed_Income, Soc_Sec, MEDICARE, and St_Income match the accounts shown on page 554, Employee Defaults/Employee Fields window.

6. Click on the Company Fields tab. These are the employer payroll tax liabilities. Notice that the accounts match the Employee Defaults/ Company Fields window shown on page 555. Click **Save & New**.

7. Click on the General tab. Enter another employee.

Employee ID:	**G001**
Name:	**Lynn Gale**

Accept the default for Employee.

Address:	**1899 North Drive**
City, ST, Zip:	**Yuma, AZ 85368**
E-mail:	**lynn@mail.com**
Home phone:	**928-555-8003**
Social Security No:	**002-00-1100**

Type:	**FULL**

Withholding Info:

Filing Status:	**Married** for Federal, State (Married/Jointly), and Local
Allow:	**2** for Federal, State, and Local
State Addl Withholding:	**5.04**

8. Ms. Gale is paid hourly. Her regular pay is $12.50 per hour and her overtime pay is $18.75. Select the Pay Info tab and record this information.

9. Save the employee information. Then, close the Maintain Employees & Sales Reps window. (If necessary, close the Sage Advisor Getting Started window.)

10. On the Employees & Payroll Navigation Center, click . The Employee list appears.

Employees				View Detailed List
Employee ID ▲	Last Name	First Name	Home Phone	Pay Method
A001	Anders	Taryn	928-555-2881	Hourly - Hours per Pay P
G001	Gale	Lynn	928-555-8003	Hourly - Hours per Pay P

BACKING UP YOUR DATA

When you backup, you are saving work completed for Shannon's [your first name] Service Merchandise in Chapters 12, 13, 14, and to this point in Chapter 15. The suggested file name is **Chapter 15 Begin**.

PAYROLL ENTRY

Once the defaults for payroll are set up, you have very little work to do. In Chapter 4, Employees, Bellwether Garden Supply already had the default information set up. Since the payroll tax tables were included for the sample company, all you needed to do for payroll was:

> ➤ Enter or select the Employee ID.
> ➤ Specify the pay period (period-ending date).
> ➤ Verify the information the window displays (name and address of employee, amount of hours, and employee/employer fields.)
> ➤ Print or post the paycheck.

In Chapter 15, you use the payroll tax tables included with the software. These tables are for example purposes only and are not meant for exact computation of payroll withholding amounts. In Sage 50, the Payroll Entry window is also the *payroll journal*. All entries saved in the Payroll Entry window are posted to the payroll journal, the General Ledger, and to the Employee file.

Payroll entry is a simple process after completing the Payroll Setup Wizard and employee and company (employer) default and maintenance information. When employee and company defaults are selected, you are setting up the payroll liability and expense accounts for payroll entry. The employee maintenance information includes the employee's name; address; social security number; Federal, State, and Local withholding allowances; and pay levels.

All entries made to the Payroll Journal are posted both to the General Ledger and to the Employee file. Once an Employee ID is selected, the rest of the employee information is completed automatically. Enough information is entered in the Maintain Employees record, Default Information, and the payroll tax tables included with the software to determine what the paycheck amount should be. If the information is correct, you print or post the paycheck and proceed to the next employee.

The check amount (or net pay) is automatically credited to Account No. 10300, Payroll Checking Account. The withholding amounts are calculated based on the

Payroll Fields which were defined in the Default Information that you previously entered. The rate and frequency of pay were set up in the Employee/Sales Rep record. For Shannon's Service Merchandise, employees are paid weekly.

1. From the Employees & Payroll Navigation Center, click >

   Enter Payroll For One Employee

2. The Select a Cash Account window displays. Select the Payroll Checking Account.

3. Click ___OK___ . The Payroll Entry window appears.
4. In the Employee ID field, select Taryn Anders.
5. Leave the Check Number field blank. Type or select **4** as the Date.
6. Make sure that Account No. 10300, Payroll Checking Account, is displayed in the Cash Account field.
7. In the Pay Period Ends field, type **4** and press **<Enter>**.
8. Accept the default for Weeks in Pay Period which is 1 week.
9. In the Hours Worked table go to the Overtime Hours field. Type **2** and press **<Enter>**.

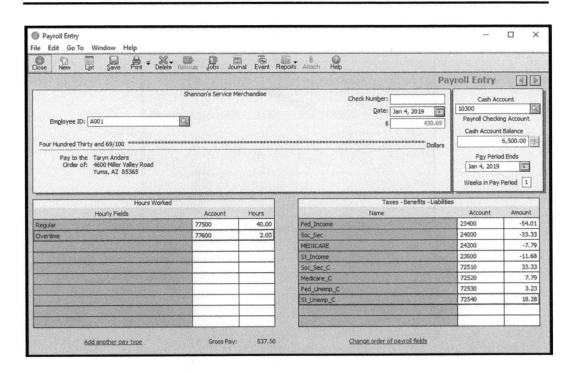

Comment: Observe that the Taxes - Benefits - Liabilities table on the Payroll Entry window includes withholding amounts. These amounts are for example purposes only and do not reflect accurate payroll taxes. For an explanation of Sage 50's payroll calculations, refer to the chart on page 546.

A separate service provided by Sage 50 at an additional cost includes payroll tax tables. More information about Sage 50's Payroll Tax Service is included on their website at https://www.sage.com/en-us/products/sage-payroll-services/.

10.   Click [Print]. (*Or,* click on the down-arrow and select Print Preview.)

11.   The Print Forms: Payroll Checks window appears. Click [Select Form]. Select OCR Multi-Purpose PR Laser.

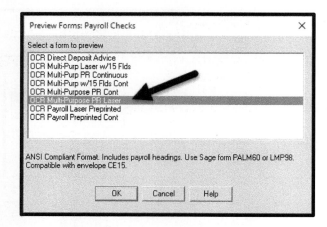

Comment: The form you select is tied to the kind of printer you are using. You may need to make a different selection depending on your printer.

12. Click OK.

13. The Print Forms: Payroll Checks window appears. Make sure that the form you chose is shown in the Use this form field.

14. Type **101** as the First check number.

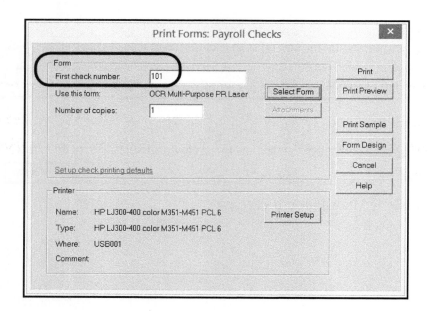

15. Click [Print] (or [Print Preview]). Your check starts to print. (*Or,* Close the Print Preview window. Then, type **101** in the Check Number field on the Payroll Entry window. Click <u>S</u>ave> to post. When you <<u>S</u>ave>, the check posts to the Payroll Journal. Printing also posts.)

Taryn Anders				Employee IC A001		
				Social Sec: xxx-xx-2325		
	This Checl	Year to Dati		Hours	Rate	Total
Gross	537.50	537.50				
Fed_Income	-54.01	-54.01	Regular	40.00	12.50	500.00
Soc_Sec	-33.33	-33.33	Overtime	2.00	18.75	37.50
MEDICARE	-7.79	-7.79				
St_Income	-11.68	-11.68				
Net Check:	$430.69	Total		42.00		537.50

Pay Period Beginnin: 12/29/18   Check Date 1/4/19
Pay Period Endin{ 1/4/19   Weeks in Pay Perio 1

Check Numbei   101   Jan 4, 2019

430.69

Four Hundred Thirty and 69/100 Dollars

Taryn Anders
4600 Miller Valley Road
Yuma, AZ 85365

16. Make the selections to pay Ms. Gale on January 4, 2019. She worked 40 regular hours. Compare your Payroll Entry window with the one shown on the next page.

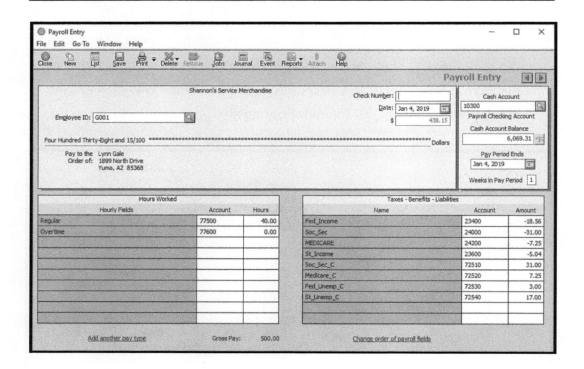

17.   Print (or display) Check No. 102. If you are <u>not</u> connected to a printer, type 102 in the Check Number field. Compare your check with the one shown on the next page.

```
    Lynn Gale                                              Employee IC  G001
                                                           Social Sec:  xxx-xx-11--

                        This Chec      Year to Dat
    Gross               500.00         500.00                  Hours      Rate        Total
    Fed_Income          -18.56         -18.56    Regular       40.00      12.50       500.00
    Soc_Sec             -31.00         -31.00
    MEDICARE            -7.25          -7.25
    St_Income           -5.04          -5.04




    Net Check:          $438.15                  Total         40.00                  500.00
                Pay Period Beginnin 12/29/18                        Check Date 1/4/19
                Pay Period Ending 1/4/19                       Weeks in Pay Perio  1



                              Check Number   102                        Jan 4, 2019


                                                                        438.15


    Four Hundred Thirty-Eight and 15/100 Dollars

        Lynn Gale
        1899 North Drive
        Yuma, AZ  85368
```

18. Make the following payroll entries for Taryn Anders and Lynn Gale.

Date	Name	Hours Worked	Overtime	Check No.
1/11/19	T. Anders	40	2	103
	L. Gale	40		104
1/18/19	T. Anders	40	2	105
	L. Gale	40		106
1/25/19	T. Anders	40	2	107
	L. Gale	40		108

After recording the paycheck information, **type the check number**, then

click [Save] to post. You do *not* need to print the paychecks.

19. Close the Payroll Entry window.

PRINTING THE PAYROLL JOURNAL

From the Recently Used Employee Reports area of the Employees & Payroll
Navigation Center, link to Print or View the Payroll Journal.

Shannon's Service Merchandise   Page: 1
Payroll Journal
For the Period From Jan 1, 2019 to Jan 31, 2019
Filter Criteria includes: Report order is by Check Date. Report is printed in Detail Format.

Date Employee	GL Acct ID	Reference	Debit Amt	Credit Amt
1/4/19	77500	101	500.00	
Taryn Anders	77600		37.50	
	23400			54.01
	24000			33.33
	24200			7.79
	23600			11.68
	24100			33.33
	24400			7.79
	23500			3.23
	23700			18.28
	72510		33.33	
	72520		7.79	
	72530		3.23	
	72540		18.28	
	10300			430.69
1/4/19	77500	102	500.00	
Lynn Gale	23400			18.56
	24000			31.00
	24200			7.25
	23600			5.04
	24100			31.00
	24400			7.25
	23500			3.00
	23700			17.00
	72510		31.00	
	72520		7.25	
	72530		3.00	
	72540		17.00	
	10300			438.15
1/11/19	77500	103	500.00	
Taryn Anders	77600		37.50	
	23400			54.01
	24000			33.33
	24200			7.79
	23600			11.68
	24100			33.33
	24400			7.79
	23500			3.23
	23700			18.28
	72510		33.33	
	72520		7.79	
	72530		3.23	
	72540		18.28	
	10300			430.69
1/11/19	77500	104	500.00	
Lynn Gale	23400			18.56
	24000			31.00
	24200			7.25
	23600			5.04
	24100			31.00
	24400			7.25
	23500			3.00
	23700			17.00
	72510		31.00	
	72520		7.25	
	72530		3.00	
	72540		17.00	
	10300			438.15
1/18/19	77500	105	500.00	
Taryn Anders	77600		37.50	
	23400			54.01

			Page: 2

Shannon's Service Merchandise
Payroll Journal
For the Period From Jan 1, 2019 to Jan 31, 2019
Filter Criteria includes: Report order is by Check Date. Report is printed in Detail Format.

Date Employee	GL Acct ID	Reference	Debit Amt	Credit Amt
	24000			33.33
	24200			7.79
	23600			11.68
	24100			33.33
	24400			7.79
	23500			3.23
	23700			18.28
	72510		33.33	
	72520		7.79	
	72530		3.23	
	72540		18.28	
	10300			430.69
1/18/19 Lynn Gale	77500	106	500.00	
	23400			18.56
	24000			31.00
	24200			7.25
	23600			5.04
	24100			31.00
	24400			7.25
	23500			3.00
	23700			17.00
	72510		31.00	
	72520		7.25	
	72530		3.00	
	72540		17.00	
	10300			438.15
1/25/19 Taryn Anders	77500	107	500.00	
	77600		37.50	
	23400			54.01
	24000			33.33
	24200			7.79
	23600			11.68
	24100			33.33
	24400			7.79
	23500			3.23
	23700			18.28
	72510		33.33	
	72520		7.79	
	72530		3.23	
	72540		18.28	
	10300			430.69
1/25/19 Lynn Gale	77500	108	500.00	
	23400			18.56
	24000			31.00
	24200			7.25
	23600			5.04
	24100			31.00
	24400			7.25
	23500			3.00
	23700			17.00
	72510		31.00	
	72520		7.25	
	72530		3.00	
	72540		17.00	
	10300			438.15
			4,633.52	4,633.52

ACCOUNT RECONCILIATION

In Chapters 12-15, you worked with Sage 50's accounts payable, accounts receivable, inventory, and payroll systems. The general ledger is integrated with the other parts of the program. For example, when a vendor is paid, that entry is recorded in *both* the general ledger, Interstate Bank *and* Accounts Payable accounts, and the individual vendor's account. In other words, the subsidiary ledger (vendor ledger) works together with the general ledger.

To see how this works, you are going to reconcile two bank statements.

- The January 31, 2019 bank statement from Interstate Bank, page 573.
- The January 31, 2019 bank statement from the Payroll Checking Account, page 574.

Then, you are going to check the accounts receivable, accounts payable, and merchandise inventory account balances against the general ledger. This assures that Sage 50's subsidiary ledgers (customer ledgers, vendor ledgers, and inventory valuation) are in agreement with the associated general ledger accounts.

Interstate Bank Statement

Statement of Account			Shannon's Service Merchandise	
Interstate Bank			3344 Milton Avenue	
January 1 to January 31, 2019		Account No. 44773-8211	Yuma, AZ 85366	
REGULAR CHECKING				
Previous Balance		12/31/18	78,500.00	
8 Deposits(+)			3,390.88	
11 Checks (-)			9,450.63	
Service Charges (-)		1/31/19	18.00	
Ending Balance		1/31/19	**72,422.25**	
DEPOSITS				
1/17/19	324.00	1/25/19	1,404.00	1/28/19	53.88
1/23/19	324.00	1/26/19	324.00	1/31/19	640.00
1/25/19	105.00	1/25/19	216.00		
CHECKS (Asterisk * indicates break in check number sequence)				
	1/3/19	Transfer	6,500.00	
	1/26/19	3030	160.00	
	1/26/19	3031	45.00	
	1/26/19	3032	107.65	
	1/25/19	3033	72.14	
	1/25/19	3034	500.00	
	1/25/19	3035	500.00	
	1/28/19	3036	370.44	
	1/30/19	3037	392.00	
	1/30/19	3038	117.60	
	1/30/19	3039	685.80	

...orded on the same day may be added together on ...indow.

$1,509.00

540.00

693.88

Payroll Checking Account Bank Statement

Statement of Account			Shannon's Service Merchandise	
Payroll Checking Account			3344 Milton Avenue	
January 1 to January 31, 2019	Account No. 7889-03289		Yuma, AZ 85366	
REGULAR CHECKING				
Previous Balance	12/31/18	0.00		
1 Deposits(+)		6,500.00		
6 Checks (-)		2,606.52		
Service Charges (-)	1/31/19	15.00		
Ending Balance	1/31/19	**3,878.48**		
DEPOSITS				
	1/3/19	6,500.00		
CHECKS (Asterisk * indicates break in check number sequence)				
	1/11/19	101	430.69	
	1/11/19	102	438.15	
	1/18/19	103	430.69	
	1/18/19	104	438.15	
	1/25/19	105	430.69	
	1/25/19	106	438.15	

Printing Reports: Account Reconciliation, Accounts Receivable, Accounts Payable, and Inventory

1. Print the Interstate Bank account reconciliation report.

```
                            Shannon's Service Merchandise
                                Account Reconciliation
                                  As of Jan 31, 2019
                                10200 - Interstate Bank
                            Bank Statement Date: January 31, 2019
 Filter Criteria includes: Report is printed in Detail Format.
```

Beginning GL Balance				78,500.00
Add: Cash Receipts				5,982.88
Less: Cash Disbursements				(3,950.63)
Add (Less) Other				(6,518.00)
Ending GL Balance				74,014.25
Ending Bank Balance				72,422.25
Add back deposits in transit				
	Jan 30, 2019	1/30/19	2,592.00	
Total deposits in transit				2,592.00
(Less) outstanding checks				
	Jan 29, 2019	3040	(500.00)	
	Jan 29, 2019	3041	(500.00)	
Total outstanding checks				(1,000.00)
Add (Less) Other				
Total other				
Unreconciled difference				0.00
Ending GL Balance				74,014.25

2. Print the Payroll Checking Account reconciliation report. (*Hint:* On the Account Reconciliation Select a Report or Form window, click Options. In the Select a filter field, select Account No. 10300, Payroll Checking Account.)

Shannon's Service Merchandise
Account Reconciliation
As of Jan 31, 2019
10300 - Payroll Checking Account
Bank Statement Date: January 31, 2019

Filter Criteria includes: Report is printed in Detail Format.

Beginning GL Balance				
Add: Cash Receipts				
Less: Cash Disbursements				(3,475.36)
Add (Less) Other				6,485.00
Ending GL Balance				3,009.64
Ending Bank Balance				3,878.48
Add back deposits in transit				
Total deposits in transit				
(Less) outstanding checks				
	Jan 25, 2019	107	(430.69)	
	Jan 25, 2019	108	(438.15)	
Total outstanding checks				(868.84)
Add (Less) Other				
Total other				
Unreconciled difference				0.00
Ending GL Balance				3,009.64

3. Print the General Ledger accounts 10200 and 10300. (*Hint:* On the General Ledger Select a Report or Form window, select General Ledger > Options. On the Modify Report - General Ledger window > select the filter GL Account ID > One or more > check the boxes next to 10200 and 10300. Click <OK>.

Shannon's Service Merchandise
General Ledger
For the Period From Jan 1, 2019 to Jan 31, 2019

Filter Criteria includes: 1) IDs: Multiple IDs. Report order is by ID. Report is printed with shortened descriptions and in Detail Format.

Account ID Account Description	Date	Reference	Jrnl	Trans Description	Debit Amt	Credit Amt	Balance
10200	1/1/19			Beginning Balance			78,500.00
Interstate Bank	1/4/19	Transfer	GEN	Interstate Bank		6,500.00	
	1/14/19	Invoice 103	CRJ	Peter Martin	324.00		
	1/21/19	Invoice 101	CRJ	Aileen Phinney	324.00		
	1/23/19	Invoice 104	CRJ	Judi Perin	105.00		
	1/23/19	Cash	CRJ	Cash sales	1,404.00		
	1/24/19	3030	CDJ	Lou Klein		160.00	
	1/24/19	3031	CDJ	U.S. Post Office		45.00	
	1/24/19	3032	CDJ	Green's Office Supplies		107.65	
	1/24/19	3033	CDJ	ILM Phone Co.		72.14	
	1/24/19	3034	CDJ	Brian Stewart		500.00	
	1/24/19	3035	CDJ	Shannon Larsen		500.00	
	1/25/19	3036	CDJ	Len Lacey Products		370.44	
	1/25/19	Invoice 106	CRJ	Aileen Phinney	324.00		
	1/25/19	Invoice 108	CRJ	Peter Martin	216.00		
	1/28/19	3037	CDJ	James Jarvis Hardware		392.00	
	1/28/19	3038	CDJ	Ronny Becker Fabrics		117.60	
	1/28/19	Invoice 105	CRJ	Betsy Bauman	53.88		
	1/28/19	Invoice 102	CRJ	Denise Cobb	640.00		
	1/29/19	3039	CDJ	CRW Mortgage Co.		685.80	
	1/29/19	3040	CDJ	Brian Stewart		500.00	
	1/29/19	3041	CDJ	Shannon Larsen		500.00	
	1/30/19	Cash	CRJ	Bertha Perkins	216.00		
	1/30/19	Cash	CRJ	Cash sales	2,376.00		
	1/31/19	01/31/19	GEN	Service Charge		18.00	
				Current Period Change	5,982.88	10,468.63	-4,485.75
	1/31/19			**Ending Balance**			**74,014.25**
10300	1/1/19			Beginning Balance			
Payroll Checking Acc	1/4/19	Transfer	GEN	Payroll Checking Accounti	6,500.00		
	1/4/19	101	PRJ	Taryn Anders		430.69	
	1/4/19	102	PRJ	Lynn Gale		438.15	
	1/11/19	103	PRJ	Taryn Anders		430.69	
	1/11/19	104	PRJ	Lynn Gale		438.15	
	1/18/19	105	PRJ	Taryn Anders		430.69	
	1/18/19	106	PRJ	Lynn Gale		438.15	
	1/25/19	107	PRJ	Taryn Anders		430.69	
	1/25/19	108	PRJ	Lynn Gale		438.15	
	1/31/19	01/31/19	GEN	Service Charge		15.00	
				Current Period Change	6,500.00	3,490.36	3,009.64
	1/31/19			**Ending Balance**			**3,009.64**

Observe that Account No. 10200, Interstate Bank; and Account No. 10300, Payroll Checking Account agree with the Ending GL Balances shown on the account reconciliation reports on pages 575 and 576: $74,014.25 and $3,009.64, respectively.

4.   Print the general ledger account balance for Account No. 11000, Accounts Receivable.

Shannon's Service Merchandise
General Ledger
For the Period From Jan 1, 2019 to Jan 31, 2019
Filter Criteria includes: 1) IDs: 11000. Report order is by ID. Report is printed with shortened descriptions and in Detail Format.

Account ID Account Description	Date	Reference	Jrnl	Trans Description	Debit Amt	Credit Amt	Balance
11000	1/1/19			Beginning Balance			
Accounts Receivable	1/7/19	101	SJ	Aileen Phinney	324.00		
	1/7/19	102	SJ	Denise Cobb	640.00		
	1/7/19	103	SJ	Peter Martin	432.00		
	1/7/19	104	SJ	Judi Perin	486.00		
	1/10/19	105	SJ	Betsy Bauman	53.88		
	1/14/19	CM103	SJ	Peter Martin		108.00	
	1/14/19	Invoice 103	CRJ	Peter Martin - Invoice: 103		324.00	
	1/18/19	106	SJ	Aileen Phinney	324.00		
	1/18/19	107	SJ	Denise Cobb	320.00		
	1/18/19	108	SJ	Peter Martin	216.00		
	1/21/19	Invoice 101	CRJ	Aileen Phinney - Invoice: 10		324.00	
	1/21/19	109	SJ	Betsy Bauman	81.00		
	1/23/19	Invoice 104	CRJ	Judi Perin - Invoice: 104		105.00	
	1/25/19	Invoice 106	CRJ	Aileen Phinney - Invoice: 10		324.00	
	1/25/19	Invoice 108	CRJ	Peter Martin - Invoice: 108		216.00	
	1/28/19	Invoice 105	CRJ	Betsy Bauman - Invoice: 105		53.88	
	1/28/19	Invoice 102	CRJ	Denise Cobb - Invoice: 102		640.00	
				Current Period Change	2,876.88	2,094.88	782.00
	1/31/19			Ending Balance			782.00

5.   Compare the general ledger's accounts receivable balance to the customer ledgers balance.

Shannon's Service Merchandise
Customer Ledgers
For the Period From Jan 1, 2019 to Jan 31, 2019
Filter Criteria includes: Report order is by ID. Report is printed in Detail Format.

Customer ID Customer	Date	Trans No	Type	Debit Amt	Credit Amt	Balance
ap001	1/7/19	101	SJ	324.00		324.00
Aileen Phinney	1/18/19	106	SJ	324.00		648.00
	1/21/19	Invoice 101	CRJ		324.00	324.00
	1/25/19	Invoice 106	CRJ		324.00	0.00
bb002	1/10/19	105	SJ	53.88		53.88
Betsy Bauman	1/21/19	109	SJ	81.00		134.88
	1/28/19	Invoice 105	CRJ		53.88	81.00
dc003	1/7/19	102	SJ	640.00		640.00
Denise Cobb	1/18/19	107	SJ	320.00		960.00
	1/28/19	Invoice 102	CRJ		640.00	320.00
jp004	1/7/19	104	SJ	486.00		486.00
Judi Perin	1/23/19	Invoice 104	CRJ		105.00	381.00
pm005	1/7/19	103	SJ	432.00		432.00
Peter Martin	1/14/19	CM103	SJ		108.00	324.00
	1/14/19	Invoice 103	CRJ		324.00	0.00
	1/18/19	108	SJ	216.00		216.00
	1/25/19	Invoice 108	CRJ		216.00	0.00
Report Total				2,876.88	2,094.88	782.00

6. Print the general ledger account balance for Account No. 20000, Account Payable. (A minus sign in front of a general ledger balance means it is a credit balance.)

Shannon's Service Merchandise
General Ledger
For the Period From Jan 1, 2019 to Jan 31, 2019
Filter Criteria includes: 1) IDs: 20000. Report order is by ID. Report is printed with shortened descriptions and in Detail Format.

Account ID Account Description	Date	Reference	Jrnl	Trans Description	Debit A	Credit Amt	Balance
20000	1/1/19			Beginning Balance			
Accounts Payable	1/3/19	56JJ	PJ	James Jarvis Hardware		300.00	
	1/14/19	112	PJ	Tom's Sales and Service		512.00	
	1/21/19	90	PJ	Len Lacey Products		432.00	
	1/21/19	210	PJ	Ronny Becker Fabrics		120.00	
	1/21/19	78JJ	PJ	James Jarvis Hardware		500.00	
	1/25/19	VCM90	PJ	Len Lacey Products	54.00		
	1/25/19	3036	CDJ	Len Lacey Products - Invoice: 90	378.00		
	1/28/19	VCM78JJ	PJ	James Jarvis Hardware	100.00		
	1/28/19	3037	CDJ	James Jarvis Hardware - Invoice: 7	400.00		
	1/28/19	3038	CDJ	Ronny Becker Fabrics - Invoice: 21	120.00		
				Current Period Change	1,052.00	1,864.00	-812.00
	1/31/19			**Ending Balance**			-812.00

7. Compare the general ledger's accounts payable balance to the vendor ledgers balance.

Shannon's Service Merchandise
Vendor Ledgers
For the Period From Jan 1, 2019 to Jan 31, 2019
Filter Criteria includes: Report order is by ID.

Vendor ID Vendor	Date	Trans No	Type	Paid	Debit Amt	Credit Amt	Balance
JJH06	1/3/19	56JJ	PJ			300.00	300.00
James Jarvis Hardware	1/21/19	78JJ	PJ	*		500.00	800.00
	1/28/19	VCM78JJ	PJ	*	100.00		700.00
	1/28/19	3037	CDJ		8.00	8.00	700.00
	1/28/19	3037	CDJ		400.00		300.00
LLP07	1/21/19	90	PJ	*		432.00	432.00
Len Lacey Products	1/25/19	VCM90	PJ	*	54.00		378.00
	1/25/19	3036	CDJ		7.56	7.56	378.00
	1/25/19	3036	CDJ		378.00		0.00
RBF08	1/21/19	210	PJ	*		120.00	120.00
Ronny Becker Fabrics	1/28/19	3038	CDJ		2.40	2.40	120.00
	1/28/19	3038	CDJ		120.00		0.00
TSS09	1/14/19	112	PJ			512.00	512.00
Tom's Sales and Service							
Report Total					1,069.96	1,881.96	812.00

8. Print the general ledger account balance for Account No. 12000, Merchandise Inventory.

Shannon's Service Merchandise
General Ledger
For the Period From Jan 1, 2019 to Jan 31, 2019
Filter Criteria includes: 1) IDs from 12000 to 12000. Report order is by ID. Report is printed with shortened descriptions and in Detail Format.

Account ID Account Description	Date	Reference	Jrnl	Trans Description	Debit Am	Credit Amt	Balance
12000	1/1/19			Beginning Balance			27,740.00
Merchandise Inventory	1/3/19	56JJ	PJ	James Jarvis Hardware - Ite	300.00		
	1/7/19	101	COG	Aileen Phinney - Item: 001ha		100.00	
	1/7/19	102	COG	Denise Cobb - Item: 003floor		216.00	
	1/7/19	103	COG	Peter Martin - Item: 002wall -		120.00	
	1/7/19	104	COG	Judi Perin - Item: 001hardwa		150.00	
	1/14/19	CM103	COG	Peter Martin - Item: 002wall -	30.00		
	1/14/19	112	PJ	Tom's Sales and Service - It	512.00		
	1/16/19	SL	INAJ	lighting		128.00	
	1/18/19	106	COG	Aileen Phinney - Item: 001ha		100.00	
	1/18/19	107	COG	Denise Cobb - Item: 003floor		108.00	
	1/18/19	108	COG	Peter Martin - Item: 002wall -		60.00	
	1/21/19	90	PJ	Len Lacey Products - Item: 0	432.00		
	1/21/19	210	PJ	Ronny Becker Fabrics - Item:	120.00		
	1/21/19	78JJ	PJ	James Jarvis Hardware - Ite	500.00		
	1/23/19	Cash	COG	Cash sales - Item: 002wall -		300.00	
	1/23/19	Cash	COG	Cash sales - Item: 001hardw		100.00	
	1/25/19	VCM90	PJ	Len Lacey Products - Item: 0		54.00	
	1/28/19	VCM78JJ	PJ	James Jarvis Hardware - Ite		100.00	
	1/30/19	Cash	COG	Bertha Perkins - Item: 002wa		60.00	
	1/30/19	Cash	COG	Cash sales - Item: 001hardw		400.00	
	1/30/19	Cash	COG	Cash sales - Item: 002wall -		300.00	
				Current Period Change	1,894.00	2,296.00	-402.00
	1/31/19			**Ending Balance**			**27,338.00**

9. Compare the general ledger's merchandise inventory account balance to the Inventory Valuation Report's item value. (*Hint:* From the Reports list, select Inventory > Inventory Valuation Report. If your reports do not agree, refer to How to Fix?, page 583.)

Shannon's Service Merchandise
Inventory Valuation Report
As of Jan 31, 2019
Filter Criteria includes: 1) Stock/Assembly. Report order is by ID. Report is printed with shortened descriptions.

Item ID Item Class	Item Description	Stocking U/M	Cost Method	Qty on Han	Item Value	Avg Cost	% of Inv Value
001hardware Stock item	hardware	each	Average	87.00	4,350.00	50.00	15.91
002wall Stock item	wall	each	Average	125.00	3,750.00	30.00	13.72
003floor Stock item	floor	each	Average	201.00	10,854.00	54.00	39.70
004lights Stock item	lighting	each	Average	131.00	8,384.00	64.00	30.67
					27,338.00		**100.00**

PRINTING THE GENERAL LEDGER TRIAL BALANCE

Shannon's Service Merchandise
General Ledger Trial Balance
As of Jan 31, 2019

Filter Criteria includes: Report order is by ID. Report is printed in Detail Format.

Account ID	Account Description	Debit Amt	Credit Amt
10200	Interstate Bank	74,014.25	
10300	Payroll Checking Account	3,009.64	
10400	Yuma Savings & Loan	22,000.00	
11000	Accounts Receivable	782.00	
12000	Merchandise Inventory	27,338.00	
13000	Supplies	1,750.00	
14000	Prepaid Insurance	2,400.00	
15000	Furniture and Fixtures	5,000.00	
15100	Computers & Equipment	7,500.00	
15500	Building	100,000.00	
20000	Accounts Payable		812.00
23100	Sales Tax Payable		429.99
23400	Federal Payroll Taxes Payable		290.28
23500	FUTA Tax Payable		24.92
23600	State Payroll Taxes Payable		66.88
23700	SUTA Payable		141.12
24000	Soc. Sec. Employee Taxes Pay		257.32
24100	Soc. Sec. Employer Taxes Paya		257.32
24200	Medicare Employee Taxes Paya		60.16
24400	Medicare Employer Taxes Paya		60.16
27000	Long-Term Notes Payable		20,500.00
27400	Mortgage Payable		74,412.05
39006	Brian Stewart, Capital		74,695.00
39007	Brian Stewart, Drawing	1,000.00	
39008	Shannon Larsen, Capital		74,695.00
39009	Shannon Larsen, Drawing	1,000.00	
40000	Sales-Hardware		2,550.00
40200	Sales-Wall		2,700.00
40400	Sales-Floor		960.00
40600	Service Fees		124.89
50000	Cost of Sales-Hardware	850.00	
50500	Cost of Sales-Wall	810.00	
57000	Cost of Sales-Floor	324.00	
57050	Cost of Sales-Lights	128.00	
59500	Purchase Discounts		17.96
62000	Bank Charges	33.00	
67500	Interest Expense	97.85	
70000	Maintenance Expense	160.00	
72510	Soc. Sec. Expense	257.32	
72520	Medicare Expense	60.16	
72530	FUTA Expense	24.92	
72540	SUTA Expense	141.12	
73500	Postage Expense	45.00	
75500	Supplies Expense	107.65	
76000	Telephone Expense	72.14	
77500	Wages Expense	4,000.00	
77600	Overtime Expense	150.00	
	Total:	**253,055.05**	**253,055.05**

PRINTING THE FINANCIAL STATEMENTS

1. Print the <Standard> Balance Sheet.

<table>
<tr><td></td><td colspan="2">Shannon's Service Merchandise
Balance Sheet
January 31, 2019</td></tr>
<tr><td></td><td colspan="2" align="center">ASSETS</td></tr>
<tr><td>Current Assets</td><td></td><td></td></tr>
<tr><td>Interstate Bank</td><td>$ 74,014.25</td><td></td></tr>
<tr><td>Payroll Checking Account</td><td>3,009.64</td><td></td></tr>
<tr><td>Yuma Savings & Loan</td><td>22,000.00</td><td></td></tr>
<tr><td>Accounts Receivable</td><td>782.00</td><td></td></tr>
<tr><td>Merchandise Inventory</td><td>27,338.00</td><td></td></tr>
<tr><td>Supplies</td><td>1,750.00</td><td></td></tr>
<tr><td>Prepaid Insurance</td><td>2,400.00</td><td></td></tr>
<tr><td>Total Current Assets</td><td></td><td>131,293.89</td></tr>
<tr><td>Property and Equipment</td><td></td><td></td></tr>
<tr><td>Furniture and Fixtures</td><td>5,000.00</td><td></td></tr>
<tr><td>Computers & Equipment</td><td>7,500.00</td><td></td></tr>
<tr><td>Building</td><td>100,000.00</td><td></td></tr>
<tr><td>Total Property and Equipment</td><td></td><td>112,500.00</td></tr>
<tr><td>Other Assets</td><td></td><td></td></tr>
<tr><td>Total Other Assets</td><td></td><td>0.00</td></tr>
<tr><td>Total Assets</td><td>$</td><td>243,793.89</td></tr>
<tr><td></td><td colspan="2" align="center">LIABILITIES AND CAPITAL</td></tr>
<tr><td>Current Liabilities</td><td></td><td></td></tr>
<tr><td>Accounts Payable</td><td>$ 812.00</td><td></td></tr>
<tr><td>Sales Tax Payable</td><td>429.99</td><td></td></tr>
<tr><td>Federal Payroll Taxes Payable</td><td>290.28</td><td></td></tr>
<tr><td>FUTA Tax Payable</td><td>24.92</td><td></td></tr>
<tr><td>State Payroll Taxes Payable</td><td>66.88</td><td></td></tr>
<tr><td>SUTA Payable</td><td>141.12</td><td></td></tr>
<tr><td>Soc. Sec. Employee Taxes Payab</td><td>257.32</td><td></td></tr>
<tr><td>Soc. Sec. Employer Taxes Payab</td><td>257.32</td><td></td></tr>
<tr><td>Medicare Employee Taxes Payabl</td><td>60.16</td><td></td></tr>
<tr><td>Medicare Employer Taxes Payabl</td><td>60.16</td><td></td></tr>
<tr><td>Total Current Liabilities</td><td></td><td>2,400.15</td></tr>
</table>

Long-Term Liabilities		
Long-Term Notes Payable	20,500.00	
Mortgage Payable	74,412.05	
Total Long-Term Liabilities		94,912.05
Total Liabilities		97,312.20
Capital		
Brian Stewart, Capital	74,695.00	
Brian Stewart, Drawing	(1,000.00)	
Shannon Larsen, Capital	74,695.00	
Shannon Larsen, Drawing	(1,000.00)	
Net Income	(908.31)	
Total Capital		146,481.69
Total Liabilities & Capital	$	243,793.89

Unaudited - For Management Purposes Only

2. Print the <Standard> Income Stmnt. Compare your Income Statement with the one shown on the next page.

How to Fix?

What if the general ledger Account No. 12000, Merchandise Inventory, does not agree with the Item Value balance on the Inventory Valuation report? If they are different, make sure that you selected inventory items on both the Sales/Invoicing window (Sales Journal) and Purchases/Receive Inventory window (Purchase Journal).

Shannon's Service Merchandise
Income Statement
For the One Month Ending January 31, 2019

		Current Month			Year to Date	
Revenues						
Sales-Hardware	$	2,550.00	40.25	$	2,550.00	40.25
Sales-Wall		2,700.00	42.62		2,700.00	42.62
Sales-Floor		960.00	15.15		960.00	15.15
Service Fees		124.89	1.97		124.89	1.97
Total Revenues		6,334.89	100.00		6,334.89	100.00
Cost of Sales						
Cost of Sales-Hardware		850.00	13.42		850.00	13.42
Cost of Sales-Wall		810.00	12.79		810.00	12.79
Cost of Sales-Floor		324.00	5.11		324.00	5.11
Cost of Sales-Lights		128.00	2.02		128.00	2.02
Purchase Discounts		(17.96)	(0.28)		(17.96)	(0.28)
Total Cost of Sales		2,094.04	33.06		2,094.04	33.06
Gross Profit		4,240.85	66.94		4,240.85	66.94
Expenses						
Bank Charges		33.00	0.52		33.00	0.52
Interest Expense		97.85	1.54		97.85	1.54
Maintenance Expense		160.00	2.53		160.00	2.53
Soc. Sec. Expense		257.32	4.06		257.32	4.06
Medicare Expense		60.16	0.95		60.16	0.95
FUTA Expense		24.92	0.39		24.92	0.39
SUTA Expense		141.12	2.23		141.12	2.23
Postage Expense		45.00	0.71		45.00	0.71
Supplies Expense		107.65	1.70		107.65	1.70
Telephone Expense		72.14	1.14		72.14	1.14
Wages Expense		4,000.00	63.14		4,000.00	63.14
Overtime Expense		150.00	2.37		150.00	2.37
Total Expenses		5,149.16	81.28		5,149.16	81.28
Net Income	$	(908.31)	(14.34)	$	(908.31)	(14.34)

For Management Purposes Only

3. Print the <Standard> Cash Flow. Compare your Statement of Cash Flow to the one shown on the next page.

Shannon's Service Merchandise
Statement of Cash Flow
For the one Month Ended January 31, 2019

		Current Month		Year to Date
Cash Flows from operating activities				
Net Income	$	(908.31)	$	(908.31)
Adjustments to reconcile net income to net cash provided by operating activities				
Accounts Receivable		(782.00)		(782.00)
Merchandise Inventory		402.00		402.00
Accounts Payable		812.00		812.00
Sales Tax Payable		429.99		429.99
Federal Payroll Taxes Payable		290.28		290.28
FUTA Tax Payable		24.92		24.92
State Payroll Taxes Payable		66.88		66.88
SUTA Payable		141.12		141.12
Soc. Sec. Employee Taxes Payab		257.32		257.32
Soc. Sec. Employer Taxes Payab		257.32		257.32
Medicare Employee Taxes Payabl		60.16		60.16
Medicare Employer Taxes Payabl		60.16		60.16
Total Adjustments		2,020.15		2,020.15
Net Cash provided by Operations		1,111.84		1,111.84
Cash Flows from investing activities				
Used For				
Net cash used in investing		0.00		0.00
Cash Flows from financing activities				
Proceeds From				
Used For				
Mortgage Payable		(587.95)		(587.95)
Brian Stewart, Drawing		(1,000.00)		(1,000.00)
Shannon Larsen, Drawing		(1,000.00)		(1,000.00)
Net cash used in financing		(2,587.95)		(2,587.95)
Net increase <decrease> in cash	$	(1,476.11)	$	(1,476.11)
Summary				
Cash Balance at End of Period	$	99,023.89	$	99,023.89
Cash Balance at Beg of Period		(100,500.00)		(100,500.00)
Net Increase <Decrease> in Cash	$	(1,476.11)	$	(1,476.11)

Unaudited - For Internal Use Only.

BACKING UP CHAPTER 15 DATA

If your reports agree with the ones shown, make a backup. If your printouts do not agree with the ones shown, make the necessary corrections. Back up. The suggested file name **Chapter 15.ptb**.

EXPORT REPORTS TO EXCEL

1. Export the following reports to Excel:

   - Payroll Journal
   - General Ledger Trial Balance
   - Balance Sheet
   - Income Statement
   - Statement of Cash Flow

2. Save. Use the file name **Chapter 15_PayJ_GLTB_BS_IS_SCF.xlsx**.
   NOTE: If your instructor would like you to save reports as PDF files, do that. The suggested file name is **Chapter 15_Payroll Journal.pdf**, etc. Your instructor may require additional reports.

ONLINE LEARNING CENTER

Complete end-of-chapter activities at www.mhhe.com/yacht2019 > select Student Edition, then Chapter 15.

1. Quizzes: Multiple Choice and True False questions. Interactive online tests that are graded and can be emailed to your instructor.
2. More Resources:
   a. QA Templates: Answer 10 multiple-choice questions and one Analysis Question.

    b. Narrated PowerPoints: Listen to the narrated PowerPoints.

    c. Going to the Net Exercises: Access the Employer Reporting website.

    d. Assessment Rubric: Complete the rubric to review Sage 50's journals, navigation centers, modules, task windows, and reports.

➤ Information Center > Sage Advisor Videos.

The OLC also includes links to the Appendixes:

- Appendix A: Troubleshooting (textbook and OLC)
- Appendix C: Review of Accounting Principles (OLC Student Edition)
- Appendix D: Glossary (OLC Student Edition)

Exercise 15-1: Follow the instructions below to complete Exercise 15-1. Exercises 12-1, 12-2, 13-1, 13-2, 14-1, and 14-2 must be completed before starting Exercise 15-1.

1. Start Sage. Open the company that you set up in Exercise 12-1, Your last name Sales and Service.
2. If necessary, restore the Exercise 14-1.ptb file which was backed up on page 542. To make sure you are starting with the correct data, display Exercise 14-2's General Ledger Trial balance (step 6, page 542).
3. Journalize and post the following General Journal entry:

    01/4/19   Transfer $5,450 from Account No. 10200, Boulevard Bank, to Account No. 10300, Payroll Checking Account.

4. Print the January 4, 2019 General Journal.
5. For setting up payroll, refer to the Payroll Setup Wizard, pages 550-553. Use the following information:

    State: GA

    State Unemployment Rate: **3.4%**

    Georgia Administrative Assessment Tax Rate: **.08%**

Company Information

Company name: Student Name Sales and Service

Federal Employer ID: 77-4422551

State Employer ID: 23-1488657

*State: GA

State Unemployment ID: 231233-5

State Unemployment Rate: 3.40000 %

Georgia Administrative Assessment Tax:

Rate: 0.08000 %

Overtime Expense: Account No. 77600, Overtime Expense

6. For entering employee and employer defaults, refer to pages 553-555. Use the Employee Fields shown below.

Field Name	GL Account
Fed_Income	23400, Federal Payroll Taxes Payable
Soc_Sec	24000, Soc. Sec. Employee Taxes Payable
MEDICARE	Account No. 24200, Medicare Employee Taxes Payable
St_Income	Account No. 23600, State Payroll Taxes Payable

Verify your Employee Fields window with the one shown on page 554.

7. Use the following Company Fields.

Field Name	Liability column	Expense column
Soc_Sec_C	24100, Soc. Sec. Employer Taxes Payable	72510, Soc. Sec. Expense
Medicare_C	24400 Medicare Employer Taxes Payable	72520, Medicare Expense

Fed_Unemp_C	23500, FUTA Tax Payable	72530, FUTA Expense
St_Unemp_C	23700, SUTA Payable	72540, SUTA Expense
St2_Unemp_C	23755, SUTA2 Payable	72545, SUTA2 Expense

Verify your Company Fields window with the one shown on page 555.
St2_Unemp_C is specific to Georgia payroll tax.

8. Refer to pages 555-559 to complete the payroll setup wizard. The Assign Company-Paid Taxes window shows ST2_Unemp_C for Other State Unemployment which is specific to GA payroll taxes.

   (*Hint:* Other State Unemployment is not shown on page 557 for the company in Arizona. For Georgia, this field is completed)

9. Add the following employees.

   Employee ID: C50
   Name: Rick Copley

Accept the default for Employee

Address:	10345 Atlantic Lane
City, ST, Zip:	Norcross, GA 30092
E-mail:	copley@email.com
Home phone:	770-555-8901
Social Security #:	002-00-0003
Type:	FULL

Withholding Info:

Filing Status:	Single for Federal, State, and Local
Allowances:	1 for Federal, State, and Local

Pay Info: Hourly - Hours per Pay Period, $12.50/hour; $18.75/hour, overtime; paid weekly

Employee ID:	M60
Name:	Mae Mandette

Accept the default for Employee

Address:	201 Wingate Avenue
City, ST, Zip:	Norcross, GA 30092
E-mail:	mandette@email.com
Home phone:	770-555-2231
Social Security #:	000-01-0001
Type:	FULL

Withholding Info:

Filing Status:	Single for Federal, State, and Local
Allowances:	1 for Federal, State, and Local

Pay Info:
Hourly - Hours Per Pay Period, $12.50/hour; $18.75/hour, overtime; paid weekly

10. Print an employee list. (*Hint:* Reports & Forms > Payroll > Employee List.)

11. Save the General Journal as a PDF file.
12. Back up. (Use **Exercise 15-1** as the file name.) Exit or continue.

Exercise 15-2: Follow the instructions below to complete Exercise 15-2.

1. Start Sage. Open your company.
2. If necessary, restore data from Exercise 15-1.
3. On January 4, 2019, issue payroll check 6050 to Rick Copley. Mr. Copley worked 40 regular hours. Issue paychecks from the Payroll Checking Account. Type **6050** in the Check Number field. To post, save after each payroll transaction.
4. On January 4, 2019, issue payroll check 6051 to Mae Mandette. Ms. Mandette worked 40 regular hours.
5. Make the following payroll entries for Rick Copley and Mae Mandette.

Date	Name	Hours Worked	Overtime	Check No.
1/11/19	R. Copley	40		6052
	M. Mandette	40		6053
1/18/19	R. Copley	40		6054
	M. Mandette	40		6055
1/25/19	R. Copley	40		6056
	M. Mandette	40		6057

After recording the paycheck information, type the check number, then post. You do *not* need to print paychecks 6050–6057.

6. Print the Payroll Journal.
7. Complete account reconciliation for Account No. 10200, Boulevard Bank.

Statement of Account Boulevard Bank January 1 to January 31, 2019			Account No. 91633-24331	Student Name Sales and Service 3814 Trinity Avenue Norcross, GA 30092		
REGULAR CHECKING						
Previous Balance		12/31/18		$67,500.00		
6 Deposits(+)				7,360.20		
8 Checks (-)				6,839.57		
Service Charges (-)		1/31/19		12.00		
Ending Balance		1/31/19		**68,008.63**		
DEPOSITS						
1/15/19		367.20	1/25/19	275.40		
1/22/19		486.00	1/30/19	972.00		
1/23/19		507.60	1/30/19	4,752.00		
CHECKS (Asterisk * indicates break in check number sequence)						
		1/3/19	Transfer		5,450.00	
		1/15/19	2020		392.00	
		1/25/19	2021		235.20	
		1/25/19	2022		125.00	
		1/25/19	2023		45.00	
		1/25/19	2024		145.72	
		1/25/19	2025		46.65	
		1/30/19	2026		400.00	

8. Complete account reconciliation for Account No. 10300, Payroll Checking
   Account. The bank statement is shown on the next page.

Statement of Account			Student Name Sales and Service	
Payroll Checking Account			3814 Trinity Avenue	
January 1 to January 31, 2019	Account No. 223-7731-44		Norcross, GA 30092	
REGULAR CHECKING				
Previous Balance	12/31/18	0.00		
1 Deposits(+)		5,450.00		
8 Checks (-)		3,142.24		
Service Charges (-)	1/31/19	15.00		
Ending Balance	1/31/19	**2,292.76**		
DEPOSITS				
	1/3/19	5,450.00		
CHECKS (Asterisk * indicates break in check number sequence)				
	1/11/19	6050	392.78	
	1/11/19	6051	392.78	
	1/14/19	6052	392.78	
	1/14/19	6053	392.78	
	1/21/19	6054	392.78	
	1/21/19	6055	392.78	
	1/28/19	6056	392.78	
	1/28/19	6057	392.78	

9. Print the account reconciliation reports for Boulevard Bank and the Payroll Checking Account.
10. Print the Customer Ledgers; Vendor Ledgers; and Inventory Valuation Report.
11. Print the General Ledger Trial Balance.
12. Print the following financial statements: Balance Sheet, Income Statement, and Statement of Cash Flow.

Check Your Figures:

Total Assets:	$194,251.39
Gross Profit	4,447.80
Net Increase in Cash	2,801.39

13. Make a backup. (Use **Exercise 15-2** as the file name.)

14. Export the following files to Excel:

- Employee List
- Customer Ledgers
- Vendor Ledgers
- Inventory Valuation Report
- Payroll Journal

- General Ledger Trial Balance
- Balance Sheet
- Income Statement
- Statement of Cash Flow

15. Use the file name **Exercise 15-2_EL_CL_VL_IVR_PayJ_GLTB_
BS_IS_SCF.xlsx.**

16. Save these reports as PDF files: Employee List, Customer Ledgers, Vendor Ledgers, Inventory Valuation Report, Payroll Journal, General Ledger Trial Balance, Balance Sheet, Income Statement, and Statement of Cash Flow.

CHAPTER 15 INDEX

Project

2 Valley Bikes

In Project 2, you complete the Computer Accounting Cycle for Valley Bikes, a merchandising business. Valley Bikes sells mountain bicycles, road bicycles, and children's bicycles. It is organized as a corporation. You purchased Valley Bikes in December 2018.

It is the purpose of Project 2 to review what you have learned in Chapters 12 through 15, Part 3 of Sage 50 for Merchandising Businesses. Accounts payable, accounts receivable, payroll, inventory transactions, and account reconciliation are included in this project. Vendors offer Valley Bikes a purchase discount of 2% 15, Net 30 days. Valley Bikes is located in OR where there is no sales tax. At the end of Project 2, a checklist is shown listing reports that you should have. The step-by-step instructions also remind you to print reports and back up.

Step 1: Start Sage 50.

Step 2: If a company opens, from the menu bar, select File > New Company > [No] for keeping another company open > click [Next >]. (*Or,* from the startup window, select Create a new Company.)

Step 3: Complete the following fields.

Company Name: Valley Bikes (your last name before company)
Address Line 1: 78 Gateway Drive, Store 32
City, State, Zip: Eugene, OR 97401
Country: USA
Telephone: 541-555-2431
Fax: 541-555-4424
Business Type: Corporation
Federal Employer ID: 78-8131355

State Employer ID:	22-8179923
State Unemployment ID:	221043-5
Web Site:	www.valleybikes.com
E-mail:	mail@valleybikes.com

Step   4:   Accept the default for Use a sample business type that closely matches your company.

Step   5:   Scroll down the list. In the **Detailed types** list, select Retail Company. (*Hint:* Account numbers have 5 digits.)

Step   6:   Accept the defaults for Accrual accounting, Real Time posting, and 12 monthly accounting periods.

Step   7:   The Choose the first period of your fiscal year window appears. If necessary, select 2019 as the year.

Step   8:   At the You are ready to create your company window, click Finish . Close the Sage Advisor Getting Started window.

Step   9:   Change the accounting period to 01-Jan 01, 2019 to Jan 31, 2019—Period 1: 01-01-19 - 01-31-19.

① Company Setup

General Ledger

1. *Delete accounts:*

10000	Petty Cash
10100	Cash on Hand
10300	Payroll Checking Account
11500	Allowance for Doubtful Account
14200	Notes Receivable-Current
15400	Leasehold Improvements
15500	Building
15600	Building Improvements
16900	Land
17400	Accum. Depreciation - Leasehold
17500	Accum. Depreciation - Building
17600	Accum. Depreciation - Bldg Imp

19000   Deposits
19200   Note Receivable-Noncurrent
19900   Other Noncurrent Assets
23000   Accrued Expenses
24200   Current Portion Long-Term Debt
60500   Amortization Expense
63000   Charitable Contributions Exp
63500   Commissions and Fees Exp
65000   Employee Benefit Programs Exp
66000   Gifts Expense
68000   Laundry and Cleaning Exp
89000   Other Expense

Change account:

10200   Regular Checking Account to State Bank
10400   Savings Account to Western Savings & Loan
12000   Product Inventory to Inventory-Mountain Bikes
14000   Prepaid Expenses to Prepaid Insurance
23300   Deductions Payable to Medicare Employee Taxes Payabl
24000   Other Taxes Payable to Soc. Sec. Employee Taxes Payab
24100   Employee Benefits Payable to Soc. Sec. Employer Taxes Payab
24800   Other Current Liabilities to Short-Term Notes Payable
27000   Notes Payable-Noncurrent to Long-Term Notes Payable
40000   Sales-Merchandise to Sales-Mountain Bikes
50000   Cost of Goods Sold to Cost of Sales-Mountain Bikes
72500   Penalties and Fines Exp to FUTA Expense
73000   Other Taxes to SUTA Expense
74000   Rent or Lease Expense to Rent-Mall Space

Add accounts:

12020   Inventory-Road Bikes   Inventory
12030   Inventory-Children's Bikes   Inventory
23350   Medicare Employer Taxes Payabl   Other Current Liabilities

40020	Sales-Road Bikes	Income
40030	Sales-Children's Bikes	Income
50020	Cost of Sales-Road Bikes	Cost of Sales
50030	Cost of Sales-Children's Bikes	Cost of Sales
73200	Soc. Sec. Expense	Expenses
73300	Medicare Expense	Expenses
73350	Local Payroll Taxes Expense	Expenses

2. Back up. Use **Valley Bikes Chart of Accounts** as the file name.

3. Record chart of accounts beginning balances as of December 31, 2018

Valley Bikes, Balance Sheet, January 1, 2019		
ASSETS		
Current Assets		
State Bank	$ 88,400.00	
Western Savings & Loan	15,000.00	
Inventory-Mountain Bikes	6,000.00	
Inventory-Road Bikes	8,250.00	
Inventory-Children's Bikes	4,050.00	
Prepaid Insurance	2,400.00	
Total Current Assets		$124,100.00
Property and Equipment: Furniture and Fixtures	6,000.00	
Total Property and Equipment and Other Assets		6,000.00
Total Assets		$130,100.00
LIABILITIES AND STOCKHOLDERS' EQUITY		
Short-Term Notes Payable	4,000.00	
Long-Term Notes Payable	5,500.00	
Total Liabilities		$9,500.00
Stockholder's Equity: Common Stock		120,600.00
Total Liabilities and Stockholders' Equity		$130,100.00

Handwritten margin note: ② Chart of Accounts

4. Print the December 31, 2018 balance sheet. Save the Project 2 Dec 31, 2018 Balance Sheet as a PDF file.

5. Back up. Use **Valley Bikes Starting Balance Sheet** as the file name.

Accounts Payable

1. Set up the following vendor defaults.

Standard <u>T</u>erms:	Due in number of days
Net due in:	30 days
Discount in:	15 days
Discount %:	2.00
Credit Limit:	15,000.00
GL Link Accounts:	
Expense Account:	12000 Inventory-Mountain Bikes
Discount GL Account:	59500 Purchase Discounts

2. Set up the following vendors.

Vendor ID:	ABC111
Name:	ABC Mountain Bikes
Contact:	Adriana Gold
Mailing Address:	7718 Fountain Avenue
City, ST, Zip:	Los Angeles, CA 90046
Vendor Type:	mountain
1099 Type:	Independent Contractor
Expense Account:	12000, Inventory-Mountain Bikes
Telephone 1:	213-555-8819
Fax:	213-555-8476
E-Mail	info@abcmountainbikes.net
Web Site:	www.abcmountainbikes.net
Purchase Info:	
Tax ID Number:	13-4838411

Vendor ID:	ERB112
Name:	Evans Road Bikes
Contact:	Michael Evans
Mailing Address:	3318 School Road
City, ST, Zip:	El Paso, TX 76314
Vendor Type:	road
1099 Type:	Independent Contractor
Expense Account:	12020, Inventory-Road Bikes
Telephone 1:	915-555-2177
Fax:	915-555-2179
E-mail:	info@roadbikes.com
Web Site:	www.roadbikes.com
Purchase Info:	
Tax ID Number:	77-5539912

Vendor ID:	TTW113
Name:	Tiny Tots Wheels
Contact:	Max Page
Mailing Address:	4200 Northeast Drive
City, ST, Zip:	Phoenix, AZ 85001
Vendor Type:	children
1099 Type:	Independent Contractor
Expense Account:	12030, Inventory-Children's Bikes
Telephone 1:	602-555-7626
Fax:	602-555-5982
E-mail:	info@tinytotswheels.biz
Web Site:	www.tinytotswheels.biz
Purchase Defaults:	
Tax ID Number:	28-3128488

4) Vendor Defaults
   + Vendor Set Up

Accounts Receivable

1. Set up the following customer defaults.

Standard Terms:	Due in number of days
Net due in:	30 days
Discount in:	0 days
Discount %:	0.00
Credit Limit:	5,000.00
GL Sales Account:	40000 Sales-Mountain Bikes
Discount GL Account:	49000 Sales Discounts

2. Set up the following customers.

Customer ID:	DB001
Name:	Donna Bryant
Billing address:	9984 Girard Avenue
City, ST, Zip:	Eugene, OR 97404
Customer type:	LANE (for Lane County)
Telephone 1:	541-555-6096
Fax:	541-555-6199
E-mail	bryant@eugene.com
Web site:	www.eugene.com/bryant
Sales Info:	
GL sales acct:	40000, Sales-Mountain Bikes

Customer ID:	RL002
Name:	Rich Lucero
Billing address:	3217 University Blvd.
City, ST, Zip:	Eugene, OR 97402
Customer type:	LANE
Telephone 1:	541-555-3393
Fax:	541-555-4117

E-mail:	rich@eugene.com
Web site:	www.eugene.com/lucero
Sales Info:	
GL sales acct:	40020, Sales-Road Bikes

Customer ID:	SW003
Name:	Sheila Welch
Billing address:	5780 East Tenth Avenue
City, ST, Zip:	Eugene, OR 97404
Customer type:	LANE
Telephone 1:	541-555-4427
Fax:	541-555-3151
E-mail:	welch@eugene.com
Web site:	www.eugene.com/sheila
Sales Info:	
GL sales acct:	40030, Sales-Children's Bikes

⑤ AR Defaults + Customer Set Up

Payroll

1. Use the following information for the Payroll Setup Wizard:

   State: OR
   State Unemployment Rate: 3.4%
   Do you have any localities for which you collect taxes in the state of OR? **Yes**

Locality: **Tri-Met**

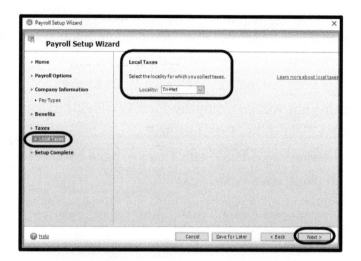

2. For entering employee and employer default information, refer to pages 553-555. Use the Employee Fields shown below.

Field Name	GL Account
Fed_Income	23400, Federal Payroll Taxes Payable
Soc_Sec	24000, Soc. Sec. Employee Taxes Payable
MEDICARE	23300, Medicare Employee Taxes Payable
St_Income	23600, State Payroll Taxes Payable

3. Use the Company Fields shown below.

Field	Liability column	Expense column
Soc_Sec_C	24100, Soc. Sec. Employer Taxes Payable	73200, Soc. Sec. Expense
Medicare_C	23350 Medicare Employer Taxes Payable	73300, Medicare Expense
Fed_Unemp_C	23500, FUTA Tax Payable	72500, FUTA Expense
Loc_Income_C	23800, Local Payroll Taxes Payable	73350, Local Payroll Taxes Expense

| St_Unemp_C | 23700, SUTA Payable | 73000, SUTA Expense |

4. Refer to pages 555-559 to complete the Payroll Setup Wizard's Taxes and Assign Tax Fields.

    a. Compare your Assign Tax Fields for W-2s to page 557.

    b. Compare your Assign Company-Paid Tax Fields to page 557. The State Special A field shows Loc_IncomeC.

    c. Compare Employee-Paid State Taxes to page 558.

5. Add the following employees.

Employee ID:	ML
Name:	Marc Livingston
Accept the default for Employee	
Address:	9934 Hillside Lane
City, ST, Zip:	Eugene, OR 97401
E-mail:	marc@mail.net
Home phone:	541-555-4591
Social Security #:	001-00-3000
Type:	FULL

Withholding Info:

| Filing Status: | Married for Federal and State Local (Married/Jointly) |
| Allow: | 2 for Federal, State and Local |

Pay Info: Salary, $500 per week.

Employee ID:	JW
Name:	Janeal Whitacre
Accept the default for Employee	
Address:	44890 West Fourth Ave.
City, ST, Zip:	Eugene, OR 97402

E-mail:	janeal@mail.net
Home phone:	541-555-2717
Social Security #:	100-00-0002
Type:	FULL

Withholding Info:

Filing Status:	Married for Federal and State
	Local (Married/Jointly)
Allow:	2 for Federal, State and Local

Pay Info: Salary, $500 per week.

6. Close.

⑥ Payroll Setup, Employee Defaults, + Employee Set up

Inventory

1. Set up the following inventory defaults. On the General Tab select Stock item as the Default Item Class.
2. Click on the GL Accts/Costing tab. For Stock item, Master Stock item, and Assembly, select LIFO as the inventory costing method
3. Set up the following Inventory items.

Item ID:	mbikes
Description:	mountain bikes
Item Class:	Stock item
Description for Sales:	mountain bikes
Price Level 1:	300.00
Last Unit Cost:	150.00
Cost Method:	LIFO
GL Sales Acct:	40000 Sales-Mountain Bikes
GL Inventory Acct:	12000, Merchandise Inventory-Mountain Bikes
GL Cost of Sales Acct:	50000, Cost of Sales-Mountain Bikes
Item Tax Type:	1
Item Type:	mountain

Stocking U/M:	each
Minimum Stock:	10
Reorder Quantity:	5
Preferred Vendor ID:	ABC Mountain Bikes
Beginning Balances:	mountain bikes
Quantity:	40.00
Unit Cost:	150.00
Total Cost:	6,000.00

Item ID:	rbikes
Description:	road bikes
Item Class:	Stock item
Description for Sales:	road bikes
Price Level 1:	150.00
Last Unit Cost:	75.00
Cost Method:	LIFO
GL Sales Acct:	40020, Sales-Road Bikes
GL Inventory Acct:	12020, Inventory-Road Bikes
GL Cost of Sales Acct:	50020, Cost of Sales-Road Bikes
Item Tax Type:	1
Item Type:	road
Stocking U/M:	each
Minimum Stock:	10
Reorder Quantity:	5
Preferred Vendor ID:	Evans Road Bikes
Beginning Balances:	Road Bikes
Quantity:	110.00
Unit Cost:	75.00
Total Cost:	8,250.00

Item ID:	cbikes
Description:	children's bikes
Item Class:	Stock item
Description for Sales:	children's bikes
Price Level 1:	90.00
Last Unit Cost:	45.00
Cost Method:	LIFO
GL Sales Acct:	40030, Sales-Children's Bikes
GL Inventory Acct:	12030, Inventory-Children's Bikes
Cost of Sales Acct:	50030, Cost of Sales-Children's Bikes
Item Tax Type:	1
Item Type:	children
Stocking U/M:	each
Minimum Stock:	10
Reorder Quantity:	5
Preferred Vendor ID:	Tiny Tots Wheels
Beginning Balances:	children's bikes
Quantity:	90.00
Unit Cost:	45.00
Total Cost:	4,050.00

4. Back up. Use **Valley Bikes Begin** as the filename.

① Inventory Defaults
+ Inventory Setup

Journalize and post the following transactions:

Date   *Description of Transaction*

1/04/19   Issued pay checks 5001 and 5002 from State Bank for Jeneal Whitacre and Marc Livingston. Type the check number on the Payroll Entry window.

1/07/19   Invoice No. 74A was received from ABC Mountain Bikes for 10 mountain bikes at $150 each.

1/07/19   Invoice No. 801 was received from Tiny Tots Wheels for 15 children's bikes at $45 each.

610 Project 2

Date	Transaction
1/07/19	Invoice No. ER555 was received from Evans Road Bikes for 12 road bikes at $75 each.
1/10/19	Deposited cash sales of $2,670: 4 mountain bikes, $1,200; 5 road bikes, $750; 8 children's bikes, $720. Cash sales are deposited in the State Bank account.
1/11/19	Deposited cash sales of $1,950: 5 children's bikes, $450; 4 road bikes, $600; and 3 mountain bikes, $900.
1/11/19	Issued pay checks 5003 and 5004 for Jeneal Whitacre and Marc Livingston. (*Hint: If necessary, complete the Check Number field.*)
1/13/19	Sold one mountain bike to Donna Bryant on account, Sales Invoice 101. (*Hint: Type the invoice number in the Invoice No. field. If necessary, select Layout, <Predefined> Product as the Invoice type.*)
1/18/19	Deposited cash sales of $1,920: 3 children's bikes, $270; 2 mountain bikes, $600; 7 road bikes, $1,050.
1/18/19	Issued pay checks 5005 and 5006 for Jeneal Whitacre and Marc Livingston.
1/19/19	Issued Check No. 5007 to ABC Mountain Bikes in payment of purchase Invoice No. 74A. Complete the Check/Reference No. field. Issue checks from the State Bank account. (Make sure that the Discount Account field shows 59500 for Purchase Discounts.)
1/19/19	Issued Check No. 5008 to Evans Road Bikes in payment of purchase Invoice No. ER555.
1/19/19	Issued Check No. 5009 to Tiny Tots Wheels in payment of purchase Invoice No. 801.
1/20/19	Issued Check No. 5010 to Robertson Rentals for $1,350 in payment of mall space rent for Valley Bikes. (*Hint: Remember to complete the Check/Reference No. field.*)
1/25/19	Issued pay checks 5011 and 5012 for Jeneal Whitacre and Marc Livingston.

④ 1/26/19 Deposited cash sales of $3,810: 6 mountain bikes, $1,800; 8 road bikes, $1,200; 9 children's bikes, $810.

1/26/19 Sold one children's bike to Sheila Welch on account, Sales Invoice 102. (*Hint: Type the invoice number in the Invoice No. field.*)

1/26/19 Invoice No. 88A was received from ABC Mountain Bikes for three mountain bikes at $150 each.

1/26/19 Invoice No. 962 was received from Tiny Tots Wheels for five children's bikes at $45 each.

1/26/19 Invoice No. ER702 was received from Evans Road Bikes for five road bikes at $75 each.

⑤ 1/28/19 Deposited cash sales of $3,240: 6 mountain bikes, $1,800; 6 road bikes, $900; 6 children's bikes, $540.

1/30/19 Issued Check No. 5013 to Marlene Schroeder for $245 in payment of Short-Term Notes Payable.

1/30/19 Issued Check No. 5014 to State Bank for $175.80 in payment of Long-Term Notes Payable.

1/30/19 Issued Check No. 5015 to City Utilities for $226.65 in payment of utilities.

 ⑧ January Transactions

5. Backup. Use **Valley Bikes January** as the file name.

6. Complete account reconciliation for the State Bank account.

Statement of Account			Valley Bikes	
State Bank			78 Gateway Drive, Store 32	
January 1 to January 31, 2019	Account No. 223-5110-890		Eugene, OR 97401	
REGULAR CHECKING				
Previous Balance	12/31/18	$88,400.00		
5 Deposits(+)		13,590.00		
12 Checks (-)		7,299.44		
Service Charges (-)	1/31/19	15.00		
Ending Balance	1/31/19	**94,675.56**		

DEPOSITS					
1/11/19	2,670.00	1/19/19	1,920.00	1/28/19	3,240.00
1/12/19	1,950.00	1/25/19	3,810.00		
CHECKS (Asterisk * indicates break in check number sequence)					
		1/9/19	5001	419.19	
		1/9/19	5002	419.19	
		1/16/19	5003	419.19	
		1/16/19	5004	419.19	
		1/23/19	5005	419.19	
		1/23/19	5006	419.19	
		1/23/19	5007	1,470.00	
		1/23/19	5008	882.00	
		1/23/19	5009	661.50	
		1/26/19	5010*	1,350.00	
		1/31/19	5013	245.00	
		1/31/19	5014	175.80	

⑨ Account Reconciliation

1. Print the General Ledger Trial Balance.
2. Print the Account Reconciliation report for the State Bank.
3. Print the Inventory Valuation Report.
4. Print the Balance Sheet, Income Statement, and Statement of Cash Flow.
5. Print the Customer Ledgers and Vendor Ledgers.
6. Back up. Use **Valley Bikes Financial Statements** as the file name.
7. Export to Excel and save PDF files: Chart of Accounts, Customer Ledgers, Vendor Ledgers, General Ledger Trial Balance, Account Reconciliation, Balance Sheet, Income Statement, Statement of Cash Flow. File name **Valley Bikes_CofA_CL_VL_GLTB_AcctRec_BS_IS_SCF.xlsx**.

		CHECKLIST OF PRINTOUTS, Valley Bikes
	1	General Ledger Trial Balance
	2	Account Reconciliation – State Bank
	3	Inventory Valuation Report
	4	Balance Sheet
	5	Income Statement
	6	Statement of Cash Flow
	7	Customer Ledgers
	8	Vendor Ledgers
		OPTIONAL PRINTOUTS
	9	Chart of Accounts
	10	December 31, 2018 Balance Sheet
	11	General Ledger
	12	Customer List
	13	Vendor List
	14	Purchase Journal
	15	Cash Disbursements Journal
	16	Sales Journal
	17	Cash Receipts Journal
	19	Payroll Journal
	19	Cost of Goods Sold Journal

_____

Student Name _____**Date**_____

CHECK YOUR PROGRESS: PROJECT 2, Valley Bikes

1. What are the total debit and credit balances on your
   General Ledger Trial Balance?   145,912.14

2. What are the total assets on January 31?   132,835.53

3. What is the balance in the State Bank account
   on January 31?   93,610.53

4. How much are total revenues as of January 31?   13,980.00

5. How much net income (net loss) is reported on
   January 31?   964.89

6. What is the balance in the Inventory-Mountain Bikes
   account on January 31?   4,650.00

7. What is the balance in the Inventory-Road Bikes
   account on January 31?   7,275.00

8. What is the balance in the Inventory-Children's Bikes
   account on January 31?   3,510.00

9. What is the balance in the Short-Term Notes Payable
   account on January 31?   3,755.00

10. What is the balance in the Common Stock account
    on January 31?   120,600.00

11. What are the total expenses reported on January 31?   6,086.61

12. Were any Accounts Payable incurred during the
    month of January? (Circle your answer.)   YES   NO

Project 2A — Student-Designed Merchandising Business

In Chapters 12, 13, 14, 15 and Project 2, you learned how to complete the Computer Accounting Cycle for merchandising businesses. Project 2A gives you an opportunity to design a merchandising business of your own. You select the type of merchandising business you want, edit your business's Chart of Accounts, create an opening Balance Sheet and transactions, and complete Sage 50's computer accounting cycle.

You should think about the kind of business you want to create. In Chapters 12, 13, 14 and 15 you worked with Shannon's Service Merchandise, a partnership form of business; and Your Last Name Sales and Service, a sole proprietorship. In Project 2, you worked with Valley Bikes, a corporate form of business. Other merchandising business types include: jewelry store, automobile dealer, furniture dealer, florist, etc. Here's what you need.

1. Company information that includes business name, address, telephone number, and form of business.
2. One of Sage 50's sample companies.
3. A Chart of Accounts: 80 accounts minimum, 110 accounts maximum.
4. A Balance Sheet for your business.
5. Transactions representing one month. Transactions should include accounts receivable, accounts payable, inventory, and payroll. A minimum of 25 transactions; a maximum of 35 transactions. Your transactions should result in a net income.
6. A bank statement.
7. Complete another month of transactions that result in a net loss.

McGraw-Hill Education, *Computer Accounting with Sage 50 2019, 21e*

After you create your business, you should follow the steps of Sage 50's Computer Accounting Cycle to complete Project 2A. After completing the Student-Designed Merchandising Business, printouts include:

CHECKLIST OF PRINTOUTS		
Student-Designed Merchandising Business		
	1	General Ledger Trial Balance
	2	Account Reconciliation Report
	3	Inventory Valuation Report
	4	Balance Sheet
	5	Income Statement
	6	Statement of Cash Flow
	7	Customer Ledgers
	8	Vendor Ledgers
OPTIONAL PRINTOUTS		
	9	Chart of Accounts
	10	General Ledger
	11	Customer List
	12	Vendor List
	13	Purchase Journal
	14	Cash Disbursements Journal
	15	Sales Journal
	16	Cash Receipts Journal
	17	Payroll Journal
	18	Cost of Goods Sold Journal

<table>
<tr><td>Part

4</td><td>Advanced Sage 50 2019
Applications</td></tr>
</table>

Part 4 includes three chapters and three projects.

Chapter 16, Customizing Forms, shows how to change the preprinted forms included with the software. Chapter 17, Import/Export, shows how to use Sage 50 2019 with a word processing program. Chapter 18, Microsoft Word and Templates, shows you how to copy Sage 50 reports to Microsoft Word, use Sage 50's write letters feature, and create templates.

Projects 3 and 4 complete your study of *Computer Accounting with Sage 50 2019, 21st Edition.* All features of the software are included for review in these projects. Project 4A gives you an opportunity to add another month's worth of transactions to any of the projects that you have completed.

The chart on the next page shows the size of the files saved and Sage 50 backups made in Part 4--Chapters 16, 17, 18, Project 3 and Project 4. You may back up or save to a USB flash drive, the hard drive, or network. *To complete work in Chapters 16-18, the Exercise 6-2.ptb file is restored.*

Chapter	Backups (.ptb), Excel (.xlsx), Adobe (.pdf)	Kilobytes	Page No.
16	Exercise 16-2.ptb	3,636 KB	641
	Exercise 16-2_Copy of Income Stmnt.pdf	8 KB	641
	Exercise 16-2_Copy of Income Stmnt.xlsx	16 KB	641
17	customer.csv	36 KB	648-649
	customer.txt	36 KB	651
	Exercise 17-1_Chart of Accounts.pdf	31 KB	659
	Exercise 17-1.Chart of Accounts.xlsx	17 KB	659
	Exercise 17-2.ptb	939 KB	659
18	Bellwether Garden Supply.docx	16 KB	663
	Customer Letters.docx	3,103 KB	665
	Bellwether Sales Special.doc	579 KB	669
	Exercise 18-1.docx	3,103 KB	672
	Exercise 18-2.docx	3,103 KB	673
Project 3	Evanston Computer Club Chart of Accounts.ptb	932 KB	680
	Evanston Computer Club Starting Balance Sheet.ptb	934 KB	681
	Evanston Computer Club January.ptb	960 KB	683
	Evanston Computer Club_CofA_ CDJ_CRJ_ GLTB_ BS_ IS_ SCF_SRE. xlsx	38 KB	683
	Project 3_Chart of Accounts.pdf	11 KB	683
	Project 3_Cash Disbursements Journal	13 KB	683
	Project 3_Cash Receipts Journal	11 KB	683
	Project 3_General Ledger Trial Balance.pdf	12 KB	683
	Project 3_Balance Sheet.pdf	10 KB	683
	Project 3_Income Statement.pdf	11 KB	683
	Project 3_Statement of Cash Flow.pdf	10 KB	683
	Project 3_Statement of Retained Earnings.pdf	13 KB	683
Project 4	CL Mftg Chart of Accounts.ptb	940 KB	687
	CL Mftg Starting Balance Sheet.ptb	957 KB	689
	CL Mftg Begin.ptb	985 KB	699
	CL Mftg January.ptb	1,103 KB	704
	CL Mftg_CofA_GLTB_BS_IS_SCF_SRE.xlsx	36 KB	704
	Project 4_Chart of Accounts.pdf	13 KB	704
	Project 4_General Ledger Trial Balance.pdf	5 KB	704
	Project 4_Balance Sheet.pdf	5 KB	704
	Project 4_Income Statement.pdf	5 KB	704
	Project 4_Statement of Cash Flow.pdf	5 KB	704
	Project 4_Statement of Retained Earnings.pdf	3 KB	704

Chapter

16   Customizing Forms

LEARNING OBJECTIVES

1. Define Sage 50 forms.
2. Customize a form (invoice).
3. Print a practice form.
4. Use design tools.
5. Use the Financial Statement Wizard.
6. Make one backup and save one PDF file.

You have used many different kinds of forms: invoices, statements, checks, etc. There may be times when you want to create your own form or customize one of the formats that come with Sage 50. You can customize forms with the Forms Designer.[1]

PRINTING FORMS

There are three types of documents that can be accessed from the Reports & Forms menu:

➢ Reports
➢ Financial Statements
➢ Forms

The rules for each type of document are different for printing and designing. This chapter will explain the rules for designing forms.

---

[1]You need a mouse to use the forms designer.

WHAT IS A FORM?

A form in Sage 50 is a document that you exchange with customers, vendors, or employees. The forms that come with Sage 50 include checks, tax forms, invoices, statements, mailing labels, quotes, and collection letters. Usually, these documents are printed on preprinted forms, but you can also design a form and print on blank paper. When you are ready to print or design a form, you select Reports & Forms, then select Forms. Select the appropriate form from the Forms Types list. The illustration below shows the Checks selection. From the Forms list, additional selections can be made.

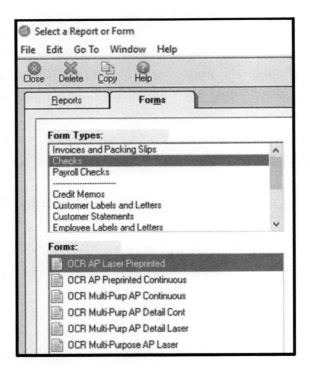

The Select a Report or Form window lists all the reports and forms currently set up in Sage 50. Reports include financial statements, aging reports, etc. Forms are usually tied to a transaction, such as an invoice or check. Letters are also listed on the Forms tab.

The following table lists the forms that can be printed or edited:

Accounts Receivable	Accounts Payable	Payroll
Collection letters	1099 Forms	Payroll checks
Credit memos	Disbursement checks	Employee mailing labels
Customer labels	Purchase orders	
Customer quotes	Vendor mailing labels	
Customer statements		
Invoices/packing slips		
Receipts		
Sales orders		

Preprinted paper forms require special attention because the forms must be aligned in the printer correctly and the printer must be configured to accommodate the form. That is why forms cannot be displayed on your screen prior to printing. You can print practice forms to test alignment and printer configuration, or you can view the layout of the form.

GETTING STARTED

In this chapter, you are going to use Bellwether Garden Supply (the sample company that you used in Chapters 1 through 7).

1. Start Sage 50.
2. Open the sample company, Bellwether Garden Supply. (The instructions in this chapter assume that you are using data from the Exercise 6-2.ptb backup made on page 202. No new data was added in Chapter 7.) If necessary, restore the Exercise 6-2.ptb file. (*Hint:* If you do not have the Exercise 6-2 backup, use any Bellwether backup.)

To verify Exercise 6-2 data, display the balance sheet. A partial balance sheet is shown below. Chapter 7's balance sheet is shown on pages 213-214. (If you restored a different Bellwether backup, your balance sheet will differ.)

Bellwether Garden Supply - Student Name		
Balance Sheet		
March 31, 2019		
ASSETS		
Current Assets		
Petty Cash	$ 327.55	
Cash on Hand	1,850.45	
Regular Checking Account	9,046.52	
Payroll Checking Account	8,836.40	
Savings Account	7,500.00	
Money Market Fund	4,500.00	
Accounts Receivable	176,026.47	
Other Receivables	7,681.84	
Allowance for Doubtful Account	(5,000.00)	
Inventory	12,386.46	
Prepaid Expenses	14,221.30	
Employee Advances	3,000.65	
Notes Receivable-Current	11,000.00	
Other Current Assets	120.00	
Total Current Assets		251,497.64
Property and Equipment		
Furniture and Fixtures	62,769.25	
Equipment	38,738.33	
Vehicles	86,273.40	
Other Depreciable Property	6,200.96	
Buildings	185,500.00	
Building Improvements	26,500.00	
Accum. Depreciation-Furniture	(54,680.57)	
Accum. Depreciation-Equipment	(33,138.11)	
Accum. Depreciation-Vehicles	(51,585.26)	
Accum. Depreciation-Other	(3,788.84)	
Accum. Depreciation-Buildings	(34,483.97)	
Accum. Depreciation-Bldg Imp	(4,926.28)	
Total Property and Equipment		223,378.91
Other Assets		
Deposits	15,000.00	
Organization Costs	4,995.10	
Accum Amortiz - Organiz Costs	(2,000.00)	
Notes Receivable- Noncurrent	5,004.90	
Other Noncurrent Assets	3,333.00	
Total Other Assets		26,333.00
Total Assets		$ 501,209.55

CUSTOMIZING A FORM

1. From the Navigation Bar, select **Customers & Sales** > in the Recently
    Used Customer Reports area, link to <u>View All Customer & Sales Reports</u>.
    The Select a Report or Form window displays.
2. Select the Forms tab. In the Form Types list, Invoices and Packing Slips is
    highlighted.
3. In the Forms list > select Invoice. Observe that the Description field shows
    Use with plain paper.

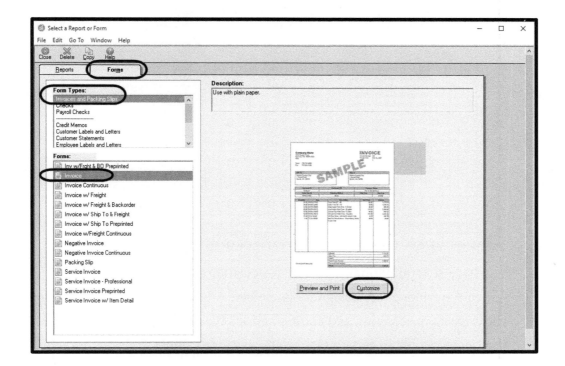

4. After selecting **Customize**, the window for designing an invoice form
    appears. A partial Invoice window is shown on the next page. This window
    allows you to create new customized forms or edit existing forms to match
    your business's needs.

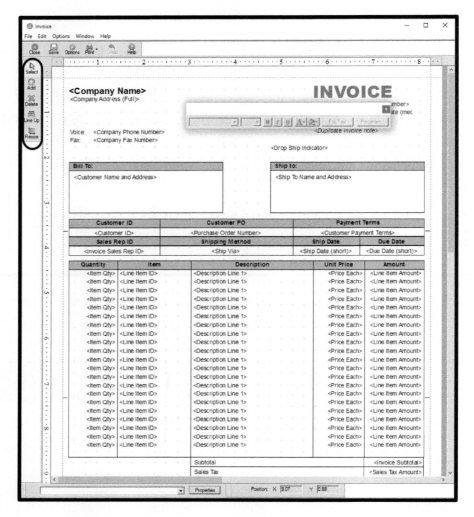

You have several options available for customizing the form. On the left side of the window are design tools: Select, Add, Delete, Line Up, Resize. These assist in selecting and adding various types of form objects. You can also design forms in certain task windows (for example, Sales/Invoicing, Payments, and Payroll Entry) by selecting the Print button, then Form Design on the Print dialog.

5. To select an object for customizing, use the Select tool [Select]. With your mouse pointer, you can drag and drop objects to move them around. Click

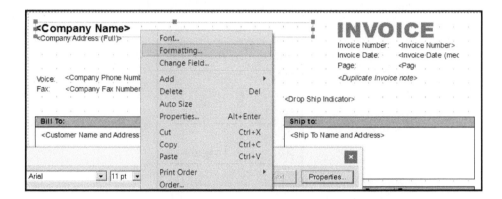

Then move your mouse cursor to the inside of the form (inside the red outline). Click on the <Company Name> field to select it (field selection is indicated by a box).

6. With the <Company Name> field selected (blue box is around it), right-click.

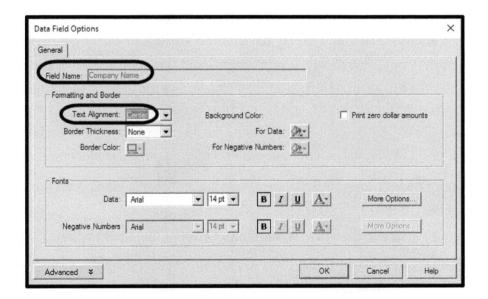

7. Left-click Formatting. The Data field Options window appears. In the Text alignment field, select Center.

8. Click [OK]. Observe that the <Company Name> field moves to the center. Right-click on the <Company Address (Full)> field and center it. You may want to Right-click on various fields and make changes such as font size, alignment, etc. You can delete a field or two as well.

9. Click [⊕ Add]. Observe that you can add a Logo or image, Data from Sage 50, Text, Shape, Line, Column to table, and Other object.

10. On the icon bar of the Forms Designer, click [⚙ Options]. The Forms Design Options window appears.

    If necessary, select the Display tab to select various display options. Select the Grid/Copies tab to adjust grid options and specify a default number of copies for this form. (*Hint:* You may also accept the default selections.)

11. Click [OK] to close the Forms Design Options window.

12. When finished designing the form, select [💾 Save]. The Save As window appears.

13. Type **Practice** in the Form Name field. Observe that the Filename field shows the path for this form. Compare your Save As window with the one shown on the next page.

14. Click 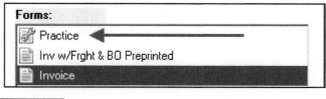 > . Observe that Practice is shown on the Forms list with a wrench next to it. A wrench indicates a Custom Sage 50 form. Select Practice.

15. Click .

PRINTING CUSTOMIZED FORMS

The Preview and Print Invoices and Packing Slips window should be displayed. Follow these steps to see the redesigned Invoice.

1. Make the following selections on the Preview and Print Invoices and Packing Slips window

   a. Type or select **3/15/2019** in the through field. Mar 15, 2019 should be displayed in the through field.

b. The Number the first invoice field shows 103. (If needed, type 103.)

c. In the Use this form field, select Practice. (*Hint:* You may need to scroll up.)

d. The Delivery method field shows Print and e-mail.

e. Click 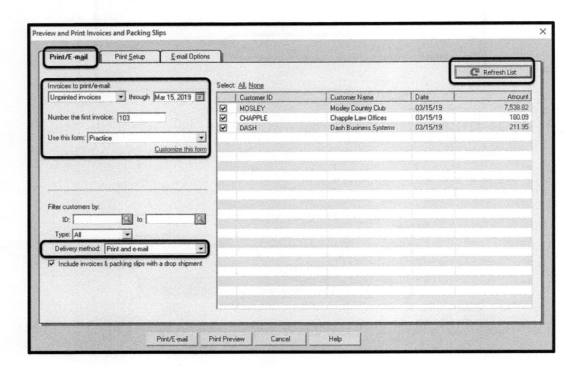.

2. After selecting Print Preview, Invoice Number 103 appears. Notice in the illustration on the next page that Bellwether Garden Supply and its address information is centered. Your Invoice may differ depending on which fields you changed. Invoice Number 103 is shown on the next page.

Bellwether Garden Supply - Student Name			INVOICE		
1505 Pavilion Place			Invoice Number: 103		
Norcross, GA 30093-3203			Invoice Date: Mar 15, 2019		
USA			Page: 1		

Voice: 770-724-4000
Fax: 770-555-1234

Bill To:	Ship to:
Mosley Country Club 1 Howell Walk Duluth, GA 30096	Mosley Country Club 1 Howell Walk Duluth, GA 30096

Customer ID	Customer PO	Payment Terms	
MOSLEY		2% 10, Net 30 Days	
Sales Rep ID	**Shipping Method**	**Ship Date**	**Due Date**
SPRICHARD	None		4/14/19

Quantity	Item	Description	Unit Price	Amount
20.00	NURS-21900	Ficus Tree 22" - 26"	55.95	1,119.00
25.00	NURS-22000	Ginko Tree 14" - 16"	49.95	1,248.75
10.00	NURS-23000	Washington Palm Tree - 5 Gallon	49.00	490.00
20.00	NURS-23010	Washington Palm Tree - 10 gallon	119.00	2,380.00
10.00	NURS-24000	Chinese Fan Palm Tree - 5 gallon	49.95	499.50
10.00	NURS-24010	Chinese Fan Palm Tree - 10 gallon	122.00	1,220.00
15.00	SOIL-34160	GA Pine Straw - wire tied 4 cubic ft. bale	6.99	104.85
1.00	TOOL-35300	Bell-Gro Wheelbarrow - Green Metal; Holds 6 cubic feet	49.99	49.99

	Subtotal		7,112.09
	Sales Tax		426.73
	Total Invoice Amount		7,538.82
Check/Credit Memo No:	Payment/Credit Applied		
	TOTAL		**7,538.82**

3. Click [Next] to see Invoice Numbers 104 and 105. Click [Print]. (*Hint:* If you do not have a printer, in the Print window's Name box, select Adobe PDF. Save the file.) When the Did the Invoices print and e-mail properly window appears, click [Yes].

4. Close the Select a Report or Form window.

EDITING A FORM DESIGN

1. From the menu bar, select Reports & Forms > Forms > Invoices and Packing Slips.
2. In the Forms list, select Practice.
3. Click [Customize]. Select the fields you want to change.
4. On the Practice window's icon bar, click [Options]. Select the Display tab to select various display options. Select the Grid/Copies tab to adjust grid options and specify a default number of copies for this form.
5. When through, click [OK].
6. Save the form. Use the same filename, Practice.

DESIGN TOOLS

The forms designer includes design tools: Select, Add, Delete, Line Up, Resize. These terms are defined as follows:

Object Toolbar

[Select]   Select: Select this to use the Selection tools to highlight or select one or more form objects.

[Add]   Add: Select Add to add an object to the form. You can add an image or logo, data field, text field, column field, shape, line or other object using this tool.

Delete: Select Delete to delete the object or objects that you have selected on the form.

Line Up: Select Line Up to align the objects that you have selected on the form. You can Line Up-Left, Right, Top, Bottom.

Resize: Select Resize to resize the objects that you have selected on the form. You can resize the width and height.

Click **Close** to return to the Select a Report or Form window. Close to return to the menu bar.

Formatting Toolbar

Use the formatting toolbar to change the format of the selected object on your form. Use this toolbar to change the font, color, and background color of the selected object. If you have selected a text object, you can click the Edit Text button to change the text. Clicking the Properties button will open the corresponding property window, where you can modify the object's properties. The Fonts section of the Data Field Options window is shown below.

You may want to experiment with the Practice form to see some of these design features.

FINANCIAL STATEMENT DESIGN TOOLS

When you design a financial statement, use the financial statement Design Tools window. It has three major areas: the toolbar at the top of the window, the design toolbar at the side of the window where you select the type of fields you want to place on the designer, and the design area where you actually create the financial statement. When you create a financial statement, you work with five areas: 1) the header; 2) lines of text; 3) columns; 4) totals; 5) footer. Follow these steps to see the designing tools that are available on the Statement of Cash Flow.

1. From the Reports & Forms menu, select Financial Statements > <Standard> Cash Flow.

2. Click Design. The <Standard> Cash Flow window includes the design tools necessary for customization. Compare yours with the one shown below.

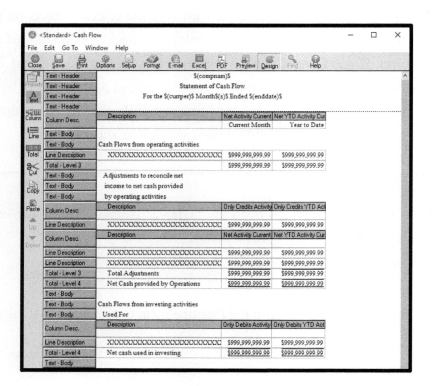

On the left side of the design window, observe that each row has a button next to it that defines the row; for example, Text – header, Column Desc., Text – Body, etc. The icon bar at the top of the window contains the following buttons: Close, Save, Print, Options, Setup, Format, E-mail, Excel, PDF, Preview, Design, and Help.

The information that follows is for explanation purposes only. You may want to experiment with some of the design tools to make changes to Sage 50's <Standard> Cash Flow.

When designing a new form or modifying an existing one, you need to save the form to record your changes. If you change one of the standard forms (those that came with Sage 50), you must rename the form before saving your changes. You cannot save changes to the standard forms using the original form name. This allows you to keep the standard form in case you make a design error and need to start over.

A custom form appears on the report list with a different icon than a <Standard> form. Predefined or standard forms and reports are included with the software.

   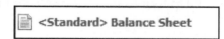

The financial statement design tools are shown below.

![Property] Use the Property tool to work with the properties window for the selected row type. For example, if you select a text row, the text window opens.

![Text] Use the Text tool to insert text that you will not change from statement to statement (for example, section headings).

Use the Column tool to define columns, enter a title for each column, select the alignment of each column title (left, right, or center) and select the style, size and color of the text.

Once the columns are defined, use the Line tool to define what data to put in each row of a column. Line objects are placed below column objects.

Use the Total tool to tell the program how to calculate totals and subtotals.

Use the Cut tool to remove the selected row and copy it to the Windows Clipboard.

Use the Copy tool to copy the selected row to the Windows Clipboard.

Use the Paste tool to insert the current row from the Windows Clipboard.

Use the Up tool to move the selected row up one position in the list of rows.

Use the Down tool to move a selected row down one position in the list of rows.

You can select multiple rows in the window and then apply the cut, copy, and paste functions to all of them. To select multiple rows, hold down the Ctrl key, and then with the cursor select the buttons that define the rows you want. When you are through looking at the <Standard> Cash Flow Design window, close it.

FINANCIAL STATEMENT WIZARD

The Financial Statement Wizard walks you through the process of designing financial statements. Follow these steps to use the Financial Statement Wizard.

1. If necessary start Sage 50. Open Bellwether Garden Supply.
2. From the Reports & Forms menu, select Financial Statements.
3. Link to <u>Financial Statement Wizard</u> (upper right side of window).

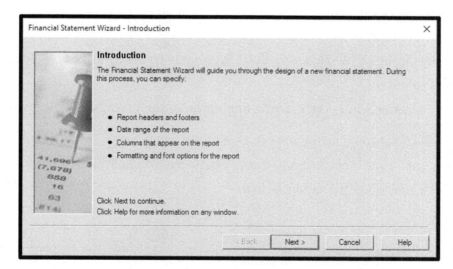

4. After reading the information on the Introduction window, click Next > .
5. Make sure <Standard> Balance Sheet appears in the Financial Statement Template field. If necessary, select it.

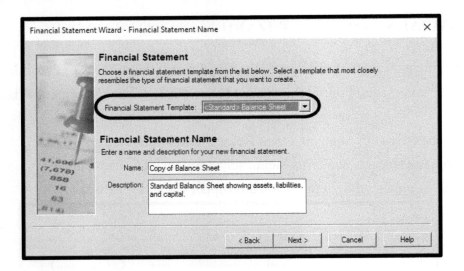

6. After reading the information on the Financial Statement window, click

    Next > . The Headers and Footers window appears.

7. The Headers and Footers window allows you to change information at the top and bottom of the balance sheet. For purposes of this exercise, click on the beginning of the Header 1 line. Type **your name** followed by a comma and a space.

8. In the Header 3 line, click on the beginning of the line, then click

    Insert ▼ (down arrow next to Insert). Select Today's Date from the drop-down list. Type a comma and a space between $(Date)$ and $(enddate)$. The Header lines are shown below.

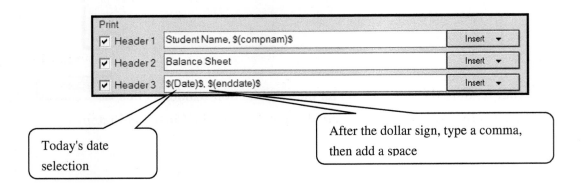

Compare your Headers and Footers window with the one shown.

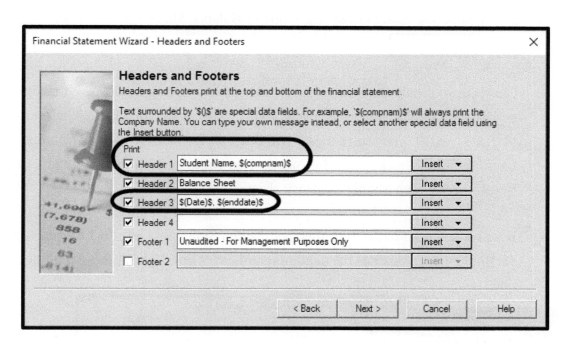

9. Click Next >. The Date Range and Account Masking window appears. Read the information in the Dates and General Ledger Account Masking sections. Accept the defaults on this window, by clicking on Next >.

10. Accept the defaults on the Column Properties window by clicking on Next >.

11. Accept the defaults on the Column Options window by clicking on Next >.

12. Unless you want to change fonts, accept the defaults on the Fonts window by clicking on Next >.

13. Accept the defaults on the Formatting and Default Printer window by clicking on Next >.

14. The Congratulations window appears. To display your new financial
    statement, click [Finish]. The Copy of Balance Sheet window appears,
    click [OK].

    Compare your balance sheet to the partial one shown below. Observe that the
    header shows your name on line one; today's date is shown on line 3 before
    March 31, 2019 (your current date will differ). This balance sheet is from the
    Exercise 6-2.ptb backup file. In Chapter 7 on pages 213-214, you printed
    Bellwether Garden Supply's balance sheet.

    If you added your name to Bellwether Garden Supply in Chapter 1 on page
    41, your name appears at the beginning of header line 1 and at the end of the
    line.

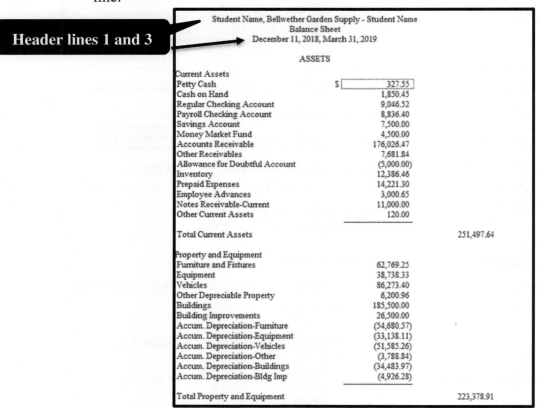

Header lines 1 and 3

Student Name, Bellwether Garden Supply - Student Name
Balance Sheet
December 11, 2018, March 31, 2019

ASSETS

Current Assets		
Petty Cash	$ 327.55	
Cash on Hand	1,850.45	
Regular Checking Account	9,046.52	
Payroll Checking Account	8,836.40	
Savings Account	7,500.00	
Money Market Fund	4,500.00	
Accounts Receivable	176,026.47	
Other Receivables	7,681.84	
Allowance for Doubtful Account	(5,000.00)	
Inventory	12,386.46	
Prepaid Expenses	14,221.30	
Employee Advances	3,000.65	
Notes Receivable-Current	11,000.00	
Other Current Assets	120.00	
Total Current Assets		251,497.64
Property and Equipment		
Furniture and Fixtures	62,769.25	
Equipment	38,738.33	
Vehicles	86,273.40	
Other Depreciable Property	6,200.96	
Buildings	185,500.00	
Building Improvements	26,500.00	
Accum. Depreciation-Furniture	(54,680.57)	
Accum. Depreciation-Equipment	(33,138.11)	
Accum. Depreciation-Vehicles	(51,585.26)	
Accum. Depreciation-Other	(3,788.84)	
Accum. Depreciation-Buildings	(34,483.97)	
Accum. Depreciation-Bldg Imp	(4,926.28)	
Total Property and Equipment		223,378.91

15. Close the Copy of Balance Sheet window. Observe a wrench is shown next to Copy of Balance Sheet, which indicates a custom form.

| Copy of Balance Sheet | Standard Balance Sheet showing assets, liabilities, and capital. |

16. Close the Select a Report or Form window. Exit Sage 50 or continue.

ONLINE LEARNING CENTER

Complete end-of-chapter activities at www.mhhe.com/yacht2019 > Student Edition > Chapter 16.

1. Quizzes: Multiple Choice and True False questions. Interactive online tests that are graded and can be emailed to your instructor.

2. More Resources:

   a. QA Templates: Answer 10 multiple-choice questions and two Analysis Questions.
   b. Narrated PowerPoints: Listen to the narrated PowerPoints.
   c. Going to the Net Exercises: On the Sage press room website, select articles to read.
   d. Assessment Rubric: Complete the rubric to review Sage 50's journals, navigation centers, modules, task windows, and reports.

➢ Information Center > Sage Advisor Videos.

The OLC also includes links to the Appendixes:

• Appendix A: Troubleshooting (textbook and OLC)
• Appendix C: Review of Accounting Principles (OLC Student Edition)
• Appendix D: Glossary (OLC Student Edition)

Exercise 16-1: Use the forms designer to customize a Service Invoice.

1. From the Customers & Sales Navigation Center, link to View All Customer and Sales Reports.
2. From the Forms list, select Service Invoice > Customize.
3. Change Company Name's font size to 16.
4. Change the font size of the Company Address to Arial 12.
5. Change the font size of the Customer Name and Address to Arial 12.
6. Save the Service Invoice as Exercise 16-1.
7. On the Preview and Print Invoices and Packing Slips window, select Printed invoices. Type **103** in the Numbered fields. Filter the customers by MOSLEY. Remember to refresh the list.

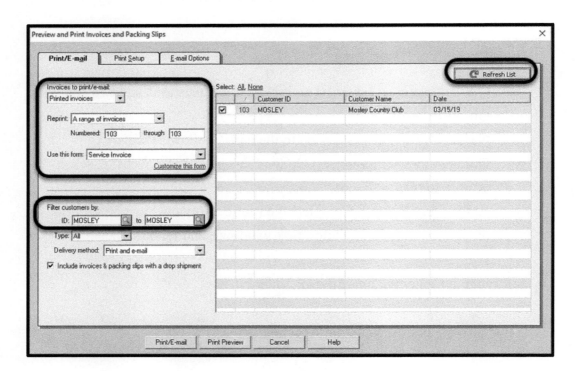

8. Preview and print the service invoice number 103 for Mosley.

Exercise 16-2: Use the Financial Statement Wizard.

1. Use the Financial Statement Wizard to add your name and today's date to \<Standard> Income Statement.
2. Print the income statement. (*Hint:* Uncheck Show Zero Amounts.) If you added your name to Bellwether Garden Supply in Chapter 1, page 38, your name appears at the beginning of header line 1 and at the end of the line.
3. Backup. The suggested file name is **Exercise 16-2.ptb**.
4. Save the Copy of the Income Statement as a PDF file and export to Excel. The suggested file name is **Exercise 16-2_Copy of Income Stmnt**. Check with your instructor to see if he or she would also like an Excel file.

CHAPTER 16 INDEX

Chapter

17   Import/Export

LEARNING OBJECTIVES

1. Export information from Sage 50 to a word processing program.
2. Select the customer list from Bellwether Garden Supply to export.
3. Import Bellwether Garden Supply's chart of accounts into a new company.
4. Save two files: a comma separated value file (.csv) and a text file (.txt).
5. Make one backup, save one Excel file, and save one PDF file.

Importing translates data from other programs into a format that Sage 50 can use. The diagram below shows how importing works. Data can be imported into Sage 50.

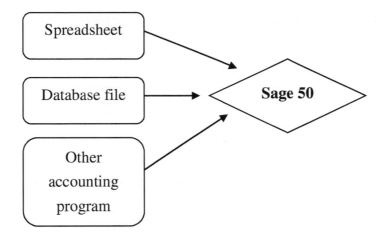

Exporting copies Sage 50 data into a format that other programs can read and use. The diagram on the next page illustrates exporting. Data is exported from Sage 50.

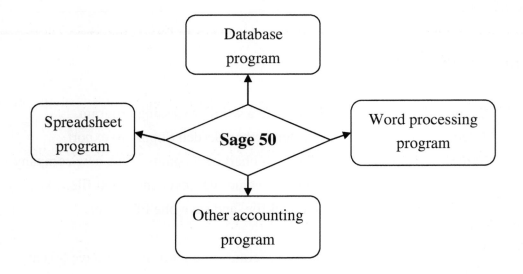

The chart below shows how Sage 50 organizes data.

Customer	**Files**	Journal	

	General Journal	Purchase Journal	Cash Disbursements Journal	Sales Journal	Cash Receipts Journal
Records					

Fields	Invoice Number	Account Number	Debit Amount	Credit Amount

➤ *Files* are a group of related records; for example, customer files and journal files.

➤ *Records* are a group of fields that contain information on one subject; for example, the general journal, purchase journal, cash disbursements journal, sales journal, or cash receipts journal.

➤ *Fields* are an individual piece of data; for example, invoice numbers, account numbers, debit amount, credit amount.

Files

When you import or export files, you use templates to format the data. The templates included in Sage 50 are:

➢ Accounts Receivable: Customer List, Sales Journal, and Cash Receipts Journal

➢ Accounts Payable: Vendor List, Purchase Journal, and Cash Disbursements Journal

➢ Payroll: Employee List

➢ General Ledger: Chart of Accounts and General Journal

➢ Inventory: Inventory Item List

➢ Job Reports: Jobs List

Records

When you select a file to export, you can define which information you want. For instance, when you select the Customer List, you can select which customers you want to export.

Fields

When export is used, you export individual fields of information. You can see what fields are exported by selecting the Format tab. You may uncheck fields to exclude them from being exported or move fields around to change their order.

When you export, the information is exported in a ***comma separated values*** (CSV) format. This means that the fields for each record are written in one line, with commas between them. You see how this looks when you export one of Sage 50's customer lists into Microsoft Word. Comma separated value files

(CSV extensions) are commonly used for transferring data between applications in a text-based format.

The file created during the export process is an *ASCII* file, which contains only text characters. Each record is on a separate line. ASCII is an acronym for American Standard Code for Information Interchange. It is one of the standard formats used for representing characters on a computer. Most word processing, spreadsheet, and database programs can read ASCII files.

GETTING STARTED: EXPORTING

1. Start Sage 50.
2. Open Bellwether Garden Supply. (In this chapter data is used from the Exercise 6-2.ptb backup file made on page 202.)
3. If necessary, restore the Exercise 6-2.ptb file. (*Hint:* Any Bellwether Garden Supply file can be used to complete work in Chapter 17.)
4. From the menu bar, select File > Select Import/Export. The Select Import/Export window appears. *Or*, from the System Navigation page, click Import/Export Data Now.
5. In the Accounts Receivable list, highlight Customer List.

6. Click . The Customer List window appears.

7. Click on the Fields tab, then click .

> **Comment:** Show All places a check mark in all the fields.

8. Click on the Options tab.

> **Comment:** The radio button next to Ask, Then Overwrite is the default.

9. Insert a USB flash drive. Click on the arrow ► below Import/Export File. The Open window appears. The File name field shows CUSTOMER.CSV

    File name: CUSTOMER.CSV. The field to the right shows Import/Export Files

    (*.CSV) Import/Export Files (*.CSV) ▼.

10. Select the location of your USB. The author's is F – 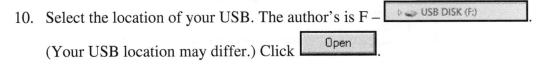. (Your USB location may differ.) Click Open.

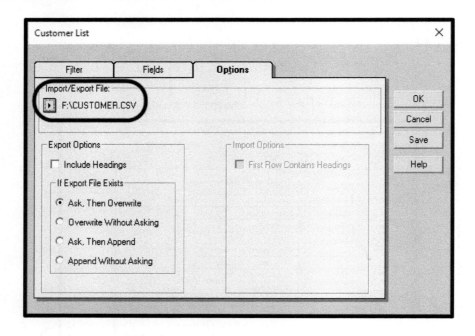

Observe that F:\CUSTOMER.CSV is shown next to the arrow ▶ under Import/Export File. (Substitute your USB location for F.)

11. Click [Save]. The Save As window appears. Type **Customers** in the Template Name field.

12. After clicking [Save], you are returned to the Customers Options window. Make sure X:\CUSTOMER.CSV is shown as the Import/Export File name. (Substitute your USB location for X.)

13. Click [OK]. The Select Import/Export window shows Customers with a red arrow. Select it. The Description field describes the custom version.

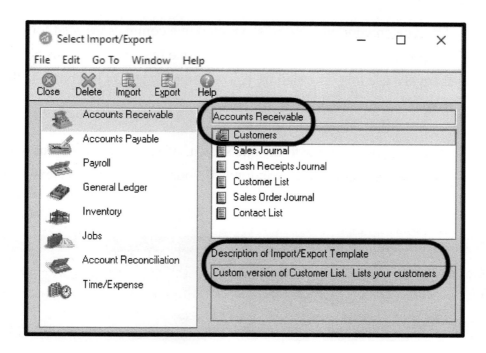

14. Close the Select Import/Export window.

15. Start your word processing program. You can use Microsoft Word, or any word processing program that supports ASCII.

16. Follow these steps to open the Sage 50 file from Microsoft Word.

    a. Start Word or other word processing program. Click [icon] (the open file icon).

    b. Select the appropriate location of the CUSTOMER.CSV file. Make sure All Files (*.*) is shown [All Files (*.*)].

    c. Highlight the CUSTOMER.CSV file. The File name field is completed

    File name: CUSTOMER.CSV   All Files (*.*)

d. Click 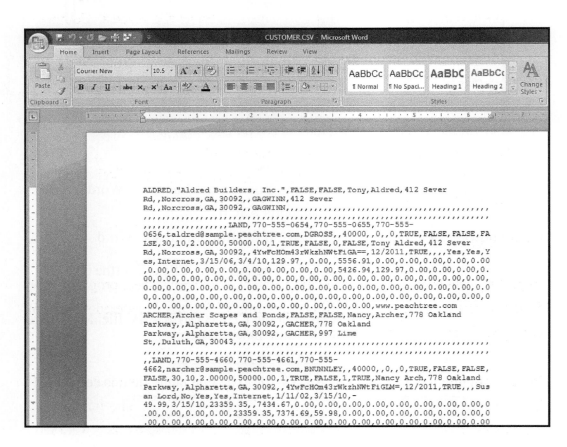. (*Hint:* If a Convert File window appears, select Plain Text, then <OK>.)

The data on your window was exported in a comma separated format. The fields for each record are written in one line, with commas between them. To use this information, you would need to edit its contents, then save it.

Compare your window to the one shown. If you used a different word processing program, your window will look different but the text portion of the data is the same.

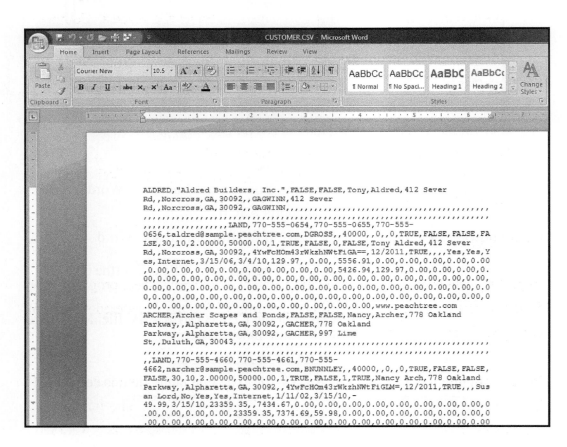

e. To keep the original ASCII file, use Word's Save <u>A</u>s command and rename the file **CUSTOMER.txt**. When you save, the file converts to a text document file from its original ASCII format. If a File Conversion – CUSTOMER.txt window appears, click .

f. Exit the word processing program.

TEXT AND COMMA SEPARATED VALUES FILES

To look at the files you just created, do this:

1. Open File Explorer. Go to the location of the CSV file.
2. Observe that the CUSTOMER.CSV file is an Excel file saved as Comma Separated Values. The CUSTOMER.txt file is a Text document.

CUSTOMER.CSV	36 KB	Microsoft Excel Comma Separated Values File
CUSTOMER.txt	36 KB	Text Document

3. Double-click CUSTOMER.CSV to see the Excel file created from Bellwether Garden Supply's customer list. Close the window.
4. Double-click CUSTOMER.txt to see the text file.
5. Exit the Notepad window and File Explorer. If the CUSTOMER.txt file is open in Microsoft Word, close it. Close MS Word.

IMPORTING

Importing data from another accounting, database, or spreadsheet program into Sage 50 works similarly to exporting. Any information that is entered in Sage 50 during setup and maintenance can be imported.

In Sage 50, the Maintain windows allow you to perform tasks associated with lists, such as the Customer List, Employee List, Chart of Accounts, etc. The Tasks windows allow you to perform tasks that consist of journalizing various kinds of transactions. When you import data, it is important to know that Sage 50 permits the importing of new transactions, for example, the information entered within the Tasks windows. Once transactions are imported they cannot be edited. In the example that follows, you are going to copy Bellwether Garden Supply's chart of accounts to another company. To start this process, you export the chart of accounts list first, then import the chart into a newly set up company.

Import a Chart of Accounts

To import the chart of accounts from Bellwether Garden Supply to another company, do the following.

1. If necessary start Sage 50 and open Bellwether Garden Supply. From the File menu > Select Import/Export > General Ledger. The Chart of Accounts Lists is the default.

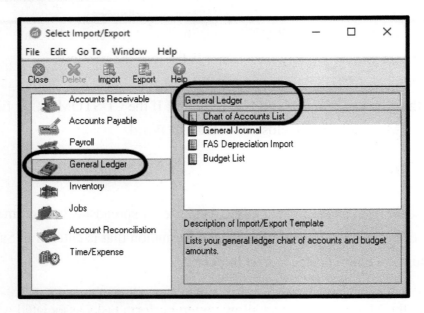

2. Click [Export]. The Chart of Accounts List window appears. Select the Options tab. Observe the default location for the CHART.CSV file. The file

will be imported from the default location. The default location is
C:\Users\[computer name]\Documents\ CHART.CSV.

3. Click [Save]. In the Template Name field, type **Chart**.

4. Click [Save]. The Chart window appears. Observe the location where
the CHART.CSV file is stored. Substitute the X's for your computer name.

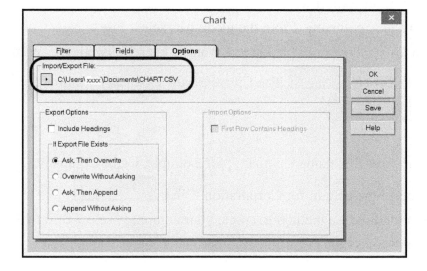

5. Click [OK]. The Select/Import Export window shows the custom
version of the Chart.

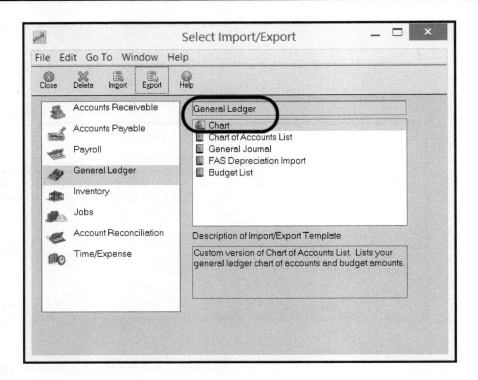

6. If a screen prompts, do you want to overwrite the file, click <No>. Close the Select Import/Export window.

7. Set up a new company. From the menu bar, select File > New Company. When the window prompts, do you want to keep Bellwether Garden Supply open, select [No]. The Create a New Company window appears. Click [Next >]

   a. Use your first name Company; for example, Carol Company.

   b. Accept the default for Corporation. Click [Next >].

   c. On the Select a method to create your company, select Build your own chart of accounts.

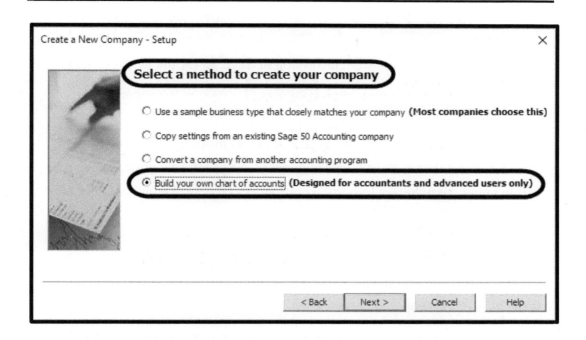

d. Click Next > until the Choose the first period of your fiscal   year window appears. Select January 2019.

e. Click 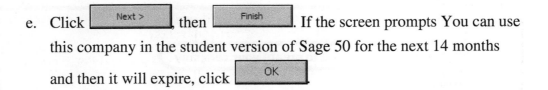, then . If the screen prompts You can use this company in the student version of Sage 50 for the next 14 months and then it will expire, click OK .

8. If necessary, close the Setup Guide and the Sage Advisor Getting Started. The title bar shows Your Name Company - Sage 50 Accounting. From the File menu, click Select Import/Export. Select General Ledger > Chart of Accounts List > Import .

9. On the Chart of Accounts List window, select Options. Observe that the file name location is the same as the illustration on page 653, step 4. (Substitute the x's for your computer name.)

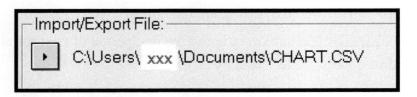

10. Click OK . When the screen prompts You should make a backup before attempting to import. Would you like to continue?, click Yes . Close the Select Import/Export window.

11. Display your Chart of Accounts (Reports & Forms > General Ledger > Chart of Accounts). Your company shows the same chart of accounts as Bellwether Garden Supply. A partial chart of accounts is shown below. The month on your chart of accounts will differ from the one shown. The month defaults to the period when the company was set up.

In this chapter, you exported and imported data. To learn more about these features, use Sage 50's Help feature. Exit Sage 50, or continue.

Carol Company
Chart of Accounts
As of Dec 31, 2019

Filter Criteria includes: Report order is by ID. Report is printed with Accounts having Zero Amounts and in Detail Format.

Account ID	Account Description	Active?	Account Type
10000	Petty Cash	Yes	Cash
10100	Cash on Hand	Yes	Cash
10200	Regular Checking Account	Yes	Cash
10300	Payroll Checking Account	Yes	Cash
10400	Savings Account	Yes	Cash
10500	Money Market Fund	Yes	Cash
11000	Accounts Receivable	Yes	Accounts Receivable
11100	Contracts Receivable	Yes	Accounts Receivable
11400	Other Receivables	Yes	Accounts Receivable
11500	Allowance for Doubtful Account	Yes	Accounts Receivable
12000	Inventory	Yes	Inventory
14000	Prepaid Expenses	Yes	Other Current Assets
14100	Employee Advances	Yes	Other Current Assets
14200	Notes Receivable-Current	Yes	Other Current Assets
14700	Other Current Assets	Yes	Other Current Assets
15000	Furniture and Fixtures	Yes	Fixed Assets
15100	Equipment	Yes	Fixed Assets
15200	Vehicles	Yes	Fixed Assets
15300	Other Depreciable Property	Yes	Fixed Assets
15400	Leasehold Improvements	Yes	Fixed Assets
15500	Buildings	Yes	Fixed Assets
15600	Building Improvements	Yes	Fixed Assets
16900	Land	Yes	Fixed Assets
17000	Accum. Depreciation-Furniture	Yes	Accumulated Depreciation
17100	Accum. Depreciation-Equipment	Yes	Accumulated Depreciation
17200	Accum. Depreciation-Vehicles	Yes	Accumulated Depreciation
17300	Accum. Depreciation-Other	Yes	Accumulated Depreciation
17400	Accum. Depreciation-Leasehold	Yes	Accumulated Depreciation
17500	Accum. Depreciation-Buildings	Yes	Accumulated Depreciation
17600	Accum. Depreciation-Bldg Imp	Yes	Accumulated Depreciation
19000	Deposits	Yes	Other Assets
19100	Organization Costs	Yes	Other Assets
19150	Accum Amortiz - Organiz Costs	Yes	Other Assets
19200	Notes Receivable- Noncurrent	Yes	Other Assets
19900	Other Noncurrent Assets	Yes	Other Assets
20000	Accounts Payable	Yes	Accounts Payable

ONLINE LEARNING CENTER

Complete end-of-chapter activities at www.mhhe.com/yacht2019 > Student Edition > Chapter 17.

1. Quizzes: Multiple Choice and True False questions. Interactive online tests that are graded and can be emailed to your instructor.

2. More Resources:

    a.   QA Templates: Answer 10 multiple-choice questions and one Analysis Question.

    b.   Narrated PowerPoints: Listen to the narrated PowerPoints.

    c.   Going to the Net Exercises: Access the Sage Knowledgebase.

    d.   Assessment Rubric: Complete the rubric to review Sage 50's journals, navigation centers, modules, task windows, and reports.

➢ Information Center > Sage Advisor Videos.

The OLC also includes links to the Appendixes:

- Appendix A: Troubleshooting (textbook and OLC)
- Appendix C: Review of Accounting Principles (OLC Student Edition)
- Appendix D: Glossary (OLC Student Edition)

Exercise 17-1: Follow the instructions below to complete Exercise 17-1.

1. Print your company's Chart of Accounts.
2. Save the Chart of Accounts as a PDF file, and export it to Excel. Use the file name **Exercise 17-1_Chart of Accounts**.

Exercise 17-2: Follow the instructions below to complete Exercise 17-2.

1. Backup. The suggested file name is **Exercise 17-2.ptb**.
2. Exit Sage 50.

CHAPTER 17 INDEX

Chapter

18 Microsoft Word and Templates

LEARNING OBJECTIVES

1. Copy Sage 50 report data to Microsoft Word.
2. Use the write letters feature.
3. Edit and save letter templates.
4. Save Word files.
5. Extract the PAWMail.zip folder.
6. Save five Word files.

Sage 50's write letters feature allows you to send information to a large number of people quickly. For example, you can send personally addressed letters to all the company's customers. The Tasks menu and the Select a Report or Forms window include a selection for write letters. Use Sage 50's write letters feature to create mailings or e-mail messages from existing or custom letter templates. A *template* is a document pattern or part of a document that is stored so that it can be used again.

You can create mailings such as newsletters, collection letters, individual letters, e-mail messages, and other types of mailings. Sage 50 integrates with Microsoft Word's mail merge feature, using Word to edit and create custom templates, then generates mailings using selected Sage 50 information.

GETTING STARTED

1. Start Sage 50. Open Bellwether Garden Supply. (*Hint:* If another company opens, select File > Open Previous Company > Bellwether Garden Supply – Student Name. Open one company.)

2. If necessary, restore the Exercise 6-2 file. This backup was made on page
    202.

> **Comment:** If you no longer have your Exercise 6-2 back up file, use starting data for
> Bellwether Garden Supply. Refer to pages 27-31, Using Sage 50's Restore Wizard, to restore
> Bellwether's starting data.

COPYING SAGE 50 REPORT DATA TO MICROSOFT WORD

A displayed report or financial statement can be copied to the Windows
clipboard. Then you can paste that data into other applications, such as Microsoft
Word or another word processing program. The steps that follow show you how
to copy and paste a report using Microsoft Word.

1. If necessary start Sage. Open the sample company, Bellwether Garden
    Supply.
2. From Bellwether's menu bar, select Reports & Forms > Financial
    Statements > <Standard> Retained Earnings > [Display]. The Statement of
    Retained Earnings displays.
3. Click [Options]. Uncheck Print Page Numbers and Show Zero Amounts >
    [OK]
4. From the menu bar, select Edit > Copy.
5. Start Microsoft Word or other word processing program. Click Paste. Or,
    right-click on the document, left-click Paste. Bellwether's statement of
    retained earnings appears. You need to format the statement in order for it
    to look like the one shown on the next page. (These account balances reflect
    data from the Exercise 6-2.ptb backup file. If you restored a different
    backup file, your account balances will differ.)

Bellwether Garden Supply - Student Name

Statement of Retained Earnings

For the Three Months Ending March 31, 2019

Beginning Retained Earnings	$	189,037.60
Adjustments To Date		0.00
Net Income		25,579.22
Subtotal		214,616.82
Ending Retained Earnings	$	214,616.82

For Management Purposes Only

The copied file was formatted with Microsoft Word.

6. Save As. In the Save in field, select the appropriate drive. Accept the file name Bellwether Garden Supply.docx. Observe that the File as type field shows Word Document (*.docx). (Some templates add the extension .doc.)

7. Click Save.

8. Exit Word.

9. Close all Sage 50 windows.

CREATE A MAILING TO CUSTOMERS

Follow these steps to use one of Sage 50's Write Letters templates.

1. From the Tasks menu, select Write Letters > Customer Letters.

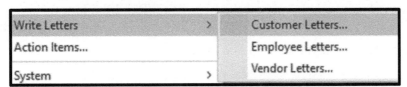

2. The Select a Report or Form window appears. Observe that the Form Types list shows Customer Labels and Letters highlighted. Select Bellwether Sales Special. The Description field shows 2nd Qtr Sales Promotion letter.

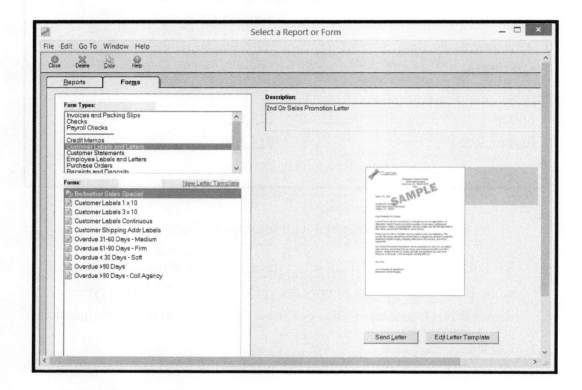

3. Click Send Letter. The Write Letters - Bellwether Sales Special window appears. Observe there are two tabs: Select Recipients and E-mail Options. Select Recipients is the default.

4. Click Word. Wait a few moments for the first customer letter to appear. Observe that the taskbar shows Page 1 of 34 – PAGE 1 OF 34. This means there are 34 customer letters. The Aldred Builders, Inc. letter is shown on your screen and on the next page. Read the letter.

GARDEN SUPPLY
1505 Pavilion Place
Norcross, GA 30093-3203
770-724-4000

BUY ONE ITEM GET THE 2nd ITEM 50% OFF PROMOTION!!!

Aldred Builders, Inc.
412 Sever Rd
Norcross, GA 30092

Dear Tony Aldred:

As one of our loyal customers, we would like to *thank you* by extending you a *special offer*. Buy any item in our catalog at the regular price and receive any 2nd item (at an equal or lesser value) for *50%* off.

This offer is also good for purchases made online!! Check us out on the web at **www.sage50accounting.com.**

Again, thank you for your continued business.

Regards,

Derrick P. Gross
Sales Representative

Go to pages 2, 3, etc. Observe that each customer receives an individually addressed letter.

5. Save the letter. The suggested filename is **Customer Letters**. If the screen prompts, You are about to save your document to one of the new file formats, click OK.

6. Close the document.

7. If necessary, go to the taskbar. Select the Sage icon and Select and Report or Form.

EDIT LETTER TEMPLATES

Follow these steps to create a letter template from the promotion letter shown on page 665.

1. From the Select a Report window, make sure Bellwether Sales Special is selected. (If necessary, select Tasks > Write Letters > Customers Letters.)

2. Click Edit Letter Template . The Edit Letter Template – Bellwether Sales Special window appears. Observe that the Letter Template Description shows 2nd Qtr Sales Promotion Letter. Compare your Edit Letter Template window with the one shown below.

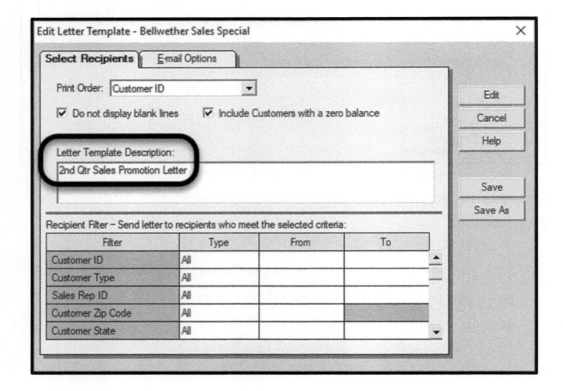

3. Review the information on the Edit Template window. Click [Edit].
   The letter appears with fields identified.

You can use this letter as a template or model to create a similar letter.
Observe that the information in the letter is the same as the customer letter
shown on page 665, *except* for the customizable information—
<<Company_Address_Line_1>>, etc.

4. To add a date to the letter, click on a line or two above

   <<Customer_Name>>. Select Date & Time [Date & Time] from
   Word's Insert selections. Select the appropriate format and the date is
   inserted.

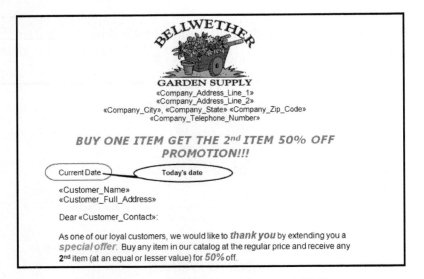

5. Select Save As. If you are using Microsoft Word 2013, your screen shows a CUSTOMER Current folder. If you open that folder, a list of letter templates appears. (*Hint:* If you do <u>not</u> see the list of customer letter templates, you may need to extract the PAWMail.zip folder. Unzipping or extracting the PAWMail.zip folder is shown on pages 669-670.)

6. To save to a USB location, select it. Accept the default file name Bellwether Sales Special.doc. (*Hint:* Sage 50's letter templates default to .doc files.) Insert your USB flash drive. Select the appropriate drive letter. Click .

PAWMail.Zip FOLDER

The letter templates are included on drive C within the Sage folder. Follow these instructions to see all the letters.

1. Open File Explorer.
2. Go to C:\Sage\Peachtree\Company\Letters.
3. Copy the PAWMail.zip folder to the desktop.
4. Extract the files. (Right-click on the PAWMail.Zip folder. Left-click Extract All. Click Extract.) Open the templates from these folders: Customer; Employee; Vendor.

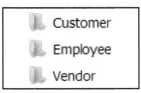

a. The Customer folder includes these documents.

Name	Type
Account Info Verification.doc	Microsoft Word 97 - 2003 Document
Collection Letter 1.doc	Microsoft Word 97 - 2003 Document
Collection Letter 2.doc	Microsoft Word 97 - 2003 Document
Collection Letter 3.doc	Microsoft Word 97 - 2003 Document
Contract Transmittal Letter.doc	Microsoft Word 97 - 2003 Document
Delivery Attempt Notification.doc	Microsoft Word 97 - 2003 Document
Detail Collection Letter.doc	Microsoft Word 97 - 2003 Document
Donation Receipt.doc	Microsoft Word 97 - 2003 Document
Fundraising Letter.doc	Microsoft Word 97 - 2003 Document
Member Fees Outstanding.doc	Microsoft Word 97 - 2003 Document
New Customer Welcome.doc	Microsoft Word 97 - 2003 Document
Pledges Outstanding.doc	Microsoft Word 97 - 2003 Document
Proposal Transmittal Letter.doc	Microsoft Word 97 - 2003 Document
Prospect Discount Offer.doc	Microsoft Word 97 - 2003 Document
Sales Reminder.doc	Microsoft Word 97 - 2003 Document
Sales Special.doc	Microsoft Word 97 - 2003 Document

b. The Employee folder includes the Employee Welcome.doc file.

c. The Vendor folder includes two documents: Disputed Charge.doc and Request Credit Increase.doc.

5. Observe that the letters end in a .doc extension which means that the Sage 50 templates were saved as Word 97-2003 files. Open the Vendor folder. Double-click the Request Credit Increase.doc.

«Company_Name»
«Company_Full_Address»

«Todays_Date_Long»

«Vendor_Name»
«Vendor_Full_Address»

Re: Request for increase in credit limit

Dear «Vendor_Contact»:

«Company_Name» has enjoyed doing business with your company for the past twelve months. We are very happy with your product, and are looking forward to a continued business relationship. After reviewing the past year's records, I would like you to consider increasing our credit limit. An increase of available credit in the amount of $500.00 should suffice.

Thank you for your consideration in this matter. If you have any questions, please feel free to contact me at my direct extension.

Sincerely,

Office Manager
«Company_Name»

6. Close the Request for increase in credit limit letter.

7. To see the Customer Templates, go to your desktop and open the Customers folder.

8. Double-click Contract Transmittal Letter.

«Company_Name»
«Company_Full_Address»

«Todays_Date_Long»

«Customer_Contact»
«Customer_Name»
«Customer_Full_Address»

Dear «Customer_Contact»:

Enclosed are two copies of the contract. If it meets with your approval, please sign both copies and return one in the enclosed, preaddressed envelope.

Please do not hesitate to contact me should you have any questions or concerns.

We at «Company_Name» are pleased to come to this agreement and look forward to working with you.

Sincerely,

«Customer_Sales_Rep_Name»
«Company_Name»
«Company_Telephone_Number»
«Company_Full_Address»

9. Look at some of the other templates.

10. Exit Word without saving documents.

11. If necessary, maximize Sage 50. Close all windows.

12. Exit Sage 50.

ONLINE LEARNING CENTER

Complete end-of-chapter activities at www.mhhe.com/yacht2019 > Student Edition > Chapter 18.

1. Quizzes: Multiple Choice and True False questions. Interactive online tests that are graded and can be emailed to your instructor.
2. More Resources:

    a. QA Templates: Answer 10 short-answer questions and two Analysis Questions.
    b. Narrated PowerPoints: Listen to the narrated PowerPoints.
    c. Going to the Net Exercises: Access the Sage Advice blog.
    d. Assessment Rubric: Complete the rubric to review Sage 50's journals, navigation centers, modules, task windows, and reports.

➤ Information Center > Sage Advisor Videos.

The OLC also includes links to the Appendixes:

*   Appendix A: Troubleshooting (textbook and OLC)
*   Appendix C: Review of Accounting Principles (OLC Student Edition)
*   Appendix D: Glossary (OLC Student Edition)

Exercise 18-1: Follow the instructions below to complete Exercise 18-1.

1. Print the sales promotion letter to Chapple Law Offices. Use March 15, 2019 as the date. (*Hint:* Use the Bellwether Special letter template. Send a letter to Chapple Law Office.)
2. Save the file as Exercise 18-1.

Exercise 18-2: Follow the instructions below to complete Exercise 18-2.

1. Print a sales promotion letter to Cummings Construction. (Use the current date.)
2. Save the file as Exercise 18-2.

CHAPTER 18 INDEX

Project

3 Evanston Computer Club

In Project 3, you complete the computer accounting cycle for the Evanston Computer Club which is located in Evanston, Illinois. The computer club is a nonprofit business organized as a corporation. Because the Evanston Computer Club is a nonprofit business, observe that there are some differences in its Chart of Accounts and some of its transactions. For example, revenues are derived from membership fees and seminars. Club members also contribute computers to local schools. This project demonstrates how these transactions are handled.

The club sponsors a trip to the Consumer Electronics Show (CES), a trade show in Las Vegas, Nevada. The trip involves expenses for bus rental, motel rooms, meals, and entrance fees to the trade show. Since so many club members attend CES, a special rate is offered to them.

In this project, you complete the accounting cycle for the month of January 2019. Evanston Computer Club's Balance Sheet, transaction register, and bank statement are provided as source documents. At the end of Project 3, a checklist is shown listing the reports that you should have. The step-by-step instructions also remind you when to print. Your instructor may ask you to turn in these reports for grading purposes. Remember to make backups at periodic intervals.

Follow these steps to complete Project 3, Evanston Computer Club:

Step 1:   Start Sage 50.
Step 2:   Make the selections to create a new company.

Step   3:   The company information for Evanston Computer Club is:

Company Name:	Evanston Computer Club (your first and last name)
Address Line 1:	6201 North First Street
City, State, Zip:	Evanston, IL 60202
Country:	USA
Phone:	224-555-5030
Fax:	224-555-9212
Business Type:	Corporation
Federal Employer ID:	28-3422118
State Employer ID:	54-4138921
State Unemployment ID:	541200-7
Web Site:	www.evanstoncomputerclub.com
E-mail:	info@evanstoncomputerclub.com

Step   4:   Accept the default to Use a sample business that closely matches your company.

Step   5:   Select Non-Profit Organizations. (*Hint:* Scroll down the Detailed types list. Chart of Account numbers have five digits.)

Step   6:   Accept the default for Accrual accounting and Real Time posting.

Step   7:   Accept the default for Choose an accounting period structure, 12 monthly accounting periods per year.

Step   8:   The Choose the first period of your fiscal year window appears. If necessary, select January 2019.

Step   9:   At the You are ready to create your company window, click
Finish . If the screen prompts You can use this company in the student version of Sage 50 for the next 14 months and then it will expire, click OK . If necessary, close the Setup Guide and Sage Advisor Getting Started windows.

Step   10:   Change the accounting period to Period 1 – 01/01/19 to 01/31/19.

Step   11:   Delete, add, and change the following General Ledger accounts in the Chart of Accounts.

Delete these accounts:

10000   Petty Cash

10100   Cash on Hand

10300   Payroll Checking Account

10500   Special Account

10600   Cash-Restricted Fund

10700   Investments

11400   Other Receivables

11500   Allowance for Doubtful Account

12100   Inventory-Kitchen

12150   Inventory-Golf & Tennis

12200   Inventory-Snack Stand

14100   Employee Advances

14700   Other Current Assets

15200   Automobiles

15300   Other Depreciable Property

15400   Leasehold Improvements

15500   Building

15600   Building Improvements

16900   Land

17200   Accum. Depreciation-Automobi

17300   Accum. Depreciation-Other

17400   Accum. Depreciation-Leasehol

17500   Accum. Depreciation-Building

17600   Accum. Depreciation-Bldg Imp

19000   Deposits

19150   Accum. Amortiz. - Org. Costs

19200	Note Receivable-Noncurrent
19900	Other Noncurrent Assets
23000	Accrued Expenses
23100	Sales Tax Payable
23300	Deductions Payable
23400	Federal Payroll Taxes Payable
23500	FUTA Tax Payable
23600	State Payroll Taxes Payable
23700	SUTA Payable
23800	Local Payroll Taxes Payable
24000	Other Taxes Payable
24100	Employee Benefits Payable
24200	Current Portion Long-Term Debt
24800	Other Current Liabilities
24900	Suspense-Clearing Account
27000	Notes Payable-Noncurrent
27100	Deferred Revenue
27400	Other Long-Term Liabilities
40200	Sales-Kitchen/Dining Room
40400	Sales-Golf/Tennis
40600	Sales-Snack Stand
40800	Sales-Other
41000	Contributions-Unrestricted
41200	Grants
41400	Program Service Revenue
41800	Investment Income
42000	Realized gain in Investment
42200	Miscellaneous Income
42400	Contributions-Restricted
42600	Investment Income-Restricted

43000 Other Income

48000 Fee Refunds

58000 Cost of Sales-Other

59000 Purchase Returns and Allowance

60000 Default Purchase Expense

60100 Grant and Allocation Exp.

61500 Bad Debt Expense

65000 Employee Benefit Programs Exp

65500 Other Employee Benefits

72000 Payroll Tax Expense

76500 Compensation of Officers

77000 Salaries Expense

89000 Other Expense

Change these accounts:

10200	Regular Checking Account	Ninth Street Bank
12000	Inventory-Bar	Inventory-Computers/Schools
14000	Prepaid Expenses	Prepaid Rent
15100	Equipment	Computer Equipment
17000	Accum. Depreciation-Furnitur	Accum. Depreciation-Furn&Fix
17100	Accum. Depreciation-Eq.	Accum. Depreciation-Comp
20000	Accounts Payable	Credit Card Payable
40000	Sales-Bar	Fees-Seminars/Classes
66000	Supplies Expense	Office Supplies Expense
67500	Occupancy Expense	Rent Expense
70000	Travel Expense	Bus Rental-CES
72500	Depreciation Expense	Depr. Exp.-Furniture & Fixture

Add these accounts:

39002	Membership Contributions	Equity-doesn't close
60000	Advertising Expense	Expenses
60400	Bank Service Charge	Expenses
70010	Meals-CES	Expenses
70020	Motel-CES	Expenses
70030	Fees-CES	Expenses
72520	Depr. Exp.-Comp Equip	Expenses

Step 12: Back up. The suggested file name is **Evanston Computer Club Chart of Accounts.ptb**.

Step 13: Use the Evanston Computer Club Balance Sheet to record the chart of accounts beginning balances.

Evanston Computer Club Balance Sheet, January 1, 2019		
ASSETS		
Current Assets		
Ninth Street Bank	$23,250.00	
Inventory-Computers/Schools	500.00	
Inventory-Office	1,500.00	
Total Current Assets		$25,250.00
Property and Equipment		
Furniture and Fixtures	1,500.00	
Computer Equipment	3,000.00	
Total Property and Equipment		4,500.00
Total Assets		$29,750.00

LIABILITIES		
Credit Card Payable	250.00	
Total Liabilities		250.00
CAPITAL		
Retained Earnings		29,500.00
Total Liabilities and Capital		$29,750.00

Step 14:   Back up your data. The suggested file name is **Evanston Computer Club Starting Balance Sheet.ptb**. To check that your beginning balances are entered correctly, display the December 31, 2018 balance sheet.

Step 15:   The transaction register provides you with the information necessary for Evanston Computer Club's Cash Receipts Journal and Cash Disbursements Journal entries for January. The Evanston Computer Club issues checks and makes deposits to Ninth Street Bank.

Evanston Computer Club, Transaction Register					
Ck. No.	**Date**	**Description of Transaction**	**Payment**	**Deposit**	**Balance**
	12/31/18				23,250.00
	1/4/19	Deposit (membership dues)[1]		2,850.00	26,100.00
8001	1/11/19	Payment - Credit Card	250.00		25,850.00
8002	1/11/19	Moore Advertising	205.00		25,645.00
8003	1/11/19	365 Office Supplies	155.65		25,489.35
8004	1/18/19	Meals-CES	800.00		24,689.35

[1]For each deposit shown on the transaction register, type the date of the transaction in the Deposit ticket ID field. For each check, use Banking > Write Checks.

8005	1/18/19	Bus Rental-CES	600.00		24,089.35
8006	1/18/19	Entrance Fees-CES	725.00		23,364.35
8007	1/18/19	Motel Rooms-CES	835.27		22,529.08
8008	1/26/19	MIL Telephone	41.76		22,487.32
8009	1/26/19	Shipping Charges	45.00		22,442.32
	1/29/19	Deposit (seminar fees)		800.00	23,242.32

Step 16: *Additional journal entry*: On January 31, a club member donated a computer system and printer to the club. The value of the computer and printer is $250. (Debit, Inventory - Computers/Schools; Credit, Membership Contributions. Use the General Journal for this entry.)

Step 17: Evanston Computer Club's bank statement is shown below. Complete the Account Reconciliation for the Ninth Street Bank.

Statement of Account Ninth Street Bank Jan. 1 to Jan. 31, 2019		Account No. 312-88741	Evanston Computer Club 6201 North Frist Street Evanston, IL 60202	
REGULAR CHECKING				
Previous Balance	12/31/17	$ 23,250.00		
2 Deposits(+)		3,650.00		
7 Checks (-)		2,887.68		
Service Charges (-)		12.00		
Ending Balance	1/31/19	**$ 24,000.32**		
DEPOSITS				
	1/5/19	2,850.00	1/29/19	800.00
CHECKS (Asterisk * indicates break in check number sequence)				
	1/14/19	8001	250.00	
	1/14/19	8002	205.00	

	1/18/19	8003	155.65	
	1/26/19	8004	800.00	
	1/28/19	8005*	600.00	
	1/29/19	8007	835.27	
	1/29/19	8008	41.76	

Step 18:   Make a backup. The suggested file name is **Evanston Computer Club January.ptb**.

Step 19:   Export these reports to Excel and save as PDF files: Chart of Accounts, Cash Receipts Journal, Cash Disbursements Journal, General Ledger Trial Balance, Balance Sheet, Income Statement, Statement of Cash Flow, Statement of Retained Earnings. Use the file name **Evanston Computer Club_CofA_CRJ_CDJ_GLTB_BS_ IS_ SCF_SRE.xlsx**.

Checklist of Printouts, Project 3: Evanston Computer Club		
1		Chart of Accounts
2		December 31, 2018 Starting Balance Sheet
3		Account Reconciliation
4		Account Register – Ninth Street Bank
5		Cash Disbursements Journal
6		Cash Receipts Journal
7		General Journal
8		General Ledger Trial Balance
9		General Ledger
10		Balance Sheet
11		Income Statement
12		Statement of Cash Flow
13		Statement of Retained Earnings

Student Name_____**Date**_____

CHECK YOUR PROGRESS: PROJECT 3
EVANSTON COMPUTER CLUB

1. What are the total debit and credit balances on your
   general ledger trial balance?   _____

2. What is the total amount of checks outstanding?   _____

3. How much are the total expenses on January 31?   _____

4. How much are the total revenues on January 31?   _____

5. How much is the net income (net loss) on January 31?   _____

6. What is the account balance in the Membership
   Contributions account on January 31?   _____

7. What are the total assets on January 31?   _____

8. What is the ending retained earnings on
   January 31, 2019?   _____

9. What is the balance in the Credit Card Payable
   account on January 31?   _____

10. What is the balance in the Office Supplies Expense
    account on January 31?   _____

11. Is there an Increase or Decrease in cash for the
    month of January?   _____

12. Was any Credit Card Payable incurred during the
    month of January? (Circle your answer)   YES   NO

Project

4 | CL Manufacturing, Inc.

In Project 4, you complete the computer accounting cycle for CL Manufacturing, Inc. This company manufactures backpacks, sleeping bags, and tents. CL Manufacturing, Inc. offers its customers a sales discount of 2% 15, Net 30 days. Vendors offer CL Manufacturing, Inc. a purchase discount of 1% 15, Net 30 days. Follow these steps to complete Project 4, CL Manufacturing, Inc.

Step 1: Start Sage 50.

Step 2: Make the selections to create a new company.

Step 3: Type the following company information:

Company Name:	CL Manufacturing, Inc. (*use your initials*)
Address Line 1:	1341 Walnut Street
City, State, Zip:	Philadelphia, PA 19122
Country:	USA
Phone:	215-555-3411
Fax:	215-555-3413
Business Type:	Corporation
Federal Employer ID:	29-7215413
State Employer ID:	38-1348577
State Unemployment ID:	381722-4
Web Site:	www.clmftg.net
E-mail:	info@clmftg.net

Step 4: Accept the default for Use a sample business type that closely matches your company.

Step 5: Scroll down the list. In the **Detailed types** list, select Manufacturing Company. (*Hint:* The Chart of Accounts has five-digit numbers.)

Step 6: Accept the default for Accrual accounting.

Step 7: Accept the default for Real Time posting.

Step 8: Accept the default for 12 monthly accounting periods.

Step 9: The Choose the first period of your fiscal year window appears. If necessary, select January 2019 as the month and year.

Step 10: At the You are ready to create your company window, click

Finish . If the screen prompts You can use this company in the student version of Sage 50 for the next 14 months and then it will expire, click OK .

Step 11: When the Sage 50 Setup Guide window appears, click on the box next to Don't show this screen at startup to place a checkmark in it. Close the Setup Guide and Sage Advisor Getting Started windows.

Step 12: Change the accounting period to 01-Jan 01,2019 to Jan 31,2019—

Period 1:
01-01-19 - 01-31-19 .

General Ledger

1. *Delete these accounts:*

   10100   Cash on Hand

   10400   Savings Account

   10500   Special Account

   10600   Investments-Money Market

   15400   Leasehold Improvements

   16900   Land

   17300   Accum. Depreciation-Other

   17400   Accum. Depreciation-Leasehol

   24800   Other Current Liabilities

2. *Change these accounts:*

   10200   Regular Checking Account to Lincoln Bank

   10300   Payroll Checking Account to Penn Savings & Loan

   14000   Prepaid Expenses to Prepaid Insurance

15100	Equipment to Computers & Equipment
15200	Automobiles to Trucks/Autos
17100	Accum. Depreciation - Equipment to Accum. Depreciation - Comp&Eq
17200	Accum. Depreciation - Automobil to Accum. Depreciation - Trks/Aut
23300	Deductions Payable to Medicare Employee Taxes Payabl
24000	Other Taxes Payable to Soc. Sec. Employee Taxes Payab
24100	Employee Benefits Payable to Soc. Sec. Employer Taxes Payab
27000	Notes Payable-Noncurrent to Mortgage Payable
40000	Sales #1 to Sales-Backpacks
40200	Sales #2 to Sales-Sleeping Bags
40400	Sales #3 to Sales-Tents
72500	Penalties and Fines Exp to Employer FUTA Expense
73000	Other Taxes to Employer SUTA Expense

3. *Add these accounts:*

Acct. ID	Acct. Description	Account Type
12010	Inventory-Backpacks	Inventory
12020	Inventory-Sleeping Bags	Inventory
12030	Inventory-Tents	Inventory
22000	Credit Card Payable	Other Current Liabilities
23350	Medicare Employer Taxes Payabl	Other Current Liabilities
23650	Employee SUI Taxes Payable	Other Current Liabilities
51050	Overtime Costs	Cost of Sales
73200	Employer Soc. Sec. Taxes Expen	Expenses
73300	Employer Medicare Expense	Expenses

4. Back up. The suggested file name is **CL Mftg Chart of Accounts.ptb.**

5. You purchased CL Manufacturing, Inc. in December 2018. Use the Balance Sheet to record the chart of account beginning balances.

CL Manufacturing, Inc. Balance Sheet. January 1, 2019		
ASSETS		
Current Assets		
Lincoln Bank	$82,650.00	
Penn Savings & Loan	31,300.00	
Investments-Cert. of Deposit	14,500.00	
Inventory-Backpacks	1,612.50	
Inventory-Sleeping Bags	1,760.00	
Inventory-Tents	2,679.60	
Prepaid Insurance	3,600.00	
Total Current Assets		$138,102.10
Property and Equipment		
Furniture and Fixtures	2,500.00	
Computers & Equipment	6,000.00	
Trucks/Autos	25,000.00	
Building	105,000.00	
Total Property and Equipment		138,500.00
Total Assets		$276,602.10
LIABILITIES AND STOCKHOLDER'S EQUITY		
Credit Card Payable	15,900.00	
Mortgage Payable	97,500.00	
Total Liabilities		$113,400.00
Stockholder's Equity: Common Stock		163,202.10
Total Liabilities and Stockholder's Equity		$276,602.10

6. Backup. The suggested filename is **CL Mftg Starting Balance Sheet.ptb**. Display the December 31, 2018 balance sheet

Accounts Payable

1. Set up the following vendor defaults.

Standard Terms:	Due in number of days
Net due in:	30 days
Discount in:	15 days
Discount %:	1.00
Credit Limit:	20,000.00

GL Link Accounts:

Expense Account:	12010 Inventory-Backpacks
Discount GL Account:	59500 Purchase Discounts

2. Set up the following vendors.

Vendor ID:	dd22
Name:	Davis Dash Fabrics
Contact:	Davis Dash
Mailing Address:	2511 Brickell Avenue
City, ST, Zip:	Hartford, CT 06109
Vendor Type:	slpg bgs
1099 Type:	Independent Contractor
Expense Account:	12020 Inventory-Sleeping Bags
Telephone 1:	860-555-9800
Fax:	860-555-9802
E-mail:	davis@ddfabrics.com
Web Site:	www.ddfabrics.com
Purchase Info:	
Tax ID Number:	12-5573322

Vendor ID:	ep33
Name:	Evans Products
Contact:	Diane Evans
Mailing Address:	4103 North Riverside
City, ST, Zip:	Cleveland, OH 44191
Vendor Type:	tents
1099 Type:	Independent Contractor
Expense Account:	12030 Inventory-Tents
Telephone 1:	216-555-2113
Fax:	216-555-3001
E-mail:	diane@evansproducts.com
Web Site:	www.evansproducts.com

Purchase Info:

Tax ID Number:	05-1991234

Vendor ID:	rk44
Name:	RK Supplies
Contact:	Rosalyn Kalmar
Mailing Address:	944 City Line
City, ST, Zip:	Trenton, NJ 07092
Vendor Type:	backpack
1099 Type:	Independent Contractor
Expense Accounting:	12010 Inventory-Backpacks
Telephone 1:	609-555-9967
Fax:	609-555-7702
E-mail:	info@rksupplies.net
Web Site:	www.rksupplies.net

Purchase Info:

Tax ID Number:	45-2448313

Accounts Receivable

1. Set up the following customer default settings:

Standard Terms:	Due in number of days
Net due in:	30 days
Discount in:	15 days
Discount Percent:	2.00
Credit Limit:	$15,000.00
GL Sales Account:	40000 Sales-Backpacks
Discount GL Account:	49000 Sales Discounts

2. Enter the following customer records:

Customer ID:	001BOS
Name:	Barlow Outdoor Suppliers
Billing address:	250 Southeast Avenue
City, ST, Zip:	Gainesville, FL 32652
Customer Type:	FL (for Florida)
Telephone 1:	352-555-1000
Fax:	352-555-2330
E-mail:	info@barlowoutdoor.biz
Web Site:	www.barlowoutdoor.biz

   Contacts:

Contact name:	Victor Barlow

   Sales Info:

G/L Sales Acct:	40000, Sales-Backpacks
Resale Number:	2331455-2

Customer ID:	002SCS
Name:	Suzy's Camping Store
Billing address:	4113 Havenhurst Avenue

City, ST, Zip:	Philadelphia, PA 19130
Customer type:	PA (for Pennsylvania)
Telephone 1:	215-555-1166
Fax:	215-555-1168
E-mail:	suzy@campingstore.biz
Web Site	www.campingstore.biz

Contacts:

Contact name:	Suzy Stricker

Sales Info:

G/L Sales Acct:	40200, Sales-Sleeping Bags
Resale Number:	9383277-3

Customer ID:	003WST
Name:	West's Store
Billing address:	4591 Hillside Road
City, ST, Zip:	Cincinnati, OH 45227
Customer type:	OH (for Ohio)
Telephone 1:	513-555-2001
Fax:	513-555-4118
E-mail:	janice@weststore.com
Web Site:	www.weststore.com

Contacts:

Contact name:	Janice West

Sales Info:

G/L Sales Acct:	40400, Sales-Tents
Resale Number:	9448812-2

Payroll

1. Use the following information for the Payroll Setup Wizard.

State: PA

State Unemployment Rate: **3.4**

Hourly Pay Type: Regular, Select
51000 - Direct Labor Costs

Overtime: Select 51050 -
Overtime Costs

Salary Pay Type: Select 77000 -
Salaries Expense

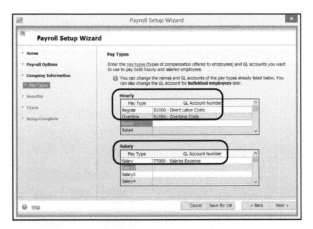

Do you have any localities for which you collect taxes in the state of PA?
Yes

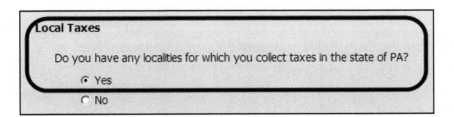

Locality: **Phila**

Tax rate: **1.0**

2. Set up these employee defaults.
    Use the Employee Fields
    information shown below.

    Field Name   *G/L Account*

    Fed_Income   Account No. 23400, Federal Payroll Taxes Payable
    Soc_Sec   Account No. 24000, Soc. Sec. Employee Taxes Payable
    MEDICARE   Account No. 23300, Medicare Employee Taxes Payable
    St_Income   Account No. 23600, State Payroll Taxes Payable

Loc_Income	Account No. 23800, Local Payroll Taxes Payable
St_Unemp	Account No. 23650, Employee SUI Taxes Payable

3. Use the Company Fields shown below.

Field Name	*Liability column*	*Expense column*
Soc_Sec_C	24100, Soc. Sec. Employer Taxes Payable	73200, Employer Soc. Sec. Taxes Expense
Medicare_C	23350 Medicare Employer Taxes Payable	73300, Employer Medicare Expense
Fed_Unemp_C	23500, FUTA Tax Payable	72500, Employer FUTA Expense
St_Unemp_C	23700, SUTA Payable	73000, Employer SUTA Expense

4. Complete the Payroll Setup Wizard's Taxes and Assign Tax Fields.

5. Add the following employees.

Employee ID:	EK40
Name:	Emily Keller
Accept the default for Employee	
Address:	23981 Arch Street
City, ST, Zip:	Upper Darby, PA 19110
E-mail:	emily@mail.net
Home phone:	215-555-7682
Social Security #:	000-01-2000
Type:	FULL

Pay Info:
Salary, $1,500. Ms. Keller is paid monthly.

Withholding Info:

Filing Status:	Single for Federal, State, and Local
Allowances:	1 for Federal, State and Local

Employee ID: JS50

Name: Jackie Sutton

Accept the default for Employee

Address: 34587 Bainbridge Street

City, ST, Zip: Philadelphia, PA 19191

E-mail: jackie@mail.net

Home phone: 215-555-3203

Social Security #: 003-00-0001

Type: FULL

Pay Info: Hourly, $13.00 per hour; Overtime, $19.50. Ms. Sutton is paid weekly.

Withholding Info:

Filing Status: Married for Federal, State, and Local

Allowances: 2 for Federal, State and Local

Employee ID: LS60

Name: Les Sanchez

Accept the default for Employee

Address: 15 Orange Street

City, ST, Zip: Philadelphia, PA 19122

E-mail: les@mail.net

Home phone: 215-555-2199

Social Security #: 000-01-0001

Type: FULL

Pay Info: Hourly, $13.00 per hour; Overtime, $19.50. Mr. Sanchez is paid weekly.

Withholding Info:

Filing Status: Married for Federal, State, and Local

Allowances: 2 for Federal, State and Local

Employee ID:	OW70
Name:	Oliver Warner
Accept the default for Employee	
Address:	4600 West Mill Road, Apt. 3C
City, ST, Zip:	Philadelphia, PA 19131
E-mail:	oliver@mail.net
Home phone	215-555-0302
Social Security #:	000-00-7000
Type:	FULL

Pay Info: Hourly, $13.00 per hour; Overtime, $19.50. Mr. Warner is paid weekly.

Withholding Info:

Filing Status:	Married for Federal, State, and Local
Allowances:	2 for Federal, State and Local

Inventory

1. Set up inventory defaults. On the General Tab, select Stock item as the Default Item Class.
2. Make sure that FIFO is the default inventory costing method.
3. Set up the following inventory items:

Item ID:	backpacks
Description:	backpacks
Item Class:	Stock item
Description for Sales:	backpacks
Price Level 1:	150.00
Last Unit Cost:	37.50
Cost Method:	FIFO
GL Sales Acct:	40000 Sales-Backpacks
GL Inventory Acct:	12010, Inventory-Backpacks

GL Cost of Sales Acct: 50500, Raw Material Purchases

Item Tax Type: 2 Exempt

Item Type: backpack

Stocking U/M: each

Minimum Stock: 10

Reorder Quantity: 5

Preferred Vendor ID: rk44, RK Supplies

Beginning Balances: backpacks

   Quantity: 43.00

   Unit Cost: 37.50

   Total Cost: 1,612.50

Item ID: sleeping bags

Description: sleeping bags

Item Class: Stock item

Description for Sales: sleeping bags

Price Level 1:   105.00

Last Unit Cost: 27.50

Cost Method: FIFO

GL Sales Acct: 40200, Sales-Sleeping Bags

GL Inventory Acct: 12020, Inventory-Sleeping Bags

GL Cost of Sales Acct: 50500, Raw Material Purchases

Item Tax Type: 2 Exempt

Item Type: slpg bgs

Stocking U/M: each

Minimum Stock: 10

Reorder Quantity: 5

Preferred Vendor ID: dd22, Davis Dash Fabrics

Beginning Balances: sleeping bags

Quantity: 64.00

Last Unit Cost	27.50
Total Cost:	1,760.00

Item ID:	tents
Description:	tents
Item Class:	Stock item
Description for Sales:	tents
Price Level 1:	175.00
Last Unit Cost:	47.85
Cost Method:	FIFO
GL Sales Acct:	40400, Sales-Tents
GL Inventory Acct:	12030, Inventory-Tents
GL Cost of Sales Acct:	50500, Raw Material Purchases
Item Tax Type:	2 Exempt
Item Type:	tents
Stocking U/M:	each
Minimum Stock:	10
Reorder Quantity:	5
Preferred Vendor ID:	ep33, Evans Products
Beginning Balances:	tents
Quantity:	56.00
Unit Cost:	47.85
Total Cost:	2,679.60

Jobs

1. Set up the following job records:

Job ID:	13-221
Description:	backpacks

For Customer:	001BOS
Start Date:	1/2/19
Projected End Date:	12/31/19
Job Type:	backpack

Job ID:	14-331
Description:	sleeping bags
For Customer:	002SCS
Start Date:	1/2/19
Projected End Date:	12/31/19
Job Type:	slpg bgs

Job ID:	15-441
Description:	tents
For Customer:	003WST
Start Date:	1/2/19
Projected End Date:	12/31/19
Job Type:	tents

2. Back up. Use **CL Mftg Begin.ptb** as the filename.

3. Exit or continue.

Journalize and post the following transactions:

1/4/19   Pay the factory employees for 40 hours of direct labor. Select Account No. 10300, Penn Savings & Loan, as the Cash Account. In the Check Number field, type **101** for Ms. Sutton's paycheck. The check numbers for Mr. Sanchez and Mr. Warner are automatically completed. (Do *not* print the payroll checks.) Cick to complete the following to make the appropriate selection.

Check No.	Employee	Job	Hours
101	Jackie Sutton	15-441	40
102	Les Sanchez	14-331	40
103	Oliver Warner	13-221	40

Click ⊟ Save *after each payroll entry.*

1/5/19 Invoice No. 315 was received from Davis Dash Fabrics for 15 sleeping bags @ $27.50 each for a total of $412.50. Post invoice 315.

1/5/19 Invoice No. 45 was received from RK Supplies for 20 backpacks @ $37.50 each for a total of $750.00. Post invoice 45.

1/5/19 Invoice No. 800 was received from Evans Products for 16 tents @ $47.85 each for a total of $765.60. Post invoice 800.

1/11/19 Pay the factory employees for 40 hours of direct labor. (Refer to the information below.) *Remember to post each payroll entry.*

Check No.	Employee	Job	Hours
104	Jackie Sutton	15-441	40
105	Les Sanchez	14-331	40
106	Oliver Warner	13-221	40

1/12/19 Sold 20 backpacks on account to Barlow Outdoor Suppliers for a total of $3,000.00, Job 13-221. In the Invoice No. field, type **101**.[1] Post sales invoice 101.

1/12/19 Sold 12 sleeping bags on account to Suzy's Camping Store for a total of $1,260.00, Job 14-331. Post sales invoice 102.

_____

[1]Since you are not printing sales invoices, it is necessary to complete this field.

1/12/19	Sold 20 tents on account to West's Store for a total of $3,500.00, Job 15-441. Post sales invoice 103.
1/15/19	Issued Check No. 1001 to RK Supplies in payment of purchase Invoice No. 45. Select Account No. 10200, Lincoln Bank as the cash account. In the Check/Reference No. field, type **1001**. Do *not* print vendor checks. In the Discount Account field, make sure that Account No. 59500, Purchase Discounts is shown. Post Check No. 1001 in the amount of $742.50.
1/15/19	Issued Check No. 1002 to Davis Dash Fabrics in payment of purchase Invoice No. 315. Post Check No. 1002 in the amount of $408.37.
1/15/19	Issued Check No. 1003 to Evans Products in payment of purchase Invoice No. 800. Post Check No. 1003 in the amount of $757.94.
1/18/19	Pay the factory employees for 40 hours of direct labor. *Remember to click on* <u>S</u>*ave after each payroll check is recorded.*

Check No.	Employee	Job	Hours
107	Jackie Sutton	15-441	40
108	Les Sanchez	14-331	40
109	Oliver Warner	13-221	40

1/19/19	Invoice No. 328 was received from Davis Dash Fabrics for 15 sleeping bags @ $27.50 each for a total of $412.50. Post invoice 328.
1/19/19	Invoice No. 900 was received from Evans Products for 20 tents @ $47.85 each for a total of $957.00. Post invoice 900.
1/22/19	Received payment from Barlow Outdoor Suppliers for sales invoice 101. Select Account No. 10200, Lincoln Bank, as the cash account. Use the date of the transaction in the Deposit ticket ID field. In the Check/Reference No. field, type **Inv. 101**. Post this receipt in the amount of $2,940.

1/22/19	Received payment from Suzy's Camping Store for sales invoice 102. In the Check/Reference No. field, type **Inv. 102**. Post this receipt in the amount of $1,234.80.
1/22/19	Received payment from West's Store for sales invoice 103. In the Check/Reference No. field, type **Inv. 103**. Post this receipt in the amount of $3,430.
1/22/19	Sold 25 sleeping bags on account to Suzy's Camping Store for a total of $2,625.00, Job 14-331. In the Invoice No. field, type **104**. Post sales invoice 104.
1/22/19	Sold 21 tents on account to West's Store for a total of $3,675.00, Job 15-441. Post sales invoice 105.
1/25/19	Pay the factory employees for 40 hours of direct labor. *Remember to click on* Save *after each payroll check is recorded.*

Check No.	Employee	Job	Hours
110	Jackie Sutton	15-441	40
111	Les Sanchez	14-331	40
112	Oliver Warner	13-221	40

1/25/19	Pay the salaried employee, Emily Keller. In the Salary Amounts table, make sure that account 77000, Salaries Expense, is shown in the Account column. If not, select that account. Post Check No. 113.
1/29/19	Issued Check No. 1004 to Lincoln Bank for $709.23 in payment of Mortgage Payable; split the mortgage payment between principal in the amount of $584.06, and interest in the amount of $125.17. In the Check number field, type **1004**. (Use the Write Checks task and the split feature. Make sure that account 10200, Lincoln Bank, is selected as the Cash Account.) Post Check No. 1004.
1/29/19	Issued Check No. 1005 to Penn Savings & Loan for $800 in payment of Credit Card Payable. Post Check No. 1005.

1/29/19 — Issued Check No. 1006 to the Hull Power Company for $204.75 in payment of utilities. (Debit Utilities Expense, Account No. 78000.) Post Check No. 1006.

1/29/19 — Issued Check No. 1007 to East Telephone for $189.10 in payment of telephone bill. Post Check No. 1007.

1/30/19 — Received payment from West's Store for sales invoice 105. In the Reference No. field, type **Inv. 105**. Post this receipt in the amount of $3,601.50.

Account Reconciliation

1. Complete the bank reconciliations.

Bank Statement: Lincoln Bank

Statement of Account		CL Manufacturing, Inc.		
Lincoln Bank		1341 Walnut Street		
January 1 to January 31, 2019	Account #45712	Philadelphia, PA 19122		
REGULAR CHECKING				
Previous Balance	12/31/18	$82,650.00		
2 Deposits(+)		11,206.30		
3 Checks (-)		1,908.81		
Service Charges (-)	1/31/19	22.00		
Ending Balance	1/31/19	**$91,925.49**		
DEPOSITS				
	1/26/19	7,604.80		
	1/31/19	3,601.50		
CHECKS (Asterisk * indicates break in check number sequence)				
	1/28/19	1001	742.50	
	1/30/19	1002	408.37	
	1/30/19	1003	757.94	

Bank Statement: Penn Savings & Loan

Statement of Account Penn Savings & Loan January 1 to January 31, 2019 Account #2310-48001			CL Manufacturing, Inc. 1341 Walnut Street Philadelphia, PA 19122	
PAYROLL CHECKING				
Previous Balance	12/31/18	31,300.00		
9 Checks (-)		3,943.26		
Service Charges (-)	1/31/19	20.00		
Ending Balance	1/31/19	**27,336.74**		
CHECKS (Asterisk * indicates break in check number sequence)				
	1/08/19	101	438.14	
	1/08/19	102	438.14	
	1/08/19	103	438.14	
	1/15/19	104	438.14	
	1/15/19	105	438.14	
	1/15/19	106	438.14	
	1/22/19	107	438.14	
	1/22/19	108	438.14	
	1/22/19	109	438.14	

2. Back up. Use **CL Mftg January.ptb** as the file name.
3. Save the reports as PDF files and export to Excel: Chart of Accounts, General Ledger Trial Balance, Balance Sheet, Income Statement, Statement of Cash Flow, and Statement of Retained Earnings. Refer to the checklist of printouts for additional reports.

CHECKLIST OF PRINTOUTS, CL MANUFACTURING, INC.		
	1	Account Reconciliation Report: Lincoln Bank
	2	Account Reconciliation Report: Penn Savings & Loan
	3	Account Register: Lincoln Bank
	4	Account Register: Penn Savings & Loan
	5	General Ledger Trial Balance
	6	General Ledger
	7	Balance Sheet
	8	Income Statement
	9	Statement of Cash Flow
	10	Statement of Retained Earnings
	11	Customer Ledgers
	12	Vendor Ledgers
	13	Job Ledger
	14	Job Profitability Report
	15	Inventory Profitability Report
	16	Payroll Register

Optional printouts, CL Manufacturing, Inc.				
	17	Chart of Accounts	25	Cash Receipts Journal
	18	December 31, 2018 Starting Balance Sheet	26	Cost of Goods Sold Journal
	19	Customer List	27	General Journal
	20	Vendor List		
	21	Payroll Journal		
	22	Purchase Journal		
	23	Cash Disbursements Journal		
	24	Sales Journal		

Student Name_____**Date**_____

CHECK YOUR PROGRESS: PROJECT 4
CL MANUFACTURING, INC.

1.   What are the total debit and credit balances on your
     General Ledger Trial Balance?   _____

2.   What are the total assets on January 31?   _____

3.   What is the balance in the Lincoln Bank
     account on January 31?   _____

4.   What is the balance in the Penn Savings &
     Loan account on January 31?   _____

5.   What is Suzy's Camping Store account balance
     on January 31?   _____

6.   What are the direct labor costs on January 31?   _____

7.   How many backpacks were sold during the month
     of January?   _____

8.   How many sleeping bags were sold during the
     month of January?   _____

9.   How many tents were sold during the month of
     January?   _____

10. What is the ending retained earnings amount on
     on January 31?   _____

11. What are the total expenses reported on January 31?   _____

12. Was any Accounts Payable incurred during the
     month of January? (Circle your answer)   YES   NO

Project 4A   Student-Designed Project

You have completed four projects: Marcia Westcott, Accounting; Valley Bikes; Evanston Computer Club; and CL Manufacturing, Inc. In each project you completed the Computer Accounting Cycle for one month.

It is the purpose of Project 4A, to have you write the next month's transactions for one of the four projects. You pick the project and complete the accounting cycle: Project 1, Marcia Westcott, Accounting, a service business; Project 2, Valley Bikes, a merchandising business; Project 3, Evanston Computer Club, a nonprofit business; or Project 4, CL Manufacturing, Inc., a manufacturing business. At the end of your month's transactions, you are required to complete adjusting entries.

Good luck! It is your turn to create the transactions for another month and complete the Computer Accounting Cycle. Remember to back up periodically.

Appendix

A

Troubleshooting

Refer to the Online Learning Center for the most recent troubleshooting information. Appendix C, Review of Accounting Principles; and Appendix D, Glossary is on the OLC at www.mhhe.com/yacht2019 > Troubleshooting Tips. The last page of each chapter is an index. Refer to the chapter index for specific troubleshooting, how to fix, comments, and Read Me boxes. Appendix A,

Troubleshooting, includes the following.

1. System Requirements Warning, pages 709-710
2. PDF Files, page 710
3. Save Excel File as a PDF, page 710
4. Inactive Excel Icon, pages 710-711
5. Spreadsheet Compare, pages 711
6. Windows Printer Settings, page 711
7. Go Green and Save, *or* No Printer, pages 711-712
8. Opening the Sample Companies, pages 712-713
9. Restoring Starting Data for the Sample Companies, page 713
10. Restoring Sage 50 2016 or 2017 Backup Files (.ptb extension), pages 713-714
11. Payroll Entry, page 714-715
12. Deleting Sage 50, page 715

SYSTEM REQUIREMENTS WARNING

If a System Requirements window warns RAM is not large enough or processing speed is too slow, you may continue installation but Sage 50 2019 it may run

---

---

slower. The minimum requirements for Sage 50 2019 installation is 2 GB of RAM for single user, 4 GB of RAM for multiple users, and 2.4 GHz of processor speed. Refer to page v for System Requirements.

PDF FILES

To convert Sage 50 reports to PDF files, you need Adobe Reader software, an Adobe Corporation product. This software lets you view, navigate, and print the contents of a file. Free Adobe Reader software is available at https://get.adobe.com/reader/.

If you are having difficulty using Sage 50's PDF feature, do the following:

1. Update to the latest version of Adobe Reader https://get.adobe.com/reader/.
2. Exit Sage 50. Insert the Sage 50 DVD and select Repair.

SAVE EXCEL FILE AS A PDF

You can also save PDF files from an Excel 2013 and higher file.

1.   Open the Excel file; for example, Chapter 1_Employee List.xlsx.
2.   Select File > Save as Adobe PDF > Convert to PDF > type the File name **Chapter 1_Employee List** > Save.

INACTIVE EXCEL ICON

In order to use Microsoft Office 365 integration features, you must have an Office 365 Business Premium account. OneDrive must be activated and configured. Refer to Integration/compatibility requirements, page v.

Display the Sage report, select Edit > Copy. Start Excel > Open a blank workbook > right-click on the sheet > left-click Paste > reformat and save.

SPREADSHEET COMPARE

Office Professional 2016: "Compare two versions of a workbook by using Spreadsheet Compare" at https://support.office.com/en-US/article/Compare-two-versions-of-a-workbook-by-using-Spreadsheet-Compare-0E1627FD-CE14-4C33-9AB1-8EA82C6A5A7E.

"What can you do with Spreadsheet Inquire in Excel 2016 for Windows," at https://support.office.com/en-US/article/what-you-can-do-with-spreadsheet-inquire-in-excel-2016-for-windows-5444eb12-14a2-4d82-b527-45b9884f98cf. For **Office Professional 2013**, go to https://technet.microsoft.com/en-us/library/dn205148.aspx.

WINDOWS PRINTER SETTINGS

If PDF files are <u>not</u> printing, do this: Go to Start > click > go to

> click > turn off Let Windows manage my default printer. When turned off, the default printer is the last used printer.

GO GREEN AND SAVE, *OR* NO PRINTER

Reminders to Go Green and Save are included within chapters of the textbook. *Or*, if your computer is not connected to a printer, you have these choices.

1. In the Print Properties field, save the file as either an Adobe PDF file or a Microsoft XPS Document Writer file. If needed, you can attach the file to your instructor.

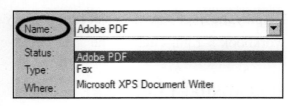

2. In the Check number field or Invoice number field, type the appropriate number. Since printing a check or invoice numbers the entry and posts it to the ledger, typing the number in the appropriate field before posting will also include the number on the journal and ledger.

OPENING THE SAMPLE COMPANIES

When selecting one of the sample companies – Bellwether Garden Supply or Stone Arbor Landscaping – the Explore a Sample Company Window does <u>not</u> show the <OK>, <Close>, or <Help> buttons.

No, <OK>, <Close>, or <Help> buttons. Press <Enter> to continue.

Screen resolution affects how Sage 50's windows look. The recommended screen resolution is 1024X768 with small fonts.

Page v includes recommended system requirements:

- At least high color (16-bit) SVGA video; supports 1024x768 resolution with small fonts required.

Higher screen resolution may be used. Higher resolution will not affect how the software functions, but the user interface might look different. For example, if you do not have an <OK> button, press <Enter> to start Bellwether Garden Supply or Stone Arbor Landscaping.

RESTORING STARTING DATA FOR THE SAMPLE COMPANIES

To start the sample companies from the beginning (before any data was added), restore these files:

1. In Chapter 1, on pages 23-26, you backed up Bellwether Garden Supply. This back up was made *before* any data was added. Restore the bgs.ptb file. Refer to Using Sage 50's Restore Wizard on pages 27-31 for detailed steps. Once the bgs.ptb file is restored you have starting (beginning) data for Bellwether Garden Supply.
2. In Chapter 8, on page 243, you backed up Stone Arbor Landscaping. Restore the Chapter 8.ptb file.

RESTORING SAGE 50 2016 OR 2017 BACKUP FILES (.PTB EXTENSION)

To restore files from earlier versions of Sage 50, use the Educational version software. The student version *cannot* be used to restore .ptb backup files from earlier Sage 50 versions. The Educational version is free to schools, does not have a time limit, is multiuser ready, and has a different serial than the student version.

If your school is a member of the Sage Education Partner Program, the new version of Sage 50 is automatically sent to schools. When installing the Educational version, use the serial number emailed by SageEducation@sage.com, 800-256-8807. The website for downloading free classroom software is http://www.sage.com/us/about-us/education-instructor.

PAYROLL ENTRY

If you are trying to use the payroll tax tables and a window prompts to register your product, you may not have installed the software with the appropriate serial number. [Peachtree is used as an example; your window shows Sage 50.]

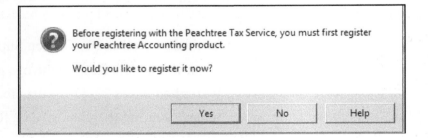

Before registering with the Peachtree Tax Service, you must first register your Peachtree Accounting product.

Would you like to register it now?

| Yes | No | Help |

If you select the Payroll Entry window and a window appears asking you to register payroll, click on the Do not display this message again box. Then click <OK>.

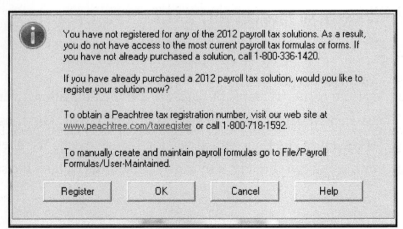

You have not registered for any of the 2012 payroll tax solutions. As a result, you do not have access to the most current payroll tax formulas or forms. If you have not already purchased a solution, call 1-800-336-1420.

If you have already purchased a 2012 payroll tax solution, would you like to register your solution now?

To obtain a Peachtree tax registration number, visit our web site at www.peachtree.com/taxregister or call 1-800-718-1592.

To manually create and maintain payroll formulas go to File/Payroll Formulas/User-Maintained.

| Register | OK | Cancel | Help |

Sage 50 educational and student versions include *example* tax tables for 50 states (File > Payroll Formulas > Sage-Maintained > select the down-arrow in the Formula ID field. Example payroll formulas are included for the 50 states.)

You may need to delete the software and reinstall, then restart Sage 50.

DELETING SAGE 50

Follow these steps to delete Sage 50 Accounting 2019. (Use similar steps to delete Sage 50 2017 or earlier version.) These steps are also shown on page xxii.

1. Go to Control Panel > Programs and Features > Uninstall Sage 50 Accounting 2019 (*or* other year). The InstallWizard window appears briefly.
2. When the Maintenance Options window appears, select <u>R</u>emove > click <Next>.
3. The Confirm Uninstall prompts This will remove Sage 50 Accounting 2019 (all versions), click <OK>. Be patient. Removing Sage 50 Accounting will take a while.
4. When the Maintenance Complete window appears, click <Finish>.
5. If necessary, remove the CD. Close Control Panel.

After removal, you may want to delete these two folders:

1. C:\Sage
2. C:\Program Files (x86)\Sage

<u>Before</u> removing the folders, backup data that you want to keep. Once the Sage folder is deleted, all company data files are removed. (In Windows Vista, the Sage folder is within C:\Program Files.)

Appendix B

Accounting Information Systems

In *Computer Accounting with Sage 50 2019, 21e,* you learn about the relationship between Sage 50 and accounting principles and procedures. Throughout the textbook, you are shown how the initial decisions for setting up a company, setting defaults, processing transactions, and generating reports relates to what is learned in other accounting courses.

Another feature of the textbook explains how Sage 50's user interface organizes and processes data. Sage 50 is an example of an accounting information system. The following section defines *accounting information systems (AIS)*.

ACCOUNTING INFORMATION SYSTEMS

An accounting information system is the method of recordkeeping a business uses to maintain its financial information. This includes purchases, sales, and other financial processes of the business. The purpose of AIS is to accumulate data and provide decision makers with information.

Key characteristics of an accounting information system include providing accurate financial information to management and external users (creditors, investors, regulatory authorities, and taxation authorities). AIS software uses various modules to record data and produce reports. Users can easily produce financial statements or obtain information to manage the day-to-day activities of a business. In the past, this was a paper-based process. Today businesses use accounting software. In an electronic financial accounting system, the steps in the accounting cycle are built by the system.

Accounting information systems not only record the financial transactions of a business but also combine the study and practice of accounting within the design, implementation, and monitoring of records. Such systems use information technology resources together with traditional accounting controls and methods to provide users the financial information necessary to manage their organizations. The key components of an accounting information system are:

Input. The input devices commonly associated with AIS include: standard personal computers or workstations, scanning devices for standardized data entry, electronic communication devices for electronic data interchange (EDI) and e-commerce. In addition, many financial systems come Web-enabled to allow devices to connect to the internet.

Process. Basic processing is achieved through computer systems ranging from individual personal computers to large-scale enterprise servers. The underlying model is the double-entry accounting system initially introduced in Italy in the fifteenth century.

Output. Output devices used include computer displays, printers, and electronic communication devices for electronic data exchange and e-commerce. The output content may encompass almost any type of financial reports from budgets and tax reports to multinational financial statements.

SAGE 50 AND QUICKBOOKS

Sage 50 and QuickBooks are two popular small business accounting software applications. Both software applications contain modules that reflect business processes. Typical business processes include sales, cash receipts, purchases, cash payments, and human resource functions such as payroll.

Sage 50

Sage 50 includes a Navigation Bar and Navigation Centers which take you to various business process areas or system modules. Another way to go to Sage 50's modules is to make selections from the menu bar. In order to show Sage 50's accounts payable system, the Vendors & Purchases Navigation Center is used.

When Vendors & Purchases is selected, the Vendors & Purchases Navigation Center appears. A task diagram shows the flow of data through the accounts payable system. Other areas on the Vendors & Purchases Navigation Center include the Vendors list, Recently Used Vendor Reports, Aged Payables, and Sage 50 solutions. This is all in Sage 50's accounts payable system or accounts payable module.

Another way to use the accounts payable system is to make selections from the menu bar. The Maintain menu is where defaults are set up. The Maintain menu includes a Vendors selection and a selection for Default Information, Vendors. The menu bar's Tasks menu is also organized by module. For example, the accounts payable selections are in one area.

The Reports & Forms menu includes an Accounts Payable selection. When the Select a Report or Form window appears, Accounts Payable: Vendors and Purchases selections are available. There are two tabs: Reports and Forms. The Forms tab allows you to select the appropriate accounts payable form. Notice that the Reports list includes each Sage 50 module: Accounts Receivable, Accounts Payable, Payroll, General Ledger, Inventory, etc.

In addition, various system controls exist to ensure the accuracy and reliability of the data recorded. For example, preformatted screens facilitate the accuracy and completeness of data entry. Fields are restricted to either text or numeric data or a specific number of characters. Values are automatically calculated. The system prompts or requests the user to enter specific data and processing will not continue until the appropriate data is entered. Drop down lists or look-up tables allow the user to access master tables.

Master tables are used to set and maintain constant data, i.e. defaults. When a user enters a specific identification code such as a vendor number, the system accesses the master table and automatically completes information about the vendor within the transaction window.

From these examples, you can see how Sage 50's accounts payable system is organized. Now let's look at QuickBooks and you will see many similarities as well as differences between the two accounting information systems.

QuickBooks Desktop

The differences between desktop, or software that is installed locally on the hard drive, and Online accounting software are disappearing. QuickBooks desktop files can be converted to QB Online. The Company menu shown on the next page shows QB Desktop's selection for exporting a company file (files ending in .qbw extension) to QuickBooks Online.

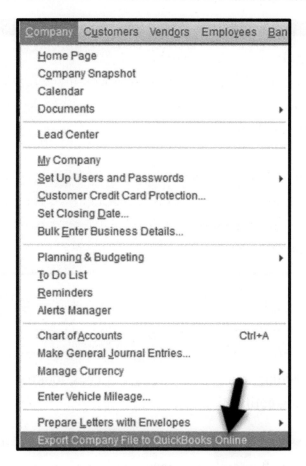

For all devices to work together – iPad, iPhone, Android, Macs or PCs – more companies use the cloud. QB Online requires an internet connection, not a specific Windows, Macintosh, or Apple operating system. This means that Macs, PCs, Chromebooks, tablets, and Smartphones can be used.

QuickBooks Online

With QuickBooks Online, you can track income, expenses, create reports, and access your data online from anywhere with a PC, Mac, Tablet or smartphone. When you start your internet browser to sign into QuickBooks Online, the user interface looks like the one shown on the next page.

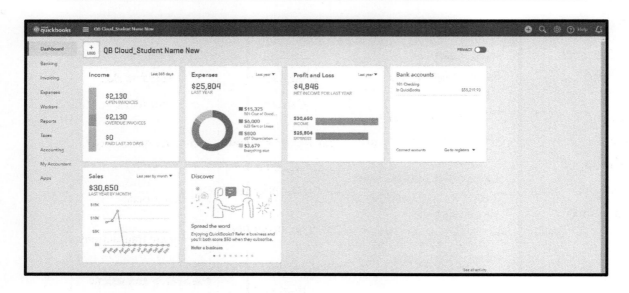

The first page you see is the Dashboard which includes a Navigation Bar on the left side of the screen and amounts and visual images of Income, Expenses, Profit and Loss, Bank Accounts, and Sales on the right side of the screen. Familiar icons are used for adding transactions, doing searches, looking at settings, using help, or reading notifications.

Plus for adding transactions.   Magnifying-glass for search.

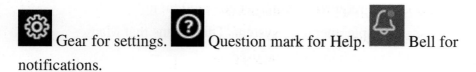

Gear for settings.   Question mark for Help.   Bell for notifications.

For more information about QuickBooks Online go online to www.mhhe.com/qbo2e and https://www.intuit.com/partners/education-program/.

The table on the next two pages summarizes the similarities and differences between Sage 50 and QB Desktop (local computer installation) and QB Online (internet delivered).

Features	Sage 50	QuickBooks Desktop	QuickBooks Online
Modules Customers (A/R) Vendors (A/P) Employees Banking Inventory	**Navigation Bar** Transaction windows include debit/credit fields LIFO/FIFO, and average inventory User-maintained payroll *or* third-party	**Icon Bar & Centers** Transaction window dr./cr. defaults cannot be changed Average inventory Intuit payroll add-on or third-party	**Navigation Bar and icons** *Same features as QB Desktop* Familiar icons: ⊕ Create transactions 🔍 Search and recent transactions ⚙ Settings
Periods/Year End	Select period/fiscal year for accounting; year-end closing process	One period or list for all entries; select new year	*Same as QB Desktop*
Journals	**GL:** General Journal **A/P:** Purchase Journal and Cash Payments Journal **A/R:** Sales Journal and Cash Receipts Journal **Inventory:** Cost of Goods Sold Journal; Inventory Adjustments Journal **Payroll:** Payroll Journal	Transaction Journal Customize and filter for expenses, income, etc.	*Same as QB Desktop*

Features	Sage 50	QuickBooks Desktop	QuickBooks Online
General Ledger **Subsidiary Ledgers** **Financial Statements**	YES	YES	*Same as QB Desktop*
Export and Save Reports	Excel and Adobe PDF	Excel and Adobe PDF	Excel and Adobe PDF
Backup/Restore/ Open Company	One file extension - .PTB - for backups/restore/open company	Backup extensions include .QBB, .QBM, .QBA. Open company, .QBW extension	Save or back up on Intuit's web server. Start browser, sign into account.

Sage 50 and QuickBooks are examples of accounting information systems that are used for small business accounting. Even though the user interface looks different, the processing of accounting data and the reports generated are the same.

QuickBooks Online is an example of **cloud computing** or **Software as a Service**. SaaS is a way of delivering applications over the internet as a service paid for with monthly or yearly subscriptions. Instead of installing software locally on the computer's hard drive, you access software via the internet.

Sage 50 Business Cloud is the online version of Sage accounting software. To learn more, go online to https://www.sage.com/en-us/.

Accounting Software

Accounting information systems use software applications like Sage 50, QuickBooks, and Microsoft Dynamics to process and manage business transactions.

The major difference between accounting software includes the depth of processing, enhanced features and functions, and the size of the database. As the database gets larger, the depth of processing increases and more features and functions are available. As companies grow in size, their accounting software needs change. The diagram compares QuickBooks Online and Desktop, Sage 50 and Microsoft Dynamics. Because of its larger database, observe that Sage 50 can be used by both small and medium-sized businesses.

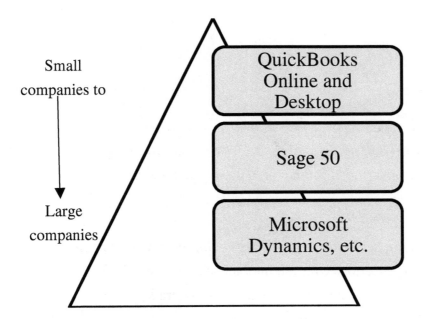

Sage 50 and QuickBooks are used by small companies. As the company grows to mid-size, Sage 50 and Microsoft Dynamics can be used. Large companies use Microsoft Dynamics, Oracle and SAP.

Company size	No. of Employees
Small business	1-50 employees
Medium-sized business	50-500 employees
Large business	500+ employees

Accounting software is available for small, medium and large businesses. The high-end accounting software applications are generally referred to as *enterprise resource planning (ERP)* systems. ERP systems are designed to integrate all of the major functions of a business to promote efficient operations. ERP systems are company-wide software applications which manage and coordinate all the resources, information, and functions of a business from shared data sources.

Index

728   Index